The Rhetorical Act

The Rhetorical Act

Thinking, Speaking, and Writing Critically

Fifth Edition

Karlyn Kohrs Campbell
University of Minnesota

Susan Schultz Huxman
Conrad Grebel University College

Thomas R. Burkholder
University of Nevada–Las Vegas

CENGAGE
Learning·

Australia • Brazil • Mexico • Singapore • United Kingdom • United States

The Rhetorical Act: Thinking, Speaking, and Writing Critically, Fifth Edition
Karlyn Kohrs Campbell,
Susan Schultz Huxman, Thomas R. Burkholder

Product Director: Monica Eckman

Senior Product Manager: Nicole Morinon

Content Developer: Larry Goldberg

Content Coordinator: Alicia Landsberg

Product Assistant: Colin Solan

Media Developer: Jessica Badiner

Marketing Brand Manager: Lydia LeStar

Rights Acquisitions Specialist: Ann Hoffman

Manufacturing Planner: Doug Bertke

Art and Design Direction, Production Management, and Composition: Cenveo Publisher Services®

Cover Image: www.gettyimages.com

Photo on chapter openers, in the boxes, Material for Analysis box is credited to dinn/Vetta/Getty Images.

For product information and technology assistance, contact us at **Cengage Learning Customer & Sales Support, 1-800-354-9706**

For permission to use material from this text or product, submit all requests online at **www.cengage.com/permissions**. Further permissions questions can be emailed to **permissionrequest@cengage.com**.

Library of Congress Control Number: 2013948730

Student Edition:
ISBN-13: 978-1-133-31379-3
ISBN-10: 1-133-31379-5

Cengage Learning
200 First Stamford Place, 4th Floor
Stamford, CT 06902
USA

Cengage Learning is a leading provider of customized learning solutions with office locations around the globe, including Singapore, the United Kingdom, Australia, Mexico, Brazil, and Japan. Locate your local office at: **international.cengage.com/region.**

Cengage Learning products are represented in Canada by Nelson Education, Ltd.

For your course and learning solutions, visit **www.cengage.com.** Purchase any of our products at your local college store or at our preferred online store **www.cengagebrain.com.**

Instructors: Please visit **login.cengage.com** and log in to access instructor-specific resources.

Printed in the United States of America
2 3 4 5 6 7 17 16 15 14

*To all those who have struggled
for the right to speak,
in the hope that what this book contains
will help to give them voice*

About the Authors

Karlyn Kohrs Campbell is Professor of Communication Studies at the University of Minnesota. She is the author of *Man Cannot Speak for Her: A Critical Study of Early Feminist Rhetoric*, 2 vols. (1989) and co-author of *Deeds Done in Words: Presidential Rhetoric and the Genres of Governance* (1990), *Presidents Creating the Presidency* (2008), *The Interplay of Influence: News, Advertising, Politics, and the Mass Media* (6th ed., 2006), and editor of *Critiques of Contemporary Rhetoric* (1997, 2003), *Women Public Speakers in the United States, 1800–1925* (1993), and *Women Public Speakers in the United States, 1925–present* (1994). Awards include a fellowship at the Shorenstein Center of the Kennedy School at Harvard, the National Communication Association Distinguished Scholar Award, the Lauren Ecroyd outstanding teacher award, the Woolbert Award for scholarship of exceptional originality and influence, Golden Anniversary Monograph Award, and the University of Minnesota 2002 Distinguished Woman Scholar in the Humanities and Social Sciences. She has taught at Macalester College, The British College at Palermo, Italy, California State University at Los Angeles, SUNY at Brockport and at Binghamton, City University of C.U.N.Y., University of Kansas, and Dokkyo University, Tokyo, Japan.

Susan Schultz Huxman (PhD, University of Kansas) is President and Professor at Conrad Grebel University College in Waterloo, Ontario. She received her undergraduate degree from Bethel College in Kansas in English and her master's and doctoral degrees in communication studies with an emphasis on rhetoric from the University of Kansas. Her first academic appointment as director of the Public Speaking program was with Wake Forest University. She has won numerous teaching awards in her twenty-year career at Wichita State University. Before accepting the presidential post in Canada, she served as Director of the Elliott School of Communication at WSU and regularly taught honors public speaking, rhetorical criticism, research methods, and strategic communication in organizations. In her current post, as time permits, she still teaches special courses and workshops in rhetorical theory and criticism and leadership and crisis communication. An active scholar, she has published in the field of rhetorical criticism and U.S. public address. A new book, *Landmark Speeches in U. S. Pacifism*, is in press with Texas A & M University press. She engages in a range of professional speaking and consulting opportunities each year to advance the discipline, develop support for the college, and showcase scholarship in action.

Thomas R. Burkholder (PhD, University of Kansas) is Associate Professor and former Chair of the Department of Communication Studies at the University of Nevada–Las Vegas. He is co-author, with Karlyn Kohrs Campbell, of the second edition of *Critiques of Contemporary Rhetoric* (1997) and co-editor, with Martha S. Watson, of *Perfecting American Society: The Rhetoric of Nineteenth Century Reform* (2007). His work has also appeared in the *Western Journal of Communication*, *Southern Communication Journal*, *Communication Studies*, and various book chapters. He teaches undergraduate and graduate courses in rhetorical theory, rhetorical criticism, and U.S. public address.

Brief Contents

Contents

PART TWO

Resources for Rhetorical Action

Chapter 4
The Resources of Evidence   86

Chapter 5
The Resources of Argument   106

Chapter 12
Understanding Visual Rhetoric   282

Chapter 13
Understanding the Medium of Transmission   298

Chapter 14
Understanding Occasion   325

Epilogue   345

Index   351

Preface

WHAT IS THE DISTINCTIVE PERSPECTIVE OF THIS BOOK?

The first edition of *The Rhetorical Act* appeared more than thirty years ago. It grew out of a course on rhetoric and social influence that I taught at the University of Kansas. Susan Huxman and Tom Burkholder were graduate students in the communication studies program, and both were teaching assistants in that class. Based on our shared experiences, we developed views of the relationship between rhetoric and criticism that inform all of the editions. Susan Huxman joined me as co-author on the third edition; fortunately for the two of us, Tom Burkholder was willing to bring his expertise to this edition. In my view, their contributions have made this edition the best so far.

The fifth edition retains the conceptual core of the earlier editions while extending the book's scope and relevance. Quite simply, this book aims to teach students how to craft and critique messages that influence. Moreover, we believe that teaching students to be effective critics is essential to teaching them to be effective communicators. This edition presents rhetorical criticism, media literacy, and strategic public speaking as an integrated skill-set, reflected in the subtitle: *Thinking, Speaking, and Writing Critically*.

This edition remains committed to the ancient idea of the interrelationship of art and practice, that you cannot improve skills such as speaking and writing without understanding the theory, concepts, and ideas on which they are based. Conversely, you cannot master the theory unless you use it and test it in practice. In our view, this ancient relationship demands that those who would learn about rhetoric must adopt the role of rhetor-critic. The rhetor initiates rhetorical action and seeks to make the choices that will make her or him the most effective moral agent. The critic describes, analyzes, and evaluates rhetorical acts to understand what they do and how and for whom they are effective. As rhetor-critics, students learn to critique their own rhetoric in order to improve it, and as critic-consumers, they learn to analyze the rhetoric of others in order to make decisions as intelligently as possible.

Consistent with the earlier editions, the fifth edition of *The Rhetorical Act* is different from traditional textbooks on criticism and public speaking in several ways. First, it treats rhetorical action as the joint creation of rhetor and audience, emphasizing the audience's active role as collaborators, as joint creators of messages, the classical concept of the enthymeme (Aristotle). Second, it approaches rhetoric in all its varieties as a "strategy to encompass a situation" (Kenneth Burke) and as "that art or talent by which discourse is adapted to its end" (George Campbell). Third, it treats all forms of rhetoric as points on a single continuum of influence; there is no separate treatment of speaking or writing to inform, entertain, or persuade. Finally, it does not rely on "schools of criticism"; rather, it concentrates on the descriptive, analytical, and evaluative tools that make up the critical process. It introduces students to a comprehensive critical "grammar" and "vocabulary."

Once again, we offer a Prologue and an Epilogue. The Prologue by Professor Huxman is addressed to a beginning student audience. The Epilogue is written for advanced students and instructor audiences by Professor Campbell. Both are designed to address larger audiences on college campuses when discussions about the centrality of speech to the liberal arts curriculum and to the general education curriculum arise.

Supplements: The book's supplements include the Instructor Companion Site where Cognero Computerized Testing and tutorial quiz and essay questions are available.

WHAT HAS CHANGED IN THE FIFTH EDITION?

In General: In each new edition we attempt to refine our analysis of the elements of the rhetorical process and to respond to the changing characteristics of the contemporary rhetorical environment. Teachers will find the basic structure familiar, but punctuated with new examples, changes in layout that make concepts clearer, and fresh illustrations. Consistent with the ways in which our communicative environment has grown and changed, we have increased our analysis of visual communication and incorporated exercises related to the new ways in which we use the tools of communication.

Major Revisions in Key Chapters

- **Chapter 5: "The Resources of Argument"** includes new material drawn from the research of classical scholars that enlarges our understanding of the enthymeme and which is illustrated by reference to the speech of Robert Kennedy referred to in the Prologue, President John Kennedy's speech in Berlin, and President Obama's speech after the shootings in Tucson, Arizona.
- **Chapter 12: "Understanding Visual Rhetoric"** incorporates analysis of the changes in technology that have made all of us visual rhetors.
- **Chapter 13: "Understanding the Medium of Transmission"** details the fundamentals of media literacy with examples and illustrates the media's high ethos appeal. It explores the implications of mediated exchanges in which who speaks is unknown, and notes the different form of "reading" that occurs on social media and the communicative paradoxes social media create. Finally, it explores the relationship between mass media and social reform and asks whether social movements can emerge out of socially mediated communication.

AN IMPORTANT NOTE TO STUDENTS AND TEACHERS

We believe that one of the major strengths of *The Rhetorical Act*, through all of its prior editions, has been the high quality of the contemporary, up-to-date examples and materials for analysis—the texts of speeches, the editorials and op-ed pieces, the photos—that bring to life the rhetorical principles and theories that are introduced and explained throughout the book. In preparing this fifth edition, however, we discovered that the cost of obtaining permission to reprint those examples and materials for analysis has skyrocketed since publication of the fourth edition. Those high permission fees threatened to raise the production costs of this edition—costs that might ultimately be passed along to the students who purchase this book.

Thus, in this fifth edition we have, reluctantly, chosen not to reprint some of the examples and materials for analysis that we had hoped to include. Rather, in selected cases we have instead included the Internet addresses (the URLs) for those materials, and we strongly encourage students and teachers to follow those Web links and obtain those materials for their own use. We understand that this decision carries with it the risk that some of those online materials may at some point become unavailable. We also believe that the effort to hold down the production cost of this fifth edition is worth that risk.

WHY DID WE WRITE A TEXTBOOK ON RHETORIC?

We wrote this new edition of *The Rhetorical Act*, like the earlier editions, because we have a passion to educate students on how to become discerning consumers and articulate practitioners of all varieties of rhetorical acts. We are committed to the humanistic approach to rhetoric—that the understanding of who we are as symbol users will foster greater appreciation of, and heighten the moral sensibilities of our students toward, our rhetorical universe. It is our fervent hope that this edition of *The Rhetorical Act* expands the relevance and scope of the previous editions and that it will continue to stimulate the kind of critical discussion so essential to developing analytical thinking, speaking, and writing skills. In Ciceronian terms, we wish to develop "citizen-orators" for our times.

WHO HELPED US?

We thank all those whose comments and criticisms have improved this edition, including the following reviewers: Paul Achter, University of Richmond; Karen Kimball, University of North Texas; Bohn Lattin, University of Portland; Audra McMullen, Towson University; Susan Millsap, Otterbein University; and Kristina Sheeler, Indiana University–Purdue University Indianapolis.

We also thank the instructors who completed the satisfaction survey about the text. We want to offer special thanks to Susan Huxman for her intensive work on visual rhetoric and to Tom Burkholder who challenged both of us by asking the hard questions and who has improved this edition significantly because of his special interests in criticism and his extensive background in argumentation. We all owe great thanks to the Department of Communication Studies at the University of Nevada–Las Vegas, and the department chair, Dr. David Henry, for providing us space in which to work and underwriting our joint efforts as we made this revision.

Prologue

WHY STUDY RHETORIC?

Welcome to the discipline of *Rhetoric*—the study of all the processes by which people influence each other through symbols (verbal, nonverbal, visual, aural). This book will help you craft and critique *rhetorical acts*—strategic symbolic attempts to overcome the challenges in a given situation to connect with a specific audience on a given issue to achieve a particular end. As a *rhetor* (a writer, speaker, or producer of a rhetorical act), you have the potential to make an enormous impact on the lives of those around you—affecting decisions large and small about what we buy, where we live, how we vote, to whom we donate money, and why we socialize with particular groups, configure our smartphones to display certain apps, and embrace certain spiritual traditions. As a *critic* (one who describes, analyzes, and evaluates rhetorical acts to understand how and for whom they work), you will learn to examine your own rhetoric in order to improve it and to analyze the rhetoric of others in order to make decisions as intelligently as possible. If you study all forms of influence, you will become aware of the available resources of persuasion and learn how people use and misuse them to advance their goals—a noble aim first advanced by the ancient Greeks and Romans who advocated that all citizens study rhetoric.

So, many moons ago Aristotle and company thought rhetoric was good for you. But why study it today? Because rhetoric often is defined as reason-given discourse, consider these three reasons why the study of rhetoric is important to you.

Intellectual Reasons

Instruction in rhetoric is central to understanding who we are as symbol-using animals. The study of rhetoric helps you appreciate the diverse ways in which discourse forms communities and sharpens your moral sensibilities regarding the power of language to affect societal values. The ability to speak or write clearly, eloquently, and effectively has been recognized as the hallmark of an educated person since the beginning of recorded history.[1] At the age of eighteen, Cicero said, "If truth were self-evident, eloquence would not be necessary." Isocrates said, "To become eloquent is to activate one's humanity, to apply the imagination and to solve the practical problems of human living."[2] The great Greek statesman Pericles said, "One who forms a judgment on any point but cannot explain it clearly, might as well never have thought at all on the subject."[3] Aristotle recommended the study of rhetoric for intellectual advancement because it prevents the triumph of fraud and injustice; instructs when scientific instruction is of no avail; makes us argue both sides of a case; and is a means of defense. One of the rhetorical acts you will read is a courageous speech by Angelina Grimké, (1838), one of the first advocates for abolitionism and woman's rights in the United States. Despite a heckling mob and the grand place where she spoke—Pennsylvania Hall—which burned to the ground after her "incendiary" message nearly thirty years before the Civil War, Grimké, the daughter of a wealthy South Carolina slave owner, argued passionately for the rights of slaves and women on intellectual grounds: "As a Southerner I feel that it is my duty to stand up here tonight and bear testimony against slavery. I have seen it—I have seen it. I know it has horrors that can never be described. I was brought up under its wing: I witnessed for many years its demoralizing influences, and its destructiveness to human happiness. . . . Man cannot enjoy [happiness] while his manhood is destroyed, and that part of the being blotted out." More contemporary rhetors in the book also use rhetoric to make sophisticated observations about the human condition: Robert Kennedy, speaking impromptu to an African American crowd on the news of Martin Luther King's assassination; Ronald Reagan comforting a nation after the loss of the *Challenger* astronauts; Steve Olson making a conservative case for gay rights; and Steve Jobs reminding us that we are indeed "homo narans"—in his compelling stories of the transforming power of education in a university commencement address. Studying their words enriches our lives and cultivates our own symbolic capacities.

Citizenship Reasons

Aristotle first argued that humans were the only animals to live in a *polis* (a city-state or political community). The root word of communication is *communis*—Latin for community. Do you remember the movie *Castaway* with Tom Hanks? What happens to him when he's stranded on the island? He almost goes crazy because he has no one to talk to. What does he do to create that communication bond to survive? He paints a face on a volleyball that has washed up onto the shore and calls it "Wilson." A similar story line, only this one with a man-eating tiger, prevails in a later movie, *The Life of Pi*.

The art of rhetoric is as much a survival skill as the mark of an educated person. I am fond of reminding students of what contemporary rhetorical theorist Kenneth Burke said about the basic human need for rhetorical competence: it is "equipment for living."[4] Cicero in his call for "citizen-orators" cemented the relationship between civic-mindedness and speech competency. Preparation for life in the modern world requires rhetorical action with a cross section of diverse people who often have conflicting needs and values. Effective speech helps maintain a sense of community and craft consensus in an increasingly diverse and complex world.[5]

Leadership demands strong rhetorical competencies. Forging alliances, resolving conflict, negotiating change, initiating policy, handling the media, meting out justice, celebrating accomplishments, these are all rhetorical skills linked to strong citizenship. The relationship between rhetoric and citizenship has been codified in our constitution: freedom of speech, freedom of the press, freedom of assembly, and freedom to dissent. Democracy and deliberation go hand in hand. A rhetoric course brings together students from across the institution and provides a town hall forum to disseminate and evaluate the "marketplace of ideas" of a diverse speech community.[6] In a rhetorical criticism, media literacy, composition, and/or strategic public speaking course like the one you are enrolled in, your professor aims to develop effective citizens and leaders for our times.

In these pages, you will be exposed to several rhetorical acts that prompt discussion about citizenship and national identity. Michael Bloomburg's speech at "ground zero" arguing for tolerance in our treatment of Muslims; Former U.S. Senator Dale Bumpers crafts a compelling history lesson persuading his colleagues to "consider the weight of history" in dealing with the grave punishment of impeachment; the great resistance to changing our national anthem whether in content, tune, or translation is examined in rhetorical pieces by Caldwell Titcomb, a music professor, Daniel Epstein, an essayist, and David Goldstein, a reporter; the demands of political power for African Americans is enunciated with passion by Malcolm X; war speeches to the nation, such as the Pearl Harbor address by Franklin D. Roosevelt, require that we understand how and why some democratic principles are suspended during wartime. Studying these rhetorical acts will help you see why proficiency in rhetoric is "equipment for living" in a "polis."

Workplace Reasons

Studies abound pointing to the centrality of speech competency in the job market. The *Wall Street Journal* reported that in a survey of 480 companies employers ranked communication skills (speaking, listening, and writing) as those most valued in any job. In a report on the fastest-growing careers, the U. S. Department of Labor stated that communication skills would be in demand across occupations well into the twenty-first century. When 1,000 faculty members from a cross section of disciplines were asked to identify basic competencies for every college graduate, skills in communicating topped the list.[7] It is little wonder then that a Carnegie report recommended not one but two courses in communication to anchor liberal arts education in our nation's colleges and universities.[8]

Rhetorical training is valuable to employers because communicating effectively is vital to success. Its omnipresence alone deserves study. Most of our waking day is spent listening, speaking, reading, and writing. Try to find a job in any field that pays a living wage, involves working with other people, and promises advancement potential that does not require a competent communicator. It's impossible in the new economy in which we live! Many rewarding careers demand special expertise in rhetoric. A four-star general and chairman of the Joint Chiefs of Staff under President Eisenhower, General Maxwell D. Taylor had this to say when asked what training had been most helpful to him in preparation for his demanding role as Chief of Staff: "I never hesitated in replying," General Taylor began. "My most valuable preparation was membership in the Northeast High School Society of Debate in my pre-West Point days in Kansas City."[9] If you aspire to rise to the top of your field as an engineer, administrator, lawyer, legislator, teacher, health care professional, business leader, or performing artist, just to name a few, you must be good at *thinking, speaking, and writing critically*—the subtitle of this book.

To help you draw the connection between rhetorical acumen and workplace achievement, you will be exposed to rhetorical acts from some of these rhetorical careerists: provocative journalists Donna Britt, Peter Shawn Taylor, Larry Bradshaw and Lorrie Slonsky, Gary Smith, and Malcolm Gladwell; social movement leaders Frederick Douglass, Angelina Grimké, and Martin Luther King Jr.; scientist Bill McKibbin; attorney Ted Olson; advertising guru Tony Schwartz; and political leaders from Ronald Reagan to Barack Obama. You will also learn how to write and speak critically by presenting articulate speeches, crafting analytical essays, and researching strategy reports. Your rhetorical acts, if assembled and executed strategically, will be preparation for successful career choices.

DOES RHETORIC MATTER?

Despite its important place in your college curriculum, your community, and your workplace, some of you may wonder how rhetoric stacks up against other skills that ostensibly require real action. In fact, you may wonder why this book uses the term rhetorical act or rhetorical action together. I mean there's talk and then there's action; those who talk the talk and those who walk the walk, right? One way to help you think about ways in which discourse doesn't take the place of deeds but is itself a vital act is through recounting a great rhetorical moment in U.S. history. Consider how rhetoric created the events that unfolded on this night.

One hour after Martin Luther King was assassinated on April 4, 1968, in Memphis, Robert F. Kennedy, then a presidential contender campaigning in Indianapolis, received the grim news. Kennedy scuttled his scheduled campaign speech in the heart of the city of Indianapolis, resisted the advice from police and his own handlers to "get out of Dodge," walked into the ghetto of that city alone, called out for people to follow him, climbed into the back of a pickup, and in the cold night with a howling wind, delivered the following impromptu remarks to an audience of around 1,000 mostly black citizens who had no idea that King was dead. Joe Klein, political columnist for *Time* magazine and author of *Politics Lost* (2006), gives us a front row seat to the riveting audience reactions to RFK delivering the news of King's tragic death. His commentary is captured in brackets and italics.[10]

> Ladies and gentlemen, I'm only going to speak to you for one or two minutes tonight because I have sad news. I have sad news for you, for all of our fellow citizens and for people who love peace all over the world. And that is that Martin Luther King was shot and killed tonight in Memphis, Tennessee.
>
> [*At this point, there were screams, wailing—just the rawest, most visceral sounds of pain that human voices can summon. As the screams died, Kennedy resumed, slowly, pausing frequently, measuring his words (p. 5).*]
>
> Martin Luther King dedicated his life to love and to justice between fellow human beings and he died in the cause of that effort.
>
> [*There was total silence now (p. 5).*]
>
> In this difficult day, in this difficult time for the United States, it is perhaps well to ask what black—considering the evidence, evidently there were white people who were responsible.
>
> [*A shudder went through the crowd at the powerful unadorned word: responsible (p. 5).*]

You can be filled with bitterness, with hatred, and a desire for revenge. We can move in that direction as a country, in great polarization—black people amongst blacks, and white amongst whites, filled with hatred toward one another.

Or we can make an effort, as Martin Luther King did, to understand and comprehend, and to replace the stain of bloodshed that has spread across our land, with an effort to understand with compassion and love.

For those of you who are black, and are tempted to be filled with hatred and distrust of the injustice of such an act, against all white people, I can only say that I feel . . . I feel in my own heart the same kind of feeling. I had a member of my family killed, but he was killed by a white man.

[This is the first time that Robert Kennedy had ever spoken publicly of the death of his brother, John F. Kennedy (p. 6).]

We have to make an effort in the United States, we have to make an effort to understand, to get beyond these rather difficult times.

My favorite poem, favorite poet, was Aeschylus. He once wrote: "Even in our sleep, pain which cannot forget, falls drop by drop upon the human heart. Until in our own despair, against our will, comes wisdom through the awful grace of God."

What we need in the United States is not division; what we need in the United States is not hatred; what we need in the United States is not violence or lawlessness but love and wisdom and compassion toward one another, and a feeling of justice for those who still suffer within our country, whether they be white or whether they be black.

So I ask you tonight to return home, to say a prayer for the family of Martin Luther King—yes, that's true—but more importantly, to say a prayer for our own country, which all of us love, a prayer for understanding and that compassion of which I spoke.

We can do well in this country. We will have difficult times; we've had difficult times in the past. And we will have difficult times in the future. It is not the end of violence; it is not the end of lawlessness; and it is not the end of disorder. But the vast majority of white people and the vast majority of black people in this country want to live together, want to improve the quality of life, and want justice for all human beings who abide in our land.

[Someone shouted YAY! There were other shouts, which melted into a warm buttery round of applause (p. 7).]

Let us dedicate ourselves to what the Greeks wrote so many years ago: to tame the savageness of man and make gentle the life of this world. Let us dedicate ourselves to that . . . and say a prayer for our country, and for our people.

[Over the next few days, there were riots in 76 American cities. Forty-six people died. 2,500 were injured, 28,000 jailed . . . Indianapolis remained quiet" (p. 7).]

Susan Schultz Huxman

NOTES

1. Friedrich, G. W. (1991). "Essentials of Speech Communication." In Morreale, S., Junusik, L., Randall, M., and Vogl, M. (eds.), *Communication Programs: Rationale and Review Kit.* (1997). Washington, DC: National Communication Association, p. 125.

2. Isocrates as quoted by Hart, R. P. (1993). "Why Communication? Why Education? Toward a Politics of Teaching." *Communication Education*, 42, 97–105.

3. Pericles as quoted by Lucas, S. (2007). *The Art of Public Speaking.* 9th ed. New York: McGraw-Hill.

4. Burke, K. (1941). *Philosophy of Literary Form: Studies in Symbolic Action.* Baton Rouge: Louisiana State Univ. Press; (1945). *A Grammar of Motives.* New York: Prentice-Hall; (1950). *A Rhetoric of Motives.* Berkeley: University of California Press.

5. Morreale, S. P., Osborne, M. M., and Pearson, J. C. (2000). "Why Communication Is Important: A Rationale for the Centrality of the Study of Communication." *Journal of the Association for Communication Administration*, 1, 1–25.

6. National Communication Association (1996). Speech Communication Association policy platform statement on the role of communication courses in general education. Annandale, VA: NCA.

7. Morreale, S. P. and Swickard-Gorman, A. (2006). *Pathways to Communication Careers in the 21st Century.* 7th ed. Washington, DC: National Communication Association.

8. Witkin, B. R., Lovern, M. L., and Lundsteen, S. W. (1996). "Oral Communication in the English Language Arts Curriculum: A National Perspective." *Communication Education*, 45, 40–47.

9. Carpenter, R. (2004). *Rhetoric in Martial Decisions and Decision-Making: Cases and Consequences.* Columbia: University of South Carolina.

10. Klein, J. (2006). *Politics Lost: How American Democracy Was Trivialized by People Who Think You're Stupid.* New York: Doubleday. See prologue, p. 1–24.

Chapter 1

A Rhetorical Perspective

Through its title, *The Rhetorical Act*, this book boldly announces that it is about rhetoric. Because media commentators often use *rhetoric* to mean "hot air" or "lies," you may well ask why you should study rhetoric in a class or read a book about rhetorical action. One way to answer this question is to encourage you to read the prologue and epilogue of this book. Another way is to define *rhetoric* properly and to show the possible value of a rhetorical perspective on human action.

For the moment, we will define *rhetoric* as "the planned use of symbols to achieve goals."[1] Although we will explain that definition in greater detail later in this chapter, you should note these key elements. Most examples of *rhetoric* are not spontaneous, spur-of-the-moment exclamations; rather, they are carefully thought-out messages. This definition is very broad in scope because the symbols that make up those carefully planned messages can be of many types—written and spoken language; nonverbal behaviors; fine arts such as paintings, drawings, and sculptures; music; visual images such as photographs, motion pictures, or television programs—in short, any form of symbol. And finally, the goal, aim, or purpose of such messages is to influence a particular group of people—an audience—in some way, usually to somehow change their thoughts or behaviors. From a rhetorical perspective, we view human communicative acts in that way.

Any "perspective" is literally a way of looking through (*per* = through; *specere* = to look), an angle of vision, a way of seeing. All perspectives are partial and in that sense distorted or biased: each looks at this rather than that; each has its particular emphasis. Put a bit differently, from any perspective we can seem some things very well, other things less well, and still other things not at all. Because someone is always doing the looking and seeing from somewhere, it is impossible to avoid taking some point of view or perspective.

Sometimes perspectives are physical—actual places from which to view material things. For example, go to the top floor of the tallest building at your university and look out through a window. What do you see? Likely, you will see the tops of trees and other smaller buildings on campus, and perhaps even a geometrical pattern of walkways crisscrossing a central quad or plaza. Then, leave the building and as you do, stop on the front steps and take another look at the campus. It is the same campus, of course, but because your perspective has changed, what you see is likely very different. You see the same trees, buildings, and walkways, but from this view point you see the trunks of the trees and the facades of the buildings rather than their tops, and the geometrical pattern of the walkways may not be apparent. From these two different physical perspectives, then, you see some things well, other things less well, and still other things not at all.

Sometimes perspectives, like a *rhetorical* perspective, are mental or intellectual rather than physical. Rather than places from which to view material things, they are orientations or attitudes that frame the way we think. Just what is the mental or intellectual perspective that we call *rhetorical*? It might best be understood by comparing it to other mental or intellectual perspectives with which you might be more familiar, such as a philosophical or scientific perspective.

Whereas scientists would say the most important concern is the discovery and testing of certain kinds of truths, rhetoricians (who study rhetoric and take a rhetorical perspective) would say, "Truths cannot walk on their own legs. They must be carried by people to other people. They must be explained, defended, and spread through language, argument, and appeal." Philosophers and scientists respond rightly that, whenever possible, assumptions should be tested through logic and experiment. In fact, they would argue that you and I should pay more attention to how scientific or philosophical conclusions are reached and tested. Rhetoricians reply that unacknowledged and unaccepted truths are of no use at all. Thus the bias of a rhetorical perspective is its emphasis on and its concern with the resources available in language and in people to make ideas clear and cogent, to bring concepts to life, to make them salient for people. A rhetorical perspective is interested in what influences or persuades people: in other words, in the planned use of symbols to achieve goals.

Those strongly committed to a rhetorical perspective argue that some scientists and philosophers delude themselves, when they claim they are not persuaders and do not use rhetorical strategies in their writings. In a review of two books reporting research on Neanderthals, for example, Stephen Jay Gould, who taught biology, geology, and the history of science at Harvard, said that humans are storytelling creatures and commented on "the centrality of narrative style in any human discourse (though scientists like to deny the importance of such rhetorical devices—while using them all the time—and prefer to believe that persuasion depends upon fact and logic alone)."[2]

When objectivity is highly valued, as it is in science and philosophy, some feel that any hint of the sort of subjectivity that usually characterizes rhetorical decision making must be denied. The folly of holding such a suspicious view of rhetoric is apparent in the evolution versus intelligent design controversy making the rounds in state school board policy debates on what should be taught about Darwin's theory of evolution in high school biology classes. In his documentary about the recent evolution debates, A *Flock of Dodos*, Randy Olson, a protégé of Professor Gould's and a twenty-year marine biologist turned filmmaker, pokes fun at his own colleagues for refusing to engage the creationists and intelligent design advocates in public forums. Scientists are their own worst enemy, Dr. Olson maintains, when they think biology and rhetoric don't mix—that explaining the importance of evolutionary theory to citizens is beneath them. He cautions half-jokingly, "If evolutionists don't learn to adapt to the new media environment, then their message could go the way of the dodo!"[3] Similarly, feminist challenges to traditional philosophy call attention to possible sources of bias in modes of philosophizing, pointing to rhetorical impulses in the works of great philosophers.[4] In other words, rhetoricians can identify persuasive elements in all discourse, including scientific and philosophical communication.

A rhetorical perspective, then, focuses on the sorts of issues on which informed and honest people can disagree. It focuses on how people arrive at social truths; that is, on the kinds of truths created and tested by people in groups and that influence social and political decisions. These truths represent what a group of people agrees to believe or accept; such truths become what the group takes to be "common sense."

Among the important social truths a rhetorical perspective might teach you to examine are the processes by which taxpayers, parents, congressional committees, school boards, and citizens respond to issues that cannot be resolved solely through objective means such as logical analysis and experimental testing. Should affirmative action programs, for example, be used to rectify past discrimination against minorities and women? Early acceptance of affirmative action as an appropriate remedy for past discrimination has shifted as doubts arise about "quotas" or "reverse discrimination." What constitutes discrimination? What remedies for past discrimination are fair to all those who compete for jobs and admission to educational programs? As another example, should air quality standards be set high enough that cars must be redesigned to use alternative energy sources, gasoline reformulated, and industries converted to use less polluting fuels? How can we balance our concern for healthy industries that create good jobs with the impact of pollution on the environment and on human health? Still another example: Will harsh penalties for convicted rapists provide better protection for women, or will such penalties increase the reluctance of juries to convict?

For social questions such as these, philosophers can point out contradictions in our thinking and spell out the implications of a given position. Social scientists can give us the best available data about the lack of women and minorities in categories of employment, about available pools of minority applicants for jobs, about causes and effects of pollution, and about the low conviction rates of accused rapists. When we have looked at the data and examined the logic of the conclusions drawn from them, we still must make decisions that go beyond the facts and make commitments that go beyond sheer logic.

Why Has Rhetoric Become a Dirty Word?

Not so long ago, the predominant meaning [of rhetoric] was "the art of expressive speech" or "the science of persuasion"; now the much-abused word, with a root related to "oratory," is laden with artificiality: empty talk is "mere" rhetoric.

But rhetoric, in its positive sense, fills a linguistic need: "The technique of articulate argument" is too much of a mouthful. If we mean "empty talk," or wish to deride the fulsome fulminations of a blowhard, we already have a large selection of sneering synonyms available: from the euphemism "bushwa" to the acronym "bomfog." ([The word] "bomfog," an acronym for "brotherhood of man, fatherhood of God," is not written in caps—because it relies on its similarity to two small words.)

The most effective way to rehabilitate "rhetoric," I think, is to offer a colorful, yet suitably pedantic term to cover its pejorative meaning. The word I have in mind is *bloviation*, a noun back-formed from the verb *bloviate*. (A verb is useful, too—you can't say "rhetoricize," and "orate" does not have the specifically spurious connotation.)

Bloviation is most often associated with the statements of Warren Gamaliel Harding—"Gamalielese," H. L. Mencken called it—but the word has deep roots as an authentic Americanism. In *Dictionary of Slang, Jargon & Cant*, Albert Barrère and Charles Leland placed *bloviate*'s origin before 1850, and defined it as "verbosity, wandering from the subject, and idle or inflated oratory or blowing, but which word it was probably suggested, being partially influenced by 'deviate.'"

So, if you mean "bloviating," get off "rhetoric's" back: We need "rhetoric" to do a job that no other word does as well.

Source: William Safire, *Safire's New Political Dictionary* (New York: Random House, 1993).

From its beginnings, this emphasis on social truths has been the distinctive quality of a rhetorical perspective. What fragmentary historical records exist seem to indicate that rhetoric was first studied and taught early in the fifth century BCE by sophists or wise men in Greek city-states around the Mediterranean. These city-states began to become more democratic, and as citizens met together to decide the laws under which they would live, as they brought suits and defended themselves against charges of wrongdoing, and as they celebrated the values that gave them a sense of identity, the need to speak cogently and clearly became increasingly important. Accordingly, men such as Gorgias of Leontini, Protagoras, Isocrates, and others began to teach male citizens (only males were allowed to speak and vote) how to present their ideas more effectively and to write about what made some speeches more persuasive and some speakers more appealing than others.

WHAT IS RHETORIC?

The oldest major treatise on the art of rhetoric that is still available to us is *On Rhetoric*, written by Aristotle in fourth-century BCE Athens. The Greek word for rhetoric comes from *rhêtorikê*, *-ikê* meaning "art or skill of," and *rhêtór*, meaning an experienced political/public speaker. Rhetoric, then, was for Aristotle the art or skill of speaking in the sorts of public forums common in ancient Athens—in the legislative assembly, in the courts, and on ceremonial occasions. The aim of such speaking was social influence, or persuasion. Thus, he defined rhetoric as "the ability, in each [particular] case, to see the available means of persuasion" (1355b).[5]

In *Rhetoric* and in his other works, Aristotle distinguished among kinds of truth. He believed that there were certain immutable truths of nature, which he designated as the province of metaphysics or science (*theoria*). He also recognized a different sort of truth consisting of the wisdom or social knowledge (*phronêsis*) needed to make choices about matters affecting communities or a whole society. These truths, not discoverable through science or analytic logic, he described as contingent; that is, as dependent on cultural values, the situation or immediate context, and the nature of the issue. They were the special concerns of the area of study he called *rhetoric*, the means of making decisions on issues where "there is not exact knowledge but room for doubt" (1356a).[6]

The contingent qualities of social truths can best be illustrated by looking at what it means to say that something is "a problem." Put simply, a problem is the gap that exists between what you think ought to be (value) and what is; it is the discrepancy between the ideal and the real, between goals and achievements. Problems come to exist because people can perceive and define them as such in interaction—that is, through rhetoric. As you will realize, what is a problem for one person (or group) may not be a problem for another person (or group). Some U.S. citizens, for example, perceive a problem with current income tax laws that they believe give an advantage to individuals with very high incomes at the expense of workers who earn much less. The problem, as they see it, is a matter of fairness (a value), and they urge lawmakers to raise the income tax rate for those with high incomes. Other citizens, however, view individuals with high incomes as "job creators" who stimulate economic growth through their investments. As they see it, raising taxes on high-income individuals would stifle that investment and harm the economy overall—especially for those with lower incomes.

Quite obviously, then, defining problems depends on goals and values, and these can change. In this same sense social truths—and thus rhetoric—are "subjective" and "evaluative"; rhetoric addresses issues that arise because of people's values, and these will change through time in the face of altered conditions.

Rhetoric is, of course, also concerned with data that establish what exists and with logical processes for drawing conclusions from facts and implications from principles and assumptions. Indeed, Aristotle considered rhetoric an offshoot of logic, and a rhetorical perspective is characterized not only by an emphasis on social truths but also by an emphasis on reason-giving or justification in place of coercion or violence. This distinction can be subtle. In general, rhetorical efforts seek to affect the free choices of groups or individuals, whereas coercion creates situations in which only one choice seems possible—the costs of any other option are too high, the pressure too great, the threat too terrible. Violence coerces by threatening bodily harm or death if any choice but that desired is made. Reason-giving assumes that by presenting the implications of the available options, one can persuade an audience to choose from among them freely, based on the reasons and evidence offered. Rhetoric presumes that audiences have some real freedom of choice.[7]

Of course not all of the reasons used by rhetors (those who initiate symbolic acts seeking to influence others) will make sense to logicians or scientists. Some rhetorical reasons are grounded in facts and logic, but many others are grounded in religious beliefs, history, or cultural values; in associations and metaphors; in hunger or desire, resentments, or dreams. A rhetorical perspective is eclectic and inclusive in its search for what is influential and why. In fact, rhetoric's concern with justification grows out of its focus on social truths tested by people in their roles as voters, property owners, consumers, workers, parents, and the like. In other words, reasons are presented to the decision makers and evaluators to whom the rhetoric is addressed, the audience.

Obviously, in some situations you can say, "Do this and don't ask any questions—just trust me," but such situations are rare. Reasons can be omitted only when your relationship to those addressed is so close and strong that the relationship itself is the reason for action or belief.

In most cases, then, even those involving your nearest and dearest, you must give reasons, justify your views, explain your position. And you must do so in terms that will make sense to others. Rhetors must "socialize" or adapt their reasons to reflect shared values. It is more acceptable, for example, to explain that you run several miles every day to maintain your weight and protect your health than to say that you run for the joy of it, for the sheer physical pleasure it gives you. Socialized reasons are widely accepted, meaning they are agreed to by most people. U.S. culture is strongly pragmatic; therefore, "good" reasons tend to show that an act is useful and practical. U.S. culture is strongly capitalistic; therefore, good reasons tend to show that an act is profitable, or assume that an action should be judged by its impact on "the bottom line." Other societies and some U.S. subcultures place greater emphasis on the sensual and aesthetic; for them, good reasons affirm behavior that is pleasurable and expressive, such as precision ice skating, acrobatic skateboarding, skillful hang gliding, dancing the tango really well, losing oneself in musical sound, singing in close harmony, rapping, or savoring and preparing unusual foods, regardless of whether or not those behaviors are pragmatic of economically beneficial.

Because rhetoric is addressed to others, it is reason-giving; and because it is social and public, it uses as reasons the values accepted and affirmed by a subculture or culture. In this way, rhetoric is tied to social values, and rhetors' statements will reflect the social norms of particular groups, times, and places (see Figure 1–1).

Because it is addressed to others, providing justifications that they will understand and feel, rhetoric is a humanistic study, and as such it examines all kinds of human symbol use, even the bizarre and perverse. From the beginnings of rhetoric in classical antiquity, rhetoricians have understood that persuasion occurs through both argument and association, through the cold light of logic and the white heat of passion, through explicit values and subconscious needs and associations. Accordingly, the field of rhetoric has come to examine all of the available means by which we are influenced and by which we can influence others. Thus modern interpretations of rhetoric go far beyond Aristotle's emphasis on the art or skill of speaking in public. As we suggested earlier in

Figure 1–1
What Is Rhetoric?

- Rhetoric is the study of what is persuasive.

- Rhetoric is the purposive use of messages to invite assent.

- Rhetoric is the craft of producing reason-giving discourse that is grounded in social truths.

this chapter, a contemporary rhetorical perspective seeks to understand the potential for social influence in all forms of symbol use—written and spoken language; nonverbal behaviors; fine arts such as paintings, drawings, and sculptures; music; visual images such as photographs, motion pictures, or television programs; and probably more.

In summary, rhetoric is the study of what is persuasive. The issues with which it is concerned are social truths, addressed to others, justified by reasons that reflect cultural values. Rhetoric is a humanistic study that examines all the symbolic means by which influence occurs.

There are seven defining characteristics of rhetoric, each beginning with the letter *p* (see Figure 1–2). First and foremost, rhetoric is *public*; that is, it is addressed to others. It is public because it deals with issues and problems that one person alone cannot answer or solve; the issues are communal; the solutions require cooperative effort. Because rhetoric is addressed to others, it is *propositional*; developed through complete thoughts. That's the case because one person's ideas must be made intelligible and salient for others whose cooperation is needed; that's also the case because much rhetoric is argumentative, making claims and offering reasons in their support. In that sense rhetoric is not random thoughts but some kind of coherent, structured statement about an issue or concern. As you will immediately recognize, rhetoric is *purposive*, aimed at achieving a particular goal, such as selling a product or influencing thought or action. Even the most apparently expressive discourse can have some kind of instrumental or purposive goal; for example, cheering for a team expresses the feelings of fans, but it raises the morale of players and may improve their performance, helping them to win. That's closely related to rhetoric's emphasis on *problem solving*. Most rhetorical discourse arises in situations in which we as audience and rhetors experience a felt need: a desire for closure (farewell address), a desire to mark beginnings and initiate a process (inaugural address), a desire to acknowledge death and to memorialize (eulogy). In some cases, of course, the problem is more concrete: how can a fair and accurate resolution be reached about eminent domain, high-tech surveillance, and access to medical records—all issues that pit privacy rights against government safeguards? Closely related to rhetoric's purposive, problem-solving qualities is an emphasis on the *pragmatic*. The Greek word *praxis* or action is the root for "practical," meaning that it can be put into effect or enacted. Pragmatic is a synonym of practical, but it also

Rhetoric is ...

- public
- propositional
- purposive
- problem solving
- pragmatic
- poetic
- powerful

Figure 1–2
The Seven Ps of Rhetoric

stresses facts and actual occurrences, but with an emphasis on practical outcomes. In this sense rhetoric is material; it produces actions that affect us materially; it is active, not just contemplative.

In what may seem to be a contradiction, rhetoric is *poetic*; that is, rhetoric frequently displays ritualistic, aesthetic, dramatic, and emotive qualities. The rhetoric of the mass, of communion, and of other religious rituals reinforces belief; what is pleasing and appealing to our senses, such as metaphor and vivid description, invites our participation and assent. Dramatic narrative captures our attention and involves us with characters, dialogue, and conflict and excites us emotionally so that we care about what happens and identify with the people we encounter. Those rhetorical works we call eloquent are good examples of these qualities, illustrated here and in subsequent chapters by speeches by Abraham Lincoln and Martin Luther King Jr. and by essays that involve us in the lives of people whose stories teach us lessons.

Finally, because rhetoric is all of these—public, propositional, purposive, problem solving, pragmatic, and poetic—it is *powerful*, with the potential to prompt our participation, invite identification, alter our perceptions, and persuade us. Accordingly, it has the potential to help or harm us, elevate or debase ideas, and make or break careers, and thus has significant ethical dimensions.

RHETORICAL ACTS

As we have described it, a rhetorical perspective takes note of the rhetorical or persuasive dimension in all human symbol-using behavior. Although all human actions can be considered implicitly persuasive, we do not wish to define "the rhetorical act" so broadly. The lines separating rhetorical acts from other acts are difficult to draw, however, and in this book we shall treat the concept of rhetoric in both its broad and its narrow senses.

The broadest view of rhetoric is expressed in the statement, "You can never not communicate," meaning that whatever you do or say (or don't do or say) can be observed and interpreted. For example, an unsmiling expression can be interpreted as evidence of sadness (rather than thoughtfulness), a young African American man walking home from work is perceived by some as menacing, or a woman walking home late from work is sometimes assumed to be extending a sexual invitation. Any behavior can become rhetorical when someone interprets or misinterprets it and is influenced by that interpretation, whatever the actor's intentions may have been.

In a more narrow sense, of course, many acts are intentionally rhetorical—advertisements, music videos, editorials, book and movie reviews, and films, essays, sermons, and speeches that declare a position and seek to defend it or make it attractive to others. When we address you as speakers or writers, we are speaking of rhetorical acts as intentional, deliberate attempts to influence others. When we act as critics or analysts and address you as critics and analysts, however, we comment on all possible persuasive effects, both intentional and unintentional. To understand rhetoric, you must fathom all the processes of influence, and as a rhetor you must come to terms with unintended and accidental effects—especially because some of them may work against your purpose.

In other words, defined most broadly, *rhetoric* is the study of all the processes by which people influence each other through symbols, regardless of the intent of the source.

A *rhetorical act*, however, is an intentional, created, polished attempt to overcome the challenges in a given situation with a specific audience on a given issue to achieve a particular end. A rhetorical act creates a message whose shape and form, beginning and end, are stamped on it by one or more human authors with goals for an audience. If you study all forms of influence, you will become aware of all the available resources for persuasion. Similarly, when you analyze your rhetoric and that of others, you must consider persuasive effects that may not have been fully under the control of or consciously intended by the source.

RHETORICAL PURPOSES

Because intention and impact are so important to a rhetorical perspective, we want to consider the range of meanings included in the words *persuasion* and *influence*. From the persuader's point of view, these meanings describe a range of purposes or intentions, not simply agreement or opposition. From the point of view of a reader, listener, or viewer, they reflect processes that constantly engage us as we experience the world, try to understand it, and decide what actions, if any, would be appropriate as responses. In other words, rhetorical purposes are conscious attempts to influence processes that are occurring in us all of the time as we come in contact with the world and the people in it.

Creating Virtual Experience

Through their use of symbols, rhetors call up ideas, pictures, and experiences in those they address. If a rhetor writes, "The burning sun beat down on the stubble in the oat field, and seen through a haze of sweat, the stalks suddenly seemed to be hair sprouting in a crew cut from the scalp of a red-haired giant," you can draw on past sensations and experiences to re-create your own mental picture. Although each reader's picture will be different, and each will reflect the reader's unique past, most will concern summer in a rural area.

Fundamentally, to act rhetorically is to communicate or to initiate an act—to express something in symbols—that someone else can translate into virtual experience. When something is virtual, it does not exist in fact; it is *as if* it existed. There is no sun, no stubble, no sweat, no scalp, no red hair, no giant on this page. But if a rhetor writes about them vividly enough, you can imagine them; it is as if you saw and heard and felt them here and now. That re-creation in your mind is virtual experience. In response to the rhetor's words, you imagine a scene, create a mental picture, and what you experience is virtual experience—experience called forth and shaped by your response to the symbols produced by someone else. Effective communication creates an image or idea in your mind that approximates the image or idea that the speaker or author wished to convey.

In other words, the fundamental rhetorical purpose, the most basic kind of influence—communicating—requires you to initiate a rhetorical act that can be translated into virtual experience by others. The most basic question in rhetoric is how to do that.

One kind of rhetorical action is intended primarily to produce virtual experience. Most works of literature, for example, are written to expand and shape our experience.

In them one sees, hears, smells, tastes, and touches vividly and concretely and feels intensely, and these sensations are shaped and formed into a satisfying and complete experience. When such works are transformed into dramas presented on stage or in film or television, the words become lived experience incarnated in actors' dialogue, movements, and feelings. In such processes, producers, directors, and actors do what all of us do each day as we translate the symbols we encounter into units of meaning based on our own experiences; the greater the range of our experiences, the greater our potential for imagining these dramas on the stages of our minds, of comprehending and identifying with the messages of others.

Altering Perception

Literary works can also have political effects by altering our perception or under-standing of situations and events. Charles Dickens's *Oliver Twist*[8] re-created the experiences of orphans in English poorhouses so movingly that readers demanded reform. Harriet Beecher Stowe's *Uncle Tom's Cabin*[9] depicted scenes of slavery so vividly that the book became a major force for its abolition. The same sensory or aesthetic stimuli that enliven good literature are a major means of persuasion. By creating virtual experience—the more vivid the better—literature can contribute to the second rhetorical purpose we want to discuss: altering perception.

George Washington wrote, "It is among the evils, and perhaps not the smallest, of democratic governments, that the people must *feel* before they will *see*."[10] Whether or not you must experience something before you can comprehend it, it is surely true that vivid experience improves our capacity to understand.

For an example of how an author can change the meaning of an experience for an audience—that is, alter perception of that experience—consider what Corlann Gee Bush does to one's experience of a series of paintings by the famous western artist and sculptor, Charles M. Russell. In her essay "The Way We Weren't: Images of Women and Men in Cowboy Art," she writes about how cowboy art has influenced viewers to believe in "the romantic West, the West of myth and legend."[11] She is particularly concerned with how women were depicted and uses five portraits of a Keeoma woman by Russell as illustrations. In these paintings an American Indian woman is shown in either a reclining or hip-slung pose as a highly sensual and spirited person. As ordinary viewers, we are likely to assume that these are portraits of a real person and take them as indications of the character of Keeoma women in the nineteenth century. To alter such a perception, Corlann Bush tells us:

> The truth is that Russell's wife, Nancy, was the model for the paintings. To pose, she dressed in buckskin and surrounded herself with artifacts. Russell painted the objects realistically; he painted her as an Indian. In this way he was able to paint his wife as the sensual woman he knew her to be while preserving her place within the moral code of white society.... This repressed sexuality was transposed onto an Indian woman who did not exist but who lived, nonetheless, deep in the subconscious of white American males. (27)

Once we have this information, we see the paintings differently; they become a visual record not of a Keeoma woman of the past but of the stereotypes of American Indian women in the nineteenth century that persist in the paintings.

Our impressions of the U.S. West have also been influenced by popular culture, including the novels of Louis L'Amour, John Wayne westerns, television series such as

Bonanza and *Gunsmoke*, and by miniseries based on Larry McMurtry's novels. If your images of the West come from such sources, your perceptions may be altered by information provided by historians. For example, although African Americans rarely have appeared in the West of popular culture, we were surprised to learn that "George W. Saunders of the Trail Drivers Association, as valid an authority as there is, estimated that about 25 percent of all cowhands were black."[12] Although they constituted only a small percentage of western settlers, Robert Haywood explains why such a large percentage of cowhands were African Americans:

> In an age when blacks were stereotyped as either foolish or primitive and where their opportunities to advance, either socially or economically, were limited, ranch-related jobs offered more dignity and more opportunity for self-expression than any other employment available. Whites in the ranching business realized the importance of the contributions of all cowboys—black, white, or Mexican—and adjusted their prejudices accordingly.... The mutual interdependence left little room for arrogant displays of racial superiority or overt discrimination, no matter how ingrained. (169)

If we accept it as true, Haywood's information may alter our perceptions of the popular culture portrait of the West, and he makes his rather surprising data more plausible by explaining why African Americans tended to congregate in this somewhat unlikely occupation.

Our perception of cowboys was also altered by the provocative western film, *Brokeback Mountain,* directed by Ang Lee. The tender, tragic love story of two men challenges western mythology about tough he-men, such as those seen in cigarette advertising or in John Wayne westerns. These lonely men, one an orphan starved for affection and the other living in the shadow of his father's disapproval, find tenderness and affection in each other in their isolated jobs as sheepherders through a long summer. As we experience the movie, perceptions of cowboys in the West, isolated from civilization under brutal conditions, as we have previously experienced them in books and movies, may subtly be changed.

Perceptions of gay men also may be affected by the example of John Amaechi, the first former professional basketball player to be openly gay, who has written an autobiography, *Man in the Middle.* The six-foot, ten-inch former center for the Orlando Magic was asked if he thought we would ever see an active male player come out. He replied: "We're asking the people with the most to lose financially, emotionally, psychologically, to fall on their sword in the hope that it will change the world.... [I]f the image of a young boy [Matthew Shepard] without his shoes being strapped to a fence and left to die doesn't end homophobia, then a gay Shaq won't either.[13]

To recapitulate, the most minimal rhetorical purpose, the smallest effect produced, is to add to the sum of your audience's experiences. If you can frame such experiences, you may be able to influence how those virtual experiences are interpreted.

Explaining

If we evaluated rhetorical acts by how much they altered beliefs, nearly all would be failures. Normal, healthy human beings whose physical environments are under their own control do not change their beliefs in response to a single message— whether the message lasts five minutes or five hours. If people are influenced to alter their beliefs, they do so over weeks, months, or even years, and in response to many different messages.

The need for explanation is most strongly felt when we encounter an intense, apparently irrational experience. Let us suppose, for example, that you read or hear news reports about Trayvon Martin, an unarmed African American teenager in Sanford, Florida, who was shot and killed by an Hispanic neighborhood watch patrolman, George Zimmerman, in February 2012. In response to this highly controversial and widely publicized incident, many editorials appeared trying to explain why it happened and what it meant, often accompanied by statements about how we should respond. As the controversy swirled, family members of both men, their attorneys, and their supporters made repeated television appearances in which they offered their explanations of events leading up to and following the killing. Like these editorial writers, attorneys, and other individuals, rhetors often provide explanations for events that have disturbed those they address. Note, however, that an encounter with a disturbing event precedes the felt need for explanation. As a result, rhetors sometimes begin by creating that kind of experience through vivid language and disturbing information and then offer and justify what they believe is the most plausible explanation.

Linda A. Fairstein, former director of the Sex Crimes Prosecution Unit in the Manhattan District Attorney's Office, began prosecuting rape cases in the mid-1970s and is the author of a book called *Sexual Violence: Our War Against Rape*.[14] Much of the book describes the changes that have occurred in rape laws, which no longer require corroboration of an alleged victim's testimony, for example. Because it is partly a memoir of her career and partly a series of real-life crime stories, the book's vivid virtual experience of how the criminal justice system treats rape victims, describes the experiences of individuals with whom we can identify. This evidence is obviously intended to alter perception. However, Fairstein goes beyond the data to explain and to argue that rape is different from other violent crimes because it is so much more intimate, which emphasizes the significance of the sexual element in this crime. Her views will find a ready audience because women, particularly the millions of rape victims, have found rape to be a special kind of outrage whose impact often persists for years in nightmares and sleeplessness. Fairstein's book provides much evidence about rape and about its treatment in the criminal justice system; it documents the horrors that occur but gives hope that legal changes have made the system better able to understand the crime and to punish those who commit it.[15]

Formulating Belief

By this time it should be apparent that rhetorical action is not a one-shot event but a process. Although there is a somewhat orderly progression from enlarging audience experience to altering perceptions, which, in turn, leads to a search for explanations, followed by efforts to determine which interpretation is most satisfactory, these are not discrete, separable processes for coming to terms with experience nor are they discrete rhetorical purposes. Virtual experience occurs within some kind of framework; new experience can alter a framework to change perception. When perceptions change, we seek explanations; sometimes we demand explanations before we consider altering our perceptual framework, perhaps even before participating in the creation of virtual experience. As these other processes overlap and intersect, so do the processes by which we formulate a belief or discard one belief for another. Similarly, the processes by which a rhetor urges us to believe arise out of prior experience and conceptualization.

As an illustration, let us return to the nineteenth-century U.S. West. Virtual experience might be created by the autobiography of Nat Love, also known as "Deadwood Dick," one of the West's most notorious African American cowboys,[16] or by reading the memoir of Charlie Siringo, the "cowboy detective" who wrote of experiences on the trail with African American trail riders,[17] or from the biography of Print Olive, one of Dodge City's toughest ranchers, whose life was saved by James Kelly during a shootout in a saloon.[18] The experiences they provide would challenge those in most popular culture. Before prior perceptions were abandoned, however, you might seek out historical works, such as *The Negro on the American Frontier* by Kenneth W. Porter, *The Black West* by Loren Katz (both cited earlier), or *Black People Who Made the Old West* by Loren Katz[19] testing whether the experiences depicted were accurate and typical and seeking explanations of why African Americans were disproportionately represented among cowhands in the West.

Once that was completed, new questions might arise. Why haven't western novels, films, and television programs reflected this reality? At this point, you are an audience member prepared to consider the claims of a rhetor who attempts to convince you that these omissions were no accident but a result of the racism that is a legacy of the history of slavery in the United States. Such a rhetor might have gone through the process we've described to reach a point at which everything seemed to fall together and a belief emerged. Many rhetorical acts attempt to produce such a "precipitating moment" in which the audience agrees, "That's it. That's the way it is." Few rhetorical acts succeed, however, in taking members of an audience through all these stages to transform their attitudes. At best, most confirm a position already being considered (somewhere between the search for explanation and the choice of one interpretation) or reinforce an explanation the audience has pondered and considers plausible. Indeed, those who achieve such modest goals have been resounding successes as persuaders.

Initiating Action

Let us suppose, however, that you are present at a rhetorical event that formulates the beliefs of a group about the misrepresentation of African American cowhands in the West. The pleased rhetor now urges action—but finds that most audience members are not ready to do anything about it. Those who share this belief may not write novels or produce films or television programs; indeed, they may not have the resources to do any of those things. Even if they share this attitude, they may not believe that action is needed; concern about misrepresentation may be a low priority.

As this example suggests, shared belief is not necessarily linked to a willingness or an ability to act. At such a moment, doubts arise about whether beliefs have really been formulated, and such doubts have merit. But an examination of rhetorical processes suggests that the situation is normal. Even when beliefs are formulated, action will not follow unless that belief is reinforced, rendered salient, and then channeled so that action seems appropriate, possible, and necessary. Note that these processes are the primary function of most religious discourse, which is designed to urge people to act on their faith, to put their beliefs into practice.

Although the audience in this case might not include writers or television or film producers, it may well include parents, perhaps even members of school boards. A skillful rhetor might want to urge the inclusion of more material about African American history in elementary and secondary schools and suggest that this misrepresentation is just one example of the lack of such material, an example that is particularly telling because it reflects a distortion that reduces the African American past to slavery, ignoring the diverse, positive images that all students need to encounter in order to form a more accurate picture of the nation's past.

The chances of success in initiating action would increase if other messages reinforced such proposals and suggested the importance of teaching more African American history. Television specials on racism include studies demonstrating that many African American children still have negative self-images, first identified in earlier studies by Kenneth Clark that formed part of the basis for the 1954 Supreme Court desegregation decision in *Brown v. Board of Education* (347 U.S. 483 [1954]).[20] Buttressed by such reinforcing messages, a rhetor who proposed action to change curriculum and textbooks would have a better chance of succeeding.

If messages and events support each other and are publicized, beliefs will be strengthened, and concerned individuals will form or join groups to formulate plans for influencing the school board and textbook publishers. Rhetorical acts aimed at initiating action will appear. An editorial will urge that units on African American history be developed and included in the curriculum; a parent group will press the school administration to act and formulate a committee to coordinate efforts to modify textbooks.

Maintaining Action

Then, when the intense interest generated by dramatic events lessens, rhetorical acts will be needed to ensure that the new units remain in the curriculum, that as history texts are revised they continue to include such materials, that teachers continue to use them in classes, that African American teachers and principals are hired, retained, and supported. Such rhetorical action perpetuates what has been institutionalized, as illustrated by the yearly report to the PTA on test scores and dropout rates that reaffirms the school's successes with its varied pupils; the Sunday sermon to the regular churchgoer, which urges continued support and attendance; the monthly ritual of prayer and reports of activities at the Phyllis Wheatley women's club that reinforces their motto of "lifting as we climb";[21] the singing of the national anthem before baseball games, which proclaims the patriotism of sport. In fact, ritualized rhetorical actions are especially pervasive examples of this rhetorical purpose. Convocation and commencement exercises, memorial services, retirement and anniversary celebrations, induction and award ceremonies, and engagement and wedding tributes all are events whose primary rhetorical purpose is reaffirming communal norms, or maintaining rhetorical action.

This progression reflects the rhetorical dimensions in all human behavior and links them to the purposes that emerge in rhetorical acts (see Figure 1–3). It should suggest to you as a prospective persuader that your choice of a purpose should reflect the prior experiences of your audience and should be attuned to the events taking place in your environment.

Creating Virtual Experience	Altering Perception	Explaining	Formulating Belief	Initiating Action	Maintaining Action
Use sensory cues to re-create an experience	Give a fresh angle on an old topic	Develop the who, what, where, why, when, and how	Prepare a one-sided case	Urge behavioral change	Rally the troops
Creates identification	Combats inattention	Satisfies the search for knowledge	Refines issues	Transforms convictions into deeds	Reinforces commmitment to causes
Film: IMAX theater experience	Bumper Sticker: Trust in God, She will provide	Book: *Kids & Guns*	Editorial: "The Problem with School Vouchers"	Website: N.O.R.M.L	Advertising: Presale savings for preferred customers

Figure 1–3
Range of Rhetorical Purposes

THE DISCIPLINE OF RHETORIC

Rhetoric is also the name of an academic discipline. A discipline is a field of study, an area of expertise, a branch of knowledge. A discipline provides theory, application, and experimentation, and criticism to test them all. *Theories* are explanations that seek to account for processes and data. Rhetorical theories seek to account for the processes in language and people that influence belief and action. *Applications* are rules for action that are developed from theory. Rhetorical applications suggest how you can use rhetorical principles to be an effective moral agent and to protect yourself—that is, to think critically and make informed judgments—as you participate in rhetorical action initiated by others. *Experimentation* seeks to isolate variables or elements in the persuasive process and to test theoretical explanations as carefully as possible. *Critical analysis* examines rhetorical acts in order to describe processes of influence and explain how they occur. Both experimentation and criticism (of theories, applications, experimental research, and rhetorical action) contribute to the modification and application of theory.[22] In the chapters that follow, we develop theory about the nature and application of rhetorical processes, which is supported by experimental research and critical analysis that qualify, refine, and illustrate these theoretical concepts.

In its theory, the discipline of rhetoric examines the symbolic dimensions of human behavior in order to offer the most complete explanations of human influence. This broad view is tested by critical analysis. Rhetorical application focuses more narrowly on rhetorical acts—written and spoken messages designed to achieve predetermined effects in an audience. Experimental studies of persuasion focus more narrowly on rhetorical acts and test the adequacy of prior explanations of them and the appropriateness of rules for application.

As a discipline, rhetoric is the study of the art of using symbols. This understanding is reflected in many well-known definitions of rhetoric: "That art or talent by which discourse is adapted to its end" (George Campbell);[23] "the use of language as a symbolic means of inducing cooperation in beings that by nature respond to symbols" (Kenneth Burke);[24] as well as the definition from Aristotle that we offered earlier in this chapter. In other words, the academic discipline of rhetoric offers theory, application, experimentation, and critical analysis. It studies the social use of words by people in groups, the political use of words to decide who shall make what kinds of decisions, and the ethical use of words to justify belief and action through cultural values. Rhetoric is related to logic and empirical validation because it uses these materials. It is different from philosophy and science because it studies all the available processes for influencing people, and it defines influence broadly. Accordingly, it considers how people use language to alter perception, to explain, to change, reinforce, and channel belief, and to initiate and maintain actions. Put in more traditional terms, it studies all the ways in which symbols can be used to teach, to delight, and to move.

This book is based on the ancient idea of the relationship between art and practice—the belief that you cannot improve a skill such as speaking or writing unless you understand the theory, the concepts, and the ideas on which it is based. Conversely, you cannot understand the theory unless you use it and test it in practice. In our view, this ancient relationship demands that those who would learn about rhetoric must take the posture of a rhetor-critic. The rhetor is an initiator of rhetorical action who tries to make the choices that will make her the most effective moral agent. As a rhetor you come to understand all the forces at work in persuasion, some of which are outside your control. The critic analyzes, describes, interprets, and evaluates rhetorical acts to understand what they are and how and for whom they work. As a critic you learn to criticize your own rhetoric to improve it, and as a critic-consumer you learn to analyze others' rhetoric in order to make decisions as intelligently as possible.

CRITICISM IS FEEDBACK

As students of communication you already know that the communicative process is not one-sided. Rather, receivers (audiences) virtually always send return messages back to sources (rhetors). Many models of communication call those return messages "feedback." When you speak or write, the immediate audience gives you useful but limited feedback. If you speak, they look at you intently, smile in amusement, frown in puzzlement, look away in annoyance or boredom, read the paper, sleep, take a note to check out a statistic, and the like. If you write a letter to the editor or an op-ed, your piece may be rejected or printed in an altered, edited form and provoke rejoinders—more feedback. If you are in a class and your instructor has other students discuss your speech or essay, you will discover that most reactions were not evident from facial reactions or movements. You will discover that the messages you could not see or misinterpreted or were only implied by editing are very important—perhaps the most important.

Similarly, when your instructors discuss your speech or essay in class or write comments, you will discover that their observations are different—less superficial, more helpful, linked to concepts you have studied and discussed in class. Such feedback is criticism—the careful analysis and evaluation by an experienced student of rhetoric who has heard and read many rhetorical acts, pondered many critical analyses, studied available theories, and read many experimental studies. Ideally, you should aspire to be such a critic, and the aim of this book is to teach you to be one. If you understand rhetorical processes, you have the best chance of steadily improving your performance and of succeeding consistently. You will know how to evaluate your own work, and you will be prepared to consider carefully and learn from the rhetoric of others.

No one can teach you rules that will apply in all cases or even predict the occasions for rhetorical action that each of you will encounter. If you are to be an effective persuader, able to communicate your experiences, to place them in interpretive frameworks, to justify your interpretation as most plausible, and to initiate and maintain action consistent with your interpretation, you will need skills that enable you to find the words that will create virtual experience in your audience, to discover a framework that is intelligible in that particular time and place, to select justifications with salience on that specific issue, and so on. As a result, this book does not try to teach you universal rules (there are none!) but instead tries to teach you to be a critic. In each case, theory and application are related to critical analysis of rhetorical acts, with the goal of teaching you how to analyze your own and others' rhetoric. To the degree that we succeed in doing that, the process of learning that begins here can continue outside the classroom and throughout your life.

 MATERIAL FOR ANALYSIS

The Real Heroes and Sheroes of New Orleans

by Larry Bradshaw and Lorrie Beth Slonsky[25]

1   TWO DAYS after Hurricane Katrina struck New Orleans, the Walgreens store at the corner of Royal and Iberville Streets in the city's historic French Quarter remained locked. The dairy display case was clearly visible through the widows. It was now 48 hours without electricity, running water, plumbing, and the milk, yogurt, and cheeses were beginning to spoil in the 90-degree heat.

2   The owners and managers had locked up the food, water, pampers and prescriptions, and fled the city. Outside Walgreens' windows, residents and tourists grew increasingly thirsty and hungry. The much-promised federal, state and local aid never materialized, and the windows at Walgreens gave way to the looters.

3   There was an alternative. The cops could have broken one small window and distributed the nuts, fruit juices and bottled water in an organized and systematic manner. But they did not. Instead, they spent hours playing cat and mouse, temporarily chasing away the looters.

4   We were finally airlifted out of New Orleans two days ago and arrived home on Saturday. We have yet to see any of the TV coverage or look at a newspaper. We are willing to guess that there were no video images or front-page pictures of European or affluent white tourists looting the Walgreens in the French Quarter.

5   We also suspect the media will have been inundated with "hero" images of the National Guard, the troops and police struggling to help the "victims" of the hurricane. What you will not see, but what we witnessed, were the real heroes and sheroes of the hurricane relief effort: the working class of New Orleans.

6   The maintenance workers who used a forklift to carry the sick and disabled. The engineers who rigged, nurtured and kept the generators running. The electricians who improvised thick extension cords stretching over blocks to share the little electricity we had in order to free cars stuck on rooftop parking lots. Nurses who took over for mechanical ventilators and spent many hours on end manually forcing air into the lungs of unconscious patients to keep them alive. Doormen who rescued folks stuck in elevators. Refinery workers who broke into boat yards, "stealing" boats to rescue their neighbors clinging to their roofs in flood waters. Mechanics who helped hotwire any car that could be found to ferry people out of the city. And the food service workers who scoured the commercial kitchens, improvising communal meals for hundreds of those stranded.

7   Most of these workers had lost their homes and had not heard from members of their families. Yet they stayed and provided the only infrastructure for the 20 percent of New Orleans that was not under water.

8   On day two, there were approximately 500 of us left in the hotels in the French Quarter. We were a mix of foreign tourists, conference attendees like ourselves and locals who had checked into hotels for safety and shelter from Katrina.

9   Some of us had cell phone contact with family and friends outside of New Orleans. We were repeatedly told that all sorts of resources, including the National Guard and scores of buses, were pouring into the city. The buses and the other resources must have been invisible, because none of us had seen them.

10   We decided we had to save ourselves. So we pooled our money and came up with $25,000 to have ten buses come and take us out of the city. Those who didn't have the requisite $45 each were subsidized by those who did have extra money.

11   We waited for 48 hours for the buses, spending the last 12 hours standing outside, sharing the limited water, food and clothes we had. We created a priority boarding area for the sick, elderly and newborn babies. We waited late into the night for the "imminent" arrival of the buses. The buses never arrived. We later learned that the minute they arrived at the city limits, they were commandeered by the military.

12   By day four, our hotels had run out of fuel and water. Sanitation was dangerously bad. As the desperation and despair increased, street crime as well as water levels began to rise. The hotels turned us out and locked their doors, telling us that "officials" had told us to report to the convention center to wait for more buses. As we entered the center of the city, we finally encountered the National Guard.

13   The guard members told us we wouldn't be allowed into the Superdome, as the city's primary shelter had descended into a humanitarian and health hellhole. They further told us that the city's only other shelter—the convention center— was also descending into chaos and squalor, and that the police weren't allowing anyone else in.

14 Quite naturally, we asked, "If we can't go to the only two shelters in the city, what was our alternative?" The guards told us that this was our problem—and no, they didn't have extra water to give to us. This would be the start of our numerous encounters with callous and hostile "law enforcement."

15 We walked to the police command center at Harrah's on Canal Street and were told the same thing—that we were on our own, and no, they didn't have water to give us. We now numbered several hundred.

16 We held a mass meeting to decide a course of action. We agreed to camp outside the police command post. We would be plainly visible to the media and constitute a highly visible embarrassment to city officials. The police told us that we couldn't stay. Regardless, we began to settle in and set up camp.

17 In short order, the police commander came across the street to address our group. He told us he had a solution: we should walk to the Pontchartrain Expressway and cross the greater New Orleans Bridge to the south side of the Mississippi, where the police had buses lined up to take us out of the city.

18 The crowd cheered and began to move. We called everyone back and explained to the commander that there had been lots of misinformation, so was he sure that there were buses waiting for us. The commander turned to the crowd and stated emphatically, "I swear to you that the buses are there."

19 We organized ourselves, and the 200 of us set off for the bridge with great excitement and hope. As we marched past the convention center, many locals saw our determined and optimistic group, and asked where we were headed. We told them about the great news.

20 Families immediately grabbed their few belongings, and quickly, our numbers doubled and then doubled again. Babies in strollers now joined us, as did people using crutches, elderly clasping walkers and other people in wheelchairs. We marched the two to three miles to the freeway and up the steep incline to the bridge. It now began to pour down rain, but it didn't dampen our enthusiasm.

21 As we approached the bridge, armed sheriffs formed a line across the foot of the bridge. Before we were close enough to speak, they began firing their weapons over our heads. This sent the crowd fleeing in various directions.

22 As the crowd scattered and dissipated, a few of us inched forward and managed to engage some of the sheriffs in conversation. We told them of our conversation with the police commander and the commander's assurances. The sheriffs informed us that there were no buses waiting. The commander had lied to us to get us to move.

23 We questioned why we couldn't cross the bridge anyway, especially as there was little traffic on the six-lane highway. They responded that the West Bank was not going to become New Orleans, and there would be no Superdomes in their city. These were code words for: if you are poor and Black, you are not crossing the Mississippi River, and you are not getting out of New Orleans.

24 Our small group retreated back down Highway 90 to seek shelter from the rain under an overpass. We debated our options and, in the end, decided to build an encampment in the middle of the Ponchartrain Expressway—on the center divide, between the O'Keefe and Tchoupitoulas exits. We reasoned that we would be visible to everyone, we would have some security being on an elevated freeway, and we could wait and watch for the arrival of the yet-to-be-seen buses.

25 All day long, we saw other families, individuals and groups make the same trip up the incline in an attempt to cross the bridge, only to be turned away—some chased away with gunfire, others simply told no, others verbally berated and humiliated. Thousands of New Orleaners were prevented and prohibited from self-evacuating the city on foot.

26 Meanwhile, the only two city shelters sank further into squalor and disrepair. The only way across the bridge was by vehicle. We saw workers stealing trucks, buses, moving vans, semi-trucks and any car that could be hotwired. All were packed with people trying to escape the misery that New Orleans had become.

27 Our little encampment began to blossom. Someone stole a water delivery truck and brought it up to us. Let's hear it for looting! A mile or so down the freeway, an Army truck lost a couple of pallets of C-rations on a tight turn. We ferried the food back to our camp in shopping carts.

28 Now—secure with these two necessities, food and water—cooperation, community and creativity flowered. We organized a clean-up and hung garbage bags from the rebar poles. We made beds from wood pallets and cardboard. We designated a storm drain as the bathroom, and the kids built an elaborate enclosure for privacy out of plastic, broken umbrellas and other scraps. We even organized a food-recycling system where individuals could swap out parts of C-rations (applesauce for babies and candies for kids!).

29 This was something we saw repeatedly in the aftermath of Katrina. When individuals had to fight to find food or water, it meant looking out for yourself. You had to do whatever it took to find water for your kids or food for your parents. But when these basic needs were met, people began to look out for each other, working together and constructing a community.

30 If the relief organizations had saturated the city with food and water in the first two or three days, the desperation, frustration and ugliness would not have set in.

31 Flush with the necessities, we offered food and water to passing families and individuals. Many decided to stay and join us. Our encampment grew to 80 or 90 people.

32 From a woman with a battery-powered radio, we learned that the media was talking about us. Up in full view on the freeway, every relief and news organizations saw us on their way into the city. Officials were being asked what they were going to do about all those families living up on the freeway. The officials responded that they were going to take care of us. Some of us got a sinking feeling. "Taking care of us" had an ominous tone to it.

33 Unfortunately, our sinking feeling (along with the sinking city) was accurate. Just as dusk set in, a sheriff showed up, jumped out of his patrol vehicle, aimed his gun at our faces and screamed, "Get off the fucking freeway." A helicopter arrived and used the wind from its blades to blow away our flimsy structures. As we retreated, the sheriff loaded up his truck with our food and water.

34 Once again, at gunpoint, we were forced off the freeway. All the law enforcement agencies appeared threatened when we congregated into groups of twenty or more. In every congregation of "victims," they saw "mob" or "riot." We felt safety in numbers. Our "we must stay together" attitude was impossible because the agencies would force us into small atomized groups.

35 In the pandemonium of having our camp raided and destroyed, we scattered once again. Reduced to a small group of eight people, in the dark, we sought refuge in an abandoned school bus, under the freeway on Cilo Street. We were hiding from possible criminal elements, but equally and definitely, we were hiding from the police and sheriffs with their martial law, curfew and shoot-to-kill policies.

36 The next day, our group of eight walked most of the day, made contact with the New Orleans Fire Department and were eventually airlifted out by an urban search-and-rescue team.

37 We were dropped off near the airport and managed to catch a ride with the National Guard. The two young guardsmen apologized for the limited response of the Louisiana guards. They explained that a large section of their unit was in Iraq and that meant they were shorthanded and were unable to complete all the tasks they were assigned.

38 We arrived at the airport on the day a massive airlift had begun. The airport had become another Superdome. We eight were caught in a press of humanity as flights were delayed for several hours while George Bush landed briefly at the airport for a photo op. After being evacuated on a Coast Guard cargo plane, we arrived in San Antonio, Texas.

39 There, the humiliation and dehumanization of the official relief effort continued. We were placed on buses and driven to a large field where we were forced to sit for hours and hours. Some of the buses didn't have air conditioners. In the dark, hundreds of us were forced to share two filthy overflowing porta-potties. Those who managed to make it out with any possessions (often a few belongings in tattered plastic bags) were subjected to two different dog-sniffing searches.

40 Most of us had not eaten all day because our C-rations had been confiscated at the airport—because the rations set off the metal detectors. Yet no food had been provided to the men, women, children, elderly and disabled, as we sat for hours waiting to be "medically screened" to make sure we weren't carrying any communicable diseases.

41 This official treatment was in sharp contrast to the warm, heartfelt reception given to us by ordinary Texans. We saw one airline worker give her shoes to someone who was barefoot. Strangers on the street offered us money and toiletries with words of welcome.

42 Throughout, the official relief effort was callous, inept and racist. There was more suffering than need be. Lives were lost that did not need to be lost.

Questions for Analysis

1. What rhetorical purposes are evident in this article? Which ones are most pronounced?
2. In what ways does this rhetorical act underscore the seven Ps of rhetoric?
3. How does the authors' use of vivid depiction invite readers to participate in the rhetorical act?
4. In what ways does language use contribute to that vivid depiction?
5. Have the authors' characterizations of government officials and agencies influenced those officials and agencies in later disasters or emergencies?

Source: http://socialistworker.org/2005-2/556/556_04_RealHeroes.

EXERCISES

Critical Thinking Exercises

1. Consider how some widely publicized events illustrate the range of rhetorical purposes described in this chapter. For example, how did the mass shootings at Columbine High School in Littleton, Colorado, Virginia Tech University, the movie theatre in Aurora, Colorado, and the Sandy Hook Elementary School in Newtown, Connecticut, influence attitudes on gun control? Media violence? Parental responsibilities? Safety on campus? The stigma of mental illness? The effects of bullying behavior? How did the events of 9/11/01 change attitudes about civil liberties? About intelligence agencies? About Arab Americans? About the threat of terrorism? About the Israeli–Palestine conflict? Do these examples illustrate the movement from one rhetorical purpose to another? How?

2. The history of rhetoric and communication is embedded in and revealed by the meanings, usage, and origins of these terms. Both the history and the varied meanings of these words can be discovered this way. Individually or in small groups, look up rhetoric and communication (or communications) in one of the following: *Encyclopedia of Rhetoric, Encyclopedia of Rhetoric and Composition, The Oxford English Dictionary, Roget's Thesaurus, Encyclopedia of Philosophy, A Dictionary of Word Origins, The Dictionary of the Social Sciences,* M. H. Abrams's *A Glossary of Literary Terms,* William Safire's *Safire's New Political Dictionary, Encyclopedia Britannica* (compare essays in different editions), or other similar references. Then, in class, compare and contrast the definitions, meanings, and information about word origins that were found. How old is the study of rhetoric? Of communication? What is the difference between *communication* and *communications*? Edward Schiappa has made a strong case in *The Beginnings of Rhetorical Theory in Classical Greece* (Yale, 1999) that Plato is the person who coined the word *rhetoric.* Given Plato's hostility to rhetoric, how might that have affected its meaning?

3. Consider the following scenarios. Which rhetorical purpose is most evident? Explain your choice:
   a. When students in a college sociology class must use a wheelchair for a full day to go anywhere and record their observations of how people interact with them, what rhetorical purpose is achieved?
   b. When food critics write such descriptions as "Taste the melt-in-your-mouth tender cuts of beef sautéed in a succulent garlic butter sauce and topped with braised scallions, spicy peppercorn, and lightly cooked whole mushrooms," they are engaged in what rhetorical purpose?
   c. When it's Girl Scout Cookie time, Girl Scouts will knock at doors asking individuals to sign their pledge cards and order. What rhetorical purpose do they hope to fulfill?
   d. When an advertisement reads "As a Target valued customer, we will offer you a 'sneak preview' of our

Fall Sale. We appreciate your continued support and hope to see you Saturday," it is hoping to achieve what rhetorical purpose?

Analytical Writing Exercises

Portfolio Project: An Overview

4. One of the best ways to make criticism a practical, marketable activity is to showcase your critical thinking and writing abilities in accessible project form to potential employers. Increasingly, portfolios are a popular way to do that. A portfolio is a collection of your best coursework assignments, arranged artfully and presented in a slick binder, three-ring notebook, or bound book. Sometimes, portfolio samples represent sustained work, such as a campaign or research project. The portfolio project suggested here is of that sort. In each chapter, you will be given a specific entry to work on. The first, careful decision you must make is to choose an issue that is important to you. Find three interesting and sufficiently complex rhetorical selections about this issue drawing from different forms of expression (newspapers, magazines, books, speeches, films, websites, TV and radio programming) created by different rhetors and fulfilling different rhetorical purposes. Selections must be cleared by your instructor. Craft an opening paragraph that explains why you are interested in this particular social issue and why you have selected these three rhetorical artifacts to represent that issue. Be sure to give full source citations for your rhetorical selections. Then proceed to the various portfolio entries. You may want to consult the three components of a good introduction outlined in Chapter 3 for more specific help.

Portfolio Entry 1: Purpose

5. Explain the ways in which each artifact fulfills different purposes on the range of rhetorical purposes. What do you learn about this issue from identifying how rhetors use rhetoric for different ends?

Strategic Speaking Exercise

6. As art forms, poetry and photography act rhetorically to create virtual experience. Bring a favorite short poem or photo to class and give a one- to two-minute oral presentation that examines how its purpose is to create virtual experience. Instructor approval required. Choose three of the seven "Ps of rhetoric," and explain how these characteristics are at work in your rhetorical artifact.

NOTES

1. James Herrick, *The History and Theory of Rhetoric: An Introduction*, 3rd edition. (Boston: Pearson Education, 2005), p. 31.

2. Stephen Jay Gould, "So Near and Yet So Far," *New York Review of Books*, October 20, 1994, p. 26.

3. Randy Olson, Watkins Distinguished Lecture Series, Wichita State University, May 7, 2007. See also his documentary: *Flock of Dodos: The Evolution-Intelligent Design Circus* (2006), available for viewing on ShowTime.

4. In "Feminists and Philosophy," *New York Review of Books*, October 20, 1994, pp. 59–63, Martha Nussbaum, a professor of philosophy, classics, and comparative literature at Brown University and a visiting professor of law at the University of Chicago, reviews a collection of essays by feminist philosophers who write in defense of reason, yet she comments: "feminists note that males who wish to justify the oppression of women have frequently made a pretense of objectivity and of freedom from bias in sifting evidence, and have used the claim of objectivity to protect their biased judgments from rational scrutiny" (pp. 60–61).

5. Aristotle, *On Rhetoric: A Theory of Civic Discourse*, trans. George A. Kennedy (New York: Oxford University Press, 1991), p. 36.

6. Aristotle, *On Rhetoric*, p. 38.

7. Some behaviorists argue that all choice is an illusion; if so, all efforts at influence are pointless. Consider whether media coverage of "terrorist rhetoric" is misnamed. Is it, rather, "terrorist coercion"?

8. Or, *The Parish Boy's Progress* (London: R. Bentley, 1838).

9. (London: J. Cassell, 1852).

10. George Washington to Henry Knox, 8 March 1787m, The Papers of George Washington, Confederation Series, 5:74–75.

11. Susan Armitage and Elizabeth Jameson, eds., *The Women's West* (Norman: University of Oklahoma Press, 1987), pp. 19–33. Cited material on p. 27.

12. J. Marvin Hunter, ed., *The Trail Drivers of Texas: Interesting Sketches of Early Cowboys* (Austin: University of Texas Press, 1985, p. 453), cited in C. Robert Haywood, " 'No Less a Man': Blacks in Cow

Town Dodge City, 1876–1886," *The Western Historical Quarterly,* May 1988, pp. 161–82, cited material on p. 169. See also Kenneth W. Porter, *The Negro on the American Frontier* (New York: Arno Press, 1971), pp. 521–22; William Loren Katz, *The Black West* (Garden City, NY: Doubleday, 1971), p. xi.

13. Dave Zirin, "John Amaechi's Timeout," *The Nation,* April 16, 2007, pp. 22, 24. Cited material on p. 24.

14. (New York: William Morrow & Company, 1993). For additional analysis of rape laws and the difficulties of prosecution, see Stephen J. Schulhofer, *Unwanted Sex: The Culture of Intimidation and the Failure of Law* (Cambridge, MA: Harvard University Press, 1998).

15. Another example of rhetorical explanation is *Reproducing Rape: Domination Through Talk in the Courtroom* (Chicago: University of Chicago Press, 1993), in which Gregory Matoesian analyzes transcripts of rape trials to show how courtroom talk by lawyers can shape or socially construct the victim's testimony to fit male standards of legitimate sexual practice, transforming the experience of rape into routine consensual sex.

16. *The Life and Adventures of Nat Love* ... (1907; Baltimore: Black Classic Press, 1988).

17. Charles A. Siringo, *Riata and Spurs* (Boston: Houghton Mifflin, 1927), pp. 17–18, 28.

18. Harry E. Chrisman, The Ladder of Rivers: The Story of I. P. (Print) Olive (Denver: Sage, 1962), p. 122.

19. See William Loren Katz, author of *Black People Who Made the Old West* (Trenton, NJ: Africa World Press, 1992) and of "The Black West," letter to the editor, *New York Times,* June 2, 1993, p. A10.

20. Kenneth B. Clark, *Dark Ghetto: Dilemmas of Social Power,* (New York: Harper & Row, 1965).

21. Phyllis Wheatley (1753–1784), a West African slave from Boston, was bought by Quakers who opposed slavery and educated her and promoted her writing talent. A collection of her poetry, *Poems on Various Subjects,* was published in 1773. She was free but penniless after her mistress died. She married, but her husband first abused, then deserted her. Impoverished, she and her three children died in an epidemic. "Lifting as we climb" is the motto of the National Association of Colored Women's and Girls' Clubs.

22. Karlyn Kohrs Campbell, "The Nature of Criticism in Rhetorical and Communicative Studies," *Central States Speech Journal,* 30 (1979): 4–13.

23. *The Philosophy of Rhetoric,* ed. Lloyd F. Bitzer (Carbondale: Southern Illinois University Press, 1963), p. 1.

24. *A Rhetoric of Motives,* (1950; Berkeley: University of California Press, 1969), p. 43.

25. Reprinted with permission from SocialistWorker.org. Copyright © Larry Bradshaw and Lorrie Beth.

Chapter 2

Reading Rhetorical Acts

In the first chapter we discussed rhetoric, the rhetorical dimension in all human action, and rhetorical acts in general. In this chapter we examine two rhetorical acts in some detail. Here we begin to act as critics rather than as ordinary observers or consumers of rhetoric.

As Chapter 1 made clear, we are all ordinary observers or consumers of the rhetorical acts that bombard us daily. We may be moved by those rhetorical acts to change our attitudes or beliefs or even to change our behaviors, or those rhetorical efforts may fail to affect us. Either way, as ordinary observers we are likely unable to explain, or perhaps we are even unaware of, *why* those messages were either effective or ineffective. As critics, however, our aim is different: it is to describe, interpret, and evaluate rhetorical acts in order to understand why they succeed or fail. Put differently, the role of a critic is to make explicit and understandable those elements of rhetorical acts that are often unnoticed by ordinary observers or consumers but that nevertheless account for their effectiveness or ineffectiveness.

However, criticism is not a matter of "being critical" or "attacking" a speech or a speaker. Rather, it is specialized feedback, a process that occurs in stages: description, interpretation, and evaluation. The critical process serves two important functions. Whether or not you aim toward a career in which writing or speaking plays a central role, you must act as a critic in order to cope in an age of information explosion that will require you to sift and evaluate massive amounts of discourse—in news reports, advertising, and entertainment programming as well as political debates and speeches at various levels of government. Thus the first important function of criticism is to serve as a form of consumer protection, protecting you as a consumer of persuasion. In addition, the feedback dimension of criticism can influence subsequent rhetorical action. That is, by identifying those elements of rhetorical acts that are effective—or ineffective—criticism functions to provide guidelines for later speaking and writing.

As a craft, criticism requires *specialized tools*, beginning with a handy lexicon or set of terms for clear and meaningful explication of rhetorical acts. Criticism also demands a certain *attitude*—an inquisitiveness or a passion to decipher symbols born out of appreciation and suspicion of the many ways rhetoric influences us. The three diagrams on the following pages illustrate the skills, attitude, and lexicon you will need to perform criticism (see Figure 2–1, Figure 2–2, and Figure 2–3).

Figure 2–1
What Is Criticism?

- An acquired thinking, speaking, and writing skill

- A process of description, interpretation, and evaluation

- A certain attitude: a passion to uncover the many ways in which rhetoric influences us

Figure 2–2
The Five Characteristics of the Critic

The Critic is ...
- knowledgeable/has expertise

- able to communicate clearly and efficiently

- passionate about what he/she critiques

- able to tell us the nonobvious

- able to educate and edify listeners about a message

Critic	Reporter
Critic	**Reporter**
How was it said?	What was said?
Why?	Where/Who/When?
Motive	Facts
Implicit	Explicit
Analysis	Paraphrase
Depth	Surface
Detective	Police officer
Color commentator	Play-by-play
Persuasive	Informative
Moral	Amoral

Figure 2–3
The Critic versus the Reporter

READING ANALYTICALLY

The first stage of the critical process, description, begins with a distinctive form of reading rhetorical acts that we call *descriptive analysis*. At this point, you are probably more familiar with other forms of reading. For example, we usually read novels, short stories, poetry, and the like for *entertainment*—for the excitement of the plot, the thrill of solving the mystery, or the beauty of the poetic verse. At other times we read for *content*, such as when we read a newspaper to learn about current events in our community, follow a recipe to cook a delightful dinner, or when we follow the directions to put together a new piece of furniture, perhaps a computer desk or shelving unit, for which "some assembly is required." Reading the textbook to prepare for a multiple-choice examination in your history class is another example of reading for *content*.

Reading rhetorical acts *analytically* is a different matter. Content and perhaps even entertainment can be important dimensions of rhetorical acts, but reading them analytically focuses attention instead on *how they are intended to work* in order to influence audiences. We have developed a *lexicon*, or set of terms, essential to descriptive analysis. These terms provide both a way of *gaining* entry into rhetorical acts—that is, they direct attention to rhetorically significant elements—and a set of labels to enable critics to talk about those rhetorically significant elements or parts of a rhetorical act. The terms name seven general categories of descriptive analysis as follows:

1. **Purpose:** the conclusion argued (thesis) and the response desired by the rhetor. Some purposes are *instrumental*; they seek a change in belief or attitude or even an overt action from the audience. Some purposes are *consummatory*; they seek appreciation, contemplation, or conferring honor or blame.
2. **Audience:** the receivers of a rhetorical act. This includes an immediate audience, a target audience, a role created by the rhetor for the audience, or specialized audiences (VIPs) with social or political power to effect change. In this initial,

descriptive phase of criticism, the aim should be to identify the audience or audiences that the rhetorical act seems to *seek*. That is, the aim should be to identify the people or sorts of people most likely to be influenced.

3. **Persona:** the role(s) adopted by the persuader in making the argument (for example, teacher, preacher, reporter, prophet, or mediator).

4. **Tone:** the rhetor's attitude toward the subject (detached, emotional, satirical, and so forth) and toward the audience (personal/impersonal, authoritative/egalitarian/supplicant, and so on).

5. **Evidence:** the different kinds of support material for the argument or claims made in the rhetorical act.

6. **Structure:** the way the materials are organized to gain attention, develop a case, and provide emphasis. Structure can be obvious or apparent, like the organizational pattern of the speech or essay. Or, it can be more subtle, such as an underlying organizational principle that unifies the rhetorical act and drives it forward.

7. **Strategies:** the adaptation of all of the above, including language, appeals, and argument, to shape the materials to overcome the challenges the rhetor faces (the rhetorical context).

These categories (and their subcategories) of descriptive analysis are a set of labels or terms that direct attention to the rhetorically significant elements of a rhetorical act in order to describe it as fully and carefully as possible, in other words, to read a rhetorical act *analytically*.

These seven terms also identify the choices speakers and writers must make as they prepare and deliver rhetorical acts. For instance, rhetors must choose their purpose and determine just whom they are addressing—that is, the *target audience* they most wish to influence—very early in the process. Rhetors must also select a method of organization and the evidence or supporting materials they will use, although as the two rhetorical acts included in this chapter indicate, there are many options. Speakers and writers must also choose the role or *persona* they will adopt. Will they assume the role of a peer of the audience? An expert on the topic? A leader? A supplicant? Rhetors must also be aware of the *tone* of their message and the attitudes toward both the subject and the audience that it reveals. The category of strategy is the most difficult and requires perhaps the most careful choices. Ideally, rhetors carefully study rhetorical theories and hear many rhetorical acts in order to discover what strategies are available to them and identify those that might be most effective in any particular case. As you will discover, these elements are always present and almost always important in understanding how and why a rhetorical act succeeded or failed in its purpose.

In sum, descriptive analysis offers a vocabulary for discussing rhetorical action and a method to identify what is distinctive about a particular persuasive effort. Both a vocabulary and a method are needed if you are to become sophisticated consumers of contemporary persuasion. Skillful rhetors understand both their own acts and those of others. Your ability to initiate rhetorical action and to control how others influence you depends in part on your accuracy in describing discourse.

The first rhetorical act that we analyze here is one of the most famous in U.S. history, the speech that President Abraham Lincoln made on November 19, 1863, at the battlefield at Gettysburg where the Union won an important but costly battle in July of that year. As the address makes clear, the war was not yet over.

MATERIAL FOR ANALYSIS I

Lincoln's Gettysburg Address

Four score and seven years ago our fathers brought forth on this continent, a new nation, conceived in liberty, and dedicated to the proposition that all men are created equal. Now we are engaged in a great civil war, testing whether that nation, or any nation so conceived and so dedicated, can long endure. We are met on a great battlefield of that war. We have come to dedicate a portion of that field, as a final resting place for those who here gave their lives that this nation might live. It is altogether fitting and proper that we should do this.

But, in a larger sense, we cannot dedicate—we cannot consecrate—we cannot hallow—this ground. The brave men, living and dead, who struggled here, have consecrated it, far above our poor power to add or detract. The world will little note nor long remember what we say here, but it can never forget what they did here. It is for us the living, rather, to be dedicated here to the unfinished work which they who fought here have thus far so nobly advanced. It is rather for us to be here dedicated to the great task remaining before us—that from these honored dead we take increased devotion to that cause for which they gave the last full measure of devotion—that we here highly resolve that these dead shall not have died in vain—that this nation, under God, shall have a new birth of freedom—and that government of the people, by the people, for the people, shall not perish from the earth.

Rhetorical Analysis of Lincoln's Gettysburg Address

To answer the question, why do criticism? we offer this analysis of Lincoln's Gettysburg Address. In using the seven elements of descriptive analysis, the critique addresses the following points: (1) why this speech has "lived" on as a rhetorical force, (2) how the speech reveals Lincoln's rhetorical artistry, (3) how the speech helps us appreciate the symbolic virtuosity of humans, and (4) how words contribute to the making of history. (See Figure 2–4.)

Elements of Descriptive Analysis Applied

Purpose

Instrumental (what action is expected?): To dedicate ourselves to complete the unfinished work to preserve the Union. ("It is for us the living, rather, to be dedicated here to the unfinished work...")

Consummatory (what feelings are prompted?): To memorialize those who fought and died here; to honor the slain soldiers. ("We have come to dedicate a portion of that field, as a final resting place for those who here gave their lives...")

Range of rhetorical purposes: Formulate belief/initiate action.

Response desired: The Union must be preserved and be constituted as a nation of free people (belief to be formulated). We must commit ourselves to advancing the cause of liberty and to preserving a unified nation (action to be initiated).

Figure 2–4
*Seven Elements
of Descriptive
Analysis*

PURPOSE (Aims) What are the **ends** of the discourse? What **means** are used to achieve these ends?

AUDIENCE (Publics) What are the **immediate, target, created,** and **VIP** audiences?

PERSONA (Role of Rhetor) What is the rhetor-audience relationship? What role does the rhetor play?

TONE (Attitude) What is the attitude toward the subject? What is the attitude toward the audience?

STRUCTURE (Organizational Pattern) What are the parts of speech? What are the organizational patterns?

EVIDENCE (Support Material) What kinds of support is used? Visuals? Analogies? Stories? Experts? Statistics?

STRATEGIES (Tactics) What are the special language, psychological appeals, and arguments used to adapt to the context to achieve purpose?

© Cengage Learning

Thesis: We must be "dedicated here to the unfinished work which they who fought here have thus far so nobly advanced" and that this nation, "dedicated to the proposition that all men are created equal…shall not perish from the earth."

Audience

Immediate: The thousands gathered for the eulogizing of the dead at the makeshift cemetery in Gettysburg, Pennsylvania. ("We have come to dedicate a portion of that field, as a final resting place for those who here gave their lives….")

Target: U.S. citizens sympathetic to abolishing slavery and maintaining a unified nation. ("Four score and seven years ago our fathers brought forth on this continent, a new nation, conceived in liberty, and dedicated to the proposition that all men are created equal. Now we are engaged in a great civil war, testing whether that nation, or any nation so conceived and so dedicated, can long endure.")

Created: A reenergized citizenry committed to carrying on the fight of those who gave their lives for their country. ("It is rather for us to be here dedicated to the great task remaining before us—that from these honored dead we take increased devotion to that cause for which they gave the last full measure of devotion—that we here highly resolve that these dead shall not have died in vain—that this nation, under God, shall have a new birth of freedom—and that government of the people, by the people, for the people, shall not perish from the earth.")

Agents-of-Change: Union military personnel ("The brave men, living and dead, who struggled here, have consecrated it, far above our poor power to add or detract. The world will little note nor long remember what we say here, but it can never forget what they did here.")

Persona

Relationship to audience: Peer (repetition of "we" and "our").

Relationship to subject: Inferior ("The brave men, living and dead, who struggled here, have consecrated it, far above our poor power to add or detract. The world will little note nor long remember what we say here...").

Role: Camouflaged presence (no "I" statements; no references to himself as president or commander-in-chief). If anything, Lincoln emerges as an apolitical figure, a moral voice, the conscience of the nation: "In a larger sense, we cannot dedicate—we cannot consecrate—we cannot hallow—this ground."

Tone

Formal, solemn: "Four score and seven years ago...."
Plain, simple, ordinary language: ("We are met on a great battlefield of that war. We have come to dedicate a portion of that field, as a final resting place....")
Moral: "...this nation, under God, shall have a new birth of freedom—and... shall not perish from the earth."

Structure

Chronology: Starts with "Four score and seven years ago..." and ends with the future, "the great task remaining before us...."

Evidence

No statistics, no stories.
One comparison: Past nation and future nation.
Authority: The Declaration of Independence ("all men are created equal").

Strategies

Language:

Birth imagery: "brought forth," "conceived," "new birth," "perish."

Repetition: "dedicate" is repeated six times; "here" recurs seven times.

Policy language: "proposition," "testing," "cause," "highly resolve."

Parallel structure: "...we cannot dedicate—we cannot consecrate—we cannot hallow."

Personification: Nation conceived in liberty.

Appeals:

Patriotism: "liberty," "freedom," "our fathers."

Sacrifice, service, duty: "...those who here gave their lives that this nation might live..."

Equality: "...men are created equal."

Religious: "...this nation, under God...shall not perish from the earth."

Arguments:

Deductive: "...proposition that all men are created equal."

Enthymeme: We should support the Union because it is most consistent with the principles underlying the nation.

Enthymeme: By using the term "proposition," Lincoln challenges the view that the "truths" enunciated in the Declaration of Independence are "self-evident."

Analogy: Our nation was conceived in liberty eighty-seven years ago and must remain committed to that noble cause.

Note that in each instance, a *claim* (or conclusion) is followed by *proof* (evidence from the speech). The third step is *analysis*: Why is this element present? What insights about the rhetoric emerge from recognizing this claim in the discourse? The following Questions for Analysis encourage you to wrestle with these critical "why" questions.

Questions for Analysis: Gettysburg Address

1. How do language strategies help Lincoln accomplish these two purposes: formulating belief and initiating action?
2. Why is Lincoln's persona so understated?
3. What is the tone of this address? Is it fitting for the occasion?
4. Who is his target audience? Why is this tricky given the occasion?
5. Considering Lincoln's daunting rhetorical challenge, why do you think this speech is still considered a masterpiece of rhetorical action?

 MATERIAL FOR ANALYSIS II

The rhetorical act we analyze below is the conclusion to the last speech of the Reverend Martin Luther King Jr. delivered in Memphis, Tennessee, on April 4, 1968. A strike by sanitation workers had begun on February 12, 1968, but little progress had been made toward resolving their grievances. A protest march led earlier by King on March 28, 1968, was poorly planned and organized and ended in violent encounters between marchers and police. The momentum of the civil rights movement as a whole had lessened, and King was struggling to be an effective leader. The need to encourage his audience of striking sanitation workers, to raise their morale, was great, but the past events were hardly cause for optimism. In the face of these challenges, King spoke, ending with a memorable peroration or conclusion that both transcended the immediate situation and placed it within the larger cause of social justice.

Conclusion of the Reverend Martin Luther King Jr.'s Speech, April 4, 1968[1]

1   And I want to thank God once more for allowing me to be here with you. You know several years ago I was in New York City autographing the first book that I had written. And while sitting there autographing books, a demented black woman came up. The only question I heard from her was, "Are you Martin Luther King?" And I was looking down writing, and I said yes. The next minute I felt something beating on my chest. Before I knew it, I had been stabbed by this demented woman. I was rushed to Harlem hospital. It was a dark Saturday afternoon. That blade had gone through and the x-rays revealed that the tip of the blade was on the edge of my aorta, the main artery. And once that's punctured, you drown in your own blood; that's the end of you. It came out in the *New York Times* the next morning that if I had merely sneezed, I would have died.

2   Well, about 4 days later, they allowed me, after the operation, after my chest had been opened and the blade had been taken out, to move around in a wheelchair in the hospital. They allowed me to read some of the mail that came in, and from all over the states and the world, kind letters came in. I read a few but there's one of them I will never forget. I had received one from the president and the vice president. I've forgotten what those telegrams said. I'd received a visit and a letter from the governor of New York, but I've forgotten what that letter said. But there was another letter that came from a little girl, a young girl who was a student at the White Plains High School, and I looked at that letter, and I'll never forget it. It said simply, "Dear Dr. King, I am a ninth grade student at the White Plains High School." She said, "While it should not matter, I would like to mention that I'm a white girl. I read in the paper of your misfortunes and of your sufferings. And I read that if you had sneezed, you would have died. I'm simply writing you to say that I am so happy that you didn't sneeze."

3   Because if I had sneezed, I wouldn't have been around here in 1960 when students all over the South started sitting in at lunch counters. And I knew that as they were sitting in, they were really standing up for the best in the American dream and taking the whole nation back to those great wells of democracy which were dug deep by the founding fathers in the Declaration of Independence and the Constitution.

4   If I had sneezed, I wouldn't have been around here in 1961 when we decided to take a ride for freedom and ended segregation in interstate travel.

5   If I had sneezed, I wouldn't have been around here in 1962 when Negroes in Albany, Georgia, decided to straighten their backs up. And whenever men and women straighten their backs up, they're going somewhere, because the man can't ride your back unless it is bent.

6   If I had sneezed, I wouldn't have been here in 1963 when black people of Birmingham, Alabama, aroused the conscience of this nation and brought into being the civil rights field.

7 If I had sneezed, I wouldn't have had a chance later that year in August to try to tell America about a dream that I had had.

8 If I had sneezed, I wouldn't have been down in Selma, Alabama, to see the great movement there.

9 If I had sneezed, I wouldn't have been in Memphis, to see a community rally around those brothers and sisters who are suffering. I'm so happy that I didn't sneeze. And they were telling me, now, it doesn't matter now, it really doesn't matter what happens now.

10 I left Atlanta this morning, and as we got started on the plane, there were six of us. The pilot said over the public address system, we're sorry for the delay. But we have Dr. Martin Luther King on the plane, and to be sure that all of the bags were checked, and to be sure that nothing would be wrong on the plane, we had to check out everything carefully. And we've had the plane protected and guarded all night. And then I got into Memphis. And some began to say the threats or talk about the threats that were out, what would happen to me from some of our sick white brothers. Well, I don't know what will happen now.

11 We've got some difficult days ahead but it really doesn't matter with me now, because I have been to the mountaintop. And I don't mind. Like anybody, I would like to live a long life; longevity has its place. But I am not concerned about that now. I just want to do God's will. And He's allowed me to go up to the mountain, and I've looked over and I've seen the Promised Land. I may not get there with you, but I want you to know tonight that we as a people will get to the Promised Land. So I am happy tonight. I am not worried about anything. I'm not fearing any man.

12 Mine eyes have seen the glory of the coming of the Lord.

Sample Critique: "I've Been to the Mountaintop"

Concepts illustrated:
a. How to apply the seven elements of descriptive analysis.
b. How to use "the critical equation" (Figure 2–5).

Figure 2–5
*The Critical
Equation "CPA"*

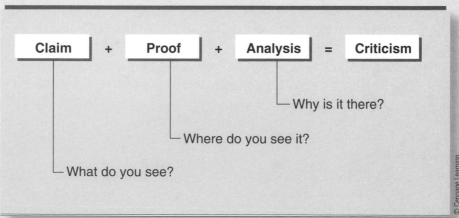

Claim + Proof + Analysis = Criticism
└ What do you see?
└ Where do you see it?
└ Why is it there?

© Cengage Learning

1. Purpose

Instrumental: King rallies the troops to action.

Consummatory: King eulogizes himself and the civil rights movement.

Continuum of rhetorical purposes: Maintaining action.

Responses desired: To inspire civil rights activists to continue the campaign for racial equality.

Thesis: Like the former Jewish slaves wandering in the wilderness, the descendants of former black slaves in the United States will reach the Promised Land.

The Critical Equation: CPA (Claim + Proof + Analysis)

King's speech aims to maintain action by inspiring civil rights activists to continue the campaign for racial equality. That is most evident in paragraphs 3–9 in which he catalogs the many past successes of the movement. Such a tactic is important at this stage in the movement when disillusionment might overwhelm idealism. King's primary argument is an enthymematic one; that is, King relies on his audience to use comparison to draw this conclusion: like the Jewish slaves in Egypt who were freed and reached the Promised Land, the descendants of former black slaves in the United States will achieve their goals. This central claim is most apparent when he says, "I want you to know tonight that we as a people will get to the Promised Land." Assuming that the audience sees the connection, that thesis is strategic because it invests the effort for civil rights with righteousness and associates it with a biblical success story. King's purpose, thus, is primarily instrumental because he wants to rally the troops to rededicate themselves to the cause. King also expresses some satisfaction about what the movement has accomplished, however, and his speech commemorates the movement and his work.

The expressive dimensions of what he says can be seen in such lines as these: "[I]t really doesn't matter with me now, because I have been to the mountaintop. And I don't mind. Like anybody, I would like to live a long life; longevity has its place. But I am not concerned about that now....I am not worried about anything. I am not fearing any man." Because King was assassinated shortly after he made this speech, the expressive value of the speech is greater now. The speech reads in places as if he had a premonition of his own death and delivered a eulogy for himself.

2. Audience

Immediate: Striking sanitation workers and their supporters.

Target: Civil rights sympathizers, particularly African Americans.

Created: You are part of a great and noble cause; rededicate yourselves to it.

Agents of change: Not addressed directly.

The Critical Equation: CPA (Claim + Proof + Analysis)

King spoke directly to striking sanitation workers in Memphis. Although this group was his immediate audience, his target audience was broader. He is trying to reach

African Americans who support the movement to achieve their civil rights. Passages to support this claim include all the abbreviated references to civil rights successes, from the sit-ins in North Carolina to the freedom rides all over the South, to the activism of "Negroes in Albany, Georgia," and the activism of "black people of Birmingham, Alabama," and supporters who came to the nation's capital in 1963 to take part in the demonstration at which King delivered his well-known "I have a dream" speech, to those fighting against injustices in Selma, Alabama, and Memphis (see paragraphs 3–9). King creates a role of activist for his target audience to play as he retells stories of heroism in the rank and file and prophesizes that the movement will succeed eventually, even if he is no longer around (see paragraph 11). Those who have the power to bring about the changes are legislators and judges. The effort to obtain full civil rights required both political and legal reform, yet in this speech excerpt, King does not address these agents of change or explain how his target audience can attract the attention of the political elite. King recognizes that the movement is in the doldrums and that his speech will be transmitted to other audiences through print and electronic media. King uses the occasion of speaking to Memphis sanitation workers to address a larger constituency and to urge them to rededicate themselves to the cause.

3. Persona

Relationship with the audience: Superior.

Role adopted: Prophet.

The Critical Equation: CPA (Claim + Proof + Analysis)

King adopts a superior relationship with his audience. There are many self-references ("I" statements), forty-five to be exact. Further, that King uses only personal examples to support his claims lets the listener/reader know that he is a powerful authority on this subject. More important, however, King cultivates the role of prophet. Prophets are people who are "called out" from the larger society by God. They stand alone. They are fearless and courageous. They are tested for their strength of character. They bring a divine message. They are visionaries. From the outset, King develops this important biblical role. He says, "I want to thank God once more for allowing me to be here with you" (paragraph 1). He then tells the story of his near-death experience (paragraphs 1–2), which like a true prophet allows us to see that he had been tested and chosen. He is a visionary because, like Moses who is allowed to glimpse the Promised Land from Mount Nebo, he has "been to the mountaintop" and done "God's will" and has "seen the Promised Land." This prophet persona is strategic for giving the cause an aura of invincibility and for giving it a biblical mandate, because if King is a modern Moses, his cause will surely succeed.

4. Tone

Attitude toward subject: (1) Reflective, intuitive, serene; (2) confident, hopeful, inspirational, visionary.

Attitude toward audience: Respectful, commendatory.

The Critical Equation: CPA (Claim + Proof + Analysis)

King's tone varies. He is reflective (past tense dominates the progression of his speech), intuitive ("I may not get there with you"), and serene ("I am not fearing any man"). This attitudinal cluster reinforces the consummatory purposes of the speech and is consistent with his prophetic persona. King is also hopeful and inspirational ("We as a people will get to the promised land."…"Mine eyes have seen the glory of the coming of the Lord.") This attitudinal cluster reinforces his prophetic persona and effectively meets the rhetorical challenge of buoying the hopes of disheartened people.

5. Evidence

Example: Two extended personal examples; several brief references to historical instances.

Statistics: None.

Authority: The speaker and the Bible.

Analogy: Enthymematic comparison of Israelite slaves and U.S. slaves.

The Critical Equation: CPA (Claim + Proof + Analysis)

King uses little evidence. Two detailed personal examples, one of his near-death experience in New York City (paragraphs 1–2), the other of his security difficulties in Atlanta (paragraph 10), compose the bulk of the supporting material. Other abbreviated examples of civil rights successes cluster in paragraphs 3–9. That King uses no other direct evidence except the example works well for his purposes. Prophets are authority figures; they do not need corroborating evidence for claims they make. Further, the example appeals to us on an emotional level. The story of the little girl's heartfelt get well letter is memorable and inspirational. Remember, too, that he is speaking to the committed, not to detractors, so the need for other forms of proof (statistics, authorities) is minimal. The analogy King develops is implicit. He does not say that U.S. blacks and Israelite slaves are similarly situated, but that is clearly the connection he wants the audience to make if they know their Bible. Hence, the analogy is enthymematic; it relies on audience participation.

6. Structure

Macro structure (Intro/body/conclusion): Conclusion is evident.

Micro structure: Chronology.

The Critical Equation: CPA (Claim + Proof + Analysis)

The speech excerpt analyzed here is the conclusion to a much longer speech. It is recognizable as a conclusion because of its foreshadowing of the end of the speech: "And I want to thank God once more for allowing me to be here with you." It also rises in intensity; hence, it is a *peroration*. It ends with a dramatic flair: "Mine eyes have seen the glory of the coming of the Lord." For the purposes of this speech, that kind of rousing ending is important. Strategically embedded in the context of that conclusion is chronological structure. King goes back to the earliest success of the movement in 1960, systematically works his way up to the present ('61, '62, '63,...'68), then ends with a visionary look into the future. Chronology is an especially good structure for showcasing the scope of a subject and gaining perspective on it. By using chronology, King is able to rekindle enthusiasm by reminding his audience of its scope and asking them to keep current troubles in perspective; the larger cause still looks good. Prophets, of course, have this ability to see the "big picture," the panoramic view.

7. Strategies

Language: Repetition, allusion, simple sentences.

Appeals: Emotional, democracy, righteousness, patriotism.

Arguments: Enthymeme.

The Critical Equation: CPA (Claim + Proof + Analysis)

King uses repetition ("If I had sneezed" is repeated seven times) to invite audience participation, contribute to his inspirational tone, reinforce his "tested" status as a prophet of the movement, and structure his message. He uses two allusions, the death of Moses after climbing Mount Nebo ("I've seen the Promised Land. I may not get there with you") and the words of the "Battle Hymn of the Republic" ("Mine eyes have seen the glory of the coming of the Lord") to associate the cause with righteousness and patriotism. The biblical connection makes the cause righteous. The line from the "Battle Hymn of the Republic" links the cause to patriotism and foreshadows success; Julia Ward Howe wrote that poem during the Civil War for the Union armies. King uses simple words throughout the conclusion, which reinforces his belief in the simplicity of his message and is an adaptation to his audience, many of whom have been deprived of advanced education.

The psychological appeals in the speech are many. An emotional appeal is made when King retells the story of the little white girl at the White Plains High School. An emotional appeal is made in the retelling of the stabbing incident, and the "if I had sneezed" refrain is a haunting reminder of the precarious circumstances of his life. King appeals to democracy and patriotism when he speaks of "those great wells of democracy which were dug deep by the founding fathers in the Declaration of Independence and the Constitution" and "the American dream" and the reference to the "Battle Hymn of the Republic." There are Christian/moral appeals in such lines as "I just want to do God's will," and "I want to thank God once more for allowing me to be here with you."

The arguments in this speech are enthymematic. This is not a logical, deductive presentation in which claims and proof and warrants are spelled out for the audience. In other words, it is not a logical speech; rather, the arguments are supplied by the audience from fragmentary clues that King provides. King claims that the civil rights movement will succeed. His proof for that claim is the sharing of his vision. The warrant for this argument is that his premonition is adequate proof for such a claim when the speaker is a prophetic figure. Another argument is that the civil rights message is a simple plea for equality; it is not a "black" demand or a "white" fear. Proof comes from the contrasting examples of the demented black woman who almost kills him and of the little white girl who admires him.

Given the length of time King had been active in the movement and that he is targeting those already committed to civil rights for all, it is appropriate that his arguments be exclusively enthymematic.

EXERCISES

Critical Thinking Exercises

1. Practice your critical abilities by using "the critical equation" (Claim + Proof + Analysis) for the following excerpts from "Madness Visible," "Hurricane Katrina—Our Experiences," the Material for Analysis from Chapter 1.

   a. Excerpt 1—Category Persona: What is the rhetor's (reporter's) relationship to her audience based on this passage?

      On Day 2, there were approximately 500 of us left in the hotels in the French Quarter. We were a mix of foreign tourists, conference attendees like ourselves, and locals who had checked into hotels for safety and shelter from Katrina. Some of us had cell phone contact with family and friends outside of New Orleans. We were repeatedly told that all sorts of resources including the National Guard and scores of buses were pouring in to the City. The buses and the other resources must have been invisible because none of us had seen them.

      We decided we had to save ourselves. So we pooled our money and came up with $25,000 to have ten buses come and take us out of the City. Those who did not have the requisite $45.00 for a ticket were subsidized by those who did have extra money. We waited for 48 hours for the buses, spending the last 12 hours standing outside, sharing the limited water, food, and clothes we had. We created a priority boarding area for the sick, elderly and new born babies. We waited late into the night for the "imminent" arrival of the buses. The buses never arrived. We later learned that the minute they arrived at the City limits, they were commandeered by the military.

   b. Excerpt 2—Category Tone: What is the attitude conveyed in this passage?

      Two days after Hurricane Katrina struck New Orleans, the Walgreen's store at the corner of Royal and Iberville streets remained locked. The dairy display case was clearly visible through the widows.

   It was now 48 hours without electricity, running water, plumbing. The milk, yogurt, and cheeses were beginning to spoil in the 90-degree heat. The owners and managers had locked up the food, water, pampers, and prescriptions and fled the City. Outside Walgreen's windows, residents and tourists grew increasingly thirsty and hungry.

      The much-promised federal, state and local aid never materialized and the windows at Walgreen's gave way to the looters. There was an alternative. The cops could have broken one small window and distributed the nuts, fruit juices, and bottle water in an organized and systematic manner. But they did not. Instead they spent hours playing cat and mouse, temporarily chasing away the looters.

   c. Excerpt 3—Category Audience: Who is the target audience in this passage?

      We were finally airlifted out of New Orleans two days ago and arrived home yesterday (Saturday). We have yet to see any of the TV coverage or look at a newspaper. We are willing to guess that there were no video images or front-page pictures of European or affluent white tourists looting the Walgreen's in the French Quarter.

      We also suspect the media will have been inundated with "hero" images of the National Guard, the troops and the police struggling to help the "victims" of the Hurricane. What you will not see, but what we witnessed, were the real heroes and sheroes of the hurricane relief effort: the working class of New Orleans. The maintenance workers who used a fork lift to carry the sick and disabled. The engineers, who rigged, nurtured and kept the generators running. The electricians who improvised thick extension cords stretching over blocks to share the little electricity we had in order to free cars stuck on rooftop parking lots. Nurses who took over for mechanical ventilators and spent many hours on end manually forcing air into the lungs of unconscious patients to keep them alive. Doormen who rescued folks stuck in elevators. Refinery workers who broke into boat yards, "stealing" boats to rescue their neighbors clinging to their roofs in flood waters. Mechanics who helped hot-wire any car that could be found to ferry people out of the City. And the food service workers who scoured the commercial kitchens improvising communal meals for hundreds of those stranded. Most of these workers had lost their homes, and had not heard from members of their families, yet they stayed and provided the only infrastructure for the 20 percent of New Orleans that was not under water.

2. Arrange for the class to attend a speech, perhaps a chapel or convocation speaker or a lecturer brought to campus for a special event. Spend the next class period describing that event analytically. What does such an analysis reveal that wasn't immediately apparent while you were listening to the speech?

Analytical Writing Exercises

3. Select an editorial from your local or school newspaper. Write a brief analysis of it using select elements of descriptive analysis that your instructor has assigned. Practice using the critical equation seamlessly—two to three pages.

NOTE

1. This is a transcription by the author of the conclusion as delivered. From "I've Been to the Mountaintop," by Martin Luther King Jr. Reprinted by arrangement with the Estate of Martin Luther King Jr., c/o Writers House

4. Locate two contrasting articles (advocating opposite positions) on one of the following topics: global warming, genetic cloning, or security in a post "9/11" world. Conduct a descriptive analysis of each. How is using the seven elements of descriptive analysis useful in discerning the rhetorical choices in each piece of scholarship? Which article is most compelling? Why? Which element of descriptive analysis is easiest to apply? Hardest? Why? What suggestions can you make for how each article might be more successful in advancing its purpose?—four to six pages.

Portfolio Entry 2: Persona/Tone

5. Compare and contrast how your three rhetorical selections use persona and tone to advance their purposes. This will require that you construct critical equations for each artifact—two to three pages.

Strategic Speaking Exercise

6. Using an element of descriptive analysis assigned by your instructor, craft a two- to three-minute "one-point" speech to alter perception of Robert F. Kennedy's impromptu speech in Indianapolis (see prologue). Practice formulating a seamless critical equation (claim + proof + analysis) to make your point.

as agent for the proprietor, New York, NY. Copyright 1968 Dr. Martin Luther King Jr., copyright renewed 1991 Coretta Scott King.

Chapter 3

Crafting Your Rhetorical Act

In Chapter 2 you learned that all rhetorical acts contain seven elements that when examined together, help you analyze how rhetors use written, spoken, or visual messages to invite assent to social truths. In this chapter we examine how you use these elements and more to craft a rhetorical act that achieves your purpose. In particular, we look at the special skills needed to speak well in public. As the prologue of this book argues, *public speaking is essential to a liberal arts education, grooms citizenship, promotes leadership, and is vital to survive and thrive in the workplace.* Surveys of CEOs indicate that the ability to express ideas verbally is the most important of the qualifications and criteria used to promote employees to positions of leadership. Good public speaking skills also are closely related to psychological well-being. One's self-esteem is directly related to how well people develop the competence and confidence to speak in front of others.

UNDERSTANDING SPEECH ANXIETY

The prospect of initiating rhetorical action is frightening even for the most skilled practitioners. In fact, one survey reported that Americans fear speaking before a group more than they fear snakes, heights, disease, or even death.[1] We suspect that is because most people believe it is more likely they will find themselves facing an audience than

41

those other alternatives. Nevertheless, people who speak regularly never overcome the fear of seeming boring, saying something foolish, or forgetting important material. Anyone can misread a situation, presenting material the audience already knows and, hence, produce a humdrum act. Anyone can forget something important, be ill prepared, or make a silly or foolish statement. Anyone can be rattled by unexpected noise or by a restless or a very large audience. The important point is that *nervousness is normal*, and the sooner you accept that (and join all the rest of us who feel as you do), the more enjoyable and relaxed your presentations will be.

In one sense feeling apprehensive about speaking is normal because speakers are the very enactment of their ideas. We sometimes feel more ownership and, thus, more vulnerability about ideas we speak than those we write. Think about this for a minute. If you were to turn in a sloppy essay on capital punishment to your teacher, only you and she would know it. On the other hand, if you were to give an unrehearsed speech on capital punishment, the whole class would witness it. Another reason speech anxiety plagues so many students is because they have so little opportunity to practice speaking in public to peers before arriving at the university. With the exception of show-and-tell in the early grades or participation in drama or speech and debate teams in high school, oral presentations are not the primary way in which elementary and secondary students are expected to demonstrate their mastery of information. No wonder students sometimes dread oral performances. The unfamiliar is scary.

Recognize, however, that nervousness can be beneficial. Like the "game day" athlete who performs better under pressure, you too can use an adrenaline surge to enliven your presentation. In fact, teachers worry more about the student who says, "I'm not the least bit nervous" than the one who says, "I get anxious when speaking in public." Speakers without any sense of trepidation tend to be lethargic and underestimate the challenges of public speaking.

Although nervousness is normal and even beneficial, high levels of speech anxiety can be counterproductive. Here are a series of tips for how to manage anxiety productively:

- *Speak on subjects you know well when possible.* We will talk more about speech topics later, but for now it is important to know that anxiety decreases if you have a strong attachment to your subject and feel comfortable with the material. If you can focus on the content of your presentation, you will be less self-conscious, and focusing on content is much easier when you speak on subjects on which you have built-in knowledge and enthusiasm.
- *Know your audience.* Gathering plenty of information about the audience will help you control for the unexpected and craft a more interesting presentation. Find out about its size, its demographic makeup, and the room configuration. If you can discover audience attitudes toward your subject, that's even better. It is startling to think you are speaking to twelve to fifteen college students in a lounge, only to arrive and see 200 students with parents in an auditorium!
- *Practice, practice, practice.* If you have practiced the speech standing up and out loud to a sympathetic friend—even a mirror—and timed it carefully, the speech will show it. If you haven't practiced (rehearsing in your head does not count), and you are "winging" it, you deserve to feel petrified!
- *Don't memorize.* Why raise the stakes any more than you have to? Memorization can lead to mental blocks and embarrassing silences if you forget what comes next. Speaking with minimal notes is preferable. Note cards are a fine "security blanket."

- *Use physical activity.* There's no need for aerobics before speaking, but if you can take slow deep breaths, clench and unclench your fists, flex your arms and shoulders, roll your neck, or even yawn repeatedly, you are working off excess levels of adrenaline to stay flexible and relaxed.
- *Check out the speaking location.* It's easier to visualize yourself giving a strong performance if you know in advance where you will be standing; what kind of sound system, if any, you will be using; what sort of podium, lighting, space, and technology you can use for visual aids; and what the room looks like. Try to arrive early and arrange to meet a technician. If that's not possible, ask the program planners about these matters.
- *Be very familiar with your opening remarks.* This may appear to contradict the "don't memorize" advice, but it shouldn't. Getting off on the right foot is critical to a smooth speech. Your confidence will carry over to the rest of your speech if your introduction (usually not more than one minute) is delivered with minimal to no notes because you know it so well.
- *Stay positive.* Immediately before speaking, think positively about the audience and reassure yourself that what you have to say is interesting. Mentally review your introduction and check to see that you have all of your notes and visual aids.

The material in the rest of this chapter is designed to provide you with more detailed insurance against nervousness when you write and speak for an audience. We divide our suggestions into four areas: picking a topic, researching a subject, organizing your material, and preparing for the final presentation.

PICKING A TOPIC

Outside the public speaking classroom, most speakers have, at best, only limited choice regarding their topics. Rather, the appropriateness of the topic is often strongly influenced—sometimes even dictated—by other factors such as the situation or the events leading up to the speech, the occasion, the nature of the audience, and the like. For example, if you are called upon to deliver a "toast to the bride" at a wedding rehearsal dinner, choosing to talk about your stamp collecting hobby would likely be considered inappropriate for the occasion. If your employer assigns you to make a sales presentation to a potential client, you would be well advised not to talk about your experience working in a local food bank. Of course, speakers with particular backgrounds, knowledge, or experiences are often invited to address groups that share those interests, but the choice of topic will nevertheless be heavily influenced by the occasion and the audience. It is useful, then, to think of your public speaking class as a training ground for those speaking situations that you will encounter outside the classroom. And, perhaps fortunately, in that training you will frequently have greater choice regarding your speech topics. The suggestions that follow are designed to help you make the most of that training and then to speak with greater confidence and success outside the classroom.

Earlier we talked about understanding and managing speech anxiety. Much of the fear you feel in a rhetorical situation arises from a sense that the situation is not under your control. Admittedly, unforeseen things can happen, even in your public speaking classroom, but they are much less likely if you choose an appropriate topic. So important is developing a good topic that the ancient Greek and Roman rhetoricians called the discovery process "invention" (from the Latin, *invenire*, to come upon or find) and identified it as the first of five "canons of rhetoric" followed by arrangement, memory, style, and delivery. Especially in the public speaking classroom, selecting a good topic is the first stage of invention.

Equally important for invention is your storehouse of knowledge (personal knowledge and received wisdom) and your repertoire of resources (rhetorical strategies) that you draw upon to select subject material and adapt in ways best suited to the audience and the occasion. Skillful invention requires that you know yourself and the role you will play, that you know just what audience you are trying to reach, and that you are familiar with the available evidence and arguments and with the cultural history of your subject. Indeed, knowledge is power, and the larger your repertoire of experiences and expertise, the greater your chances for rhetorical success. In Part Two of this book you will be introduced to the resources of evidence, argument, organization, and language—chapters that aim to build on the ideas presented here and further develop your arsenal of invention for rhetorical action.

The most basic advice to the rhetor is: Speak and write from your own knowledge and experience! If you do, you will prepare with greater ease and confidence because you are working from familiarity. You will have general knowledge against which you can test information from other sources. Your experiences will provide a stock of examples that will make the subject more personal and vivid for the audience. If you share values and experiences with audience members, your relationship to the topic will make it easier to connect them to the topic. In addition, research will be easier because you will have access to firsthand information from people who work with or experience the topic directly every day. Here are some general questions to help you find suitable topics for speeches or essays:

1. *Where did you grow up?* Each of you has special knowledge from growing up on a farm, in the inner city, on army bases, in a mining town, in the mountains, or in the desert. These experiences can be the starting point for a speech or essay. In the past, students who have grown up on farms have spoken on government programs to support the price of farm commodities, insecticides, fertilizers, beef imports; students from cities have written about red lining, street repair, and variations in police protection in areas of the city. In no case was the personal experience of the student sufficient, but in each case, the research was easier, and familiarity with the subject increased the rhetor's confidence.

2. *What are your parents' occupations?* As the child of a plumber, a lawyer, an assembly line worker, or the owner of a hardware store, you have access to a source of firsthand information. For example, in the past, students have used this background to explain how plumbers are licensed and why they command such high pay, the feasibility of converting factories from oil to coal (a parent sold such machinery), medical malpractice, carpal tunnel syndrome, awards from juries, and the high cost of credit card debt (the child of a bankruptcy lawyer). The daughter of a prison guard who was murdered by an inmate already serving a life sentence for murder spoke in support of capital punishment. Once again, your experience can be the starting point for your rhetorical act, and you will write and speak with familiarity.

3. *What jobs have you done?* Even temporary or part-time work teaches you a lot. For instance, a grocery clerk discussed the arguments for and against automated checkout equipment; a student who had worked as a building inspector wrote about city laws governing apartments and how to make complaints to

compel landlords to meet the requirements of the building code; a student who had worked as the manager of a fast food restaurant discussed the pros and cons of franchises.

4. *What are your hobbies and interests?* A member of the track team talked about why some shoes increase your speed and last longer; a collector of Barbie dolls argued for their value as an investment; a foreign exchange student explained the special learning experiences that come from studying in another country; a yoga instructor showed how proficiency in yoga translates to better overall mental health.

5. *Have you family or friends with special problems, distinctions, or unusual characteristics?* Many rhetorical acts spring from tragedy. An alcoholic father prompted a speech on organizations that help the families of alcoholics; a schizophrenic sister prompted a speech on megavitamin therapy—what it is and how it works; the suicide of a friend's brother prompted an essay on suicide among college students; an epileptic brother occasioned a speech on misconceptions about epilepsy; a father's death from a shot of penicillin inspired an essay on the perils of allergies.

   Success and honor can also be the source of topics: the daughter of a mother who patented a new chemical process talked about how patents are acquired; a basketball player used the career of Jackie Stiles—a star of women's basketball at Southwest Missouri State University, the first NCAA Division I woman player to score more than 1,000 points in a season—to write about the limited opportunities for extraordinary women athletes; a scholarship student in ballet demonstrated and explained the basic movements of ballet as part of a speech to increase appreciation of ballet performances.

6. *Have you had unusual experiences?* The survivor of a severe automobile accident wrote vividly of seat belt safety; a girl who was threatened by a drunken boy with a loaded gun argued for gun control; a news intern spoke about witnessing the total destruction of a small town from an F5 tornado. Speaking or writing from your own experience has additional benefits. In most cases, you will be deeply involved in your topic and your sincerity will be contagious—the audience will care too. When you draw on personal experience, your audience will find you knowledgeable and credible, worthy of being believed. Your rhetorical act will not seem to be an exercise for a class; rather, the audience experiences you telling them something you know about firsthand, that you care about, and they will consider what you write or say seriously and with respect. You will be on the way to a successful presentation.

If you have considered these questions carefully, you will recognize some weak approaches. Don't write from research you did for last semester's term paper unless you can personalize the topic for yourself and your audience. A similar warning goes for a rhetorical act drawn from articles in newspapers, magazines, or on the Internet. Don't pick a topic just because you happen upon it in a Google search or a Facebook post. Again, do pick a subject that is close to you, one you know about personally.

Firsthand experience and personal knowledge alone, however, are not sufficient to reap the benefits of invention. You must be familiar with sources that captivate audiences, know the guidelines for adapting the range of rhetorical purposes (Chapter 1) to actual speaking situations, and test your experience and broaden your knowledge with information drawn from other sources.

WAYS TO CAPTIVATE AN AUDIENCE

A captivated audience is engaged in a speaker's presentation because of its substance and style. By *ways to captivate an audience*, we refer to the kind of subject matter that, owing to its intrinsic nature, tends to capture the attention of listeners. The following captivating sources, adapted from Alan Monroe et al., are important to attract audiences for any kind of speech.[2]

1. *Movement*. Expressed most simply a speech should impart a sense of movement. The more active your speech is the more intently an audience will listen. A speech will move or become active if it has two or three main ideas and develops several lines of reasoning. Signposting or foreshadowing the destination of a speech assists a speech in showing activity. Transitions from one point to the next indicate activity as well. If a speech is not active—if it only covers one point—then it remains static and can become redundant. Like taking your audience on a journey, a speech should treat a subject in a way that expands an audience's horizons.

2. *Reality*. Talking in abstract or vague terms will not convince an audience that your subject is based on real-life situations. All explanation should be clear and vivid. Chapter 7 introduces you to language strategies that refine this source of audience animation. Examples, in particular, should be relayed to an audience in terms of real-life people, events, and places. Good speakers are good storytellers—entertainers who can create virtual experience for listeners.

3. *Proximity*. Attention can often be commanded by making a direct reference about an audience member, or to some object near at hand, or to some event that has recently occurred in your area, or to the immediate occasion in which the speech is being made. Make a special point to refer to happenings on campus or in your communication classroom in order to add the appeal of proximity—of what is "close to home"—to your classmates.

4. *Novelty*. There is an old saying that "when a dog bites a man, it's an accident. When a man bites a dog, it's news." What is new or seen from a unique angle attracts us. The bizarre news story, the extraordinary feat, the "outside the box" perspective, the disarming bumper sticker—all work to alter perception in refreshing ways and minimize audience boredom.

5. *Suspense*. Listeners are attentive when they must mentally predict the outcome of a story. A speaker may, for example, relate pieces of a mysterious story at the outset of a speech and explain that the story will come together as the speech progresses. Or a speaker may use a series of startling statements that force the audience to draw a conclusion. The speaker then may promptly end the suspense by providing the "bombshell" or keep the audience guessing for a while. Piquing audience interest is tantalizing.

6. *Humor*. Judicious use of humor will hold an audience's attention any time. People enjoy a good chuckle or laugh and like to be put at ease by a speaker. Humor is an excellent way to create identification with your audience (see Chapters 5, 6, and 7) as it capitalizes on shared experience. It is a good pacing device too; in providing a light moment, the speaker allows an audience release. However, relevancy and good taste must be kept uppermost in a speaker's mind.

7. *The Vital*. Audience members pay attention to those things that vitally and directly affect their lives. Health and wellness, life-threatening issues, financial matters, success, happiness—all are of critical importance to us. Topics that relate to vital aspects of our well-being and address our most basic needs have a built-in attention factor.

The same principles are developed in Chip Heath and Dan Heath's book *Made to Stick: Why Some Ideas Survive and Others Die*.[3] Using many examples, they develop a "Velcro theory of memory" to argue that if you want what you say or write to remain in the memories of your audience, make it Simple, Unexpected, Concrete, Credible, Emotional, and tell a short story—principles they sum up as SUCCESS. Our approach to the thesis statement, explained later in this chapter, emphasizes simplicity. Creating suspense as you develop your topic is the basis of the unexpected. Concrete elements include details and specific examples. The credible comes from the kind of evidence you use and your link to your subject. The emotional is what has salience, what people care about. Finally, of course, what sticks in our minds is what is told to us as a story. Remember, captivating messaging is summed up in a memorable acronym: SUCCESS. Effective communication is Simple, Unexpected, Concrete, Credible, Emotional and in the form of Short Stories!

PRESENTATION GUIDELINES

Inventiveness in speech is not free-form creativity. In other words, selecting a topic shrewdly and knowing ways to captivate an audience is only half the battle. One's inspiration still needs to be tempered by the demands of the occasion. You will learn more about how invention and convention intersect in some well-defined rhetorical genres in Chapter 14, but all speech occasions, even those outside a classroom, have "assignment specifics" to satisfy the expectations of audiences. Here, we introduce you to six primary purposes of crafting your rhetorical act that conform to the six rhetorical purposes outlined in Chapter 1. Additional guidelines that your instructor may use to make actual speech assignments are included in the exercise portion of this chapter.

Storytelling Rhetorical Act. The primary purpose of the storytelling presentation is to create virtual experience. You learn how to tell a rhetorical narrative that is coherent, authentic, and highly descriptive. Your narrative must contain the elements of a good story. Your aim is to show your audience that you are a gifted narrator by telling them a captivating story that makes a timely point in a novel, memorable way. You will need to understand the instrumental and consummatory purposes of a rhetorical act.

Definitional Rhetorical Act. The primary purpose of the definitional presentation is to alter perception. You learn how to define an unfamiliar or often misinterpreted concept in familiar, clear terms. Your aim is to shape audience knowledge by defining a term clearly, accurately, and imaginatively. You will need to understand the parts of speech, outlining techniques, how to use and cite evidence, and the ten definitional strategies outlined in Chapter 4 in order to give depth and precision to your chosen term for this rhetorical act. (See Figure 4–4 for an inventional resource related to defining terms.)

Instructional Rhetorical Act. The primary purpose of the instructional presentation is to explain. You learn how to define, explain, and analyze the who, what, where, when, why, and how of a subject in an objective way. Your aim is to give the audience new, comprehensive information in order to expand their awareness and understanding of your subject. You will need a strong understanding of how evidence, argument, and organization work to help you meet the objectives of this rhetorical act.

Public Service Rhetorical Act. The primary purpose of the public service presentation is to formulate belief. You learn how to move your audience to accept a point of view and support a person, place, program, or product. Your aim is to shape audience belief around a "question of value" (see Chapter 5) by developing a convincing promotion similar to a public service announcement. You will need to understand all the resources for rhetorical action, especially argument strategies, and the contexts of rhetorical action (especially Chapter 8) in order to be successful with this rhetorical act.

Policy Rhetorical Act. The primary purpose of the policy presentation is to initiate action. You learn how to create dissonance by presenting a pressing social problem and then consonance by proposing a workable solution. Your aim is to construct a case around a controversial "question of policy." You will need to understand cognitive dissonance, problem-solution structure, the motivated sequence (see Chapter 6), and all the contexts of rhetorical action (audience, subject, and rhetor challenges) in order to achieve results with this rhetorical act.

Ceremonial Rhetorical Act. The primary purpose of the ceremonial presentation is to maintain action. You learn how to offer an inspirational tribute to an idea, person, institution, or an event. Your aim is to "rally" your audience to reflect, admire, and honor their commitment to your subject. You will need to understand how to use language poetically, and other resources of the nondiscursive, and the special constraints of rhetorical action, especially Chapter 14, where the demands of epideictic address are examined, in order to fulfill the expectations of this rhetorical act. Although these presentation guidelines grow more complex as they move along the rhetorical purposes continuum, note that in many ways the ceremonial speech comes full circle in embracing the nondiscursive elements of storytelling and the demands of creating virtual experience.

For each of these presentations, your instructor will make specific assignments regarding topic clearance, time, types of sources and research expectations, outlines, strategy reports, note cards, visual aids, types and amount of resources for rhetorical action, attention to contexts of rhetorical action, and other special grading criteria.

RESEARCHING A SUBJECT

If you want to be an effective speaker or writer, you must make the library, the Internet, and area professionals your helpful friends. They are primary resources for testing personal experience, refining understanding of the subject, and collecting concrete material that will explain and prove your claims and make your subject vivid.

General Sources

There are three types of basic general sources to help you: encyclopedias, dictionaries, and almanacs and statistical yearbooks. The least specialized and most general sources are large encyclopedias such as the *Encyclopedia Britannica,* now available online, or the *Encyclopedia Americana.* These will give you general and historical information on people, places, concepts, and events. The articles are written by experts, and each ends with a list of books and articles that offer additional information. Many of you probably use *Wikipedia* as a convenient Web resource. Although popular, this Web-based encyclopedia is not edited by experts exclusively, so it's a "hit or miss" proposition to use it as a reliable source. Nevertheless, *Wikipedia* can be a useful *starting point* for your research by providing you with information and ideas that can then be tested or verified by consulting other, potentially more reliable, sources. Those might include slightly more specialized but still encyclopedic references, such as the *Encyclopedia of Philosophy,* the *Encyclopedia of Social Work,* or the *American Negro Reference Book.* Once again, these will give you background plus a list of more detailed sources.

You are familiar with general dictionaries such as *Webster's International Dictionary* and the *Oxford English Dictionary* and their more compact and abridged versions. You can check the meanings of terms in them, the history of changes in meanings, and the etymology or the linguistic origin of meanings. As with encyclopedias, specialized dictionaries may be helpful. For example, the *Dictionary of the Social Sciences* explains terms peculiar to or with special meanings in the social sciences; the *Oxford Classical Dictionary* focuses on figures from ancient Greece and Rome and on concepts needed to study classical literature and philosophy. There are similar dictionaries for medicine, law, sociology, psychiatry, and the like.

If you need more recent information, particularly quantitative information, turn to almanacs and statistical yearbooks. These contain information, usually covering one year, compiled by agencies usually named in the titles—the *CBS News Almanac,* the *New York Times Almanac,* the *Reader's Digest Almanac, World Almanac, Information Please Almanac,* among others. These sources are usually current within a few months of the events you may be researching. Similarly, the *Statistical Abstract of the United States* provides quantitative information of all sorts for a single year (often with comparisons to other, recent years).

Other key general sources include computerized databases subscribed to by your university libraries. Bibliographic databases contain citations and abstracts of published print literature and online journals. Those of special interest to communication students are Readers Guide to Periodical Literature, ComIndex, ComAbstracts, ERIC (Educational Resources Information Center), PsycINFO (Psychological Abstracts), Sociological Abstracts, Wilson Business Abstracts, Social Science Abstracts, Humanities Abstracts, and Education Abstracts.[4]

The Internet is a research tool full of promise and peril. Its special strengths and weaknesses are discussed in Chapter 13. Without some basic guidance, excursions into cyberspace can be daunting. The Web is cluttered with hundreds of millions of sites, which means you need navigational tools. Search engines or Web directories, the most familiar being Google and Yahoo!, are specialized computer programs that catalog Web content. Beware, however. They are not all created equal. According to a recent study by the Research Institute in Princeton, New Jersey, not one of the top eleven major Internet search engines indexed more than 16 percent of the Web.

Because none of the search engines is keeping up with Web growth, multiple searches with several engines are necessary, say the researchers. Further, most Web content is commercial, such as company home pages, which make up a whopping 82 percent! Trailing far behind are other noncommercial sites (often with .org, .net, or .edu URL addresses).[5]

Most students have a greater comfort level with finding specific Internet resources. Remember, as discussed earlier in the chapter, not to overestimate the amount and relevance of information on the Web. At the risk of listing websites that may no longer be available once this book is in print (the dynamic feature of the Web allows for timely postings that may last only a short time), you may find the sites in Figure 3–1 useful for preparing rhetorical acts of interest to college students and, in particular, students with an interest in communication issues.

Figure 3–1
Sources of Research

General Sources	www.refdesk.com
	www.britannica.com
Government Sources	www.access.gpo.gov
	www.firstgov.gov
	www.thomas.loc.gov
Media Literacy and Consumer Advocacy	www.medialit.org
	www.mediachannel.org
	www.publiccitizen.org
	www.consumerreports.org
	www.filmcritic.com
	www.rottentomatoes.com
Communication	www.natcom.org
	www.AEJMC.org/abstracts
	www.rhetoricsociety.org/
	www.americancomm.org
	www.AmericanRhetoric.com
	http://blog.umd.edu/ncapublicaddress/ vibrant-voices-of-public-address/
	http://voicesofdemocracy.umd.edu/
	www.ngsw.org
	www.historicalvoices.org
	www.aaf.org
	www.Poynter.org
	www.prsa.org
News & Information	www.c-span.org
	www.NewYorkTimes.com
	www.totalnews.com

	www.tvnews.vanderbilt.edu
	www.votesmart.org
	www.studentpress.org
	www.assignmenteditor.com
	www.ire.org
	www.cnn.com
	www.newsbank.com
	www.altpress.org
	www.realclearpolitics.org
	www.newslibrary.com
History	www.historyplace.com
	www.greatwomen.org
	http://www.history.com/
	www.biography.com

Once you have decided to use a website for evidence, you must carefully evaluate it, much more so than traditional library sources, because there is no gatekeeper, no editor of the World Wide Web. Everything from science to scams, from fact to fiction competes for your attention, often with no ratings, citations, authorship, or seals of approval. If you're not vigilant, it's highly likely you'll be duped into thinking a study is valid when on closer scrutiny it turns out to be the ranting of a nonexpert. Some of the most fear-mongering messages come from unsubstantiated websites masquerading as news. Consider the supposed link between vaccines and autism; the infiltration of the Muslim Brotherhood in the White House; or the illegitimacy of the U.S. president's birth certificate. All of these "news stories" gained substantial following precisely because they were billed as news.

The check sheet in Figure 3–2, courtesy of Michigan State University Libraries (http://www.lib.msu.edu),[6] itemizes what is necessary to confirm the value of your website.

✓ **AUTHORITY**
✓ **VERIFIABLITY**
✓ **TIMELINESS**
✓ **RELEVANCE**
✓ **BIAS**
✓ **ORDERLINESS**
✓ **CLARITY**
✓ **VALIDITY**

Figure 3–2
Assessing Internet
Sources

© Cengage Learning

In Chapter 11 you will be exposed to four general standards of evaluation for all rhetorical acts (effects, truth, ethics, and aesthetics); here the evaluative tips are more evidence-centered. You must ascertain what expertise (*authority*) the author of your website has. Sometimes this is tricky and requires a larger Google search to learn more. You must try to corroborate (*verify*) the information on your site by using links to other sites that claim much the same thing. You must discover when the site was last updated (*timeliness*) to know whether data, especially statistical data, are still valid. You must articulate how your website is appropriate (*relevant*) for the topic under investigation. Is it one that scholars or enthusiasts visit with some frequency? You must keep an eye out for hidden agendas (*bias*). Although the site may have an authoritative name, such as "Government Action," the domain name may be purchased by an advocacy group with interests that slant the content presented. You must make some judgment on navigational ability (*orderliness*) and ease of digesting material (*clarity*). Some sites are maddeningly frustrating to browse. This lack of artistry is more than a cosmetic distraction. It should make you suspicious about the authenticity (*validity*) of its content and the sophistication of its authors.

As a credible rhetor, you will also need to know the qualifications and experience of persons you quote as authorities from printed library sources. Among the special references that can help you are the *Directory of American Scholars, American Men and Women of Science*, and *Who's Who in America*. In some cases, an Internet search for the author's name will lead you to reliable sources, such as government agencies, university faculty directories, or even corporate personnel directories, that can provide useful information about that person's background and qualifications. Sources such as these will help you judge the authority and credibility of a source and indicate to the audience how much weight should be given to a person's statement. As you expand your knowledge of library and Internet resources, you will find that you are expanding your abilities as a rhetor.

In addition to the library and Internet, don't overlook the relevance and practicality of interviewing professionals in your area and even your peers on campus. Quoting experts or peers from an interview that you conduct gives you enhanced credibility. It showcases your investigative prowess and your creativity. If you want an area professional, begin with the phonebook. If you want a faculty member, consult a campus directory and your university's media guide or website, and, of course, use faculty from your own classes. Keep in mind the following tips for successful interviewing in person, over the phone, or by email:

- Identify yourself and your intention clearly.
- Have prepared a focused, short set of open-ended questions.
- Check the credentials of your source.
- Thank the people you interview for their time.

Remember to be respectful in your requests for information from area experts, and recognize that they are busy people who may not be able to assist you at your convenience. Following up with a note or call of appreciation shows your professionalism in the research transaction. One of the best ways to involve classmates in the research process is to formulate a brief survey for in-class distribution. This does two things: (1) it is a great way to tailor your rhetorical act to the needs of your specific audience; and (2) it adds relevance to the evidence gathering process because it is highly personalized. Students are curious about what others like them think and believe.

ORGANIZING YOUR MATERIAL

Chapter 6 discusses organization and outlining in detail. You may wish to consult that chapter when you have finished reading this material. What follows are some preliminary and general considerations to use in limiting your topic and in planning the structure of your rhetorical act.

Narrowing or Limiting Your Topic

Most assignments in public speaking or writing classes require rhetorical acts that are relatively brief, a five- to seven-minute speech or a 1,500-word essay, for example. Our culture is fast-paced; even most presidential addresses are no longer than a half hour for transmission by television or radio. Your first concern, then, is to narrow your topic to something you can adequately develop in the time or space available. Three questions will help you do this:

1. What parts of this topic are most significant and interesting for this audience?
2. What parts of this topic are most important, serious, or have the broadest implications?
3. What aspect of the topic is most easily explained, or what aspect can be discussed most fully in the time or space allotted?

The first question focuses your attention on the audience. What aspects of the topic will be new to them? What parts of the topic touch their lives or are directly related to their immediate circumstances? As an example, imagine that you want to talk about energy problems. Most college students do not pay utility bills directly, and some do not own cars, so the price of gas may not be salient. Few live in houses heated by solar energy; in most cases, few will have the necessary expertise to compare coal and gas as sources of energy. If there is no nuclear plant in the area and none proposed, even the dangers of nuclear power may not be particularly relevant.

Assume, however, that student activity fees have been raised because of the increased costs of heating and cooling the student union, and that fees for board and room in dormitories have been raised for the same reason. Some research leads to the discovery that these buildings waste energy because of the way they were built. Perhaps your topic should be narrowed to the relationship between architecture and construction and energy consumption. Recognize that you are trying to alter the perceptions of this particular audience and that your first concern should be to approach the topic so that its significance for them is apparent.

The second question is designed to fit your subject to the particular circumstances of the audience. Consider here what any audience should know about this subject. On the basis of your research, you may decide that the problems of nuclear energy are the most pressing despite their remoteness from the immediate concerns of the audience. If so, you need to think carefully about how you can make this facet of the energy question significant for the audience. You might decide to begin with the nuclear plants built more than twenty years ago, which are now obsolete, but no one knows how to protect, make safe, or dismantle them. Such dangers can be made concrete and personal for a community and for individuals. Members of the audience can identify with dangers to people like themselves and to communities similar to their own.

Whatever facet of the subject you choose, this second question will help you explain to the audience why you have chosen it. If you decide to discuss the relationship between building construction and fossil fuel consumption, you may need to explain briefly why you are not discussing nuclear power but instead have selected what may appear to be a less important part of the subject of energy. (Obviously, the need for energy in general and for nuclear energy in particular would be lessened if consumption dropped. You might argue that that makes the question of construction an important one.)

The third question, what aspect of the topic can be treated fully in the time or space allotted, is designed to call the rhetor's attention to clarity and intelligibility. In Chapters 8 through 10, which examine the rhetorical problem, we discuss the problems created by the complexity of some topics and purposes. The decision you make on this question is intended to simplify appropriately so the audience will understand what you are discussing.

For example, the problems of energy are many, and each is complex. The problems of nuclear power alone cannot be discussed in five minutes or in 1,500 words. In order to make sense of the subject, you might decide to limit your discussion entirely to the problem of what to do with existing outdated nuclear plants. This choice ignores a great deal—whether there is sufficient uranium, whether nuclear wastes can be disposed of, whether the products of breeder reactors can be kept from terrorists, whether alternative energy sources exist, and on and on. But it focuses on an existing concrete problem: By the year 2000 there were hundreds of inactive atomic plants, and smaller nuclear installations, such as nuclear medicine facilities and navy ship reactors, have ceased to operate. All of them will stay radioactive for hundreds or even thousands of years, and they remain a serious threat.

A rhetorical act on this subject could be a case study of the problems of nuclear power as a concrete way for you to explore the existing problems in the use of atomic energy. It's important, it's concrete, and it's sufficiently limited to be explained and explored in a relatively short rhetorical act. In other words, the third question should bend your energies toward finding a facet of the subject that you can cover thoroughly and clearly in the time or space allotted.

In sum, narrowing the topic should take into consideration the ways in which the subject is significant for the audience, the most important facets of the topic, and which aspects of the subject can be treated fully and carefully in a limited time or space.

Choosing a Thesis

Narrowing your topic leads naturally into the most important decision you make about organization: the selection of a thesis. Ordinarily, the general purpose of a rhetorical act is determined by the occasion or assignment. For example, editorials, feature stories, and general news stories have rather clearly defined general purposes, but writers must choose how they will translate the general purpose into a specific purpose. Occasions for speeches also usually define a general purpose—commencement speakers are expected to praise the new graduating class and talk about their future; sermons are intended to reinforce belief; reports are expected to provide information and create understanding. In each case the rhetor must decide just how he or she will translate the general purpose into a specific thesis.

Deciding on a thesis or central idea is difficult, and you should expect to find it troublesome. First, it represents a commitment that is hard to make—"I want the audience to know and understand precisely this: 'Storage facilities for nuclear wastes cannot be guaranteed safe for longer than twenty years.'" When you choose such a thesis, you make a claim to knowledge; in effect you say, "I have researched this topic, and I stake my credibility and authority on the accuracy of my research." In addition, you eliminate material and limit yourself drastically. In this case, all research that does not bear directly on storage of nuclear wastes must be discarded, so the choice of a thesis is a decision that specifies the precise claim you want to make and represents a drastic limitation of the topic. The thesis should be a grammatically simple, declarative sentence that answers the question, "Just what do I want the audience to know or understand (or believe or do) when I finish?"

Here are some examples of good theses:

Building a solar home or converting a home to solar energy are practical solutions to the energy crunch for individuals.

Note that the topic is narrowed in two ways: to solving the energy problem for individuals (not industry, for example) and to solar energy. It is a good thesis because it focuses on practicality. As the audience for this rhetorical act, we would expect to hear about costs of building and conversion, availability of materials, ease of construction, availability of materials and knowledge for maintenance, climatic conditions needed, and so forth. It is also good because the claim of the rhetor is explicit and clear, and we know how to judge whether or not the claim is adequately supported.

Nuclear breeder reactors are unsafe.

This is a larger and more difficult claim that is aimed at a speech to formulate belief. It is good, however, because it narrows the topic to breeder reactors and because it narrows the perspective to questions of safety. As an audience, we would expect such a rhetorical act to focus on the problems of disposing of plutonium wastes and of preventing nuclear material suitable for explosive devices from falling into unauthorized hands.

Here are some poor thesis statements:

The deregulation of natural gas.

This is poor because it isn't a sentence (there is no verb!) and doesn't make a claim. It isn't clear what we are to know or understand about deregulation. That makes it a poor thesis, although it narrows the subject to natural gas and to questions about the relationship between price, availability, and government controls. Contrast this statement with a more explicit version:

The deregulation of natural gas will increase both the supply and the price.

Here is a poor statement that reflects a common error:

How a nuclear plant runs.

It is not a sentence (again, there is no verb) and does not state a purpose or a goal. One may rightly ask, why should I know or care about how a nuclear plant runs? The thesis ought to give an answer. Contrast this statement with a more explicit one:

A nuclear power plant has a major impact on the environment.

This claim cannot be substantiated without explaining how a plant runs, but it also says, Here's why you should know how it runs.

Recall that you, as rhetor, must always concern yourself with relevance and significance. Just as you may ask about classes and lecture materials, Why should I learn that? Your audience always asks, Why should I know? Why should I care? What difference does it make to me? Your thesis should be a statement that gives an answer.

People should drive more carefully.

This statement is a sentence, and it has a purpose, but it's hard to imagine how anyone could disagree. It's also hard to see how it could be developed or argued. No matter how careful drivers are, they could still drive more carefully. This seems to put the statement beyond argument. Just what is meant by "more carefully"? That general phrase, open to many interpretations, ought to be translated into more concrete terms: not driving while sending or receiving text messages, while on medication, while ill, while drunk, or in a car with poor brakes. A speech or essay on a particular kind of carelessness would come to grips with an issue that should challenge you and the audience.

People drive too fast.

This statement is a sentence, and it has a purpose. Its problems arise from its generality. The rhetor who uses this thesis will be all right if she narrows and specifies in the speech or essay just what benefits are to be derived from slower driving, although "too fast" is vague. Contrast it with a more specific statement:

You can save lives and money by obeying the speed limit.

The following sentence is a problem because it contains two theses and implies two different rhetorical acts:

We must build nuclear power plants and wind farms.

Each claim is adequate separately, but the rhetorical act that combines them will be at odds with itself. Choose one or the other. "There is no economically feasible alternative to nuclear power," for example, or "Wind farms are the future of environmental sustainability."

A good thesis statement should

- Be short. (Think: Can I tweet it in 140 characters?)
- State a specific claim. (Think: What's your positioning statement?)
- Express a single unified purpose. (Think: What's my one aim?)
- Indicate significance and relevance. (Think: Why will my audience care?)

You will have conquered many of the problems of organizing your material when you have decided on a thesis and stated it clearly. As will be evident from the examples we have given, clearly stated theses imply the internal organization of the speech or essay. The structure of your rhetorical act is the development of your thesis. The main points of the rhetorical act should be statements (sentences making claims) that prove and explain the thesis. These main points should answer the questions: Why? or How do I know? For example, the thesis "The deregulation of natural gas will increase both the supply and the price" implies a two-part development:

A. It will increase the supplies available across state lines.
B. It will raise the interstate price to the level of the intrastate price.

The statement "Nuclear breeder reactors are unsafe" implies that the main points will give reasons such power plants are unsafe.

A. There are no safe methods for storing plutonium wastes.
B. There is no way to prevent the theft of plutonium.

Note that these reasons will need to be developed, in turn, by statements that show how the rhetor knows these things to be true or highly probable.

For your initial speech preparation you should do only two additional things to organize your material: indicate how you will develop these main points, and plan an introduction and conclusion.

Outlining

What follows are outlining guidelines and an outline form to help you think logically about the arrangement of ideas—the second canon of rhetoric. Outlining takes on special significance in the oral mode because audiences do not have a blueprint of your speech. They cannot see your indentations and subheadings as they can in an essay. Audiences soon lose interest in speakers who are disorganized or who are difficult to follow. We would add that although these suggestions for outlining are intended primarily to help you prepare for an oral presentation, they can apply equally well to the outline that you should develop in the initial stage of writing an essay.

Outlining Guidelines

1. Use complete sentences for main ideas and major subdivisions. Use phrases and key words for minor subdivisions.
2. Each part of speech (Introduction, Body, Conclusion) should be in the outline and clearly labeled; Do not number these parts.
3. Every sentence or indented passage should have a symbol, not a dash or star, and only one symbol.
4. Use Roman numerals for main ideas only.
5. Indent according to the importance of the symbol.
6. Subdivisions should have three characteristics:
   a. Subordination. Subdivisions should be ideas of smaller scope than the claim that they support.
   b. Coordination. Subdivisions should be of relatively equal scope and importance.
   c. Mutual exclusiveness. Subdivisions should cover different aspects of the larger idea; content should not overlap.

Sample Outline Form for Student Speeches
Title

Thesis Statement
Introduction (15 seconds to 1 minute)

Attention Step
  I. (A statement designed to gain attention and reveal the purpose.)

Need Step

II. (A statement designed to explain why the audience needs to listen.)

Signposting Step

III. (A statement designed to preview the main points.)

Body: (approximately 3–5 main ideas, 3–5 minutes)

I.   (Main Point. Make this a complete sentence.)

    A.   (Subpoint. Make this a complete sentence.)

       1. (Supporting material. Make this a phrase or key word.)

       2. (Supporting material.)

          a. (Sub-subpoints using key words for further detail.)

          b.

II. (Second Main Point.)

    A.

       1.

       2.

    B.

III. (Third Main Point.)

    A.

    B.

(And so forth . . .)

Conclusion (15 seconds to 30 seconds)

I.   (A statement designed to foreshadow the end of the speech and reinforce the audience's understanding of the main points.)

II. (An optional final appeal.)

INTRODUCTIONS AND CONCLUSIONS

In the fields of Communication and Psychology, persuasion and cognition have been studied from several angles. One has been to determine what people remember most in a speech. Primacy and recency effects theory stipulates that audiences tend to remember what they heard first and last in a speech. Researchers are divided on which is most important, introductions or conclusions. The lesson to take from these research findings is go in with a bang and out with a flash! Introductions and conclusions must be well crafted and well delivered. Don't tack them on in a perfunctory way to fulfill the requirements of form. What follows are some tips for how to craft the three components of a good introduction and some tips for how to remain concise and clear in your conclusion.

The introduction should get the attention of the audience, indicate the significance of or need for the topic, and signpost the development of the speech. In other words, a good introduction

- Gains attention.   Hook interest
- Shows relevance.   Relate to audience
- Previews main points.   Sets expectations

Attention steps win attention and establish interest in your topic. Attention steps are important because audiences want to know, Why should I pay attention? So, for example, don't just announce, "My speech is about global warming," or "I want to talk about requiring a comparative world religions class at our university." You need to bait your audience with a flashy spinner not a metal hook! Here are some good ways to get attention:

Rhetorical Questions. No direct answers are sought when you ask a rhetorical question. They stimulate audiences to think, and you establish ties with the audience by recognizing them.

Startling Statements. Sometimes it's appropriate to jar the audience into attention. Use this technique with serious subjects but avoid hyperbole. Startling statements make a dramatic impact on the audience.

Pithy Quotation. Beginning with a memorable quote can be a simple and succinct way to introduce your speech. Don't begin a speech with a quotation just because someone famous said it. A pithy quote can enhance your credibility, legitimize the importance of the topic, and depending on the context of the quote, may evoke an audience's frame of reference.

*Humorous Anecdote.*Humor can not only captivate the audience but can also help you establish friendly rapport with listeners right off the bat. It can be an especially shrewd strategy if you are speaking to a suspicious or hostile audience. Resist the urge, however, to tell a joke just to get laughs. The humor needs to be related directly to your topic.

*Real or Hypothetical Example.*Beginning with a story, real or hypothetical, is one of the best ways to get attention. Your examples need to be clear, vivid, interesting, and tied directly to the purpose of your speech. Stories invite participation; they involve the audience on an emotional level. Detailed examples also make your subject matter more real and personal.

The second step of the introduction—the need step—explains why the audience needs to listen. How does the subject affect them? Although you should have thought along these lines when selecting a topic, you need to make a statement that answers directly the question: What's in it for me? The need step should be placed right after the attention step. Resources for the need step include basic human appeals such as: the vital, prevalence of a topic, increased knowledge, better health, success, fun, financial rewards, altruism, adventure, and so forth. Be careful not to overdo it and turn your speech into a full-blown sales pitch. One or two sentences will suffice.

The third step of the introduction—the signposting step—is a brief synopsis or overview of your main points. This statement should resemble your thesis statement. A good preview sets expectations for the audience (audiences like to know where a speaker is going), reflects favorably on the speaker (we are impressed by well-organized speakers), and is an appropriate transition from the introduction to the body.

When you put the three steps of the introduction together, they should flow together seamlessly and be concise. Introductions that go over a minute in a five- to six-minute speech present balance problems for speakers and promise more than they can deliver. Here is a simple fifteen-second example of an introduction from a speech to explain:

(Attention Step) I. How many of you can say with confidence: "I know how to change a tire?"
(Need Step) II. As often as we all drive cars, this is a skill worth learning. It is easy to learn, and you could save up to $50 on a towing bill.
(Signposting Step) III. Today, I would like to show you the tools you will need and the four easy steps involved in changing a tire.

Here is a slightly longer example of an introduction from a speech to formulate belief:

(Attention Step) I. Raise your hand if you care about your grade. Those who raised your hand will especially care about my topic. Those of you who didn't, you're about to find out why you should!
(Need Step) II. Our university uses a grading scale that makes it harder for all of you to get good grades. Here, all A's does not always equal a 4.0; or all C's does not always equal a 2.0, though it would at other schools that use the traditional five-letter grading scale.
(Signposting Step) III. Today, I want to examine what the problems are with the plus/minus grading scale and, second, propose why we should return to the traditional five-letter scale.

Our final suggestion is that the introduction (and the conclusion, too, for that matter) should not be prepared until *after* the body of the speech has been developed. The function of the three parts of the introduction, after all, is to prepare the audience for the main part of the message—the body. You will be better prepared to do that if you know what that message will be.

The conclusion of a rhetorical act is good if it is such that the act ends rather than stops. Your summary sentences here must be clear and concise and project completeness or a sense of finality. Ideally, a conclusion should do two things:

- Summarize the major ideas.
- Fix the specific purpose in the audience's mind.

You need to plan carefully just how you will end. First, you need to signal the end of the speech with a clear transition. Some obvious—albeit perhaps abrupt—ways of doing that would be to say: "In conclusion," "In closing," "In summary," "So remember," "Finally," "So the next time," "Now you know," and the like. As you gain experience as a speaker, however, you should be able to develop equally clear but less abrupt transitions to signal the end of the body and the start of the conclusion. The second thing you need to do is choose a good way of ending. Two common methods include a summary of main points and referring back to your introduction. The latter, often referred to as a "circular effect" provides psychological unity to a speech. So, for instance, if you began with a quotation, end with one from the same source; if you began with a rhetorical question, end with some questions and now provide answers; if you began with a story, especially one that involved some suspense, end with a story that provides closure. As we suggested earlier, doing any of those things will be easier if you compose the conclusion *after* the body and the introduction have been developed.

Conclusions can create problems if the following rules are not observed:

1. **Do not introduce new information**. Conclusions are wrap-ups, reminders, and statements of reaffirmation. They are by nature repetitive of information in the body of your speech.
2. **Don't be long-winded**. Don't say, "In conclusion," and then ramble. When audiences sense the conclusion, they do not want to be irritated by waiting too long for closure. Conclusions are almost always shorter than introductions. For in-class speeches, aim for thirty seconds.
3. **Don't stop abruptly**. Let us know you are ending. Abrupt conclusions are oxymoronic.
4. **Don't speed up**. Nonverbal indicators of closure are equally important as verbal indicators. Write SLOW DOWN on your note cards. Conclusions are a winding down not a winding up.
5. **Don't read.** Deliver your conclusion with minimal notes. Like the introduction, the conclusion should be well rehearsed.

PREPARING YOUR PRESENTATION

The quality of your final presentation depends on your skill at implementing what you have learned about rhetoric and your willingness to practice or rewrite. You can develop and refine your rhetorical skills through preparing the strategy report described at the end of the chapter. A strategy report is a written analysis of the choices you made in preparing your rhetorical act, in light of the challenges you faced and your purpose. In addition, if the act is oral, you must practice it aloud, standing, and, at the same time, try to imagine yourself as a member of the audience. If your act is written, you must learn to polish and refine your efforts through rewriting, a process made much easier if you use a word processor.

At this point you have an outline that states the specific purpose, lists the main points, and cites the evidence you will use to explain and prove your assertions. You have made some rough notes for what you will say in the introduction and conclusion. You now need to move from the outline toward the composition of a complete and finished rhetorical act. Your first concern should be clarity. Focus your attention on two areas: the clarity of the relationships among ideas and the clarity of each piece of evidence you will present.

The clarity of the relationships among the main ideas depends on the soundness of the argument's structure and on the kinds of transitions or bridges made between ideas. If you have prepared your outline carefully and have made certain that your main points answer the questions Why? and How do I know? the relationships among the main points should be clear. There is a relatively simple test you can apply to deter-mine the adequacy of your argument. If your main points are A, B, C, and D, then, if the argument is sound, the following should apply:

If A is true, if B is true, if C is true, and if D is true, then it should follow that the claim you make in your specific purpose is true.

Transitions

Transitions or connectives are statements made to ensure that the audience understands and recognizes the relationships among ideas. Transitions or connectives are like road-maps. They tell your audience where you have been, where you are, and where you intend to go. Transitions are needed most at the completion of a main idea or major subpoint (a Roman numeral or capital letter in your outline). Although some members of your audience will listen actively, others will listen more passively and will not see relationships unless you make them explicit. Here are some examples of transitions:

Numerical. "The first cause...The second cause...The third cause..." "First, let's examine...Second, let's examine..." "The first step toward...The final step toward..."

Preview. "In discussing the challenges of climate change, I will define the phenomena, identify its magnitude, and describe its effects on our ecosystem."

Summaries. "In short, remember that..." "In summary, the primary treatments are..." "Let's pause to reexamine what experts have found thus far...." "And so you can see that..."

Rhetorical Questions. "Now you may be asking who is responsible for the funding?" "This last point raises a question..." "Why should you care about how this organization is funded?" "What was the result? Just this..."

Internal Connectives. "Above all, you need to know..." "Be sure to keep this in mind..." "And so you can see that..." "We have seen...yet it remains for us to observe..." "In addition to...there is another outstanding reason..."

Practicing and Editing

Practicing aloud and editing/rewriting are the processes by which rhetors prepare oral and written rhetorical acts, respectively. Both are essential to produce a good final product. Practicing aloud has two purposes. First, it creates a physical memory of what you intend to say that will help you speak smoothly. It prevents your oral presentation before the audience from being especially frightening because it is the first time you make your speech. Part of the fear associated with speaking is the fear each of us has about doing things that are new and different and in which we feel unskilled. You can diminish that by oral practice. Stand up as if you were before the audience, hold your notes as you intend to, and deliver your speech as you plan to on the actual occasion. If there are tongue twisters, you'll find them and be able to overcome them or make changes. If there's complicated material that's hard to explain, you'll discover it and have time to make some changes. Moreover, by the time you give your speech, it won't be the first time—it will be the ninth or tenth—and the material will feel familiar when you begin your speech.

Second, practicing aloud is the means for refining and reorganizing. For example, you practice your five-minute speech aloud, and it runs fifteen minutes; or what was supposed to run 1,500 words actually runs 3,000. Clearly, you haven't narrowed the topic enough, and you need to do some cutting. Or, as you listen to yourself or read what you've written, you realize that to be clear you have to add something—and you figure out how to add it and how to make the idea clearer. Please note, however, that none of these benefits occur unless you read your work with the critical eye of a stranger or practice aloud exactly as if you were presenting the speech to your audience and listen to yourself critically. You must pretend to be your own audience, listening to the speech or reading the essay as someone unfamiliar with the subject. It is such listening and reading that enables you to catch problems and make needed changes. (Of course, you can snag a cooperative roommate or friend and ask that person to respond candidly about questions and problems that arise in reading or listening to what you say. But such a person is only a poor substitute for developing your abilities as your own best listener and editor.)

Your speech should be presented from notes, not from a manuscript on which you have written out, word by word, what you intend to say. Presenting a speech from a manuscript is a difficult skill reserved for highly skilled rhetoricians on specialized time-sensitive occasions as illustrated by the varying abilities of presidents reading from a teleprompter. Do not add to your problems by attempting this in the communication classroom. Tailor your notes to your personal needs. You might decide to memorize the introduction and write only one or two words from it on a card. You may need a chain of terms to create associations to help you remember all the elements of the story you want to tell and the order you want to follow.

After these terms, write a phrase or word that will suggest the transition into the thesis or specific purpose and then write out the purpose in full. Next write a word or phrase suggesting the transition into the first main point and write this main point out in full. You should depart from outline or key term form only for evidence that should be written out in full so you can cite it accurately and completely, along with its source.

As you practice, add whatever notes you need for changes or additions. Be sure that what you have written on the cards is easily legible. Hold your notes slightly above waist level, and use them every time you practice. Do not try to avoid looking at them (you will lose your place, fail to shift the cards as you progress, and have to search desperately if you need to consult them). Practice looking at them regularly, and plan to consult each card, moving the top card to the bottom as you finish the ideas it covers. Stand up firmly, speak aloud, and try to imagine the audience in front of you. Practice until you can present the whole speech smoothly and easily. When your moment arrives, you will be well prepared to make a competent presentation.

The suggestions in Figure 3–3 include tips designed to help you remember that effective rhetorical acts must be poetic and pragmatic.

Figure 3–3
Message Tips

- Avoid information overload
- Establish a unifying theme
- Develop a memorable phrase
- Introduction should be "catchy" and signpost the speech
- Conclusion should be concise and aim for closure
- Tell at least one story or anecdote
- Repetition aids memory recall for audience members
- Avoid generalizations: be concrete

DELIVERING A SPEECH

Concerns about delivery are closely related to communication apprehension or stage fright. As we said at the outset of this chapter, fears about speaking are normal and appropriate. Speaking involves a social risk, and we fear isolation from and rejection by others. In most speaking situations, the audience clusters together in comfortable anonymity while the speaker stands alone. Nonverbally, it feels as if it's you against them. Because rhetorical action asks for and requires the participation of others, every speaker risks rejection. In face-to-face situations, the evidence is immediate and unavoidable. Audience members send hundreds of nonverbal messages registering their responses. All good speakers, even those with much experience, feel some apprehension. On every occasion, a speaker takes responsibility for a commitment, is partially isolated from the audience, and chances a rebuff. Apprehension is recognition of what is involved in acting as a rhetor.

Such fears are inherent in any form of public performance, and most performers—whether they are athletes, singers, actors, comedians, or public speakers—agree that those fears diminish greatly with practice. If you have prepared your speech carefully and practiced aloud so that you are in command of your material, your fears will be manageable after a few sentences. Human beings are symbol using creatures, and despite our fears, we take pleasure in communicating with others, in expressing our ideas and feelings. You will enjoy the experience even more if you consider the following bits of advice.

Preparing the Scene

Insofar as possible, take control of the scene. If you are speaking, arrive early and case the joint. If possible, move chairs so you lessen your distance from the audience. This will make you more comfortable and create an environment in which participation by the audience is easier. If the audience is scattered over a large area, ask them to move forward so that they are closer together. Unless the occasion is extremely formal, be sure that lights are arranged so that you can see the audience. Stage lighting separates you from the audience and alters the situation in ways that can limit your rhetorical efforts.

In general, avoid the use of a lectern and stand in front of tables or desks. A lectern shuts off much of your nonverbal communication and reduces your immediacy. Both lessen ease of audience participation. Use a lectern or table if you will feel more comfortable behind one or if you are in a rare situation in which you must use a manuscript, but do everything you can to minimize the barrier between you and the audience. Try standing next to the lectern. In this way you will be able to rest one hand on the lectern, and yet you won't be as "fenced off" from the audience.

Check to ensure that all materials you need are present and working. Test the microphone and computer/projection system if you have a PowerPoint, Prezi, or media clip. Nothing destroys your efforts more quickly than a projector or audio that won't work, an incompatible laptop, or denial of Internet access. Your textbook authors have each learned this lesson the hard way!

If there are problems that can't be solved, acknowledge them to the audience in good humor. Try to make them your confederates in struggling to cope with a cold room, a noisy radiator, a defective mike, or whatever. Your role as rhetor requires you to take charge of the scene and to be responsive to what goes on in it (see Figure 3–4).

Figure 3–4
Preparation Tips

- Check out speaking location, sound system, platform
- Know where you are in the program and who introduces you
- Time your speech carefully to meet program restrictions
- Use large note cards; write large
- Don't memorize
- Be most familiar with opening and closing remarks
- Nervousness is normal
- Know your audience (composition, disposition, size)

Using Visual Aids

Visual aids include such items as PowerPoint, Prezi, digitized film clips, You Tube, websites, charts, maps, pictures, posters, actual objects, demonstration assistants, and handouts. They can be powerful tools to increase the recall of a speech by more than 40 percent! But visual aids also can create special problems. Pictures, for instance, should not pop like popcorn in a presentation. There are limitations. It is easy to become drunk on technology—to overindulge on computer slides. It can be comforting to let visual aids upstage the speaker, but remember that they are *aids* and not the main element of the presentation. In other words, you must resist the urge to play "the Wizard of Oz"—to hide behind the curtain, dim the lights, pull the levers, and click the buttons. A Harvard Business School study found that PowerPoint slides have become crutches for boring or disorganized speakers and that PowerPoint presentations cluttered with too many visuals creates competition for the audience's attention between the eye and the ear. In our public speaking classes, the rule is no more than four to six slides in a five- to seven-minute speech. The key is to use visual aids as aids, as sidelights not the spotlight of a presentation. Use them only when they contribute something essential to your presentation, and prepare them carefully. Visual aids are essential when presenting large amounts of statistical material or when ideas and relationships are difficult to explain verbally—for example, locations on maps.

As you prepare such aids, follow the general guidelines in Figure 3–5.

Figure 3–5
Visual Aid Tips

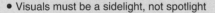

- Visuals must be a sidelight, not spotlight
- Limit visuals if you want them to be memorable
- Practice with visuals so delivery is seamless
- Do not talk to your visual aids!
- Position visuals so all audience members can see
- Don't clutter words on visuals
- Point specifically to key features of your visual aids
- Use visual aids when you need them, then remove them promptly
- Be prepared to give speech without visuals in the event of technological malfunction
- Avoid using a chalk or marker board or passing out items while you are speaking

Visual Aid
Tips

NONVERBAL PRESENTATION GUIDELINES

As you will learn in Chapter 10, researchers have discovered that audiences form first impressions about speakers instantaneously based on nonverbal evidence, such as what they are wearing, how they move, how poised they are, and their facial expressions. We often hear "Good athletes are poetry in motion." Well, good speakers are poetry in motion too. How you look, move, gesture, and make eye contact should complement not distract from the nature of your message. Audiences pay more attention to non-verbals than you might think because nonverbals don't lie. So avoid "double-binds" where you say one thing ("Trust me"), but are doing another (looking down or failing to maintain eye contact). What follows are aspects of nonverbal communication especially important to public speakers.

Appearance

Dress with due consideration for the occasion, the role you will play, your purpose, and the expectations of the audience. Clothing is a major source of messages for the audience, and it can distract. Follow these simple rules:

- Dress for comfort and ease of movement. Avoid tight, stiff clothing, high heels that wobble, or climbing shoes that squeak.
- Dress to avoid distraction. Avoid bright, busy, loud patterns that attract attention away from your message. Eliminate any item that can rattle, such as coins, keys, or bracelets.
- Dress in an outfit that complements the occasion. Minimize the time the audience will spend remarking on your clothes.

Facial Expression

Related closely to dress in conveying one's overall appearance is facial expression. How you position your mouth, eyebrows, and eyes especially accentuates a message and shows your overall interest in a topic. Beginning speakers sometimes forget that unless their face is animated, audiences may assume erroneously that you are not really interested in your speech. Avoid the deadpan expression in which your face appears frozen and emotionless. If you are happy, smile; if concerned, be tense. In other words, if we were to turn off the sound of your recorded speech, we should still be able to interpret your emotional state. One good way to determine how animated your facial expressions are is to practice in front of a mirror. Alternatively, because digital audio/video recording devices have become common and relatively inexpensive—even some "smart-phones" have video recording capability—you might consider recording your practice sessions and then viewing them through a critic's eye in an effort to improve delivery.

Posture

Before you begin to speak, walk slowly to the front of the room and position yourself comfortably. Do not begin to speak until you are standing firmly on both feet. You will create anticipation for what follows, and you will take charge of the scene. Avoid standing on one foot, crossing your legs, rocking back and forth, slouching, placing your hands in your pockets, or using the podium to prop yourself up. Standing straight infuses energy into your speech, aids in projection, and conveys confidence. Arrange your hair so that it does not fall into your face, and avoid repetitive motions flicking it back. All of these distract from your message and suggest discomfort and lack of involvement.

Gesture

Gestures are to be used judiciously. No gestures are better than poor ones. Gestures do three things: (1) describe, (2) emphasize, and (3) signal a change. Remember the following guidelines for using gestures properly: keep gestures natural, keep them close to your body, and keep gestures waist high. Hold your notes at chest level in one hand for easy reading and gesturing. Do not clasp your hands in front of you or behind you, fold your arms, play with your notes, or grip the podium tightly. Avoid pointless or repetitious gestures. Never take a pen or pencil with you; it's easy to play with such an item without thinking, making it a major distraction, especially if you click it open and shut!

Eye Contact

Your eyes are a major source of contact with the audience. Shakespeare said the eye is the window to the soul. To establish your involvement and to hold attention, you will be most effective with most U.S. audiences if you look at them directly. Be sure to include everyone. For the audience, your gaze is a primary indicator of immediacy, and, of course, you can't respond to messages from the audience unless you are looking at them. Common problems for speakers in making eye contact with audiences include the "bobbing effect"—looking down so frequently at your notes yet wanting to look up to see your audience that it appears you are nodding "yes" repeatedly; talking to one person or one half of the room; talking to empty chairs or the back of the wall; or talking to the camera. Remember that your introduction and conclusion need to be delivered in such a way that you hold a steady gaze with your audience.

Movement

Kinesics, the study of bodily movement, is important in public speaking. Although not an aerobic activity, dynamic public speaking requires movement with purpose. We call this kind of purposive movement "transitional walks." Moving between points helps organize your speech, helps relieve tension, and keeps audience attention. Recall that movement or activity is a source of captivating audiences. As you move from point to point, be aware of the size of the room, camera restrictions, and keep your body facing the audience as you walk. Whenever possible, don't stand so far away as to connote fear or disdain for the audience or so close to the front row that listeners become uncomfortable. Of most importance, remember that movement should be intentional; it should not be pacing back and forth to reduce excess nervous energy.

VERBAL PRESENTATION GUIDELINES

Imagine writing an article without punctuation. Imagine music without a musical score. When playing an instrument, one must know when the music should become soft or loud, is repeated, changes rhythm, changes pitch, and how long the rests are.

We also need to prepare speeches with directions about verbal delivery. Public speaking is an art form, and we invite you to treat your voice as a musical instrument. Think for a moment that if your speech were monitored on an EKG machine, it should show many peaks and valleys, not a straight horizontal line signifying code blue! Generally, you need to use your natural voice and be conversational. This is the idea that you are talking *with* an audience not *at* an audience. Understanding how the components of verbal delivery work will enhance your message in dramatic ways and contribute mightily to a persona and tone that fits your purpose.

Rate

The speed at which you talk has important implications for the pacing of your speech. The extremes to avoid are plodding, halting delivery or racing, and rapid-fire delivery. Beginning speakers most often err in racing through their speeches as time cards tick away. You need to be conscious that although you have practiced this speech several times and know it inside and out, your audience is hearing it for the first time. You need to give your audience time to absorb your arguments. When using a microphone, you must be especially sensitive to speed owing to the echo effect of amplification. Think about where your speech warrants going slow and where it would be best to speed up. The rate of speed should change (fast, slow, moderate) throughout a presentation.

Volume

Volume or projection determines how well an audience hears what you say without working too hard. Projection comes from your diaphragm, not the back of your mouth. Speaking with a strong voice requires practice like any muscle conditioning. It is a misnomer that you must have a large frame to have a voice that projects. Lucy Stone and Ernestine Rose, two nineteenth-century women's rights speakers, were noted for their strong, articulate voices in speaking outdoors to large crowds despite slender physiques. And this in an era before microphones could aid projection! You will need to adjust your volume to the size and the acoustics of the room. Like rate, you must adjust your volume for emphasis. If you are speaking too loudly, audiences will think you are insensitive or boorish. If speaking too softly, they won't understand you or they will perceive you as timid.

Pitch

Pitch or intonation is the highness or lowness of a speaker's voice. Although it is important to use your natural voice (e.g., don't try to sound sophisticated or try to imitate important people), you can also train your voice to exhibit vocal variety. A speech should register hills and valleys, not straight lines. Some speakers are unaware of distracting pitch problems such as a monotone delivery, where every word is delivered at the same pitch so everything is of equal importance, or sing-song delivery, where every sentence follows a repetitive pitch alteration. Good pitch in a speech does not call attention to itself. As with rate and volume, pitch must be varied to reflect the various mood changes of the speech. Think how pitch is affected if you want to convey seriousness, joy, urgency, anger, fear, or unfairness, for example.

Enunciation

Enunciation is composed of two features: pronunciation and articulation. Nothing lowers credibility faster than a mispronounced word. Pronunciation is tricky given all the regional dialects, but if you are worried about tripping over difficult to pronounce words, substitute easier ones. Articulation refers to clarity of delivery. In a public speech, you must pay greater attention to opening your mouth and formulating your words in the front of your mouth, not in your throat. Here is where a formal speech and a casual conversation differ the most. In conversation we tend to "swallow" our words at the end of sentences. In speaking in public, you cannot afford to be an amateur ventriloquist. Lots of teeth must show to be an articulate speaker. Some common problems include dropping the ends of sentences and laziness with common words ("fer," "dunno," "didja," becuz," "ta"). If you have your tongue pierced, your challenges with enunciation are especially great.

Dramatic Pause

A dramatic or pregnant pause is not a lapse in memory, but strategic silence. Timing is key to its use. Like the other components of verbal delivery, the dramatic pause contributes to mood, pacing, variety, and especially impact. Mark Twain once said, "The right word may be effective, but no word was ever as effective as a rightly timed pause." An intentional pause should always be used after a rhetorical question. Your aim is to stimulate audience interest and even suspense. If you do not pause after asking a question, you ruin its effect. The pause can also be used for dramatic effect and to signal the end of a thought unit. Pauses are often used before a transition. Like rate, this is one of the more difficult verbal cues to remember, so write DRAMATIC PAUSE at the appropriate place on your note card. Otherwise you may butcher the best line of your entire speech!

Taken together (see Figure 3–6), the ideal speaker is easy to hear, pleasing to listen to, and not distracting to watch. As a rhetor, your goal is participation by the audience. Initiating joint action requires dynamism on your part. These nonverbal and verbal guidelines compose the canon of delivery. Even the ancient Greeks recognized that

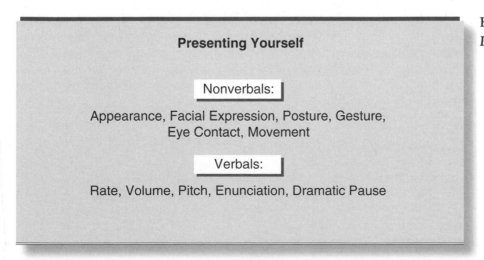

Presenting Yourself

Nonverbals:

Appearance, Facial Expression, Posture, Gesture, Eye Contact, Movement

Verbals:

Rate, Volume, Pitch, Enunciation, Dramatic Pause

Figure 3–6
Presenting Yourself

Figure 3–7
Delivery Tips

- Take a slow, deep breath to begin on a strong note
- Aim for vocal variety
- Enthusiasm is contagious
- Don't abandon a conversational style
- To be articulate, lots of teeth must show
- Stand on balls of feet, knees slightly bent, thrust shoulders back to project confidence
- Locate friendly faces in your audience from various sections of the room, and make sustained eye contact
- Allow sufficient pause time for audience response
- Are you having fun yet?

how you speak should never be emphasized over what you say. Invention and arrangement were given precedence over style, delivery, and memory. Nevertheless, the Roman Cicero, perhaps the greatest orator of the ancient world, called delivery "the sole and supreme power in oratory; without it, a speaker of the highest mental capacity can be held in no esteem; while one of moderate abilities, with this qualification, may surpass even those of the highest talent."[7] So the ancient rhetoricians were also well aware of the importance of presentation skills. Good delivery (see Figure 3–7) does not call attention to itself, but it is essential to invigorate and enhance your message. This section on how to present yourself has supported the idea that if rhetorical action is your goal, you must seek it both verbally and nonverbally.

STRATEGY REPORT

At this point you have the preliminaries to craft your first rhetorical act and to do it with some competence. In the next chapters we explore the resources available to you as a speaker or writer.

We strongly suggest that, for each rhetorical act that you are assigned, whether a speech or an essay, you prepare a written strategy report to be turned in at the time of your presentation. The report makes explicit at least part of the process you go through in preparing for rhetorical action. As such, it is not an end in itself but a tool for learning. It should help make you aware of the choices you make in initiating rhetorical action.

The strategy report has seven parts, some of which can be quite short:

1. Purpose
2. Persona (role) and tone
3. Audience
4. Outline
5. Source sheet
6. Strategies
7. Special remarks

1. *Purpose*: Define the rhetorical purpose of your speech or essay in terms of the general response you seek from the audience: to alter perception, to explain, to formulate belief, to initiate action, to maintain belief or action. Recall that each purpose is related to assumptions you are making about what your audience knows, feels, and believes.

   Then, state as briefly and precisely as you can what you would like the audience to know, feel, believe, or do when you have finished. In other words, indicate what you would consider ideal responses from your audience.

2. *Persona (role) and tone*: A speaker or writer assumes a persona or role in relation to the audience, and the tone of the language reflects his attitude toward the subject and relationship to the audience. Indicate whether you will speak as a peer or as an expert and if you will shift roles during the act. Similarly, indicate whether your tone will be relatively impersonal and objective (appropriate for an expert, for instance) or personal and conversational (appropriate for a peer) or ironic (appropriate for a skeptic).

3. *Audience*: Discuss whether the exposed audience is your target audience and whether it includes agents of change—people who have the capacity to act on your purpose (see Chapter 8). If there are discrepancies between those exposed and those you seek to reach or who can act, discuss some specific obstacles you face from this audience in transforming them into an ideal audience. Consider how you might appeal to them to play a real role that would lead them to respond as you desire.

4. *Outline*: With some practice, most students have little difficulty in making outlines. Look at the examples in Chapter 6, and be sure that your outline is in complete sentences, particularly as it expresses your thesis and your main points. Leave a wide margin on the left in order to label what you are doing at each point, such as kinds of evidence, transitions, organizational patterns, and strategies.

5. *Source sheet*: In preparing a speech or essay, your personal experience and your imagination are important sources from which to draw material and shape it for your audience. But almost no one's personal experience is so broad or insight so penetrating that she cannot benefit from the knowledge in secondary sources or the challenge of responding to the ideas of others. For each rhetorical act, supply a list of annotated sources—that is, sources with a short paragraph for each describing the nature of the source and what you used it for.

   Sources may be of four types. Use all these types in rhetorical acts throughout this course so you become familiar with different kinds of resources.

   a. Popular sources. Mass circulation newspapers and magazines are popular sources. Articles in *People* or *Time* or your local newspaper are intended for general audiences. They provide useful evidence and often stimulate thinking. Most Internet material, such as Google or Yahoo! News, falls into this category.

   b. Specialized sources. Periodicals (such as academic journals) intended for limited audiences of experts are specialized sources. They present articles by experts for specialists, and they analyze more thoroughly topics that are discussed generally or superficially in popular sources. In the *Quarterly Journal of Speech, Rhetoric & Public Affairs, Communication Quarterly,* or the *Journal of Applied Communication Research*, for example, you can gain greater understanding, gather data, and verify claims made in popular sources about communication issues. You should learn to do research that takes you beyond the popular press. Your instructor can give you suggestions here.

    c. Interviews. The world is full of all kinds of experts, and you should take the opportunity to talk to those available in your area on your subject. Such interviews, including the person's credentials, should be listed as part of your source materials.

    d. Personal experience. You may have direct knowledge of your subject that goes beyond the ordinary. If you have such experience, and it is relevant to your subject, cite your own expertise and describe its nature. Be reminded, however, of the importance of testing your experience against data gathered by others and the opinions of experts.

Cite your sources in proper bibliographic form. Here are examples for a periodical and a book:

Trottier, Daniel. "Interpersonal Surveillance on Social Media." *Canadian Journal of Communication* 39 (2012): 319–332.

Turkle, Sherry. *Along Together: Why We Expect More From Technology and Less From Each Other*. New York: Basic Books, 2011.

Here is an example from a URL address on the Internet:

Schramm, C. "Are we thwarting medical innovation?" Forbes online. 8 Mar. 2011. http://blogs.forbes.com/carlchramm/2011/03/08are-we-thwarting-medical-innovation/.

If your source is an interview with an expert or personal experience, simply make note of the nature of the interview or the experience. For example:

On January 31, 2011, I interviewed Caitlin Linshied, a maternal and fetal immunology researcher at the University of Kansas. She explained to me that cord blood is thought to be a minimal source for stem cells but they are noncontroversial because these cells cannot reproduce or clone a baby human.

6. *Strategies:* It may take you only a sentence or two to describe your purpose, your persona and tone, and your audience, but it will take you several paragraphs to describe your strategies adequately. In this section, you must discuss the means you will use to achieve your purpose and the choices you will make to overcome the obstacles you face. Your statement should have two parts.

First, given your subject and purpose, how is your audience likely to respond? Here you should explore the rhetorical obstacles of complexity, cultural history, cost, control, and reasons that the audience might be hostile or indifferent to your subject or to what you propose (see Chapter 9).

Second, discuss specific choices you made in regard to language, arguments, and appeals. In addition, discuss your choice of perspective, evidence, organizational patterns, and introductory and concluding remarks to indicate your relationship to the subject. Strategies should reflect the ways that you have adapted materials to your audience in order to achieve your purpose.

7. *Special remarks:* Use this section to discuss anything you believe significant that does not fit into the other sections. It may be that you have no special remarks, but many rhetorical acts are unusual, and you may need this section to talk about elements you believe are unique or out of the ordinary.

MATERIAL FOR ANALYSIS I

Rhetorical Act to Alter Perception: The Definitional Essay

It Is Your Basic Human Right to Agree with This Column[8]

By Peter Shawn Taylor

1   You can't swing a cat without hitting a basic human right or two these days.

2   Last week, for example, Danish bicycling advocate Mikael Colville-Andersen was in Kitchener telling local planners how to make Waterloo Region friendlier to bicyclists.

3   Judging from coverage in The Record, Colville-Andersen's suggestions range from the sensible (separated bike lanes) to the silly (reducing speed limits to 30 km/h). But his most preposterous argument came in summing up his overall philosophy: "urban mobility is a basic human right," he said.

4   However one may define urban mobility, and I suspect Colville-Andersen has in mind fewer cars and more bikes, it is certainly not a basic human right.

5   Then again, Colville-Andersen has plenty of company in making outlandish claims about basic human rights. Going back several years in The Record's archives, I found numerous references to the term. Most of them ludicrous.

6   Alleged "basic human rights" include (big breath) fluoridation of the region's drinking water, unlimited special-needs education, access by federal prisoners to a Buddhist spiritual adviser, wearing a niqab, access to clean water, a place to call home, universal sex education and something called "food freedom."

7   With such a diverse and curious list of basic human rights on offer, perhaps it's worth taking another big breath and considering what the phrase actually means. And how such an important notion has come to be so widely misused.

8   In contract law, a right is something you possess that cannot be taken away without your consent. It might be the right to buy a certain number of shares at a particular time or price. Or right of first refusal on a house. These kinds of rights are reliable and defendable.

9   Human rights, on the other hand, are a much looser concept. While often couched in near-religious terminology, even those so-called human rights enshrined in legislation, outlined in international treaties or described as "inalienable" are frequently denied or proscribed.

10   Consider the Canadian Charter of Rights and Freedoms, which this year marks its 30th anniversary. What does the very first section of the charter say? It isn't a list of all

those things we might consider important, such as free speech, freedom of religion or freedom of peaceful assembly. Those come in the next section. Rather, section 1 makes it clear that every right about to be listed is subject to "reasonable limits" as defined by government and the legal system.

11   In other words, even the charter's list of so-called basic human rights can be taken away under a wide variety of conditions. Regardless of how rights advocates may phrase it, rights are something governments give to us (or we give ourselves), not something we're born with or innately possess.

12   As outrageous as it may seem to have rules imposed on us regarding what we can eat or wear, these are not violations of basic human rights. In a democracy, such rules are the result of governments we freely choose.

13   Consider that residents of Waterloo recently voted to remove fluoride from its water supply. This despite the fact the Ontario Dental Association claims having fluoride added to your water is a basic human right. Apparently not.

14   Further confusing things, the United Nations' Universal Declaration of Human Rights even declares a right of children to compulsory education. But how you can have the right to be forced to do something remains a bit of a mystery.

15   There's really only one truly universal and basic human right that can never be curtailed or removed. That's the right to independent thought. And it has survived Hitler, Stalin, Mao and countless other despots who successfully obliterated every other basic human right you might name. It is this fundamental and inalienable right that makes possible free speech, freedom of religion and all the other components of a free and democratic life.

16   The real problem with the current proliferation of the term basic human rights, as economist Thomas Mayer has pointed out, is that people use the term "right" when they really mean "should."

17   There's nothing wrong with arguing everyone should have access to clean (or fluoridated) water, affordable housing or sex education. These are all statements of political belief. As such they're open to debate, criticism and competing interests.

18   But when people claim there is a "basic human right" to whatever pet project they happen to be promoting, what they're really saying is that they're not interested in debating the matter. It's a right. End of discussion.

19   This sort of rhetorical legerdemain cheapens the underlying concept of human rights by turning it into an ideological battle, in the same way provincial and federal human rights commissions have been hijacked by special interest groups.

20   Free speech, freedom of religion and free assembly are all great and important things that must continually be protected because they form the basis of our democracy.

And only within a functioning democracy can we debate and decide on a whole range of other "non-basic" facets of our lives.

21 Democracy does not depend on bike lanes on our streets, fluoride in our water or Zen masters in our prisons. The presence or absence of such things is the product of democratic decisions. Stop calling them basic human rights.

Questions for Analysis

1. How well does this essay fulfill the rhetorical purpose of altering perception? For a short piece, does it adequately shape audience knowledge by defining a term clearly, accurately, and imaginatively? Is the term frequently misunderstood? How does it involve another rhetorical purpose: to formulate belief?

2. How does this piece illustrate suggestions made in this chapter for how to captivate an audience? Are there some sources of audience captivation that could have been used but are not? Explain.

3. Examine the "definitional strategies" in Chapter 4, "The Resources of Evidence" (see Figure 4–4). Definitional strategies are directly related to the rhetorical purpose of altering perception. Which definitional strategies are evident in this essay? Imagine other definitional strategies that this essay might have used if it were addressing a different kind of audience (say, a student audience) in a different context (such as a U.S. University Communication class)?

 MATERIAL FOR ANALYSIS II

Rhetorical Act to Explain: The Speech to Inform[9]

"Schizophrenia"

By Jarod Acquistapace

1 Adam "was a wonderfully, sweet young man," his mother said. He was a high school athlete and captain of his soccer team, active in his college fraternity, a good student. He had graduated from college and started working while studying for a professional certification exam when something inside him changed.... Adam stopped being careful about his personal appearance. He told his parents he suspected them of communicating with each other in secret ways, such as in sign language, which he couldn't understand. He began to hear his mother's voice in his head, and he asked her why she was sending him messages.... Adam was diagnosed with schizophrenia.

2 According to Dr. E. Fuller Torrey's book, *Surviving Schizophrenia*, 1 out of every 100 people will be directly affected by schizophrenia in their lifetime, yet far too often this disease goes undiagnosed and unnoticed.

3 I for one never thought I would ever have any kind of mental illness, let alone something like schizophrenia; I was in the gifted program since the sixth grade, wrote music and played guitar, and was well liked in school. Certainly, I was exempt from this "bizarre" illness. Yet this is far from the truth. No one is invulnerable to this illness, as I have learned the hard way.

4 Today, I want to explain to you what schizophrenia is, how it affects those afflicted, and what treatments are available.

5 So, what exactly is schizophrenia? First, we must know what schizophrenia is not. Those afflicted are not homicidal (January 2001 "Schizophrenia Update"). Those afflicted are not retarded; hopefully, I am evidence of this.

6 Now that we know what schizophrenia is not, we can effectively state what it is. According to PsychLaws.org, Schizophrenia is a neurological brain disorder that affects 2.2 million Americans today, or approximately 1 percent of the population. Schizophrenia can affect anyone at any age, but most cases develop between ages sixteen and thirty. Since the early 1980s, with the availability of brain imaging techniques and other developments in neuroscience, the evidence has become overwhelming that schizophrenia is a disease of the brain, just as multiple sclerosis, Parkinson's disease, and Alzheimer's disease are diseases of the brain.

7 The brains of individuals with these diseases are measurably different from individuals who do not have these diseases, both structurally and functionally. Look at these brain images to see the differences (show visuals on computer slide). Notice the enlarged ventricles of the brain. Notice the reduced volume of gray matter in the brain. If you look over here you will see an enlarged part of the brain known as the amygdala. Finally, you will see from this image an increased amount of white matter. (Put away visual aid.)

8 Now we know what schizophrenia is on a clinical level. How does it affect those afflicted? Again from psychlaws.org, schizophrenia interferes with a person's ability to think clearly, manage emotions, make decisions, and relate to others. Specific abnormalities with schizophrenia include: Delusions and hallucinations (sometimes I think people are plotting against me); Alterations of the senses (sometimes I experience what can best be described as "emotional flatness"—a kind of numbness to pain or joy); An inability to respond appropriately (you've seen me in class have trouble sitting still or staying engaged for long on a topic; some have erroneously concluded that I suffer from attention deficit disorder).

9 Now that we know how people are affected by schizophrenia, how can schizophrenia be treated? Hospitalization is often necessary in cases of acute schizophrenia.

This is not the *One Flew over the Cuckoo's Nest* experience. Rather, such treatment ensures the safety of the affected person and allows for observation by trained mental health professionals to determine whether schizophrenia is the appropriate diagnosis. According to a friend of mine, who requested to remain anonymous, the structure of mental hospitals is usually tailored specifically to the individual and allows for a little or a lot of social interaction depending on his or her current mental state. Medication is also a common and effective treatment for schizophrenia. In an article on schizophrenia.com, I learned that antipsychotic drugs (also called *neuroleptics*), available since the 1950s, can dramatically improve the functioning of people with schizophrenia. Once the most troubling symptoms are controlled by medication, the person often does not require hospitalization. Medication also prevents harsh relapses by regulating symptoms that could otherwise get out of hand. I know this firsthand!

10 I want you all to remember what Josh Lyman, Adult Compeer Coordinator, Mental Health Association of Central Kansas, told me, "While there is no cure for schizophrenia, it is a highly treatable disorder." In fact, he says, the treatment success rate for schizophrenia is comparable to the treatment success rate for heart disease!

11 I hope I have helped everyone understand what schizophrenia is, how it affects people, and how it can be treated. If anyone has any questions about this illness or is worried about him or herself or loved ones, or would like more information on Schizophrenics Anonymous (I have brochures), don't hesitate to ask me in private, and I'll be happy to address your concerns.

Questions for Analysis

1. How well does this speech fulfill the rhetorical purpose of explaining? Does it adequately address the who, what, where, when, and why questions that such a purpose demands?

2. Is this topic one that needs explaining? For whom? Is it frequently misunderstood? Mysterious? Complex? How have current events made the topic of mental illness of particular interest for general audiences? What subject-related rhetorical obstacles (see Chapter 9) are evident with this topic? What is the thesis? How does it involve another rhetorical purpose: to alter perception?

3. How does this speech illustrate suggestions made in this chapter for how to pick a topic, research a subject, and prepare your presentation, including how and when to use visual aids? Analyze content carefully for strengths and weaknesses.

4. Can you label the parts of speech (introduction, body, conclusion) and outline the main points and subpoints in the body of the speech? Can you spot transitions? Do they help to organize the speech and provide pacing for the development of ideas? Do the introduction and conclusion meet the criteria outlined in this chapter for what these parts of speech should accomplish? How?

5. What specific "Message Tips" do you see in this speech? Is the speech a strong example of how rhetoric should be poetic and pragmatic?

MATERIAL FOR ANALYSIS III

Rhetorical Act to Formulate Belief: Essay to Support a Communal Value

"Always Go to the Funeral"[10]

By Deirdre Sullivan

1 I believe in always going to the funeral. My father taught me that.

2 The first time he said it directly to me, I was sixteen and trying to get out of going to calling hours for Miss Emerson, my old fifth-grade math teacher. I did not want to go. My father was unequivocal. "Dee," he said, "you're going. Always go to the funeral. Do it for the family."

3 So my dad waited outside while I went in. It was worse than I thought it would be: I was the only kid there. When the condolence line deposited me in front of Miss Emerson's shell-shocked parents, I stammered out, "Sorry about all this," and stalked away. But, for that deeply weird expression of sympathy delivered twenty years ago, Miss Emerson's mother still remembers my name and always says hello with tearing eyes.

4 That was the first time I went unchaperoned, but my parents had been taking us kids to funerals and calling hours as a matter of course for years. By the time I was sixteen, I had been to five or six funerals. I remember two things from the funeral circuit: bottomless dishes of free mints, and my father saying on the ride home, "You can't come in without going out, kids. Always go to the funeral."

5 Sounds simple—when someone dies, get in your car and go to calling hours or the funeral. That, I can do. But I think a personal philosophy of going to funerals means more than that.

6 "Always go to the funeral" means that I have to do the right thing when I really, really don't feel like it. I have to remind myself of it when I could make some small gesture, but I don't really have to and I definitely don't want to. I'm talking about those things that represent only inconvenience to me, but the world to the other guy. You know, the painfully underattended birthday party. The hospital visit during happy hour. The shiva call for one of my ex's uncles. In my humdrum life, the daily battle hasn't been good versus evil. It's hardly so epic. Most days, my real battle is doing good versus doing nothing.

7 In going to funerals, I've come to believe that while I wait to make a grand heroic gesture, I should just stick to the small inconveniences that let me share in life's inevitable, occasional calamity.

8 On a cold April night three years ago, my father died a quiet death from cancer. His funeral was on a Wednesday, middle of the workweek. I had been numb for days

when, for some reason, during the funeral, I turned and looked back at the folks in the church. The memory of it still takes my breath away. The most human, powerful and humbling thing I've ever see was a church at 3:00 on a Wednesday full of inconvenienced people who believe in going to the funeral.

Questions for Analysis

1. How well does this essay fulfill the rhetorical purpose of formulating belief? How does it build upon another rhetorical purpose: creating virtual experience? Why is crafting a rhetorical act to formulate belief often more of a challenge for a rhetor than those primarily aimed to create virtual experience, alter perception, or explain?

2. How does this essay illustrate suggestions made in this chapter for how to pick a topic, research a subject, and prepare a presentation?

3. How does the essay illustrate suggestions made in this chapter for how to captivate an audience? Are there some sources of audience captivation that could be here but are not? Explain.

4. Do the introduction and conclusion meet the criteria outlined in this chapter for what these parts of a rhetorical act should accomplish? How does a written rhetorical act change the expectations for introductions and conclusions compared to an oral rhetorical act?

 ## MATERIAL FOR ANALYSIS IV

Rhetorical Act to Initiate Action: Speech to Advocate Policy

"The Valley of Death" 11

By Julia Huxman

1 By the time Suzanne Herbert's breast cancer was discovered, it had spread to her spine. Metastatic cancers, her doctors explained, multiply aggressively and prove fatal in 9 out of 10 patients. So Suzanne, a single mother of two young children, Dominic and Grace, promises to make the most of her estimated 26 months; she has a lot of mothering left to do.

2 This story, reported in the New York Times on January 17th 2011 strikes a nerve with those of us who are reminded of a close family member or friend who struggled through a terminal illness (New York). But imagine the added turmoil in knowing that in 2004 the journal *Cancer Research* reported the discovery of a peptide that blocked the metastasis process in various organs of lab animals. Today, seven years later, that

breakthrough in cancer research has nothing more to show for itself than a publication, collecting dust on a shelf somewhere while Suzanne struggles to explain to her children that there is no cure.

3 There is a great divide, called the Valley of Death, between medical research and tangible cures for patients. Too often when the potential for a cure is discovered, it is not translated into medicine. So today, I'd like to first alert you to the disturbing problem of the divide between research and cures, second point out two causes for this crisis, and finally offer some solutions; because our health care system cannot heal its patients until it has gone through some rehab of its own.

4 So how does a country that produced cures for Polio and Smallpox have a valley of death between research and medicine? Slate Magazine asks, "Are the cures really coming?" In an August 24th 2010 article, and in typical Slate fashion journalist Emily Yoff asserts, "Adding to the frustration is an endless stream of laboratory animals that are always getting healed. Mice with Parkinson's have been successfully treated with stem cells, as have mice with sickle cell anemia. Dogs with hemophilia and muscular dystrophy have been made disease-free. But humans keep experiencing suffering and death. Why?"(Yoff). Keith Yamomoto the Chairman of the Board on Life Sciences explains it best by saying, "results from basic research in the life sciences, typically are not advanced beyond publication in a scientific journal, suggesting that there is a growing mass of untapped scientific knowledge with great potential for humanitarian and economic benefit" (Cures). Say, for sake of an oversimplified analogy, you went into a restaurant to order food. But the waiter comes out and informs you that the cook only comes up with recopies, he doesn't actually make the food for you to eat, so you'll just have to go hungry tonight. But we could give you some bread and butter to tide you over? Obviously there would be outrage in this situation, partly because Americans love their food, but mostly because a restaurant is set up for an order to transition smoothly from the cook to the waiter to the customer. But why, why is there not a connection between our medical researchers, doctors and patients?

5 There are two main causes for our biomedical valley of death; first, a lack of communication between the researchers and the producers, and secondly, frightening little incentive for that communication to exist. First, the lack of communication accounts for a bulk of this crisis. For example, Biologist Hans Keirstead discovered a way to cure paralysis in lab animals, and decided to make the lonely treck across the Valley of Death. He soon found, that he didn't have the skills to do it alone, and had to hire a specialist to handle practical roadblocks, such as inventing specialized injection instruments, or obtaining monkeys for testing. As he remarked to Newsweek magazine on November 1st 2008, "what do we academics know about developing medical devices?" (Begley 2008). You see, a specialist is required for each translational step of biomedical research, so there needs to be collaboration among each component, not isolation.

6 Secondly, there is little incentive for communication because the old adage "publish or perish" is alive and well in academia. Because most biomedical researchers are academics whose main goal is publication, momentum stops once this goal is met.

Sharon Begley, writing in the afore [mentioned] issue of Newsweek writes that our country's biomedical system is focused on research because "THAT is what gets them published in leading journals, and THAT is what gets them grants from the [National Institute of Health]"(Begley 2010). Getting published is a high honor and expectation in academia, but the tedious and often fruitless work required to turn what was discovered in that research into something even testable on humans has become such a tangled mess of approvals from the Food and Drug Administration which the Wall Street Journal of February 28th 2011 calls: "The bureaucratic assault on cancer treatments" (FDA).

7 Plus, grants for transitional work are nearly impossible to receive because they are rarely successful on the first attempt. And if it's difficult to earn funding, indicating that the larger "system" doesn't value such work, who would want to waste time trying to collaborate? John Adler of Stanford University, and the inventor of the cyberknife radiation therapy, tells the afore mentioned Newsweek, "Basic research is healthy in America. But patients aren't benefiting. Our understanding of diseases is greater than ever"(Begley 2010). An xconomy.com article published September 2nd 2010 reports of the $879 million in grants the NIH provided last year, "less than 15% was directed at new therapies or clinical trials"(Iadonato).

8 This is a scary problem. And though its causes lie at an institutional level, it has become a very real crisis on a personal level. Considering that according to the American Cancer Society's website posted July 2010, each of us in this room carries a 41% chance of developing some type of cancer in our lifetime, perhaps the personal danger will spur us to action. There are two levels at which change can occur: the governmental and individual.

9 First, legislative action has already been taken but not funded. Former Pennsylvania senator, Arlen Specter initiated the Cures Acceleration Network or CAN act. On his website, Specter explains, "my CAN Act" specifically addresses the "Valley of Death"(Cures). This piece of legislation mandates acceleration in the development of distributable cures, and most importantly establishes regular communication between the NIH and the Food and Drug Administration, which approves the research for human use. If authorized, CAN would have a 500 million dollar budget to award to outcome-driven research (Cures). CAN was added to and passed with the health care bill passed last spring. At the time, bundling CAN with the Health Care bill seemed like a good idea to move it through congress. But now, the fact that it is bundled with the Health Care bill is the very roadblock it faces.

10 As you are aware, debates about funding have turned into a congressional game of tug-o-war. Which is why I am advocating that the Senate approves funding for the Cures Acceleration Network as a separate section of the bill. Forbes.com of March 8th 2011 agrees, "A better 'repeal' agenda would focus on undoing, and re-thinking, much of the FDA regulatory regime and other barriers to innovation in health care" (Schramm). Francis Collins, director of the NIH explains to Science Magazine on January 28th 2011,

11 "I [...] want to see the scientific opportunities that relate to translation approached in a very bold way" (Kaiser). This is where we can help on an individual level. At the end of this round, please pick up one of my information cards, where I have listed a website that is actively pushing for the CAN act. I mapped out the proper mouse clicks that will take you to each of your state senators' pages where there is an update of their position on the CAN act along with a link to send them a letter or e-mail right on the spot. Not sure what to say? Join my facebook group and copy and paste something I've already written for you. Now that Senator Specter is retired from the political arena, we cannot let this bill lose momentum!

12 I know you'll hear a lot of persuasions that encourage you to write your legislator, which seems like a solution that requires change to start from the top down. But in response to my question at a press conference on March 8th 2011, former congressman and current ambassador Tony Hall explained to me that if there's one thing politicians are afraid of, it's voters, because they have to make them happy. Let's enact the democratic process here! When we're talking about funding cures for terminal illnesses, the playing field is equalized across party lines by a common vulnerability. Tribune Media Columnist Cal Thomas calls it a "failure of political leadership" and reminds us of a time when "the political and medical communities united and led the public toward a cure for polio.[...] And look at the money saved from no longer having to treat victims of polio" (Thomas).

13 After being alerted to the problem, its causes, and possible cures it is clear that the Valley of Death must be bridged. Chances are, before Suzanne's children are even teenagers, she will join the 40,000 that lose their battle with breast cancer each year. "People like the pretty story with the happy ending," Suzanne says. "We don't have the happy ending." How do we justify a dusty database of cancer research, when that untapped medical knowledge could be the difference between life and death? We have the technology and the resources to fix this problem and allow our health care system and its patients to heal.

Works Cited

Begley, Sharon. "Where are the Cures?" 1 Nov. 2008 Newsweek Online. http://www.newsweek.com/2008/10/31/where-are-the-cures.html

Begley, Sharon and Mary Carmichael. "Desperately Seeking Cures." Newsweek Magazine May 24th & 31 2010: 38-42.

"Cures Acceleration Network Act." Specter for the Cure.com 2009-2011. http://www.specterforthecure.com/the-initiative.php

"The FDA and Slower Cures." Wall Street Journal 28 Feb 2011: A18

Iadonato. Shawn. "The feds need to start supporting early-stage drug development." Xconomy.com. 2 Sept. 2010 www.xconomy.com

Kaiser, Jocelyn. " Collins Sparks Furor With Proposed NIH Reshuffling." Science Magazine Online. 28. Jan 2011 http://www.sciencemag.org/content/331/6016/386.full

New York Times. Jan 17th 2011 "A Pink Ribbon Race, Years Long". Roni Caryn Rabin http://www.nytimes.com/2011/01/18/health/18cancer.html

Schramm, Carl. "Are We Thwarting Medical Innovation?" Forbes online. 8 Mar. 2011
http://blogs.forbes.com/carlschramm/2011/03/08/are-we-thwarting-medical-innovation/
Thomas, Cal. "U.S. Should Make Curing Diseases a Top Priority." Tribune Media
Services. Wichita Eagle Dec 8 2010.
Yoff, Emily. "The Medical Revolution." Slate Magazine Online 24 Aug. 2010. http://
www.slate.com/id/2264401/

Questions for Analysis

1. How well does this speech fulfill the rhetorical purpose of initiating action? How does it build upon the rhetorical purpose of formulating belief?

2. Is this topic one that creates adequate dissonance (psychological discomfort) for audiences to contemplate action (see Chapter 6)? For whom?

3. How well does this speech follow the Motivated Sequence (Attention, Need, Satisfaction, Visualization, and Action), the organizational pattern tailored specifically for speeches to initiate action (see Chapter 6)?

4. How does this speech illustrate suggestions made in this chapter for how to pick a topic, research a subject, and prepare your presentation?

5. Can you label the parts of the speech (introduction, body, conclusion) and outline the main points and subpoints in the body of the speech? Can you spot transitions? Do they help to organize the speech and provide pacing for the development of ideas? Do the introduction and conclusion meet the criteria outlined in this chapter for what these parts of speech should accomplish? How?

6. What specific "Message Tips" do you see in this speech? Is the speech a strong example of how rhetoric can be poetic and pragmatic?

7. In comparing the four rhetorical acts in this chapter, which has the strongest ethos appeal (credibility of the rhetor)? Logos appeal (soundness of argument and evidence)? Pathos appeal (emotional impact)? How is your judgment affected by subsequent events (Chapter 11) related to these topics?

EXERCISES

Critical Thinking Exercises

1. Assign each member of the class one of the "ways to captivate audiences." Locate the Top 100 Speeches of the twentieth century at www.news.wisc.edu/misc/speeches/ as voted on by 137 leading rhetoric professors in the United States and tabulated by speech professors at the University of Wisconsin and Texas A & M. Find a speech from this list where your assigned method of captivating is used. Bring the speech to class and read aloud the passage where you find this particular inventional quality. Ask members of the class to identify the means of captivating an audience that is at work in the passage. Were some of these ways of captivating easier to find than others? Why do you think that is the case?

2. The choice of a thesis is a decision that specifies the precise claim you want to make, and it represents a drastic limitation of the topic. In choosing a thesis, speakers take into consideration not only their own interests and goals, but also the potential benefits for their audience. Here is an exercise to walk you through the process of selecting a topic and deciding on your position and purpose. Select a controversial

topic that is currently being discussed in the media but for which you can say, "I am unable to take a stand on the issue of…" Consider drafting a proposal for a new course that will educate students on this controversial topic. Start by answering these three questions: What is the topic you wish to explore? Why are you interested in it? Why do you think other students should be paying attention to it (i.e., what do you think is at stake in the debate)? And, Why can't you make up your mind at this time? Gather information about the different concerns and interests involved in the controversy. Identify the major point of disagreement. Draft a syllabus that reflects the anatomy or history of the debate—who is involved? what are their concerns? what are the origins of the controversy? What is the central idea you would like students to retain upon completing your course? Considering all the points and counterpoints that you have collected, can you now take a stand on the controversy? What arguments and evidence turned out to be most persuasive in helping you make your stand? Why?

Analytical Writing Exercises

3. Prepare a 1,500 word essay that applies a fable, tale, myth, or story to a current problem in order to formulate belief. Use such stories as Aesop's fables, Greek and Roman mythology, the fairy tales of Hans Christian Anderson or the Grimm Brothers, books by Dr. Seuss, or a religious parable.

4. Write an op-ed to your school newspaper that formulates belief on a compelling current problem on campus. Utilize the tips for the public service rhetorical act to craft value appeals that pique readers' interest and engage their convictions. Consult an opinion-writing text from award-winning journalists, such as *Beyond Argument: A Handbook for Editorial Writers*, produced by the National Conference of Editorial Writers, or *The Book of Writing*, by Paula LaRocque, for additional guidance on how to get opinion writing published.

5. Write a 1,200 word essay as a tribute to your favorite class, instructor, or extra-curricular activity. Utilize the tips for the ceremonial rhetorical act to craft epideictic discourse that venerates the object of affection, unifies your campus community, and maintains the normative actions of the community. How might you turn this tribute into a feature story that could be published in your local newspaper or magazine? Consult a feature-writing text such as *Feature Writing for Newspapers and Magazines*, 5th edition, by Edward Friedlander and John Lee

or *At the Heart of It: Ordinary People, Extraordinary Lives*, by Walt Harrington, or *This I Believe: The Personal Philosophies of Remarkable Men and Women*, edited by Jay Allison and Dan Gediman in association with NPR, to gain additional techniques for translating spoken tributes into publishable feature stories.

Strategic Speaking Exercises

6. One of the best ways to reduce high levels of speech anxiety is to speak in front of your classmates often in thirty-second to one-minute impromptu performances. These are low-key, low-risk speaking exercises that help you practice critical thinking and delivery skills. Your instructor may want to prepare an envelope full of topics ranging from "Famous Proverbs" to "Current Events" to "Reading Checks." Each day three to five students can practice public speaking skills. The following keys will guide you to an effective impromptu speech—one that does not wander or turn into a comic routine: (1) state your point clearly; (2) illustrate your point with a brief explanation and a few examples; and (3) restate your point. The more "unadorned" the better for these one-minute speaking exercises.

7. Another very good way to reduce speech anxiety is to speak from experience in the form of a story. Craft a two- to three-minute storytelling speech about "My adventure with or in…" A storytelling speech is essentially a rhetorical act to create virtual experience. Utilize the tips from the storytelling rhetorical act guidelines to craft a coherent, authentic, and highly descriptive speech that unfolds in narrative form.

8. Prepare a four- to five-minute speech to alter perception that includes a visual aid or an excerpt from a novel, short story, or poem as a major piece of evidence. You will be evaluated based on preparation, message, presentation, and visual aid tips presented in this chapter. Utilize the tips from the definitional rhetorical act guidelines to craft a speech that takes a new angle and presents a novel approach on a misunderstood topic. See the "Basic Human Rights" material for analysis in this chapter as a building block for this kind of larger altering-perception speech assignment.

9. Prepare a five- to seven-minute speech to explain some concept, event, or process that includes detailed personal experience and research from secondary sources. Utilize the tips from the instructional

rhetorical act guidelines to craft an interesting, well-researched speech that gives new information on your topic in an unbiased way.

10. Look up topics such as the war on terror, health care reform, climate change, stem cell research, immigration reform, alternate energy sources, the "Arab Spring," or the "Fiscal Cliff." Imagine that you are a member of an academic committee on campus that is in possession of limited funds for putting on a special lecture series. The program will involve offering a series of free workshops to students and invite prominent guest lecturers. Your funds will be sufficient for coverage of only one of the above topics.

Which topic should be considered the most significant, urgent, or beneficial to students? Draft a short policy speech (5–6 minutes) in which you address the committee and make your recommendation for allocating the money. You need to offer clear arguments and to demonstrate that you have in mind the best interests of the student body. Utilize the tips from the policy rhetorical act guidelines to craft a speech that initiates action by overcoming points of audience resistance. See the "Valley of Death" material for analysis in this chapter as a model for this shorter problem-solution or comparative advantage policy speech.

NOTES

1. "The Only Thing We Have to Fear Is Speaking Before a Group," 1988, *Psychology Today*. Reprinted, [Minneapolis] *Star Tribune*, 19 March 1991.

2. Material adapted from Monroe et al. *Principles and Types of Speech Communication* 8th edition. (Glenview, IL: Scott Foresman, 1978).

3. New York: Random House, 2007.

4. For an excellent book on research for communication students, see R. B. Rubin, A. M. Rubin, and L. J. Piele, *Communication Research: Strategies and Sources*, 6th edition. (Belmont, CA: Wadsworth, 2005).

5. "Wanted: Search Engines with Uncommon Sense." *Kansas City Star*, August 10, 1999, p. D16.

6. See also Esther Grassian, *Thinking Critically About World Wide Web Resources*, UCLA College Library; "Evaluating Information Found on the Internet," from Johns Hopkins University Library.

7. Cicero, *On Oratory and Orators*, trans. J. S. Watson. (Carbondale: Southern Illinois University Press, 1970), p. 255.

8. Peter Shawn Taylor, "It Is Your Basic Human Right to Agree With This Column." *Waterloo Region Record*, November 29, 2012, p. A13. Reprinted with permission from the Author. Available online at http://www.therecord.com/opinion/columns/article/844633--it-is-your-basic-human-right-to-agree-with-this-column Accessed 1/4/13; paragraph numbers added.

9. Reprinted with permission by Jarod Acquistapace.

10. Deirdre Sullivan, *This I Believe: The Personal Philosophies of Remarkable Men and Women*, ed. Jay Allison and Dan Gediman. (New York: Holt). In association with National Public Radio, *All Things Considered, Morning Edition*, 2006, pp. 235–237.

11. Reprinted with permission of Julia Huxman, Forensics circuit speech, Bethel College, 2011.

Chapter 4

The Resources of Evidence

No public speaking class or any textbook can totally prepare you for the occasions on which you will be expected to present materials, make a case, defend a conclusion, or memorialize a beloved friend. What both can do is prepare you to think about what symbolic resources you have to respond to the circumstances in which you find yourself. Accordingly, the chapters that follow explore the four primary resource fields that you have to cope with different kinds of situations and the kinds of challenges that you are likely to face because of the subject or purpose of your rhetoric, because of the attitudes and characteristics of audiences, and because of your personal history. In the next four chapters we explore four important resources you have as a rhetor—the evidence or supporting materials you can use, the arguments you can develop, the organization or structure of your discourse, and the language or style of your rhetoric. This chapter explores the resources of evidence, the most basic building blocks of rhetorical action.

Writing long ago in *On Rhetoric*, Aristotle said, "There are two parts to a speech; for it is necessary [first] to state the subject and [then] to demonstrate it" (1414a.30).[1] Aristotle emphasized the role of a central claim or thesis, buttressing arguments, and data in persuasion. As Aristotle also noted in the *On Rhetoric*, however, proof comes in different forms. He wrote about three sources of persuasion arising out of the discursive (definitional or logical) qualities of language (*logos*), out of the feelings, attitudes, or states of mind of the audience (*pathos*), and out of the audience's perceptions of the rhetor (*ethos*). Aristotle was also concerned with the resources in language, particularly the resources of figurative language or metaphor to make ideas visual and vivid.

Although Aristotle's ideas are still useful, we cannot discuss evidence or supporting materials solely in logical or empirical terms. We must also consider its psychological impact on the audience—whether evidence makes ideas lively and clear or affects attitudes toward the rhetor.

In practical terms, every piece of evidence must be judged by two criteria:

1. What are its logical or empirical strengths and limitations?
2. What are its psychological powers?

[handwritten: ↑ how we judge every piece of evidence]

Ideally, good supporting materials show the truth of a claim; they are clear, vivid, and concrete; and they present the rhetor as competent and trustworthy.

To illustrate the resources of evidence, we use selections from an evidence-rich essay titled "A Special Moment in History"[2] by Bill McKibben, an environmentalist, author, and Schumann Distinguished Scholar at Middlebury College in Ripton, Vermont. It's a good source to explore the resources of evidence because it deals with an important but difficult and controversial subject—climate change—and it argues that we U.S. Americans have to change our ways now if we are to avert a worldwide catastrophe. In other words, it is targeted at us, and it asks us to do things we don't particularly enjoy doing, such as cutting back drastically on burning fossil fuels. We use excerpts from the essay to talk about how the author attempts to use supporting materials—all kinds of evidence—in an effort to persuade us to take this issue seriously, to recognize the threat that it poses, and to take action despite our cultural attachment to gas-guzzling cars, for instance.

Rhetors have five categories of evidence as resources: *stories* or examples, *statistics* or numerical data, *experts* (or testimony from authority), *analogies* or comparisons, and *visuals* or pictorial representations and presentations (see Figure 4–1). These different types of evidence rarely occur in isolation, as the examples we use will show, because each has weaknesses that can be offset by combining it with other kinds of evidence. In the next sections the strengths and weaknesses of each type will be explored and illustrated.

[handwritten: Stories, statistics, analogies, experts, visuals.]

Types of Evidence (VASES)	Visuals	Analogies	Statistics	Experts	Stories
Psychological Appeal	✓	✓			✓
Rational Appeal		✓	✓	✓	
Primary Strength	Package ideas holistically	Alter perception	Amplify & scope	Enhance credibility	Invite empathy
Primary Weakness	Over-simplified	Irrelevant	Incomprehensible	Distorting	Unrepresentative

Figure 4–1
Types of Evidence (VASES)

STORIES

In "A Special Moment in History," McKibben argues that we now face a special kind of pollution problem:

> It's not that we're running out of stuff. What we're running out of is what the scientists call "sinks"—places to put the by-products of our large appetites. Not garbage dumps (we could go on using Pampers till the end of time and still have empty space left to toss them away) but the atmospheric equivalent of garbage dumps....New kinds of pollution come...from normal human life—but there are so many of us living these normal lives that something abnormal is happening. And that something is so different from the old forms of pollution that it confuses the issue even to use the word.
>
> Consider nitrogen, for instance. Almost 80 percent of the atmosphere is nitrogen gas. But before plants can absorb it, it must become "fixed"—bonded with carbon, hydrogen, or oxygen. Nature does this trick with certain kinds of algae and soil bacteria, and with lightning. Before human beings began to alter the nitrogen cycle, these mechanisms provided 90–150 million metric tons of nitrogen a year. Now human activity adds 130–150 million more tons. Nitrogen isn't pollution—it's essential. And we are using more of it all the time. Half the industrial nitrogen fertilizer used in human history has been applied since 1984. As a result, coastal waters and estuaries bloom with toxic algae while oxygen concentrations dwindle, killing fish; as a result, nitrous oxide traps solar heat. And once the gas is in the air, it stays there for a century or more. (64)

According to McKibben, the general problem or claim is that we now face new kinds of pollution, and the example used to illustrate that claim is nitrogen, a naturally occurring, harmless gas and element. In order to make that example more powerful, however, he makes a statistical comparison of the amount of nitrogen bonded or "fixed" through natural processes with the additional amount that is now being produced. The example of the increased use of nitrogen fertilizer is a way to make this problem more concrete—this is a kind of bonded nitrogen that we use in agricultural production in huge corporate farming operations, on small family farms, even in our own backyard gardens. At the end of the second paragraph, there are examples of the kinds of problems created by increasing amounts of nitrogen—toxic algae blooms that we probably have read about and a reference to the ability of nitrogen to trap solar heat. Because these are specific, they help us to understand the kinds of effects that increased uses of nitrogen can produce. Although the nitrogen example is detailed and although statistical data are provided to indicate the extent of the change in amount of nitrogen produced, it still has the weaknesses that are typical of examples: it is just one case. So, you say, there are problems with nitrogen, but that's just one thing, and with experimentation we probably can find substitutes that will enable us to reduce our use of nitrogen fertilizer without making major changes in our overall use of fossil fuels.

There is another example in this material—the reference to Pampers, a brand of disposable diapers. McKibben is drawing a sharp contrast between finding space for such waste and the special problems posed by the special forms of pollution he describes. The contrast helps us to understand the difference between the pollution he is talking about and the kinds of wastes we put into garbage bags. Note, too, that there is a figurative analogy in the opening of this material, a reference to the need for "sinks" in which to dispose of these special kinds of pollution. That familiar term makes it easier for us to understand the kind of disposal systems that are needed.

As this excerpt illustrates, an example is a *story* of a case or an instance, real or hypothetical, detailed or not detailed, used to illustrate an idea or to prove that a particular kind of event has happened or could happen. Nevertheless, such an example is a potentially weak form of evidence when judged logically or empirically. It merely shows that something happened once or is true in one case, and if the example is hypothetical or imaginary, it does not even do that.

The weakness of the example as proof is illustrated in the true story of a woman who was killed instantly by the fall of a large meteor while asleep in her bed. No matter how dramatically the story is told or how detailed its devastation, those who hear it are never frightened. From their personal experience, from the experience of others, and from news reports and astronomical data, they know that meteors rarely fall all the way to the ground on our planet, especially in sizes that would be harmful, and that they rarely strike people or animals. Audience reaction is, "OK, it happened once. The odds are that it won't ever happen again, and the chances of its happening to me are infinitesimal."

On the other hand, the rhetorical force of an example lies in its capacity to promote visualization: to make us imagine a scene, imagine ourselves in it, and identify with the people and events. The more detailed the story—and the more skillfully the details are chosen—the more we identify with the problem or situation and participate in it. This capacity for stimulating identification makes examples extremely powerful pieces of evidence psychologically. They clarify through detail; they engage us by creating the bases for identification or by making a problem concrete and real.

The effectiveness of stories lies on a continuum. In most cases a real example of an actual event or person is better than a hypothetical or imaginary case, but real examples are not always available. To the best of our knowledge, no terrorist has yet acquired a nuclear device. If a rhetor is to describe such an event, it will be necessary to develop a hypothetical example, and events of this kind already have become the subjects of works of fiction. As proof, both logically and psychologically, a hypothetical example is strongest when it seems most plausible to the audience, when it has, in literary terms, the greatest verisimilitude (the appearance of truth or likelihood)—when it creates virtual experience. In other words, the details of the example should conform to what is known—imaginary presidents must behave like their real-life counterparts; imaginary nuclear accidents must take account of all the levels of protection in real-life nuclear plants, and so forth. Television films based on real-life events, such as the capture by terrorists of the airplane United flight 93 on 9/11/2001 (*United 93*) or the impact on Queen Elizabeth II of Princess Diana's death (*The Queen*) capitalize on (exploit?) the feelings and excitement the original event aroused in order to attract large audiences.

Real examples too—indeed all examples—are judged by three conditions:

1. What is their degree of plausibility?
2. What is their degree of verisimilitude?
3. What is their degree of engagement?

Although no example by itself can demonstrate its own representativeness, it should conform to common knowledge of what is plausible and likely. In addition, our willingness to accept examples is heightened by the amount of detail that is offered or that we can provide from our experience. Plausibility is not just a function of the example itself, it is a result of the similarity between what happens in the example and the experiences of the audience. If an example is to engage the audience—that is, if it is to create identification and induce participation by the audience—it must fit their experience; otherwise you as rhetor must be prepared to show through other evidence that the case you provide is representative or relatively common.

In addition, you should note that a number of examples will strengthen an individual instance so that as a series they suggest that each is typical or representative of a larger number of instances. After the previously cited material about nitrogen, for instance, the author immediately presents another example, that of carbon dioxide, in order to strengthen the point he is making.

Examples also contribute to the ethos (credibility) of the rhetor. They suggest that the rhetor is concerned with real people and events and imply that she or he has had firsthand experience with the situation. Very often, examples demonstrate the goodwill of the speaker and the expertise that comes from combining practical experience with theoretical knowledge.

In summary, then, the example is psychologically a vivid evocation that clarifies the meaning of an idea or problem. When details are given and when the audience finds an example plausible because of detail or conformity to their experience, it becomes highly effective in creating identification and in involving the audience with the problem. Real examples are stronger than hypothetical ones. To be effective, a hypothetical case must establish its similarity to real-life situations. Examples are stronger when they are relatively detailed and when a series of them is used. Examples are weak as proof because they are single instances that may be atypical and unrepresentative. They are also weak if they are not detailed and if they contradict the experiences of the audience.

Their precise opposite in terms of strengths and weaknesses is statistical or numerical data.

STATISTICS

Here is another excerpt from the article by Bill McKibben in which he talks about what is happening to population growth:

Around the world people are choosing to have fewer and fewer children—not just in China, where the government forces it on them, but in almost every nation outside the poorest parts of Africa. Population growth rates are lower than they have been at any time since the Second World War. In the past three decades the average woman in the developing world, excluding China, has gone from bearing six children to bearing four. Even in Bangladesh the average has fallen from six to fewer than four; even in the mullahs' Iran it has dropped by four children. If this keeps up, the population of the world will not quite double again; United Nations analysts offer as their mid-range projection that it will top out at 10 to 11 billion, up from just under six billion at the moment. The world is still growing, at nearly a record pace—we add a New York City every month, almost a Mexico every year, almost an India every decade. But the rate of growth is slowing; it is no longer "exponential," "unstoppable," "inexorable," "unchecked," "cancerous." If current trends hold, the world's population will all but stop growing before the twenty-first century is out....

Will the drop continue? It had better. UN mid-range projections assume that women in the developing world will soon average two children apiece—the rate at which population growth stabilizes. If fertility remained at current levels, the population would reach the absurd figure of 296 billion in just 150 years. Even if it dropped to 2.5 children per woman and then stopped falling, the population would reach 28 billion.

But let's trust that this time the demographers have got it right. Let's trust that we have rounded the turn and we're in the home stretch. Let's trust that the planet's population really will double only one more time. Even so, this is a case of good news, bad news. The good news is that we won't grow forever. The bad news is that there are six billion of us already, a number the world strains to support. One more near-doubling—four or five billion more people—will nearly double that strain. Will these be the five billion straws that break the camel's back? (56)

The United States is a highly technological, scientific society. Accordingly, we use a great many statistics, and we tend to trust numerical measures more than most other kinds of evidence. A *statistic* is a numerical or quantitative measure of scope or of frequency of occurrence; that is, statistics tell us "how many" or "how often." In the excerpt from Bill McKibben's essay, there are many statistics—the drop in birthrates among women in many countries, the projection that world population will top out at 10 or 11 billion from its current level (now over 6.7 billion). That calculation is based on the assumption that women in the developing world will soon average two children apiece, and the projection about the incredible population surge that would occur if it stayed at current levels as well as the data about what the population would be if the average remained at 2.5 children per woman. That is, they are all measures of size, extent, or frequency of occurrence.

As you will have recognized, most of these statistics are comparisons that enable us to have a sense of their significance. When we know that the average woman in the developing world now has four rather than six children, we have a sense of the size of the drop that has occurred. If we were told only that such women now have four children, we would have little basis for assessing the meaning of that data. That world population will nonetheless nearly double from its current level is apparent from the world's present population of some 6 billion and the estimates that population will stop growing at somewhere around 10 to 11 billion. The estimates about what world population would be if current levels continued or if childbearing stabilized at 2.5 children per woman are predictions or extrapolations from present data.

All of these give us a sense of size, scope, and extent. Note, however, that these numbers, no matter how specific, remain quite remote from us. We do not have a real sense of what it means for the world population to be over 6 billion at present, and we have a hard time imagining just what it will mean when that number doubles. And that is precisely the weakness with statistics. The author has some awareness of that problem, and he uses an important and useful strategy to counteract the remoteness of numerical data. At the end of the first paragraph, he writes that "we add a New York City every month, almost a Mexico every year, almost an India every decade." This is a strategy of translation; instead of giving us numbers (we add some 8 million people every month), he substitutes or translates those numbers into something that is more meaningful, more within our experience. The psychological impact of saying that we add a New York City is that it gives us an existential sense of what such growth means, and the idea that we add an India, soon to be the most populous nation in the world, every decade is awe-inspiring. This strategy of translation is one of the most effective ways to counteract the abstraction and remoteness of numbers.

Statistics are strong logically and empirically because they are measures of frequency, but even as proof, they pose some problems. As the subtle cliché puts it,

"Figures can't lie but liars can figure." In other words, numbers can be used to distort and misrepresent. At least two questions should be asked about every statistic:

1. What counts as an instance of what is being measured?
2. How was the whole population sampled to obtain these data?

Such problems are less important for the example on population. In most countries, births and deaths are recorded fairly reliably. But these problems can loom large in other kinds of statistics.

As an example, let us suppose that the state highway department reports speeding as the major cause in one-third of all fatal automobile accidents. It is easy to determine what a fatal auto accident is, but it may be hard to decide just what "speeding" is. Is it exceeding the posted speed limit? If so, how do we know that was happening? Was someone clocking the speed? Is speeding traveling faster than is safe for the conditions? A fatal accident would seem to be proof that the driver exceeded the safe speed, but mechanical problems might cause such an accident even at low speeds. In addition, how do we decide what is the *major* cause? Suppose we know that someone was driving faster than the speed limit but was also legally drunk or on medications that slowed reactions. Which is the major cause? If you ask such questions, you will realize that this statistic is a rough approximation of what state troopers believe is a major factor in serious auto accidents based on their reading of the signs (skid marks, damage, distance traveled after impact, Breathalyzer tests) and on their extensive experience.

Other statistics are gathered through survey research, however, the kind of technique through which George Gallup, Louis Harris, Elmo Roper, and other pollsters question a random sample whose views are then taken to be representative of the views of all U.S. Americans "with a margin of error of plus or minus 5 percent" or some similar figure. What is called a "sampling" error occurs when this smaller population—the group questioned—is unlike the larger population it is meant to represent. In the past, the accuracy of the Nielsen ratings of television viewing, for example, was questioned because few African American or Hispanic viewers were included in their samples, far below their representation in the population. In the 1948 presidential election when pollsters predicted that Thomas Dewey would beat Harry Truman, for example, one major error seemed to come from sampling that included only people with telephones—people who were, at least in 1948, more affluent and apparently more sympathetic to Republican candidates. A similar error might be made today if we sampled only those with mobile phones or personal computers.

Many cigarette ads illustrate another kind of statistical distortion—the suggestion that a measurable difference is important in terms of harmfulness. Brands of cigarettes have been advertised as having only one or four or seven milligrams of "tars" or nicotine, implying that smoking these brands is somehow less dangerous. There is, however, no evidence of any medically significant advantage from smoking brands with lower levels of these ingredients as currently measured. Smoking any cigarette is bad for one's health. The undesirable effects of smoking may even arise, not from the amount of "tars" or nicotine, but from the products of combustion—carbon dioxide, nitrous oxide, sulfur dioxide, and the like. But the statistic makes it seem "safer" and "better" to smoke some brands than others, and if we fear the effects of smoking but cannot bring ourselves to stop, we may go along with the pretext that a numerical difference makes a medical difference.

The willingness to make such an assumption calls attention to a psychological asset of statistics: the appearance of objectivity and precision, which invites us to treat them as factual and true. Our scientific, technical society reveres the empirical and "objective" so much that, as members of audiences, we are likely to be particularly impressed by statistical evidence.

This psychological strength is offset in part, however, by a psychological problem: statistics are hard to understand and remember. An audience confronted with a series of statistics is likely to become confused and lost; special efforts must be made to translate large numbers remote from personal experience into more familiar terms. In this case, for example, McKibben translates the rates of increase in population into entities that have more meaning than numbers alone—"we add a New York City every month, almost a Mexico every year, almost an India every decade." Think how much less vivid it would be if the author used the actual numbers.

You can compensate for the weaknesses of statistical evidence by combining numbers with analogies, another kind of evidence discussed next. Biologist Stephen Jay Gould, for example, claims that "Joe DiMaggio's fifty-six-game hitting streak is the greatest accomplishment in the history of baseball, if not in modern sport." Gould explains that, despite the belief in "hot hands," or streaks, they just don't exist. They can all be explained statistically; better players have longer runs of success because they are better players, and less talented players have shorter runs. "There is one major exception, and absolutely only one—one sequence so many standard deviations above the expected distribution that it should not have occurred at all: Joe DiMaggio's fifty-six-game hitting streak in 1941.... He beat the hardest taskmaster of all, a woman who makes Nolan Ryan's fastball look like a cantaloupe in slow motion—Lady Luck." In this case, Gould has used analogies to make the significance of the statistics clearer. How hard is it to beat the odds? When compared to Nolan Ryan's fastball, which gave that pitcher one of the winningest records in baseball, it makes his achievements appear to be nothing, as if his fastball had been so slow that it looked like a cantaloupe in slow motion, a pitch even the least talented of us probably could hit.

Gould explains that we have problems appreciating DiMaggio's feat "because we are so poorly equipped, whether by habits of culture or by our modes of cognition, to grasp the workings of random processes and patterning in nature." He argues that we cannot bear to accept the randomness of chance: "We believe in 'hot hands' because we must impart meaning to a pattern—and we like meanings that tell stories about heroism, valor, and excellence." He argues that DiMaggio's accomplishment was "a unique assault upon the otherwise unblemished record of Dame Probability." His feat combined extraordinary luck with great skill. Gould, a biologist, draws an analogy between DiMaggio's accomplishment and the biological entities that interest him:

> The history of a species, or any natural phenomenon that requires unbroken continuity in a world of trouble, works like a batting streak. All are games of a gambler playing with a limited stake against a house with infinite resources. The gambler must eventually go bust. His aim can only be to stick around as long as possible.... DiMaggio's hitting streak is the finest of legitimate legends because it embodies the essence of the battle that truly defines our lives. DiMaggio activated the greatest and most unattainable dream of all humanity, the hope and chimera of all sages and shamans: he cheated death, at least for a while.[3]

Several analogies are at work in this example. All attempts, Gould argues, to overcome the laws of probability, the power of chance, are like gambling. Thus, the efforts of species to survive are like a batting streak, and just as the gambler must lose eventually, and the batting streak must end, he implies that species die out. Hence, beating the laws of chance at the gaming table or in the batting box is like beating death—which you can do only for a little while. Notice that these analogies are considerably more powerful because they come from a renowned biological scientist and a student of the statistical lore of baseball (and other sports). In other words, the potential rhetorical power of the analogies, and perhaps even of the statistics on which they are based, comes in part from the credibility of the source, something we will discuss later in this chapter in the section on authority evidence. Note, too, that the analogies also confer meaning on a pattern, ironically doing just what he has chided us humans for wanting to do!

(handwritten note in margin: Credibility of the source very important in these instances)

Incidentally, sports fans are extremely reluctant to give up the belief in "hot hands" and "streaks," which is in and of itself a strong bit of evidence of the human need to perceive patterns and to make meaning out of random events, part of the psychological power of statistics.[4]

In the article from the *Atlantic Monthly* cited at the beginning of this chapter, Bill McKibben uses examples to highlight the difficulties of explaining why population growth is slowing. Those examples, that the women in Oman who know about contraception still average six or more children each and the contrast between childbearing by women in Turkey and Japan who use contraceptives at the same rate, call into question the reasons offered by experts for the decline in childbearing. Note, too, that these problems of explanation emphasize just how speculative predictions about future population growth really are.

In summary, statistics are a strong form of evidence that you can use to convey how often something happens or the size and scope of a problem. To interpret statistics, you need to know how the raw data were gathered, how measurements were made, what counted as an instance of this event, how sampling was done, and what kinds of error might be involved.

Psychologically, statistics are strong because of the empirical and scientific bias of our society and our respect for objectivity, for "hard cold facts." Despite this general attitude, however, statistics are a difficult form of proof to use effectively. Lists of numbers are hard to understand and remember. Speakers and writers must make special efforts to translate numerical measures into more familiar terms, into proportions and relationships that are within our personal experience. Often this is done through visuals, another form of evidence used in rhetorical acts.

VISUALS

As a form of evidence, visuals are unusual in that they can function in one of two ways: as reinforcement (a visual aid) or as stand-alone presentation (visual rhetoric). Chapter 3 provided some basic guidelines for using visual aids, and Chapter 12 explores the nondiscursive power of visual rhetoric. Because of the problem of absorbing and recollecting a series of numbers, you may want to use visual aids when you present statistics. Statistical evidence often makes better sense to both readers and listeners if it is in the form of charts and graphs that depict quantitative relationships in *visual terms*; in effect, you are presenting the same material through two sensory channels. President Ronald Reagan, for example, was praised for using charts and graphs innovatively to illustrate his State of the Union addresses, speeches that are not particularly easy to present because they often discuss complex problems and solutions, the kinds of problems and solutions that most often involve statistical evidence.

The Ad Council advertisement (see Figure 4–2) "Adoption Cake" is an example of a visual aid that reinforces another form of evidence, the analogy, in conveying its purpose. Both visually and verbally, the ad urgently forces us to reexamine a major point of resistance many people feel when weighing whether or not to join a cause: what is its *cost* to me in time, energy, finances, social status, and so forth (one of four subject obstacles we examine in Chapter 9). Implicitly, the ad makes two comparisons. First, it compares the urgency of placing thousands of older children into adopted homes with a drooping near flop of a birthday cake for a sixteen-year-old. Second, it debunks idealized notions of good parenting by stating: "You don't have to be perfect to be a perfect parent. There are thousands of teens in foster-care who would love to put up with you." The drooping cake now can be seen as funny. Hey, so the cake didn't bake right; we still decorated it pretty and, it's the thought that counts! Most parents can identify with this "Roseanne Barr over June Cleaver" moment because that's real parenting these days. The dramatic picture is both a negative and positive image. If you find the double-layered meaning of the cake compelling, then the visual has worked its persuasive magic; it has relied on an argument we call an enthymeme (explored more fully in Chapter 5).

Courtesy of Adopt Us Kids and the Ad Council

You don't have to be perfect to be a perfect parent.
There are thousands of teens in foster care who would love to put up with you.

1 888 200 4005 · adoptuskids.org

Figure 4–2
*Ad Council
Advertisement:
Adoption Cake*

In the Bill McKibben's article from the *Atlantic Monthly*, the strength of visuals as aids is especially apparent. Pictorial representation is used in an entertaining, efficient way to simplify many complex ideas about depleting natural resources. Here visual evidence takes the form of vibrantly colored modernized drawings, six of which take up the better part of a double-page magazine spread. Each accentuates the tone of urgency in McKibben's plea for conservation. The reader's gaze is drawn to a series of disturbing pictures: a luxurious, red Queen Anne chair crammed with identical faces all over it; a skeleton of a fish—its guts made to look like smokestacks; a water faucet with four spouts turned on full blast; and the most eye-opening—four missiles increasing in size from bottom to top with the largest two missiles looking like babies! The enthymeme suggested by this picture is a powerful one: It's not nuclear missiles that will destroy us; it's overpopulation! In addition, on every page in the right-hand corner stands an alarm clock with a chunk (a quarter) of its numbers missing—reminding us of McKibben's primary thesis: between now and the year 2050 is "a special moment in history" for us to reverse global warming and its deleterious effects.

The other kind of visual evidence is illustrated in the NYC flag raising by firefighters on the afternoon of September 11 in the wreckage of the World Trade Center (see Figure 4–3). This is a real photo (unlike the visuals of most ads). It stands alone as a piece of evidence. (It needs little if any text to convey its message—at least for those who remember the events of 9/11.) It has become iconic (which means, in part, that it is "brimming" with instant meaning for viewers; it is enthymematic on many levels).

Figure 4–3
9/11 Flag Raising

2001 The Record (Bergen Co. NJ)/Getty Images News/Getty Images

good way to convey something complex

When visuals are used in this way, not as aids to some other form of evidence, but as stand-alone pieces of evidence, they are presentational and performative. This piece of visual rhetoric says that even from the depths of one of the nation's darkest moments of terror, the national values of honor, duty, courage, teamwork, patriotism, and optimism rise. It is also eerily reminiscent of another iconic photo for U.S. Americans of the World War II generation: the flag raising at Iwo Jima. That photo's similarity to this one is explored more fully in Chapter 12, along with many other examples of visual rhetoric.

Whether used for reinforcement or solo performance, visuals are an enthymematic, efficient, and emotional form of evidence. Visuals package ideas quickly and holistically in ways that fit our fast-paced, information-saturated age. Increasingly, many scholars argue that we are becoming a society of visual learners, so this form of evidence is increasingly common. On the other hand, visuals tend to oversimplify and thus distort issues because they lack context. Recognizing that visual rhetoric deserves specialized treatment, Chapter 12 examines its nondiscursive features.

[handwritten margin note: Visuals tend to oversimplify and thus distort issues because they lack context]

ANALOGIES

Analogies are likenings or comparisons between things, processes, persons, or events. They come in two varieties: literal analogies (usually simply called comparisons) and figurative analogies (usually called metaphors).

Literal Analogies *[handwritten: 2 colleges, 4 rivers]*

Literal analogies focus on the similarities between items that are obviously alike in some way: two colleges, three hair styles, eight field hockey players, four rivers, and so on. Literal analogies are comparisons among items that are alike in detail and similar in explicit and obvious ways. The demands made on two professional tennis players are similar, for example, and you might compare their records of points on first serves and numbers of unforced errors in order to state that one is more skillful or talented than another. In the essay cited earlier, the author compares the birthrates among women in different countries and world birthrates at different periods.

Such comparisons are made for the purposes of evaluation and prediction. One compares in order to evaluate just how serious and extensive the drop in rates of child-bearing has been. One compares in order to judge which team or player is better or to predict which will be more successful in a future encounter. It is risky, however, to predict a pitcher's success, because her success also depends on the skill of her outfield and on the hitting power of her teammates. These complexities suggest the critical factor in the power of literal analogies as proof: the extent of relevant similarities and the presence of relevant differences. As a rule, the greater the number of relevant similarities between two cases, the better the basis for evaluation or prediction; the existence of relevant differences (differences directly related to the evaluation or prediction being made) lessens the strength and force of any claim. Baseball teams are just that—teams. The skill of a pitcher is only one element in its success, and the differences in talent and experience of other members of the teams being compared are significant for evaluating the performance and predicting the success of any one member.

[handwritten margin note: useful for evaluation + prediction]

Literal analogies enable us to go from what is known and tested and in operation to what is unknown, untested, and not yet working. In one high crime neighborhood, for instance, traffic patterns are altered to prevent through traffic, and a crime control unit to report suspicious events is set up. The burglary rate drops 45 percent during the year after these changes are made. If we can replicate this success in other neighborhoods, people and property will be much safer. Careful analysis of such a project and determination of how similar—how analogous—any two neighborhoods really are should help us determine whether what worked in the one area will work in another.

Figurative Analogies

The process by which we go from what is known and familiar to what is unknown and unfamiliar is accentuated in the figurative analogy, a comparison of items that are unlike in obvious ways, that are apparently totally different if looked at with literal and practical eyes. The *figurative analogy* asserts a similarity that is metaphoric or that is a similarity in principle. For example, there are no obvious similarities between playing blackjack and batting a baseball except for the interrelationship of skill and chance common to both, and there is no similarity between a baseball and a cantaloupe except their generally round shape. There are no obvious similarities between the earth's capacity to sustain human life and the back of a camel, yet the question, "Will these be the five billion straws that break the camel's back?" dramatizes the threat represented by increasing population.

The figurative analogy is one means by which a concept or problem can be made more vivid and dramatic. A later section of McKibben's article illustrates this process:

> Throughout the 10,000 years of recorded human history the planet—the physical planet—has been a stable place. In every single year of those 10,000, there have been earthquakes, volcanoes, hurricanes, cyclones.... But these have never shaken the basic predictability of the planet as a whole....
>
> Among other things, this stability has made possible the insurance industry—has underwritten the underwriters. Insurers can analyze the risk in any venture because they know the ground rules. If you want to build a house on the coast of Florida, they can calculate with reasonable accuracy the chance that it will be hit by a hurricane and the speed of the winds circling that hurricane's eye. If they couldn't, they would have no way to set your premium—they'd just be gambling. They're always gambling a little, of course: they don't know if that hurricane is coming next year or next century. But the earth's physical stability is the house edge in this casino. As Julian Simon pointed out, "A prediction based on past data can be sound if it is sensible to assume that the past and the future belong to the same statistical universe."
>
> So what does it mean that alone among the earth's great pools of money and power, insurance companies are beginning to take the idea of global climate change quite seriously? What does it mean that the payout for weather-related damage climbed from $16 billion during the entire 1980s to $48 billion in the years 1990–1994? What does it mean that top European insurance executives have begun consulting with Greenpeace about global warming? What does it mean that the insurance giant Swiss Re, which paid out $291.5 million in the wake of Hurricane Andrew, ran an ad in the *Financial Times* showing its corporate logo bent sideways by a storm?
>
> These things mean, I think, that the possibility that we live on a new earth cannot be discounted entirely as a fever dream. (63)

In an effort to explain the changing character of the earth, the author in this case compares insurers to casino owners who are able to make a profit by calculating the odds and making sure that the payouts are smaller than the premiums. The house edge, like the favorable odds built into slot machines and roulette wheels, is the stability of the planet. The point of that comparison is made with a statement from an authority, Julian Simon, who sets forth the basic assumptions underlying predictability. Readers may not be mathematical geniuses; they may not know about the kinds of tables used by insurance companies to calculate odds, but most U.S. Americans are now familiar with casinos and gambling, and the figurative analogy makes the point much clearer.

The main weakness of the figurative analogy, however, is that in logical and empirical terms it gives no proof, makes no demonstration. But figurative analogies are not all equivalent in rhetorical force; some are stronger and more persuasive than others. As a rule, a figurative analogy is more powerful when it is more comprehensive; that is, when there are many points of similarity. Here, for example, the comparison is powerful because the laws of chance and the rules of predictability are at work in both cases.

the more points of similarity the more comprehensive the analogy.

In his essay, McKibben uses analogies to appeal for action to reverse the problems that have developed:

> If we can bring our various emissions quickly and sharply under control, we *can* limit the damage, reduce dramatically the chance of horrible surprises, preserve more of the biology we were born into. But do not underestimate the task. The UN's Intergovernmental Panel on Climate Change projects that an immediate 60 percent reduction in fossil-fuel use is necessary just to stabilize climate at the current level of disruption. Nature may still meet us halfway, but halfway is a long way from where we are now. What's more, we can't delay. If we wait a few decades to get started, we may as well not even begin. It's not like poverty, a concern that's always there for civilizations to address. This is a timed test, like the SAT: two or three decades, and we lay our pencils down. It's *the* test for our generations, and population is part of the answer. (72)

The analogy of the time allotted to respond to the problems of pollution and global warming to the time allotted to take the SAT is a vivid figurative analogy. For most students, the SAT is a milestone in determining what college they can go to, and it is a somewhat frightening moment when one's performance is vital to one's future. The author hopes that young people especially can respond to that comparison and feel a sense of the pressure we are under to respond to these problems.

feel the pressure

Weaker figurative analogies rest on one or few similarities of principle; for example, as illustrated by the comparison of the world's capacity to sustain life and the back of a camel or describing the need for "sinks" to dispose of the special wastes that are developing. Consider how weak or how strong you consider the comparison to the SAT in the above excerpt. Is the comparison strengthened by the contrast drawn between poverty, a recurring and enduring problem, and the special character of the threat posed by global warming?

The strengths of the figurative analogy are, like the power of a metaphor or the force of a slogan, somewhat difficult to describe. When the analogy is a fresh comparison that strikes the audience as highly apt, it has considerable persuasive force. The comparison of DiMaggio's hitting streak to the fate of species, for example, is disturbing and thought-provoking, especially from this source.

originality

In sum, the analogy derives its strength from its originality, its ability to make us see things from a new angle; from its aptness, its capacity to evoke an "ah-ha" reaction; and from its brevity, its ability to crystallize a whole range of problems into a single phrase or image. That, too, is the power of the slogan, the brief phrase that expresses a position or idea in a vivid, unforgettable image. "Pro-Choice" and "Forced Motherhood" struggle against the power of "Right to Life." "A Woman's Place is in the House—and Senate!" turns the stereotypic view of women on its head to express another point of view. This tactic of turning things around to express the opposite view is the best defense against a figurative analogy or slogan in argumentative terms.

EXPERTISE OR AUTHORITY

In some of the material quoted previously, an expert's view was cited, and in McKibben's essay there are good examples of the strengths and weaknesses of this kind of evidence.

Authority evidence is a strong way to bolster a claim and enhance the credibility of the rhetor. The contrast between a lay and an expert witness in a courtroom is a helpful way to define the special function of this kind of evidence. If we, as ordinary people or lay witnesses, testify in a court of law, we can testify only to what we actually know from personal experience. (We give testimony, a form of the example.[5]) We are not allowed to draw conclusions, and lawyers are not allowed to "lead" us, that is, to ask us to draw conclusions or interpret evidence. In contrast, the expert witness comes to court specifically to draw conclusions and interpret raw data. A ballistics expert draws on his experience and training to conclude that two bullets were shot from the same gun; a psychologist draws on her experience with the defendant and on her training to interpret the defendant's mental capacity. The functions of the expert witness are the same functions performed by authority evidence.

Authority evidence appears in two forms in the material we have quoted. In the McKibben essay, an expert named Julian Simon was quoted about the soundness of predictions. We have no information about his qualifications, and we are likely to accept that statement primarily because it fits our general knowledge about predictability. The second kind of authority is that of the author. This essay is strong evidence of the quality of the research that has been done. In the course of the essay, McKibben writes: "Ten years ago I wrote a book called *The End of Nature,* which was the first volume for a general audience about carbon dioxide and climate change, an early attempt to show that human beings now dominate the earth" (65). McKibben has written half a dozen books about environmental degradation and how to live in less destructive ways. His concern for the fate of the earth and the people on it is evidence of one kind of ethos, the demonstration that one has the good of the community at heart.

Evidence from authority, like evidence from statistics, discussed earlier in this chapter, can be misused. Perhaps the most common sort of misuse is to cite experts in one area as if they were experts in another, which happens often in advertising. You should pay attention to this common distortion problem, for example, when a highly successful professional golfer appears in ads for watches or cars. He is not only a winning professional golfer but also an astute analyst of equipment and courses. When advertisers try to suggest that he speaks as an expert on consumer products unrelated to golf, however, you should be skeptical. Why should we believe him when he endorses automobiles or watches? What knowledge does he have in those areas? Similarly, we doubt the claims of actors on the benefits of a particular brand of dog food or garden fertilizer, but we listen seriously to them when they talk about television and film acting because that is where they have demonstrated their abilities in performance. No one is an expert in all areas; the strength of authority evidence as proof is directly related to the authority's degree of expertise in the area in question.

Authoritative evidence is strongest when

1. We know the credentials of authorities—their training and experience.
2. We know the explicit relationship between the expertise of the authority and the subject.
3. We know details about the data used by the authority to make interpretation.
4. We know whether authorities are self-interested, that is, whether the conclusions drawn will benefit them.

Authority evidence is weakened when we do not know details about credentials, when the relationship of the authority to the subject is indirect or unclear, or when we do not know what data, principles, or experiences were used in drawing conclusions or making interpretations. Our experiences with research scientists who receive grants from drug companies should make us wary of claims made by those who will benefit from the products they endorse.

McKibben is well aware of the strengths and weaknesses of authority evidence and of the need to compare the views of various experts. In one section of his essay, he talks about the difficulties of predicting the impact of population on the world's resources by acknowledging that some experts believe the Reverend Thomas Malthus was wrong in 1798 when he predicted that the growth of population would outstrip the supply of food. In fact, McKibben notes that there is a whole group of experts who take the opposite point of view:

> This group's intellectual fountainhead is a brilliant Danish economist named Ester Boserup—a sort of anti-Malthus, who in 1965 argued that the gloomy cleric had it backward. The more people, Boserup said, the more progress. Take agriculture as an example: the first farmers, she pointed out, were slash-and-burn cultivators, who might farm a plot for a year or two and then move on, not returning for maybe two decades. As the population grew, however, they had to return more frequently to the same plot. That meant problems: compacted, depleted, weedy soils. But these new problems meant new solutions: hoes, manure, compost, crop rotation, irrigation. Even in this century, Boserup said, necessity-induced invention has meant that "intensive systems of agriculture replaced extensive systems," accelerating the rate of food production. (59)

Here the expertise is focused on reinterpreting the available historical data to emphasize that "necessity is the mother of invention." As the author points out, these experts have been right so far: despite dire predictions about the effect of population growth, technological developments have produced increased resources rather than starvation. As a transition, he asks, "Will Malthus still be wrong fifty years from now?" (60) and offers some additional authority evidence:

> In 1986 [Stanford biologist Peter] Vitousek decided to calculate how much of the earth's "primary productivity" went to support human beings. He added together the grain we ate, the corn we fed our cows, and the forests we cut for timber and paper; he added the losses in food as we overgrazed grassland and turned it into desert. And when he was finished adding, the number he came up with was 38.8 percent. We use 38.8 percent of everything the world's plants don't need to keep themselves alive; directly or indirectly, we consume 38.8 percent of what it is possible to eat. "That's a relatively large number," Vitousek says. "It should give pause to people who think we are far from any limits.... There's a sense among economists that we're so far from any biophysical limits. I think that's not supported by the evidence." (60)

It's very likely that you have never heard of Peter Vitousek. That he is a biologist is an indicator of his expertise regarding the conditions of life, and that he is connected with Stanford University, one of the leading research institutions in the country, suggests that he is a person of above average competence. McKibben uses this material to respond to the anti-Malthusians, and this material is more persuasive because the author explains how Vitousek went about calculating how much humans consume— almost 40 percent of what it is possible to consume—before quoting his statement that we are closer to the biophysical limits of our planet than many economists seem to believe. We don't just have to take his word for it; we have some idea of how he reached that conclusion, and if we think that process is sensible, we are more likely to accept the claim that follows.

These contrasting viewpoints emphasize the limits of authority evidence. Both experts are unfamiliar figures; we have no experience with them that allows us to judge their competence. We have only brief references to their areas of expertise and the institutions/nations with which they are associated. Each is interpreting a body of data, and as is so often the case, the experts disagree. In each case we have some basis for understanding how they arrived at their conclusions. Neither can provide us with definitive evidence; all they can do is suggest the ways in which we might interpret the available evidence. Quite possibly, audience members will choose to believe one or the other based on their prior attitudes on this topic.

Another, potentially powerful, form of evidence is what we call *reluctant* authority. Rhetors sometimes quote their opponents, who happen to be authorities, in ways that damage their opponents' case. The quotation may be a statement by the opponent/ authority that has been proven untrue. It may be a statement that is inconsistent with something else the opponent/authority has said. Regardless, the quotation is reluctant authority because the quotation works against the best interest of the opponent/author- ity. For example, in the nineteenth century, some opponents of woman suffrage in the United States argued that women should not have voting rights because their proper role was to stay at home and protect their children rather than to engage in politics. Woman suffrage advocates countered that women could not fulfill that role without the ability to influence, through their votes, the political decisions that directly affect children and families. In effect, by using reluctant authority evidence, suffrage advocates turned the argument back on their opponents. Contemporary political candidates frequently use reluctant authority in television ads featuring statements from their opponents that have been proven false or that contradict other statements from that opponent. Especially in public debates over political issues, reluctant authority is a potentially powerful form of evidence because it can influence listeners or readers to suspect that the opponent/author- ity is uninformed, a "flip-flopper," or perhaps even dishonest.

Based on this discussion, how can you use evidence most effectively in your rhet- oric? Combine the different forms of evidence so the limitations of one kind are compensated for by the strengths of another—compensate for the impersonality of statistics with the vivid, concrete drama of an example or visual; compensate for the lonely example with more instances buttressed by statistical measures showing frequency of occurrence; compensate for the complexity of data with analyses and interpretations of experts; predict specific cases, as you cannot with statistics, through detailed comparisons. Summarize an essential principle through the figurative analogy or visual; contrast the generalizations of an expert with examples of testimony from people who have actually experienced the problem.

Figure 4–4
Definitional Strategies

Name	Function	Example
Dictionary Definition	Defining from a dictionary	"According to Webster's 10th Edition: 'Rhetoric is the art of oratory.'"
Stipulative Definition	Defining in your own particular way	"As many of you know, I like to define rhetoric by its seven P's: rhetoric is discourse that is purposive, poetic, problem-solving, public, propositional, pragmatic, and powerful."
Authoritative Definition	Defining from an expert on the subject	"Aristotle has defined rhetoric as 'the faculty of discovering the available means of persuasion in any given case.'"
Negative Definition	Defining by what it is not	"By the term rhetoric, I do not refer to its pejorative, misunderstood usages such as bombast, hot air, bloviation, mere words, or deceptive speech."
Etymological Definition	Defining from original sources	"*Ethos*, a Greek word and key constituent of rhetoric, comes from two words: ethics and ethnic; hence, rhetoric is always concerned with a speaker's moral conduct and his/her ability to reflect the norms of a given community."
Exemplar Definition	Defining by using examples	"To help you understand the scope of rhetoric, let me share with you some examples: The President's Inaugural Address is rhetoric; George Will's political commentary in *Newsweek* is rhetoric; Tracy Chapman's folk music is rhetoric; the Doonesbury comic strip is rhetoric."
Contextual Definition	Defining by tracing its usage through various times in history	"In the 4th century BCE, rhetoric referred to the full range of communicative interaction; in the 1st century distinctions were first made between informative and persuasive speaking; in the 14th century rhetoric became relevant to the sacred sphere; in the 19th century the scientific aspects of rhetoric were studied and rhetoric was transformed into the study of eloquence."
Analogical Definition	Defining by comparing the known with the unknown	"The study of rhetoric is akin to the study of literature; both involve a heightened sensitivity of the power and artistry of words."
Synonym Definition	Defining by words that can be used interchangeably	"Rhetoric is equated with the terms *persuasion*, *oratory*, *social influence*."
Operational Definition	Defining by describing its process or procedures	"Rhetoric is a process involving a source, a receiver, a message, feedback, channel, situation, and noise."

Source: Susan Schultz Huxman, *Public Speaking: A Repertoire of Resources* (New York: McGraw-Hill College Custom Series, 1992).

The functions of evidence are three: to prove, to make vivid, and to clarify. To fulfill their functions, they must be combined into larger units, into arguments and organizational patterns, which are the subjects of Chapters 5 and 6.

All of these forms of evidence can be adapted to definitional strategies, a related "building block" of learning to support your ideas. The ability to define a term clearly and craftily is a sign of an accomplished rhetor. It requires knowledge of the various ways in which support material can be utilized. In Figure 4–4, you will find ten definitional strategies that will help you think about using evidence carefully.

MATERIAL FOR ANALYSIS

Bill McKibben published a second essay, "Global Warming's Terrifying New Math," in the July 19, 2012, edition *Rolling Stone*. It is available online at http://www.rolling-stone.com/politics/news/global-warmings-terrifying-new-math-20120719. Retrieve the essay and use it to respond to the following questions for analysis.

Questions for Analysis

1. Identify each type of supporting evidence that appears in the essay.

2. How does McKibben compensate for the weaknesses of each of those types of supporting evidence?

3. Discuss the role of the audience's enthymematic reasoning in this essay. What background knowledge must the audience bring to this?

4. The power of the essay relies on enumeration of details. Could this essay be shortened to the length of a typical op-ed and still have a similar impact?

5. How does McKibben's own language heighten the effect of the supporting evidence?

EXERCISES

Critical Thinking Exercises

1. Consider the following general claims:

   The dot-com industry has been built almost overnight on a very shaky foundation; hence, one should not hope for its miracle to live on.

   After-school, summer, and other part-time jobs are beneficial to teenagers; hence, local communities should consider ways to encourage employers to hire teenagers.

   The diet industry should be regulated because currently too many shady companies use misleading advertisements and provide dangerous advice to their clients.

   What kinds of personal experiences would support any of these claims? What kinds of evidence would you use if you were to defend any of the above positions in front of (a) your communication class; (b) a city council committee investigating the relationships between large, multinational corporations and local communities; (c) a student group dedicated to raising the civic engagement of students on campus; and (d) your family. What considerations should guide your choice? What are the strengths and limitations of each type of evidence?

Analytical Writing Exercises

Portfolio Entry 3: Evidence

2. Compare and contrast how your three rhetorical selections use evidence (VASES) to advance their purposes. What are the strengths and weaknesses of each? In one or two pages, work on using critical equations smoothly.

Strategic Speaking Exercises

Adapting Evidence to Definitional Strategies

3. In Figure 4–4 you will find ten "definitional strategies" that will help you think about using evidence carefully. Prepare a one- to two-minute definitional speech designed to *alter perception* in which you carefully unpack a term using three to five definitional strategies. Choose a concept sufficiently large in scope that you can define it in several different ways. Choose a concept that is unfamiliar to your audience or one that has several confusing meanings. Choose a concept that you think your audience needs to know. Consider such words as *wisdom, justice, obscenity, myth, agape,* and so forth. Consider such ideas as *postfeminism, renaissance, chaos theory, postmodernism, compassionate conservatism,* etc.

4. Prepare a four- to five-minute speech designed to *explain* or to create understanding about something unfamiliar to the audience. Plan the speech carefully to run not more than five minutes. Build in "Are there any questions?" at each strategic point in the process. The audience is expected to take notes and then to ask the speaker only two kinds of questions: (1) what do you mean? (a request for explanation, clarification, or definition), and (2) how do you know? (a request for data). No one should be allowed to argue with the speaker or to refute claims or challenge evidence; however, active audience participation is essential.

After completing the exercise, discuss problems of clarity (vocabulary, explanation) and audience needs for evidence that speakers did not recognize. Discuss the problems of delivery created when your presentation is interrupted by questions from the audience.

Discuss why the speaker needs to solicit questions to make this exercise work (Why won't you interrupt when you don't understand or want proof for an assertion? What communication norms are involved?). What factors seemed to make some speakers more effective than others in doing this assignment?

5. Prepare a four- to five-minute speech to *create virtual experience* that mandates the use of visuals. (Your instructor may suggest additional rhetorical purposes.) Consider such topics as the styles of radio disc jockeys, methods of musical arrangement, a detailed statistical analysis, an explanation of a form or map, or a comparison of television commercials. Ideally, you should seek to use a variety of visuals: pictures, graphs, charts, audio- and videotapes, transparencies, slides, films, PowerPoint, demonstration assistants, and others.

NOTES

1. Aristotle, *On Rhetoric: A Theory of Civic Discourse,* trans. George A. Kennedy (New York: Oxford University Press, 1991), p. 258.

2. Bill McKibben, "A Special Moment in History," *Atlantic Monthly,* May 1998. Reprinted by permission of the author.

3. Stephen Jay Gould, "The Streak of Streaks," *New York Review of Books,* August 18, 1988, pp. 8–12.

4. See also Thomas Gilovich, *How We Know What Isn't So: The Fallibility of Human Reason in Everyday Life* (New York: The Free Press, 1991).

5. For a detailed analysis of the many problems with this form of evidence, see Elizabeth F. Loftus, *Eyewitness Testimony* (Cambridge, MA: Harvard University Press, 1980).

Chapter 5

The Resources of Argument

No fact has any meaning by itself. To be significant, to have impact, evidence must become part of an argument, and arguments, in turn, must be combined into larger rhetorical wholes (the subject of Chapter 6). Our concern in this chapter is with arguments, a key building block of rhetorical action. Just what is an argument?

In common, everyday terms, we may think of an argument as a quarrel between two or more people because arguments usually express differing viewpoints or disagreements, sometimes vehemently. In a more academic sense, however, we can speak of the argument of a novel, referring to the principle or pattern of its development and the kind of experience it attempts to create. This usage reflects an understanding that arguments, at least in this academic sense, are structures, ways of organizing material. In this chapter, argument is used to refer to the process of giving reasons for or against some position. Thus, for rhetorical purposes, an *argument* is a claim or a conclusion backed by one or more reasons or justifications.

Based on that definition, here are some arguments:

Capital punishment should be abolished because it is an ineffective deterrent against violent crime.

Teenagers should receive sex education and contraceptive information because they are not yet equipped to be good parents.

State lotteries should be abolished because they are a regressive and inefficient way to raise revenue.

These are arguments because each makes a claim and then provides a justification or reason in support of that claim.

These examples also illustrate the role of evidence in argument. Appropriate responses to these arguments are: How do you know that capital punishment is an ineffective deterrent against homicide? How do you know that many or most teenagers engage in sexual intercourse and that they are not equipped to be good parents? How do you know that lotteries are regressive and inefficient? For these arguments to be sustained, each question must be answered with evidence. Although some arguments, like the previous examples, omit the evidence on which they are based, all arguments are based on evidence because they at least imply that evidence exists and could be presented.

Because evidence was discussed in Chapter 4, let's now turn to the other two elements: claims and reasons or justifications.

CLAIMS

The shape or character of an argument is determined by the kind of claims it makes, the conclusion it draws. A *claim* or *conclusion* is an assertion. Here are some examples: That is a dog. You are in good health. Smoking causes lung cancer. Affirmative action damages the self-esteem of those it is designed to help.

Notice that each of these examples is a statement or assertion—a conclusion drawn by the speaker or writer—but no evidence or justification for that conclusion is provided. In other words, the *reasoning process* that led to the conclusion is not explained. Rather, that reasoning process involves a logical or inferential "leap" or interpretation. For instance, when you make a claim as simple as "That is a dog," you "jump" to a conclusion based on a few surface characteristics that seem to indicate that the creature standing before you is a particular kind of canine. Nevertheless, when we make such a claim, few of us have either the necessary data or the biological expertise to back up our statement by distinguishing canines from other mammals or domestic dogs from other types of canines, such as coyotes, dingoes, foxes, or wolves. Many times, the issues involved are not particularly serious and the claim is readily accepted; the creature probably is a dog.

Other situations are more serious, however, and even when the person who makes the claim is an expert with lots of data, such a leap is present. During the summer of 1993, Reggie Lewis, a Boston Celtics basketball player, died while shooting baskets with a friend at the team's training center at Brandeis University.[1] Earlier, on April 29, during the opening game of the NBA playoffs, Lewis had collapsed. After tests were conducted, the team physician and a group of a dozen heart specialists concluded that Lewis was suffering from cardiomyopathy, a life-threatening condition that would have ended his athletic career. In other words, these highly trained experts *interpreted* the data from the medical tests and made the *inferential leap* from that data to their diagnosis—their conclusion. But a second team of physicians at another hospital disputed those findings and concluded that Lewis had a benign neurological condition known as neurocardiogenic syncope, a condition that causes fainting but rarely is fatal. This second team of experts also made an *inferential leap* from the available data but reached quite a different conclusion. Each conclusion was informed by empirical evidence drawn from echocardiograms, magnetic resonance imaging of the heart, monitoring of his heart rhythm while he ran a treadmill, and electrical stimulation of his heart to learn whether it was vulnerable to bursts of potentially fatal rhythms. It is important to note, however, that those facts—the data from the very sophisticated medical tests—did not "speak for themselves." Rather, those test results were interpreted in light of the physicians' long training and years of medical practice.

Lewis's death was a dramatic and tragic reminder that the physicians' conclusions, like all argumentative claims, are inferential leaps that go beyond the available evidence. Obviously, none of these cardiologists wanted to put Lewis in mortal peril, and which conclusion to accept was a hard choice for the team and the player. Tragically, however, the inferential leap made by the group that Lewis and the Celtics chose to believe was wrong. Note, too, how belief—accepting one claim rather than another—follows self-interest: Lewis did not want to give up a satisfying and lucrative career in professional basketball, and the Celtics did not want to lose their six-foot seven-inch captain. The outcome, however, is dramatic evidence of the discrepancy between data (the test results) and the claim (that he did or did not have a life-threatening heart condition).

The special character of an argument is precisely this: it makes a leap from data to a claim. That is why it is a fundamental building block in rhetorical action. That is also what gives an argument its force, and, as the example shows, it is what makes arguments risky and open to challenge.

REASONS

The leap made in an argument ordinarily is not a blind leap made in ignorance. As indicated in the story of Reggie Lewis, we go from evidence or data to a claim via a justification or reason. A reason is an authorization or *warrant* for the leap made in an argument. In other words, reasons are grounds or bases for drawing conclusions. They are justifications for claims.

To illustrate this process, let us return to the Reggie Lewis example. In making tests, cardiologists gather all kinds of data about the heart—its muscle, its pumping efficiency and that of the vessels that feed it, its performance under stress, and so forth. When the results are in, they are measured against certain standards or norms established for identifying people who have different kinds of heartbeat variations and problems. By comparing the data from these tests with these standards, a cardiologist can decide whether or not someone has a life-threatening problem. Several reasoning processes are involved. It is assumed that (1) all reliable tests of heart activity were made; (2) they were made by competent cardiologists using accurate instruments; and (3) the results were compared to standard indicators of a potentially lethal or a relatively benign heart arrhythmia (variations in the rhythm of heartbeats) for persons of the patient's age and physical condition. Each of these is a reason a cardiologist might use to support a conclusion about the health of an individual's heart: all essential tests were made; these tests were made and interpreted by experts; the results were compared to established standards for a given group of people with the characteristics of the individual being tested.

These reasons are related to medicine and cardiology; thus, such reasons are sometimes called *field-dependent* because they belong to a particular field or area of expertise, and they rely on the authority of persons skilled in that field. (Recall that in Chapter 4 an authority was defined as a person thought competent to interpret data and to decide what conclusions could be drawn from it.) That reasons often arise out of the knowledge accumulated in a field of knowledge means that the reasons appropriate for one subject may not be appropriate for another.[2]

ISSUES

An *issue* is a fundamental point in dispute, a question crucial in making a decision, choosing a stance, or selecting a course of action. Most issues fall roughly into these three types: questions of fact, of value, and of policy.[3] Issues distinguish kinds of arguments and reveal the resources of each.

Questions of Fact

A *question of fact* is a dispute about what evidence exists and how it should be interpreted. Several issues about capital punishment, for example, are really questions of fact: Does capital punishment deter others from committing murder? (What evidence of deterrence exists? What is reliable evidence of deterrence? How can it be gathered?) Are a disproportionate number of poor nonwhites executed, and does the ethnicity of the victim affect such sentencing? (What proportion of capital crimes are committed by poor nonwhites? What kinds of data exist about the socioeconomic status and race of executed persons? Are there data to show that those who kill whites rather than nonwhites are more likely to be executed?) What kind of legal representation did those accused of capital crimes receive? (Was that representation competent, and what kind of evidence is needed to establish competence or incompetence?) If there was DNA evidence, was it made available to the jury? How is such evidence to be interpreted? Such disputes are not simple, as the conflicting evidence about deterrence demonstrates, but they do reflect some fundamental agreements: that deterrence is an important goal; that penalties should be applied without class, ethnic, or other bias; that the ultimate punishment should be applied only after a fair trial based on the best available evidence and in which the defendant receives competent legal representation.

In other words, when you address a question of fact, the issues focus on the quality, accuracy, and adequacy of the evidence. As just illustrated, disputants agree on a common goal—deterrence—and proceed to examine the evidence to determine whether a specific policy, such as capital punishment, meets that goal. The dispute will focus on the amount and quality of evidence and its appropriate interpretation, and most of the warrants will be field-dependent. Authoritative evidence will be particularly important because such evidence presumably represents the interpretation of raw data (facts) by highly qualified, unbiased individuals.

Questions of Value

A *question of value*, by contrast, is a dispute about what is good, desirable, useful, or perhaps even about what is ethical or moral. Obviously, then, questions of value can reflect more fundamental disagreements than questions of fact. Some of the issues about capital punishment are questions of value: Should we avenge premeditated murder or obey absolutely the biblical injunction against killing? What are the ethical implications of killing by the state? Is our goal to rehabilitate those who commit crimes or to protect society from murderers? Is our moral standard "better that ten guilty persons go free than that one innocent person die"? Are there circumstances under which killing another person is justified (such as self-defense or the battered-woman syndrome)? Such issues reflect fundamental, often deeply held commitments, and no single rhetorical act is likely to change them.

Disagreements over values often define target audiences (those who share a fundamental value with the rhetor and who the rhetor most wants to reach). They may be a measure of audience hostility, one kind of obstacle or aspect of the rhetorical problem. Conflicts between the values held by individual members of the audience may be a resource for initiating rhetorical action. Such conflicts may be used to provoke individuals to reconsider their priorities and to seek ways to reestablish internal consistency within their value systems.

Values arise from our basic needs, from cultural norms, and from our peculiarities as individuals (see Chapter 8). All of these values are resources for arguments because each value is a reason or justification. Such reasons are not field-dependent; they depend on cultural norms and social mores. Reasons or justifications drawn from such values are sometimes called *motivational* because they are grounded in our motives as human beings, as members of a culture, or as unique individuals.[4]

When we are urged to act to ensure our survival, for example, when we are pressed to buy a year's supply of food to protect ourselves against the devastation of nuclear attack, economic depression, or millennial meltdown, a motivational reason is at work. Such reasons are also present in many arguments that appeal to our need for esteem (vote for Barack Obama or Mitt Romney because he shares our values), for love (avoid dandruff and have shiny, sexy hair by using ABC shampoo), and for self-actualization (buy *Women and Money: Owning the Power to Control Your Destiny*). When arguments appeal to basic needs, cultural values, or to personal achievement, motivational justifications are being used.

Questions of Policy

A *question of policy* always involves a course of action—what we should do or not do. The issues in questions of policy are so universal that they are known as involving stock issues (they are commonplace, always "in stock"). According to Aristotle, the central issue of what he called deliberative rhetoric, which treats questions of policy, is expediency—that is, "appropriateness to the purpose at hand" or the most efficient and effective means to an end. Stock issues arise from what a rhetor must do to make a good case for changing current policy or the means to achieve our goals now in use. These issues can be stated as follows:

1. Is there a compelling need to change the current policy? To demonstrate this, show that
   a. Someone is harmed or injured.
   b. The harm or injury is of sufficient scope to be of social concern.
   c. The harm or injury is a direct consequence of the policy presently in effect (what has been called inherency).
2. Is there an alternative policy? (More than one may need to be considered.)

3. Is the alternative policy under consideration practical and beneficial?
   a. Do we have the resources and expertise to put it into effect; does it require what we consider an appropriate amount of resources?
   b. Will the results of the policy improve the situation, or is it likely to have side effects—unintended consequences, if you will—that would make it, on balance, undesirable?

Each of these stock issues in a policy dispute combines questions of fact and questions of value.

A policy is a way of doing something. It is a systematic way of dealing with a particular kind of situation or event. Because we do not assume that change is good in itself, when you advocate policy changes, you assume an argumentative responsibility that is called *the burden of proof*. If you fulfill its requirements, however, as described next, then supporters of current policies are obligated to respond to your arguments and evidence. That is, once you have met your burden of proof in advocating a change in policy, opponents face a *burden of rejoinder* or *burden of rebuttal* if they wish to maintain the current policy.

To meet the burden of proof, you must first show that someone is harmed by the current policy (a question of fact and of value). A fact by itself does not demonstrate harm. The fact must be measured against a standard (or value) to show that what exists is harmful. Consider, for example, the startling fact that over 440,000 people in the United States die each year from the effects of smoking, a figure that dwarfs the nearly 4,500 U.S. service men and women killed since 2003 in the Iraq War. Those deaths have generated national debate over U.S. military policy and over setting a date for the removal of U.S. troops. The deaths from smoking have been an accepted part of our culture for many years, and until quite recently little had been done to reduce those numbers. As these examples illustrate, a claim that some situation is harmful combines data with a justification drawn from a value.

Demonstrating harm is not enough, however. The harm must have a certain scope or magnitude. This measurement moves from injuries to individuals to harm affecting the well-being of society. A student did this well in a speech arguing that measles vaccinations should be required for all children. She transformed that topic from triviality to significance by citing evidence to show how many unvaccinated children would get the measles, how many of those children would be permanently brain damaged, and what would be the cost to society. Suddenly, a rather unimportant, previously remote childhood disease became a significant social problem with important financial implications for each of us.

As these examples suggest, scope or magnitude is usually demonstrated with statistics, but that is not always the case. A single innocent person who is executed through capital punishment is likely to raise serious questions, not only because of the importance of one human life, but also because that one instance is a sign that all the procedures designed to ensure justice were not sufficient to prevent its most serious miscarriage. Similarly, a single nuclear accident like that at Chernobyl or Fukushima in which substantial amounts of radioactive materials were released into the air (something many thought never could happen) may be significant enough to call into question current policies governing nuclear power plant construction and maintenance.

Harm and scope are not enough by themselves, however; you must also demonstrate that these problems are the direct result of the present policy. In other words, you must prove that harm of this magnitude is intrinsic to, an inevitable part of, the current procedure. As an illustration, suppose that, using your current method of study (the policy), you receive a final course grade of D in your nutrition class. That grade, which most students would consider clearly harmful, does not automatically mean that you will conclude that your current method of study is at fault. Perhaps you were not adequately prepared for this kind of science course and are really proud that you passed it in spite of your lack of preparation. Perhaps your teacher was unskilled at explaining ideas, inaccessible for conferences, and absentmindedly asked questions on the tests about material that wasn't covered in the text or lectures. Perhaps you were seriously ill during a major part of the semester, and any course you were able to pass was a victory over your health problems. Note that, in these cases, the cause lies outside the policy. Change, if any, needs to occur somewhere else—in your preparation for the course, in the teacher's approach, in your health, but not in your mode of study.

This stock issue, which some call inherency, is part of a question of policy because no policy is ever presumed to be perfect. All policies are carried out by imperfect humans who have bad days and who can create any number of problems for which the policy itself cannot be held responsible, and all of us have had experience with individuals who seem determined to make some procedure as difficult as possible! As a result, the issue of whether or not the problem is intrinsic to the policy is a demand that you show that it is the policy itself, not the persons who carry it out or some special set of circumstances, generating the problem.

If you can demonstrate significant harm and that the harm is an inevitable part of the current policy, you must still show that an alternative course of action exists. In most cases this is easy—several alternatives will seem obvious. But the issue exists because if we are to change, there must be something to change to. To return to the example of your final grade in your nutrition class, for instance, many students do not consider changing the way they study because they are not aware of any alternative. Most students are not taught how to study or exposed to various approaches and so do not see any other way to do it. Conditions must exist that make change possible. In a more serious case, after a certain number of heart attacks, a person no longer has the opportunity to change lifestyle. Given a certain amount of damage, exercises to improve heart action and circulation are no longer effective. If you are over age sixty-five or if you do not have strong family support for the postoperative period, it is unlikely that you will be able to receive a heart transplant no matter how serious the condition of your heart. Those who mourn the effects of aging are often called up short by someone who says, "Consider the alternative!"

And if you demonstrate that an alternative exists, you still must show that it is practical. That is, you must show that the resources—personnel, expertise, time, money, and materials—are available to institute the new procedure. If these resources are not available or are difficult to obtain, or if the allocation of those resources to solve one problem would divert them from another equally serious problem, the policy is not a realistic alternative. If the cost of the policy is too high, we may decide to live with the current level of harm. For example, many students consider the cost involved in following a method of study that would produce an A grade average too high. They place higher priorities on time spent in recreation with friends or in extracurricular activities such as debate or athletics.

Finally, you must demonstrate that the alternative policy is, on balance, beneficial. This issue reflects a recognition that all policies, no matter how wonderful, are not panaceas; they have undesirable as well as desirable effects. If we change our procedure, we want to be assured that we shall come out ahead. In the face of data that increasing numbers of Americans are without health insurance, the president may propose measures to Congress, such as programs to provide health care for poor children, that will ensure that more people receive adequate health care; but such programs are costly, and they require either additional taxes or shifting appropriations from other programs to this one in order to be put into operation. Political leaders will try to determine, to the extent they can, whether the benefits of reducing the numbers of people without health insurance by expanding Medicaid coverage, for example, outweigh the evils of higher taxes or lower spending in other areas.

Each of these issues combines questions of fact and questions of value. Questions of harm and scope measure facts against values. Evaluation of the current policy depends on how clearly we can establish that it, rather than other factors, is responsible for the problem. That an alternative policy exists must be demonstrated before we can evaluate its practicality (what costs we are willing to bear combines facts and values) or benefits (evaluation of predicted effects). Policy questions are treated separately here, not because they differ from questions of fact and value, but because certain demands must be met by any rhetor who advocates policy change. The values used to judge these questions may differ among people or cultures, but these same issues are addressed whenever anyone evaluates policies.

INVENTION

The ancient Greek and Roman rhetoricians called the process of preparing for rhetorical action *invention* (from the Latin *invenire*, to come upon or find). The term reflects their understanding that, ordinarily, rhetors do not create arguments from scratch, but rather appropriate and adapt ideas and materials they discover in their research, in the course of their training, in reports of research by others, in other speeches or essays, in cultural ideas. These ideas and materials are used to construct arguments adapted to new circumstances, and invention refers to the choice from among available argumentative options. Invention also reflects the creative role of rhetors in selecting and adapting arguments and evidence in ways best suited to the occasion and audience and to their purpose, and in organizing these into an effective whole.

Skillful invention requires that you know yourself and the role you will play, that you know just what audience you are trying to reach, and that you are familiar with the available evidence and arguments and with the cultural history of your subject. Once again, an understanding of your specific rhetorical context is essential to making wise choices in preparing your materials.

Some clues about the importance of arguments and evidence in rhetoric come from a body of research that is called *persuasive arguments theory*. This research was based on observation of decision making in small groups, and the results suggest that arguments have more to do with attitude change than peer pressure, the influence of the attitudes of others on the positions we take.[5]

Persuasive arguments theory assumes that there is a culturally given pool of arguments available on any issue (what we have called the cultural history of the subject; see Chapter 9). In order to decide what position to take, consider the arguments that are available. Arguments vary in accessibility (the chance that they are known or will come to mind), direction (pro and con), and persuasiveness (impact on or salience for an individual). According to this research, people take positions on issues because of the balance of arguments; that is, they decide where they stand based on the number of pro or con arguments that they know about or are exposed to and that have force for them personally. As a result, novel or unfamiliar arguments presented by a rhetor become especially important because such arguments may tip the balance and change an individual's attitude. This research also demonstrates the significance of cultural history as part of the rhetorical problem, because in these studies attitude change was least likely to occur when all members of the group were familiar with the entire pool of arguments (that is, the entire cultural history of the subject was known to them).

Testimony from authorities assumes special significance. When individuals encounter an unexpected position in a statement by a recognized authority, they tend to search for reasons that would explain why the authority would take such an unexpected position. These potentially novel arguments, constructed by members of the audience, can also shift the balance and change attitudes. Imagine, for example, that you are a committed conservative with high regard for a particular conservative political candidate. You discover, to your surprise, that this candidate supports a policy toward immigration that would allow persons who have come to the United States illegally to seek citizenship if they have lived and worked here for over ten years, paid taxes, and committed no other crimes. You then begin to think about the reasons that the candidate might have for that position (perhaps this is a realistic response to the fact that there are millions of people in this category in the United States, all of whom cannot reasonably be deported; perhaps this reflects a compassionate conservative's recognition of what these people have contributed to the U.S. economy, or that deportation would risk breaking up families; perhaps inclusion of this provision is the only way it will be possible gain enough votes in Congress to pass comprehensive immigration reform legislation to make our borders more secure and to deport those who now are caught attempting illegally to cross the border). The arguments you construct will be good reasons for you—sensible, salient, forceful. Such arguments are ideally adapted to their audience (you) and have a unique capacity to influence you.

This research suggests that evidence and arguments with which the audience is unfamiliar are particularly potent because they can prompt those exposed into rethinking a position and alter the balance of arguments to shift opinion. Audiences may construct highly potent novel arguments when confronted with an unexpected stance from a respected authority. The research underlines the rhetorical obstacles created by the cultural history of a subject; that is, attitude change is unlikely when the audience is familiar with the entire pool of arguments. In effect, we tune out when we recognize arguments that are familiar to us.

Some of the reasons that arguments are the building blocks of rhetorical action are now apparent. Arguments are essential units in rhetoric because they combine facts and values to advance claims that express our knowledge, understandings, and commitments. As such, they harness together the power of our knowledge and our values. Arguments are building blocks because they address the fundamental issues of fact and value that are part of all choices. They focus on essentials, the grounds for belief and attitude. They are structures that make sense of the world. For all of these reasons, arguments are powerful rhetorical resources.

Another way of thinking about arguments comes from the theorizing and research of Richard Petty and John Cacioppo.[6] Their *Elaboration Likelihood Model* (ELM) emphasizes self-persuasion—that is, the likelihood that audience members will be stimulated to participate in creating a message, to process or interpret it, to develop, clarify, or embellish it, and consider its implications.

Note that from this perspective a better, stronger argument is one that engages audience members, one that they collaborate in creating, translating it into their own words, attempting to clarify what seems ambiguous, and amplifying what the rhetor has voiced by recalling their own personal experiences, thinking up relevant questions, and the like. In other words, a good argument is one that the audience digests and makes its own.

According to their research as well as that of others, the single most important variable affecting one's desire or willingness to digest and amplify an argument is salience or personal relevance, the expectation that the issue it addresses is vital or will have significant consequences for one's life. Put differently, personal relevance is the single greatest motivator prompting audience members to involve themselves in a message. That underscores the importance of adapting arguments to the audience and how essential it is to point out the relevance of issues for those you seek to reach and influence.

A number of other variables affect an audience member's propensity and willingness to elaborate. Some people are natural "noodlers" who love to play around with ideas; they are relatively easy to tempt into argumentative engagement. In addition, we are more willing to participate in messages that reflect our values and beliefs, our ways of looking at the world. Obviously, such messages speak to us in familiar language and offer justifications that we already accept as valid. The fields we choose or the professions we practice reflect such preferences: engineers respect statistical proofs and practical applications; economists respond particularly to claims based on economic principles, and so on.

As noted, ELM theory recognizes that persuasion does not occur solely on the basis of the quality of the evidence and the argument. We sometimes use what they call a *peripheral route*, a kind of shortcut, to avoid the hard work involved in exploring the implications of arguments and evidence. Instead of doing the work yourself, for example, you might turn to *Consumer Reports*, a magazine that sells no advertising; on that basis, you might ignore the details of their testing and the assumptions from which they worked and simply look for the bottom line, accepting whatever they say is the best brand of running shoes, which you then go out to buy. In that case, you judge the source and use it as a peripheral cue on which to make a decision, a highly efficient way of making a choice. Arguments themselves may be peripheral cues; for example, we can be influenced by the sheer number of arguments offered—a peripheral cue—in effect, concluding that because there are many reasons given for it, it must be the best choice.

The accumulated evidence of research on persuasion is quite consistent with the ELM view that there is a trade-off between participating in messages—exploring and evaluating arguments and evidence—and relying on peripheral cues. In general, anything that reduces a person's ability and/or motivation to interpret, test, and amplify issue-relevant arguments also increases the likelihood that simple peripheral cues from the source, occasion, or context will influence the outcome.

Indeed, some rhetorical acts exploit that fact and attempt to force audiences to take the *peripheral route* when processing arguments. For example, the popular sport drink Gatorade was developed in the mid-1960s by researchers at the University of Florida who were concerned about the health effects of strenuous workouts under the blazing Florida sun for their "Gator" football team. Those researchers actually collected the sweat from the players bodies, analyzed it in the laboratory to determine what nutrients—salts, carbohydrates, electrolytes, and the like—in addition to water were lost due to heavy perspiration, and then formulated a drink designed to replenish those nutrients. The resulting product was Gatorade.

Thus, there are logical reasons, supported by credible scientific evidence, for people to purchase and consume Gatorade. But television advertisements for the product rarely present those reasons and evidence. Rather, they typically feature well-known, successful athletes—often NFL or NBA players—drinking Gatorade. The advertisements force the audience to take the *peripheral route* in processing the argument, to ignore those logical reasons and scientific evidence, and instead ask them to purchase the product because a celebrity has endorsed it.

Yet another way of thinking about arguments was described by Aristotle in *On Rhetoric*. He wrote about what he called *topos* (singular; *topoi*, plural). These were places or locations in which to look for what Aristotle called the "available means of persuasion" or "strategies of argument" to make your position credible and cogent. Aristotle identified two types: (1) *common topics* or lines of argument that are universal—they appear in discourse on every subject; and (2) *special topics*, or "field-dependent" arguments, meaning that available arguments emerge out of a particular discipline, such as medicine or economics or genetics or physics or even from subfields such as cardiology, illustrated by the Reggie Lewis case cited earlier in this chapter. The special topics or field-dependent arguments emerge out of your research, just as the arguments McKibben uses about the effects of pollution arise directly out of the issues that environmentalists address (see Chapter 4).

By contrast, the following common topics or universal arguments are so general, even obvious, that it is easy to discount them:

1. *More or less.* This is an argument about magnitude, importance, weight—how serious, how widespread, how important or, conversely, how exaggerated, miniscule, trivial, or limited something is. More or less arguments are important in policy questions: How serious and widespread is the problem? How significant are the benefits of change or the undesirable side effects? In law, these are arguments about the seriousness of a crime and the length of the sentence that should be imposed, with a consideration of mitigating circumstances that suggest that juries and judges should be merciful. Ceremonial discourse is typified by amplification, with repetition and detail that asks us to give greater weight to national values or to commit ourselves to carrying out the work begun by the person who died. How can we agree about how to assess the magnitude of this problem, issue, or event? Here, interestingly enough, Aristotle urges rhetors to turn to details and particulars. Be concrete!

2. *Possible/impossible.* This kind of argument prompts us to think about alternatives (e.g., if war is possible, so is peace). This is central to proposed policy changes that assess practicality and expediency, and to consider whether the opposite of what we hoped and dreamed might be the outcome of our actions. For example, we hoped and believed that the Iraqis would greet us with open arms when we invaded and removed Dictator Saddam Hussein, but if that was possible, unfortunately, so was the reverse! This is an argument designed to curb unexamined optimism.

3. *Past fact.* This kind of argument questions whether some action has or has not occurred, not just a question of empirical verification, but a question of likelihood or probability. What would have been more natural in these conditions, what usually occurs in these circumstances, are important considerations. Circumstantial detail arguments are of this sort. A prosecutor has no direct

evidence against someone indicted, but she tells a story of criminal behavior that fits all that is known and tries to convince the jury that this is the most likely scenario for what has occurred. It assumes that what seems to be the best explanation is usually right, which of course can reflect our stereotypes and prejudices. Generally, this is an argument about plausibility. How to respond?

4. *Future fact*. This is an argument about prediction—what is going to happen in the future? Here arguments based on comparison (literal analogy) are prominent; quite simply, we assume that the future will be like the past. We make predictions based on the past record of a tennis player against a particular opponent or based on past experience, and the greater our knowledge of what happened under similar circumstances, the better our predictions will be. Again, this is an argument about likelihood or probability, such as will Barry Bonds beat Hank Aaron's home run record, and if he does, will his record have an asterisk because of clear evidence that he used steroids to enhance his performance? In some cases this argument rests on knowledge of motive or character (e.g., if someone has the desire to shoplift an item and no one is watching, will he steal it?). Here motives and character play a significant role; here we ask questions about future behavior based on the enjoyment of power, the significance of greed, the possibility of envy, all of which affect our predictions about human behavior.[7]

Thus far, we have considered arguments as rational structures that make explicit claims backed by reasons and evidence. But arguments, even rational arguments, are often implicit, subtle, and fragmentary, especially when they appear in the statements of real human beings in contrast to neat diagrams in logic textbooks. The most basic kinds of arguments found in rhetoric are outlined in Figure 5–1: (a) *enthymeme*, (b) *induction/deduction*, (c) *causal*, and (d) *analogy*. Here, the attention will focus on enthymemes, argumentative resources that lie outside the field of logic and emphasize the importance of audience participation in the process of persuasion.

Once again, Aristotle and other ancient rhetoricians considered the *topoi* or topics to be "places to look" for arguments during the invention stage. On any topic, rhetors were encouraged to take an inventory of the arguments that were available in that given case and then select those that seemed to be the strongest and most salient for their audiences.

ENTHYMEMES

One of the most difficult rhetorical concepts to explain and illustrate is the *enthymeme*, a Greek word that Aristotle used to identify what he called the central principle of all rhetorical art. There is no English equivalent. Enthymeme is derived from the word *thumos* or heart, which in all its forms is linked with some element of emotion in the perceiver or the perceived, plus the prefix *en*, meaning in, and the suffix *ma*, meaning the result of action. Classical scholar Caroline Caswell says this of its use in early Greek epic: "*thumos* of the perceiver recognizes the nature of the emotion in another person; unity with another is expressed.... verbs of perception and verbs of emotion could be connected with *thumos* . . . [it is] frequently in passages for the purpose of indicating the simultaneous presence of emotion and cognition."[8] In other words, the basic concept from which enthymeme is derived involves feeling, a sense of identification with

Figure 5–1

Reasoning Types (or General Assignments)

Name	Function	Example	Value
Enthymeme	An abbreviated kind of argument. Audiences must complete the argumentative cues provided by the rhetor.	The classic negative campaign ad of 1968, "The Daisy Spot," never explicitly says "Goldwater will push the nuclear button." But audiences draw that conclusion from the sequencing of powerful visual and aural cues (see Chapter 11).	Invites participation Audiences like drawing their own conclusions
Induction/ Deduction	In inductive argument, a rhetor details examples in order to arrive at a larger claim; in deductive argument, a rhetor presents a claim as presumed truth or fact and then proceeds to document how that claim is true.	"I've Been to the Mountaintop" is organized inductively. King gives many brief and poignant examples of civil rights successes before concluding that it is a righteous cause and it is God's will for the movement to prevail. "The Gettysburg Address" is organized deductively. Lincoln begins with an established truth: "all men are created equal." The rest of the address buttresses this truth.	Inductive = seductively draws audiences to accept rhetor's conclusions Deductive = straightforward appearance of logical rigor
Causal	Establish necessary relationships between two phenomena.	McKibbin writes in "Global Warming's Terrifying New Math," "So far, we've raised the average temperature of the planet just under 0.8 degrees Celsius, and that has caused far more damage than most scientists expected. (A third of summer sea ice in the Arctic is gone, the oceans are 30 percent more acidic, and since warm air holds more water vapor than cold, the atmosphere over the oceans is a shocking 5 percent wetter, loading the dice for devastating floods.)"	Adheres to the scientific method
Analogy	Compare two phenomena in order to evaluate, predict, or dramatize the rhetor's point.	"You know, it's got to be just as nice, if you're a gun collector, to see that $3,000 semi gleaming under glass as it is for a baseball fan to see a Mickey Mantle card, but here's what I don't get—how that can possibly trump everyone else's right to go to the movies without ending up in a lake of 70 people's blood?"	Adheres to the jurisprudence (courtroom) model

another person, and the ability to see evidence of emotion in another. Caswell concludes that *thumos* describes a kind of mutual, interpersonal interaction that involves perception, feeling, and a sense of unity.

This description recalls President Obama's eulogy after the shooting that killed several people and severely wounded Representative Gabrielle Gifford in Tucson, Arizona. In that speech he said: "We mourn with you for the fallen. We join you in your grief." These are simple statements of unity and shared feeling. Later, he personalized the pain when he spoke of a young girl who was killed:

And in Christina...in Christina we see all of our children. So curious, so trusting, so energetic and full of magic. So deserving of our love....Christina was given to us on

September 11th, 2001, one of 50 babies born that day to be pictured in a book called "Faces of Hope." On either side of her photo in that book were simple wishes for a child's life. "I hope you help those in need," read one. "I hope you know all of the words to the National Anthem and sing it with your hand over your heart. I hope you jump in rain puddles."

Those details link Christina to the tragedies of 9/11 and to our feelings about that awful day, and they create a vivid sense of what her death means, a perverse reenactment of the horrors of that earlier tragedy, because she comes alive for us as she is linked to generosity, patriotic feelings, and the joy of children's play. The speech does not tell us what to do; instead, it powerfully seeks to unite us in profound fellow-feeling.

Classical scholar Jeffrey Walker contests the view that the enthymeme is just another kind of logical argument. He writes that "if one assumes that 'syllogism' means formalized, propositional reasoning, such as Aristotle outlines in his logical treatises, . . . then . . . it is difficult to see how, even for Aristotle, such a limited construct could be conceived as the central principle of all rhetorical art or could account for all real-world argumentative procedures."[9] He notes that in "Against the Sophists" (7-8), Isocrates, the preeminent Athenian teacher of rhetoric, uses the verb "syllogize" to refer "to the way that ordinary, private persons (*idiôtai*) intuitively derive an inference or judgment from a bundle of observations."[10] Accordingly, Walker concludes that "rhetoric is to dialectic, not merely its 'counterpart' or loose equivalent, but its *antistrophos*, its differing sister," reinterpreting the meaning of the famous opening line of Aristotle's *Rhetoric*.[11] He also points to its early use by playwright Sophocles in "Oedipus at Colonnus" as a name for a piece of "heartfelt reasoning," or something "taken to heart" or pondered in the heart.[12] In other words, Walker concludes, the enthymeme is not a device invented by rhetoricians any more than a metaphor is; rather, "it is an everyday discursive practice, an existing feature of human behavior."[13] Moreover, he writes,

> it cannot be reduced to or stated as a formal syllogism . . . because it may include among its "premises" such things as sense perceptions, mental imagery, memories, cognitive schemata, deepset beliefs and values (ideologies), bodily states, the aesthetic effects of music or drugs, and existing emotional predispositions (the "habits" of response that Aristotle considers to constitute *êthos*) as well as propositions or "ideas" overtly present to the psyche. . . . [And] the operation of such diverse "premises" depends on no linear, propositional sequencing but is "simultaneous and quick" and may not be especially accessible to consciousness. . . . The word *enthymemata* [plural] refers to emotively charged reasons *felt by an audience* for responding in a certain way.[14]

For example, the background music and sound effects in a film illustrate "emotively charged reasons" to accept tragic or comic happenings, invite viewers to sense danger, anticipate an unexpected turn of events. Each of us brings to rhetorical situations such as ads, speeches, documentaries, discussions with friends, appeals to teachers, and songs our memories, our past experiences, our beliefs about human behavior, our knowledge about particular subjects, and the like, and these are part of the process by which we all reach conclusions.

Obviously, understood in this way, a rhetorical argument or enthymeme doesn't refer to the kind of reasoning that we associate with a formal syllogism. Rather, it seeks to persuade an audience by appealing to what speaker and audience share culturally, to memories, beliefs and values, to beloved music, emotional predispositions (to respond to the flag, to certain phrases, with deep cultural roots), and such linkages may produce responses that are "simultaneous" or immediate, and "quick," not requiring much thought.

Enthymemes emerge out of the shared cultural beliefs, attitudes, and values of an audience; it is jointly created by source and audience; it is an elaborated argument in the ELM sense and has force because audience members fill in details or add their experience as evidence. Obviously, a rhetor can prepare carefully to try to prompt, direct, and shape such responses, but the enthymeme comes into being only if readers, listeners, or viewers participate in it and amplify its message(s).

As noted, the concept of the enthymeme comes from ancient writers, but contemporary theorists also refer to transacts or interacts as basic units of communication. These concepts emphasize that you cannot commit a rhetorical act alone. Rhetoric is a transaction (*trans* means across or over or through) or an interaction (*inter* means between or among). Each of us bring a store of experience, feelings, beliefs, values, and concepts to every encounter with a speech, article, advertisement, TV or radio program, visual, piece of music, tweet, or poke. These are the raw materials through which we participate in all these forms of rhetorical action.

The dynamics of the enthymeme are evident in the consciousness-raising that was an essential part of second-wave feminism. As women and men discovered, feminist awakenings can happen in many different ways, although the most common arise out of personal experiences. Sometimes they happen in response to reading feminist materials, when the reader feels that the author seems to be writing about her life. Sometimes if comes from watching a film that dramatizes sexist behaviors; sometimes from a classroom moment in which people share their experiences; sometimes it is evoked by a bad joke or a comment in a TV program or a movie. Such moments are called "clicks," when you suddenly realize or recognize a pattern that you had not noticed before, when you put a lot of things together and say, "Aha, now I see it." Because sexist attitudes are deeply entrenched in culture and because we are all enculturated—in school, at work, in books, plays, humor—we don't notice the patterns of behavior that make assumptions about girls and women, assumptions about what they can and can't do, what their roles in life are supposed to be, and so on.

Obviously, as the earlier material on enthymemes indicates, such "clicks" don't just happen to nascent feminists. Clicks are just examples of moments when any and all of us suddenly recognize a pattern, make a connection, look at some event or moment differently. Feminist "clicks" are good examples of the dynamics of one kind of rhetorical building block—the enthymeme. If you use feminist clicks as an example, you'll realize that enthymemes only happen when those involved have lots of prior experience—an enthymeme, like a click, is a recognition of a pattern, a connection that you hadn't made before. Based on your past, some event, some work, some comment, some picture, prompts you to make a linkage that you hadn't made before. In other words, enthymemes are special kinds of persuasion grounded in large amounts of shared experiences, in a common culture, and background that prepares you or me to make a leap—to jump from what is part of our past to a conclusion based on this particular experience. In a way, what creates an enthymematic moment may be the comment or joke or happening that is "the straw that breaks the camel's back," that is, the one more small thing that prompts a conclusion.

The character of the enthymeme places a premium on the *inventional* stage of the rhetorical process because it is there that rhetors must take pains to discover and select those arguments or "means of persuasion" most likely prompt participation and amplification by the specific audience involved.

This element of audience participation and amplification is why Aristotle called the enthymeme "the substance of rhetorical persuasion." What distinguishes rhetorical reasoning is the use of *endoxa*—the opinions, beliefs, ideology, experiences, and knowledge of the audience—as the basis for arguments. These can be the premise for the argument, the evidence used as proof, or the warrant that links the premise and conclusion. Of special importance is that this kind of argument relies on the active participation of, or collaboration by, audience members. Such is not the case with other forms of reasoning, such as the formal logic represented by the syllogism. Informed and honest individuals cannot dispute either the premises or the conclusions of true and valid syllogisms. Socrates was mortal, and proved it when he drank the hemlock.

Here are two examples of enthymemes at work in memorable speeches. The prologue to this book includes the text of Robert F. Kennedy's speech on March 4, 1968, in Indianapolis, interspersed with commentary by Joe Klein. Here I focus on the role the enthymeme plays in it.

When he arrived at the rally, the crowd was happy, excitedly anticipating Kennedy's appearance, and when he climbed onto the flatbed of a truck to speak, he knew he would be bringing them terrible news. There was no script; he had to improvise. Much of what he said was ordinary, reporting the awful news, then offering a brief eulogy commemorating and celebrating Martin Luther King's life and work. Kennedy also attempted to shift the crowd's focus on grief and anger to the future.

Kennedy understood, however, that this transition would be exceedingly difficult for some of his audience, and he addressed them directly: "For those of you who are black—considering the evidence evidently is that there were white people who were responsible—you can be filled with bitterness, and with hatred, and with a desire for revenge." He acknowledged white responsibility, and he voiced what he believed his black listeners were feeling—bitterness, hatred, and an intense desire for revenge.

Then he offered a stark choice: immediate powerful anger and separation or following in the footsteps of Martin Luther King and substitute compassion and love for violence.

But why should they listen to him? Isn't that what whites are always asking of blacks, that they swallow and then transcend terrible injustices? In what followed, Kennedy did an extraordinary thing, for the first time, he spoke of his intense reaction to the killing of his beloved brother, and he built a personal bridge to his black listeners: "For those of you who are black and are tempted to be filled with hatred and mistrust of the injustice of such an act, against all white people, I would only say that I can feel in my own heart the same kind of feeling. I had a member of my family killed, but he was killed by a white man." With those words, he became the exemplar of what he was asking of his audience, to do as he has done in the face of terrible personal loss.

The personal reference was very painful, and Kennedy could not bring himself to express his intense feelings publicly, so he appropriated the words of Aeschylus in the *Agamemnon*: "Even in our sleep, pain which cannot forget falls drop by drop upon the heart until, in our own despair, against our will, comes wisdom through the awful grace of God." Those words are terrifying; they speak of a pain that never stops, even in sleep, until, in despair, "against our will, comes wisdom through the awful grace of God." Those words invite the audience to acknowledge the terrible pain of a loss that, finally, transcends anger and hatred in a kind of wisdom that emerges by "grace of God." It was a transcendent and transformative moment.

Kennedy assumed another responsibility, to prevent an explosion by asking his hearers "to return home, say a prayer for the family of Martin Luther King, yeah that's true, but more importantly to say a prayer for our own country, which all of us love—a prayer for understanding and that compassion of which I spoke." (And, as noted in the prologue, they seemed to have followed his advice.) Finally, he returned to the Greeks, saying "Let us dedicate ourselves to what the Greeks wrote so many years ago: to tame the savageness of man and make gentle the life of this world." That reference suggests the unending challenges that humans face; thus, he invited all to dedicate themselves "to that, to say a prayer for our country and our people."

Rhetorical critics included this speech among the one hundred greatest speeches of the twentieth century.[15] Much of what Kennedy said is familiar, even pedestrian. Appeals to heal our divisions, not to react with hatred and despair to terrible events, are commonplace. What makes the speech so moving and startling is the speaker's use of the poetry of Aeschylus as a means to communicate the incommunicable, to invite us to believe that out of the unending pain comes wisdom. Why should we believe him? Because he was the living example of what he said. Thus, enthymemes exemplify moments in which we take "to heart" the statements of others, we recognize and share their pain; through special circumstances, what they say ceases to be just "words" and instead are "written on our hearts."

Here is a different speech, illustrating how a statement, an assertion, becomes enthymematic, that is, arouses deep emotion, becomes memorable, and stands as the symbol for an idea. In *Kennedy in Berlin*,[16] Andreas W. Daum tells the story of the key line in John F. Kennedy's speech delivered at Schoëneberg City Hall in West Berlin on June 26, 1963.[17]

Kennedy's speech was unusual in several ways. At the outset, he ignored the prepared text and improvised. Originally, he was supposed to recall the dramatic events of post-war history: the Berlin blockade, the 1953 uprising in East Germany, Khruschev's 1958 ultimatum, and the building of the Berlin Wall, but he did not say any of those things. Indeed, he only briefly referred to those on the platform, West Berlin Mayor Willy Brandt, West German Chancellor Konrad Adenauer, and General Lucius Clay, who managed the Berlin Airlift and responded with U.S. tanks to the Soviet challenge at Checkpoint Charlie, was mentioned only as having been "in this city during its greatest moments of crisis and will come again if ever needed." But when the huge crowd roared, Kennedy beckoned Clay to the podium, to wave to the crowd. "These spontaneous moments," Daum writes, "made the occasion much more relaxed and popular in tone than the film excerpts that became familiar in later years would suggest" (141).

Kennedy then uttered the sentence that, Daum comments, would "remain indelible in the memory of generations to come" (141). He prepared the audience for it by making a powerful comparison: "Two thousand years ago the proudest boast was '*civis Romanus sum.*' Today, in the world of freedom, the proudest boast is '*Ich bin ein Berliner.*'"[18] Heinz Weber translated what he had said, and now all of the audience understood just what he had claimed, and the crowd cheered. Kennedy then thanked Weber for improving his German, and Weber translated that compliment for the crowd, and Kennedy grinned. He had made a declaration of a common identity and a special relationship between U.S. Americans and West Berliners. Not one word of this key sentence was on the typed cards Kennedy held.

Where did that sentence come from? John F. Kennedy, who was well educated, liked to use quotations from antiquity or classical modern literature in his speeches. He was particularly eager to find appropriate quotations for his trip to Berlin. On May 4, 1962, Kennedy visited New Orleans, where he was made an honorary citizen of the city. In his speech responding to the honor, he said: "Two thousand years ago the proudest boast was to say, 'I am a citizen of Rome.' Today, I believe, in 1962, the proudest boast is to say, 'I am a citizen of the United States.'" On June 26, 1963, Kennedy used the first part of that statement, word for word, in his speech to the West Berliners. He altered the second half to fit the immediate situation.

The next paragraph of the speech illustrates the more common understanding of the enthymeme as an argument that must be completed by the audience. Kennedy began, "There are many people in the world who really don't understand, or say they don't, what is the great issue between the free world and the Communist world. Let them come to Berlin." In this case, the refutation of the claim is the city itself—and the proof is evident to anyone who sees conditions in Berlin. The same pattern followed in the next argument: "There are some who say that communism is the wave of the future. Let them come to Berlin." Once again, the hearer's experience of the city is all the proof needed to reject the claim. Next he said, "And there are some who say in Europe and elsewhere we can work with the Communists. Let them come to Berlin." Again, the falsity of the assertion would be apparent to any visitor. Finally, "And there are even a few who say that it is true that communism is an evil system, but it permits us to make economic progress. *Lass' sie nach Berlin kommen*. Let them come to Berlin." In effect, Kennedy was saying, do as I have done, come see for yourself, and in this case, Kennedy was even more emphatic. He underscored his argumentative challenge by repeating the line in German and English. No one, no German or anyone else, he seemed to say, could come to this city and believe these arguments.

Now Kennedy added: "Freedom has many difficulties and democracy is not perfect, but we have never had to put up a wall to keep our people in, to prevent them from leaving us," words that reflected the impact on him of seeing the Berlin Wall for the first time. Now he emphasized that he spoke for the entire U.S. public: "I want to say, on behalf of my countrymen, who live many miles away on the other side of the Atlantic, who are far distant from you, that they take the greatest pride that they have been able to share with you, even from a distance, the story of the last 18 years." The identification between Berliners and U.S. Americans was explicit, and Kennedy now praised qualities that his constituents admired: "I know of no town, no city, that has been besieged for 18 years that still lives with the vitality and the force, and the hope and the determination of the city of West Berlin." Here West Berlin is the metonym, the physical embodiment, of the Cold War and of the qualities of character that will enable the West to endure and prevail in "the long twilight struggle" of which Kennedy spoke in his inaugural address. Kennedy acknowledged that the wall was only "the most obvious and vivid demonstration of the failures of the Communist system," but he enriched its meaning by enumerating its personal impact, as "an offense not only against history but an offense against humanity, separating families, dividing husbands and wives and brothers and sister, and dividing a people who wish to be joined together."

Kennedy reaffirmed the special relationship of Berlin to larger Cold War issues: "What is true of this city is true of Germany—real, lasting peace in Europe can never be assured as long as one German out of four is denied the elementary right of free men, that is to make a free choice." These statistics underscored his earlier enumeration of those who were separated by the wall and reaffirmed a basic U.S. value—free choice. Kennedy then said that Berliners "live in a divided island of freedom," a vivid image that linked to an allusion in the words that followed, "but your life is a part of the main," a reference to John Donne's poem that links each person to every other, words used by Ernest Hemingway as the title of his novel about the Spanish civil war, *For Whom the Bell Tolls*.[19] It is doubtful that many Berliners recognized an illusion to a line from seventeenth-century English poetry, but for the English-speaking audience, those words powerfully expressed the belief that all humanity is interconnected. Having established Berlin as epitomizing the larger East-West conflict, he now asked his listeners "to lift your eyes beyond the dangers of today, to the hopes of tomorrow, beyond the freedom merely of this city of Berlin, or your country of Germany, to the advance of freedom everywhere, beyond the way to the day of peace with justice, beyond yourselves and ourselves to all mankind." Note the repetition at the beginning of each phrase of "beyond...to," a use of anaphora that in each case shifted the argument from the specific case to a general principle.

The words of Donne's poem were reaffirmed in his conclusion: "Freedom is indivisible, and when one man is enslaved, all are not free," so, he ended, "All free men, wherever they may live, are citizens of Berlin, and, therefore, as a free man, I take pride in the words, "*Ich bin ein Berliner*," a reaffirmation of his symbolic citizenship of Berlin.

Kennedy's famous declaration, "*Ich bin ein Berliner*" surprised his immediate audience, and it surprised politicians from the West and the East; this was confrontational language.[20] What some believed was a grammatical error became a joke, as if Kennedy had claimed to be "a jelly donut." Daum refers to the work of linguist Jürgen Eichhoff who notes that saying "*Ich bin ein Berliner*" is grammatically correct if the claim is metaphorical, that is, Kennedy was symbolically expressing his solidarity with West Berlin, with "America's Berlin."[21] In Daum's words, "It was a rhetorical intensification of a symbolic common identity linking Americans and Berliners" (148).[22]

Kennedy's whole speech was devoted to establishing West Berlin as the embodiment of the Cold War, of the conflict between the East and the West. Much of the speech asserted that directly in words that express all the ways in which the experiences of its citizens epitomized the form of this ongoing conflict, but many of these words were familiar, even commonplace. The challenge he faced was to find a way to make those ideas living, vivid, memorable, and he did so with a single sentence that invited all those who struggled against communism and who sought freedom to make a simple claim, that they, too, symbolically, were citizens of Berlin.

In summary, then, rhetorical arguments come into being in the minds of members of the audience through direct and indirect means. In fact, all rhetorical action combines elements that are discursive (logical, formed out of propositions and evidence) and nondiscursive (nonlogical, formed by associations and connotations, prompted by juxtapositions, frequently visual and nonverbal). In order to understand the nature of argument, we have to step back to take a broader view of rhetorical action.

DIMENSIONS OF RHETORICAL ACTION

As we wrote in Chapter 1, rhetoric is the study of all the processes by which people are influenced, and as the preceding discussion of enthymemes suggests, some of these processes are logical, some are not. The dimensions of rhetorical action reveal the mixture of qualities found in it (see Figure 5–2). Each of these dimensions is a continuum; that is, each dimension is formed by a pair of qualities related in such a way that one

Figure 5–2
Dimensions of Rhetorical Action

	Discursive (logical links)	Nondiscursive (nonlogical)
Purpose	Instrumental (a tool)	Consummatory (purpose in action itself)
Argument	Justificatory (offers reasons)	Ritualistic (participatory, performative)
Structure	Logical (necessary links)	Associative (learned, from personal experience)
Language	Literal (describes world)	Figurative (describes internal state)
Evidence	Factual (verifiable)	Psychological (appeals to needs, drives, desires)

of them gradually becomes the other. The ends of each continuum represent extreme forms of the same quality or characteristic. Each dimension focuses on the mixture of qualities involved in each facet of rhetorical action: purpose or argument or structure or language or evidence.

Instrumental—Consummatory

Something instrumental is a tool, a means to an end. Something consummatory is its own reason for being—the purpose is the action itself; the end is the performance or enactment, "singing sweet songs to please oneself," as in singing in the shower. Most rhetoric is primarily instrumental because it seeks to achieve some goal outside itself: to alter perception, to share information or understanding, to change attitudes, or to induce action. But rhetorical action is also consummatory. Senator Zell Miller of Georgia, a Democrat, spoke at the Republican National Convention in the summer of 2004. He made a powerful speech, but of equal importance was that a Democrat was endorsing the reelection of George W. Bush. The son of former Republican President Ronald Reagan spoke at the 2004 Democratic National Convention in support of stem cell research, which was opposed by many Republicans. Just what he said in his speech was probably less important than that someone so closely linked to a Republican icon was willing to appear and speak at the Democratic convention. Similarly, the boasts of victorious athletes during championship competitions are consummatory in celebrating their prowess. They are often instrumental, however, in spurring their opponents to new efforts, a reason that such boasting is discouraged by coaches. These are instances in which instrumental and consummatory purposes are mixed and interrelated.

Some rhetorical acts are primarily consummatory. If you were to attend a football or basketball game at the University of Kansas, you would see the Kansas fans rise and begin to murmur what sounds like a Gregorian chant while waving their arms slowly over their heads. They repeat, at an ever-increasing speed, the words "Rock Chalk. Jayhawk. K.U." Unless you are a member of the University of Kansas community, the words and gestures are meaningless.[23] But if you belong to the community, you chant and wave to affirm or reaffirm your membership in it. There is also an instrumental component. The chant expresses, indirectly, support for Jayhawk athletic teams, which represent the community on these occasions. Because morale affects play, the chant may increase the team's likelihood of winning.

Most rhetorical acts are a combination of these purposes, with the emphasis on instrumental ends. Consummatory purposes are often revealed in introductions and conclusions that express shared values and affirm membership in a community.

Justificatory—Ritualistic

An act that is justificatory gives reasons; it explains why something is true or good or desirable, why we should do something or not do it. Ritual refers to the prescribed form or order of an act (usually a ceremony), to the way it is performed. For this reason, ritualistic elements are often nonverbal or involve the sheer repetition of verbal elements, as in a chant. Ritual involves formal practices, customs, and procedures. Rituals do not justify or explain, they affirm and express. Some common ritualistic acts are pledging allegiance to the flag, standing to sing the national anthem, taking communion, or participating in the "Rocky Horror Picture Show." Participating in a ritual requires behaviors such as standing, putting your hand over your heart, wearing a costume or uniform, kneeling, throwing rice, eating, or drinking. Rituals are performed by members of a community; they are repeated over and over again; the form of their performance is very important. Many Roman Catholics, for example, were dismayed when the Latin liturgy was abandoned; many Protestants were unhappy when the King James Version of the Bible was supplanted by translations using more contemporary language. By contrast, justificatory acts imply an absence of shared belief, which requires the presentation of arguments and evidence. Note that the enthymeme illustrates the degree to which rhetorical action falls between these two extremes.

Examples of the use of ritual to make a rhetorical point include silent vigils protesting deaths of U.S. military personnel and Iraqi civilians in the Iraq War, sometimes by standing quietly in symbolic spaces, sometimes by marching at night with candles, sometimes alongside fields of white crosses commemorating each death. Ritualistic arguments can also be made positively. We affirm our love of country as we sing the national anthem and say the pledge of allegiance. The conflict over school prayer is, in part, a conflict over the force of ritualistic appeal. Just how much pressure is put on a child when a teacher says, "Let us pray," and many of her schoolmates bow their heads?

Logical—Associative

Logical relationships are necessary relationships, such as effect to cause or cause to effect. Logical structures reflect such relationships; they express necessary or asserted connections. By contrast, associative relationships are learned through personal experience or are based on cultural linkages or social truths. Associative relationships are based on personal experiences and subjective reactions, but, as illustrated by stereotyping, they can be shared by many individuals.

Associative structure is like juxtaposition—two things are placed in relation to each other, and because they are positioned that way, a relationship is inferred. Rorschach tests are associative, asking individuals to divulge what pops into their minds when they see giant ink blots. Thematic Apperception Tests (TATs), asking individuals to finish stories, are examples of associative structure. Commercials that show beautiful, young, sexy people in attractive locales drinking a soft drink are trying to create associations between the advertised brand and the qualities of the models who appear in the ad. Tobacco companies continue to be blamed for deaths from smoking, despite warnings on cigarette packages, because of the power of their advertising to prompt links between smoking and health, beauty, and sexual appeal.

The power of association is tested in studies of the influence of the size of a package on how much we eat. "The bigger the plate, the larger the spoon, the deeper the bag, the more we eat," according to the research of Professor Brian Wansink, who directs the Cornell University Food and Brand Lab. For example, in one study moviegoers were given free stale popcorn, some in large, some in medium-size buckets. Afterward, what remained was weighed, and the people who received larger buckets ate 53 percent more than those with smaller buckets. Wansink argues that they didn't eat the popcorn because they liked its taste; instead, he claims, "They were driven by hidden persuaders: the distraction of the movie, the sound of other people eating popcorn, and the Pavlovian popcorn trigger that is activated when we step into a movie theater."[24]

Logical structure is ordinarily explicit and overt. Claims are stated as propositions. The connections between ideas are made clear to us, and we can examine claims, evidence, and reasons, testing them against other evidence and the like. Associative structure is usually implicit and oblique. Links are suggested to us, indirectly, by juxtaposing ideas or events or pictures/videos, and we test these connections against our personal experience and subjective response. Note that the associations prompted by juxtapositions can act as substitutes for formal arguments.

The power of arguments based on personal relevance links these two concepts. Prior to the late 1960s, the argument that "if you're old enough to fight, you're old enough to vote" was dismissed as illogical. The qualities needed to fight are quite different from those needed to vote intelligently, so the implied literal analogy was rejected. During the Vietnam War, however, large numbers of men under the age of 21 were drafted and sent to fight in Vietnam, and the argument came to have greater force. Should those who would be asked to risk their lives have a right to choose those who would make that decision? Suddenly, the argument was heard as analogous to "no taxation without representation," that no government should have the right to tax you unless you can vote to decide who will represent you. Now the analogy was between choosing those who would have the power to take away what is your own, whether it be your property in taxes or your life in war. Note that the same basic argument can be seen as illogical or logical depending on which analogy is emphasized. That choice, of course, was deeply affected by personal relevance, and in 1971 the United States lowered the voting age to eighteen.

Many of the strategies discussed in Chapter 7 use the resources of language to make associative connections. Repetitions of sounds, words, and phrases create structures based on association. Relationships based on logic are only one kind of form that appears in rhetorical action. Other forms are based on relationships that emulate patterns in nature and in our experience: repetition, crescendo and decrescendo, and the like.[25]

Rhetorical action combines forms based on logic and on association. Both kinds of form prompt the creation of arguments in the minds of listeners. Television advertising is an excellent source of examples of the use of associative form to support claims.

Literal—Figurative

Literal language is prosaic and factual; it is intended to describe the world. Figurative language is poetic and metaphorical, and it reveals the person who uses it. Literal language deals with external reality; in some cases it can be tested empirically for accuracy. Figurative language reveals the experiences and feelings of the rhetor. One poet calls the moon "the North wind's cookie"; another calls it "a piece of angry candy rattling around in the box of the sky." These statements reveal the feelings of the authors but tell us little about the moon. As critics, we look for metaphors to discover how a rhetor perceives the world. For example, in his famous "I Have a Dream" speech in 1963, Dr. Martin Luther King Jr. construed civil rights for Americans, including African Americans, as a promissory note and efforts to obtain them as analogous to attempting to cash a check on a substantial bank account and being told that there were insufficient funds. That metaphor captures the sense of legal obligation inherent in fundamental citizen rights and the profound injustice in being told by a bank that you had no right to the money on deposit there for you.

Rhetorical acts combine the literal language of factual statements with metaphors and other poetic devices. In her 1988 keynote address to the Democratic National Convention, Texas Governor Ann Richards used a figurative analogy to describe women's ability to perform well in situations usually associated with men, such as delivering keynote addresses: "After all, Ginger Rogers did everything that Fred Astaire did; she just did it backwards and in high heels."

In a column criticizing President George W. Bush's commitment to the war in Iraq, Nicholas Kristof wrote that "the single best guide to Mr. Bush's presidency may be *Moby Dick*. Melville's book is, of course, about much more than Captain Ahab's pursuit of the white whale—a 'nameless, inscrutable, unearthly' symbol of all that is dark and unknown in the world. Rather, it is an allegory about the cost of obsession. Ahab has a reasonable goal, capturing a whale, yet he allows this quest to overwhelm him and erode his sense of perspective and balance. Ignoring warnings, refusing to admit error, Ahab abandons all rules and limits in his quest.... The fanaticism becomes self-destructive, eventually destroying Ahab and his ship."

Kristof uses a figurative analogy to criticize the president's policy in the Iraq War. The power of that analogy will be greatest for those who share Kristof's views, but the comparison adds powerful connotations to the criticism, particularly for those who have read the novel or seen the movies made from it starring Gregory Peck (1956) or Patrick Stewart (1998). The columnist uses the analogy as a story with a moral: "Melville's lesson is that even a heroic quest can be destructive when we abandon all sense of limits."[26] Chapter 7 explores these and other dimensions of language and their role in rhetorical action.

Factual—Psychological

These qualities of evidence are explored in Chapter 4. The factual dimension of evidence can be verified to determine its accuracy or truthfulness. Psychologically, evidence appeals to our needs, drives, and desires. Evidence can be fictive or hypothetical, inducing us to imagine and speculate. Evidence can pander to our prejudices or reflect our opinions and beliefs, which may be wrong. Rhetorical evidence is both data about the world and our perception of the world in terms of ourselves, a process that transforms the "facts" of what exists into instruments for our use and into obstacles that frustrate us.

These continua express the discursive and nondiscursive dimensions of rhetorical action. Although the concept of argument emphasizes discursive or logical processes, rhetorical argumentation includes all kinds of cues that stimulate us to treat our associations as evidence, to construct reasons, to draw conclusions. Many of these cues are nondiscursive. The characteristics of the enthymeme reflect the ways in which rhetorical action combines these dimensions.

Strategies of Proof

Strategies of proof resemble or mimic logical arguments. Through the identification and participation of the audience, they invite the audience to provide material that will justify a claim or conclusion. Figure 5–3 identifies seven common strategies of proof, several of which are illustrated more fully.

Rhetorical Questions. A *rhetorical question* is, in fact, an enthymeme. The rhetor who asks the question does not expect a verbal answer from the audience. Rather, the question is intended to prompt a mental response based on the audience's beliefs, background, values, experiences, and the like. If the rhetor asks the right question—or asks the question in the right way—the mental response of the audience completes the argument that the rhetor intends. Presidential campaigns often include rhetorical questions. In 1952 Dwight D. Eisenhower said, "The Democrats say you never had it so good. Do you want it any better?" That's a particularly effective rhetorical question because few people would answer no, but it was a highly strategic choice for Ike in this campaign. It allowed the audience to supply from their own memory what they perceived as the defects of the Democrats' policies so that the heroic leader of the allied forces in Europe in World War II did not have to stoop to making nasty charges. In 1980 Ronald Reagan asked, "Can anyone look at the record of this administration and say, 'Well done'? Can anyone compare the state of our economy when the Carter administration took office with where we are today and say, 'Keep up the good work'? Can anyone look at our reduced standing in the world today and say, 'Let's have four more years of this'?"[27] Once again, the questions need no answer. Note that they also presented Reagan as merely reminding us of what we all knew rather than as making charges against a sitting president, and that the questions direct our attention to economic and foreign policy issues, areas in which the Carter administration was particularly vulnerable because of the Americans then held hostage by the Iranians.

A Fortiori. A *fortiori* is a Latin phrase that means "to the stronger," and it is an organizational strategy. It connects two claims so that if we accept the first, it becomes more likely we will accept the second. If it can be shown that a politician betrayed his spouse or a close friend who trusted him, for example, it becomes more plausible that he would betray his constituents. Early in the contemporary women's movement, political scientist Jo Freeman wrote an essay designed to show the subtle forces at work that limit women's achievement by teaching women not to take risks or deviate from traditional patterns. She structured her essay following *a fortiori* principles. The opening sections of the essay document the history of discrimination against women in law, followed by sections that document the effects of socialization on

Figure 5–3
Strategies of Proof

Name	Function	Example	Value
Rhetorical Question	Probative, sometimes confrontational way to stimulate the audience to support the rhetor's position	Former Russian President Boris Yeltsin urged Americans to support his plea for mutual cooperation. "After all, what sense does it really make to reinvent the bicycle? Why do we have to pursue parallel efforts doing exactly the same thing in Russia and the United States? Why can't we put our unique expertise together and when I say expertise I mean both research, development and basic and applied research? Why couldn't we join our hands and then we will be able to work miracles?"	Invites audience participation; encourages pseudo-dialogue
A *fortiori* "to the greater"	A specialized analytical argument that says if something happened in one case how much more likely would it happen in another	Angelina Grimké: "If God punished his own peculiar people [the Jews] for their transgressions of slavery, how much more likely will He subject His wrath on our transgression of slavery."	Logical force
Enumeration	A long list of particulars designed to give overwhelming support to a claim	In Reagan's tribute to the Challenger crew, he said: "There will be more shuttle flights, more shuttle crews and yes, more volunteers, more civilians, more teachers in space. Nothing ends here."	Emphatic proof
Refutation	Rhetors state opposing argument and then show why their opponent's case is flawed	Angelina Grimké says: "It is admitted by some that the slave is not happy under the *worst* forms of slavery. But I have never seen a happy slave. I have seen him dance in his chains, it is true; but he was not happy. There is a wide difference between happiness and mirth."	Showcases rhetor's expertise
Definition	A rhetor sets the terms for the debate	In an RJR Tobacco campaign on secondhand smoke, one ad reads: "Since we have discussed scientific aspects of the passive smoking controversy in previous messages, we'd like to focus here on the social questions."	Allows rhetor to argue from position of strength
Enactment	Rhetor is living proof of the claim she/he is making	Angelina Grimké argues women are competent, articulate persons capable of bringing about reform in the public arena. Her very presence as a public speaker in 1838 in the great hall in Pennsylvania, her very ability to talk down her detractors, her bold, scolding tone, her eyewitness expertise on slavery, are all visual and aural proof of the claim that she is making.	Difficult to deny because disagreement means you discount the authority of the rhetor
Turning the tables	Taking an opponent's argument and turning it against him/her	The Budweiser Image ad promoting the WNBA uses All-star Cynthia Cooper to disarm those who think disparagingly of women's sports. She compliments two men for their basketball skills with the line: "You play like a girl."	Disarms opposition

women's ambition. If it can be shown that women are discriminated against overtly in law, it becomes much more plausible that they face covert discrimination based in socialization. Again, the strategy aims at proof. Where arguments are in an *a fortiori* relationship, the claim in the second is made more likely by proof of the first.

Enumeration. *Enumeration* means a long list of particulars is specified. If done well, we are swamped with a mass of details, and each particular or example gains force from all those preceding it. In one of the most powerful examples of enumeration from a classic American speech, "What to the Slave Is the Fourth of July?" Frederick Douglass, the nineteenth-century abolitionist, debunked the argument that slavery was acceptable because the African Americans were not equal to the white race:

> Is it not astonishing that, while we are ploughing, planting, and reaping, using all kinds of mechanical tools, erecting houses, constructing bridges, building ships, working in metal of brass, iron, copper, silver, and gold; that while we are reading, writing and ciphering, acting as clerks, merchants and secretaries, having among us lawyers, doctors, ministers, poets, authors, editors, orators, and teachers; that, while we are engaged in all manner of enterprises common to other men, digging gold in California, capturing the whale in the Pacific, feeding sheep and cattle on the hillside, living, moving, acting, thinking, planning, living in families as husbands, wives and children, and above all, confessing and worshipping the Christian's God, and looking hopefully for life and immortality beyond the grave, we are called upon to prove that we are men!

That withering critique using enumeration, while potent in writing, is even more forceful as argument in speaking, much as a few other strategies of proof are, such as rhetorical questions and enactment. You will have an opportunity to explore other artistic features of Douglass's speech in Chapter 7. Note also, however, that enumeration isn't always so brilliantly constructed; it can often become a dull laundry list of particulars that bore the audience. That has sometimes occurred in presidential State of the Union addresses, for example.

Refutation. Answering and rebutting the arguments of the opposition is one of the commonest but most important strategies. In an organizational pattern that examines arguments pro and con, it can work strategically to answer questions in the minds of the audience and to inoculate them against competing persuaders. One form of refutation, however, deserves special mention. *Debunking* refutes opposing positions by making fun of exaggerated claims. Debunking is a process of deflating pretense, of shrinking opposing arguments to their "proper" size. It is often done through names that serve as labels. For example, in an essay that appeared in *The Nation*, Alexander Cockburn used figurative analogies (that function as derrogatory labels) to debunk concerns over global warming. With those analogies, Cockburn compares the case for global warning to claims, made in the tenth century, that human sinfulness was leading the world to ruin and proposals for selling carbon credits to the Pope's selling of indulgences that supposedly absolved wealthy parishioners of their sins.[28]

Like Kristof's comparison of President Bush to Captain Ahab, Cockburn uses figurative analogies, but unlike Kristof's comparison, this one is intended to debunk those whom Cockburn calls "fearmongers" and "Greenmongers" by comparing them to those who ignorantly predicted doom at the end of the tenth century because of human sinfulness, and by comparing those selling "carbon credits" to those who profited from the sale of indulgences that fraudulently claimed protection against the consequences of sin.

Once again, note that the strategy depends on the beholder. The strategy is most evident to those who believe that human use of fossil fuels is a prime cause of global warming and is least evident to those who share the author's views.

Definition. Those with experience in debate quickly learn that definitions are strategic. Chapter 4 includes a chart of definitional strategies (Figure 4–4) because definitions are critical elements in determining just what must be proved in order to establish a claim. The dialectical definitions discussed earlier are also examples of strategic definitions. *Definitions* explain highly abstract terms, and they are often used in an attempt to change the perceptions of the audience. Bernice Sandler, for example, used this strategy in a 1991 speech at Illinois State University in Normal to explain the meaning of an unfamiliar and technical sociological term.

> At a very early age, boys learn to use girls as what the sociologists call a "negative reference group." In other words, the boys define themselves by comparing themselves favorably to girls, the lesser group, the females. After all, what is the worst thing you can call a little boy? A sissy—which means he is acting like a girl. By teasing girls a boy begins to feel good about himself—he is better than they are, and teasing them makes him feel like a "real boy." Moreover, by putting down girls and females he can get closer to his buddies. They can all put down the girls, and feel better and bigger than the girls. Harassment, and even sexual assault, can be, for many men, the way in which they show other men how "manly" they really are. We see this in its extreme in the case of gang rape, where psychologists have noted that the men are not raping for sexual reasons but are really raping for each other. This is how they show their friends how strong, how virile, how manly, how wonderful they really are.[29]

Sandler's statement combines a number of strategies. It defines by enumerating the various activities that illustrate the meaning of the phrase "negative reference group." The illustrations are arranged in a climax construction that works from the least to the most harmful manifestation, from teasing girls to gang raping them. The phrase, its definition, and the illustrations are all part of an effort to demonstrate the harmful effects of sexism in our society and to make us more willing to intervene to prevent the earliest indications of such attitudes among boys. Note that the final sentence uses the terms "strong," "virile," "manly," and "wonderful" in a sarcastic way.

Other strategies aid the rhetor in making arguments and substantiating claims, but these are the most important. Strategies described here and in Chapter 7 often appear in combination and depend on the participation of the audience.

Other argumentative strategies that invite audiences to behave in less than rational ways are called *fallacies.* Fallacies are potent persuaders because they mimic legitimate kinds of argument. Fallacies short-circuit the critical thinking process. This kind of "slick" argument trades in knee-jerk reactions; its reasoning is anathema to nuance, complexity, and careful deliberation. Nonetheless, fallacies are not treated here as uniformly unethical or improper (they're just not logical). Try telling an editorial columnist not to use fallacies and see how many readers he'll keep! In other words, fallacies can be a clever strategy for entertaining. Knowing when a fallacy has crossed an ethical line can be difficult. For example, name-calling mimics the strategy of definition. When is a label descriptive and defining, and when does it become an instance of name-calling? You will be invited to examine more of these tricky questions about fallacies in the exercise section. (See Figure 5–4.)

Figure 5–4
Argumentative Fallacies

Name	Function	Example
Straw Argument	Presents the weakest point of an opponent's position as if it were the strongest.	Why should we support affirmative action? All these people want is a quota system.
Begging the Question	A speaker assumes as already proven the very point he or she is trying to prove.	Everyone ought to be free because it is a real value in a society when there is liberty for all.
Non Sequitur	Arguments that advance claims that do not logically follow from the premises.	She must wear Levi's—she's got sex appeal.
Appeal to Ignorance	An argument that a speaker asks the audience to accept solely because it has not been proven false.	No one can prove there was any vote buying in the last election; thus, there clearly was none going on.
Argumentum ad Populum	Assumes that just because a position is popular, it must be good and right.	Both presidential candidates supported keeping Elian Gonzales with his Miami relatives rather than returning him to his father in Cuba because many Americans saw it as the patriotic thing to do.
Faulty Cause and Effect	Asserts a cause-and-effect relationship where one may not exist.	Since sexually transmitted diseases (STD) go up when beer is cheap, if we tax beer, STDs will go down.
Appeal to Inertia	Assumes that what has been practiced since anyone can remember, must necessarily be true, right, and good.	My great-grandfather was a Republican, I'm a Republican, therefore, you should be a Republican.
False Analogy	When two things are compared that are not alike in significant ways.	Why should car makers complain about working more than ten hours a day? After all, professors work at least that many hours a day without any apparent harm.
Name-Calling	Substitutes name-calling for discussing the issues.	The Strategic Defense Initiative is called "Star Wars"; the Estate Tax is called "the Death Tax." The teaching of evolution is called "secular humanism"; the Death Penalty is called "barbarism."
False Dilemma	Presenting only two options as if they are the only two that exist.	Senator Smith is either lying about campaign financing or he is covering it up.
Hasty Generalization	A position that has been reached based on insufficient grounds.	Asians are studious people.
Glittering Generalities	Feel-good phrases that seek immediate agreement.	Democrats are committed to peace, prosperity, and equality for all.
Guilt or Glory by Association	Transfers positive or negative feelings from a known phenomenon to a product, group, person, or idea.	George W. sometimes shows a blank Dan Quayle look, sometimes speaks with the creative grammar of George Sr., and has the worldview of Ronald Reagan.
Slippery Slope	If we allow this one thing to happen, we will soon see many other things we don't want to happen.	Tighter gun control legislation will ultimately mean a complete erosion of the 14th Amendment and the slow but systematic disarming of the citizenry.

Source: Susan Schultz Huxman, *Public Speaking: A Repertoire of Resources* (New York: McGraw-Hill College Custom Series, 1992). Reprinted with pemission from Susan Schultz Huxman.

■ MATERIAL FOR ANALYSIS

Dale Bumpers, High Crimes and Misdemeanors, Testimony at Impeachment Trial[30]

On January 21, 1999, Senator Dale Bumpers, a Democrat from Arkansas, made the final speech for the defense in the impeachment trial of President W. J. Clinton. This is an excerpt from the speech that addresses the difficult constitutional argument about the meaning of the phrase "high crimes and misdemeanors," a phrase whose meaning has been a matter of dispute in all three impeachment cases (Andrew Johnson, Richard Nixon, and W. J. Clinton).

1 Impeachment was debated off and on in Philadelphia [at the Constitutional Convention] for the entire four months, as I said. The key players were Governor Morris, ... a brilliant Pennsylvanian.

2 George Mason, the only man reputedly to have been so brilliant that Thomas Jefferson actually deferred to him. And he refused to sign the Constitution, incidentally, even though he was a delegate, because they didn't deal with slavery and he was a strict abolitionist.

3 And then there was Charles Pinkney ... from South Carolina, just a youngster, 29 years old, I believe.

4 Edmund Randolph from Virginia, who had a big role in the Constitution in the beginning—the Virginia Plan. And then there was, of course, James Madison, the craftsman.

5 They were all key players in drafting this impeachment provision. And uppermost in the mind during the entire time they were composing was [that] they did not want any kings. They had lived under despots, they had lived under kings, they had lived under autocrats, and they didn't want any of that. And they succeeded very admirably. We've had 46 presidents, and no kings.

6 But they kept talking about corruption, maybe that ought to be the reason for impeachment, because they feared some president would corrupt the political process. That's what the debate was about. Corrupt the political process and ensconce himself through a phony election, maybe as something close to a king.

7 They followed the British rule on impeachment, because the British said, the House of Commons may impeach, and the House of Lords must convict. And every one of the colonies had the same procedure: House, Senate. Though, in all fairness, House members, Alexander Hamilton was not very keen on the House participating.

8 But here was the sequence of events at Philadelphia that brought us here today. They started out with "maladministration," and Madison said that's too vague. What

does that mean? So they dropped that. They went from that to "corruption" and they dropped that. Then they went to "malpractice." And they decided that was not definitive enough. And they went to "treason, bribery and corruption." And they decided that still didn't suit them. But bear in mind one thing. During this entire process, they are narrowing—they are narrowing the things you can impeach the president for. They were making it tougher. Madison said if we aren't careful, the president will serve at the pleasure of the legislature—the Senate, he said.

9 And then they went to "treason and bribery" and somebody said that's still not quite enough.

10 And so they went to treason, bribery, and George Mason added "or other high crimes and misdemeanors against the United States." And they voted on it, and on September 10 they sent the entire Constitution to a committee.

11 They called a committee on style and arrangement, which was the committee that would draft the language in a way that everybody would understand; it would be well-crafted from a grammatical standpoint. But that committee, which was dominated by Madison and Hamilton, dropped "against the United States." And historians will tell you that the reason they did that was because of redundance, because that committee had no right to change the substance of anything. They would not have dropped it if they hadn't felt that it was redundant.

12 And then, they put in for good measure—we can always be grateful—the two-thirds majority.

13 Now this is one of the most important points of this entire presentation: The term—first of all—"treason and bribery," nobody quarrels with that, and we're not debating treason and bribery here in this chamber. We're talking about "other high crimes and misdemeanors.". . .

14 And where did "high crimes and misdemeanors" come from? It came from the English law, and they found it in an English law under a category which said, "distinctly political offenses against the state." Let me repeat that. They said "high crimes and misdemeanors was to be," because they took it from English law, where they found it in the category that said, "offenses distinctly political against the state."

15 So colleagues, please, for just one moment, forget the complexities of the facts and the tortured legalisms. And we've heard them all brilliantly presented on both sides, and I'm not getting into that. But ponder this. If "high crimes and misdemeanors" was taken from English law by George Mason, which listed high crimes and misdemeanors as political offenses against the state, what are we doing here?

16 If, as Hamilton said, it had to be a crime against society or a breach of the public trust, what are we doing here?

17 Even perjury, concealing or deceiving an unfaithful relationship does not even come close to being an impeachable offense.

18 Nobody has suggested that Bill Clinton committed a political crime against the state. So, colleagues, if you honor the Constitution, you must look at the history of the Constitution and how we got to the impeachment clause. And if you do that and you do that honestly, according to the oath you took, you cannot—you can censure Bill Clinton, you can hand him over to the prosecutor for him to be prosecuted, but you cannot convict him. And you cannot indulge yourselves the luxury or the right to ignore this history.

Questions for Analysis

1. How does Bumpers create identification between the founders and members of his audience?

2. In his speech, Bumpers admits as fact the behaviors with which President Clinton was charged. Then he develops this argument as a story about how the founders came to define what would be impeachable offenses. What kind of an argument is this? Why might this way of structuring these materials be effective in a speech delivered orally? Compare an outline of the argument to the story Bumpers tells.

3. The Supreme Court sometimes turns to "legislative intent" as a way to decide just what Congress intended when it passed a particular law. In what ways is this argument similar? Why is this form of argument particularly well adapted to an audience of Senators, who are the jurors in an impeachment trial?

4. What are other ways in which the phrase "high crimes and misdemeanors" might be defined? Consult a law dictionary, for example.

5. In 1974, when articles of impeachment were voted against Richard Nixon, the House Committee on the Judiciary rejected an article based on evidence that Nixon had fraudulently backdated the donation of his vice-presidential papers to the national archives in order to gain a tax write-off. In what ways is that decision similar to the argument that Bumpers is making?

6. Do you see any fallacies in Bumpers speech? If so, how are they used?

EXERCISES

Critical Thinking Exercises

1. Drawing on the fallacies identified in Figure 5–4, find examples of these strategies from a website or blog with a decided political slant. Are the fallacies used primarily for entertainment purposes, or do they raise troubling ethical questions? (See Chapter 11 for more specific ways to evaluate rhetoric on ethical grounds.)

2. Think about a joke that uses an enthymeme particularly well. Write it down and submit it to your teacher. Your teacher will then select a "top five" humorous enthymeme list. Vote on a class winner. Discuss the two levels of argument (one overt; the other covert) that make the joke funny.

3. Identify the five most compelling current issues on your campus. Then decide if these issues are examples of questions of fact, questions of value, or questions of policy. Does the kind of issue affect its level of controversy? Explain.

Analytical Writing Exercises

4. In segments of an editorial "Vouchers a Threat to Public Schools" by Joe Murray of the *San Francisco*

Examiner, analyze how arguments and fallacies work together. Prepare a 1,500-word essay that specifically considers these points:

   a. How do analogical arguments work in this piece? How does enumeration of the analogies contribute to the tone and purpose of the piece?

   b. How are rational and psychological appeals evident in the analogical argument?

   c. Does the reasoning by analogy turn into a slippery slope fallacy? Explain. What other fallacies do you detect?

   d. What enthymemes can you make from this piece? Is there a causal argument? Is the editorial arranged inductively or deductively?

   e. There are many strategies of proof (or specific arguments) in this piece. Try to identify at least four. Consult Figure 5–3 in this chapter for help.

Vouchers a Threat to Public Schools[31] (an excerpt)

1. I happen to have an opinion about public education: that no other institution has contributed more to democracy in America.

2. And now we're going to whittle it down into a bunch of splinter groups?

3. People who want their kids to go to private or church schools, or who want to school them at home, think they ought to be able to spend their tax money for education the way they please. After all, it's *their* kids.

4. That sort of argument may sound like it makes sense. The truth is, it's talking silly.

5. You might as well argue that people whose kids are out of school, or people who never had children, shouldn't have to pay school taxes, that government should give back their money so they can spend it as best benefits them.

6. But that's not the issue, what's best for you or what's best for me. Rather, it's what's best for America.

7. Every citizen has an investment in public education. Our nation's children represent our nation's future. As they succeed, we all succeed. It's not by luck that America enjoys the most advanced technology and healthiest economy.

8. You like the idea of school vouchers? Then why not these ideas:

9. Park vouchers for parents who'd rather take their children to Disneyland instead of public parks.

10. Road vouchers for motorists who prefer toll roads to the public highway system.

11. Water vouchers for those of us who drink bottled water instead of city water.

12. Zoo vouchers for animal lovers who enjoy their own personal menagerie over the public zoo. (With eight dogs and two cats, I could use the money.)

13. Protection vouchers for private police and firemen who would come to the aid of only those who subscribe to their services.

14. And, while we're at it, arms vouchers for militia groups who don't trust the U.S. military to defend the nation.

15. Why not, indeed? Because it's silly, that's why.

16. But the proposals for school vouchers aren't silly. Such ideas…are serious—a serious threat to our public education system.

17. You want to home-school your children? Fine.

18. You want to send your children to private schools? Fine.

19. But not at the expense of our public schools.

Portfolio Entry 4: Argument

5. Compare and contrast how your rhetorical selections use general and specific arguments to advance their purpose. Do you see argumentative fallacies? In two or three pages, use critical equations (c+p+a) to formulate your answers.

Strategic Speaking Exercises

6. Public Forum Debate and Lincoln Douglas Debate are two popular forms of scholastic debate competition in this country. Look up their respective websites for the rules of engagement; one is more value oriented; the other more policy oriented. Form into teams of two. Your instructor will have a list of debate topics from which you will choose and decide which debate format works best based on class size, time constraints, and so forth. You will need time to research evidence for your case once you are assigned a position: pro or con. Your goal is to draw upon the general and specific argument types presented in this chapter and construct a persuasive case on the affirmative or negative side of the question. After the mini-debate tourney in your class, vote on a class winner. Consider what arguments made for the most persuasive case. What arguments were suspect? What teams seemed most prepared? Are these the teams that had the best evidence? The best delivery? The best organization? Consider also: how does teamwork factor into the persuasiveness of a debate round?

NOTES

1. Lawrence K. Altman, "Autopsy Expected to Give Answers," *New York Times*, July 29, 1993, p. B7; Dave Anderson, "Lewis's Death on Celtics' Conscience," *New York Times*, July 29, 1993, p. B6.

2. For a more complete discussion of argument claims, warrants, conclusions, and argument fields, see Stephen E. Toulmin, *The Uses of Argument* (Cambridge: Cambridge University Press, 1969).

3. Aristotle classified issues into four types: being (fact or conjecture), quantity (scope or definition), quality (value, mitigating circumstances), and procedure (including jurisdiction). See *On Rhetoric: A Theory of Civic Discourse*, trans. George A. Kennedy (New York: Oxford University Press, 1991), p. 273, 1417b. 21–28.

4. For a discussion of the complex interrelationship between our basic biological needs and their cultural modification through language, see Kenneth Burke, "Definition of Man," *Language as Symbolic Action* (Berkeley: University of California Press, 1966), pp. 3–24.

5. See Eugene Burnstein and Amiram Vinokur, "Testing Two Classes of Theories about Group Induced Shifts in Individual Choice," *Journal of Experimental Social Psychology* 9 (March 1973): 123–137, and "What a Person Thinks upon Learning He Has Chosen Differently from Others: Nice Evidence for the Persuasive-Arguments Explanation of Choice Shifts," *Journal of Experimental Social Psychology* 11 (September 1975): 412–426. Also see Amiram Vinokur and Eugene Burnstein, "Effects of Partially Shared Persuasive Arguments on Group-Induced Shifts: A Group-Problem-Solving Approach," *Journal of Personality and Social Psychology* 29 (March 1974): 305–315; and Amiram Vinokur, Yaacov Trope, and Eugene Burnstein, "A Decision-Making Analysis of Persuasive Argumentation and the Choice-Shift Effect," *Journal of Experimental Social Psychology* 11 (March 1975): 127–148. A critique of this theory is found in Glenn S. Sanders and Robert S. Baron, "Is Social Comparison Irrelevant for Producing Choice Shifts?" *Journal of Experimental Social Psychology* 13 (July 1977): 303–314.

6. Richard E. Petty and John T. Cacioppo, *Communication and Persuasion: Central and Peripheral Routes to Attitude Change* (New York: Springer-Verlag, 1986). For more information, see Shelly Chaiken and Yaacov Trope, eds. *Dual-Process Theories in Social Psychology* (New York: Guilford, 1999).

7. As an illustration of analysis based on Aristotle's *topoi*, see: Forbes Hill's critique of Nixon's Vietnamization Address: "Conventional Wisdom—Traditional Form—The President's Message of November 3, 1969," *Quarterly Journal of Speech* 58 (1972): 373–386.

8. Caroline P. Caswell, *A Study of Thumos in Early Greek Epic* (Leiden, Kobenhavn, Köln: E. J Brill, 1990), p. 33.

9. Jeffrey Walker, *Rhetoric and Poetics in Antiquity* (Oxford: Oxford UP, 2000), p. 170.

10. Walker, 170–71.

11. Walker, 171.

12. Some of you may hear an echo of the words in Luke 2:19, which says that, after she gave birth, Mary was visited by the shepherds who told her of the angels who had appeared to them, and "Mary kept all these things, and pondered them in her heart."

13. Walker, 171.

14. Walker, 174.

15. Contrast this speech with the speech he delivered at the City Club of Cleveland, Ohio, on April 5, 1968. http://www.rfkmemorial.or/lifevision/onthemindlessmenaceofviolence

16. Trans. Dana Geyer (Washington, D.C.: German Historical Society and Cambridge UP, 2003, 2008).

17. The origin of the key sentence is unclear. On June 18, Kennedy summoned Robert H. Lochner, who had been recommended by Lucius D. Clay as an interpreter, to the White House. Also present were McGeorge Bundy and Margarete Plischke, a language instructor at the State Department's Foreign Service Institute. Several sentences to be uttered in German were suggested, but none pleased the president. On the lower half of the sheet along with other phonetically spelled German sentences, Kennedy wrote several lines in English, and in the lower right-hand corner Kennedy had written in blue ink: "I am a Berliner" (Daum, 150).

18. The figure who memorialized the statement, "I am a Roman citizen," was Marcus Tullius Cicero, for whom that line was a claim to the rights, privileges, and protection that citizenship in the Roman republic and, later the empire, carried, in particular "protection from bodily harm and persecution by foreign or local jurisdictions" (Daum, 151). Cicero used it to attack Verres for his brutal treatment of Roman

19. citizens in Sicily (Cicero, *The Orations of Marcus Tullius Cicero*, trans. C.D. Yonge, vol 1. London: G. Bell, 1893, pp. 528, 534). See also Acts 16: 37–38 and Acts 22: 25–29 for the Apostle Paul's appeal to this principle.

19. The poem reads:
No man is an island,
Entire of itself.
Each is a piece of the continent,
A part of the main.
If a clod be washed away by the sea,
Europe is the less.
As well as if a promontory were.
As well as if a manor of thine own
Or of thine friend's were.
Each man's death diminishes me,
For I am involved in mankind.
Therefore, send not to know
For whom the bell tolls,
It tolls for thee.

20. Kennedy's words in Berlin seemed to contradict the words of his Commencement Address at American University, delivered in June, which proposed a new relationship between the United States and the Soviet Union.

21. "To take a common example, the sentence "*Er ist schauspieler*" (He is an actor) is a statement of fact about a man's profession; the sentence '*Er ist ein Schauspieler*' means that the man is putting on an act" (148). Similarly, "*Ich bin Berliner*" would assert actual citizenship, whereas "*Ich bin ein Berliner*" is an expression of identification with the citizens of Berlin.

22. Moreover, Daum adds, Berliners and people living in the eastern regions of Germany refer to jelly donuts as *Pfannkuchen* (literally, pancakes); *Berliner* is the name used in western Germany. "In sum, it is safe to say that the jelly donut jokes can be relegated to the realm of legend."

23. They are also meaningless to many K.U. students who do not know that the waving arms symbolize waving wheat or that "rock chalk" refers to quarries in which skeletons of prehistoric animals were discovered by K.U. geologists, whose students originated the chant.

24. Kim Severson, "Seduced by Snacks? No, Not You," *New York Times*, October 11, 2006, pp. D1, D4, material cited on D4. See also Brian Wansink, *Mindless Eating: Why We Eat More Than We Think* (New York: Bantam, 2006).

25. Kenneth Burke, "Psychology and Form," *Counter-Statement* (Berkeley: University of California Press, 1968), pp. 29–44, discusses form as the psychology of the audience. Kinds of form and their appeal are discussed on pp. 124–149.

26. Nicholas D. Kristof, "Et Tu, George?" *New York Times*, January 23, 2007, p. A19.

27. "Acceptance Speech," *New York Times*, July 18, 1980, p. A8.

28. See Alexander Cockburn, "Is Global Warming a Sin?" *The Nation*, May 14, 2007, p. 8.

29. Bernice Sandler, "Men and Women Getting Along: These Are the Times That Try Men's Souls," in *Contemporary American Speeches*, 7th edition, ed. Richard L. Johannesen, R. R. Allen, and Wil A. Linkugel (Dubuque, IA: Kendall/Hunt, 1992), pp. 228–229.

30. Reprinted by permission from the *San Francisco Examiner*, December 1999.

31. Joe Murray, "Vouchers a Threat to Public Schools," *Wichita Eagle*, March 19, 1999, p. 11A. Reprinted by permission.

Chapter 6

The Resources of Organization

"Organizational patterns just provide a nice backdrop for an essay or speech."

"It doesn't really matter what organizational pattern you choose."

"No one can see an organizational pattern, so it is not central to an audience."

Like many beginning critics or public speakers, you may share some of these misconceptions about the importance of choosing an appropriate organizational pattern for your rhetorical acts. If so, consider the following phrases: "a striking young man," "a young man striking," "striking a young man." The same four words, organized three different ways, for three different meanings: the first refers to physical appearance, the second to a labor dispute, and the third to an act of violence. If organization makes such a dramatic difference in a simple, four-word phrase, it certainly makes a difference in a speech or essay.

How you organize a rhetorical act is not a matter for casual attention. It is integrally related to the type of audience you are addressing, the clarity of your thesis, and the cogency of your arguments. In fact, this chapter will argue that organization itself makes a statement to your audience about what they need to know. Organization reveals the relationships that the rhetor sees between ideas and asks listeners or readers to see those same relationships. In short, *organization is a kind of argument*. It is a process of structuring materials so ideas are clear and forceful for readers or hearers. Ideally, the pattern of development should reflect a consistent point of view on a subject, clarify the relationships among ideas, and make a case effectively. That's a tall order! And that is exactly why organizational patterns should not be considered inconsequential.

As noted earlier, Aristotle wrote, "There are two parts to a speech; for it is necessary [first] to state the subject and [then] to demonstrate it....Of these parts, the first is the statement [*prothesis*], the other is the proof [*pistis*]" (1414a.30–1).[1] This is good advice for starters, but as Aristotle also recognized, you need to adapt your ideas to an audience. Our purpose is to show you how thinking strategically about organization assists rhetors in adapting ideas to people. First, we talk about formulating a thesis and developing an outline. Second, we discuss the three basic types of organizational structure, their function, and strategic value. Third, we provide some more in-depth guidelines for introductions and conclusions that help you adapt these to your audience.

THE THESIS

The key to organizing ideas rhetorically is a clear central idea or thesis. In Chapter 3 you learned that constructing a good thesis begins with narrowing your topic to support one of the six primary rhetorical purposes. As you consider more carefully what makes for clear organization, know that a good thesis statement has these qualities:

1. *It is a simple sentence* (states one and only one idea). For example, "Heavy television viewing inclines children toward violence and stereotyping" is a problematic thesis, especially for a short essay or speech, because it involves two quite distinct claims—that television viewing is related to *both* violence *and* stereotyping—that are related only indirectly. Either claim by itself would take a good bit of time to develop.
2. *It is a declarative sentence* (a statement, assertion, or claim; for example, "Mandatory sentencing for drug-related crimes should be abolished,") *or an imperative sentence* (a command; for example, "Join the Peace Corps!").
3. *It limits your topic* (narrows your subject). The subject must be limited to what you can manage in the time or space you will have. This reinforces the first point, but note that even one of the two claims above about television might be too large for a short rhetorical act.
4. *It suggests your purpose* (implies the kinds of response you want: understanding, belief, or action).
5. *It is a capsule version of everything you will say or write.* That is, it should sum up your purpose, and everything in the rhetorical act should be related to it.

Please note that you may never state your thesis quite as bluntly as it appears in your outline. That is why it is acceptable in your outline to have the thesis statement stand alone and not be considered a main point represented with a Roman numeral in the body of your speech or essay. Nonetheless, the central idea ought to be clear to your audience when you have finished.

OUTLINING

An outline is a visual representation of the relationships among the ideas you will present. Accordingly, it is a useful tool for testing the consistency of your approach and the strength of your case. To understand how outlining is the "DNA" of the second canon of rhetoric (arrangement), review the six outlining guidelines in Chapter 3 and consider this standard outline skeleton:

Your thesis or central idea is stated at the top of your outline in one complete sentence.

Introduction:

I. Your inventive use of rhetorical resources to get attention and reveal purpose.

II. Your capsulated appeal to show the relevance and importance of your thesis for your target audience.

III. Your statement that previews the main ideas of your rhetorical act. (This will look or sound much like the thesis statement.)

Body of Speech:

I. Your first main point (subordinate to the thesis; coordinate with II)

   A. Subpoint of and subordinate to I; coordinate to B.

   B. Subpoint of and subordinate to I; coordinate to A.

II. Your second main point (subordinate to the thesis; coordinate with I)

   A. Subpoint of and subordinate to II; coordinate to B.

      1. Subpoint of and subordinate to A; coordinate to 2.

      2. Subpoint of and subordinate to A; coordinate to 1.

   B. Subpoint of and subordinate to II; coordinate to A.

And so forth . . .

Conclusion:

I. Your statement to foreshadow the end of the rhetorical act and reinforce the audience's understanding of the main points.

II. Your final appeal to rouse the audience to understand, affirm, reaffirm, or act (an optional closing technique called the "peroration" in classical times).

Now to see how an outline skeleton translates to real rhetorical action, consider the outline of the body of a speech given by a student who argued for legalization of the growing of industrial hemp, a practice widely prohibited by anti-marijuana laws.

Thesis Statement: Growing industrial hemp should be legalized.

Body of Rhetorical Act:

I. Hemp cannot be used as a substitute for marijuana

   A. Hemp has only traces of the psychoactive ingredient, tetrahydrocannabinol or THC, found in marijuana

   B. Growing hemp is illegal because it is treated as identical to marijuana in the federal Controlled Substances Act.

II. Hemp is beneficial for the environment.
    A. It reseeds itself in forests.
    B. Oil from hemp seeds has many commercial uses, particularly as a substitute for petroleum.
    C. Fibers in the stem can be used for textiles.
        1. Natural fibers are less damaging to the environment than synthetics.
        2. Hemp fibers are stronger than cotton fibers.
III. Hemp has important nutritional uses.
    A. Hemp seeds have more protein than soybeans.
    B. Hemp seeds are more nutritious than alternatives for animal feed.

Note that each point is subordinate to the thesis; each sets forth a reason for legalizing production of industrial hemp. The points are relatively coordinate in explaining the confusion of hemp with marijuana and in exploring its environmental and nutritional benefits.

Main points such as these develop, divide, explain, and prove the thesis. Main points can explain just what the thesis means. Main points can try to demonstrate the truth of the thesis. The subdivisions of a thesis or of any point in an outline usually answer one of these questions:

- What do you mean?
- How do you know?
- How does it work?
- Why?

In other words, there is a necessary relationship between a main point and its subdivisions. For example:

    I. Capital punishment should be abolished. (Why?)

    (Because) A. It does not deter would-be murderers.

    (How do you know?)

    I. Comparisons of similar jurisdictions reveal that those with capital punishment have murder rates as high as those without.
    II. Most murders are crimes of passion and lack the thought and planning that might make a deterrent effective.

In other words, an outline is a way to plan how you will develop your ideas, a way to lay them out so you can examine the relationships among them, and a way to make relationships among ideas clear to your audience.

Although some outlines used for other purposes need not be composed of sentences, it is essential that rhetorical outlines be composed of complete sentences. The reason is simple: the building blocks of rhetoric are arguments, and arguments only exist in sentences. Put a bit differently, as Chapter 5 explained, arguments are complete thoughts consisting of a claim and a reason or warrant for that claim. A claim must be an assertion, a declarative sentence; and summaries of evidence and statements of justification (reasons or warrants) require expression in sentences. Accordingly, you cannot make the sort of outline you need or use the outline to test the coherence of your ideas unless you use sentences. In addition, to emphasize a main idea or thesis, as you construct your sentences, especially the main points of the outline, you should use the same pattern of wording. The industrial hemp outline does this well. This practice is especially critical for oral presentations, but even strong writers understand the power of repetition as it applies to the main ideas that support their commentaries.

Here is an outline that served as the basis for an excellent short speech that illustrates these principles of outlining:

Thesis: Traumatic shock is a dangerous condition for which every injured person should be treated. (General rhetorical purpose is to alter perception of the condition known as shock and to create understanding in order to affect behavior.)

(Why? Because)

I. Traumatic shock is potentially fatal. (What do you mean?)
   A. Shock is a substantial reduction in the vital functions of the body caused by a decrease in the volume of circulating blood. (defines and explains shock)
   B. If shock is allowed to persist, the person will die. (details results of shock on an injured person)

(Why treat every person?)

II. Traumatic shock can result from almost any injury.
   A. Common household accidents can produce shock.
   B. Psychological factors may speed the onset of shock.
III. Traumatic shock has no reliable indications that it is present.
   A. The symptoms of shock can be misinterpreted or misunderstood.
   B. A person can experience shock without showing any of the usual symptoms.
IV. Traumatic shock can be treated simply. (feasibility)
   A. Keep the person in a prone position.
   B. Keep the person warm but not overheated.
   C. Try to reduce contributing psychological factors by reassurance.

This outline leaves out a number of things that happened in the actual presentation, but it is nevertheless strong because it divides the topic and explains its dimensions, and the main points prove that the thesis is true (if A and B and C and D, then I must follow). The similar wording of main points aids the audience in understanding there are four main points. In effect, the outline says you treat every injured person for shock because shock is life-threatening, it can result from any injury, you can't tell whether or not it is present, and it is relatively easy to treat.

FORMS OF ORGANIZATION

There are three basic ways to develop your thesis, central idea, or major claim: through *sequence structures*, *topical structures*, and *logical structures*. Each of these general patterns can be varied in several ways, and all three patterns may be used to develop parts of a single piece of rhetoric.

Sequence Structures

Chronological sequence is one type of sequence structure. It organizes an idea in terms of its development through time or in a series of ordered steps (see Figure 6–1). This may involve division in terms of historical periods or by phases or stages. Chronological

Figure 6–1

Sequence Structure

Sequence	Function	Example	Value
Chronological	Treats a subject by tracing its development over time.	To explain the seven steps to performing CPR	Well suited for "how to" speeches. Amplifies a subject. Presumes little audience knowledge.
Narrative	Treats a subject in story form.	To formulate the belief that diligence pays, with a timely version of Little Red Hen	Teaches in nonlogical ways. Induces audience participation. Transcends cultural barriers.
Spatial	Treats a subject in a directional pattern.	To explain what the new science building will look like by giving a simulated guided tour of the first three floors	Helps audiences visualize subject. Audiences can anticipate sequence.

organization is most appropriate when the topic is best understood in terms of how it develops or unfolds through time, or to demonstrate that you cannot achieve a goal without following a certain sequence. The most obvious form of chronological structure follows historical development. For example:

I. Contemporary feminism has gone through a series of ideological changes.
   A. Until 1968 it was a relatively conservative, reformist movement.
   B. From 1968 until 1977, it divided into conservative and radical factions.
   C. Since the Houston Conference of 1977, the factions have unified into a less conservative but highly political coalition.
   D. Following the Anita Hill–Clarence Thomas hearings in 1991, political activity escalated.
   E. During the late 1990s, a backlash developed that produced what some call "post-feminism."

Chronological organization is also used to develop the steps or stages in a process. For example:

I. Follow a sequence in preparing for rhetorical action.
   A. Choose your subject.
   B. Research available materials.
   C. Select a thesis.
   D. Structure your ideas.
   E. Produce a first draft (orally from notes or in writing).
   F. Edit your work through rewriting or oral practice (rehearsal).

Spatial structure is another, less common form of sequence structure. Spatial sequence organizes an idea in terms of its development through direction or space. This may involve moving from left to right or top to bottom to describe a building, an outfit, a geographical site, or a surgical procedure. For example, architects commonly give presentations that follow this sequence. They explain the blueprint of a building project by giving a simulated guided tour of each floor, sometimes even illustrated with elaborate, computer-generated visual aids that provide a "virtual tour" of the building. Beauty consultants sell makeovers by starting with options for eyebrows and ending with variations of lip liner, following a "top-to-bottom" spatial pattern. Geologists explain the intricacies of earth layers using similar "top-to-bottom" spatial patterns of organization. Spatial sequence argues that audiences must visualize and anticipate the directional progression of ideas for them to be memorable. Like a time sequence, a directional sequence requires a rigid adherence to its operating principle. Once you begin a time or directional developmental line to your topic, you must be faithful to that form to fulfill the expectations of your audience.

Narrative sequence is a third, highly poetic sequence structure that is more difficult to illustrate with a traditional outline even though most narratives develop chronologically. When speakers or writers tell stories to make their point, they argue ever so subtly. Because stories entertain by inviting audience participation, we sometimes forget that they do more than create virtual experience; they work to alter perceptions and even initiate action. An example of such a story is James Thurber's "The Little Girl and the Wolf," one of his *Fables for Our Times*. The story relies on cultural history in two ways. First, it adopts the form of the fable, a story with a moral, most familiar from Aesop's fables or Jesus's parables, and it assumes that we are already familiar with this form. Second, it assumes our familiarity with the plot of the fairytale about Little Red Riding Hood, which it revises and parodies.

The Little Girl and the Wolf
by James Thurber[2]

One afternoon a big wolf waited in a dark forest for a little girl to come along carrying a basket of food to her grandmother. Finally a little girl did come along and she was carrying a basket of food. "Are you carrying that basket to your grandmother?" asked the wolf. The little girl said yes, she was. So the wolf asked her where her grandmother lived and the little girl told him and he disappeared into the wood.

When the little girl opened the door of her grandmother's house she saw that there was somebody in bed with a nightcap and nightgown on. She had approached no nearer than twenty-five feet from the bed when she saw that it was not her grandmother but the wolf, for even in a nightcap a wolf does not look any more like your grandmother than the Metro Goldwyn Mayer lion looks like Calvin Coolidge. So the little girl took an automatic out of her basket and shot the wolf dead.

Moral: It is not so easy to fool little girls nowadays as it used to be.

This revision is humorous because it pokes fun at the original story, but it also forces us to look anew at the old story and to consider the unstated moral that it implies. In the original story, Little Red Riding Hood is naive, incapable of defending herself against the evil in the world, and she, like her grandmother before her, is eaten by the wolf. Only when a hunter comes to their rescue can she and her grandmother be saved. Although both stories develop chronologically, neither the story nor the moral of either version can be easily reduced to outline form. They are nondiscursive or nonlogical structures, and they follow a different pattern of development. This pattern is followed by most stories, dramas, and jokes, and it looks something like Figure 6–2.

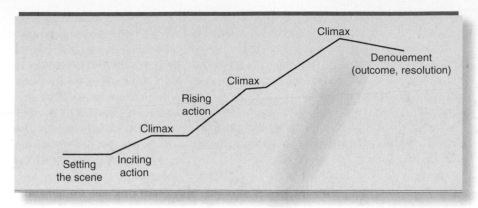

Figure 6–2
Story Diagram

comparison

James Thurber's fable follows this pattern. The first paragraph sets the scene and alerts us that this is a retelling of a familiar fairytale about a little girl, a wolf, and a grandmother; it introduces us to the wolf and the threat he implies, and to the other main characters in the familiar story. The inciting action is the appearance of the little girl. There is rising action as the wolf and she carry on a brief dialogue, which escalates the possible threat. A new pattern of rising action begins when the little girl arrives at her grandmother's house, sees that there is someone in her grandmother's bed, and recognizes that it is not her grandmother. The climax, the height of the conflict, occurs when she takes an automatic out of her basket and kills the wolf. The resolution or denouement is the moral, a comment that interprets the meaning of the story.

This story is a useful illustration for several reasons. First, as a fable it is intended to teach and persuade. Second, it teaches and persuades in an entirely nondiscursive way. There are no arguments, and no data are presented. The story is wholly outside logical and empirical reality (wolves, after all, cannot talk!). If it teaches us and gains our assent, however, it does so because it is a revision that exploits our familiarity with the original story of Little Red Riding Hood. The humor arises out of our surprise at what happens in this version and in response to the highly original figurative analogy and a point made by the second meanings lurking in "little girls" and "wolves." It also works because it teaches by contrast, forcing us to think about the assumptions in the original story. How could we ever have believed that a little girl would mistake a wolf for her grandmother? Why did we assume that the little girl wouldn't have prepared herself to cope with the dangers of the forest?

Good stories have certain qualities. They follow certain patterns and develop through details that we can see or imagine, and the plot has universality or general application (fairytales deal with the hopes and fears of all of us; fables such as those of Aesop comment on common human failings, made more palatable by being presented as the failings of animals, for example, the stories of the fox and the grapes or the dog in the manger). These stories usually develop one or more characters with whom we can identify, or they describe a situation in which we can imagine ourselves. They are organized around a conflict that increases in intensity so that we are drawn into the story and come to care about how it is resolved or "comes out." The rhetorical strength of many stories comes from their *verisimilitude*, that is, their formal resemblance to events and persons in our world of experience. In the case of The Little Girl and the Wolf, the verisimilitude arises out of the story's resemblance to a familiar tale (Little Red Riding Hood), out of a structure that follows the familiar form of the fable, and situations in which wolves wait to prey upon little girls.

A work that is structured as a dramatic narrative exploits the literary and poetic resources of language or the plot lines with which we are familiar. On the simplest level, such a story is an extended example, with all of the strengths and weaknesses of this kind of evidence, but dramatic narratives have compensating strengths. They can reach out to the audience to prompt identification and participation. They are easy to follow and pleasing, and so invite involvement. In a dramatic narrative we are invited to share the point of view of the narrator, to imagine ourselves in the experiences described. The rhetor's claim is expressed as a series of concrete experiences or dramatic encounters, and the conclusion is the meaning of the tale. If the story is well constructed, it is hard to reject such "claims." They become part of our experience, not simply an idea or an argument.

Narrative dramatic development is less common than other forms of organization in rhetorical discourse, but when it appears, it illustrates these resources. The most famous examples are the parables of Jesus, stories he told to illustrate truths.

There are more contemporary examples. Rachel Carson's *Silent Spring*[3] is often credited with initiating environmental activism with its vivid evocation of a world polluted by DDT. The film *Saving Private Ryan* memorialized the sacrifices of U.S. soldiers in World War II and revived interest in that period. Ken Burns's PBS documentary *The War* did the same for that war from the perspective of how various minority groups in the United States contributed. The testimony on Capitol Hill by Jessica Lynch, the U.S. Army Private First Class who was kidnapped, abused, and rescued in the early stages of the Iraq war in 2003, was a dramatic warning about how media are manipulated by the Pentagon's version of events. In each of these cases, a dramatic narrative transcends the obstacles created by cultural history or diminishes hostility toward a controversial group or idea or reaches across the chasm of cultural differences to create identification between rhetor and audience. Incorporating a detailed example into a speech is one way to use the resources of narrative.

The dramatic narrative is not above suspicion, however. Witness the fall of the memoir as a genre of authentic first-person accounts. Two recent bestsellers, James Frey's *A Million Little Pieces*, the story of the author's struggles with drug addiction, and Augusten Burroughs's *Running with Scissors*, the story of the author's trauma with abuse by his adopted family, turned out to contain major sections that were fraudulent or contested by others close to the rhetors.

You should choose some form of sequence structure if you wish to emphasize development over time or in steps or stages. It is a good choice if the audience knows little of your subject because it is a pattern ideally suited to provide background and to develop relationships among events. It is also a kind of structure easily adapted to hold the attention of the audience because it emphasizes progress through time, completion of a process, or movement toward a climax.

Topical Structures

Topical structures develop a subject in terms of parts or perspectives (see Figure 6–3). Sometimes the divisions are integral *parts* of the subject, such as the executive, judicial, and legislative branches of the U.S. government. Frequently, however, the topics are familiar *perspectives* we take on many subjects—the economic, legal, and social implications of, say, requiring a national identification card, reauthorizing the

Topical	Function	Example	Value
Parts	Treats a subject by subtopics	To explain the three basic shots in tennis: forehand, backhand, half-court Volley	Flexibility Emphasis Narrowing
Perspectives	Treats a subject by familiar divisions	To explain the economic, legal, and social implications of affirmative action	Familiarity of perspectives

Figure 6–3
Topical Structures

Patriot Act, or discontinuing low-interest student loans. The outline about legalizing production of industrial hemp is a rather typical example of a topical outline. Note that the student considers hemp in terms of environmental and food benefits. Topical organization is ideally suited for selecting some parts of a subject for discussion or emphasis.

Topical organization can explore natural divisions of a subject (fiction and nonfiction, regular and cable television, print and electronic media, for example). It can explore selected parts of a subject (soap operas and situation comedies as outstanding examples of kinds of television programming). Or it can apply familiar perspectives to a subject (the legal, economic, psychological, social, and medical aspects of state-run lotteries or mandatory prison sentences or nuclear power).

Because there usually is no necessary relationship between the points in a topical structure, this kind of organization can also be put to nondiscursive use. In such a case, the work develops associatively, in a manner analogous to the structure of the lyric poem by exploring the aspects of an attitude or feeling. Such organization is uncommon in rhetorical acts. When topical organization is used well, it divides a subject into parts that seem appropriate to the audience, parts that reflect a clear appraisal by the rhetor of what is important, what is typical. In addition, these parts should be arranged into some sort of hierarchy so the speech moves from one point to another with a sense of progression. The outline on legalizing industrial hemp, for example, could be rearranged into a crescendo or climax pattern moving from smaller benefits to larger ones.

Consider how these distinctive features of topical structure work in approaching the topic of New Media. Nontraditional or digital media is a burgeoning "new frontier" in communication technology. Trying to keep up with all its possibilities and all its implications is mind-boggling. Tackling this subject topically allows a rhetor to narrow and manage a complex subject in terms of parts.

Thesis: New Media is distinctive in at least five major ways from "Old Media."[4]

Body:
    I. New Media is interactive.
        A. The content of a media system is selectable or customized.
            1. Computer games that get harder as you score more points.
        B. Feedback from the receiver is used by the source.
            1. Online novels that allow readers to select new alternative plot developments.

II. New Media is asynchronous.
- A. Communication that is distributed across time so that not all participants have to attend at a particular point in time.
  1. Digital video recorders (DVRs) are a popular method of asynchronous communication.

III. New Media empower users in production.
- A. The influence of media organizations has diminished as "end users" play increasingly active roles in determining content.
  1. Desktop publishing of an electronic newsletter.
  2. An iPod recording of a local band.
  3. iMovie of your graduation party.
  4. A YouTube or Facebook post.

IV. New Media converges technologies.
- A. Separate media systems (phone, calendar, mail) are no longer needed; one platform can perform multiple functions.
  1. Personal Data Assistants (PDAs).
  2. Teleconferencing.
  3. The iPhone.

V. New Media narrowcasts its audiences.
- A. Smaller audiences (or niche users) are sought via new technologies.
  1. Websites.
  2. Blogs.
  3. Chat rooms.
  4. Streaming Radio Stations on the Internet.

Think about how this subject could be examined topically from familiar perspectives. There are troubling social, economic, and legal issues surrounding New Media use. Identify some of these. Can you formulate a main point from each of these perspectives? Note that as you move from parts to perspectives so too can your rhetorical purpose, from explaining to formulating belief.

Whether from a parts or a perspectives vantage point, topical structure is an ideal pattern for narrowing a broad subject to a manageable size. It is also a method of emphasis by which you can indicate what parts of a subject are most important.

Logical Structures

Logically linked structures assert that ideas or situations stand in some necessary relationship to each other (see Figure 6–4). These patterns express processes of *cause and effect* or define a *problem and its solution*. As you might guess, such organization often is used to develop questions of policy. The relationship between questions of policy and logically linked structure is illustrated by most television commercials (commercials ask you to change policy by buying a new product or by switching brands or to resist the appeals of competing products). Many ads are little problem-solution dramas. For example, a man in a commercial is shown anxiously discussing the lack of interest his girlfriend is showing in their relationship. His friend suggests the solution of a toothpaste for sparkling teeth and sweet breath. We then see the man with his sexy

Logical	Function	Example	Value
Causal	Treats a subject by showing a cause-and-effect relationship.	To explain the effects of deforestation and its three principal causes	Reflects necessary, not arbitrary, relationships. Streamlines subject.
Problem-Solution	Treats a subject in two parts: the first showing harm and scope, the second showing remedy.	To initiate the action of random drug testing of students at registration	Ideal for policy speeches. Capitalizes on cognitive dissonance theory.

Figure 6–4

Logical Structure

girlfriend in a scene that leaves no doubt that his romantic problems are over (this is also an enthymeme). In other words, if you have a problem being attractive to someone, solve it by brushing with Brand X toothpaste.

Here is an example of a problem-solution outline taken from a news article.[5]

Thesis: The FDA must better regulate the dangerous unregulated tissue transplant businesses.

Body:

I. Unregulated tissue transplants are a significant and dangerous practice in the United States.

    A. Tissue transplant operations are growing across the medical spectrum.

        1. Over a million surgeries were performed last year that required tissue from donated dead bodies.

        2. The number of tissues distributed for transplants rose from 350,000 in 1990 to 650,000 in 1999 and to 1.3 million in 2003.

        3. Business is booming for tissue companies—even the nonprofits.

            a. The biggest is the Musculosketal Transplant Foundation Inc. of New Jersey.

            b. In 2004 that company had $243 million in revenue and paid its chief executive $542,212.

    B. Tissue transplant complications are also growing.

        1. Each year an estimated 500 cases of serious heart inflammation and 200 deaths occur from fungus-contaminated heart valves alone.

        2. Hospitals and doctors can buy from unaccredited suppliers that offer tissue quicker or cheaper.

        3. Tissue isn't tested as thoroughly as blood is for infectious diseases.

        4. There is no regulation setting limits on age or health of donors or how long after death tissue can be taken.

        5. Funeral homes don't have to report deaths to organ procurement groups, leaving them outside a regulatory system and able to cut side deals to supply body parts if they want to.

        6. There is no medical training required to run a tissue bank or procure tissue.

II. The FDA must take a stronger approach to regulating businesses that trade in tissue transplants.

    A. Current FDA regulations are inadequate.

        1. A three-month investigation by the Associated Press found inadequate testing for potentially deadly germs.

        2. The same investigation revealed a lack of any system for tracking tissues as they travel from donor to recipient.

    B. The FDA must increase its funding and oversight of tissue transplant regulation.

        1. Currently, it spends just $5.4 million a year on tissue regulation—less than two days' revenue for the industry.

        2. Inspection of tissue business is actually down even as the number of companies has risen from 1,235 two years ago to 2,030 today.

    C. The FDA must formulate a specific industry-wide standard for inspection of tissue transplants.

        1. The broad goals of FDA regulation must be "transplanted" with commonsense regulations that we require for other industries.

        2. Several specific regulations should be adopted.

            a. Patients must know if they are receiving tissue from a reputable tissue bank.

            b. Doctors and hospitals must know the origins of the tissue they use.

            c. Medical certification must be required for someone to acquire a tissue bank license.

            d. Tissue banks must be seriously penalized, including revoking licenses, when basic sanitation measures are not followed.

The advantage of a problem-solution pattern is that the structure always calls for two main ideas: a problem and a solution. As you begin collecting evidence for a problem-solution speech, put what you find into two folders: one addressing the significance and the harms of the problem; the other addressing ways to fix the problem, both personal and structural. The Tainted Tissue outline is in the early stages of problem-solution outline. Note that very little evidence is included that personalizes the topic. But the full sentences in the outline enable you to read the outline and get a rather complete sense of what a speech or essay developed from it might say. In a sense, such an outline becomes the notes from which you could write a first draft of an essay or begin to practice your speech. However, the outline has not been adapted to create an introduction or conclusion nor has it been shaped for a particular target audience. As you think about adapting such material to an audience, consider what you might use to attract attention, and what might leave an indelible impression on the audience in your conclusion.

Cause-effect structure is a variation of problem-solution structure. Cause-effect structure ordinarily focuses on the first *stock issue* of a question of policy, the need for a change. Emphasis is placed on effects (the scope of the harm) and their cause (intrinsic to the current policy). For example:

Thesis: High rates of minority unemployment are caused, in part, by a lack of skills.

    I. Unemployment among racial minorities is consistently higher in this country than for Caucasians.
        A. Census data has consistently supported this disparity for decades.
        B. Welfare rolls in every state continue to swell with minorities, not whites.
        C. When you factor in the employment picture in the skilled labor force, those unemployed from minority groups grow even more alarming.
    II. Education in urban ghettoes and in the rural South does not provide basic reading and arithmetic skills.
        A. Few vocational training programs are available.
        B. Minorities are denied access to union apprenticeship programs.
        C. Federal programs do not teach marketable skills.

Like problem-solution structure, this cause-effect outline requires two main points and combines topical and logical structure. The thesis asserts a cause-effect relationship, but the main points are a topical list of the major causes of the problem—lack of skills.

As these examples illustrate, using logical structures to organize your outline is ideal for treating questions of policy. It allows you to meet the requirements for defending a change of policy, and it can be used to explore causal relationships. In all cases, logical structures reflect necessary relationships between ideas or events.

Each form of organization is a kind of argument. Each structure offers a particular kind of perspective on a subject. You can combine these different forms in a piece of rhetoric, but in each case you should choose the kind of structure best suited to the kind of argument you are trying to make.

ADAPTING STRUCTURE TO THE AUDIENCE

In the early part of this century, U.S. philosopher John Dewey published a book entitled *How We Think*.[6] The book laid out the *stages in reflective thinking*, the processes by which we recognize problems and then go about solving them. These stages included:

1. Perceiving a felt difficulty or recognizing that a problem exists.
2. Analyzing the problem, including attempts at definition.
3. Exploring possible solutions and evaluating them.
4. Selecting the best solution.
5. Discovering how to implement the selected course of action.

Dewey's analysis reflects the stock issues of a question of policy, especially in Stages 2, 3, and 4. But the first and last steps are additions, and they are clues to one kind of structural adaptation that needs to be made in presenting material to an audience. Stage 1 is introductory; it establishes the facts and values that suggest that we ought to be concerned about something, that we ought to find out what sort of problem this is and whether and how it can be solved. Stage 5 goes beyond the stock issues to ask how we can go about setting in motion the change we have decided would be a good one. It concerns concrete action.

Dewey's book was probably the stimulus for *the motivated sequence* that Alan H. Monroe developed.[7] This structural form illustrates the adaptation of logical organization for presentation to an audience. The steps in the motivated sequence are as follows:

1. *Attention:* call attention to the problem; in Dewey's terms, make the difficulty felt.
2. *Need:* demonstrate that a need exists (that is, develop the first issue of a question of policy to prove there is harm, of significant scope, arising out of current practice).
3. *Satisfaction:* show the audience that the need can be met (that is, that there is a practical and beneficial alternative policy).
4. *Visualization:* describe vividly and concretely what will happen if the problem is or is not solved (that is, picture good or bad consequences).
5. *Action:* call for immediate action from the audience; show them how to bring about the solution.

The motivated sequence is based on *cognitive dissonance theory*, a theory of persuasion first proposed by psychologist Leon Festinger.[8] As the terms *cognitive* (thought) and *dissonance* (imbalance) suggest, a rhetor's task is to create psychological discomfort by showing that a major problem exists. Then the rhetor's task is to create consonance (balance) by suggesting a remedy (a policy) that will solve the problem. The theory asserts that persuasion is more likely to occur if you first experience dissonance because psychological discomfort motivates the acceptance of a new belief or action (see Figure 6–5).

As you examine this sequence, you will see that Steps 2 and 3 develop the stock issues of a policy question. In other words, the motivated sequence is a form of logical organization that is appropriate only for advocating a course of action. Steps 1, 4, and 5, however, are structural elements designed to adapt materials for presentation to an audience. Step 1 precedes the thesis in order to involve the audience in the

Figure 6–5
The Motivated Sequence and Cognitive Dissonance Theory

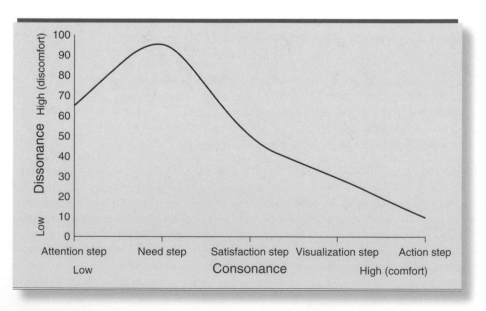

subject. Step 4 is designed to increase the motivation of the audience by vividly depicting what their world will be like with or without the policy proposed. In ads for exercise machines or diet aids, for example, "before" and "after" photographs are juxtaposed to perform this function. Step 5 presumes that the audience needs specific instructions on how to bring a solution about—where to go, what to do, who to write or call, and so on. It is designed to bring the proposed policy or course of action closer to reality. In sales, it becomes the closing. Steps 4 and 5 also require additions to the outline forms described earlier. They require special sections that make your ideas vivid and concrete and that give the audience assistance in implementing policy change.

The motivated sequence is an excellent pattern to follow in adapting logical organization for presentation to an audience, especially in cases when the desired response is a specific action on the part of listeners. But all rhetorical action requires similar adaptations. At a minimum, it is necessary to begin with an introduction and to end with a conclusion.

Introductions

The basic functions of an introduction are to gain attention, to create accurate expectations in the audience for what follows, and to suggest the relationship between the subject and the audience (see Chapter 3). These functions are good general touchstones for anyone preparing for rhetorical action. But the introduction also serves a vital purpose in overcoming the rhetorical obstacles that you face on any given occasion. For this reason, the introduction is the first attempt to cope with these difficulties. The choices a rhetor makes should be guided by the answers to these questions:

1. *What is the relationship between the rhetor and the audience?* Do they share many experiences and values, or is the rhetor seen as an alien or outsider?
2. *What is the attitude of the audience toward the subject and purpose?* Will the audience perceive the subject as overworked and complex or as fresh, vital, and intelligible? Is the reaction to the purpose likely to be hostile and indifferent or sympathetic and interested?
3. *What is the rhetor's relationship to the subject?* Is the rhetor an expert or an interested amateur?

As these questions indicate, introductions should be adapted to the attitude of the audience toward your subject and purpose, to the relationship between you and your audience, and to the relationship between you and your subject. It is in light of these considerations that you need to gain attention, create accurate expectations, and develop connections between the subject and the audience.

Kenneth Burke wrote, "Only those voices from without are effective which can speak in the language of a voice within."[9] His statement emphasizes the importance of *identification* between a rhetor and audience and emphasizes the role that the rhetor plays in the rhetorical process. One of the most important functions of an introduction, therefore, is to create common bonds between author and audience; that is, to overcome the perception that the rhetor is different, not like the members of the audience. Very often, personal experience is used to create connections and to establish common ground. Here, for example, is the opening paragraph of the Tainted Tissue newspaper story:

> Don't worry, the doctor told Brian Lykins' parents as he prepared to use cartilage from a cadaver to fix their son's knee.
>
> A million people a year have operations that use tissue from donated dead bodies. The nation's largest tissue bank had supplied this cartilage. It was disinfected and perfectly safe, he assured them.
>
> But it wasn't.
>
> Four days after this routine, elective surgery, Lykins—a healthy 23-year-old student from Minnesota—died of a raging infection.
>
> He died because the cartilage came from a corpse that had sat unrefrigerated for 19 hours—a corpse that had been rejected by two other tissue banks. The cartilage hadn't been adequately treated to kill bacteria. The Georgia-based tissue bank, CryoLife Inc., knew all of this and released the tissue anyway.
>
> None of this broke a single federal rule. And it could happen again today—likely is still happening today—because of shoddy practices by some in the billion-dollar body parts business and the lack of government regulation.

Note from this gripping beginning how different kinds of evidence are attention-getting. The article uses a dramatic example to get attention and raise dissonance. It contains enough specificity that readers cannot discount it as unrealistic, and it uses suspense creatively to pull the reader further into the story. As you think about preparing an introduction, look at the evidence you have gathered and consider which of it might work as introductory material.

Introductions may be composed of almost any of the resources available to a rhetor—examples, visuals, analogies, statistics, quotations from authority, a literary reference, personal experience, explanation, description, and so forth. What an introduction needs to do in a given case depends on the specific challenges you face. You always need to gain attention, create appropriate expectations, and seek to involve the audience with your subject. But how you accomplish these depends on the audience's attitude toward your subject and purpose, your relationship to the audience, and the nature of your expertise on the subject.

Conclusions

You should remember from Chapter 3 that a good basic conclusion (1) summarizes the major ideas that lead to the claim that is your thesis, and (2) fixes the specific purpose in the audience's mind. In addition, the conclusion ought to be both an ending and a climax. It should be an ending in the sense that it provides a sense of closure, a feeling of completion. Rhetorical action should end, not just stop or peter out. A conclusion can be an ending in the simplest and most obvious way—as a summary that recalls the processes by which rhetor and audience drew a conclusion. Unless the act is unusually short or the structure is very simple, a review of the arguments is highly desirable and probably necessary. If you doubt this advice, listen closely to some television commercials and note the amount of repetition that occurs even in these relatively short bits of rhetoric.

Ideally, the conclusion ought also to be the climax or emotional highpoint, and the material in the conclusion should epitomize (typify, embody) the thesis. Such a conclusion might include a story that captures the essence of what you are saying. It might present a metaphor or analogy that represents the idea. Obviously, a literary allusion or quotation, a citation from an authority, or other kinds of resources might be used as well. Recall from Chapter 2 King's stirring conclusion ("I've Been to the Mountaintop") in the last speech he would ever make.

In order to appreciate how conclusions provide context and closure for a complete rhetorical act, here is an example of both the introduction and the conclusion from Kate Michelman's Testimony to the Senate Judiciary Committee during the Judge Samuel Alito Confirmation Hearings on January 12, 2006. In her introduction she begins with the appropriate formal acknowledgments, sets the terms for her role (she is not speaking as the former president of the National Abortion Rights Action League, but as a woman), and shares a very personal story:[10]

> Mr. Chairman, Senator Leahy, members of the committee: Many of you have known me in my professional capacity over the past twenty years. I want to speak with you today in a capacity that, at this historic and decisive moment, matters far more: as one woman—a woman very much like the millions whose lives could be indelibly shaped by this nomination.
>
> In 1969, I was a young, stay-at-home mother of three girls, a practicing Catholic who had accepted the Church's teachings about birth control and abortion. The notion that abortion might be an issue I would face in my own life never occurred to me until the day my husband suddenly abandoned our family. In time, with nothing to live on, we were forced onto welfare. Soon after he left, I discovered I was pregnant. I knew instinctively that another child would turn a crisis into a catastrophe. After a long period of searching—of balancing my moral and religious values about the newly developing life with my responsibilities to my three young daughters—I decided to have an abortion. Mr. Chairman, I might add parenthetically that of the countless women I have encountered and known over the course of my career, not one has made a decision about abortion—either for it or against it—without first contemplating the gravity of that choice. Not one needed the tutelage or supervision of the state to understand her own ethical values, much less to be reminded to consult them. And every one of them deserved the respect and protection afforded by Roe v Wade.
>
> Because this all occurred prior to Roe, I was legally prevented from acting privately on my decision. I was compelled to submit to two interrogations before an all-male panel of doctors. They probed every aspect of my private life—from what kind of sex life my husband and I had to whether I was capable of dressing my children in the morning. Eventually, they gave their permission. I had been admitted to the hospital and was awaiting the procedure when a nurse arrived to tell me that state law imposed yet another humiliating burden. The government required me to obtain my husband's consent. I was forced to leave the hospital, find where he was living and ask him to give me his permission.
>
> Mr. Chairman and Senators, I do not tell this story to ask your sympathy. It was a humiliating experience, but one that also awakened me to a life of activism devoted to ensuring no other woman ever would be required to endure such humiliation. I tell you this story because we stand at the threshold of millions of women—women doing their very best to do what is right for themselves and their families—once more facing the dreadful choice between the degradation of the review board and the danger of the back alley. This is neither hyperbole nor hype. It is the simple, demonstrable reality of the situation. . . .

Michelman's introduction is her strategic effort to adapt to the occasion, the audience, and the subject. Senators can be insulated from real-world implications. Senate hearings can focus on legalisms. Views of pro-life and pro-choice adherents have become so narrow, predictable, and entrenched, it is difficult to see more complex points of view or real people holding them. Michelman's story of vulnerability gives a raw, unfiltered look at what privacy can really mean for a woman who possesses a strong moral compass when faced with life's tragedies. Enthymematically, the story also argues that Judge Samuel Alito is unfit to sit on the U.S. Supreme Court because of his dangerous views on abortion and the Fourteenth Amendment and that his confirmation would tilt the court to overrule *Roe v. Wade*, sending millions of women to review boards and, perhaps, to back alleys.

Her conclusion more emphatically makes the case that Judge Alito cannot be entrusted to rule on privacy issues and that his confirmation would be a huge injustice to women everywhere. Note, however, how Michelman attempts to avoid alienating her audiences by drawing comparisons to outgoing Justice O'Connor. Conclusions often include final appeals to convince audiences to act. See how she uses appeals to fairness, individual rights, and dignity to make the case against confirmation.

> Mr. Chairman, I have been involved in many Supreme Court nominations. But none more important than this one—or as dangerous. For the contrast between Judge Alito and the Justice he would replace is stark. As the first woman to serve on the Court, Justice O'Connor has brought a unique perspective to the law that is evident in her opinions upholding a woman's right to choose, protecting women from discrimination and defending affirmative action. Quite often, she has been the decisive vote in 5–4 cases whose balance Judge Alito would now tip the other way. And here, Senators, it is important to note that Justice O'Connor is a judicial conservative, and she has not always fully protected Constitutional rights and liberties. But she has been the Justice more than any other who has crafted legal approaches that retained some meaningful protections for rights that other Justices sought to deny completely. Judge Alito stands far to her right in every one of these areas and more. Still, the most disturbing difference between these two jurists is not simply the conclusions at which they arrive, but also how they reach them: Justice O'Connor assesses each case with careful attention to what the law means and who it affects, for she knows that is where the essence of justice lies. In Judge Alito's approach to the law, there are no individuals, there is no privacy—and without them, there can be neither justice nor human dignity.

Finally, here is the conclusion to the speech that Elizabeth Cady Stanton made at the first woman's rights convention at Seneca Falls, New York, in 1848. The speech was long and complex, setting forth arguments to respond to all of the major justifications offered for women's special and limited place in society. At the end, she wished to rouse her listeners to action:

> "Voices" were the visitors and advisers of Joan of Arc. Do not "voices" come to us daily from the haunts of poverty, sorrow, degradation and despair, already too long unheeded. Now is the time for the women of this country, if they would save our free institutions, to defend the right, to buckle on the armor that can best resist the keenest weapons of the enemy—contempt and ridicule. The same religious enthusiasm that nerved Joan of Arc in her work nerves us to ours. In every generation God calls some men and women for the utterance of truth, a heroic action, and our work to-day is the fulfilling of what has long since been foretold by the Prophet—Joel 2:28: "And it shall come to pass afterward, that I will pour out my spirit upon all flesh, and your sons and your daughters shall prophesy." We do not expect our path will be strewn with the flowers of popular applause, but over the

thorns of bigotry and prejudice will be our way, and our banners will beat the dark storm-clouds of opposition from those who have entrenched themselves behind the bulwarks of custom and authority, and who have fortified their position by every means, holy and unholy. But we will steadfastly abide the result. Unmoved we will bear it aloft. Undaunted we will unfurl it to the gale, for we know that the storm cannot rend from it a shred, that the electric flash will but more clearly show to us the glorious words inscribed upon it, "Equality of Rights."[11]

At the time of this speech, women were not allowed to speak in public, and when they married, they ceased to exist in law—they could not sue or bear witness, own property, including their own earnings (or even their own clothing!), and had no guardianship rights in their children. Cady Stanton knows that it will be very difficult for women to pay the costs in ridicule or to face the intense hostility of most men and women to their cause. She seeks to raise their morale, to give them courage to pursue this cause. She does so in the high style of nineteenth-century U.S. public address, but her appeal is powerful, particularly to an audience with deep religious commitments. Joan of Arc is a model of a woman who stepped out of her traditional place in order to pursue a moral cause; the words of the prophet Joel foresee a time when women will speak for moral causes. She also ends with an appeal to the nation's fundamental values. Thus, in the face of what she knows will be great obstacles, she energizes her audience with religious and patriotic appeals that may enable them to withstand fierce resistance.

These examples illustrate the basic functions that conclusions should perform. They are competent, real illustrations of experienced public speakers trying to end their rhetorical acts effectively.

ADAPTING YOUR OUTLINE TO THE AUDIENCE

If you were to follow the form of your outline in presenting your ideas to the audience, your rhetorical action would be presented through *deduction*, which means starting from a general conclusion and moving to illustrations and applications of it. In fact, all outlines are deductive in starting from a thesis and moving to its divisions. But such a pattern may not be the ideal way to present your ideas under all circumstances. For example, if an audience is hostile to your purpose, or if the subject is controversial, announcing your thesis (forewarning) might stir up resentment and prevent the audience from hearing or considering your ideas. In such a case you might want to present your ideas inductively.

Deductive Structure

The advantages of presenting your ideas in deductive order, as in your outline, are that such a structure avoids ambiguity and possible misinterpretation, and that such a procedure is perceived as honest and straightforward. The disadvantages are that hostility may be created or increased by a blunt statement of the thesis near the beginning of the speech and by a failure to acknowledge opposing viewpoints or arguments. The problems of hostility can be handled to some extent through the introduction. The clarity of this pattern is a strong advantage. As you will note below in the section on two-sided structure, it is possible to incorporate a deductive approach into a two-sided presentation of the pro and con arguments on an issue. In all cases, however, your choice of the pattern in which you present your materials should be a conscious one that you make after having considered carefully the obstacles that you face and the strengths and weaknesses of alternative modes of presentation.

Inductive Structure

Logically, *induction* is a process of going from specifics to a general conclusion. In fact, in traveling from data or evidence to a claim, induction involves the "leap" described in Chapter 5. You will probably follow such a pattern of thinking in the preparation of your speech or essay. But it would be strange indeed if you were to operate inductively while you were speaking to or writing for an audience. That would mean that you were drawing your conclusions and deciding on your thesis at the same moment you were presenting them to the audience. As a thoughtful rhetor, you will have reached conclusions before you present your ideas to an audience. An inductive structure, however, is an attempt to re-create for the audience the process by which you arrived at your conclusions. Obviously, you cannot replicate that process exactly. But you might shorten and streamline the process you went through while giving the listener or reader a sense of how you came to draw the conclusions you are advocating.[12] The inductive format has several advantages. It is likely to increase audience involvement, as they will participate more directly in the processes by which conclusions are drawn. This form of presentation also minimizes hostility. The audience has fewer opportunities to disagree, fewer chances to dispute the positions taken by the author. But there are disadvantages. Inductive presentation takes more time or space for development. Also, unless the audience participates very actively—listens acutely or reads intently—they may miss the point, fail to draw the conclusion, and misunderstand your purpose.

Two-Sided or Refutative Structure

As described, an outline is a brief or series of arguments developing reasons for taking one position rather than another. But many subjects of rhetorical action are controversial issues. There will be arguments on both sides that need to be considered and examined. When speaking about such an issue, you might wish to use *refutative structure* by exploring the opposing arguments as part of the process of explaining why you have decided to advocate another position. In effect, you look at the pool of available arguments in order to show that the weight of the evidence and of available arguments falls on one side or the other. A two-sided presentation also can present you as a mediator who has examined more extreme positions and who seeks to find a compromise between them. Compromise or finding "third" and "fourth" ways to view controversy is, in fact, a more sophisticated way to handle many issues that do not divide neatly into "pro" and "con" sides. Unfortunately, the "for" and "against" format is used so gratuitously in media to inflame controversy, oversell division, and conflate complicated policy, that it is little wonder that we have "blue state" and "red state" gridlock. As a rhetor, if you can present a "three-sided" structure, for instance, you can gain credibility by putting yourself "above the fray."

Two-sided or refutative structure is also more appropriate for certain audiences. A two-sided presentation allows you to incorporate refutation into your presentation. That is essential under several conditions:

1. When you know that the audience is familiar with opposing arguments or will be exposed to competing persuaders.
2. When a one-sided presentation may motivate the audience to seek out opposing views.
3. When a one-sided view of an issue may need to be corrected.
4. When your opposition is also a significant part of your audience.

In the first situation, opposing arguments are already in the minds of the audience, or they soon will be. As a result, it is essential that you respond to questions they have in their minds or that you prepare them for the arguments they will hear from competing persuaders. When arguments already exist in the minds of audience members, you ignore them at your peril, as they are competing with you whether you know it or not. When the audience will eventually be exposed to opposing arguments, you can *inoculate* them by suggesting weaknesses in the arguments, which will make them less susceptible to the appeals of competing persuaders. Without such inoculation, the arguments of opponents may become the novel arguments that shift the balance and alter opinion.

As discussed in more detail in Chapter 8, there are three conditions in which audiences seek information that challenges their beliefs or values: when audience members are of generally higher levels of education, when the information is very useful, and when the audience members' history of exposure leads them to believe they have heard a biased or one-sided presentation. Thus, two-sided presentations are desirable with knowledgeable audiences—a slanted or one-sided presentation can create a desire on the part of the audience for competing information. That is particularly true when the position you take is extreme or unusual. If you claim that ingesting almonds cures AIDS but don't acknowledge contradictory views, you may drive your audience to seek out competing medical studies. If you claim that there is no evidence that smoking is dangerous to health or that the amount of cholesterol in foods we eat has no effect on heart condition, you are likely to send your audience off to competing persuaders to look at the opposing evidence. At a minimum, you will need to qualify your claims. At best, you will acknowledge opposing arguments.

Finally, there are situations in which those holding opposing views are part of your target audience. One of the finest examples of two-sided or refutative structure is an essay on the birth of the "Black Power" slogan written by Dr. Martin Luther King Jr.[13] King's opposition included civil rights activists who were using the slogan and a more militant approach to civil rights protest. But those same people were part of his primary audience because he sought to reconcile these competing groups and to unify the effort for civil rights. However successful his efforts at persuasion might have been, he would have failed if he had not demonstrated to his opponents that he understood their position and respected it. As a result, the essay is both a persuasive statement for a nonviolent approach and a moving statement of why the slogan and a more militant approach became attractive to civil rights workers. The essay is so balanced that it is an excellent source of information about the motivation of more militant civil rights groups. Despite his fair treatment of the opposition, King makes a powerful case for his own point of view. But a two-sided presentation was ideally suited to the condition in which he found himself: competing with those whom he needed to persuade. When your opposition is also your audience, not only must you make a two-sided presentation, but you must also present opposing arguments fairly and sympathetically.

MATERIAL FOR ANALYSIS

On June 12, 2005, Steve Jobs, co-founder and CEO of Apple Computers and founder of NeXT, Inc. and Pixar Animation Studios, delivered the commencement address at Stanford University. Given the enormous impact that Apple products and Jobs himself have had worldwide, it is understandable that he would be invited to be the commencement speaker at a major university. In another sense, however, his presence in that role was a bit surprising because he never graduated from college. Since its delivery, and especially since Jobs's death in October 2011, his speech has received considerable attention by the press if for no reason other than, somewhat ironically, it includes a discussion of death and the pancreatic cancer that eventually ended Jobs's life.

Both a video recording and the text of his speech are available online at http://news.stanford.edu/news/2005/june15/jobs-061505.html. Retrieve the text of the speech and use it to respond to the following questions for analysis.

Questions for Analysis

1. Examine the ways in which topical structure works in this speech. Why is this organizational pattern a strategic choice given the occasion?

2. How does a narrative substructure interact with topical structure to give the audience a humanized view of Steve Jobs?

3. How do evidence and language fulfill the requirements of form—the inspirational occasion of a commencement?

4. Among business associates, Steve Jobs had the reputation of sometimes being impatient and perhaps even abrasive. Does this speech support or contradict that reputation? Why?

5. What rhetorical purposes does this act fulfill? Are these purposes aligned with the needs of a ceremonial occasion?

6. How do the introduction and conclusion work to meet the requirements of form? Of the occasion?

7. How do transitions sharpen the speaker's organization and reflect on his ethos?

8. The commencement speech is part of the larger epideictic genre (see Chapter 14). Generally, this means audiences expect commencement speeches to be inspirational, unifying, and invoke traditional American values. They are not to be divisive, nor tackle issues of policy that could be perceived as controversial. How does Jobs fulfill those expectations?

9. Why would a logical structure, such as a problem-solution pattern, be inappropriate for this occasion?

EXERCISES

Critical Thinking Exercises

1. Divide into groups. Each group will be asked to design a brief outline of major points on the topic "McDonald's" using a different organizational pattern assigned by your instructor to advance your group's claims. Designate someone from your group to present your case. What do you learn about the way structure complements purpose? How is the value of each organizational pattern realized in your group's use of it?

2. Think about an ad that you know well. Does it conform to the motivated sequence? In what ways? Share your observations with the class.

Analytical Writing Exercises

3. Create copy for a one-minute radio spot on why students should attend your college or university. Use the motivated sequence to structure your ad. Vote for a class winner.

Portfolio Entry 5: Organization

4. Examine your rhetorical acts for the type of organizational patterns they use. How do these organizational patterns illustrate the value of such patterns as indicated in the chapter reading? How does the organizational pattern advance the purpose of the act? Is one pattern more striking than others in advancing the cause? Why? Explain in one to two pages.

Strategic Speaking Exercises

5. Two-sided presentations: Prepare a speech or write an essay organized to present two sides of a controversial topic. Select one of these obstacles as your focus:

   a. Inoculating the audience against the arguments of competing persuaders, or refuting the major arguments of the opposition.

   b. Moderating the views of extremists, for example, urging extreme conservatives to moderate their demands on politicians, urging abortion foes to permit abortions in cases of rape, incest, or where there is a threat to the mother's life, or urging pro-choice advocates to limit their appeals to the first trimester, and the like.

   c. Presenting arguments from another perspective to an audience likely to be familiar with only one side of an argument, such as minority or women's points of view to majority/male audiences.

   d. Acknowledging the justice of arguments on both sides while taking a point of view; for example, acknowledging the problems of censorship while arguing that the linkage of sex and violence in pornography is more significant, or acknowledging the evils of pornography while arguing that the evils of censorship are more significant.

   Focus attention on the strengths and weaknesses of this form of organization and attempt to locate the particular rhetorical situations in which it is likely to be most effective.

6. Prepare a two- to three-minute storytelling speech to create virtual experience. Be sure your story follows the narrative dramatic form and is plausible.

7. Prepare a six- to eight-minute policy speech to initiate action. Use the motivated sequence and capitalize on cognitive dissonance.

NOTES

1. *On Rhetoric: A Theory of Civic Discourse,* trans. George A. Kennedy (New York: Oxford University Press, 1991), p. 273.

2. James Thurber, "The Little Girl and the Wolf," Copyright © 1940 James Thurber. © 1968 Helen Thurber, originally published by HarperCollins and reprinted by permission of the Barbara Hogenson Agency.

3. (New York: Summit Books, 1977).

4. For a more complete examination of the subject matter for the New Media outline, see Joseph Straubhaar and Robert LaRose, *Media Now: Understanding Media, Culture, and Technology,* 4th edition (Belmont, CA: Thomson/Wadsworth, 2004).

5. See "With tainted tissue, transplants turn deadly," AP reporters Marilynn Marchione and Seth Borenstein, in *The Wichita Eagle,* June 12, 2006, p. 1A.

6. (Boston: D.C. Heath, 1910).

7. *Principles and Types of Speech*, 2nd edition (Glenview, IL: Scott, Foresman, 1939). Both were probably influenced by Francis Bacon's *Advancement of Learning* in which he developed the concepts underlying faculty psychology and in which he wrote that "the duty and office of rhetoric is to apply reason to the imagination for the better moving of the will."

8. *A Theory of Cognitive Dissonance* (Evanston, IL: Row, Peterson, 1957).

9. *A Rhetoric of Motives* (1950; reprint ed., Berkeley: University of California Press, 1969), p. 39.

10. Michelman's testimony reprinted with permission.

11. Elizabeth Cady Stanton, "Speech at the Seneca Falls Convention, 1848," *Man Cannot Speak for Her: Vol. 2: Key Texts of the Early Feminists*, ed. K. K. Campbell (Westport, CT: Greenwood Publishing, 1989), pp. 69–70.

12. An exceptionally fine example of this is Virginia Woolf's *A Room of One's Own* (1929; reprint ed., New York: Harbinger, 1957).

13. "Black Power," the second chapter of King's book, *Where Do We Go from Here: Chaos or Community?* (New York: Harper and Row, 1967). It is reprinted in Robert L. Scott and Wayne Brockriede, *The Rhetoric of Black Power* (New York: Harper and Row, 1969), pp. 25–64.

Chapter 7

The Resources of Language

The language of a rhetorical act may be casual (It just blew my mind...) or formal ("Four score and seven years ago"), vague (Just Do It!) or precise (Only two calories in an eight-ounce glass), figurative ("America has given the Negro people a bad check; a check which has come back marked insufficient funds") or literal ("The only thing we have to fear is fear itself"); but whatever its style and whatever strategies are used, language is a powerful and significant resource.

However else it may be defined, rhetoric is the art of using symbols. All the resources of rhetorical action have their foundation in language. Given its importance, students of rhetoric need to understand the characteristics of language that allow it to play such a special role in rhetorical action.

THE CHARACTERISTICS OF LANGUAGE

In its ordinary sense, language refers to verbal symbol systems such as Sindebele or Hmong, English or Portuguese. Language also includes other symbol systems based on space, movement, sound, pitch, time, color, and so on. In their most developed forms, such symbol systems are dance, music, sculpture, painting, architecture, and the like. Through symbol systems, we order our experiences and assign them meaning. Instead of being bombarded by billions of distinct stimuli, language enables us to make sense of the chaos so that we can perceive and respond to a world of recognizable objects and events.

Language has three primary dimensions: *naming, abstracting,* and *negating.*

Naming

The first dimension of language is *naming*—the process by which we notice, recognize, and label certain elements or qualities in ourselves and in our world. Names permit us to identify and isolate significant events. For this reason, the vocabulary of an individual or a community is a rough index of what is or has been important to that person or group, a relationship reflected in the "verbal ability" sections of college entrance examinations.

Naming is a process of ordering the world and of focusing our attention. Many names do not label single things but rather categories of relatively similar objects or events. As labels that refer to categories, names permit us to ignore the differences among objects and events and to lump them together into groups to which we can respond similarly. If you identify an object as a "chair," for example, you respond to it as a humanly created object with arms or a back, intended for a category of actions labeled "sitting" (the definition of a "chair") and ignore its unique characteristics— color, shape, wood or plastic, size. If this process of labeling and responding is to work well, however, there must be standards to determine when a particular object, person, or event may be included in a particular category—that is, when it may properly be labeled with a particular name. Such standards are set by definitions.

A definition specifies the essential qualities that something must have to be labeled in a particular way in a given linguistic community. Definitions collected in dictionaries give words a special meaning called *denotation*. People do not learn meanings from dictionaries, however. They learn meanings in real life situations, by having experiences with words and with the persons, events, and objects to which words are applied. In these real, concrete situations, people not only learn denotative meanings (definitions), they learn to associate the feelings they experience in these situations with the words. Such meanings are called *connotations* (con = together with, notate = to mark or note), and they refer to the associations a word calls up.

A graduate student named Lin-Lee Lee wrote in a chapter of her dissertation on the 1996 presidential election in the Republic of China that presidential candidate Chen Li-an had urged Taiwanese citizens to view each of their homes as a *baldachin.* Because English was her second language, she had searched the dictionary for an English counterpart to an unusual Chinese noun. A baldachin is a canopy of cloth or wood or stone used to protect the image of a saint or an altar in a procession or in a church. Her choice of that word baldachin was delightful because it was an apt metaphor for a candidate whose campaign emphasized moral values. If you have ever visited churches in Italy, you may have seen the same word there, written *baldachino* in Italian. Accordingly, in this case, baldachin not only refers to a protective religious canopy, but it also means one of the unusual words that crop up when a foreign student is struggling with translation, an apt metaphor for the importance of moral values in the home, an experience with such canopies in Italy, and a good example to use in this book explaining how connotative meanings develop. If you remember the word, one part of your connotative meaning will be related to reading about it in this book.

Semanticists (students of meaning) say that meaning is in people, not in things or even in words. The connotative meanings associated with all symbols illustrate this idea. They also show that names are not just factual or descriptive. Words are labels for our experiences so that names are valuative as well as descriptive. Meanings include subjective qualities such as associations and connotations.

Names are valuative at the most basic levels because they are signs of interest and relevance. If you already knew the meaning of baldachin, for example, your knowledge would indicate past experience with the word. You may have encountered it in a church or novel, you may be a student of religious architecture or pageantry, you may even have run across it in the dictionary. But it is unlikely the term produces strong reactions because it is unlikely to be a word that you associate with intense or disturbing experiences.

Contrast *baldachin* with *masturbation*. The latter term is, for many, associated with disquieting sexual feelings and taboos. (Consider that a U.S. Surgeon-General was forced to resign her post after suggesting that masturbation should be taught to teenagers as an alternative to more dangerous and consequential forms of sexual activity!) In a class on the psychology of sex at the University of Kansas, students asked their professor not to use that word because it was so upsetting. The students decided they preferred *self-pleasuring*. Denotatively, masturbation and self-pleasuring are identical, but connotatively they are not. Masturbation calls up many highly charged associations and taboos, but self-pleasuring, a less familiar term, is unlikely to have been used to label forbidden feelings and behaviors. As a result, hearing and using it are less disturbing. Recently, Pfizer, the drug company that markets Viagra, "insisted on calling the problem 'erectile dysfunction,' and not 'impotence.'" A successful marketing campaign involves managing the pitfalls of connotation: "Part of that is giving them [potential customers] language that is not emotionally charged," said David Brinkley, the worldwide team leader for Viagra at Pfizer.[1]

A successful marketing campaign also can exploit product recognition to create enthymemes. In an ad shown only in Canada at this time, two middle-aged men are talking: "Viagra spanglecheff?" says a man to a friend at a bowling alley. "Spanglecheff?" his friend asks. "Minky Viagra noni noni boo-boo plats!" the first man replies. Maxine Thomas, an executive at Taxi, the agency in Toronto that produced the campaign, said the ad takes advantage of Viagra's name recognition. "It's not as though we need to tell people what it does because they already know," she said. "Consumers can fill in the blank for themselves."[2] Now the advertiser has avoided using any words with powerful connotations, although once you've encountered the ad, even these words will have developed associations.

When we speak of *loaded language*, we are referring to words that provoke strong feelings; the person who hears or reads them has vivid, intense associations because of emotion-laden experiences with them. No term understood by a person is simply neutral or factual. It is always bound up with experiences and will always contain evaluations resulting from feelings associated with those experiences. Fittingly, mothers who have lost their children to drunk drivers have channeled their anguish and outrage into the name of their organization MADD (Mothers Against Drunk Drivers) to toughen laws against these senseless acts. In some cases, however, the response is so strong that it interferes with communication. For many people, it is not possible to talk calmly about abortion or rape or condoms or homosexuality or AIDS. Think, for example, about euphemisms we use to talk about such subjects as death, money, and sexual intercourse, among others. Euphemistic terms are one strategy we use to avoid such powerful reactions. The passionate responses to the words Don Imus used to disparage the women's basketball team from Rutgers illustrates the power of connotations and the use of emotionally powerful terms by "shock jocks" to attract listeners who find such "forbidden" but evocative language exciting.

The use of *loaded language* can also be a powerful rhetorical strategy in political contexts. For example, the Patient Protection and Affordable Care Act, passed by Congress in 2010, was quickly relabeled "Obamacare" by its opponents. Students of argumentation will immediately recognize "Obamacare" as an *ad hominem* fallacy, an attack on a person (in this case, President Barack Obama who championed the bill) rather than an attack on the policy itself. Despite that fallacy, the new label carried powerful, negative connotations for many, especially for "birthers" (another naming or labeling strategy!), those who believed that Obama is not a natural born citizen of the United States.

As Aristotle observed, such powerful emotional appeals (*pathos*) function to put audiences into the "frame of mind" desired by the rhetor. In turn, that frame of mind influences how the audience responds to the rest of the rhetor's message (*logos*) because "our judgements when we are pleased and friendly are not the same as when we are pained and hostile" (Aristotle, *On Rhetoric*, 1356a). So, members of the audience who experienced that powerful, negative reaction to the label "Obamacare" were also much more likely to believe other claims made by the bill's opponents, such as former Alaska Governor Sarah Palin's assertion that the bill established "death panels" that would determine who would receive health care and who would not based on their "level of productivity in society" (no such provision is included in the law).[3]

Despite the potential rhetorical force of connotative meanings, those meanings can change with time. For example, at the beginning of the 1960s, *Negro* had positive connotations as a term of respect, and *black* was considered a term of disrespect. In the course of that decade, protestors changed those connotations so that Negro was associated, negatively, with persons who sought approval from whites and who were ashamed of their culture, their past, and their physical characteristics. By contrast, *Black,* now capitalized, became associated with racial pride. *African American* is now the preferred term (formerly, but no longer, hyphenated) because it has become associated with ethnic history and ethnic pride.

Naming, the first dimension of language, enables us to order, call attention to, focus, define, and evaluate. Names have denotative meanings, found in dictionaries, that define the accepted conditions for their use. Names have connotative meanings that reflect our experiences and associations with a term and its use. The connotations of terms can change for us as individuals and for us as members of a culture as our experiences with terms change.

Abstracting

The second dimension of language is abstracting. *Abstracting* leaves out details; the most basic kind of abstracting occurs with names. As a title for a category, names leave out all the distracting particulars. You call what you sit in a desk, ignoring its color, the gum underneath the seat, the initials carved in its surface or inscribed in ink, the difference between it and the desks your professors have in their offices. The most basic element in abstracting is omission—leaving out or ignoring details in order to treat different objects in similar ways.

Abstracting moves us further and further from concrete, specific details. In fact, we can go on and on leaving out more and more details. The word *abstract* is defined as "not concrete or specific, without reference to a specific instance, theoretical, not easily understood, abstruse." That definition alerts you to problems in communication that arise from abstracting. As we move further from concrete detail, an idea or concept becomes more and more difficult to grasp, and the chances of misunderstanding and disinterest increase. Abstracting is also a major linguistic resource, however.

Symbols are abstractions that permit us to talk about an absent world. We write books about the remote past, most of whose details have vanished; we read books and talk about places we have never seen or that are created entirely out of our imaginations; we argue about a future that is outside our experience; we explore concepts we can never see or touch. Figure 7–1 provides an example of abstracting as a process of including more and more experience but omitting more and more detail.

Even at the most concrete level in the here and now, abstraction occurs. It occurs as we label our experiences, as for example, when we ignore individual differences and label people as "students" and "teachers." As we move up each level, we include greater amounts of experience as we omit more and more details. Level 2 lumps together many hours of varied activity under a single label. Level 3 lumps together all the courses offered to students and orders them into one giant pattern. And so on.

The advantages of abstracting are evident: they enable us to combine, for thinking and talking, ever-larger areas of experience while ignoring varied and complex detail. As we move up the ladder of abstraction, it becomes more and more difficult to understand these abstractions—they are further and further from our personal experience. It is also easy to ignore significant differences—to forget that students differ in background, age, social skills, verbal ability, maturity, and so on; and to treat them stereotypically, as if they were all identical. Abstraction allows us to manipulate great hunks of the world verbally; it tempts us to forget that these chunks are made up of highly varied concrete events, objects, and individuals. Westerners are tempted to lump together "Asians," despite the enormous cultural differences between Japanese, Chinese, Koreans, Indians, and Filipinos, among others, as well as the subcultural differences among groups in these cultures. Foreigners are tempted to lump

Most Abstract	Level 5	All of the activities and experiences involved in obtaining knowledge and skills.	"An education"
	Level 4	All of the activities, academic and nonacademic, of this institution.	"The university"
	Level 3	All classes offered to students leading to degrees at this institution.	"The curriculum"
	Level 2	All of the classroom experiences on T, Th at 9:30 in Elliott 111, Spring 2013.	"Rhetoric 535"
Least Abstract	Level 1	Concrete experiences with the individuals now in this classroom.	Abstracted by labels such as "students" and "teachers"

Figure 7–1
Abstracting: Most Abstract to Least Abstract

together "Americans," despite the great differences among those who live in southern California and those who live in northern Maine. The capacity of language to abstract permits us to talk about the absent, the past, and the future, and it enables us to conceptualize ideas such as love, truth, beauty, and rhetoric that lie far beyond our concrete experience.

Abstracting is a powerful source of identification and has great potential to prompt participation. Politicians exploit this potential by speaking in less concrete, more general terms, hoping that listeners will interpret such language in different ways, enabling them to appeal to diverse groups. In the 2000 presidential campaign George W. Bush promised not to engage in nation-building, but given his decisions about Iraq, his idea of what was nation-building and some voters' understanding of it seem to have been quite different. Is anyone opposed to "family values," for example? But what does the person espousing them really mean by that phrase? Reducing or eliminating abortion? Opposing sex education in schools? Providing family leave to parents of newborn or newly adopted children? Providing tax write-offs for child care services? Opposing gay marriage? All of these might be part of whatever someone might mean by that phrase.

Negating

Negating is the third dimension of language. Definitions are based on negating because when we say what something is, we are also saying what it is not. The rhetorical power of negation is reflected in the Judeo-Christian cultural heritage. As seven of the Ten Commandments state, "Thou shalt not..." But negation is very tricky, because such prohibitions imply their opposites. Whenever you say to a teenager, for instance, "Don't fall in love with a high school boyfriend!" you are at the same time suggesting an enticing possibility! Organizational crisis communicators understand this dilemma all too well as rumors that tarnish their reputations infiltrate rogue websites and mass emails. Rather than "set the record straight" with a vigorous denial of the outrageous rumor, the new PR rules say to resist that urge as more damage can be done by giving the rumor free publicity. Even positive commands imply their opposite, suggesting the option not to do whatever it is that we are being told to do.

Negation also is involved in abstracting. To abstract is to omit (negate) details and ignore (negate) differences. In fact, the ability to use symbols at all requires an understanding of negation. Whatever a name is, it is *not* what it stands for. "Cat" is a bit of black ink or a few sound waves, not this sable-colored, furry creature that meows and purrs, bites and scratches, grooms by licking, and growls as it carries off a stuffed toy.

Negation underlies all comparisons and contrasts, including those involved in literal and figurative analogies. As discussed in Chapter 4, literal analogies allow us to evaluate and to predict. But comparisons are also involved in definitions.

A dialectical definition defines by contrast. If you wish to define capitalism, for example, you might compare it to socialism and conclude that what is distinctive about it is the private ownership of the means of production. Such a definition uses socialism as a perspective through which to look at capitalism; it ignores similarities and emphasizes differences. We can also compare capitalism and democracy. In this case, the focus shifts to assumptions made about individuals. Capitalism presumes that some will have more economic power (capital) and, in all likelihood, more influence on policy, whereas democracy affirms the right of each individual, regardless of economic or other differences, to an equal voice in how he or she is governed. If we compare capitalism and feudalism, the focus shifts to the reciprocal obligations of liege lord and vassal and the absence of such mutual obligations between capitalist/employer and laborer/employee. Comparisons between capitalism and communism might emphasize the difference between production controlled by the market and production determined by state planning. In each case negation, in the form of contrast, directs our attention and shapes the definition that emerges. Dialectical definitions are effective ways to delineate the specific meanings of highly abstract terms.

Negation is also the basis for the figurative analogy and for metaphorical language generally. The moon is not "the North Wind's cookie" or "a piece of angry candy" or "a ghostly galleon tossed upon cloudy seas" as it has been described by poets. We can understand and use such metaphors precisely because we recognize that they are not literally true. This form of the negative extends the range of our symbols to include comparisons between anything and anything. In addition, the negative allows us to use irony (to say one thing but mean something else), develop satire and parody, and speak in a sarcastic tone.

These, then, are the three fundamental dimensions of language: the capacities to *name,* to *abstract,* and to *negate.* From them come all the powers of language to influence our perceptions and our attitudes. And from them arise the specific resources of style and strategy.

STYLE

Style is what is distinctive about the language of a rhetorical act. Style reflects the attitudes and character of the rhetor and hints at feelings about the subject being explored or advocated; in other words, it is closely related to tone. The style of an act can vary. It can be more or less formal, more or less precise, more or less literal, and more or less redundant.

Formality/Informality

Whenever we speak or write, we make certain assumptions about what kind of language is appropriate to the situation at hand. Basically, this amounts to deciding how formal or informal to be. Rhetorical style ranges from the formality of a presidential address or a scholarly article on one hand to the informality of a radio or TV interview or a conversation—perhaps even a text or twitter message—with a friend on the other. Generally speaking, as style becomes more informal, it becomes more conversational or colloquial.

Informality may be a way of expressing intense feelings or identifying with those from whom you seek support. In response to the attacks on 9/11/01, President George W. Bush said, "Bring 'em on!" and referring to Osama bin Laden, he said he was, "Wanted Dead or Alive." This is not the usual level of presidential language, and the president later said that he regretted using those words. At the same time, when he said them, he was reflecting his history as a Texan and his feelings as a person who wanted to find a way to punish the perpetrators. He also was reaching out to others who were as angry as he at suicide attacks aimed at economic and military symbols that killed thousands of people.

The factors influencing the degree of formality will be discussed in Chapters 8, 9, and 10 as parts of the rhetorical context: the audience, the purpose, and the rhetor. Whatever is serious and important will be presented in a more formal style. The more authoritative the rhetor is or wishes to appear, the more formal the style. The relationship between rhetor and audience also affects formality. Formal prose creates distance between rhetor and audience while informality minimizes distance.

The differences between formal and informal prose are chiefly matters of grammar, sentence structure, and vocabulary. Formal prose is strictly grammatical and uses complex sentence structure and precise, often technical vocabulary. Informal prose is less strictly grammatical and uses short, simple sentences and ordinary, familiar words. Informal style may include sentence fragments, such as the truncated style of text messaging ("sup?" "ruok?" "g2g," "ttyl") and some colloquialisms or slang, such as is common in rap music ("grill," "bling," "crib," "ice").

How formal or informal should you be? Obviously the answer depends on your subject and purpose, the role you will play, and your relationship to your audience. Most public rhetorical action observes conventional niceties of grammar, is modestly complex in sentence structure, and avoids an excessive use of colloquialisms (words or phrases found more frequently in conversation than in writing). That is, it is relatively formal, although the rhetor must determine just where on the continuum from highly formal to informal a particular rhetorical occasion should be placed.

Precision/Ambiguity

Language can be highly precise, specific, and verifiable, or it can be ambiguous and vague. Precise language expresses ideas clearly and distinctly. It is exact and sometimes technical. Ambiguous language is open to more than one interpretation, and vague language is inexplicit and indefinite. For the most part, good style aims for precision and avoids ambiguity.

Precise language is a symptom that a rhetorical act is emphasizing empirical evidence and logical proof. Only clearly stated arguments can be evaluated logically; only exact statements are capable of verification. Precision in language reflects the rhetor's purpose and assumptions about the audience. More complex, technical subjects require the use of formal, technical vocabulary. In addition, precision reflects the expertise of the speaker or writer.

Some apparently precise terms, however, can be highly ambiguous. Many advertisements illustrate the ways that technical terms can confuse and mislead. For instance, a brand of skin care lotion advertises itself as "oxygen therapy," although all skin is constantly exposed to oxygen in the air, and no externally applied product can introduce oxygen into skin cells. Similar instances can be drawn from military jargon. "Collateral damage" in war, for example, refers to civilians killed unintentionally by missiles or bombs that missed their primary target. In such a case, apparently precise terms turn out to be vague, even deceptive. This phrase took on grim connotations in 1995 when terrorist Timothy McVeigh referred to the children killed by the bomb he placed at the Murrah Federal Building in Oklahoma City as "collateral damage."

The persuasive advantages of vagueness are illustrated in many advertisements. Commercials tell us that a brand of heating and air conditioning equipment is an "Rx prescription for home comfort," that we should "Just do it," that a particular makeup "acts like skin care" or that "X is more than a mouthwash." These are *pseudo-claims*, statements that sound like conclusions, but assert nothing. What is a prescription for home comfort? What should we "just do"? What does it mean to "act like skin care" (like washing one's skin, like putting on lotion)? More *what* than a mouthwash?[4] In these cases, imprecise statements are used as cues to suggest arguments to or evoke memories in viewers, and if the ads are successful, viewers participate to embellish these statements to create arguments—*enthymemes*—in their minds.

Some imprecision in language is inevitable. No word (except some proper nouns) refers to only one thing. The abstraction of language makes ambiguity inevitable. We need some vague terms, such as "middle-aged," to refer to conditions that have no definite boundaries. We require the ambiguity of euphemism (substituting an inoffensive term such as passed away or self-pleasuring, for ones considered offensively explicit) to deal with some highly controversial, emotionally charged subjects. We need figurative language to make concepts vivid and to enlarge the bases for comparison.

Stylistic precision is good for complex subjects and for exact proof. Precision implies that the rhetor is an expert. The ambiguities of abstraction, euphemism, and figurative language are important resources for persuasion, but at the same time they open wide vistas for confusing, misleading, and deceiving audiences.[5]

Literal/Figurative

The style of a rhetorical act can vary in its use of figurative or metaphorical language. Figurative language grasps and defines the intangible qualities of experience. Such language can be used to explain or illustrate a difficult concept. Although it may not be verifiable, it involves another kind of precision—the vividness of immediate sensory experience. In a parody of the clichés mouthed to college graduates, Tom Lehrer wrote a song that told them, "Soon you'll be sliding down the razor blade of life." Such an image is painfully vivid.

Figurative language holds our attention and sticks in our memories. Detergent ads, for example, claim to make clothes "as fresh and clean as sunshine," or show a picture of a measuring cup filled with blue sky. In this case, sunshine is compared to clean clothes, echoing the good smell of clothes dried in the sun. To persuade you that a cleaner named POW attacks stains, an ad could use a metaphor such as "POW: Stain Grenade," or a picture of a bottle of POW next to a hand grenade, or "POW: Dirt Bulldozer" next to a picture of one. Another cleaner was advertised as a "white tornado." Like the figurative analogy, the metaphor connects what are familiar shapes and known power with a product that is unknown and unfamiliar.[6]

Metaphors reflect attitudes. If life is a dance, it follows a pattern and is influenced by individual artistry. If life is a chess game, it is a competitive struggle of wits. If life is a crap game, it is ruled by chance. If "life is a banquet and most poor suckers are starving to death," as Patrick Dennis's Auntie Mame claimed, then it's time to dig in and eat up!

Metaphors evaluate. Sensory images express our values. Bad books are dry. A conservative refers to "hemophiliac" liberals bleeding for every cause; liberals, on the other hand, sometimes call conservatives ice cold and heartless.

There is an ongoing tension between literal and figurative language in rhetorical action. Literal language is more precise and exact, but it often is less vivid and engaging. Literal language is part of accurate description and an effort to produce careful proof. Metaphorical language enlivens ideas and arouses participation. Rhetoric is made effective by both.

Economy/Redundancy

Style varies in its use of repetition or restatement. Advice to writers usually suggests that they aim for economy of language, avoiding wordiness and circumlocutions. The amount of repetition needed depends on the complexity of the subject and argument and on the knowledge of the audience.

Oral style, whether in live public speeches or in radio and television commercials, differs from written style. Most commercials repeat their claims at least three times and usually many more. Highly creative ads reiterate their central idea in several amusing ways, frequently in oral, visual, and nonverbal terms. All repeat the product's name many times over. Engaging ditties and the attractive faces and graceful or humorous actions of skilled actors help to relieve the monotony.

Oral style must be more redundant than written style. Because you can reread material and pause to think between paragraphs, a writer need not repeat and restate, at least not as often. Listeners do not have such options. As discussed in Chapter 3, successful speaking requires internal summaries, transitions connecting ideas, repetition of the major steps in the argument, and the like. Such redundancy increases comprehension and the impact on listeners. Used in print, such devices become irritating under all but the most unusual circumstances.

No other quality so consistently distinguishes oral and written style. Both oral and written rhetoric range along the other dimensions. Both can be formal or informal. Both reflect the possibilities of precision and ambiguity, although formulations demanding the most precision appear in writing. Both exploit the possibilities of figurative language and require literal expression for careful proof. Because oral style is often related to informality, it is likely to be more personal, with greater use of personal pronouns; but the impersonality and formality of presidential addresses, for example, indicate that such qualities are not an inevitable part of oral discourse.

Evaluating Style

Good style is clear, vivid, appropriate, and consistent.

Clarity. To say that style has clarity is to say that it is immediately intelligible to the audience. There is no delay in understanding it; no translation is required. The vocabulary is familiar, the syntax meets the norms of listeners and readers, and the discourse develops according to a pattern that can be followed easily. Obviously, if you write or speak on a technical subject, however, all of your language will not be immediately clear to most audiences, who will not be experts. The standard simply requires that unfamiliar terms and concepts be defined and illustrated so they can be understood by nonexperts or by the diverse members of the audience you are addressing. No rhetorical act can achieve its goals if it leaves the audience puzzled, confused, at sea.

Vividness. Good style is vivid. It comes alive. It makes us see and hear and imagine and feel. It creates virtual experience. Vividness is essential to catch and hold the attention of the audience, a prerequisite to successful rhetorical action. It also speaks to the psychological dimension of proof—we must give assent, not just recognize facts. Vivid style depicts, dramatizes, personifies, and describes. It employs the resources of language to focus and emphasize, to make ideas memorable. Vivid style fills our eyes, noses, ears, mouths, and muscles with associations and enriches the connotations of words and ideas with sights, smells, sounds, tastes, memories, and movements.

Figurative language attracts and surprises us. In a review of the *Selected Letters of Rebecca West*, Francine Prose quoted from an account of a talk by the editor Frank Harris. West wrote, "His manner was foully offensive: a barking arrogance with oily declensions at the points where he was moved to speak of the necessity of the artist to feel pity and love—awful passages as though the Sermon on the Mount had kittened, and these were its progeny."[7] In those words one hears a vivid description of the voice and attitude of the speaker Frank Harris; in addition, one hears the intense reaction of the writer and critic. The coined verb, 'kittened,' is a shock—a vivid evocation through metonymy of sloppy sentimentality!

Appropriateness. Like all other elements of rhetorical action, style is contingent on the audience, subject and purpose, occasion, and rhetor. Your style should reflect the formality of the occasion and the seriousness of your purpose. It should be suitable for the complexity of the subject, and it should be adapted to the expertise and attitudes of the audience and to them as members of a linguistic community. Your style must be appropriate to you—to your expertise on the subject, to your relationship to the audience, to the persona you present in this situation. Determining appropriateness requires understanding how style and delivery intersect. The materials on verbal and nonverbal delivery in Chapter 3 address a rhetor's ability to assess the rhetorical context and project one's authentic voice.

Consistency. Good style is consistent. All elements fit together so your discourse is a unified whole. Your language should reflect your tone, your persona, your purpose, and your relationship to the audience. Style may vary, but avoid contradictions among the elements of your rhetoric or major shifts in your perspective.

The importance of consistency should focus attention on introductions. Opening lines establish tone and create expectations. As a result, stylistic choices made at the outset become important commitments that should be reflected in what follows.

Strategies are one route by which speakers and writers achieve some of their stylistic goals.

LANGUAGE STRATEGIES

A *strategy* is a plan of action, a maneuver designed to overcome the obstacles in a particular rhetorical situation. Strategies are part of rhetorical invention. They are discovered or found in your materials as you prepare for rhetorical action, and they are part of the creativity of your role as a rhetor. Strategies are used to cope with controversial and complex issues, with hostile and skeptical audiences, and with difficulties in establishing your credibility and expertise as a source. Every rhetorical situation is as different as every athletic competition, and successful persuasion, like successful play, involves assessing the obstacles you face and the resources at your disposal.

Many of the resources already discussed can and should be used strategically. Evidence should be selected and presented strategically to be salient for the audience, to refute competing persuaders, to present your subject and perspective clearly. Each organizational pattern is a strategic way of unfolding your position. The arguments you select should be chosen strategically for the response you seek and the audience you want to attract and influence. Introductions and conclusions are particularly important as strategic responses to the rhetorical problem. In the speeches and essays you analyze, consider how speakers and writers have used opening and closing statements to respond to the obstacles in a particular situation.

Despite the strategic character of most rhetorical choices, specific strategies are usually devices that exploit the capacities of language. Although their purposes overlap, strategies are designed to assist in proof, to make ideas vivid, and to create connotations. All strategies require participation by the audience and illustrate that rhetorical action is jointly constructed by rhetor and audience.

Language Strategies to Animate and Vivify

Nearly all strategies catch and hold attention and, in that sense, make ideas more vivid, but some strategies have this as their chief function. They are intended to make people and events come alive before our eyes, to create virtual experience by allowing us to see and hear and feel what the rhetor is talking about.

Description. Providing the detail that makes a scene or person come alive before our eyes is the function of description. It creates the sensation that you are there watching events as they occur. An editorial by physician Mark DePaolis describes in detail a videotape of the procedures involved in liposuction, with narration, to warn readers about what occurs during this method of removing fat from thighs or abdomen. According to his report of the videotape, the following occurs after areas of the patient's body are marked for removal and a sharp metal tube like a curtain rod is inserted under the skin:

> ...the powerful suction machine is turned on.... Suffice it to say that the tube is moved back and forth in "a piston-like motion" to suck up the fat....Meanwhile, the patient's skin, which has evidently grown accustomed to those fat deposits, is putting up a valiant fight to keep them. This requires several burly assistants to keep the patient on the table while the surgeon works.... In the next hideous scene, as the narrator puts it, "fat can be seen moving through the transparent tube....No more than 2,000 ccs are removed at any one time," the doctor says finally, showing us what looks like an extremely heavy two-liter soda bottle.... The tube is removed, the incision is sewn shut and several miles of gauze is wrapped around the patient. This is to hide the fact that her thighs now look like gallons of ice cream with one scoop taken out...[8]

Note that the description incorporates figurative analogies ("like a curtain rod"; "piston-like"; "like gallons of ice cream with one scoop taken out") and emotive-language that reflects his reaction ("suffice it to say"; "hideous"). He also personifies the patient's skin, which he describes as "putting up a valiant fight" to keep the fat, a struggle intensified by describing the assistants who are holding the patient down as "burly." He translates the statistic 2,000 ccs by explaining that that is an amount that would fill a two-liter bottle of soda. These details help to create virtual reality which, he hopes, will deter readers from opting for this procedure.

Dr. Helen Broinowski Caldicott, a founder of the group Physicians for Social Responsibility, was a nuclear freeze activist in the 1980s whose work advocating an end to construction and deployment of nuclear weapons by the United States and the Soviet Union culminated rhetorically with "This Beautiful Planet," the annual Phi Beta Kappa oration, delivered during Commencement Week of 1981 to an audience of 700 in Sanders Theatre at Harvard University. *Harvard Magazine* called the speech "powerful" and "chilling" (July–August 1981:50, 52, 53). Based on a series of articles published in the *New England Journal of Medicine*, she described the horrors of nuclear war in vivid detail, as adapted to a Cambridge, Massachusetts, audience:

> A 20 megaton bomb is equal to 20 million tons of TNT. That is four times the collective size of all bombs dropped during the Second World War. It is a small sun. It explodes with the heat of the sun. It will do this to Boston: It will carve out a crater about half a mile to a mile wide and 300 feet deep.... Every human being within a radius of six miles from the hypocenter will be vaporized.... Concrete and steel will burn. Out to a radius of 20 miles, most people will be dead.... If you happen to glance at the blast from 35–40 miles away, the flash would instantly burn the retina and blind you. It will create a fire storm of 15,000 to 30,000 square miles ... creating a holocaust fanned by hurricane winds, so if you were in a fallout shelter, you would be pressure cooked and asphyxiated as the fire used all the oxygen.[9]

Dr. Caldicott uses descriptive language to make statistics vivid and real. The literal analogy to the bombs dropped in World War II helps us to grasp the existential size of a twenty-megaton bomb. The figurative analogy to a small sun gives us a sense of its brightness, which is heightened by her description of what would happen should a person be unfortunate enough to look at the blast even from a distance of over thirty miles away. It is plausible that there would be a firestorm, like that seen during powerful forest fires, that would cover many square miles. Its power and devastation are heightened by comparing the winds to those in a hurricane, and the lack of safety in a fallout shelter is made vivid by the analogy to what happens to food in a pressure cooker and the reminder of how much oxygen such a fire would consume. Here description serves primarily to dramatize the size and impact of a catastrophic event.

Another function of description comes from an earlier event. A great deal of controversy was aroused when the Walker Report labeled the behavior of Chicago police officers at the 1968 Democratic National Convention a "police riot." Most Americans view police officers as helpful protectors and believe that if they misbehave, they must have been provoked. In combating such attitudes, the Walker Report used eyewitness accounts such as this one to describe the kinds of confrontations that occurred between Chicago police and antiwar demonstrators:

> A federal legal official relates an experience of Tuesday evening.
>
> I then walked one block north where I met a group of 12–15 policemen. I showed them my identification and they permitted me to walk with them. The police walked one block west. Numerous people were watching us from their windows and balconies. The police yelled profanities at them, taunting them to come down where the police would beat them up. The police stopped a number of people on the street demanding identification. They verbally abused each pedestrian and pushed one or two without hurting them. We walked back to Clark Street and began to walk north where the police stopped a number of people who appeared to be protesters and ordered them out of the area in a very abusive way. One protester who was walking in the opposite direction was kneed in the groin by a policeman who was walking towards him. The boy fell to the ground and swore at the policeman who picked him up and threw him to the ground. We continued to walk toward the command post. A derelict who appeared to be very intoxicated, walked up to the policeman and mumbled something that was incoherent. The policeman pulled from his belt a tin container and sprayed its contents into the eyes of the derelict, who stumbled around and fell on his face.[10]

This instance illustrates the convergence of evidence and strategy. The cited material is testimony (an eyewitness account) that provides a series of examples of police behavior. Because the eyewitness is described as "a federal legal official," his observations shift toward authority evidence rather than mere testimony: He may be competent to judge what is improper behavior, and his status gives his report greater credibility. But the descriptive details give this evidence its force. The police "yell," "taunt," "abuse," and "push." As described, the attack on the "boy" is wholly unprovoked, and because it is an attack on a *boy*, it is doubly offensive (note that the police officer's ability to pick him up and throw him to the ground lends credence to this label). The description gives us the sense of walking down the street with this group and watching what occurs. We come to see the events as the observer does and to judge them, unfavorably, with him. Such descriptions are particularly effective ways to induce readers to participate in creating the proofs by which they are persuaded.

Depiction is an intensified form of description. To represent in a picture or sculpture or to portray in detail is what depiction literally means. It is a particularly vivid form of description, and it usually involves dramatization, presenting material as a story, a drama of characters in conflict. If successful, it should create virtual experience. Woman suffragist Anna Howard Shaw used detailed examples in refuting arguments of anti-suffragists. In a speech delivered in New York in 1915, for instance, she responded to the argument that if women voted, it would cause conflict and destroy happy homes. She refuted this claim:

> Then they will tell you all the trouble that happens in the home. A gentleman told me that in California—and while he was talking I had a wonderful thing pass through my mind, because he said he and his wife had lived together for twenty years and never had a difference of opinion in the whole twenty years, and he was afraid if women began to vote that his wife would vote differently from him and then that beautiful harmony which they had had for twenty years would be broken, and all the time he was talking I could not help wondering which was the idiot—because I knew that no intelligent human beings could live together for twenty years and not have differences in opinion. All the time he was talking I looked at

that splendid type of manhood and thought, how would a man feel being tagged up by a little woman for twenty years saying, "me too, me too." I would not want to live in a house with a human being for twenty hours who agreed with everything I said. The stagnation of a frog pond would be hilarious compared to that. . . . Now it may be that the kind of men . . . that the anti-suffragists live with is that kind, but they are not the kind we live with and we could not do it. Great big overgrown babies! Cannot be disputed without having a row! While we do not believe that men are saints, by any means, we do believe that the average American man is a fairly good sort of fellow.[11]

The overall strategy is refutation of the argument that voting will cause friction between spouses. To do so, she tells the story in some detail of a particular man who raised this objection so her listeners can assess the objection in a particular case. This depiction is rather unusual because it also includes a description of what goes on in Shaw's mind as she listens to what he says, through which she invites us to join her in treating this objection as absurd, and she dramatizes that absurdity by imagining the wife going around after the husband saying, "me too, me too." The comments following the story are important because the depiction of this man is an effort to isolate him, to present him as a special case, quite unlike other men who can tolerate differences of opinion without starting a row. Isolating this man as unusual allows Shaw to help to create the audience of male agents of change that she must persuade in order to obtain the ballot for women. Consider how pleasing it likely was for men to see themselves as she describes them and how effective this must have been in creating a role that her male auditors would have been happy to play, a role that would make them more likely to support suffrage. She not only refutes but also debunks fears about political conflicts between spouses as unrealistic, which is more effective as the story she tells is real, not hypothetical. Note, too, that strategies often come in groups. Depiction here includes refutation, a figurative analogy ("the stagnation of a frog pond"), and an effort to create the audience—to invite them to see themselves in ways that are helpful to her purpose. The example also is a vivid case of Shaw's ability to use humor that debunked her opposition while making them laugh. Finally, this example is from a stenographic record of a stump speech, and the informal style and the small grammatical errors reflect its extemporaneous delivery and its orality.

The most famous example of depiction in rhetorical literature occurs in a speech by Senator Daniel Webster of Massachusetts given in reply to Senator Robert Y. Hayne of South Carolina in 1830. The crux of the debate was the issue of slavery and the power of the federal government to regulate it. Hayne advocated state nullification, that is, that states should have the right to strike down or "nullify" acts of the federal government, and Webster argued that this doctrine must inevitably lead to war. But Webster chose to make his case, not through logical argument, but through depicting what must happen if a state should nullify a federal law. He used the tariff law and nullification by South Carolina as his example:

> We will take the existing case of the tariff law. South Carolina is said to have made up her opinion upon it. . . . She will, we must suppose, pass a law of her legislature, declaring the several acts of Congress, usually called the tariff laws, null and void, so far as they respect South Carolina, or the citizens thereof. So far, all is a paper transaction, and easy enough.

(At this point, Webster has set the scene for his depiction.)

But the collector at Charleston is collecting the duties imposed by these tariff laws. He, therefore, must be stopped. The collector will seize the goods if the tariff duties are not paid. The State authorities will undertake their rescue, the marshal, with his posse, will come to the collector's aid, and here the contest begins.

(*The depiction includes a drama, and Webster prepares us for conflict.*)

The militia of the State will be called out to sustain the nullifying act. They will march, Sir, under a very gallant leader; for I believe the honorable member [Hayne] himself commands the militia of that part of the State. He will raise the nullifying act on his standard, and spread it out as his banner! It will have a preamble, setting forth, that the tariff laws are palpable, deliberate, and dangerous violations of the Constitution! He will proceed, with his banner flying, to the custom-house in Charleston,

All the while,
Sonorous metal blowing martial sounds.

Arrived at the custom-house, he will tell the collector that he must collect no more duties under any of the tariff laws. . . . But, Sir, the collector would not, probably, desist, at his bidding. He would show him the law of Congress, the treasury instruction, and his own oath of office. He would say, he should perform his duty, come what might.

Here would ensue a pause; for they say that a certain stillness precedes the tempest. The trumpeter would hold his breath awhile, and before all this military array should fall on the custom-house, collector, clerks, and all, it is very probable some of those composing it would request of their gallant commander-in-chief to be informed a little upon the point of law; for they have, doubtless, a just respect for his opinions as a lawyer, as well as for his bravery as a soldier. . . . They would inquire, whether it was not somewhat dangerous to resist a law of the United States. What would be the nature of their offence, they would wish to learn, if they, by military force and array, resisted the execution in Carolina of a law of the United States, and it should turn out, after all, that the law was constitutional? He would answer, of course, Treason. No lawyer could give any other answer. . . . How, then, they would ask, do you propose to defend us? We are not afraid of bullets, but treason has a way of taking people off that we do not much relish. How do you propose to defend us? "Look at my floating banner," he would reply; "see there the nullifying law!" Is it your opinion, gallant commander, they would then say, that, if we should be indicted for treason, that same floating banner of yours would make a good plea in bar? "South Carolina is a sovereign State," he would reply. That is true; but would the judge admit our plea? "These tariff laws," he would repeat, "are unconstitutional, palpably, deliberately, dangerously." That may all be so; but if the tribunal should not happen to be of that opinion, shall we swing for it? . . .

Mr. President, the honorable gentleman would be in dilemma, like that of another great general. He would have a knot before him which he could not untie. He must cut it with his sword. He must say to his followers, "Defend yourselves with your bayonets"; and this is war—civil war.[12]

This excerpt from Webster's speech is justly famous as an outstanding example of the depiction of a hypothetical encounter, and like many strategies, it combines animation and demonstration. As proof, it spells out the consequences of Hayne's position, but the proof depends on the plausibility of the scene for the listener. It is highly effective refutation that shows that, contrary to Hayne, state nullification means civil war. The humor of the depiction debunks Hayne's position, reduces it to absurdity. Webster also uses an allusion to the story of Alexander the Great cutting the Gordian knot as a figurative analogy to illustrate that Hayne's position must end in violence. Webster's depiction is structured as a drama. He sets the scene, presents characters, sets forth the conflict, presents the dialogue between Hayne and his militia, and even provides the theatrical spectacle of banners and trumpets. The conflict within the doctrine, dramatized in the dialogue, escalates to a climax, which is followed by a denouement that draws his conclusion: "This is war—civil war."

The detail Webster provides is worth noting. The marshal and his posse, supporting the federal customs collector, confront Hayne and the state militia. The acts of the collector are detailed. The dialogue between Hayne and the militiamen spells out the internal contradiction in Hayne's position.

Webster might easily have chosen to set forth these consequences in a logical argument, but depicting this scene animated his claim, a process that was essential if civil war was to be averted at this time. He attempted to create virtual experience, to allow his audience to imagine a scene in all its detail, so they would perceive, in human terms, the results of Hayne's stance.

Personification and Visualization. Closely allied to description and depiction are the strategies of personification and visualization. Personification treats an object or an abstract idea as if it were a human being or had human capacities. Advertisers personify products as characters or cartoon figures, such as the Energizer Bunny or the Geico Gecko. The longevity of a battery or the value of insurance cannot be seen or experienced directly, so the bunny and the gecko are intended to represent those qualities. Even a highly successful computer advertisement personifies its product by pitting a young, brash computer geek (the Macintosh) against a stressed and frumpy corporate man (the PC). The strategy of personification attempts to compensate for the lack of attachment we feel toward inanimate products. Visualization puts an idea into visual form. A long-running series of commercials showed someone drinking a glass of iced tea and then falling backward into a swimming pool. The ad visualized how refreshed and cool you would feel after a sip of iced tea.

Enactment. When there is enactment, the speaker or writer is proof of the claim that she or he is making. Enactment is both proof and a way to present evidence vividly. For example, Representative Barbara Jordan gave the keynote address at the Democratic National Convention in 1976. In her speech she said, "And I feel that, notwithstanding the past, my presence here is one additional piece of evidence that the American dream need not forever be deferred."[13] That she, an African American woman, had achieved the stature to be asked to give the address was proof that minorities and women can reach the highest levels of achievement in the United States. A similar move was made by Geraldine Ferraro in her vice presidential nomination acceptance address for the Democratic ticket in 1988, and in Ruth Bader Ginsburg's 1993 speech accepting nomination to be an associate justice of the Supreme Court. By the time Sonia Sotomayor won a contentious nomination to be the first Hispanic associate justice on the Supreme Court sixteen years later, she was forced to back away from enactment strategies she had used in confirmation appointments for lesser judgeship appointments. Barack Obama, on the other hand, exercised enactment in his keynote address to the 2004 Democratic National Convention, and again in both his first and second Inaugural speeches, reminding us in 2013, for instance, that "what binds this nation together is not the colors of our skin or the tenets of our faith or the origins of our names." Enactment is powerful evidence because members of the audience directly see and hear the evidence for themselves. The references to the mob outside in Angelina Grimké's 1838 speech (the rhetorical act you will analyze in the next chapter) are additional examples. This form of proof is particularly vivid—it is alive in front of and around the audience! Examine the way in which enactment works in the Frederick Douglass speech in the Material for Analysis section later in this chapter.

Alliteration. Alliteration is the repetition of initial consonants, a strategy advertisements and speech writers use effectively. One of the most memorable alliterative phrases in history was uttered in 1969 by Vice President Spiro Agnew, Nixon's embattled vice president at the height of the deep divisiveness in the country over the Vietnam War. He derisively referred to those who opposed the war, including the media, as "nattering nabobs of negativism."[14] One of the most memorable and provocative lines of President Obama's second Inaugural was alliterative. In making the case that gay rights deserved the same attention as civil rights and women's rights, Obama cleverly referred to the defining places of each movement that began with the letter "s." He said: "We the people declare today that the most evident of truth that all of us are created equal is the star that guides us still; just as it guided our forebears through Seneca Falls and Selma and Stonewall"[15]

Assonance. Assonance is the repetition of a vowel sound, and it produces a kind of rhyme. In his inaugural address, for example, John F. Kennedy spoke of "the steady spread of the deadly atom." The repetition made the phrase memorable and the creeping vowel seemed to mirror the creeping danger.

Rhymes. Although they are a staple of children's literature and many genres of music, rhymes occur less frequently in both oral and written rhetoric. Interestingly, the highly rhetorical rap form not only trades in rhyme but often appropriates nursery rhymes (as examples consider how London Bridge and Do Your Ears Hang Low have been used). Or consider the lyrics to Pink's "Stupid Girls":

Where, oh where have the smart people gone?
Oh where, oh where could they be?[16]

Rhymes are also common in advertising as slogans. A slogan is a verbal logo, another way to establish a brand. So, for example, a brand of British snacks is advertised this way: "The flavour of a Quaver is never known to waver." A travel agency says, "Don't just book it, Thomas Cook it," and as a traveler, you are invited to "Savour the flavour of Belgium." Such rhymes not only make products come alive, but they also attempt to influence audience attitudes.

Parallelism. Parallelism is a strategy that creates rhythm in prose. It can also enhance the precision of language and create an impression that the rhetor thinks in a very orderly fashion. Perhaps the most famous example is the repeated "I Have a Dream" in Dr. Martin Luther King Jr.'s famous speech of that name. Like King's speech, it may take the form of a series of sentences or paragraphs, all of which begin or end with the same phrase. In Obama's second inaugural, clearly crafted with the echoes of King's "I Have a Dream Speech" in mind, Obama repeats "we, the people" five times and "together" is coupled with action words seven times: "Together, we determined... Together, we discovered... Together we resolved...."[17] Such parallelism creates easy-to-follow patterns, and such patterns help fix ideas in our minds. They are particularly well suited to oral rhetoric and epideictic occasions, a form of speech that will be examined carefully in Chapter 14.

Parallelism can also create contrast and emphasis. *Antithesis* is a kind of parallelism that contrasts one idea with another. Two examples in contemporary speeches have proved particularly memorable. In 1960 John F. Kennedy said, "Ask not what your country can do for you: Ask what you can do for your country." In 1964 Barry Goldwater accepted the Republican nomination for the presidency and said, "I would remind you that extremism in the defense of liberty is no vice! And let me remind you also that moderation in the pursuit of justice is no virtue!" Republican strategist William Kristol rang a change on this in 1994 when he said of health care reform, "we should make clear now that there will be no deal. 'Obstructionism,' when it comes to protecting our health care system, is no vice."[18] As these examples illustrate, rhetoric builds on prior rhetoric, and the memorable antithesis remains a resource. Antitheses juxtapose two ideas, and the contrast aptly defines the speaker's position and animates it with emphasis.

Climax constructions are also a form of parallelism. In a climax construction, repetition builds to a high point of excitement or tension, a *climax*. The conclusion of the last speech of Dr. Martin Luther King Jr. discussed in Chapter 2, is an excellent example.

Finally, recall that parallelism also appears in patterns of organization. Ideally, main points in an essay or speech will be stated in parallel form so that major ideas will stand out for the reader or listener. Once again, these are only some of the strategies that can be used to make ideas vivid.

Language Strategies to Change Connotations

The strategies described in this section are directed at our attitudes. They are attempts to change associations so that we will feel more positive or negative toward an idea or position. Successful rhetorical action changes verbal behavior. Our speech reflects our perceptions, understandings, and attitudes, and if these change, our speech will change. But the reverse is also true: If we change the way we talk, changes in perception and attitude will follow. Consider, for example, the impact of calling taxes on the estates of wealthy people (currently $4 million can be sheltered from such taxes by a married couple) a "death tax"!

The claim that changes in the way we talk will produce changes in perception and attitude is controversial, but the protest movements of African Americans and Chicanos (or Latinos or Hispanics or *La Raza*) illustrate the power of a name change to mobilize a social movement.[19] The argument is at the heart of disputes over whether or not the pronoun "he" or the word "man" can function generically to include both men and women. Feminists present examples to show that they cannot, as in "Man, being a mammal, breast-feeds his young." Or "All men are mortal; Sophie is a man; therefore, Sophie is mortal." They also argue that shifts in words, such as the use of chair or chairperson, and in pronouns, "s/he" or "he and she," raise consciousness about the sexism of our society.[20] Rather than use he and she, our copyeditor has chosen to alternate these pronouns. In all these cases, all the parties involved behave as if the words we use are very, very important.

Labeling. The commonest strategy used to alter attitudes is labeling, which is often related to debunking. A label is a name or epithet chosen to characterize a person, idea, or thing. "Climate change" sounds less threatening than "global warming"; "undocumented workers" is softer than "illegal aliens." The extremes of the political spectrum have been labeled "bleeding heart liberals" versus "Right-wing wackos." As the examples illustrate, such labels work by creating associations.

At the beginning of the woman's rights movement in the nineteenth century, women activists were told that if they spoke in public, they would be "unsexed"; that is, they would lose their femininity. In the 1960s, at the beginning of the second wave of the women's movement, women activists were called lesbians or dykes, once again implying that women who sought to improve their status were not feminine, not real women. These are powerful attacks because success for women has long been defined as attracting a male and marrying, which presumably places a high value on traditional femininity. Note that even contemporary advertisements showing women in settings outside the home continue to reinforce the beauty myth by presenting women as sex objects and showing women primarily as mothers, which reinforces traditional concepts of femininity.[21] Accordingly, being attacked as unfeminine is a strong deterrent to feminist identification and activism.

Slogans. Labels expanded become slogans. They are highly effective because they condense into a single phrase or sentence a whole world of beliefs and feelings. This power to sum up is illustrated in enduring phrases such as "the American dream," "the personal is political," and "rugged individualism" and in more contemporary expressions such as "Support the Troops" and "One Nation Under Surveillance." They are powerful unifiers because, although individuals have their own ideas of just what they mean, the level of abstraction is such that disputes over meaning are avoided. Because of their broad appeal, they are especially attractive to advertisers and politicians who seek to reach the widest possible audiences. An effective slogan draws together a whole world of ideas in a short, cleverly expressed phrase or sentence. Advertisers seek such catchphrases: "Just Do It." "You're in good hands with Allstate." "Nothing runs like a Deere." Every political campaign manager tries to find such a slogan, because, as noted earlier, a short, memorable phrase can sum up many associations and evoke strong reactions.

Metaphors. Many labels and slogans also are metaphors. Figurative language not only makes ideas vivid but changes our attitudes toward them, and it clarifies meaning. A particularly famous example comes from the speech Booker T. Washington made at the Atlanta Exposition in 1895. Washington, an African American, tried to allay the hostility of racist whites while urging them to support the economic and educational development of his people. The metaphor he used illustrates how metaphors can clarify, vivify, and change connotations. He said, "In all things that are purely social we can be as separate as the fingers, yet one as the hand in all things essential to mutual progress."[22]

In his famous "I Have a Dream" speech of 1963, Dr. Martin Luther King Jr. translated the issues of civil rights into terms every listener could understand. He said, "In a sense we have come to our nation's Capitol to cash a check. When the architects of our republic wrote the magnificent words of the Constitution and the Declaration of Independence, they were signing a promissory note to which every American was to fall heir. . . . Instead of honoring this sacred obligation, America has given the Negro people a bad check; a check which has come back marked 'insufficient funds.' But we refuse to believe that the bank of justice is bankrupt."[23] The idea of civil rights is abstract, and many statements about it were not known and familiar. The imagery King used made the abstract concrete and familiar, yet the metaphor was original, making his appeal fresh and vivid. Elizabeth Cady Stanton's speech, "The Solitude of Self" (a rhetorical act you will analyze in Chapter 9), is an extended illustration of the use of *metonymy*, a trope that finds a physical counterpart for abstract notions, such as a heart for the idea of love, as in "I © New York."

Allusion. Closely related to metaphors are allusions to items from our shared cultural knowledge, such as references to history, the Bible, Greek and Roman mythology, Shakespeare's plays or other works of literature, or to elements of popular culture such as television programs, films, comic books, national advertising, or images on YouTube.

When he was running for the governorship of Minnesota in 1998, Jesse Ventura needed to counter the charge that he was unprepared for that office. He had not completed college, and his résumé consisted chiefly of his experiences as a professional wrestler and a talk show host on a local radio station. Bill Hillsman, an advertising genius, prepared an ad that showed a flesh-colored Jesse Ventura in the position of Rodin's famous sculpture, *The Thinker*, which is among the most familiar sculptures in existence. Against the sound of classical music, and introduced by large classical lettering of "THE BODY," the voice-over recited Ventura's personal history as a Navy SEAL, union member, volunteer high school football coach, outdoorsman, husband of twenty-three years, and father of two children. As the camera panned to the statue and focused on Jesse Ventura's face, the letters "THE MIND" appeared, and the voice-over indicated his positions: "A man who will fight to return Minnesota's budget surplus to the taxpayers. A man who will fight to lower property and income taxes. A man who does not accept money from special interest groups. A man who will work to improve public schools by reducing class sizes." At this point, the camera zoomed back to show us the entire statue with the words "Jesse Ventura Our Next Governor" superimposed on it. At that point, the camera zoomed in on Ventura's face, and he smiled and winked.

The ad exploits the ambiguity of Rodin's statue, which presents a beautiful male body in a position of deep thought. It subtly counteracts voters' tendency to think of Ventura solely as a body, a wrestler, and writes a different meaning on his past by listing facts about his life (note that it omits his history as a wrestler). Then, exploiting the statue as an expression of intellectual effort, the ad presents the positions Ventura presumably has arrived at after thoughtful deliberation. The end of the ad—the smile and the wink—invites us not to take all this too seriously while encouraging us in a warm and charming way to participate in the ad and reject efforts by opposing candidates to suggest that Ventura is unqualified.

Much of this process is nondiscursive. Our familiarity with Rodin's statue means that we already have its dual meaning in our mind, which makes it easy to extend it to candidate Ventura. The ad is also discursive, providing basic information about Ventura and about his positions. Visually and musically, the ad is high-brow—a famous sculpture viewed against the sound of classical music. The ending counteracts that quality with the smile and the wink, letting us all know that Jesse is a regular guy. Consider how much more effective this rebuttal is compared to an ad that provided this information without this ad's metaphorical and visual appeal.

Biblical materials are also common sources of allusion. Such materials are frequently used to demonstrate that God is on our side or we are doing God's will. In defending U.S. involvement in Vietnam, for example, Richard Nixon said, "Let historians not record that when America was the most powerful nation in the world we passed on the other side of the road and allowed the last hopes for peace and freedom of millions of people on this earth to be suffocated by the forces of totalitarianism,"[24] language also used by George W. Bush in his first inaugural address. The allusion is to the story of the Good Samaritan, and as used by Nixon, it was intended to convince us that in Vietnam we were behaving as good neighbors.

Allusions can be used to perform acts that would not be acceptable to an audience if they were done directly and explicitly. Most audiences, for example, do not take kindly to being threatened. Yet in what is surely one of the most controversial of all Fourth of July addresses, on July 5, 1852, the African American abolitionist orator Frederick Douglass used the story of Samson in Judges 16:23–30 to confront his audience:

> The Fourth of July is yours, not mine. You may rejoice, I must mourn. To drag a man in fetters into the grand illuminated temple of liberty, and call upon him to join you in joyous anthems, were inhuman mockery and sacrilegious irony. Do you mean, citizens, to mock me by asking me to speak today? If so, there is a parallel to your conduct. And let me warn you that it is dangerous to copy the example of a nation whose crimes, towering up to heaven, were thrown down by the breath of the Almighty, burying that nation in irrevocable ruin![25]

If you know the story of Samson (stripped of his prodigious strength by the cutting of his hair, captured by the Philistines, blinded, taken to Gaza, brought to the temple for sport on the feast day of their god Dagon, praying for strength, pulling down the temple, and killing more Philistines in death than he had in life), there are powerful parallels between it and the situation of Frederick Douglass on July 5, 1852. If you do not know the story, you may not recognize the allusion, much less feel its impact. Allusions work only if the audience recognizes them and can fill in the necessary details. Thus, Biblical allusions are powerful, if the audience recognizes them, because our culture is Judeo-Christian, and many Americans accept the Bible as the word of God. For contemporary readers who may not be familiar with stories from the Old Testament, that is only half the problem. To appreciate the parallels one must know biographical facts about Douglass (an escaped former slave speaking in Rochester, New York, at a time when slavery was still a fact in much of the country). These problems illustrate the limitations of allusions. In essence, they function like *enthymemes*, which depend for their impact on knowledge in the minds of the audience.

Identification. Finally, the strategy of identification uses language to create positive associations between the rhetor and the audience; it suggests shared experience or common viewpoints. Speakers and writers traditionally identify ties of kinship, shared beliefs, and common experience as ways to create bonds between themselves and the audience.

Barack Obama was the keynote speaker at the 2004 Democratic National Convention. This is how he began his speech:

> Tonight is a particular honor for me because, let's face it, my presence on this stage is pretty unlikely. My father was a foreign student, born and raised in a small village in Kenya. He grew up herding goats, went to school in a tin-roof shack. His father—my grandfather—was a cook, a domestic servant to the British.
>
> But my grandfather had larger dreams for his son. Through hard work and perseverance my father got a scholarship to study in a magical place, America, that shone as a beacon of freedom and opportunity to so many who had come before.
>
> While studying here, my father met my mother. She was born in a town on the other side of the world, in Kansas. Her father worked on oil rigs and farms through most of the Depression. The day after Pearl Harbor my grandfather signed up for duty; joined Patton's army, marched across Europe. Back home, my grandmother raised a baby and went to work on a bomber assembly line. After the war, they studied on the G.I. Bill, bought a house through F.H.A., and later moved west all the way to Hawaii in search of opportunity.
>
> And they, too, had big dreams for their daughter. A common dream, born of two continents.
>
> My parents shared not only an improbable love, they shared an abiding faith in the possibilities of this nation. They would give me an African name, Barack, or "blessed," believing that in a tolerant America your name is no barrier to success. They imagined—They imagined me going to the best schools in the land, even though they weren't rich, because in a generous America you don't have to be rich to achieve your potential.

Although he begins by describing differences, based on his Kenyan father, Obama creates identification through shared values. His grandfather, like so many Americans, had a dream for his son, and he saw this nation as a place of opportunity in which that dream could be realized. Like many Americans, his grandparents and parents were poor and worked at unskilled jobs; his grandfather fought for the United States in World War II and followed the paths of many veterans. His parents, too, believed in the possibilities of this country. His name "Barack," which changes its connotations when we know that it means "blessed," also is a badge, not of difference, but of faith in equal opportunity. In what ways is this speech an example of the strategy of enactment? How are difference and identification linked in this speech?

Figure 7–2 captures many of the language strategies discussed in this chapter. Pay particular attention to the function and example used to illustrate each. Use it as a handy resource in constructing your own rhetorical acts.

These are some of the strategies available for rhetorical action. Strategies are techniques that use language to prove, vivify, and alter attitudes. Each of these functions is a central element in rhetoric. Strategies provide important resources for rhetors to overcome obstacles in a rhetorical situation.

Figure 7–2
Language Strategies

Name	Function	Example
Metaphor	Creates an image by comparing two dissimilar things that share certain properties.	Columnist Ellen Goodman characterizes cell phones as "the boom boxes of the 90's," as "a status symbol on a par with the S.U.V.," and as "promoting a verbal gated community."
Metonymy	Idea evoked or named by means of a term designating some associated notion, often more concrete.	Referring to royal authority as "the sceptre" or to military action as "the sword," or the heart in "I © NY."
Onomatopoeia	The tendency in certain words to imitate by their very sound the actions they symbolize.	Words such as buzz, hiss, bump, meow, trudge. Budweiser ad: "Waaas Uuuuuup?"
Parallelism	The use of the same initial wording in a sequence of statements or phrases to add emphasis, order, and climax to an idea.	Martin Luther King Jr.: "If I had sneezed... If I had sneezed... If I had sneezed."
Antithesis	The succinct juxtaposition of opposing expressions to make an idea more memorable, distinctive, and sloganistic.	President John F. Kennedy said in his inaugural address: "Ask not what your country can do for you, but what you can do for your country."
Rhyme	Repetition of the final vowel and consonant sound of words to imprint a key message of your speech either for emphasis or as a mnemonic device to help your audience remember important points.	Johnny Cochran, defense attorney in the O. J. Simpson trial, reminded jurors: "If it doesn't fit, you must acquit."
Depiction	Choose highly descriptive, sensory words to catch the interest of your audience.	Frederick Douglass in "What to the Slave Is the 4th of July," says: "O! Had I the ability, and could I reach the nation's ear, I would, to-day, pour out a fiery stream of biting ridicule, blasting reproach, withering sarcasm, and stern rebuke. For it is not light that is needed, but fire; it is not the gentle shower, but thunder. We need the storm, the whirlwind, and the earthquake."
Personification	A representation or abstraction of an inanimate object or idea that is endowed with personal or human qualities.	The Energizer Bunny, Scrubbing Bubbles, Mr. Clean.
Alliteration	Repeat the initial consonant sounds in words to capture attention and to make clever slogans.	Spiro Agnew's referring to the press as: "nattering nabobs of negativism."
Slogan	Wise, compact sayings that summarize the beliefs of a people.	Susan B. Anthony: "Resistance to tyranny is obedience to God." Nike ad: "Just Do It." Causes: "It's a life, not a choice." "Think Globally, Act Locally."
Allusion	Indirect references to our shared cultural knowledge, such as the Bible, Greek and Roman mythology, or our history.	To defend U.S. involvement in Vietnam, Richard Nixon said: "Let historians not record that when America was the most powerful nation in the world we passed on the other side of the road and allowed the last hopes for peace and freedom of millions of people on this earth to be suffocated by the forces of totalitarianism."
Identification	Use of language to create perceived similarity between rhetor and audience; includes humor, stroking, and appeal to shared values.	Barack Obama: "My parents shared...an abiding faith in the possibilities of this nation. They would give me an African name, Barack, or 'blessed,' believing that in tolerant America your name is no barrier to success. They imagined me going to the best of schools in the land, even though they weren't rich, because in a generous America you don't have to be rich to achieve your potential."
Labeling	A name or epithet chosen to characterize a person or thing.	"Climate change" is preferred to "global warming" by many "conservatives." "Undocumented workers" is preferred to "illegal aliens" by many "liberals." The gaming industry has tapped our capitalistic spirit in their "Say, yes, to local control" campaign to expand casinos.

MATERIAL FOR ANALYSIS I

In 1852 the Rochester, New York, Ladies Anti-Slavery Society invited one of the city's most famous residents, Frederick Douglass, a former slave, to deliver the Fourth of July oration. Douglass accepted, and on July 5, 1852, (July 4 was a Sunday that year) he delivered one of the most memorable antislavery discourses in U.S. history. The speech illustrates vividly the ways in which the speaker responded to the rhetorical problem and used all of the resources available to him, including all of the resources of language. Following is an excerpt from that speech.

What to the Slave Is the Fourth of July?

by Frederick Douglass[26]

1   FELLOW-CITIZENS—Pardon me, allow me to ask, why am I called upon to speak here to-day? What have I, or those I represent, to do with your national independence? Are the great principles of political freedom and of natural justice, embodied in that Declaration of Independence, extended to us? and am I, therefore, called upon to bring our humble offering to the national altar, and to confess the benefits and express devout gratitude for the blessings resulting from your independence to us?

2   Would to God, both for your sakes and ours, that an affirmative answer could be truthfully returned to these questions! Then would my task be light, and my burden easy and delightful. For who is there so cold, that a nation's sympathy could not warm him? Who so obdurate and dead to the claims of gratitude, that would not thankfully acknowledge such priceless benefits? Who so stolid and selfish, that would not give his voice to swell the hallelujahs of a nation's jubilee, when the chains of servitude had been torn from his limbs? I am not that man. In a case like that, the dumb might eloquently speak, and the "lame man leap as an hart." [Isaiah 35:6]

3   But such is not the state of the case. I say it with a sad sense of the disparity between us. I am not included within the pale of this glorious anniversary! Your high independence only reveals the immeasurable distance between us. The blessings in which you, this day, rejoice, are not enjoyed in common. The rich inheritance of justice, liberty, prosperity and independence, bequeathed by your fathers, is shared by you, not by me. The sunlight that brought light and healing to you, has brought stripes and death to me. This Fourth of July is yours, not mine. You may rejoice, I must mourn. To drag a man in fetters into the grand illuminated temple of liberty and call upon him to join you in joyous anthems, were inhuman mockery and sacrilegious irony. Do you mean, citizens, to mock me, by asking me to speak today? If so, there is a parallel to your conduct. And let me warn you that it is dangerous to copy the example of a nation whose crimes, towering up to heaven, were thrown down by the breath of the Almighty, burying that nation in irrevocable ruin! I can to-day take up the plaintive lament of a peeled[27] and woe-smitten people!

4   By the rivers of Babylon, there we sat down. Yea! We wept when we remembered Zion. We hanged our harps upon the willows in the midst thereof. For there, they that carried us away captive, required of us a song; and they who wasted us required of us mirth, saying, Sing us one of the songs of Zion. How can we sing the Lord's song in a strange land? If I forget thee, O Jerusalem, let my right hand forget her cunning. If I do not remember thee, let my tongue cleave to the roof of my mouth. [Psalm 137:1–6]

5   Fellow-citizens, above your national, tumultuous joy, I hear the mournful wail of millions! Whose chains, heavy and grievous yesterday, are, to-day, rendered more intolerable by the jubilee shouts that reach them. If I do forget, if I do not faithfully remember those bleeding children of sorrow this day, "may my right hand forget her cunning, and may my tongue cleave to the roof of my mouth!" To forget them, to pass lightly over their wrongs, and to chime in with the popular theme, would be treason most scandalous and shocking, and would make me a reproach before God and the world. My subject, then, fellow-citizens, is AMERICAN SLAVERY. I shall see this day and its popular characteristics from the slave's point of view. Standing there identified with the American bondman, making his wrongs mine. I do not hesitate to declare, with all my soul, that the character and conduct of this nation never looked blacker to me than on this 4th of July! Whether we turn to the declaration of the past, or to the professions of the present, the conduct of the nation seems equally hideous and revolting. America is false to the past, false to the present, and solemnly binds herself to be false to the future. Standing with God and the crushed and bleeding slave on this occasion, I will, in the name of humanity which is outraged, in the name of liberty which is fettered, in the name of the Constitution and the Bible, which are disregarded and trampled upon, dare to call in question and to denounce, with all the emphasis I can command, everything that serves to perpetuate slavery— the great sin and shame of America! "I will not equivocate; I will not excuse"; I will use the severest language I can command; and yet not one word shall escape me that any man, whose judgment is not blinded by prejudice, or who is not at heart a slaveholder, shall not confess to be right and just.

6   But I fancy I hear some one of my audience say, "It is just in this circumstance that you and your brother abolitionists fail to make a favorable impression on the public mind. Would you argue more, and denounce less; would you persuade more, and rebuke less; your cause would be much more likely to succeed." But I submit, where all is plain there is nothing to be argued. What point in the anti-slavery creed would you have me argue? On what branch of the subject do the people of this country need light? Must I undertake to prove that the slave is a man? That point is conceded already. Nobody doubts it. The slaveholders themselves acknowledge it in the enactment of laws for their government. They acknowledge it when they punish disobedience on the part of the slave. There are seventy-two crimes in the State of Virginia which, if committed by a black man (no matter how ignorant he be), subject him to the punishment of death; while only two of the same crimes will subject a white man to the like punishment. What is this but the acknowledgment that the slave is a moral, intellectual, and responsible being? The manhood of the slave is conceded. It is admitted in the fact that southern statute books are covered with enactments forbidding, under severe fines and penalties, the teaching of the slave to read or to write. When you can point to any such laws in reference to the beast of the

field, then I may consent to argue the manhood of the slave. When the dogs in your streets, when the fowls of the air, when the cattle on your hills, when the fish of the sea, and the reptiles that crawl, shall be unable to distinguish the slave from a brute, then will I argue with you that the slave is a man!

7   For the present, it is enough to affirm the equal manhood of the Negro race. Is it not astonishing that, while we are ploughing, planting, and reaping, using all kinds of mechanical tools, erecting houses, constructing bridges, building ships, working in metals of brass, iron, copper, silver, and gold; that, while we are reading, writing and ciphering, acting as clerks, merchants and secretaries, having among us lawyers, doctors, ministers, poets, authors, editors, orators and teachers; that, while we are engaged in all manner of enterprises common to other men, digging gold in California, capturing the whale in the Pacific, feeding sheep and cattle on the hill side, living, moving, acting, thinking, planning, living in families as husbands, wives and children, and, above all, confessing and worshiping the Christian's God, and looking hopefully for life and immortality beyond the grave, we are called upon to prove that we are men!

8   Would you have me argue that man is entitled to liberty? That he is the rightful owner of his own body? You have already declared it. Must I argue the wrongfulness of slavery? Is that a question for republicans? Is it to be settled by the rules of logic and argumentation, as a matter beset with great difficulty, involving a doubtful application of the principle of justice, hard to be understood? How should I look to-day, in the presence of Americans, dividing, and subdividing a discourse, to show that men have a natural right to freedom? Speaking of it relatively and positively, negatively and affirmatively. To do so, would be to make myself ridiculous, and to offer an insult to your understanding. There is not a man beneath the canopy of heaven that does not know that slavery is wrong *for him*.

9   What, am I to argue that it is wrong to make men brutes, to rob them of their liberty, to work them without wages, to keep them ignorant of their relations to their fellow men, to beat them with sticks, to flay their flesh with the lash, to load their limbs with irons, to hunt them with dogs, to sell them at auction, to sunder their families, to knock out their teeth, to burn their flesh, to starve them into obedience and submission to their masters? Must I argue that a system thus marked with blood, and stained with pollution, is wrong? No! I will not. I have better employment for my time and strength than such arguments would imply.

10   What, then, remains to be argued? Is it that slavery is not divine; that God did not establish it; that our doctors of divinity are mistaken? There is blasphemy in the thought. That which is inhuman, cannot be divine! Who can reason on such a proposition? They that can, may; I cannot. The time for such argument is passed.

11   At a time like this, scorching irony, not convincing argument, is needed. O! Had I the ability, and could I reach the nation's ear, I would, to-day, pour out a fiery stream of biting ridicule, blasting reproach, withering sarcasm, and stern rebuke. For it is not light that is needed, but fire; it is not the gentle shower, but thunder. We need the storm, the whirlwind, and the earthquake. The feeling of the nation must be

quickened; the conscience of the nation must be roused; the propriety of the nation must be startled; the hypocrisy of the nation must be exposed; and its crimes against God and man must be proclaimed and denounced.

12   What, to the American slave, is your 4th of July? I answer; a day that reveals to him, more than all other days in the year, the gross injustice and cruelty to which he is the constant victim. To him, your celebration is a sham; your boasted liberty, an unholy license; your national greatness, swelling vanity; your sounds of rejoicing are empty and heartless; your denunciation of tyrants, brass fronted impudence; your shouts of liberty and equality, hollow mockery; your prayers and hymns, your sermons and thanksgivings, with all your religious parade and solemnity, are to Him, mere bombast, fraud, deception, impiety, and hypocrisy—a thin veil to cover up crimes which would disgrace a nation of savages. There is not a nation on the earth guilty of practices more shocking and bloody than are the people of the United States, at this very hour.

13   Go where you may, search where you will, roam through all the monarchies and despotisms of the Old World, travel through South America, search out every abuse, and when you have found the last, lay your facts by the side of the everyday practices of this nation, and you will say with me, that, for revolting barbarity and shameless hypocrisy, America reigns without a rival.

Questions for Analysis

1. What language strategies do you see in this speech? How do they contribute to tone? Persona?
2. What is the structure of this speech? What kinds of arguments are embedded in the structure?
3. A Fourth of July speech is designed to venerate the nation, its heroes; it is designed to be uplifting, inspiring, and patriotic. Why does Douglass violate these expectations? What purpose is he trying to achieve?
4. How does the speech indicate the author's awareness of the rhetorical obstacles that he faces? (For a detailed discussion of obstacles, see Chapters 8, 9, and 10.)
5. Identify an important enthymeme in the speech.

 MATERIAL FOR ANALYSIS II

A One-Word Assault on Women

by Donna Britt[28]

1   A few years ago I saw a black teenage girl with a delicate necklace clasped around her throat. I've forgotten her features but remember what sparkled in rhinestones around her neck:

2 "BITCH BITCH BITCH"

3 My immediate reaction was to weigh how offensive it would be to approach this child with one obvious question: "Why are you wearing that?"

4 I never asked. But the necklace proved something I'd doubted: There really are women who want to be identified as female dogs by all who encounter them—which is good news for the rappers, rockers, and regular guys who call all women by that epithet.

5 Frankly, some women refer to each other that way. On a recent 60 *Minutes*, a female lawyer mouthed the word to describe a female judge she disliked.

6 Still, most women hate being called that. One widely publicized proof: the reaction of female journalists last summer to rapper Bushwick Bill's defense of his use of the B-word at a national African American journalists' convention.

7 Maybe you read about it. One of several hiphoppers on a music panel, Bill—a dwarf who supposedly lost his eye in a gunfight with a girlfriend—was asked by a woman why he and other rappers routinely call women "bitches" and "ho's" (whores) in their music.

8 Not all women qualify, Bill said. He'd never describe his mother that way, he continued, because he isn't having sex with her. But, he told the woman, "if I was [having sex with] you, you'd be a ho."

9 Hmmmmmmmmm.

10 I see why dozens of incensed women stalked out, why several columnists deplored Bill's comments. Yet months later—in the midst of a national debate over the violent words and images characteristic of a small segment of rap music known as "gangsta" rap—the whole thing still makes me sad. Why? Because it makes too much sense.

11 It makes sense that a less-than-handsome young man who lost half his sight tussling with a woman—and who now, if he's like other rich male celebrities, combs groupies out of his hair—would be contemptuous of all women.

12 It's also undeniable that almost every name-calling rap or rock video is decorated with the bodies of hip-grinding young women. Even the faintest promise of fame remains as much an incentive for girls to strip for the camera as it was 40 years ago, when young starlet Marilyn Monroe posed nude.

13 Years later, Monroe said she posed only for the money, because "she was hungry."

14 But what is it that the name-calling male performers are hungering for? While contempt for women isn't new, entertainers' constant, public use of "bitch," aired on radio and TV, is.

15   Perhaps it's a genuine expression of increased male resentment or of certain singers' willingness to disrespect women in hopes of stirring controversy—and increasing record sales.

16   Are young performers reflecting a harsh world's reality? Or is real life—as in innocent kids parroting epithet-laden songs—reflecting the performers' influence?

17   Some rappers say they're just being honest. They say nice women—those who are neither sluts nor skeezers (women who use men for money)—should take no offense to names that don't apply to them. They're just dissing the women who deserve it.

18   Cool. So that means these same brothers would make allowances for a white politician who was revealed to routinely call black folks "niggers" if he only explained, "I use that term only in reference to black people who kill others, you know, criminals. The rest of you—take no offense."

19   The worst thing about the B-word—and the N-word and every denigrating term—is what is assumes. It assumes that everybody—all women, all black men, all members of any group—are alike. The brother who disses all women because of the actions of some is as unenlightened as the racist who denies all black people's humanity because some black acts inhumanely.

20   But I keep going back to Bill—who later apologized to the group for "being myself."

21   It's no accident that the most negative feelings the rapper revealed weren't directed at women, but at himself: Only a man with a twisted self-concept would assume that any woman who'd have sex with him should require payment.

22   But maybe, like so much else, it all boils down to money. The fellas who make millions singing their contempt for women—and who at the same time pride themselves for slamming racism in their music—are actually in the business of selling racism's most destructive lies. Singers who wave their Glocks, grab their crotches, and dis their women—while thousands of us pay to watch and listen—do more than make themselves and record producers rich.

23   Too often they tell the world—and the young whites who reportedly are gangsta rap's biggest consumers—what morgues overflowing with the bodies of black men suggest: how deeply some African Americans have internalized the racism they deplore.

24   The messages many are selling to—and about—blacks:

25   You don't deserve to live. Your women are sluts and animals. You kill without remorse, and copulate without love or responsibility.

26   Sure, that's all a lie. But slap a beat on it, apply a coat of glamour, and someone, somewhere will dance to it.

27   Or clasp it in rhinestones around her neck.

Questions for Analysis

1. Consider how the author uses examples to invite readers to participate in drawing conclusions.
2. In what ways are Britt's reactions unexpected? Consider the ways that such moves create mystery that keeps you interested.
3. How does Britt link the use of derogatory terms to economic conditions such that young women are prompted to "sell out" to make money?
4. How does Britt use comparison as a basis for criticizing the derogatory terms applied to women?
5. Britt suggests many reasons that rappers and hip-hoppers or women might use such derogatory terms. Which does she suggest is likely? Why might this reversal have an impact on attitudes?
6. How does Britt's persona as an African American columnist for the *Washington Post* allow her to use "in your face" language in ways that are less likely to offend readers?
7. Identify what language strategies you see in this speech? How do they contribute to tone?

EXERCISES

Critical Thinking Exercises

1. Fill-in-the-blank exercise. Choose the correct language strategy (as illustrated in chapter readings) for each sentence below.

   a. "America: Love It or Leave It"; "Just Do It"; "Question Authority"; "Have you hugged your kids today?" "Shit Happens." What type of language strategy are these examples of? _____

   b. "Ask not what your country can do for you, but what you can do for your country" (John F. Kennedy) is an example of what language strategy? _____

   c. "We've come from disgrace to amazing grace"; "Doctors are now more concerned with public health than personal wealth" (Jesse Jackson) are examples of what language strategy? _____

   d. "Take it from me, Mr. Clean, I am a cleanser with scrubbing bubbles" is an example of what language strategy? _____

   e. "Peter Piper picked a peck of pickled peppers" is an example of what language strategy? _____

   f. "If I had sneezed, I wouldn't have been here in 1961.... If I had sneezed, I wouldn't have been able to tell a nation about a dream I'd had.... if I had sneezed,..." (Martin Luther King Jr.) is an example of what language strategy? _____

   g. "The steady spread of the deadly atom" (John F. Kennedy) is an example of what language strategy? _____

   h. "I will lift up my voice like a trumpet and tell the people of their transgressions"; "Deluded beings they know not what they do" (Angelina Grimké) are examples of what language strategy? _____

   i. "There will be more shuttle flights, more shuttle crews, more volunteers, more civilians, more teachers in space" (Ronald Reagan) is an example of what language strategy? _____

2. Bring the lyrics to your favorite song, or jot down the words of a memorable bumper sticker, billboard, or poem. What language strategies are at work? Why must these forms of rhetoric exploit the resources of language?

3. What is the correct word for an unshaven man, wearing shabby clothes, lying on a pile of cartons in an off-street alley and drinking from a bottle hidden in a paper bag? Consider the following terms: a person on welfare, a panhandler, a homeless person, a hobo, a skid row "wino," a beggar, a pauper, a drunkard. Do you see a connection between the term being used by the writers and what they perceive as the causes for the person's condition?

Analytical Writing Exercises

4. Select your favorite advertisement (print or broadcast) to analyze in terms of the style and strategies resources outlined in this chapter. Write a two- to three-page

paper where you identity, describe, and evaluate how its distinctive style and strategies work to overcome challenges in a particular rhetorical situation.

Portfolio Entry 6: Language

5. What resources of language are used strategically in your rhetorical acts? Are they particularly well-crafted in the use of words or not? What might explain why some selections use word choice better than others? Answer in two pages.

Strategic Speaking Exercises

6. Language strategies and delivery work hand in hand to accentuate the artistic dimensions of rhetoric. Select a reading from a Dr. Seuss book or a Mother Goose Nursery Rhyme book to read aloud to the class. How do rhyme, rhythm, alliteration, onomatopoeia, work with rate, pitch, volume, and vocal variety to create a memorable piece of rhetorical action? Have the class vote on the best performance of integrating style and delivery.

NOTES

1. Gina Kolata, "Impotence Is Given Another Name," *New York Times,* April 18, 2000, p. D6.

2. Alex Berenson, "Minky Viagra? Pfizer Doesn't Want You to Understand It, Just Buy It," *New York Times,* April 30, 2007.

3. See "Sarah Palin's 'Death Panel' Claim Rises from the Grave," http://www.latimes.com/news/politics/la-pn-sarah-palins-death-panel-claim-rises-from-the-grave-20120625,0,7057615.story

4. For almost one hundred years, ads for Listerine claimed that the product prevented colds and sore throats. It does not. In 1977 the court upheld the Federal Trade Commission requirement that the next $10 million of Listerine's regular advertising include the corrective statement, "Listerine will not prevent colds or sore throats or lessen their severity" (*Warner-Lambert Co.* v. *FTC*, 562 F.2d 762 [1977]).

5. See M. Lee Williams, "The Effect of Deliberate Vagueness on Receiver Recall and Agreement," *Central States Speech Journal* 31 (Spring 1980): 30–41, for empirical evidence about the advantages and disadvantages of precision and vagueness.

6. See http://www.acrwebsite.org/topic.asp?artid=291. Accessed May 11, 2007.

7. *Lingua Franca,* April 2000, pp. 30–31.

8. Mark DePaolis, "A Power-Tool Approach to Weight Loss," [Minneapolis] *Star Tribune,* July 16, 1993, p. 19A.

9. "This Beautiful Planet," Phi Beta Kappa Oration. *Speak Out,* ed. Herbert Vetter (Boston: Beacon Press, 1992), pp. 85–93.

10. Daniel Walker, "A Summary of the Walker Report," in *Counterpoint: Dialogue for the 70s,* ed. Conn McAuliffe (Philadelphia: J. B. Lippincott, 1970), p. 153.

11. Anna Howard Shaw, "The Fundamental Principle of a Republic," in *Man Cannot Speak for Her: Key Texts of the Early Feminists,* vol. 2, ed. K. K. Campbell (Westport, CT: Greenwood Press, 1989), p. 451.

12. Daniel Webster, "Reply to Hayne," in *Famous Speeches in American History,* ed. Glenn R. Capp (Indianapolis: Bobbs-Merrill, 1963), pp. 57–58.

13. Barbara Jordan, "Democratic National Convention Keynote Address," July 12, 1976. Available at: http://www.americanrhetoric.com/speeches/barbarajordan1976dnc.html. Accessed 1/30/January 30, 2013.

14. *New York Times,* July 15, 1976, p. 26. Columnist William Safire was the author of the line "nattering nabobs of negativism," which was used in a 1969 speech by then Vice President Spiro Agnew to characterize those who opposed the Vietnam War. See also *New York Times,* August 5, 1993, p. A15.

15. Barack Obama, "Second Presidential Inaugural Address," January 21, 2013. Available at: http://www.americanrhetoric.com/speeches/barackobama/barackobamasecondinauguraladdress.htm. Accessed January 30, 2013.

16. http://www.lyricstop.com/s/stupidgirls-pink.html

17. Obama, "Second Presidential Inaugural Address."

18. *New York Times,* July 3, 1994, p. E3.

19. See Karlyn Kohrs Campbell, "The Rhetoric of Radical Black Nationalism," *Central States Speech Journal* 22 (Fall 1971): 151–160; Richard J. Jensen and John C. Hammerback, "Radical Nationalism among Chicanos: The Rhetoric of José Angel Gutierrez," *Western Journal of Speech Communication* 44 (Summer 1980): 191–202.

20. See, for example, Wendy Martyna, "Beyond the 'He/Man' Approach: The Case for Nonsexist Language,"

Signs: Journal of Women in Culture and Society 5 (Spring 1980): 482–493.

21. See Anthony J. Cortese, *Provocateur: Images of Women and Minorities in Advertising* (Lanham, MD: Rowman & Littlefield, 2004); John B. Ford and Michael S. Latour, "Contemporary Female Perspectives of Female Role Portrayals in Advertising," *Journal of Current Issues and Research in Advertising* 18 (Spring 1996): 81–95; M. A. Masse and K. Rosenblum, "Male and Female Created They Them: The Depiction of Gender in the Advertising of Traditional Women's and Men's Magazines," *Women's Studies International Forum* 11 (1988): 127–144. For broader analyses of how advertising and mass media treat women, see Erving Goffman, *Gender Advertisements* (Cambridge, MA: Harvard University Press, 1976); Jean Kilbourne, *Can't Buy My Love: How Advertising Changes the Way We Think and Feel* (New York: Simon & Schuster/Touchstone Book, 1999); and Liesbet van Zoonen, *Feminist Media Studies* (London: Sage Publications, 1994).

22. Booker T. Washington, "Atlanta Exposition Address," *Famous Speeches in American History*, ed. Glenn Capp (New York: Bobbs-Merrill, 1963), p. 115. Washington may have heard this metaphor in a speech President Rutherford B. Hayes delivered in 1880 at Hampton Institute, where Washington was on the faculty.

23. "I Have a Dream. . . ." in *Selected Speeches from American History*, ed. Robert T. Oliver and Eugene E. White (Boston: Allyn and Bacon, 1966), pp. 291–292.

24. Speech delivered November 3, 1969, *Congressional Record*, Vol. 115, Part 24, pp. 32784–32786.

25. *The Frederick Douglass Papers: Series One: Speeches, Debates, Interviews: Volume 2: 1847–54*, ed. John W. Blassingame (New Haven: Yale University Press, 1982), pp. 359–388. Cited material is on p. 368.

26. Reproduced from Douglass's autobiography, *My Bondage and My Freedom* (New York: Miller, Orton & Mulligan, 1855), pp. 441–445.

27. The *Oxford English Dictionary* defines *peeled* as "stripped of possessions, plundered, reduced to destitution."

28. "A One-Word Assault on Women," by Donna Britt, *Washington Post*, November 30, 1993, p. B1. Copyright © 1993, The Washington Post. Reprinted by permission.

Chapter 8

Challenges Arising from the Audience

The rhetorical context is composed of all the elements of the rhetorical process. The interaction of those elements—audience, subject, rhetor—poses special challenges for rhetorical success. In rhetorical action, a rhetor often confronts an audience that perceives, understands, believes, or acts in one way and wants that audience to perceive, understand, believe, or act in another way. The *rhetorical context* is an umbrella concept that covers all of the challenges rhetors face. Part Three examines *challenges* arising from the audience (Chapter 8), from the subject (Chapter 9), and opportunities and challenges arising from the rhetor (Chapter 10).

In practice, of course, challenges arising from audience, subject, and rhetor cannot be separated so neatly. For example, suppose your subject was the history of oats as a cash crop. Even if your purpose were merely informative (and not efforts to increase the acreage devoted to raising oats), you would have a fairly hard time holding the interest of audiences made up of teenagers or lawyers. But your rhetorical problem would be much smaller if your audience was a group of Midwestern farmers, preferably sprinkled with dedicated horse breeders and trainers (oats is the best grain to feed horses). In other words, whether or not your subject and purpose create challenges depends partly on the nature of your audience. In fact, challenges are only obstacles if the audience perceives them that way.

Think of these three aspects of the rhetorical context as forming a triangle. These interrelationships can be expressed in three questions:

1. What will be necessary to induce the audience to take part in rhetorical action?
2. What does the subject or purpose demand of the audience?
3. What demands are made on the credibility (ethos) of the rhetor by the subject or purpose and the audience?

Beginning rhetors tend to make two common errors in thinking about audiences. First, they assume that most audiences (particularly classmates, friends, colleagues) are just like themselves, with the same experiences, values, religious beliefs, political preferences, and life goals. They are shocked to discover—within the same culture or community or even in the same communication class—wide divergences in belief. But people differ. All audiences, even close friends, need explanation, adaptation, and effort to see the importance and significance of the issue and the purpose.

Your assumption that members of the audience are just like you, the rhetor, takes several specific forms. Sometimes, for example, you might take for granted that those you address are, like you, rational, impartial, interested, informed, and concerned. Although people can be all of these some of the time, we are also creatures of deep feeling who are, at the same time, likely to be apathetic toward issues of great importance to others. And your audiences are people. As a rhetor, you must treat them as many-faceted with experiences that may surprise you, but you must not assume they are well informed and curious unless you make an effort to provide information and arouse curiosity. In this sense, you create or construct your audience—you provide the materials that enable them to become the ideal respondents to your message.

The second common error rhetors make is to transform the audience into vicious monsters eagerly waiting to jeer at them and to discredit their messages. Assuming that those for whom you write or speak are different from you can help when you try to imagine yourself as a member of the audience. But this feeling can be carried too far. Audience members are like you. Although not identical, they have needs and fears similar to yours. You and they have many values in common. Generally, an audience can share your experience and come to understand a differing point of view.

To be successful as a rhetor requires that you induce the audience to participate, indeed, to collaborate in creating the rhetorical act. You and the audience must identify with each other and come to some kind of common understanding if the message you produce is to be a communication. With some experience, you will discover that one of your assets as a rhetor is your individuality—your special experiences, biases, and fallibilities, especially as you are able to recognize them and share them with the audience.

Your goal as a rhetor, then, is to avoid both these errors: to recognize differences between yourself and members of the audience and yet create common bonds between you from what you do share. In other words, prepare your rhetorical act to minimize the challenges represented by these differences.

Beliefs about persuasion are also relevant to the rhetorical challenges arising from the audience. At various times in U.S. history we have demonstrated our fears of the power of persuasion. We have banned certain books and movies as heretical or obscene and have forbidden Muslims and Marxists to speak in certain forums, as if exposure to a book, a movie, or a speech could cause good Christians to lose their faith and become ravening sex fiends, or patriotic U.S. Americans to become traitors or converts to a dramatically different ideology. As this chapter indicates, normal people are not transformed by a single rhetorical act. Audiences, in fact, show considerable resistance to persuasion in all forms. Indeed, considering all of the resistance to persuasion that arise from audiences, you may well marvel that any persuasion ever occurs.

THE AUDIENCE

There are at least four ways to understand what is meant by an "audience" (see Figure 8–1). An audience can be those exposed to the rhetorical act, the *empirical audience*; it can be the *target audience*, the ideal audience at whom the act is aimed; it can be the *agents of change*, or VIP audience who have the capacity to do as the rhetor wishes, who can make changes; and it can be the role the audience is invited to play by the rhetor, the *created audience*.

The Empirical Audience

In the most simple sense, the empirical audience is all those exposed to the rhetorical act, whether it be in a face-to-face encounter or through the print, electronic, or New Media. Obviously, if people do not encounter the rhetorical act, they will not be influenced by it. The channels through which rhetorical acts are transmitted select and limit the potential empirical audience. An essay printed in *Ms.*, a feminist magazine, reaches a relatively small audience of subscribers and others—at a friend's house or the women's clinic—who pick up the magazine and read it. Some of those who read *Ms.* are likely to be different from those who read *Ebony*, a magazine targeted at African Americans, or *Road and Track*, a magazine for car lovers. The empirical audience is even more segmented in cyberspace. Narrowcasting (or reaching niche audiences) is a defining characteristic of New Media. For example, if you get your news of the day from www.rightwingnews.com or from www.moveon.org you are likely part of a particular group of people who share a particular political viewpoint. Even more generalized websites such as www.craigslist.com or www.salon.com cater to different audiences. Rhetors who wish to reach the appropriate audience must try to find the channel that will expose their ideas to the ideal or target audience.

The Target Audience

Realistically, you cannot address everyone. All rhetorical acts are shaped and planned to reach people with certain characteristics. These people are the target audience. They are the ones most likely to be responsive. The target audience

Figure 8–1
Types of Audiences

Type	How Defined
• Empirical (Immediate) Audience	• Who is exposed to the rhetorical act?
• Target (Most responsive) Audience	• Who are you most trying to reach?
• Agents of Change (VIPs)	• Who are the movers and shakers?
• Created Audience	• Who are you trying to empower?

is likely to share basic assumptions with the rhetor; ideally, they have common experiences and shared longings. Patterns of television advertising illustrate this concept. For example, the demographic analyses of television viewers made by the Nielsen Company indicate that a large proportion of viewers of network news are older people (over age forty-five). Accordingly, if you watch the news on any broadcast network, you will see advertisements for such products as laxatives, denture adhesives, and vitamins because older viewers are thought more likely to suffer from constipation, have loose false teeth, or need vitamin supplements. Similarly, razor blades and aftershave lotions are advertised on broadcasts of football games because Nielsen studies indicate that a majority of viewers of such programming is male. In each case, the ads are targeted at audiences most likely to have needs these products can fill.

The Agents of Change

Only some members of your potential audience have the capacity to do what you desire—to buy an expensive product, to provide a service, or to enact a change in policy. Generally, you should target those who have the power to act, those with the political ability, the economic power, the numbers, or the social influence to alter the situation. Effective rhetors aim their messages at those who can do what they desire— who have the political power (the vote), the economic power (the money), or the numbers (to march, petition, vote) or other resources (expertise, technology, or whatever) to act. We often refer to such influential persons as VIPs—very important persons. For example, elected officials, judges, teachers, parents, administrators, a board of directors, religious leaders, and celebrities are all examples of agents of change; they have clout economically, socially, politically, or religiously.

Such a description of the audience seems to make it a power elite, but other factors are also at work. Advertisers, for example, have learned that they can be effective if they reach those who can influence the agents of change. Pokémon cards, monster-shaped vitamins, sugar-coated cereals, toys, and video games are advertised on children's television programs although few children make independent purchasing decisions.[1] Children, however, can influence the decisions of their parents. The agents of change are not only those with the power to act but also those who can influence them. Lobbyists and constituents may not be able to vote on legislation, but they can influence members of the House and Senate.

The Created Audience

Rhetorical action is participatory; it involves a reciprocal relationship between those involved. Just as the rhetor plays a role and takes on a persona, audiences are invited to play roles and take on one or more personas.[2] Advertising, for example, creates appealing scenarios that invite us to imagine ourselves playing roles in them. Playing roles in these scenarios, however, requires us to purchase products. Cosmetic ads invite viewers to imagine themselves as glamorous, seductive women with long, bouncy hair (buy our shampoo), glistening lips (buy our lipstick or lip gloss), and sultry eyes with long dark lashes (buy our eye shadow and mascara). If and only if we can be prompted to see ourselves in such roles, will we buy the products they advertise.

The importance of creating the audience, of inviting them to play a role, is illustrated by the challenges posed by female audiences. An audience must not only have the power to act, but it must also believe that it has that power. A number of studies seem to indicate that women, especially young women, have low self-esteem and lack confidence in their ability to succeed in areas not traditionally identified as female.[3] In fact, they can act as agents of change. As they have demonstrated, they can sue for admission to all-male institutions; they can use affirmative action to gain entry to areas from which women have been excluded; they can start businesses as well as vote, work as volunteers, and donate money to candidates; they can write letters to influential people and outlets; they can influence businesses through purchasing decisions; they can form groups that will influence school policy, television programming, and police actions. They can run for office and be elected. But they can do these things if and only if they come to believe that they can. Their economic power to affect political campaigns had always been there, but the Anita Hill–Clarence Thomas hearings mobilized many women to exercise that power in 1992. The so-called consciousness-raising groups in the women's liberation movement can be seen as transforming women into audiences—that is, into people who believe that they can act effectively to become agents of change.

In other words, if a rhetorical act is to have any chance of succeeding, audience members must participate in it from beginning to end. They must perceive its ideas accurately and internalize the "virtual experience" presented. They must see the information and arguments as coming from an informed and trustworthy source,[4] and the rhetorical act as relevant to their needs. In addition, the audience must see the purpose of the act and the means to achieve it as consistent with their values, and they must come to believe that they can take action, here and now, that can reasonably be expected to achieve the goal desired. These requirements suggest the dimensions and the facets of the obstacles that arise from the audience.

AUDIENCE-RELATED RHETORICAL CHALLENGES

The common kinds of *audience-related rhetorical challenges* are (1) inattention, (2) misperception and misinterpretation, (3) lack of motivation, and (4) inertia (see Figure 8–2).

Figure 8–2
Audience-Related
Rhetorical
Challenges

Audience-Related Challenges

- Inattention
  - Insulated from exposure
- Misperception
  - stereotyping/distortion
- Lack of motivation
  - no salience
- Inertia
  - resistance to change/powerless

Inattention

Although you may not appreciate it, as a student you are in a rare and highly privileged rhetorical situation: you have a captive audience. Your teacher is paid to read and comment on your essays or to listen and evaluate your speeches, and your classmates are required to attend class. Unlike most rhetors, you do not need to struggle to gather an audience, to have your name recognized, or to gain media coverage.

College teachers also have more or less captive audiences. Yet as college professors, we compete directly in any given lecture with local newspapers, letters from parents and friends, and assignments for other classes. When students use laptops in class, we compete with email, Facebook, and with other sites on the Internet. Until students read our syllabi regarding classroom policies, we must also compete with the annoyance of cell phones and pagers.

And like all other rhetors we compete indirectly with the hundreds of eager persuaders our students encounter daily: newspaper editorials and letters to the editor; television, radio, and magazine advertising; telephone and door-to-door solicitors; billboards; political candidates; family and friends. If this bombardment does not create resistance to persuasion by its sheer volume, it may outclass us in slickness or entertainment quality. Although we come in three dimensions and the mass media persuaders do not, and though we are in "living color," we cannot make eight retakes, do a dissolve, edit the tape, or cut to an animated cartoon when attention flags.

If our students could choose whether or not to come to class, we would encounter another audience-related challenge. Let us call it limited or *selective exposure*. Audiences selectively expose themselves to messages and selectively attend to those they see or hear. Students do this to some degree in their choices of electives. In other words, audiences control their exposure to rhetorical acts. In general, we tend to expose ourselves to messages that meet our physical, psychological, or social needs. The young woman about to be married suddenly begins to seek out *Bride* magazine; the student faced with the need to buy a car suddenly seeks out *Consumer Reports* for information on reliability and repairs to maximize her purchase. We routinely read those publications and watch those programs that reflect our general interests and styles. The messages we encounter here are likely to be reassuring and reinforcing. If you are an investor or running a small business, you are likely to read the *Wall Street Journal*, and its editorial columns are likely to take positions congenial to people like you, for example, opposing an "employer mandate" in proposed health care reforms. If you are such a person, you are less likely to read *Mother Jones* and be exposed to editorials and articles with strong commitments to environmentalism, some parts of which may be costly to businesses. In other words, our patterns of viewing and reading are related to topics and subjects important to satisfying our needs for information and advice, and these patterns tend to expose us primarily to supportive or unchallenging viewpoints. When faced with a choice, however, especially an important choice, we seek out wider sources of information. We watch debates among prominent candidates and deliberately expose ourselves to conflicting views. In other words, our interests and needs limit our exposure to rhetoric, and to some extent, such limits filter in supportive or reassuring messages. You know this from your own experience. Although they hear both sides represented, committed conservatives are more likely to watch and listen to such programs as *The O'Reilly Factor* where the conservative viewpoint is well and strongly represented. Such exposure is pleasant because it does not threaten our views, and it reinforces our sense that we have made the right choices. On the other hand, as these examples indicate, ordinarily we do not avoid exposure to alternative points of view.

As a rhetor, however, you need to know that under certain circumstances people actively seek out information that conflicts with what they know and with views that challenge their own. At least three factors significantly modify the commonsense picture just presented: the audience's level of education, the usefulness of the information to be presented, and the audience's history of exposure. One early study concluded: "Clearly the most powerful known predictor of voluntary exposure to mass communications of an information or public-affairs sort is the general factor of education and social class."[5] Put simply, people with more education and higher incomes choose to expose themselves to more news and information on public affairs in the mass media. They buy more magazines and newspapers; they watch more public affairs programs on radio and television (and they can more easily afford cable hookups that give them access to more outlets); they are more likely to be active in groups that spread such information; they are more likely to have personal computers and use the Internet for information, entertainment, and shopping. In fact, education and social class may be a more significant factor in exposure than ideological agreement.

As suggested previously, another factor influencing exposure is the immediate usefulness of the information to the recipient; in some studies, subjects preferred what they saw as more useful information to what they saw as less useful, regardless of which of these supported their previous beliefs.[6] Ideological differences or a lack of shared beliefs and attitudes are serious barriers, but ones that can be breached by relevance, that is, if the recipients see a direct, personal use for the information provided now.

Finally, past exposure to the issue influences a person's reaction to future exposure in ways that are not necessarily related to the compatibility of beliefs. Some studies have found that when individuals initially were exposed to one-sided or biased information, they later preferred opposing information regardless of whether it supported their initial position.[7] Such studies, along with others indicating tolerance for and interest in new and challenging data, suggest that it would be a mistake to assume that audiences will not read or listen to information that conflicts with their beliefs and attitudes.

The first challenge you face as a rhetor in relation to an audience, then, is gaining and maintaining attention. As indicated here, the individual rhetor competes for attention with many other persuaders and meets obstacles having to do with the selection of messages by members of the audience. A tendency to be exposed to information compatible with our interests and needs and, hence, views we already hold is balanced by the generally high level of interest in information evident among the more educated and affluent, by a desire for useful information, and by a desire for opposing information if the initial exposure seems to have been one-sided or biased.

Misperception and Misinterpretation

Selective perception names a second kind of audience-related challenge you face. It refers to the human ability to function rather like a radio—to tune one channel in and another out, turn the volume down or up, fade the sound in and out, or turn the set off entirely. We do not perceive all the stimuli to which we are exposed—we would go crazy if we did. We sort out what we believe is relevant, for example, and ignore the rest. The basis for this ability remains largely a mystery. There is evidence, however, that our attitudes influence what we perceive and how we interpret it.

Attitudes

No one has ever seen an attitude. *Attitude* is a concept developed by researchers to describe some of the mental (emotional/affective and rational/cognitive) processes and behaviors of human beings. The concept is particularly difficult because it is complex, and not all researchers agree on how to define attitudes or on whether and how they can be distinguished from *beliefs* and *values*.

Attitudes are likes or dislikes, affinities for or aversions to situations (liking to speak publicly or hating to talk on the phone), events (weddings), objects (motorcycles), people (children), groups (Methodists), or any identifiable aspect of one's environment (humidity). Attitudes are a mental readiness or a predisposition to react that influences a fairly large class of one's valuative responses consistently or over a significant period of time.

Attitudes are expressed in statements like these: I don't like big parties; I love ginger ice cream; I like assertive people; the *New York Times* is the best newspaper in the United States. Presumably, as a result of direct experience (at parties, eating ice cream, making choices, reading many newspapers) and other kinds of learning (from school, parents, and peers, among others), people develop valuative categories so they are prepared to respond, favorably or unfavorably, with varying degrees of intensity (strongly or mildly favorably or unfavorably) to the items they encounter.

Attitudes are relatively generalized (they tend to refer to categories or classes rather than to individual items), and they are enduring (they persist over time). They also are learned. People probably learn likes and dislikes as they learn nearly everything else, and they categorize their valuative experiences in order to simplify the world. If you have an aversion to cats, for example, it is likely that you were frightened or scratched by a cat as a child or had a reaction to cat dander or have a parent, friend, or sibling with a strong dislike for felines. In most cases, the attitude will apply to most or all cats, and probably if you dislike them today, you will continue to dislike them next week and next month, although change is possible based on new experiences and learning.

In addition, your aversion to cats would probably influence reactions to related areas: to cat shows, to cat owners, to prohibitions against pets in apartments, and so on. Obviously, the rhetor who tries to alter audience attitudes like this one or whose purposes run counter to intensely held attitudes of audience members will run into trouble. Attitudes are learned over a period of time from experiences or credible sources; they are reinforced by later experiences; they are also patterns of response that make it easier to cope with the world. This rhetorical challenge is compounded because attitudes influence what we perceive and how we interpret it.

A famous study of the influence of attitudes on perception used a particularly controversial football game between Dartmouth and Princeton as its raw material. The researchers showed students from both schools the same film of the game and tested their perceptions of who broke the rules how many times and in what ways. From the test results, you might have thought the two groups of students had seen two different events. For example, Princeton students "saw" the Dartmouth team break the rules more than twice as many times as the Dartmouth students "saw" their team do so. The researchers concluded that the same data transmitted in the same way create different experiences in different people, and that the significance of an event depends on the purposes different people bring to it and the assumptions they have about the purposes of other people involved. They wrote, "It is inaccurate and misleading to say that different people have different 'attitudes' concerning the same 'thing.' For the 'thing' simply is not the same for different people whether the 'thing' is a football game, a presidential candidate, Communism, or spinach."[8]

You can probably think of many similar examples from the sports world in which partisanship strongly influences what the fans see. The most striking example is when your team is playing in a championship series. On close, contested plays, the difference between the live local media coverage of the game and the national coverage can be so incredibly different you wonder if the announcers are calling the same game! And such responses are not surprising, given the nature of attitudes.

And what happens in sports can easily happen in other areas. An attitude is a readiness to respond favorably or unfavorably. It represents an expectation of favorable or unfavorable qualities and behaviors. In other words, we tend to "see" the qualities and behaviors in objects, events, persons, and so forth that we expect to be there. Accordingly, our attitudes influence our perceptions and our interpretations of events.

Beliefs

The influence of attitudes on perception and interpretation suggests that there is a close relationship between information and evaluation. A *belief* is a judgment about what is true or probable, real or likely. Beliefs may refer to the past (guns were involved in 66 percent of the 14,249 murders in 2004, more than any other weapon[9]), the present (school shootings are still increasing in the United States), or the future (so many guns already are owned by U.S. Americans that gun control legislation cannot reduce their role in violent crime). Our beliefs may assert a causal relationship or evaluate the credibility of sources of information.

Insofar as attitudes are learned from our own experiences or those of others, they are based on beliefs, on what we consider true, or likely. For example, if you strongly dislike dogs, you probably believe that they bite many people each year, that they often bite without provocation, and that they are the source of some serious diseases of children. These beliefs not only describe dogs, as you may see them, but also predict future situations.

Note that insofar as attitudes rest on beliefs, they can be influenced by future learning. Hence, the rhetor who wants to change attitudes tries to alter perception (and beliefs) through virtual experience. Conversely, as the Dartmouth–Princeton football game example shows, attitudes influence perception in ways that undermine this process, and even conflicting information can be perceived as compatible with the perceiver's attitudes.

Decoding

Attitudes influence perception and interpretation so strongly that rhetors cannot be sure their audiences will perceive information as they do. In fact, the interpretation of information and argument is a problem with all audiences, however well intentioned they may be. *Decoding* is a term used to refer to this interpretive process by which listeners or readers translate and interpret messages from outside, assign meanings, determine relationships, and draw out implications.

Audiences obviously find decoding hard to do. Thus, much of the impact of a rhetorical act is lost unless rhetors make special efforts to organize material, to state conclusions, and to show the relationships among ideas. In one study, for example, an audience of bright college students became confused when the conclusions of a message to which they were exposed were not stated explicitly. Other studies confirm this finding.[10] Audiences resist or botch decoding unless claims are presented clearly and made explicit. At a minimum, the rhetor must state conclusions, organize materials clearly, and provide transitions that show relationships if the audience is to interpret accurately what is being said.

The Elaboration Likelihood Model (ELM). As we explained in Chapter 5, researchers Richard Petty and John Cacioppo developed a theory they call the *Elaboration Likelihood Model* (ELM),[11] which emphasizes the central role of the audience in persuasion. Their theory, as its name implies, focuses on the likelihood that audience members will be stimulated not only to attend to and decode a message but also to develop or elaborate it—that is, to process or interpret it, to amplify, clarify, or embellish it, and to consider its implications. By this standard, the most effective rhetorical act is one that produces the greatest amount of cooperative message-building by members of the audience. Under ideal circumstances, audience members collaborate with the rhetor in creating the discourse by which they are influenced.

ELM is useful in understanding the role of the audience in persuasion. As a theory, ELM postulates two routes through which persuasion occurs: a *central route* and a *peripheral route*. The central route is rationalistic and argumentative; that is, it is directly related to cooperative message-building prompted by the quality of the argument and the evidence on which it rests. Based on many research studies, it seems that changes in attitude that occur via this route require more work, more thought, on the part of the reader or listener; however, research studies also suggest that attitude changes resulting from this process last longer, are more resistant to counter persuasion from opponents, and are more predictive of actual behavior. In other words, a good case can be made for the importance of argument and evidence if audience members respond to, participate in, and collaborate in creating a message that is initiated by a rhetor.

As its label suggests, the peripheral route is less direct; mostly, we use it for efficiency—we cannot investigate thoroughly all issues on which we must make decisions. Some snap judgments are necessary. Decisions made via this route are shortcuts; instead of the hard work involved in interpreting the argument and evidence, we use some element in the persuasive context or situation as a cue or sign by which to assess the message. It could be linked to the person who carries it—positively or negatively. It could be linked to a belief system with which audience members agree or disagree. Whatever the association, it allows audience members to make a relatively simple leap from the cue to the position being advocated; for example, someone who is intensely disliked supports a position that is rejected because of that association—that is, because of feelings about the source (e.g., "If Bill Maher favors it, it must be bad—or good").

According to this research, the most important variable affecting audience members' willingness to work at this special kind of decoding—the motivation actively to participate in and interpret a persuasive message—is its *personal relevance*; that is, a belief that the topic or issue is vital and will affect them personally. The greater its possible personal consequences for the audience, the greater will be the importance of forming an opinion based on the most accurate and complete information. As one author can attest, younger women are less likely to work at understanding messages about osteoporosis, for example, but women who are approaching menopause are likely to pay close attention to messages about the pros and cons of estrogen- or hormone-replacement therapy; in fact, they may even seek out such messages! That's unfortunate because younger women need to eat foods with lots of calcium (and do weight-bearing exercises) to build up their bone mass, which is the best protection against bone loss later in life. When there are immediate and vital personal consequences, people are likely to be motivated to engage in the mental work—the interpretation and decoding—necessary to evaluate the true merits of a proposal. This strongly suggests the importance of showing why your message is vital for those you hope to reach.

The willingness to collaborate in creating the rhetorical act is also affected by one's worldview. Those who view the world legalistically, such as lawyers, for example, find messages that are justified on legalistic grounds to be more persuasive, whereas those who see the world in religious terms are more likely to be persuaded by messages that are justified on religious or moral grounds.

In sum, the ELM if delete "model" then needs another descriptor such as "theory" suggests that there is a trade-off between the brainwork involved in participating in messages—exploring and evaluating arguments and evidence—and the importance of peripheral or external cues. In general, anything that reduces someone's ability or motivation to interpret and amplify issue-related arguments also increases the likelihood that external cues in the source, message, recipient, or context may affect response. On the other hand, all of us use such peripheral cues to make a great many decisions because we haven't the time or inclination to scrutinize all the arguments and evidence relevant to every choice we have to make. For example, one might buy bleach or laundry detergent impulsively by the color of the bottle or box, but make a detailed study of evaluations of cars in *Consumer Reports* and other outlets before spending thousands of dollars on a new car.

Lack of Motivation

Needs

People act for reasons. They pursue goals, they are motivated, they try to satisfy their needs. The significant role of needs and goals has already been indicated by people's willingness to expose themselves to messages containing information they believe will be useful to satisfy needs. What are these "needs"? Among the many catalogs of human needs, one of the most useful was developed by Abraham Maslow.[12] Maslow, a psychologist, postulated a *hierarchy of needs*, which suggests that some needs may be more intense and basic than others under some circumstances. The most fundamental needs are *physiological*—for food, water, sleep, and protection from exposure to the elements. Only when these are relatively well satisfied do needs for *safety* (stability, order, freedom from violence and disease) begin to predominate. When these, in turn, are relatively well met, needs for *love and acceptance* (affection, giving and receiving love, touching and being touched) emerge. And when these are satisfied, needs for *esteem* (recognition, respect from others and for ourselves) surface. Finally, we aspire for transcendence or *self-actualization*—to be all that one is capable of being, to develop one's unique potential. All humans experience all of these needs and seek to have them met. This pyramid of needs can help us to understand the successes and failures of some kinds of rhetorical processes. We may wonder why parliamentary democracy has not attracted more Third World nations, but most citizens of these countries do not have their physiological and safety needs met. They need to find ways to meet the needs at the more basic levels of the pyramid, whereas democracy is an ideology that emphasizes satisfying individual needs for esteem and self-actualization, needs nearer to the top of the pyramid.

Likewise, the successes of charismatic and mystical religious movements should not be too surprising in our culture. We are a nation of transients (one of four families moves every five years) with a diminishing sense of community; our families are a less stable source of love and acceptance—at present, between 40 and 50 percent of marriages end in divorce. In such a climate, a community of believers becomes very attractive; if no one else loves you or cares for you, God does. The vogue for books on self-development in the 1980s reflected a society in which the basic needs of many people were relatively well met, so that interest focused on self-actualization; the changed conditions of the 1990s shifted interest to therapeutic books on how to cope with the results of changing economic conditions, changing marital roles, or how to deal with stress. In the twenty-first century, increasing investment in the stock market has made books on buying stocks and on handling wealth more popular, and increasing concerns with time management has created a cottage industry of personal trainers, domestic coaches, and family planners.

Because the concept of "needs" focuses on deprivation and because it does not take into account the extent to which our needs are modified by socialization and acculturation, values also need to be considered.

Values

Attitudes, our predispositions to respond favorably or unfavorably to elements of the environment (including invitations to rhetorical action), are influenced not only by beliefs about what is true or probable but by goals or values. Like attitude and belief, *value* is a construct describing a pattern of human behavior. It cannot be touched or seen. Values are usually defined as judgments about what is moral (good or right), important (worthy, significant), or beautiful (moving, expressive, pleasing), or as fundamental preferences for certain ends (such as equality, freedom, self-actualization) or for certain modes of conduct (such as honesty, courage, or integrity). In other words, values express strong, basic, and very general views of how one should act or what goals one should seek (what goals are worthy of seeking). The ideal of self-government, for example, strongly implies that all citizens should enter into policy deliberations and should involve themselves actively in discourse related to choosing those who represent them in government. These are views that positively value rhetorical action.

Values seem to arise from three sources: our biology, our cultures, and our distinctive qualities as individuals. These sources suggest the relationship between values and needs. Some values arise from biological needs or genetic characteristics (birds need to fly; salmon need to swim upriver to spawn). Despite the many catalogs in psychological works or Maslow's hierarchy of needs (leading to a hierarchy of motives), there is no list of needs that satisfactorily describes human motivation. Consider Maslow's hierarchy. It cannot explain artists who are driven to paint or sculpt even though they cannot buy enough food to eat and are scorned by others. Nor can it explain religious figures, such as Mother Teresa or Dorothy Day, who devoted their lives to acting altruistically. Maslow himself recognized these exceptions and discussed the problems involved in establishing any needs as basic or in describing motivation as arising from deprivation. As he noted, rats seem to run mazes as fast out of curiosity as out of hunger, thirst, or sex drive.

Obviously, human beings need nutrition, safety, shelter from exposure, and affection, but we have modified these needs culturally and socially—creating a second source of values. The Masai of Africa, for example, seem to thrive on a diet composed largely of the milk and blood of their cattle, a diet that would nauseate most Americans. Dwellers in tropical and even Mediterranean climates meet part of their sleep needs by the siesta, a practice unintelligible to those from more temperate climates. In other words, what begin as organic or biological needs are shaped by culture and society.

In every community there are norms about what is good and proper to eat, and what is a delicacy to one group may be revolting to another. Values arise, then, not only from biological requirements but also from the norms of the groups we belong to, groups ranging in size from the nation to the gang on the block. Group values are expressed in such statements as, "That is unpatriotic or disloyal." "This is the Chinese way." "Seventh Day Adventists do not eat meat." "That's sissy." These values, affecting every facet of life, are so fused with biological needs that no one can say just where biology stops and socialization begins.

A third source of values is idiosyncrasies, the unique qualities of the individual. Each of us is physiologically different. If you have an unusually acute sense of smell, you may have a strong aversion to many perfumes; if tobacco smoke gives you headaches, you may support regulations creating smoke-free areas. Epileptics place a special value on sleep (seizures are more likely if they are deprived of it). Those who suffer from migraines dislike strobe lights and avoid television programs with lots of jump cuts because these can provoke headaches. Some people have intense aesthetic needs, some have few sexual needs, some relish food, and others eat only to survive. As you will note from these examples, such individual values are refinements or modifications of cultural values and biological needs. Values arising from the special qualities of individuals may account for some unusual responses to rhetorical efforts. Individual values are also a source of variation in the importance or priority given to a particular social value.

Attitudes, our predispositions to respond, are a product of values and beliefs. The emotive and affective component of attitudes (reflecting our desires) and goals comes from our values; the cognitive component of values (based on information and inference) comes from our beliefs. Clearly, however, these concepts and the processes they represent are inseparable because evaluations are based on what we believe to be true, and our evaluations, in turn, influence what we perceive and how we interpret its *salience*, or relevance in our lives. In sum, as a rhetor you must recognize that lack of motivation will likely plague your audience unless you can answer the question posed at the beginning of this chapter ("What will be necessary to induce the audience to take part in rhetorical action?") by saying, "I know my audience's needs and values."

Inertia

The concept of *inertia* is by now a familiar one. Inertia is the tendency of an object to continue doing whatever it has been doing—to rest if it has been resting, to move in a straight line unless disturbed by an outside force, and so on. When applied to people, inertia refers to an audience's resistance to the rhetor's purpose. Inertia is a complex psychological matter, but from a rhetorical viewpoint, it usually has to do with resisting demands on our time and energies or with a feeling of powerlessness. Audiences will resist changing their ideas and ignore calls to action unless the proposed action is both vital enough to engage their energies as well as within their capabilities, capable of being done here and now, and has a reasonable chance of being effective.

The problem of persuading people to practice "safer sex" is illustrative. Many sexually active people have not used condoms in the past; as a result, "safer sex" involves a change in behavior. Condoms cost money, and buying them can be embarrassing and expensive, especially for many teenagers. Accordingly, those promoting safer sex provide condoms free of charge to make using them easier and try to convince the sexually active not only that they face life-threatening dangers from unprotected sex but also that using condoms is easy, effective, and consistent with sexual pleasure.

Those who write about attitudes argue that they have three parts: cognitive (beliefs), affective (values), and behavioral. Attitudes do not exist apart from behaviors, but the relationship between them is complex. There is no simple correlation between an attitude and a particular behavior. One can agree that unprotected sexual intercourse is dangerous, for example, and behave in various ways. One can act as if that belief had nothing to do with you—for example, as if only gay males were at risk of contracting HIV, the virus that leads to AIDS—screening out data about increasing risks to heterosexuals and women. One can believe in the danger but also espouse the value that premarital sex is wrong (value). Taking precautions would contradict that value. In such instances if sex occurs, pregnancy, a sexually transmitted disease, or exposure to the HIV virus are risked, perhaps as punishment for flouting the value. Or, one can carefully plan to enjoy sexual activity safely. Attitudes and behaviors either correlate very poorly, or people's reported attitudes differ from their actual attitudes.

Just as attitudes can influence behaviors, so behaviors can also influence attitudes. Studies comparing listening to a speech or reading an essay by someone else with composing one's own speech or essay or with recording the arguments made by others are illustrative. In the studies, even for those hostile to the specific purpose of the speech or essay, there was considerable change in attitudes with greater participation.[13] Advertisers who promote contests in which participants write "Why I like X in twenty-five words or less" are using behavior to influence attitudes. This process is sometimes called self-influence, and it may occur because the people involved try to make their attitudes consistent with their behaviors.

At a minimum, an action is a commitment, often a public commitment, to an attitude. It expresses the recipients' participation in the persuasive process and involves them in the process of influence. Participation in the rhetorical act may be a most effective way of influencing attitudes, and inducing a specific action may be just the reinforcement needed to ensure that a belief will persist. In all cases, as just mentioned, rhetorical acts that propose specific, feasible, and immediate actions for the audience will be the most successful.

These, then, are the rhetorical challenges arising from the audience: inattention, misperception and misinterpretation, lack of motivation, and inertia. Thankfully, most rhetors never have to face all these obstacles simultaneously. Those that do rarely succeed in combating them all. A marvelous exception was the courageous true story of a woman named Angelina Grimké. Her compelling story and impassioned speech are provided in Material for Analysis I.

MATERIAL FOR ANALYSIS I

Angelina Grimké (1805–1879) was an unlikely reformer. Born into privilege in 1805 in Charleston, South Carolina, to a wealthy slaveholding family, Angelina had every comfort imaginable. She was the youngest of fourteen children, educated by private tutors, raised as a devout Episcopalian, and doted on by her parents and siblings. And yet she was restive. She and her older sister Sarah were particularly disturbed by the practice of slavery. So, even though the laws of South Carolina forbade teaching slaves to read or write, the sisters created an underground school on their own plantation. Angelina's diary describes these sessions with supreme satisfaction. "The light was put out, the keyhole screened, and flat on our stomachs, with the spelling book under our eyes, we defied the laws of South Carolina." The girls were discovered by their father and severely lectured. Rather than submitting as dutiful children, they ran away, took up residence in Philadelphia, and joined the Quakers and the antislavery cause. Here, in 1836, at the age of thirty-one, Angelina published a letter titled "Appeal to the Christian Women of the South" wherein she urged southern women to do the unthinkable: "to persuade your husband, father, brothers, and sons that slavery is a crime against God and man." That sentiment was considered heretical. As pamphlets were disseminated in South Carolina, the Charleston authorities warned Angelina that she would be arrested if she ever returned to her hometown, and the postmaster burned copies of the "letter."

Undaunted, Angelina turned to public speaking, even though in the 1830s it was considered unseemly for women to speak to men in public places. In 1837, in Amesbury, Massachusetts, Angelina engaged in a series of debates on the slavery question—the very first public debates between a man and a woman in the United States.

A hot May evening in Philadelphia in 1838 became the setting for Angelina's swan song in her struggle for human rights. Two days after her marriage to Theodore Weld, a fellow reformer in the antislavery cause, Angelina accepted an invitation to speak at the dedication of Pennsylvania Hall—a splendid structure with the motto "Virtue, Liberty, Independence" carved in gold letters over the stage. In publicity leading up to the event, she was denounced in the papers by the Massachusetts clergy as "a Godless woman," a "he-woman," even "the devil incarnate." Before the ceremonies could unfold, an angry, howling mob formed in the streets. When a black woman, Maria Chapman, got up to introduce Angelina Grimké, the crowd inside booed and yelled; the mob outside threw bricks and rotten tomatoes through the windows. Maria fainted and the crowd erupted with laughter and ridicule. Calmly, Angelina arose from her seat, gazed around the large hall with such unnerving intensity the crowd momentarily quieted. She began: "Men, brethren, and fathers—mothers, daughters, and sisters, what came ye out for to see? A reed shaken with the wind? Is it curiosity merely, or a deep sympathy with the perishing slave, that has brought this large audience together?" At this, someone yelled, "Fire." People ran. Heavy stones thudded against the windows. Angelina Grimké kept speaking. She continued, "Deluded beings! They know not what they do....Do you ask, 'What has the North to do with Slavery?' Hear it—hear it. Those voices without tell us that the spirit of slavery is here!" Amidst the hostile crowd, Angelina spoke for over an hour. Later that evening, the mob burned the new hall to the ground.

Address at Pennsylvania Hall, 1838[14]

by Angelina Grimké

1   Men, brethren and fathers—mothers, daughters and sisters, what came ye out for to see? A reed shaken with the wind? [Matthew 11:7] Is it curiosity merely, or a deep sympathy with the perishing slave, that has brought this large audience together? (*A yell from the mob without the building.*) Those voices without ought to awaken and call out our warmest sympathies. Deluded beings! "They know not what they do" [Luke 23:34]. They know not that they are undermining their own rights and their own happiness, temporal and eternal. Do you ask, "What has the North to do with slavery?" Hear it—hear it. Those voices without tell us that the spirit of slavery is here, and has been roused to wrath by our abolition speeches and conventions: for surely liberty would not foam and tear herself with rage [Mark 9:18], because her friends are multiplied daily, and meetings are held in quick succession to set forth her virtues and extend her peaceful kingdom. This opposition shows that slavery has done its deadliest work in the hearts of our citizens. Do you ask, then, "What has the North to do?" I answer, cast out first the spirit of slavery from your own hearts, and then lend your aid to convert the South [Matthew 7:5]. Each one present has a work to do, be his or her situation what it may, however limited their means, or insignificant their supposed influence. The great men of this country will not do this work; the church will never do it. A desire to please the world, to keep the favor of all parties and of all conditions, makes them dumb on this and every other unpopular subject. They have become worldly-wise,[15] and therefore God, in his wisdom, employs them not to carry on his plans of reformation and salvation. He hath chosen the foolish things of the world to confound the wise, and the weak to overcome the mighty [1 Corinthians 1:27–28].

2   As a Southerner I feel that it is my duty to stand up here to-night and bear testimony against slavery. I have seen it—I have seen it. I know it has horrors that can never be described. I was brought up under its wing: I witnessed for many years its demoralizing influences, and its destructiveness to human happiness. It is admitted by some that the slave is not happy under the *worst* forms of slavery. But I have never seen a happy slave. I have seen him dance in his chains, it is true; but he was not happy. There is a wide difference between happiness and mirth. Man cannot enjoy the former while his manhood is destroyed, and that part of the being which is necessary to the making, and to the enjoyment of happiness, is completely blotted out. The slaves, however, may be, and sometimes are, mirthful. When hope is extinguished, they say, "let us eat and drink, for to-morrow we die" [Isaiah 22:13]. (*Just then stones were thrown at the windows—a great noise without, and commotion within.*)

3   What is a mob? What would the breaking of every window be? What would the leveling of this Hall be? Any evidence that we are wrong, or that slavery is a good and wholesome institution? What if the mob should now burst in upon us, break up our meeting and commit violence upon our persons—would this be anything compared with what the slaves endure? No, no: and we do not remember them "as bound with them" [Hebrews 13:3], if we shrink in the time of peril, or feel unwilling to sacrifice ourselves, if need be, for their sake. (*Great noise.*) I thank the Lord that there is yet left enough to feel the truth, even though it rages at it—that conscience is not completely seared as to be unmoved by the truth of the living God.

4   Many persons go to the South for a season, and are hospitably entertained in the parlor and at the table of the slave-holder. They never enter the huts of the slaves; they know nothing of the dark side of the picture, and they return home with praises on their lips of the generous character of those with whom they had tarried. Or if they have witnessed the cruelties of slavery, by remaining silent spectators they have naturally become callous—an insensibility has ensued which prepares them to apologize even for barbarity. Nothing but the corrupting influence of slavery on the hearts of the Northern people can induce them to apologize for it; and much will have been done for the destruction of Southern slavery when we have so reformed the North that no one here will be willing to risk his reputation by advocating or even excusing the holding of men as property. The South know it, and acknowledge that as fast as our principles prevail, the hold of the master must be relaxed. (*Another outbreak of mobocratic spirit, and some confusion in the house.*)

5   How wonderfully constituted is the human mind! How it resists, as long as it can, all efforts made to reclaim from error! I feel that all this disturbance is but an evidence that our efforts are the best that could have been adopted, or else the friends of slavery would not care for what we say and do. The South know what we do. I am thankful that they are reached by our efforts. Many times have I wept in the land of my birth, over the system of slavery. I knew of none who sympathized in my feelings—I was unaware that any efforts were made to deliver the oppressed—no voice in the wilderness was heard calling on the people to repent and do works meet for repentance [Isaiah 40:3; Matthew 3:3]—and my heart sickened within me. Oh, how should I have rejoiced to know that such efforts as these were being made. I only wonder that I had such feelings. I wonder when I reflect under what influence I was brought up, that my heart is not harder than the nether millstone [Psalm 95:8; Hebrews 3:15]. But in the midst of temptation I was preserved, and my sympathy grew warmer, and my hatred of slavery more inveterate, until at last I have exiled myself from my native land because I could no longer endure to hear the wailing of the slave. I fled to the land of Penn; for here, thought I, sympathy for the slave will surely be found. But I found it not. The people were kind and hospitable, but the slave had no place in their thoughts. Whenever questions were put to me as to his condition, I felt that they were dictated by an idle curiosity, rather than by that deep feeling which would lead to effort for his rescue. I therefore shut up my grief in my own heart. I remembered that I was a Carolinian, from a state which framed this iniquity by law. I knew that throughout her territory was continual suffering, on the one part, and continual brutality and sin on the other. Every Southern breeze wafted to me the discordant tones of weeping and wailing, shrieks and groans, mingled with prayers and blasphemous curses. I thought there was no hope; that the wicked would go on in his wickedness, until he had destroyed both himself and his country. My heart sunk within me at the abominations in the midst of which I had been born and educated. What will it avail, cried I in bitterness of spirit, to expose to the gaze of strangers the horrors and pollutions of slavery, when there is no ear to hear nor heart to feel and pray for the slave. The language of my soul was, "Oh tell it not in Gath, publish it not in the streets of Askelon" [2 Samuel 1:20]. But how different do I feel now! Animated with hope, nay, with an assurance of the triumph of liberty and good will to man, I will lift up my voice like a trumpet, and show this people their transgression [Isaiah 58:1], their sins of omission toward the slave, and what they can do towards affecting southern mind [*sic*], and overthrowing Southern oppression.

6   We may talk of occupying neutral ground, but on this subject, in its present attitude, there is no such thing as neutral ground. He that is not for us is against us, and he that gathereth not with us, scattereth abroad [Matthew 12:20]. If you are on what you suppose to be neutral ground, the South look upon you as on the side of the oppressor. And is there one who loves his country willing to give his influence, even indirectly, in favor of slavery—that curse of nations? God swept Egypt with the besom of destruction [Isaiah 14:23] and punished Judea also with a sore punishment, because of slavery. And have we any reason to believe that he is less just now?—or that he will be more favorable to us than to his own "peculiar people?" (*Shouting, stones thrown against the windows, etc.*)

7   There is nothing to be feared from those who would stop our mouths, but they themselves should fear and tremble. The current is even now setting fast against them. If the arm of the North had not caused the Bastille of slavery to totter to its foundation, you would not hear those cries. A few years ago, and the South felt secure, and with a contemptuous sneer asked, "Who are the abolitionists? The abolitionists are nothing"—Ay, in one sense they were nothing, and they are nothing still. But in this we rejoice, that "God has chosen things that are not to bring to nought things that are" [1 Corinthians 1:28]. (*Mob again disturbed the meeting.*)

8   We often hear the question asked, "What shall we do?" Here is an opportunity for doing something now. Every man and every woman present may do something by showing that we fear not a mob, and, in the midst of threatenings and revilings, by opening our mouths for the dumb and pleading the cause of those who are ready to perish.

9   To work as we should in this cause, we must know what Slavery is. Let me urge you then to buy the books which have been written on this subject and read them, and then lend them to your neighbors. Give your money no longer for things which pander to pride and lust, but aid in scattering "the living coals of truth" [Isaiah 6:6–8] upon the naked heart of this nation—in circulating appeals to the sympathies of Christians in behalf of the outraged and suffering slave. But, it is said by some, our "books and papers do not speak the truth." Why, then, do they not contradict what we say? They cannot. Moreover the South has entreated, nay commanded us to be silent; and what greater evidence of the truth of our publications could be desired?

10   Women of Philadelphia! allow me as a Southern woman, with much attachment to the land of my birth, to entreat you to come up to this work. Especially let me urge you to petition. Men may settle this and other questions at the ballot-box, but you have no such right; it is only through petitions that you can reach the Legislature. It is therefore peculiarly your duty to petition. Do you say, "It does no good?" The South already turns pale at the number sent. They have read the reports of the proceedings of Congress, and there have seen that among other petitions were very many from the women of the North on the subject of slavery. This fact has called the attention of the South to the subject. How could we expect to have done more as yet? Men who hold the rod over slaves, rule in the councils of the nation: and they deny our right to petition and to remonstrate against abuses of our sex and of our kind. We have these rights, however, from our God. Only let us exercise them: and though often turned away unanswered, let us remember the influence of importunity upon the unjust judge

[Luke 18:1–6] and act accordingly. The fact that the South look with jealousy upon our measures shows that they are effectual. There is, therefore, no cause for doubting or despair, but rather for rejoicing.

11   It was remarked in England that women did much to abolish Slavery in her colonies.[16] Nor are they now idle. Numerous petitions from them have recently been presented to the Queen, to abolish the apprenticeship with its cruelties nearly equal to those of the system whose place it supplies. One petition two miles and a quarter long has been presented. And do you think these labors will be in vain? Let the history of the past answer. When the women of these States send up to Congress such a petition, our legislators will arise as did those of England, and say, "When all the maids and matrons of the land are knocking at our doors we must legislate." Let the zeal and love, the faith and works of our English sisters quicken ours—that while the slaves continue to suffer, and when they shout deliverance, we may feel the satisfaction of *having done what we could.*

Questions for Analysis

1. Angelina Grimké speaks to all four audience types in this speech: empirical, target, agents of change, and created. Find passages in the speech to support each audience conception.

2. Identify the ways in which Angelina Grimké experiences all four challenges arising from the audience: inattention, misperception, lack of motivation, and inertia.

3. Prophets are individuals who are "chosen"; they are high authority figures who have "a direct line" to the Almighty. Prophets tend to be courageous and tested. Their duty is to lead a people from their destructive path to a righteous path (recall how Dr. Martin Luther King Jr. played this role). How does Grimké assume the role of a prophet? What audience challenges does this role overcome? Why is it a risky role for her to play? How is it linked to the tone of the speech?

4. Locate the following kinds of argument in Grimké's speech: rhetorical questions, analogy, enactment, *a fortiori*, refutation, and turning-the-tables. What challenges do these arguments help Grimké overcome?

 MATERIAL FOR ANALYSIS II

The second rhetorical act that we analyze is the speech delivered by U.S. Senator and presidential candidate Barack Obama on Sunday, June 15, 2008, at the Apostolic Church of God in Chicago, Illinois, his hometown. It is an excellent model for analysis because it is particularly rich in rhetorically significant elements. The occasion for the speech was ostensibly ceremonial, Father's Day, on which we typically honor fathers for their role in nurturing their children and building strong families, much as we honor mothers on Mother's Day. In Aristotle's terms, such ceremonial speeches are usually characterized as *epideictic* in that they praise their subjects—be they fathers or mothers. However, Obama's speech is distinctive because he used the occasion to address the emotionally charged topic of absentee African American fathers who neglect or abandon their families. In large part, rather than praising fathers, Obama chastises them. The speech is distinctive also because Obama adopts the rhetorical form of a sermon, or perhaps even a prophetic message (certainly appropriate for the venue in which he spoke) to urge African American fathers to fulfill their obligations to their families. The speech also merits analysis because it was widely reported in the national media and, as we might expect, it generated considerable controversy.

We acknowledge that this speech might also be productively viewed as a campaign address. Just twelve days earlier, on June 3, 2008, Obama won the Democratic presidential nomination with a victory in the Minnesota primary and any public speech by the new nominee surely had implications for the general election campaign. Nevertheless, because neither the nomination nor the campaign are mentioned in the speech, we believe it is most appropriate to take the speech at face value, as a Father's Day address.

Barack Obama's Father's Day Address[17]

1   Good morning. It's good to be home on this Father's Day with my girls, and it's an honor to spend some time with all of you today in the house of our Lord.

2   At the end of the Sermon on the Mount, Jesus closes by saying, "Whoever hears these words of mine, and does them, shall be likened to a wise man who built his house upon a rock: and the rain descended, and the floods came, and the winds blew, and beat upon that house, and it fell not, for it was founded upon a rock." [Matthew 7: 24-25]

3   Here at Apostolic, you are blessed to worship in a house that has been founded on the rock of Jesus Christ, our Lord and Savior. But it is also built on another rock, another foundation—and that rock is Bishop Arthur Brazier. In forty-eight years, he has built this congregation from just a few hundred to more than 20,000 strong—a congregation that, because of his leadership, has braved the fierce winds and heavy rains of violence and poverty; joblessness and hopelessness. Because of his work and his ministry, there are more graduates and fewer gang members in the neighborhoods surrounding this church. There are more homes and fewer homeless. There is more community and less chaos because Bishop Brazier continued the march for justice that he began by Dr. King's side all those years ago. He is the reason this house has stood tall for half a century. And on this Father's Day, it must make him proud to know that the man now charged with keeping its foundation strong is his son and your new pastor, Reverend Byron Brazier.

4   Of all the rocks upon which we build our lives, we are reminded today that family is the most important. And we are called to recognize and honor how critical every father is to that foundation. They are teachers and coaches. They are mentors and role models. They are examples of success and the men who constantly push us toward it.

5   But if we are honest with ourselves, we'll admit that what too many fathers also are is missing—missing from too many lives and too many homes. They have abandoned their responsibilities, acting like boys instead of men. And the foundations of our families are weaker because of it.

6   You and I know how true this is in the African-American community. We know that more than half of all black children live in single-parent households, a number that has doubled—doubled—since we were children. We know the statistics—that children who grow up without a father are five times more likely to live in poverty and commit crime; nine times more likely to drop out of schools and twenty times more likely to end up in prison. They are more likely to have behavioral problems, or run away from home, or become teenage parents themselves. And the foundations of our community are weaker because of it.

7   How many times in the last year has this city lost a child at the hands of another child? How many times have our hearts stopped in the middle of the night with the sound of a gunshot or a siren? How many teenagers have we seen hanging around on street corners when they should be sitting in a classroom? How many are sitting in prison when they should be working, or at least looking for a job? How many in this generation are we willing to lose to poverty or violence or addiction? How many?

8   Yes, we need more cops on the street. Yes, we need fewer guns in the hands of people who shouldn't have them. Yes, we need more money for our schools, and more outstanding teachers in the classroom, and more afterschool programs for our children. Yes, we need more jobs and more job training and more opportunity in our communities.

9   But we also need families to raise our children. We need fathers to realize that responsibility does not end at conception. We need them to realize that what makes you a man is not the ability to have a child—it's the courage to raise one.

10   We need to help all the mothers out there who are raising these kids by themselves; the mothers who drop them off at school, go to work, pick up them up in the afternoon, work another shift, get dinner, make lunches, pay the bills, fix the house, and all the other things it takes both parents to do. So many of these women are doing a heroic job, but they need support. They need another parent. Their children need another parent. That's what keeps their foundation strong. It's what keeps the foundation of our country strong.

11   I know what it means to have an absent father, although my circumstances weren't as tough as they are for many young people today. Even though my father left us when I was two years old, and I only knew him from the letters he wrote and the stories that my family told, I was luckier than most. I grew up in Hawaii, and had two wonderful grandparents from Kansas who poured everything they had into helping my mother raise my sister and me—who worked with her to teach us about love and respect and the obligations we have to one another. I screwed up more often than I should've, but I got plenty of second chances. And even though we didn't have a lot of money, scholarships gave me the opportunity to go to some of the best schools in

the country. A lot of kids don't get these chances today. There is no margin for error in their lives. So my own story is different in that way.

12   Still, I know the toll that being a single parent took on my mother—how she struggled at times to the pay bills; to give us the things that other kids had; to play all the roles that both parents are supposed to play. And I know the toll it took on me. So I resolved many years ago that it was my obligation to break the cycle—that if I could be anything in life, I would be a good father to my girls; that if I could give them anything, I would give them that rock—that foundation—on which to build their lives. And that would be the greatest gift I could offer.

13   I say this knowing that I have been an imperfect father—knowing that I have made mistakes and will continue to make more; wishing that I could be home for my girls and my wife more than I am right now. I say this knowing all of these things because even as we are imperfect, even as we face difficult circumstances, there are still certain lessons we must strive to live and learn as fathers—whether we are black or white; rich or poor; from the South Side or the wealthiest suburb.

14   The first is setting an example of excellence for our children—because if we want to set high expectations for them, we've got to set high expectations for ourselves. It's great if you have a job; it's even better if you have a college degree. It's a wonderful thing if you are married and living in a home with your children, but don't just sit in the house and watch "SportsCenter" all weekend long. That's why so many children are growing up in front of the television. As fathers and parents, we've got to spend more time with them, and help them with their homework, and replace the video game or the remote control with a book once in awhile. That's how we build that foundation.

15   We know that education is everything to our children's future. We know that they will no longer just compete for good jobs with children from Indiana, but children from India and China and all over the world. We know the work and the studying and the level of education that requires.

16   You know, sometimes I'll go to an eighth-grade graduation and there's all that pomp and circumstance and gowns and flowers. And I think to myself, it's just eighth grade. To really compete, they need to graduate high school, and then they need to graduate college, and they probably need a graduate degree too. An eighth-grade education doesn't cut it today. Let's give them a handshake and tell them to get their butts back in the library!

17   It's up to us—as fathers and parents—to instill this ethic of excellence in our children. It's up to us to say to our daughters, don't ever let images on TV tell you what you are worth, because I expect you to dream without limit and reach for those goals. It's up to us to tell our sons, those songs on the radio may glorify violence, but in my house we live [sic] glory to achievement, self respect, and hard work. It's up to us to set these high expectations. And that means meeting those expectations ourselves. That means setting examples of excellence in our own lives.

18 The second thing we need to do as fathers is pass along the value of empathy to our children. Not sympathy, but empathy—the ability to stand in somebody else's shoes; to look at the world through their eyes. Sometimes it's so easy to get caught up in "us," that we forget about our obligations to one another. There's a culture in our society that says remembering these obligations is somehow soft—that we can't show weakness, and so therefore we can't show kindness.

19 But our young boys and girls see that. They see when you are ignoring or mistreating your wife. They see when you are inconsiderate at home; or when you are distant; or when you are thinking only of yourself. And so it's no surprise when we see that behavior in our schools or on our streets. That's why we pass on the values of empathy and kindness to our children by living them. We need to show our kids that you're not strong by putting other people down—you're strong by lifting them up. That's our responsibility as fathers.

20 And by the way—it's a responsibility that also extends to Washington. Because if fathers are doing their part; if they're taking our responsibilities seriously to be there for their children, and set high expectations for them, and instill in them a sense of excellence and empathy, then our government should meet them halfway.

21 We should be making it easier for fathers who make responsible choices and harder for those who avoid them. We should get rid of the financial penalties we impose on married couples right now, and start making sure that every dime of child support goes directly to helping children instead of some bureaucrat. We should reward fathers who pay that child support with job training and job opportunities and a larger Earned Income Tax Credit that can help them pay the bills. We should expand programs where registered nurses visit expectant and new mothers and help them learn how to care for themselves before the baby is born and what to do after—programs that have helped increase father involvement, women's employment, and children's readiness for school. We should help these new families care for their children by expanding maternity and paternity leave, and we should guarantee every worker more paid sick leave so they can stay home to take care of their child without losing their income.

22 We should take all of these steps to build a strong foundation for our children. But we should also know that even if we do; even if we meet our obligations as fathers and parents; even if Washington does its part too, we will still face difficult challenges in our lives. There will still be days of struggle and heartache. The rains will still come and the winds will still blow.

23 And that is why the final lesson we must learn as fathers is also the greatest gift we can pass on to our children—and that is the gift of hope.

24 I'm not talking about an idle hope that's little more than blind optimism or willful ignorance of the problems we face. I'm talking about hope as that spirit inside us that insists, despite all evidence to the contrary, that something better is waiting for us if we're willing to work for it and fight for it. If we are willing to believe.

25   I was answering questions at a town hall meeting in Wisconsin the other day and a young man raised his hand, and I figured he'd ask about college tuition or energy or maybe the war in Iraq. But instead he looked at me very seriously and he asked, "What does life mean to you?"

26   Now, I have to admit that I wasn't quite prepared for that one. I think I stammered for a little bit, but then I stopped and gave it some thought, and I said this:

27   When I was a young man, I thought life was all about me—how do I make my way in the world, and how do I become successful and how do I get the things that I want.

28   But now, my life revolves around my two little girls. And what I think about is what kind of world I'm leaving them. Are they living in a country where there's a huge gap between a few who are wealthy and a whole bunch of people who are struggling every day? Are they living in a country that is still divided by race? A country where, because they're girls, they don't have as much opportunity as boys do? Are they living in a country where we are hated around the world because we don't cooperate effectively with other nations? Are they living a world that is in grave danger because of what we've done to its climate?

29   And what I've realized is that life doesn't count for much unless you're willing to do your small part to leave our children—all of our children—a better world. Even if it's difficult. Even if the work seems great. Even if we don't get very far in our lifetime.

30   That is our ultimate responsibility as fathers and parents. We try. We hope. We do what we can to build our house upon the sturdiest rock. And when the winds come, and the rains fall, and they beat upon that house, we keep faith that our Father will be there to guide us, and watch over us, and protect us, and lead His children through the darkest of storms into light of a better day. That is my prayer for all of us on this Father's Day, and that is my hope for this country in the years ahead. May God Bless you and your children. Thank you.

Sample Critique: Barack Obama's Father's Day Address

To illuminate Barack Obama's Father's Day Address we again turn to the Critical Equation (CPA) explained in Chapter 2 (see Figure 2–5). As you recall, the Critical Equation consists of a Claim + Proof + Analysis. It illustrates the essential components of reading rhetorical acts *analytically*. The first component, "Claim," names the rhetorically significant element (usually one of the elements of descriptive analysis) that you have identified in the rhetorical act. The second component, "Proof," supports or illustrates that claim, usually with evidence (a direct quotation) from the rhetorical act itself. The third component, "Analysis," explains how the proof illustrates the claim as well as the rhetorical significance of this element of the rhetorical act. Concepts illustrated:

How to apply the seven elements of descriptive analysis.

How to use "the critical equation"

1. Purpose

In what ways does the speech illustrate consummatory purpose? What action by African American fathers does he urge? What response is desired? State the thesis in a sentence.

2. Audience

Identify the different audiences.

Immediate: The primarily African American Congregants of the Apostolic Church of God.

Mediated: Those who view or read the speech or accounts of it in the media.

Target: African American fathers who have neglected their responsibilities.

Created: Not a factor.

Agents of Change: African American fathers.

The Critical Equation: CPA (Claim + Proof + Analysis)

Obama directly references the immediate audience, the congregants of the Apostolic Church of God, in the first and third paragraphs. That the immediate audience is predominantly African American is evident as Obama chastises absentee fathers and then adds, "You and I know how true this is in the African-American community" (paragraph 6). Obama further narrows the audience to those he targets, the agents of change, in the thirteenth paragraph. There he says that there are "certain lessons that we must strive to live and learn as fathers," and then follows that with the three specific actions discussed earlier as a part of Purpose. However, it may be unlikely that the miscreant fathers he targets are part of his immediate audience. Rather, because Obama was a U.S. senator and presidential candidate at the time of the speech, it seems likely that he relies on media coverage of the event to relay the message to that target audience.

3. Persona What personae does Obama enact?

Relationship with the audience: Superior.

Role adopted: African American father; minister or perhaps a prophet.

The Critical Equation: CPA (Claim + Proof + Analysis)

Obama begins to take on the role of an African American father in the first paragraph when he says, "it is good to be home on this Father's Day with my girls." That role is reemphasized later in the speech when he asks his predominantly African American audience, "How many times have our hearts stopped in the middle of the night with the sound of a gunshot or a siren? How many teenagers have we seen hanging around on street corners when they should be sitting in a classroom?" (paragraph 7), and in paragraphs twelve and thirteen he again assumes the role of father. Assuming the role of father undoubtedly makes Obama the peer of many in the immediate and target audiences. Nevertheless, he relates to those audiences as a superior in at least two ways. Unlike his target audience, he makes it a personal goal to fulfill the responsibilities of fatherhood: "I resolved many years ago that it was my obligation to break the cycle—that if I could be anything in life, I would be a good father to my girls; that if I could give them anything, I would give them that rock—that foundation—on which to build their lives. And that would be the greatest gift I could offer" (paragraph 12). He also relates to that audience as a superior when he chastises them for "acting like boys instead of men" (paragraph 5), and then urges them to take the three specific actions that we described in the section on Purpose. Finally, Obama assumes the role of preacher or perhaps even a prophet in that the speech takes on the form of a sermon or prophetic message. In the Bible, Old Testament prophets were frequently members of a community who are selected or "called out" by God to chastise the community for failing to follow God's commandments and thus bringing hard times on the community. The prophesy ends with a promise of better times if the community will only "get right" with God. Prophets were also frequently attacked by the indignant community as a result of their efforts. We discuss that form further in this analysis in the sections on structure and strategies.

4. Tone

What is Obama's attitude toward the subject? Toward the audience(s)?

Attitude toward subject: alarmed; serious.

Attitude toward audience: respectful; admonishing; encouraging.

The Critical Equation: CPA (Claim + Proof + Analysis)

Obama's respect for the immediate audience is evident in his praise for their pastor, Bishop Arthur Brazier. Obama says: "Here at Apostolic, you are blessed to worship in a house that has been founded on the rock of Jesus Christ, our Lord and Savior. But it is also built on another rock, another foundation—and that rock is Bishop Arthur Brazier. In forty-eight years, he has built this congregation from just a few hundred to more than 20,000 strong . . ." (paragraph 3). That tone quickly shifts to seriousness, perhaps even alarm, as he recounts the impact of absentee fathers on the African American community (paragraphs 5–6) and then asks: "How many times in the last year has this city lost a child at the hands of another child? How many times have our hearts stopped in the middle of the night with the sound of a gunshot or a siren? How many teenagers have we seen hanging around on street corners when they should be sitting in a classroom? How many are sitting in prison when they should be working, or at least looking for a job? How many in this generation are we willing to lose to poverty or violence or addiction? How many?" (paragraph 7). Obama's tone is stern when he admonishes his target audience, absentee fathers: ". . . what makes you a man is not the ability to have a child—it's the courage to raise one," (paragraph 9); ". . . don't just sit in the house and watch 'Sports Center' all weekend long. That's why so many children are growing up in front of the television," (paragraph 14); "[Your children] . . . see when you are ignoring or mistreating your wife. They see when you are inconsiderate at home; or when you are distant; or when you are thinking only of yourself. And so it's no surprise when we see that behavior in our schools or on our streets" (paragraph 19). By the end of the speech, Obama's tone becomes hopeful, encouraging: "And what I've realized is that life doesn't count for much unless you're willing to do your small part to leave our children—all of our children—a better world.... That is our ultimate responsibility as fathers and parents. We try. We hope. We do what we can to build our house upon the sturdiest rock. And when the winds come, and the rains fall, and they beat upon that house, we keep faith that our Father will be there to guide us, and watch over us, and protect us, and lead His children through the darkest of storms into light of a better day" (paragraphs 29–30). The shift in tone reinforces Obama's thesis: when fathers fulfill their responsibilities, families flourish and communities are strengthened.

5. Evidence

What kinds of evidence does Obama use? Which seem most important?

Examples: personal narrative; allusions to contemporary culture.

Statistics: data on single-parent African American families, school dropout rates, poverty rates, crime, etc.

Authority: the Bible (Matthew 7: 24-25).

Analogy: figurative comparison between the "rock" on which faith is founded and fatherhood.

The Critical Equation: CPA (Claim + Proof + Analysis)

Obama uses a significant amount of supporting material in his speech. In the second paragraph, he quotes the conclusion of Jesus's "Sermon on the Mount" that appears in Matthew 7: 24–25: "Whoever hears these words of mine, and does them, shall be likened to a wise man who built his house upon a rock: and the rain descended, and the floods came, and the winds blew, and beat upon that house, and it fell not, for it was founded upon a rock." Such authority evidence is obviously appropriate for the location and occasion—in a church on a Sunday—but echoes of the quotation are also woven into other sections of the speech to perform strategic functions. For example, echoing Jesus, Obama says: "Here at [The] Apostolic [Church of God], you are blessed to worship in a house that has been founded on the rock of Jesus Christ, our Lord and Savior. But it is also built on another rock, another foundation—and that rock is Bishop Arthur Brazier." Because of Brazier's leadership, Obama says, the church "has braved the fierce winds and heavy rains of violence and poverty; joblessness and hopelessness." Praise for Brazier's accomplishments functions strategically to ingratiate Obama with the immediate audience. Moreover, Obama continues to draw an analogy between the "rock" upon which faith is founded and the role of fathers in families and in the community. He says, "Of all the rocks upon which we build our lives, we are reminded today that family is the most important. And we are called to recognize and honor how critical every father is to that foundation" (paragraph 4), and later, "We should take all of these steps to build a strong foundation for our children. But we should also know that even if we do; even if we meet our obligations as fathers and parents . . . we will still face difficult challenges in our lives. There will still be days of struggle and heartache. The rains will still come and the winds will still blow. And that is why the final lesson we must learn as fathers is also the greatest gift we can pass on to our children—and that is the gift of hope" (paragraphs 22–23). Obama also uses statistical evidence to demonstrate the impact of absentee fathers on the African American community: "We know that more than half of all black children live in single-parent households, a number that has doubled—doubled—since we were children. We know the statistics—that children who grow up without a father are five times more likely to live in poverty and commit crime; nine times more likely to drop out of schools and twenty times more likely to end up in prison. They are more likely to have behavioral problems, or run away from home, or become teenage parents themselves. And the foundations of our community are weaker because of it" (paragraph 6). Obama uses a personal narrative to both identify with the topic and to establish one dimension of his persona. He explains that he knows "what it means to have an absent father" because his own father "left us when I was two years old, and I only knew him from the letters he wrote and the stories that my family told" (paragraph 11). Although he acknowledges that his childhood in a single-parent family was better than many others who find themselves in that situation, he nevertheless knows "the toll that being a single parent took on my mother—how she struggled at times to the pay bills; to give us the things that other kids had; to play all the roles that both parents are supposed to play." Because of that experience, he says, "I resolved many years ago that it was my obligation to break the cycle—that if I could be anything in life, I would be a good father to my girls; that if I could give them anything, I would give them that rock—that foundation—on which to build their lives. And that would be the greatest gift I could offer" (paragraph 12). Near the end of the speech he offers a second personal narrative, recounting the story of a recent "town hall meeting" during which a young man asked him, "What does life mean to you." Obama admits struggling with his answer and explains that eventually he said: "When I was a young man, I thought life was all about me," but that now he has "realized that life doesn't count for much unless you're willing to do your small part to leave our children—all of our children—a better world. Even if it's difficult. Even if the work seems great. Even if we don't get very far in our lifetime" (paragraphs 25–29). Those personal narratives help to build Obama's persona as a father and to strengthen his credibility on the topic. Finally, Obama uses references (allusions) to contemporary culture to enliven his message. He urges fathers not to "watch 'SportsCenter' all weekend long," and to help their children "with their homework, and replace the video game or the remote control with a book once in awhile" (paragraph 14). Later he says: "It's up to us—as fathers and parents—to instill this ethic of excellence in our children. It's up to us to say to our daughters, don't ever let images on TV tell you what you are worth, because I expect you to dream without limit and reach for those goals. It's up to us to tell our sons, those songs on the radio may glorify violence . . ." (paragraph 17).

6. Structure

How is the speech organized? In what ways is its structure affected by its delivery in a church on Fathers' Day?

Obvious or apparent: problem/solution.

Organizing principle: the speech takes the form of a sermon or perhaps a prophetic message.

The surface-level structure or organizational pattern of Obama's speech is problem/solution. He first identifies the problem, fathers who have "abandoned their responsibilities" (paragraph 5), and then explains that "the foundations of our community are weaker because of it" (paragraph 6). Then, he urges three specific actions to solve that problem. Fathers must: set examples of excellence for their children (paragraph 14); they must teach their children to empathize with others rather than to be self-centered (paragraph 18); and they must instill hope in their children (paragraph 23). However, a more subtle, less noticeable, but nevertheless more important organizing principle is also present: Obama's speech appropriates the form of a sermon or prophetic message. That form begins with the quotation from Matthew 7:24–25 in the second paragraph. In that quotation, Jesus says "whoever hears these words of mine, and does them, shall be likened to a wise man who built his house upon a rock" making it safe from storms and trouble. In paragraph 4, that "rock" becomes a metaphor for true fatherhood. Obama says: "Of all the rocks upon which we build our lives, we are reminded today that family is the most important. And we are called to recognize and honor how critical every father is to that foundation. They are teachers and coaches. They are mentors and role models. They are examples of success and the men who constantly push us toward it." Metaphorically, then, true fatherhood becomes God's commandment—fathers must be the "rock" upon which families and the community are founded. However, in paragraph six, Obama chastises the community because "too many fathers are . . . missing from too many lives and too many homes;" they have failed to heed God's command, and the result is the hard times enumerated in paragraphs six and seven. To relieve this suffering, fathers must "get right" with the commandment for true fatherhood by taking the specific actions described in paragraphs fourteen, eighteen, and twenty-three. And when they do, better times will follow. Obama says: "That is our ultimate responsibility as fathers and parents. We try. We hope. We do what we can to build our house upon the sturdiest rock. And when the winds come, and the rains fall, and they beat upon that house, we keep faith that our Father will be there to guide us, and watch over us, and protect us, and lead His children through the darkest of storms into light of a better day." We must add that, like Old Testament prophets, Obama was criticized harshly by some members of the African American community following his prophetic message.

7. Strategies

Identify strategies based on language, appeals, references to the Bible and to the pastor of the church. What language strategies are noteworthy?

Repetition; antithesis; metaphor.

Appeals: ingratiation; spiritualization; refutation; rhetorical questions.
Obama draws on the biblical quotation in the second paragraph to ingratiate himself with the immediate audience by praising their pastor, Bishop Arthur Brazier, as the "rock" upon which their church is founded. Obama uses the language strategy of antithesis to enumerate Brazier's accomplishments: "Because of his work and his ministry, there are more graduates and fewer gang members in the neighborhoods surrounding this church. There are more homes and fewer homeless. There is more community and

less chaos . . ." (paragraph 3). Earlier, in the section on Evidence, we explained that the "rock" from the biblical quotation also becomes a metaphor for true fatherhood. That biblical reference also serves strategically to lend a spiritual dimension to Obama's case for true fatherhood—like Jesus's words forming the foundation of the church, true fatherhood forms the foundation for families and communities. Obama also uses the language strategy of repetition in two significant passages. In the seventh paragraph, he enumerates the fears of parents when he asks: How many times in the last year has this city lost a child at the hands of another child? How many times have our hearts stopped in the middle of the night with the sound of a gunshot or a siren? How many teenagers have we seen hanging around on street corners when they should be sitting in a classroom? How many are sitting in prison when they should be working, or at least looking for a job? How many in this generation are we willing to lose to poverty or violence or addiction? How many?" Repetition of the phrase "How many" builds a rhythm or cadence that emphasizes the seriousness of the problems he enumerates. The passage also consists of a series of rhetorical questions, to which Obama invites the audience to respond: "Too many times." He uses the language strategy of repetition again near the end of the speech when he says, "But now, my life revolves around my two little girls. And what I think about is what kind of world I'm leaving them. Are they living in a country where there's a huge gap between a few who are wealthy and a whole bunch of people who are struggling every day? Are they living in a country that is still divided by race? A country where, because they're girls, they don't have as much opportunity as boys do? Are they living in a country where we are hated around the world because we don't cooperate effectively with other nations? Are they living a world that is in grave danger because of what we've done to its climate?" Again, repetition of the phrase "Are they living" emphasizes the problems with which fathers, families, and communities must struggle.

EXERCISES

Critical Thinking Exercises

1   In the paragraphs below, identify the most likely audience challenges (choose from inattention, misperception, lack of motivation, inertia).

a. A college student attempts to persuade her speech class that horrible injustices exist in Iraq. She is concerned that her subject holds little salience for this group.

b. An ad agency is given an account with Royal Caribbean Cruise Lines to create a mass mailing campaign targeted at corporate executives. The ad agency is concerned, however, that their mailer will be wrongly viewed as "just another flimsy sales pitch."

c. Angelina Grimké wants to share her compelling story of the horrors of slavery, but she is constrained by the presence of a disruptive audience and a loud, angry mob of detractors outside. She wonders if she can even be heard.

d. MTV wants to launch an educational "Rock-the-Vote" campaign designed to get its young listeners to register to vote. Those producing the radio spots are concerned that if their listeners have never taken part in the electoral process, they may be inclined to resist any message for the simple reason that registering involves a behavioral change.

2.   Design an interviewing schedule (a series of planned and interrelated questions on a subject) and use it to interview three people on the subject of your rhetorical act: a student, a professor, and a community member. Do not interview friends or roommates; try to interview complete strangers.

   The exercise has three purposes: (1) to give you experience with the problems involved in developing questions that elicit accurately what others know, believe, and feel; (2) to give you experience in creating an atmosphere in which others are willing to tell you what they know, believe, and feel; and (3) to provide you with information about the knowledge, beliefs, and attitudes of others to help you adapt a rhetorical act to a general or heterogeneous audience.

The intent of the interviews is to gather information that would help you, as a rhetor, prepare a rhetorical act more likely to be attended to and to be influential for a general audience. You are attempting to discover the causes of resistance to your purpose and the sorts of challenges you might face. You are also trying to find out what bases there are for appeals that might cause this audience to give your point of view a fair and open hearing. In order to be an effective interviewer, you need to be well informed on the subject yourself.

You need to plan an opening that introduces you, indicates what you are doing and why, introduces the subject, and tells the person to be interviewed how much time will be involved and why it is important that he or she participate. Plan a series of questions that progress through the areas of the subject you think most important. Begin with basic questions to determine just what the person knows. Plan a closing that expresses appreciation and that will end the interview comfortably.

Avoid these problems: not knowing the questions well enough or reading them mechanically, lack of warmth and eye contact suggesting disinterest, speaking too softly or too quickly, rushing the interview so that answers are superficial, apologizing, asking biased questions, suggesting answers if the person hesitates, mentioning how others answered, taking too many notes, and taking too much for granted (such as how much the person knows about the subject or how familiar he or she is with the vocabulary of your topic).

a. Turn in a copy of the questions you used, together with an evaluation of them as a means of getting useful and accurate information about knowledge, beliefs, and attitudes.

b. Briefly evaluate your strengths and weaknesses as an interviewer and indicate what kinds of things were successful and unsuccessful in creating an atmosphere in which people were willing to be interviewed and to take the questions seriously. What places were the best for doing the interviews?

c. Briefly evaluate the information you obtained in terms of using it for a rhetorical act on this subject for a general audience. Indicate what assumptions were confirmed or disconfirmed; consider how your class differs from this wider audience; indicate some ways you might proceed that you think would be effective in gaining a hearing for your point of view.

Analytical Writing Exercise

Portfolio Entry 7: Audience Obstacles

3. Identify and explain the audience challenges that are evident in your rhetorical acts. Using relevant elements of descriptive analysis, detail how each rhetor tries to combat these audience challenges. Is one more successful than another? Explain in one to two pages.

Strategic Speaking Exercises

4. In preparation for your next speaking assignment, conduct a brief survey of your classmates to locate where the points of audience resistance are in terms of your topic and thesis. In what ways might inattention, misperception, lack of motivation, or inertia be a challenge? Once you have collected this information, indicate briefly how you will attempt to minimize this challenge strategically with various elements of descriptive analysis. For a refresher on this assignment, revisit the "Strategy Report" in Chapter 3. As you become a more sophisticated speaker, conducting these kinds of surveys will become standard operating procedure. Your instructor may elect to make this a featured component of the grading criteria.

5. Give a two-minute impromptu speech (claim + support + restatement) in which you sell a person, place, product, or idea to an assigned audience provided by your instructor (e.g., sixth graders at YMCA camp; active seniors at a fitness center; Rotary club members; Moms-Day-Out group). Ask the class if they can identify which audience you were assigned. How do your strategies for selling change depending on audience type? What do you assume about their attitudes, beliefs, and values regarding your topic?

NOTES

1. According to professor of marketing James U. McNeal at Texas A&M University, as reported in an article in *American Demographics* in April 1998, children under age twelve spent more than $24 billion of their own money in 1997, while directly influencing the spending of $188 billion more. He estimates that by 2001, children's spending may reach $35 billion. "In the 1990s, children aged 2–14 directly influenced about

$5 billion in parental purchases," McNeal wrote. "In the mid-1970s, the figure was $20 billion, and it rose to $50 billion by 1985. By 1990, kids' direct influence had reached $132 billion, and in 1997, it may have peaked around $188 billion. Estimates [have] shown that children's aggregate spending roughly doubled during each decade of the 1960s, 1970s, and 1980s, and tripled so far in the 1990s." Reported by Miriam H. Zoll, "Psychologists Challenge Ethics of Marketing to Children," *American News Service,* April 5, 2000. http://www.mediachannel.org/originals/kidsell.shtml. Accessed June 6, 2002.

2. Edwin Black, in "The Second Persona," *Quarterly Journal of Speech* 56 (April 1970): 109–119, discusses the persona of the audience. See also Michael McGee, "In Search of the People," *Quarterly Journal of Speech* 61 (October 1975): 235–249.

3. See K. K. Campbell, "The Rhetoric of Women's Liberation: An Oxymoron," *Quarterly Journal of Speech* 59 (February 1973): 74–86, for evidence of some changes in women's self-images produced by contemporary feminism. See "The Glass Half Empty: Women's Equality and Discrimination in American Society," a report by the NOW Legal Defense and Education Fund, New York City, 1994, for data on young women's attitudes. In addition, a 1991 study by the American Association of University Women, "Shortchanging Girls, Shortchanging America," found substantial problems of self-esteem among teenage women. See also Peggy Orenstein, *School Girls: Young Women, Self Esteem and the Confidence Gap* (New York: Doubleday, 1994).

4. This part of the rhetorical problem is the subject of Chapter 10.

5. D. O. Sears and J. L. Freedman, "Selective Exposure to Information: A Critical Review," *Public Opinion Quarterly* 31 (1967): 175. See also I. L. Janis and L. Mann, *Decision Making: A Psychological Analysis of Conflict, Choice and Commitment* (New York: Free Press, 1977).

6. L. K. Canon, "Self-confidence and Selective Exposure to Information," in *Conflict, Decision and Dissonance,* ed. L. Festinger (Stanford, CA: Stanford University Press, 1964); J. L. Freedman, "Confidence, Utility and Selective Exposure: A Partial Replication," *Journal of Personality and Social Psychology* 2 (1965): 778–780.

7. J. L. Freedman and D. O. Sears, "Selective Exposure," in *Advances in Experimental Social Psychology,* vol. 2, ed. L. Berkowitz (New York: Academic Press, 1965); D. O. Sears and J. L. Freedman, "Effects of Expected Familiarity with Arguments upon Opinion Change and Selective Exposure," *Journal of Personality and Social Psychology* 2 (1965): 420–426; D. O. Sears, J. L. Freedman, and E. F. O'Connor, "The Effects of Anticipated Debate and Commitment on the Polarization of Audience Opinion," *Public Opinion Quarterly* 28 (1964): 617–627.

8. A. Hasdorf and H. Cantril, "They Saw a Game: A Case Study," *Journal of Abnormal and Social Psychology* 49 (1954): 133.

9. http://64.233.167.104/custom?q=cache:-fCiOR-YMvQkQJ:www.census.gov/compendia/statab/tables/07s0299.xls+Guns+used+in+murders& hl=en&ct=clnk&cd=7&gl=us&client=pub-3255643703350154

10. The original study was done by C. I. Hovland and W. Mandell, "An Experimental Comparison of Conclusion Drawing by the Communicator and the Audience," *Journal of Abnormal and Social Psychology* 47 (July 1952): 581–588, and its findings have been confirmed in subsequent studies. The results emphasize the importance of the thesis, organization, and transitions in your rhetoric; they are the subject of Chapter 6, on the structuring of a rhetorical act.

11. Richard E. Petty and John T. Cacioppo, *Communication and Persuasion: Central and Peripheral Routes to Attitude Change* (New York: Springer-Verlag, 1986).

12. Abraham Maslow, *Motivation and Personality* (New York: Harper, 1954).

13. O. J. Harvey and G. D. Beverly, "Some Personality Correlates of Concept Change Through Role Playing," *Journal of Abnormal and Social Psychology* 63 (1961): 125–130.

14. The comments in parentheses are by the contemporary reporter and describe the scene inside and outside the hall during the speech. Biblical allusions are identified in brackets. The text is from *History of Pennsylvania Hall, Which Was Destroyed by a Mob on the 17th of May 1838,* ed. Samuel Webb (1838), pp. 123–126.

15. The character of Worldly-Wise appears in John Bunyan's *Pilgrim's Progress* (originally published 1683; printed in the United States in 1789), the story of a man struggling to find salvation despite many obstacles and temptations.

16. "Anti-slavery reached its climax in the 1830s, sending over 4,000 petitions to Parliament during three separate sessions, a feat unequalled by any other national movement. . . . Women began to petition en masse at the beginning of the 1830s. . . . In 1833 a single petition of 187,000 'ladies of England—a huge featherbed of a petition' was hauled into Parliament by four sturdy members" (Seymour Drescher, "Public Opinion and British Colonial Slavery," in *Slavery and British Society, 1776–1846*, ed. James Walvin [Baton Rouge: Louisiana State University Press, 1982], pp. 30, 33).

17. The text of Barack Obama's speech is available at http://www.huffingtonpost.com/2008/06/15/obamas-fathers-day-speech_n_107220.html. Accessed March 28, 2012. Paragraph numbers added.

Chapter 9

Challenges Arising from the Subject and Purpose

Although audience obstacles are central in an analysis of the rhetorical context, *subject and purpose* challenges are almost equally important. Actually, of course, the issues discussed here arise out of the interrelationship between the audience and the issue: the subject the audience is invited to consider and the purpose, the response the rhetor wishes to evoke from the audience. Again, no subject is without interest for some audience, and no subject is of interest to everyone.

To give you a feeling for the kind of rhetorical challenges discussed in this chapter, consider this paragraph from the essay on global warming by Bill McKibben cited several times in Chapter 4. At this point the author is exploring the conflicting views of experts, some of whom are positive, some fearful, about the carrying capacity of the earth:

> But we can calculate risks, figure the odds that each side may be right. Joel Cohen made the most thorough attempt to do so in *How Many People Can the Earth Support?* Cohen collected and examined every estimate of carrying capacity made in recent decades, from that of a Harvard oceanographer who thought in 1976 that we might have food enough for 40 billion people to that of a Brown University researcher who calculated in 1991 that we might be able to sustain 5.9 billion (our present population), but only if we were principally vegetarians. One study proposed that if photosynthesis was the limiting factor, the earth might support a trillion people; an Australian economist proved, in calculations a decade apart, that we could manage populations of 28 and 157 billion. None of the studies is wise enough

Figure 9–1
Subject-Related
Rhetorical
Challenges

Subject-Related Challenges

- Complexity
  - no firsthand experience
  - too difficult to understand
- Cultural History
  - taboos on subject
  - boredom/overkill
- Cost
  - too much time, money, effort
- Control
  - lack of enforcement

to examine every variable, to reach by itself the "right" number. When Cohen compared the dozens of studies, however, he uncovered something pretty interesting: the median low value for the planet's carrying capacity was 7.7 billion people, and the median high value was 12 billion. That, of course, is just the range that the UN predicts we will inhabit by the middle of the next century. (62–63)[1]

The complexity of this issue arises from several sources. One is that there are so many variables involved that it is almost impossible to predict accurately the carrying capacity of the earth. In addition, experts disagree widely. Finally, all of this involves fairly sophisticated mathematical models that are the bases of the prediction. In the face of that kind of complexity, audience members are likely to feel overwhelmed and abandon the subject.

The challenges facing anyone writing or lecturing about global warming are great indeed: the audience's limited personal experience, the formidable technical and scientific vocabulary as well as the disagreements among experts, and the mind-boggling statistics. Resistance of this sort arises from the subject and from the rhetor's purpose. One of the reasons Al Gore's *An Inconvenient Truth* won the Oscar for Best Documentary is that the film cleverly addressed many of these subject-related challenges endemic to global warming. In this chapter we discuss the four "Cs" of subject and purpose obstacles (Figure 9–1).

SUBJECT-RELATED OBSTACLES

Two major areas of resistance are created by subjects or topics: resistance created by *complexity* and resistance created by the *cultural history* of the issue.

Complexity

Some subjects are complex or, more to the point, the audience sees them as complex. In such cases you will meet a special kind of audience resistance that is definitely a barrier to joint rhetorical action. (Of course, there might also be an obstacle in your own capability to handle certain kinds of complex subjects. Even if you were speaking from personal experience, the preparation time would be far longer. But let's assume you can handle the subject.)

Subjects are complex or seem so under these conditions:

1. They are remote from the audience's personal experience.
2. They require technical knowledge or some other kind of special expertise.
3. They are bound up with many other difficult issues.

That is, audiences resist participation in rhetorical acts for which they have no touchstone in their ordinary lives. They are uncomfortable with subjects demanding decisions that they do not feel competent to make, and they are often overwhelmed by subjects with broad ramifications.

Subjects that lie outside the personal experiences of the audience create special difficulties. The audience feels unfit to make judgments. This is the case with most foreign policy decisions. Despite a great increase in world travel by U.S. Americans, few of us have been in Afghanistan, Syria, or Iran, and even fewer have been in Mali in Africa or have had experiences that would make us feel comfortable about deciding military or economic policies for those areas. By contrast, farmers have considerable experience with acreage allotments, storage facilities, insecticides, crop failure, and the like, and they bring a good deal of familiarity to decisions on such issues. Women who have delivered children in hospitals have experience they bring to proposals for birthing rooms; parents have had personal experiences with teachers relevant to educational decisions; and so forth. But when a subject is outside our personal experience, we are at the mercy of others. We have to rely on data gathered by others and on interpretations made by experts. Because experts rarely agree, we must try to decide who is more reliable and credible. Because we have to rely on others, we are more vulnerable to manipulation: It is easier to fool those without personal experience because they have no basis on which to test the data or claims of others. That is one reason we feel helpless about foreign policy decisions and why we can be deceived more easily about what really is happening in Syria or Mali or Pakistan.

Subjects are also complex when they require technical knowledge or a special kind of expertise. Subjects that demand a lot of economic knowledge from the audience are particularly dangerous. Making decisions about global warming, for example, requires many kinds of knowledge from audience members. People must know something about the factors influencing agricultural production and causing salinization and the creation of deserts. They need to know about factors affecting population growth, and they have to be able to understand the dynamics created by special kinds of pollution. Audiences faced with such demands are likely to resist participation—unless their livelihoods, say, as owners of ski resorts, have been directly affected by climatic changes—because basic information is outside their personal competence. In such a situation, rhetors must become educators, and under such circumstances, they are likely to use the entire range of rhetorical purposes in a persuasive campaign. Rhetors will begin by creating virtual experience, including altering the audience's perception of its own competence. This will be followed by efforts to explain that link and interpret the data. Only then can rhetors try to formulate beliefs in the audience about such things as the degree to which different kinds of pollution are responsible for diminishing the ozone layer, the responsibility of businesses and government for the levels of pollution, how pollution-eliminating technology can be paid for, and what kinds of regulation are needed to prevent this problem from worsening.

Subjects like global warming also are complex because they are bound up with many other difficult issues with broad ramifications. Decisions about pollution controls cannot be separated from issues of rapid transit, highways, car manufacture and costs, agriculture, and the losses of jobs and comforts in altering our lifestyle. The result is a sense that the problem is so large and its implications so extensive that no one can understand it or begin to solve it.

The history of the civil rights movement illustrates the complexity of another problem with broad ramifications. Initial efforts to attack the denial of civil rights involved eliminating clearly defined evidences of oppression—segregated waiting rooms, water fountains, and bathrooms, and barriers to voter registration, for example. When these basic battles were largely won, however, other issues emerged that were not so easy to define or solve: providing quality education, decent housing, and good jobs. Housing cannot be separated from employment or employment from education. Hence, in order to solve one problem, all the problems apparently have to be addressed. Such efforts take time and involve cultural dislocations (reflected, for example, in disputes over school busing and integration plans), and clear evidence of progress may be hard to see.

In summary, a subject may create challenges because of its real or perceived complexity. A subject is complex when the audience has no firsthand experience with it, when technical knowledge or special expertise is required, and when the subject is part of an interrelated set of problems or issues.

Cultural History

The second set of challenges arising from the subject has its roots in events that happened long before you take the stage. Let us call them the *subject's cultural history* to indicate that the obstacle's resistance comes from ideas or concepts about the subject formed during past discussions in your culture. Obstacles arising from cultural history include these:

1. Boredom or indifference owing to familiarity with existing arguments.
2. Closed minds about public discussion of some taboo topics.
3. Conditioned responses to emotionally loaded subjects.
4. Conflict with cultural values.

No subject exists in a void. Every subject has a context and meaning consisting of past experience with the subject and the issues surrounding it. This context is the residue of past rhetorical action. It is the subject's cultural history. If your topic has a long and rich cultural history, beware! Here is an example of the problems for change created by cultural history. Consider how the author tries to combat the rich cultural history that is associated with our national anthem:

The Star-Spangled Earache: What So Loudly We Wail
by Caldwell Titcomb[2]

1   Not so long ago Representative Andrew Jacobs Jr. of Indiana filed a bill to replace "The Star-Spangled Banner" with "America the Beautiful" as our national anthem. Many people have long advocated just such a change, and for a number of reasons the bill deserves wide support.

2   "The Star-Spangled Banner" has been the official national anthem only since March 3, 1931. Most people assume that it has been the anthem virtually from time immemorial and that

it is thus now sacrosanct. But clearly there is nothing wrong with supplanting something that has been in effect for only 50-odd years.

3   The music is by an Englishman, John Stafford Smith (1750–1836), who wrote it as a drinking song for a London social club, the Anacreontic Society. Is our nation so poverty-stricken that we must rule out home-grown music?

4   The tune is a constant stumbling block. Technically, it covers a span of a twelfth—that is, an octave plus a perfect fifth. Not only is it difficult for the general public to sing, but it has repeatedly caused trouble even for professional opera singers. Some people assert that this problem could be solved by selecting the right key for performance. But the point is that *all* 12 possible keys are poor. No matter what the key, the tune goes either too high or too low (and both, for some people). What's more, the tune is irregular in its phrasing and does not always fit the text well. In "Whose broad stripes," for instance, assigning "broad" to a tiny sixteenth note is bad.

5   Finally, Francis Scott Key's poem (1914) is not suitable. It is of low quality as poetry, and its subject matter is too specific and too militaristic, dealing with a one-day incident in a war. Are glaring rockets and bursting bombs the essence of the nation? I wonder how many people have really read through all four stanzas and thought about the words. The third stanza is particularly offensive: "Their blood has wash'd out their foul footsteps' pollution./ No refuge could save the hireling and slave/ From the terror of flight or the gloom of the grave." When a bank celebrated the last Independence Day by buying a full page in the *New York Times* to print the tune and text of the anthem, not surprisingly the dreadful third stanza was entirely omitted. The poem has little to recommend it except for the single line, "The land of the free and the home of the brave."

6   Why not choose "America the Beautiful" in its place? Consider, for a moment, why such a change might be resisted and the kinds of arguments that might be mounted in defense of retaining the present national anthem. Are virtually all such arguments examples of our attachment to cultural history?

In response, essayist Daniel Mark Epstein chose to accept the claim that the "Star-Spangled Banner" is hard to sing but argued that this was a good thing! Consider the way in which cultural history is used to respond.

"The Star-Spangled Banner" is a sublime anthem, democratic and spacious, holding at least one note for every American. The tune is a test pattern not only for the voice but for the human spirit. The soul singer, the rock star, and the crooner—all are humbled by the anthem. We have heard world-famous tenors and sopranos choke upon the low notes and cry out in pain at the high ones. We have seen the great Mahalia Jackson tremble . . . . The anthem perfectly suits our collective spirit, our ambition and national range. So it ought to be sung by a crowd of Americans, to guarantee that all of the notes will be covered . . . .

This leads us to the next argument against "The Star-Spangled Banner": that it is too difficult for schoolchildren to sing. An editorial in the *New York World* of March 31, 1931, answered this charge with logic and eloquence. "What if schoolchildren could sing it? We should be so sick of it by now that we could not endure the sound of it." . . . The virtues of "The Star-Spangled Banner" are that it does require a wide compass, so that schoolchildren cannot sing it, and that it is in three-quarter time, so that parades cannot march to it. So being, it has managed to remain fresh, not frayed and worn, and the citizenry still hear it with some semblance of a thrill, some touch of reverence.[3]

The ritualistic power of the national anthem was demonstrated in a recent controversy over its Spanish translation. As it turns out, the government gave its blessing in 1919 when the U.S. Bureau of Education prepared a Spanish version of the "Star-Spangled Banner." (There are translations in many other languages as well.) The controversy grew in part because, during the heated debate in Congress over immigration policy, some Latin pop stars released a Spanish version with some different lyrics ("The time has come to break the chains.") called "Nuestro Himno"— "Our Anthem." Critics insist that the song should be sung only in English, and Senators Jim Talent (R-MO), Pat Roberts (R-KS), Lamar Alexander (R-TN), and Representative Jim Ryun (R-KS) introduced legislation requiring that the anthem never be recited or sung in a foreign language.[4]

Capital punishment is another example. The death penalty for certain crimes (usually murders) has been defended and attacked so often that the arguments on both sides almost have become clichés. Virtually any audience will have been exposed to them before. Everyone has heard the argument that capital punishment deters people from committing murder (the deterrence argument), and everyone also knows the counterargument—that most murders are committed in the heat of passion when the part of the mind affected by deterrents is simply not in control. On and on go the arguments and counterarguments—from cruel and unusual punishment, unequal protection of the law (many more nonwhites and poor people are executed than whites and the wealthy), the likelihood of rehabilitation, to the haunting possibility of executing the innocent. Death, as one anti-capital-punishment argument reminds us, is so final.

Because everyone knows these arguments, the first challenge you face may be *boredom*. Thus, unless you can find a fresh approach to the subject, you might be better off avoiding it. You might argue that the issues are far from settled. Not long ago, the Governor of Illinois suspended executions after investigations by a group from Northwestern University exonerated convicts on death row and revealed the incompetence of the attorneys who had been assigned to defend those facing capital charges. At present, 200 prisoners have been exonerated by DNA evidence, and 14 of them were on death row.[5] Public argument about the death penalty reminds us that even much-argued, familiar issues can become lively once again, particularly when new and disturbing evidence of its misuse emerges. Note that this is an illustration of the dynamics of persuasive arguments theory.

Another rhetorical challenge that may lurk in a subject's history is a *taboo* against discussing it. Consider, for example, almost any subject having to do with sexuality in the United States, dramatically illustrated by public policy disputes over the prevention and treatment of AIDS (acquired immune deficiency syndrome). The virus causing AIDS is spread primarily through sexual contacts, and AIDS cases in the United States initially appeared predominantly among the gay male community. As a result, AIDS involved two areas considered taboo by many—sexual acts and homosexuality—and policy makers and physicians found it difficult to discuss them; accordingly, actions to enhance prevention and to improve treatment were adopted slowly. Even now, with more detailed information about AIDS all over the world and an increasing number of cases caused by heterosexual contacts, proposals to provide sex education in elementary schools and condoms to high school students in order to provide safer sex remain controversial. Despite a rising incidence of AIDS among African Americans, most churches that serve these communities have resisted supporting such programs because of strong religious taboos against homosexuality and public discussion about sexual behavior; recently, that has been changing. Many of us seem to want to deny that teenagers or preteens tend to be sexually active and find blatant reminders of their sexuality deeply disturbing, even when providing condoms that, if used, would protect them from sexually transmitted diseases and AIDS and would lower rates of abortion by preventing unwanted pregnancies. Discussion of issues such as pornography, venereal disease, rape, incest, and domestic abuse arouse resistance among some audiences. Some of these taboos are breaking down, the subjects are beginning to be aired, and the victims are beginning to gain help. But if you talk about these subjects, you must choose your audiences and your words carefully, or minds will be so tightly closed against you that no rhetorical action can occur, not even the sharing of basic data.

The cultural history of a subject may also include *highly charged emotional reactions*. Most taboo subjects have such emotional loads. Arab-Israeli relations are highly charged subjects in Jewish and Arab communities; racism and its remedies, homosexual rights generally, or policies toward gay marriage and amnesty for illegal aliens are hot-button issues in the United States. These topics produce intense emotional reactions in audiences. If you choose such a subject, you can expect to face several challenges falling under the general headings of conditioned responses and closed minds.

One sure sign of a "hot" subject is to have a loaded slogan associated with it. In recent debates over legalized abortion in the United States, opponents have chanted "right to life." This slogan provokes a strong conditioned response and effectively closes minds to any discussion because it puts opponents in the position of defenders of life and proponents of legal abortion in the position of murderers. Thus proponents have been forced to come up with a slogan of their own, "pro-choice" (or sometimes "voluntary motherhood"), which moves the debate to different ground.

With any such emotionally loaded subject, your problem is to structure the discussion so issues can be treated apart from predictable and intense emotional responses—in short, to open closed minds, if only a little way.

Closely related to highly charged emotional reactions is the intense resistance created by subjects that are in conflict with revered cultural values. Anyone who chooses energy conservation as a subject will have to contend, for example, with the U.S. love affair with the automobile. Independence and personal autonomy have been ultimate goods in our culture for many decades; their value is part of our history. Bigger was better, greater speed and power were symbols of personal power and wealth, and driving bigger, faster, and more powerful cars and SUVs that used more gas was a symbol of success. Faced with rising gas prices, some argue for a return to smaller cars; others argue that we should support "fracking" as a way to increase oil and gas production, which would lower prices, and reduce the federal tax on gasoline to make it even more affordable. Others argue for policies to encourage the construction and use of rapid transit systems. But until such energy-sensitive values establish themselves, efforts to persuade people to limit their energy consumption, to pollute less, and to protect the environment will run head-on into the value of independence and the long cultural history of the automobile as the symbol of success. And if minds are not actually closed to policies to conserve energy through reduced driving, they are certainly resistant, as reflected in the number of pickups, vans, and SUVs on U.S. highways, most of which are gas guzzlers. The new marketing of hybrid vehicles has been a promising breakthrough to this formidable cultural history challenge.

The second major set of rhetorical challenges arising from your subject and purpose, then, lie in what we have called cultural history. Specifically, they are boredom, taboos, and emotional loads and the closed minds that can result, and conflicts with cultural values.

PURPOSE-RELATED CHALLENGES

As a rhetor, you will not just be dealing with a subject; you will also be trying to induce a certain kind of participation from the audience. The kind of response that you seek may create resistance. The two kinds of challenges that arise from rhetorical purposes are resistance to the *cost* of responding and audience perception that it has no *control* over the issue in question (audience members do not see themselves as agents of change).

Cost

Just what is the audience expected to do, and what is the cost in time, energy, money, inconvenience, or ridicule? The greater such costs to audience members, the smaller the chance that they will do what you ask. If you are typical college students, some of you smoke and few of you exercise enough, and many of you eat lots of junk food. In the face of medical evidence, no one argues that smoking is good for your health, that exercise is unnecessary, or that junk food will lengthen your life. Why, then, do so many U.S. Americans smoke, live sedentary lives, and eat junk food? The answer is that doing otherwise would cost them too much—too much agony or at least considerable discomfort to quit smoking, too much sustained thought and effort to fit exercise into their way of life, and too many withdrawal pains from butter-drenched popcorn and french fries. Thus, if your purpose is to change any one of these habits, you will meet solid resistance in the form of the costs the audience sees in what you are suggesting. In fact, no single rhetorical act is likely to achieve this kind of purpose, although many people in the United States are extremely vulnerable to advertising for products that promise that you can stop smoking without discomfort, exercise painlessly, or lose weight without changing eating habits. Smoking clinics, exercise programs, and diet groups that do succeed have long-term contact with participants and supply consistent support from people struggling with similar problems or toward similar goals.

Time is another cost that may obstruct your rhetorical purpose. It is much faster (and easier) to write a check to a political candidate than to telephone all the Democrats, Republicans, or Independents in a precinct; this telephoning, in turn, is easier than going door to door to distribute literature and discuss a candidate. The greater the time, the energy, or the commitment demanded by your purpose, the greater the resistance you will meet.

Still other costs may be involved in your purpose—costs in money and expertise. Your audience may not have to contribute either one directly but may feel the burden in other ways, such as higher taxes or smaller amounts of money or expertise available for other projects.

Finally, cost is closely related to cultural values; these are the social costs of some subjects and purposes. Some beliefs bring down ridicule and other social sanctions on the believers. Because all of us want to be liked and respected by our friends, neighbors, and family, a subject or purpose that would separate us exacts a cost that few are willing to pay, and then only if the rewards are substantial. For example, nineteenth-century woman's rights activists recognized that what came to be called the "bloomer" costume was both healthy and comfortable. Its loose harem-style pants under knee-length skirts were far better for parenting or housework than fashionably long dresses whose skirts trailed in the dirt and weighed up to twenty pounds and whose narrow waists, cinched by stays, cut off breath and circulation. Yet even the most stalwart gave up the bloomer costume because the ridicule heaped on them was so consistent and so great that it threatened their cause. Similarly, it is hard for a Roman Catholic to espouse pro-choice on abortion, a car manufacturer to support rapid transit, or an evangelical Christian to endorse the Supreme Court decision outlawing prayer in public schools. There are exceptions, of course, but those who take such stances often pay a high social price.

The rhetorical context of cost, then, measures the price the audience must pay in time, energy, inconvenience, commitment, money, expertise, or social pressure for espousing your purpose. The more you demand from the audience in such costs, the larger your rhetorical challenge.

Control

The second obstacle arising from purpose is what we call *control*—that is, the audience's perception that it has at least some ability to affect the outcome—whether those addressed believe they can effect changes. Challenges arise when members of the audience cannot see what they as individuals can do, or do not believe that their actions will have any appreciable effect—in short, when they feel they have no control. Many U.S. citizens, for example, fail to vote because they think their votes make no difference—all politicians are alike, no one vote counts, they don't know how to nominate and elect officials who will do what they want, or they fear that, through manipulation, their votes will not be counted. Such feelings illustrate the rhetorical problem of control.

Lack of a sense of control can have other undesirable side effects. Some commentators, for example, have argued that because antiabortion activists have not been able to prevail through nonviolent tactics, some have come to accept violence, including condoning the murder or attempted murder of physicians who perform abortions. Deep commitment plus loss of control may lead to extremism.

Issues of control are closely related to the context of the audience—specifically, the audience as agents of change and as created through rhetorical action (see Chapter 8). If rhetors are to overcome challenges to control, they must ensure that rhetorical action engages those who are or can be agents of change. But the resistance to control that exists in the perceptions of the audience is difficult to overcome. How does one convince women who are socialized to passivity and deference that they should act aggressively to take the initiative? How does one counteract the social influence of generations that has taught African American children that they are inferior and ugly? Given the presidential power to deploy hundreds of thousands of troops prior to congressional approval, how does one convince members of Congress to vote against an authorization to fund a troop surge in Iraq? The rhetorical efforts of politicians, religious leaders, protesters, and reporters writing and speaking on the "war on terrorism" are examples of attempts to overcome the challenge of control and to empower the citizenry.

Challenges related to control—and also to cost—exist for all audiences. It is easier to act once and be done with it than to commit yourself to a long-term course of action. If an audience feels unable to make a long-term commitment, it may refuse to act at all. Usually, it is easier to act alone than to organize a group. If a rhetorical act demands group action, individual audience members may not believe that others will join them in the effort. It is also easier to act if a problem is relatively limited and sharply defined than if the problem is complex and calls for varied and sustained actions.

Rhetorical resistance arising from control is partly a function of the characteristics of the audience. If rhetors are to deal with the context of control, they not only must target the audience carefully, but they also must ensure that the target audience includes agents of change or those who can influence agents' decisions.

Challenges arising from purpose are related to challenges arising from the subject. For example, the problem of control will be greater if the issue is diffuse and complex, and if its ramifications are so great that achieving results requires the concerted and varied efforts of a large group of people over a long period of time.

 MATERIAL FOR ANALYSIS I

On August 3, 2010, New York City Mayor Michael Bloomberg, City Council Speaker Christine Quinn, New York Governor David Paterson, and ten religious leaders of various faiths journeyed to Governors Island in New York Harbor to show their support for the proposed mosque and community center to be built near the World Trade Center site. With the Statue of Liberty in the background, the mayor delivered a stirring declaration of principle. He ended with a dramatic statement that "Political controversies come and go, but our values and traditions endure—and there is no neighborhood in this City that is off limits to God's love and mercy, as the religious leaders here with us today can attest."

He delivered his speech amid growing hostility to the proposed mosque and community center. Conservatives were particularly vocal in their opposition. For example, on her Twitter account, Sarah Palin wrote: "Peace-seeking Muslims, pls understand, Ground Zero mosque is unnecessary provocation; it stabs hearts."[6] In July, Newt Gingrich commented, "There should be no mosque near Ground Zero in New York so long as there are no churches or synagogues in Saudi Arabia."[7] Two Democrats, New York Senator Charles Schumer and New York Representative Anthony Weiner, were silent on the issue; the Jewish Anti-Defamation League opposed the construction, and President Obama was reluctant to support it; his spokesman "politically declined to take a position on the planned Muslim community center in Lower Manhattan, calling it a local issue."[8] A Pew Research Center poll found that in August 2010 only 30 percent of U.S. citizens held a "favorable opinion" of Islam, compared with 41 percent five years earlier.[9] The stated platform of the Tea Party focused on economic issues and fiscal responsibility, but its rise was tied to growing national anti-Muslim sentiment.

Bloomberg's speech was significant because of the heated climate in which it was delivered, but also because of his use of his position and audience to take a stand in support of the construction of the proposed mosque. Bloomberg was elected and reelected in 2002 and 2005 but left the Republican Party in 2007 and was reelected in 2009 as an Independent. He also self-financed his campaigns out of his large personal fortune, so his financial and party independence meant that he faced fewer political restraints than many other politicians and was freer to take a strong stand in favor of the proposed mosque and cultural center.[10]

Bloomberg also made good use of location. As New York City mayor, his constituent base was rich with ethnic and religious diversity, which could be used to prompt a more tolerant attitude from the city's residents than is seen in the nation as a whole. The history of the city's ethnic and religious diversity was linked to the history of Ellis Island, a gateway to the United States for more than 12 million immigrants between 1892 and 1954.[11] Moreover, at the time of the speech, it was estimated that 36 percent of the city's population was foreign born.[12] Timing was also a factor that aided Bloomberg. He spoke after a unanimous decision by the Landmark Preservation Commission to allow the demolition of the building that sat on the site of the proposed mosque, which removed the last legal roadblock to construction.[13]

Address in Support of Religious Tolerance and New York City Mosque[14]

by Michael Bloomberg, August 3, 2010, Governors Island, New York

1   It is, by my watch, one minute before noon, but I will still say, good afternoon.

2   We've come here to Governors Island to stand where the earliest settlers first set foot in New Amsterdam, and where the seeds of religious tolerance were first planted. We've come here to see the inspiring symbol of liberty that, more than 250 years later, would greet millions of immigrants in the—this harbor, and we come here to state as strongly as ever: This is the freest City in the world. That's what makes New York special and different and strong.

3   Our doors are open to everyone—everyone with a dream and a willingness to work hard and play by the rules. New York City was built by immigrants, and it's sustained by immigrants—by people from more than a hundred different countries speaking more than two hundred different languages and professing every faith. And whether your parents were born here, or you came yesterday, you are a New Yorker.

4   We may not always agree with every one of our neighbors. That's life and it's part of living in such a diverse and dense city. But we also recognize that part of being a New Yorker is living with your neighbors in mutual respect and tolerance.

5   It was exactly that spirit of openness and acceptance that was attacked on 9/11, 2001. On that day, 3,000 people were killed because some murderous fanatics didn't want us to enjoy the freedoms to profess our own faiths, to speak our own minds, to follow our own dreams, and to live our own lives.

6   Of all our precious freedoms, the most important may be the freedom to worship as we wish. And it is a freedom that, even here in a City that is rooted in Dutch tolerance, was hard-won over many years. In the mid-1650s, the small Jewish community living in Lower Manhattan petitioned Dutch Governor Peter Stuyvesant for the right to build a synagogue—and they were turned down.

7   In 1657, when Stuyvesant also prohibited Quakers from holding meetings, a group of non-Quakers in Queens signed the *Flushing Remonstrance*, a petition in defense of the right of Quakers and others to freely practice their religion. It was perhaps the first formal, political petition for religious freedom in the American colonies, and the organizer was thrown in jail and then banished from New Amsterdam.

8   In the 19…In the 1700s, even as religious freedom took hold in America, Catholics in New York were effectively prohibited from practicing their religion—and priests could be arrested. Largely as a result, the first Catholic parish in New York City was not established until the 1780's—St. Peter's on Barclay Street, which still stands just one block north of the World Trade Center site and one block south of the proposed mosque and community center.

9   This morning, the City's Landmark Preservation Commission unanimously voted to extend—not to extend landmark status to the building on Park Place where the mosque and community center are planned. The decision was based solely on the fact that there was little architectural significance to the building. But with or without landmark designation, there is nothing in the law that would prevent the owners from opening a mosque within the existing building. The simple fact is this building is private property, and the owners have a right to use the building as a house of worship. And the government has no right whatsoever to deny that right, and if it were tried, the courts would almost certainly strike it down as a violation of the U.S. Constitution.

10   Whatever you may think of the proposed mosque and community center, lost in the heat of the debate has been a basic question: Should government attempt to deny private citizens the right to build a house of worship on private property based on their particular religion? That may happen in other countries, but we should never allow it to happen here. This nation was founded on the principle that the government must never choose between religions, or favor one over another.

11   The World Trade Center Site will forever hold a special place in our City, in our hearts. But we would be untrue to the best part of ourselves, and who we are as New Yorkers and Americans, if we said "no" to a mosque in Lower Manhattan.

12   Let us not forget that Muslims were among those murdered on 9/11 and that our Muslim neighbors grieved with us as New Yorkers—and as Americans. We would betray our values and play into our enemies' hands if we were to treat Muslims differently than anyone else. In fact, to cave to popular sentiment would be to hand a victory to the terrorists—and we should not stand for that.

13   For that reason, I believe that this is an important test of the separation of church and state as we may see in our lifetimes—as important a test—and it is critically important that we get it right.

14   On September 11th, 2001, thousands of first responders heroically rushed to the scene and saved tens of thousands of lives. More than 400 of those first responders did not make it out alive. In rushing into those burning buildings, not one of them asked, "What God do you pray to?" "What beliefs do you hold?" The attack was an act of war, and our first responders defended not only our City but our country and our Constitution. We do not honor their lives by denying the very Constitutional rights they died protecting. We honor their lives by defending those rights, and the freedoms that the terrorists attacked.

15 Of course, it is fair to ask the organizers of the mosque to show some special sensitivity to the situation—and in fact, their plan envisions reaching beyond their walls and building an interfaith community. B[y] doing so, it is my hope that the mosque will help to bring our City even closer together and help repudiate the false and repugnant idea that the attacks of 9/11 were in any ways consistent with Islam. Muslims are as much a part of our City and our country as the people of any faith and they are as welcome to worship in Lower Manhattan as any other group. In fact, they have been worshiping at the site for better—the better part of a year, as is their right.

16 The local community board in Lower Manhattan voted overwhelming to support the proposal and if it moves forward, I expect the community center and mosque will add to the life and vitality of the neighborhood and the entire City.

17 Political controversies come and go, but our values and our traditions endure—and there is no neighborhood in this City that is off limits to God's love and mercy, as the religious leaders here with us can attest.

Questions for Analysis

1. How does Bloomberg incorporate New York City's history into his argument? Is this speech a kind of history lesson?
2. How does he link the issue of the mosque and community center to basic constitutional rights?
3. The decision by the Landmark Preservation Commission removed a legal roadblock to the mosque; in what ways might their decision aid Bloomberg's cause?
4. Identify the lines in which Bloomberg characterizes New York City and its residents. In what ways do these lines contribute to "creating" his audience?
5. What language in the speech presents Bloomberg as a peer rather than as the mayor?
6. In what sense does Bloomberg characterize the proposed mosque and community center as an affirmation of the values attacked on 9/11?
7. Why is it strategic for Bloomberg not to refer to this geographic area as Ground Zero?
8. How does Bloomberg's ethnic background strengthen his argument?

 MATERIAL FOR ANALYSIS II

Following is an article by Gary Smith, senior writer at *Sports Illustrated*. Smith has received many awards for his writing including the National Magazine Award for nonfiction—the magazine equivalent of the Pulitzer Prize—a record four times; he also was a finalist for the award a record ten times.[15] Some of his literary peers have called him "the best magazine writer in America" and "America's best sportswriter."[16] However, in this essay, published on the heels of the mass murders at Sandy Hook Elementary School in Newtown, Connecticut, Smith steps outside his customary role to address the extremely controversial issue of gun control.

After Newtown: Change Has *Gotta* Come[17]

by Gary Smith

1   Thirty-two years, one month and six days ago, I decided I was done living in 850-word boxes like this one. I'd grow claws, if that's what it took. I'd scratch my way out.

2   I'd just finished coming to a conclusion about a man I'd never spoken to in my life. I'd just written, in two hours of moist deadline panic, an 850-word judgment on Dick Howser's vacillation over returning to manage the 1981 Yankees. Hamlet Howser, I'd called him, a man hemming and hawing over whether to be or not to be. Very cute. Very clever. Very wrong. Dick, it turned out, was a dignified man trying to find some dignified way to stand up to George Steinbrenner's backroom bullying, a hundred cogs whirring behind the curtains that I couldn't see.

3   That was it for me and sports columns. I went right on applauding the masters of the high-wire sprint. I just knew I didn't have the fast-twitch muscles for it. I needed two months and 8,500 words, not two hours and 850, so I exited the box.

4   Until last Thursday morning, over breakfast, reading what a rookie basketball coach from low-lying Winthrop University had just done. Walked to the microphone after a 10-point loss to an Ohio State team ranked fourth in preseason polls, politely answered the age-old questions about X's and O's and Davids and Goliaths, then hesitated, as everyone began to scatter and someone muttered, "Anything else, Coach?"...and said, Well, yes, he did have one more thing.

5   And suddenly Pat Kelsey was talking about these two pink bedrooms back home in South Carolina and these two little girls that he was going to give the biggest hugs of his life...and about those twenty empty bedrooms in Newtown, Conn.

6   "I didn't vote for President Obama," he said. "But you know what? He's my president now. He's my leader. I need him to step up. Mr. Boehner, the speaker of the House... he needs to step up. Parents, teachers, rabbis, priests, coaches, everybody needs to step up. This *has* to be a time for change. And I know this microphone's powerful right now, because we're playing the fourth-best team in the country. I'm not going to have a microphone like this the rest of the year, maybe the rest of my life.

7   "I'm proud to grow up American. I'm proud to say I'm part of the greatest country ever.... And it'll stay that way if we change. But we *gotta* change."

8   Then I read, in the next paragraph, that Jim Boeheim—after talking for 15 minutes about his 900th victory at Syracuse last week—had done it too. "If we in this country," he said, "cannot get the people that represent us to do something about firearms, we are a sad, sad society."

9   And I looked up from my French toast and started reading their words to my wife, and started wondering out loud what would happen if this became contagious, if every coach and every athlete....

10   *Why'd you switch to the 2–3 zone in the last three minutes, Coach?* "Their point guard was killing us off the dribble, we weren't getting any weakside help, and I've got

one more thing, a question for you: How long can 300 million people keep letting a rifle club's money and fears steamroller all their common sense and humanity?"

11 *Who's your quarterback this Sunday?* "Well…uh…that depends on Michael's concussion test on Wednesday, on what the doc says, and one more thing: You know, it's got to be just as nice, if you're a gun collector, to see that $3,000 semi gleaming under glass as it is for a baseball fan to see a Mickey Mantle card, but here's what I don't get—how that can possibly trump everyone else's right to go to the movies without ending up in a lake of 70 people's blood?"

12 *So you still like your chances against Oklahoma City once all your teammates are healthy?* "Give us a month to get a little chemistry going, and yeah, I do, but meantime, help me get something straight: So we're saying that a target shooter's right to squeeze a trigger 30 times and make 30 holes in a target 60 feet away without reloading matters more than every six-year-old's right *not* to end up in a pile of bodies under a 27-year-old teacher full of bullets?"

13 And then I began wondering out loud what would happen if all of us, when our wives call from the grocery to see if we're out of peanut butter, reminded each other that banning assault weapons might not prevent every massacre, like the rifle club says, but it would surely prevent at least one.

14 And if every time our mothers finished updating us on the weather back home, we added that one more thing: "Did you write to your congressman and senators again this week, Mom, because like Coach said, we *gotta* change."

15 My wife looked at me across the breakfast table. "You need to write a column," she said.

16 And I knew she was right, because I was twitching. Fast.

Questions for Analysis

1. How does Smith's earlier decision not to write short pieces like this one add to the power of the essay?
2. How does Smith's background as an award-winning sportswriter affect his credibility (ethos) in this essay? Is his ethos enhanced or diminished as a result? Why?
3. How is the evidence used in this essay best characterized? In what sense is it "reluctant evidence"?

EXERCISES

Critical Thinking Exercises

1. In the following passages, identify the most likely subject/purpose challenges (choose from complexity, cultural history, cost, control):

   a. You have been given six minutes to summarize for your introductory economics class the difference between preferred stock and common stock.

   b. As coordinator of the athletic department, you have been asked to approach local alumni for significant (six figures) financial contributions to the program.

   c. As the public relations coordinator for Planned Parenthood, you are launching a community information campaign in a predominantly Catholic neighborhood on a form of birth control, Norplant, now available at your clinic.

2. Roger Fisher and William Ury, authors of *Getting to Yes*,[18] argue that getting past difficult subjects requires reconciling interests, not positions. "Interests motivate people; they are the silent movers behind the hubbub of positions" (41). Reconciling interests rather than positions works because for every interest there are usually several positions that could satisfy it, and behind opposing positions lie more interests than conflicting ones. Identify a subject that creates an impasse for you and your parents, spouse, or significant other. Share these tips with them and see if together you can negotiate a truce when you discuss the subject. How difficult is it to follow this advice?

Analytical Writing Exercises

Portfolio Entry 8: Subject Obstacles

3. Identify and explain the subject and purpose challenges relevant to your rhetorical acts. What do the rhetors do to combat these tricky subject and purpose challenges? Use relevant elements of descriptive analysis to discuss their strategic choices. Two pages.

Strategic Speaking Exercises

4. The class will be divided into two groups. One group will prepare a list of topics they believe most of their classmates will find uninteresting, such as technical or specialized subjects. The other group will prepare a list of topics they think will arouse intense hostility from two or more class members, such as highly controversial issues. Each group should compose three or four introductions for their list of topics to be presented by group-designated speakers.

The introductions for the uninteresting topics should seek to arouse interest, perhaps by presenting a novel point of view, a startling fact, or the like. However, the subject of the speech should be clear to the audience from the introduction.

The introductions for the highly controversial topics should seek to gain a fair and open hearing for a disliked point of view, perhaps by an appeal to self-interest or to the threat of biased or limited exposure, or the like. The controversial point of view should be clear to the audience from the introduction.

Present the introductions from each group. Discuss the strategies that were used, and suggest other possibilities. Discuss which approaches seemed more effective, and why.

NOTES

1. Bill McKibben, "A Special Moment in History," *Atlantic Monthly*, May 1998.

2. *The New Republic*, December 18, 1985, pp. 11–12. The author was a professor of music at Brandeis University. Reprinted by permission of The New Republic, © 1985, The New Republic LLC.

3. Daniel Mark Epstein, *Star of Wonder: American Stories and Memoirs*. (Woodstock, NY: Overlook Press, 1986), p. 14; cited in Robert J. Branham, *Debate and Critical Analysis: The Harmony of Conflict* (Hillsdale, NJ: Erlbaum, 1981), p. 125.

4. David Goldstein, "Spanish Version of U.S. National Anthem First Appeared in 1919," Knight Ridder Newspapers, *The Wichita Eagle*, May 6, 2006, p. 8A.

5. Chris Conway, "The DNA 200," *New York Times*, May 20, 2007, Section 4:14.

6. Dan Harris, "Sarah Palin Riles Up NYC Mayor Michael Bloomberg Over Mosque Tweets." *ABCNews.com*. ABC News, 20 March 2011. Accessed 3/20/11. http://abcnews.go.com.GMA/sarah-palin-riles-nyc-mayor-michael-bloomberg-mosque/story?id+11203590.

7. Justin Elliott, "Gingrich Aide: Mosque at Ground Zero is like the Statue of Marx at Arlington," *War Room*, Salon.com, 30 July 2010. Accessed 3/20/11. http://www.salon.com/news/politics/war room/2010/07/30/mosque_like_marx_at_arlington/index.html.

8. Justin Elliott, "Democrats Startlingly Silent on 'ground Zero Mosque'," *War Room*. Salon.com, 4 August 2010. Accessed 3/21/11. http://www.salon.com/news/politics/war_room/2010/08/04/democratic_silence_on_mosque.

9. Joe Garofoli, "Anti-Muslim Sentiment Grows 9 Years Later." *Featured Articles*. SF Gate, 11 Sept. 2010. Accessed 3/20/11. http://articles.sfgate.com/2010-09-11/news/23998489_1_muslims-and-islam-anti-muslim-sentiment-islamic.

10. Sewell Chan, "Bloomberg Leaving Republican Party," *Metro City Blog* NYTimes.com. *New York Times*, 19 June 2007. Accessed 4/2/11. http://cityroom.blogs.nytimes.com/2007/06/19/Bloomberg-leaving-republican-party/.

11. "Ellis Island History—A Brief Look." *Nps.gov.* 2 April 2011. National Park Service. Available online athttp://www.nps.gov/ellis/historyculture/loader.cfm?csModule=security/getfile&PageID=294652.

12. "The Newest New Yorkers 2000." New York City Department of City Planning, 2000. Available online at http://www.nycgov/html/dcp/pdf/census/nny_briefing_booklet.pdf.

13. The cited research was done by Aaron Seegmiller, an undergraduate at the University of Minnesota, who gave us permission to use his work.

14. http://www.americanrhetoric.com/speeches/michaelbloombergdefenseofnymosque.htm Accessed 5/5/11; paragraph numbers added. At a dinner on August 24, 2010, at Gracie Mansion with Muslim leaders preparing to celebrate Ramadan Isfar, Bloomberg made a second short speech about religious freedom and the debate regarding building a mosque and community center in Lower Manhattan.

15. Spencer Broome, "The Athletic Standard: Sports Illustrated's Gary Smith of Charleston Profiles Big Game and Big Picture," *Charleston Mercury*, 10 March 2009. Accessed 3/16/09; Richard Perez-Pena, "The Sports Whisperer, Probing Psychic Wounds," *New York Times*, 15 September 2008. Accessed 9/23/08.

16. Ben Yagoda, "How Gary Smith Became America's Best Sportswriter," *Slate*, 30 June 2003. Accessed 9/23/08.

17. http://sportsillustrated.cnn.com/vault/article/magazine/MAG1206666/1/index.htm. Accessed 1/4/13; paragraph numbers added.

18. Roger Fisher and William Ury, *Getting to Yes: Negotiating Agreement Without Giving In* (New York: Viking Penguin, 1991).

Chapter 10

Opportunities and Challenges Arising from the Rhetor

Ideas do not walk by themselves; they must be carried—expressed and voiced—by someone. Who that "someone" might be, however, can vary from one situation to another.

In every interaction with another human being, each of us plays a role. Some are ordinary, such as the repeated sharing of morning chores as spouses or engaging in the ordinary commercial transactions of buying gas, getting groceries, or greeting the bus driver as you go to school. We learn these basic roles at home as parents and children and spouses and, hence, learn how to speak as mothers (as women did in the Million Mom March for gun control), as fathers (as President Obama did in response to the school shootings at Newtown), and as "children" who need help and guidance from those more experienced in making basic choices. We learn other roles that we can imitate in school or at our jobs as we are exposed to the roles in our communities of political leaders such as mayors and governors (listening to New Jersey Governor Chris Christie respond to the devastation of Hurricane Sandy). Of course, online we also assume "avatars," particularly in our changing Facebook profiles, status updates, chat rooms, and video gaming. These roles, real and virtual, are expanded or constricted in peer groups, and all are part of processes by which we develop a vast array of possibilities.

In other words, we make sense of others and make sense to others by adopting roles. As part of critical analysis, we expect you to identify the personas or roles adopted by a rhetor who attempts to influence others, roles perceived by the audience that are a crucial part of any rhetorical act. These roles may be ordinary in the sense of being familiar, but they are important as they are choices of an attitude, of a way of presenting yourself through language and in action, that becomes a key part of the rhetorical effort. Sometimes more than one persona is involved. When Robert Kennedy spoke in Indianapolis, for example (see prologue and Chapter 5), he spoke first in the persona of a presidential candidate, a role consistent with the occasion of a rally. Once he began to speak, however, his role changed. Next, he was a reporter of bad news, that Martin Luther King had been shot and killed; then he became a eulogist who commemorated King's life and urged what all eulogists urge—that those who heard him would celebrate King's life by following King's example rather than erupt in anger and hatred and seek to imitate what King had done. Given the intensity of the moment and the enormous demand he was making of a largely African American audience, Kennedy's role shifted again. He now spoke as someone who had faced terrible loss caused, like the death of King, by the violence of a white man. There is no easy way to name that role. Then he spoke the words of the poet who had helped him to deal with his anger and pain at the death of his brother, and for a moment, perhaps, he was a character in a play by Aeschylus, uttering the moral of the terrible story of the *Agamemnon*. Then he again became a leader, urging the audience to go home, to pray for the King family, and to commit themselves to follow in King's footsteps. It isn't possible to identify a single persona in this case because the events and the occasion required the speaker to shift from one role to another to achieve his purpose: to commemorate our murdered leader and to focus the energies of those who heard him in nonviolent directions.

We can often identify the roles of eulogist who responds to death, commemorates and celebrates the life of the person or persons who died and asks us to make that person live on by pursuing the goals of that person's life. But each eulogist's persona is different. Compare Obama's speech in response to the shooting in Tucson, Arizona (see Chapter 5), to Robert Kennedy's speech, and you will be able to identify important differences as well as similarities. Then consider the unusual persona of Lincoln in the Gettysburg Address (see Chapter 2), another eulogy, in which he suppresses his personal role and never refers to himself directly.

By contrast, speaking in Berlin, President John F. Kennedy adopted a persona as the leader of the United States (his office) in which he assumed the right to identify the city of West Berlin as the representative, the epitome, of the struggle between communism and freedom, and invited all members of the U.S. public to join him in avowing a profound personal identification with it, to say with him that they declare themselves honorary citizens of that besieged city. It is easier to describe what he does than to identify a particular persona because his speech is unusual, out of the ordinary.

Former Senator Dale Bumpers adopted the role of advocate in defending President Clinton against the charges in the articles of impeachment (see Chapter 5). In part of that speech, he spoke as a lawyer of long experience; in the section of the speech we have included, he became a historian and teacher in order to recount the story of how the impeachment clause came into being, what was included, what excluded, and based on that history, he invited his audience to understand that clause as he does and, hence, to exonerate President Clinton. It's not possible to separate

Bumpers's persona as a former senator who was well known to his Senate audience (who were the only folks with the power to decide this case) from his persona as a lawyer who tried many divorce cases in which individuals lied about their sex life, from his persona as a historian who seeks to teach us what the Founders intended by the impeachment clause.

In other words, the persona of a given rhetor will reflect position (elective, professional, experiential), occasion, specific purpose(s), relationship to the audience, and the inventional choices that have been made as the best way to influence the audience. We ask you to analyze the personas of different speakers and writers in order to learn by a process that Greco-Roman teachers called *imitatio*; that is, by learning to recognize the personas adopted by various rhetors, you as a rhetor, in turn, learn what is possible for you.

Of the three major elements of the rhetorical context (audience, subject, and rhetor), it is the rhetor that can be best understood as both an opportunity and a challenge for rhetorical action. The importance of the rhetor in the persuasive process has been recognized since people first began to think and write about the discipline of rhetoric. In the treatise on rhetoric he wrote in the fourth century BCE, Aristotle described three paths through which ideas were made persuasive for an audience. One of these he called *ethos* (Figure 10–1), the character of the rhetor:

> [There is persuasion] through character whenever the speech is spoken in such a way as to make the speaker worthy of credence; for we believe fair-minded people to a greater extent and more quickly [than we do others] on all subjects in general and completely so in cases where there is not exact knowledge but room for doubt....character is almost, so to speak, the controlling factor in persuasion. (1.2.1356a.4)[1]

In other words, one way we are influenced is through our impressions of the rhetor—we accept the idea or believe the claim because we trust and respect the person who presents it. Moreover, says Aristotle, this is particularly true of rhetoric because it deals with social truths, what people in groups agree to believe and value when certainty is impossible and controversy is likely. Aristotle even suggests that the character of the rhetor may be the most potent source of influence, even more powerful than the arguments and evidence or the needs and motives of the audience!

The power of the rhetor's character, or ethos, becomes more understandable if we comprehend the meaning of the ancient term. *Ethos* is a Greek word that is closely related to our terms *ethical* and *ethnic*. In its widest modern usage, ethos refers not to the character or personality of an individual but to "the disposition, character, or

Figure 10–1
Definitions of Ethos

Ethos = Credibility

- One of the three paths to persuasion (along with logos and pathos)
- The character of the rhetor
- The way a rhetor mirrors qualities valued by a particular culture or group
- The attitude members of an audience have toward the rhetor

attitude peculiar to a specific people, culture, or group that distinguishes it from other peoples or groups."[2] When understood this way, its relationship to the word *ethnic* is obvious, for ethnic means "characteristic of a religious, racial, national, or cultural group." In other words, ethos refers to the distinctive culture of an ethnic group, and the ethos of an individual depends on how well he or she reflects the qualities valued in that culture. Put differently, your ethos does not refer to your idiosyncrasies or peculiarities as an individual but to the ways in which you mirror the characteristics idealized by your culture or group. Similarly, *ethics* is "the study of the . . . specific moral choices to be made by the individual in his [or her] relationship with others." In other words, we judge the character of another by the choices that person makes about how she or he will live with other members of the community. What is ethical is right conduct in relation to other persons in one's community or society. Ethical principles are the norms or values in a culture that describe what its members believe are the right relationships between persons. The ethos of a rhetor refers to the relationship between the rhetor and the community as reflected in rhetorical action.

When he described what contributed to the ethos of a rhetor in a rhetorical act, Aristotle wrote that it arose from demonstrated wisdom about social truths (*phronêsis*), from virtuosity or competence (*aretê*), and from evidence that rhetors were well intentioned (*eunoia*) toward their communities. In other words, he believed that members of the community were influenced by evidence of good sense on practical matters of concern to the community, by indications of the rhetor's ability or expertise, and by manifestations that the rhetor had the best interests of the community, not just self-interest, in mind. In more contemporary terms, your good sense or common sense is a measure of one kind of expertise or competence on an issue, your excellence is a measure of your ability or skill (based on competence and expertise), and your good-will is a measure of your concern for the community's interests not just how much you or your family and friends will gain.

Consider how these concepts have affected attitudes toward recent presidents. Jimmy Carter, for example, is viewed as a person of high moral principle and considerable expertise as an engineer who is dedicated to the good of others. Despite his high intelligence, his wisdom on social matters came to be doubted as he fumbled efforts to influence members of Congress, and later diplomatic efforts in North Korea and Haiti in 1994 were questioned for similar reasons, a sense that he is too trusting of those whose past behavior raises doubts. Ronald Reagan was seen as someone well intentioned toward the community, but, especially in retrospect, as a man who lacked social wisdom, particularly in delegating too much to subordinates, illustrated by the problems that arose in relation to what is called the Iran-Contra affair. Bill Clinton is seen as a man of great intellectual ability and charisma but someone prone to startling moral lapses. George W. Bush is seen as one with whom you can identify but whose stubbornness in the face of failed policy or poorly performing appointees provoked outcry from Republicans and Democrats alike.

Modern research has demonstrated that Aristotle's views of ethos were remarkably apt. In contemporary studies, ethos is usually defined as the attitude a member of the audience has toward the rhetor (the source of the message) at any given moment. Experimental studies demonstrate that the source of the message has considerable effect on its impact. The earliest studies compared the effects of messages attributed to different sources, and they found that sources with high prestige for an audience had a significantly greater effect. Thus, for example, similar audiences were more favorable toward a message supporting group health care when it came from the surgeon general of the United States than when it was attributed to a university sophomore. Studies like these focused on *prior ethos*, or the attitude that members of the audience have toward the rhetor (the source) before the rhetorical act. Note, however, that ethos is affected by elements of the rhetorical context. When the original surgeon general's report on the harmful effects of smoking first appeared in 1964, for example, it had little immediate impact on behavior. The decrease in smokers in the United States from more than 46 percent of the population to under 25 percent at present has occurred slowly. Moreover, no decline has occurred as yet in the percentages of teenagers who smoke despite increasing evidence of its dangers.

PRIOR ETHOS

Attitudes toward the rhetor prior to the rhetorical act originate in five areas:

1. The rhetor's reputation or track record.
2. The rhetor's appearance.
3. How the rhetor is introduced to the audience.
4. The context in which the rhetorical act occurs.
5. The occasion of the rhetorical act.

Because the attitude of the audience toward the source is so important, it is worth noting how each of these can create opportunities and challenges (Figure 10–2).

Reputation

Although you may not be famous, you have a reputation and a track record that can be as troublesome as that of a famous athlete, politician, or scholar. Two stories about the problems that Jesus had in his hometown of Nazareth are illustrative. On one occasion Jesus went home and preached in his local synagogue. According to the reports in three gospels, he did a superb job, but those in his local community were not impressed. In effect, his neighbors asked how a local boy could know and do such things—wasn't this the carpenter's son, the son of Mary, whose brothers and sisters they knew? They were offended that an ordinary person from their community should presume to preach and teach. When Jesus heard what they said, he responded,

Figure 10–2
*Rhetor-Related
Rhetorical
Opportunities and
Challenges*

Rhetor-Related Opportunities and Challenges

- Prior ethos
  - reputation, appearance, introduction, occasion, context
- Ethos from the rhetorical act
  - expertise, trustworthiness, dynamism, identification

"A prophet is not without honor, except in his own country, and in his own house" (Matthew 13:54–58; Mark 6:1–6; Luke 4:16–24).

It is quite likely that, as in this story, you will initiate rhetorical action in your local community or in a place where you are personally known well. One student reported a difficult and embarrassing experience he had when he returned from a year of study abroad and was asked to speak at a convocation at his high school. As he walked to the podium, his friends laughed. This was little Andy Smith with whom they had grown up. What could he know about the world? The student described his struggle to gain attention and to be taken seriously, and he admitted that he never quite succeeded. As his story illustrates, you face a serious rhetorical challenge when you try to establish your competence to speak to an audience in your local community, club, place of work, or neighborhood.

The second story is similar. The Gospel of John describes the process by which Jesus chose his disciples. One of them, Philip, tells another man, Nathaniel, how wonderful Jesus is. But Nathaniel responds, "Can any good thing come out of Nazareth?" And Philip answers, "Come and see" (John 1:46). Many of us come from places that, like Nazareth, are unknown and undistinguished. (One of the authors grew up on a small farm near Blomkest, Minnesota, a metropolis of some 147 residents.) Audiences may well ask how can someone from a little town in Minnesota know anything about rhetoric or criticism or the analysis of discourse? When you are outside your local community, you will have the problem of establishing your credentials and of convincing audiences that people from unusual places or small places or unknown places or places with bad reputations do have the knowledge to discuss an important subject.

Both ordinary and famous persons encounter another challenge—the difficulties that arise from inconsistent behavior. We trust those whose behavior demonstrates a systematic commitment to principles, and we are wary of those who make dramatic shifts of position. For example, when the so-called Watergate tapes were published, many were shocked at the language used privately by President Nixon who was publicly sanctimonious, suggesting inconsistency between his public and private selves. In an essay titled "Understanding Richard Nixon: A Psycho-Rhetorical Analysis," Ted Windt, a sophisticated analyst of political communication, explores the apparent "mass of contradictions" of this fascinating president. In contrast to others, Windt argues that "It was the consistent structure of Nixon's rhetoric that gave form to his politics and his political personality." Windt distinguishes between the private self that some see as full of contradictions, partly a result of the release of the Watergate tapes, and the coherent public self that emerged out of persistent patterns in Nixon's public rhetoric.[3] With the advent of websites such as YouTube, the chances increase that similar inconsistencies will be seen and heard by large audiences. Your track record as a rhetor (what you have said in the past) and as a citizen (what you have done on social issues) are analogous to your driving record or credit record. Just as you will pay higher insurance premiums if you've had accidents, or have difficulties getting credit if you have not paid your bills in the past, as a rhetor you must make a greater effort if your past statements or your past actions cast doubt on your sincerity or commitment. If what you urge appears to conflict with your past record, you will encounter a serious rhetorical problem.

In rare instances, however, deviation from the past can be an asset. When a person deviates from a lifetime of commitments, that message is important and becomes informed criticism by an insider. High-ranking military officials who come out strongly against a particular plan for war, for instance, have a special kind of credibility. There action is called *reluctant testimony* because it is given reluctantly, against their apparent interests. In such a case inconsistency can actually heighten credibility: why would these people lie if it only hurts them?

In general, one's reputation can be a real asset to a rhetor. If you are well known and well liked by your audience, it's as if you can do no wrong! Sometimes referred to as "the halo effect," rhetors who have an extraordinary bond with particular audiences often can say just about anything and receive a favorable response. Think about why candidates running for office sometimes scramble to find (and even pay) celebrities just to show up on the same stage with them! Even in the classroom, if you have given some dynamite speeches or excelled in a critical analysis, your reputation as a budding rhetorical scholar may pay dividends for you in your next assignment.

Appearance

Research on how humans form impressions of others indicates that we make initial decisions about an individual in a matter of seconds based on clothing, movement, posture, and facial expressions. Obviously, if the appearance of the rhetor (or of his discourse) creates negative impressions in the audience, a point of resistance has been created that the rhetor must overcome to be heard, much less to influence. As a result, we believe that rhetors need to make careful choices about appearance. All of us are many different people or, if you will, we play many different roles.

Depending on the audience and the occasion, rhetors try to adopt a persona that will create the least resistance in an audience. If a professor talks to students in a dormitory lounge about a film on the history of women's rights such as *Iron-Jawed Angels* on a weekday evening, she would be wise to wear a favorite pair of jeans and a comfortable shirt, sit casually on the floor, and talk informally. If she speaks at a scholarship dinner at a sorority, she would be wise to wear a favorite fashionable out-fit, stand straight, and speak more formally. If she moderates a debate before students, faculty, and townspeople between a local feminist and a psychiatrist on one hand and a gay rights leader and a psychologist on the other, she would be wise to wear neat, relatively unobtrusive clothes and speak, stand, and move with an authority and formality that bespeaks a desire to be fair. Recognize that the professor is all of these people—these are not false fronts that she puts on. But if they are shifted around, problems will arise. If she is formal in the dorm lounge, students will not feel free to talk easily and ask questions. If she is casual at the sorority, its members will feel that she is not doing honor to the occasion and will be offended. If she goes casually to the debate, her dress will be taken as a visual sign of favoring one side, and she will be suspected of bias.

Appearance is less of an issue for writers, although the different looks of student papers also create good and bad impressions. A paper written in pencil suggests a first draft, not a finished product. Handwriting that is hard to decipher suggests a rather casual approach and minimal concern for the reader. Numerous spelling and typing errors suggest that the author didn't care enough to proofread; malapropisms, such as a "feudal attempt" that was not "worth wild" call your command of your subject into question; tiny margins suggest a refusal to edit down to the specified length. It is no accident that those who make presentations in person or on paper in commercial situations try hard to have them look as professional as possible—reports are in sleek covers, nicely bound, and professionally printed; visual aids are large, printed, and colorful. The impression created is of careful planning, great concern for the result, and considerable care for the comfort of the audience.

The special styles of some famous writers illustrate the impact of the visual. African American feminist bell hooks, for example, uses no capital letters in the name that she writes under, and her decision affects the way one interprets her words and imagines her persona. Some imagist poets laid out their work to make the visual form resemble the content. Most poetry is laid out in a special kind of format, which facilitates how one understands it, although it may make it harder to read well aloud. Most newspapers have shifted from an eight- to a six-column layout, for example, to make reading them easier, and most have now introduced color in photographs and in some areas of print and advertising.

As an alert and sensitive rhetor, you must consider the demands of the situation, the subject, and the audience. You must consider which look is most appropriate and choose from your repertoire of selves so that you will not create unnecessary challenges that prevent your message from reaching the audience or that violate the occasion. Unless you are making a rhetorical point, as activists sometimes wish to do, you should choose a style of dress, posture, and speech that is appropriate to the occasion and the subject, and one that will not prevent the audience from approaching your speech with interest and a willingness to listen. Note that such choices should be closely related to the persona or role that you adopt in your speech.[4]

Your Introduction

The famous French philosopher Jean-Paul Sartre commented that one of the terrifying things about human life is that when we die our lives become the property of others to do with as they will. If you have listened to the eulogies given at funerals, you will understand how frightening that can be. In a less permanent but no less fearful way, the rhetor's ethos becomes the property of the person who introduces him to the audience, and a potential rhetorical problem is in the making. The person who introduces you creates the climate in which you will begin to speak and can be significant in determining the initial attitude of the audience. Consider carefully what you would like to have said about yourself, and if the introducer asks you, be sure to be prepared to tell her. Similarly, when you introduce someone else, think about the climate you will create. A really thoughtful introducer tells the rhetor what he plans to say or write and asks if the rhetor would like any changes or additions. You, as a rhetor, will not be able to control all the possible problems that may arise, but you need to be aware of them.

The Context

Our initial impressions of a rhetor are influenced by context. We are likely to assume, until contrary evidence appears, that those whose articles appear on the op-ed page of the *New York Times* are knowledgeable and interesting and that those who write for *Ms.* are feminist experts in some aspect of life of particular significance for women. In such cases and in many others, audiences will form initial impressions from the process by which you came to be speaking or writing at this time or in this place. Although you may be totally unknown, you will have positive prior ethos if you participate in the DePauw University Undergraduate Honors Conference because participants are selected competitively. If a well-liked member of a sorority invites her professor to speak at a scholarship dinner, the audience, to whom the professor is unknown, will probably assume that she is a professor who is often dynamic and interesting and who may be so on this occasion.

The context can also create a significant problem, however. A famous example of this involves the circumstances under which Henry Grady made a speech titled "The New South" at a dinner of the New England Society in New York City in 1886. Grady was a newspaper editor from Georgia, and he was the first southerner to speak before this group after the Civil War. He wanted to convince his audience that there was a new South developing with which New Englanders and northerners generally could form an economic partnership. But imagine his rhetorical problem when it turned out that the speaker who preceded him was none other than General William Tecumseh Sherman, who was famous for his ruthless march through Georgia, and who "waved the bloody shirt," that is, gave a speech that was most unsympathetic to the South!

The Occasion

Still other difficulties can arise from the event of which a rhetorical act is a part. Every rhetorical act is limited by the occasion, by the kind of happening or place in which it occurs. Effective rhetorical action, which reaches the audience, must be appropriate to its context. The opportunity and the challenge of the rhetor is to select a purpose that is consistent both with her beliefs and desires and with the time and place in which it occurs. Think for a moment about inappropriate rhetorical acts you have experienced, such as a commencement address on research into dread diseases that featured a large visual of a diseased tonsil or a highly partisan political speech given in a campus chapel service. Just as audiences have purposes (the needs they wish to satisfy), occasions have functions, and an effective rhetorical act must be consonant with it. If the purpose of the occasion is entertainment, your rhetorical act must be entertaining—among other things, perhaps. If the purpose of the occasion is to do honor, your act must be consistent. So important is the understanding of the demands that occasions create, we treat it in more depth as a "special constraint" on rhetorical action in Chapter 14.

Rhetorical opportunities and challenges also may arise even before you as the rhetor begin to write or speak. These may arise from your past, from your appearance, or the role you choose to play, from the way in which you are introduced to the audience, and from a conflict between your purpose and the purpose of the occasion.

ETHOS FROM THE RHETORICAL ACT

Ethos is an attitude—the impressions or images people have of the source of a message. Like all attitudes, those about the credibility of a rhetor (or the source of the message, whether it is an individual or a medium or an institution) are general and evaluative. However, unlike most other attitudes, which are unidimensional (that is, determined by only one factor), ethos is multidimensional, affected by four factors (Figure 10–3). One of these is *authoritativeness* and a second is *trustworthiness*.[5] For a rhetor to be authoritative for an audience means that she is perceived as informed,

Classical Ethos	Contemporary Ethos
• Phronesis (social truths)	• Competence
• Arete (moral excellence)	• Trustworthiness
• Eunoia (community good-will)	• Identification
• No classical equivalent	• Dynamism

Figure 10–3
*Ethos from the
Rhetorical Act*

expert, qualified, intelligent, and reliable. This cluster of attributes is similar to those characterizing a person who, in the classical sense, showed practical wisdom and expertise on matters of social concern. For a rhetor to be trustworthy means that he is perceived as honest, friendly, pleasant, and more concerned with the good of the community than with personal goals. This second factor seems to combine the Aristotelian view that a rhetor must be perceived as having moral excellence and as being well intentioned toward the community. A third factor, *dynamism*, appears in some studies. This means that, in some cases, the attitude toward the rhetor is affected by the degree to which he is emphatic, aggressive, forceful, bold, active, and energetic; but this factor functions less predictably and uniformly in diverse situations and it is a factor that may work either positively or negatively for women speakers, depending on the audience. A fourth, overarching factor, is *identification*—the perceived similarity between the rhetor and the audience—a term so central to ethos formation that it receives special attention in the next section.

The rhetor's ethos and the message do not have fixed, unchanging meanings for the audience; they interact. Once it was presumed that only the evaluation of the message was influenced by the prestige of the source from which it supposedly comes. S. E. Asch criticized this assumption and argued that authorship did not function as a source of prestige but as a context that influenced the meaning statements had for members of the audience. Such a perspective holds that meaning is in people, and when the context of a message is changed, its meaning will be interpreted differently.[6] A statement about revolution from the Declaration of Independence when attributed to Thomas Jefferson, for example, has a different meaning than if the same statement were attributed to Karl Marx. In other words, the source of an act, the rhetor or the medium in which a rhetorical act appears, are contexts that influence how the audience decides what the message means. The nature of the message itself will be influenced significantly by the source because the source is a major part of its context.

Identification

The impact of the rhetor on meaning is related to two processes with special significance for persuasion: *identification* and *participation*. In Chapter 7 identification was examined as a language strategy. Here its meaning is expanded in the context of ethos. To identify means "to establish the identity of . . . to consider as identical, equate; . . . to associate or affiliate (oneself) closely with a person or group." The word is related to identity: "the set of characteristics by which a thing is definitively recognized or known" or "the quality or condition of being exactly the same as something else."[7] If you look closely at these definitions, you will notice they are apparently contradictory or at least ambiguous. On one hand, these words refer to the set of characteristics that make something or someone unique, distinctive. On the other hand, these words refer to what is alike, even identical, about two or more things or persons. In other words, they are terms about the relationship between similarities and differences. Identification is possible because of similarities—we are all students and U.S. citizens interested in understanding how to use communication in order to be effective moral agents. These are possibilities for identification despite the many ways in which we may be different—based on sex, ethnicity, religious beliefs, or political commitments. You can identify with us if our behavior as authors of this book consistently embodies shared goals and interests, but we can become real people for you, rather than impersonal authors, only as you become aware of the qualities that make us different. As audiences, we do not identify with generalities but with general characteristics embodied in specific ways in an individual. Persons identify with each other, and it is as an individual that the audience will respond to you, specifically as an individual who illustrates and represents general qualities and characteristics you and they share.

Research on the development of trust helps explain this further. Trust arises out of a reciprocal pattern of interrelationships. We learn to trust by sharing, by mutual exchange, and by sensitivity to the other person. Trusting and risk-taking are two sides of the same coin because a trusting relationship requires a willingness to engage in trusting acts of self-disclosure. Thus, within limits, others trust us to the degree that they know details about us; we are trusted as we emerge for them as unique individuals. There are limits, of course, but they are often broader than you may think.

Similarity is important in persuasion. Kenneth Burke, a contemporary rhetorical theorist, wrote, "Only those voices from without are effective which can speak in the language of a voice within."[8] At its simplest, this statement recognizes that we are most influenced by those whose voices are most like the voices we use in talking to ourselves, and the more the rhetor shares with the audience, the greater the chance she will have of being able to speak in ways the audience will hear and understand and feel. Empirical studies reveal that rhetors increase their influence when they announce at the outset that their personal views (attitudes) are similar to those of the audience, that members of the audience more readily accept a rhetor's view of an issue if common ground has already been established on previous issues, and that the audience is more susceptible to influence if its members decide that the intentions of the rhetor are consistent with their self-interests.[9]

A cynical view of such findings would suggest that the rhetor should lie—tell the audience what they want to hear in order to gain the effects desired. That is good advice for only one kind of rhetorical situation: the one-shot effort at a quick payoff. The unscrupulous seller of, say, imaginary cemetery plots, who plans to hit town once, then take the money and run, may use this effectively. But most of us act as rhetors in quite different circumstances. You will be in a class for a quarter or a semester, and some of your classmates will know you in other contexts; so, even as nomadic students, it is difficult for you to wear a false face easily. It becomes even more difficult in a community in which you live and work over a period of time—the consistency of your behavior will be a test of your trustworthiness. In addition, most rhetorical acts are parts of persuasive campaigns. In such cases, you will be judged, over time, in different rhetorical actions with different audiences; and it would not only be difficult, but also most unwise to try "to fool all of the people all of the time."

The moral of the story is to find real areas of similarity that you share with the audience. Do not try to be what you are not, but make sure that they know what you share with them. If you are to be effective, you must find common grounds—yet you must also remain a unique individual who is, in fact, different from anyone else.

Social Power

Ethos is also influenced by the relationship between the rhetor and the audience. In a rhetorical context, *power* refers to the rhetor's potential for social influence—that is, influence that arises from the degree to which the audience depends on the rhetor and the rhetor depends on the audience. The classroom is a good example. As students, you depend on your instructor in significant ways; your instructor has power, and your relationship is between unequals. Your ability to graduate and your grade point average, in part, depend on your teacher, and this additional power may increase his ability to influence your attitudes—at least for the duration of the class. An instructor, however, also depends on the students. Any one of you can disrupt the class so it cannot continue, and the course continues period after period because you as a group permit it to do so. Because of this power, you have the ability to influence your instructor or, at least, limit her behavior. The rhetorical acts of students and professors are influenced and limited by their relative power. These limits are evident in any relationship involving the potential for social influence—between spouses, partners, employer and employee, homeowner and plumber, landlord and tenant, dean and department head, coach and player, sorority member and pledge, parent and child, and so on.

Obviously, such interdependent relationships are a facet of identification. As employees we may dislike the boss but recognize that our livelihood depends on the health of the business. As students we may dislike a teacher but recognize that the class must continue if we are to learn what we need and gain essential credits.

Participation

The ethos of the rhetor is also related to participation by the audience in the rhetorical act. To understand this process, we must return once again to the wisdom of Aristotle. As noted in Chapter 5, he described a species of argument that he called the *enthymeme,* a form of argument that he believed was peculiar to rhetoric. Recall that this kind of argument is unusual because it assumes a collaborative effort by the rhetor and the audience. In effect, the audience fills in details, makes connections based on their experiences, or draws conclusions based on knowledge and understandings they share with the rhetor. Sometimes they do that because of a common context, from what they know of a particular time or place. Sometimes they do it because of assumptions or values they share. Sometimes it occurs in response to a word or phrase that evokes vivid, salient associations. The new one- to three-second "blink" ads trade on this kind of instant participatory connection with media audiences. Sometimes it occurs in response to a visual cue, such as a smirk, a sigh, or looking at one's watch in the midst of a presidential debate, for example. The perceived character of the rhetor influences whether audience members will collaborate in creating the rhetorical act because such perceptions are signs of shared experience, attitudes, and values, which, in turn, lead to identification, which facilitates active participation in creating and elaborating the arguments offered by the rhetor. Again, note how similar these concepts are to the Elaboration Likelihood Model discussed earlier.

An enthymeme is relatively easy to describe but harder to illustrate because it relies on audience participation and requires a good bit of adaptation. The enthymeme was introduced in Chapter 5 as a general argument type that rests on what is already known and accepted by those addressed. Accordingly, audience members can fill in details that are omitted or only alluded to in passing, or the argument evokes not just assent but elaboration because it fits their personal experiences or speaks to what they believe is likely or probable. Many jokes based on current events illustrate the process. The bumper sticker "1/20/09: End of an Error" capitalizes on George W. Bush's record-setting low approval ratings (30 percent) and a play on words noting when the president's era mercifully ends. Tony Schwartz, an advertising genius, wrote a book arguing that powerful advertising works by prompting an enthymematic response, what he called a "responsive chord," in viewers or listeners.[10] In fact, Schwartz argued that no advertiser could "put" anything into audiences' minds; all that could be done was to evoke what was already there. In such cases, the rhetor produces cues that prompt audience members to collaborate in creating the rhetoric by which they are persuaded.

The process by which the ethos of the source increases our participation is most evident in commercials made by well-known actors. Because we know little about them as individuals, we tend to believe they are like the characters they play. Della Reese, for instance, is best known as a jazz and gospel singer and actor and for her role as Tess in the television series *Touched by an Angel*. She appears in commercials for a drug to treat adult diabetes. The advertiser hopes that we will confuse actor Della Reese with the warm, caring role of Tess; and if we do so, we are more likely to accept her endorsement of this drug.

In sum, the character of the rhetor is directly related to two important rhetorical processes: identification based on perceptions of similarity and participation based on clues provided by the rhetor's words that suggest shared experiences and knowledge. Both of these influence the ways in which audience members interpret messages and the extent to which they are willing to fill in details or draw inferences based on statements in the rhetorical act.

These, then, are the kinds of opportunities and challenges that may arise in rhetorical action. Some of these considerations arise out of the rhetor's background, appearance, the ways she is introduced, and the context or occasion. More important challenges arise out of the relationship between the rhetor and the message. For an act to be effective, a rhetor must be perceived by the audience as competent, practical, and trustworthy. This is particularly significant because the rhetor is a context that affects how audience members will translate and interpret a message. Specifically, ethos influences audience identification—that is, the degree to which audiences see the rhetor as an individual is closely related to trust. In addition, as the rhetor emerges as a unique person, there is an association with, or an affinity for those qualities, attitudes, and characteristics that form a common ground between rhetor and audience. This process is central to ensuring that the audience will hear the message and translate it with the greatest possible fidelity. In addition, ethos influences participation—the degree to which the audience is willing to involve itself in rhetorical action, to draw conclusions, or to fill in details implied by or to embellish the suggestions made by the rhetor.

THE RHETORICAL CONTEXT: INTERRELATIONSHIPS

By this time the interrelationships among the facets of the rhetorical context should be apparent. For example, the decisions made by an audience member about the competence of the rhetor result from decisions that the rhetor makes about the treatment of the subject and the purpose selected. The opportunities and challenges the rhetor has in establishing credibility arise from the characteristics of a specific audience. The rhetorical possibilities on a given occasion are a function of the interaction among these three elements: audience, subject/purpose, and rhetor. Earlier chapters have explored the resources of evidence, argument, organization, and language that are available to overcome these challenges.

 MATERIAL FOR ANALYSIS

Theodore B. Olson is an internationally known attorney with impeccable conservative credentials. A founding member of the Federalist Society,[11] Olson was Assistant Attorney General in charge of the Office of Legal Counsel from 1981 to 1984 during Ronald Reagan's first administration. In 2000, he successfully argued the case of *Bush v. Gore* before the United States Supreme Court, the case that put George W. Bush in the White House, and then served as Solicitor General of the United States from 2001 to 2004 during Bush's first administration. He also served as private counsel to two presidents, Ronald Reagan and George W. Bush. He is currently a partner in the Washington, D.C., office of the national law firm, Gibson, Dunn, and Crutcher.[12]

Given his background, some might have been surprised when Olson challenged the California law banning same-sex marriage. His case against that law, based on strict constitutional standards, was summarized in an essay, titled "The Conservative Case for Gay Marriage," published in *Newsweek* in January 2010 and available online at http://www.thedailybeast.com/newsweek/2010/01/08/the-conservative-case-for-gay-marriage.html. Retrieve Olson's essay from that website and use it to respond to the following questions for analysis.

Questions for Analysis

1. In what ways does Olson explain his decision to be an advocate for same-sex marriage?
2. How does Olson use analogies drawn from U.S. history as evidence for his position?
3. How does Olson appeal to values shared by conservatives and liberals?
4. How does Olson use scientific evidence in support of his position?
5. According to Olson, what would be the benefits of legalizing same-sex marriage?
6. How, if at all, does this essay affect your perceptions of Mr. Olson?

EXERCISES

Critical Thinking Exercises

1. Imagine you are the campaign manager for an underdog politician in your community. Identify such a candidate and create a "score card" for your candidate's ethos, both in terms of prior ethos and ethos from the rhetorical act. What can you suggest to improve your candidate's ethos appeal?

2. Discuss the impact of ethos on your judgment of your peers' in-class presentations. How do such things as appearance, punctuality, disposition, nonverbals, prior speech performances, topic selection, class attendance and participation, and so on contribute to the formation of strong or weak credibility?

3. Corporate ethos is an important consideration for airlines. Listen closely to the in-flight announcements and indicate the ways in which they influence your response to the airline. Have you been on a flight when the attendants use humor to spice up the usual information? How did you react? Consult a source on voice and diction, such as *Is Your Voice Telling on You?* by Daniel Boone (Thomson Learning/Singular Publishing Group). How is ethos affected by vocal qualities?

4. For over two years a California woman by the name of Cindy Sheehan picketed the Iraq War, including a lengthy vigil outside the president's home in Crawford, Texas. After losing her son, Casey, in the war, and not receiving satisfactory answers as to what he had died for, she went on a campaign to avenge her son's senseless death. What can be said about Sheehan's ethos? How was her appeal constrained by her age, values, appearance, behavior, reputation, and style of talking? Who could and who could not identify with her or her actions? Why? How was her ethos constrained by the goals of her protest and by the topic of antiwar demonstration itself? How was her ethos affected by the occasion on which she initiated her protest? How was her ethos constrained by the form of protest she chose? What do all these considerations tell us about the challenges and possibilities of social protest? What should an activist be mindful of in designing a protest strategy?

Analytical Writing Exercises

5. Corporate ethos is an important consideration for business today. Choose a local company and write an analysis that describes the ways in which it communicates its ethos through image advertising. Why must businesses work extra hard at humanizing themselves to their customers? Does your company use personification to create identification? If not, what other language strategies help form favorable ethos?

Portfolio Entry 9: Rhetor Obstacles

6. Identify and explain in one to two pages how rhetor-related opportunities and challenges arise in your rhetorical acts. What do the rhetors do to combat these ethos challenges and capitalize on ethos opportunities?

Strategic Speaking Exercises

7. Give a two- to three-minute speech of introduction to a member of your class. Your instructor may want to divide the class into pairs for this exercise. Share a mini-résumé with your paired classmate, and indicate the kind of topic you'd like to speak to the class about. As you prepare your impromptu remarks, consider the best ways to maximize your partner's prior ethos. What are some strategies for navigating between a "roast" and excessive praise? How can you use elements of ethos from the rhetorical act to enhance your performance and in so doing raise the profile of the student you are introducing?

NOTES

1. Aristotle, *On Rhetoric: A Theory of Civic Discourse*, trans. George A. Kennedy (New York: Oxford University Press, 1991).

2. The definitions used in this chapter are taken from the *American Heritage Dictionary of the English Language* (Boston: Houghton Mifflin, 1969).

3. Theodore Otto Windt Jr., *Presidents and Protestors: Political Rhetoric in the 1960s* (Tuscaloosa: University of Alabama Press, 1990), pp. 106–135. Cited material on 107.

4. There is some evidence that appearance affects jury decisions about guilt. A study at Bath Spa University found such a correlation, but the evidence is far from conclusive. See Nic Fleming, "The Ugly Truth About Juries," Telegraph.co.uk. 22 March 2007. http://www.telegraph.co.uk/connected/main.jhtml?

view=DETAILS&grid5&xml5/connected/2007/03/22/njury22.xml. Accessed 6/14/07.

5. Admittedly this is an oversimplification. Using factor analysis as a technique, a number of other factors have been found, but these two are the most stable and generalized across studies.

6. S. E. Asch, "The Doctrine of Suggestion, Prestige, and Imitation in Social Pshchology," *Psychological Review* 55 (1948): 250–78; see Wallace Fotheringham, *Perspectives on Persuasion* (Boston: Allyn and Bacon, 1966, pp. 90–92, for a discussion of this research.

7. William Morris, ed., *American Heritage Dictionary of the English Language* (Boston/New York: American Heritage Publishing Co. and Houghton Mifflin, 1969).

8. Kenneth Burke, *A Rhetoric of Motives* (1950; Berkeley: University of California Press, 1969), p. 39.

9. Ellen Berscheid reviews this research in "Interpersonal Attraction" in *Handbook of Social Psychology*, 3rd ed. (New York: Random House, 1985), vol. 2, pp. 413–484.

10. Reports about focus group reactions to the ad are found in K. H. Jamieson, *Dirty Politics* (New York: Oxford University Press, 1992), pp. 97–100.

11. James Oliphant, "Giuliani Hitches Star to Conservative Legal Group," *Chicago Tribune*, September 6, 2007. Accessed 6/24/13. http://www.chicagotribune.com/news/nationworld/chi-070905giuliani,0,1519010.story.

12. See http://www.gibsondunn.com/lawyers/tolson. Accessed 6/24/13.

Chapter 11

Understanding Evaluation

What is the difference between people like Dan Balz, Jeff Greenfield, and Bob Costas and guests on *The Daily Show* or *The View?* The first group is trained to make critical evaluations in their field of expertise: politics, media, and sports, respectively; the second group is expected to "sound off" on cultural potpourri. Critical evaluations are marked by thoughtful scrutiny; sounding off displays personal opinion or gut reaction. Recalling the Elaboration Likelihood Model (ELM) of persuasion, one might say that statements such as "The film was masterfully produced given its genre and budget" and "I liked it" illustrate the road to reflection versus the road to efficiency. Put a bit differently, the first statement tells us something about the film (an informed judgment), the second statement tells us something about the person who said it (a personal reaction). Perhaps unfortunately, some called critics have also learned to condense their informed judgments to meet the demands of a media age with rating systems like thumbs up or down, awarding stars, and ten-point scales that, again, tell us something about what the critic thinks but nothing about the film.

We have come to rely on the judgments of trained critics or consultants because we are bombarded by rhetoric every day and know how difficult it is to make careful assessments. The aim of this chapter, then, is to give you the building blocks to form your own intelligent judgments of rhetorical acts. It outlines standards of evaluation necessary to complete the critical process of description, interpretation, and evaluation. Evaluation is a natural outgrowth of the two steps you have learned thus far. Your first task is one of descriptive analysis—full and detailed understanding of the rhetorical act. Your second task concerns the rhetorical context: What opportunities and challenges did the rhetor face, and what resources were used to overcome points of resistance? Your third and final task is evaluative. The standards of evaluation introduced here should remind you of the seven Ps of rhetoric, first introduced in Chapter 1. Because rhetoric is powerful, purposive, problem solving, poetic, pragmatic, public, and propositional, we need ways to harness and brand it.

STANDARDS FOR EVALUATION

Four standards can be used alone or in combination to judge rhetorical discourse: (1) an *artistic* standard, focused on producing an aesthetically satisfying discourse; (2) a *response* standard, focused on achieving desired effects; (3) an *accuracy* standard, focused on presenting as truthful and complete an account of the issue as is possible; and (4) a *moral* standard, focused on using ethical means and advancing ethically desirable ends for society and for rhetorical practice (Figure 11–1). Each is relevant to rhetorical action. Each has important strengths and limitations.

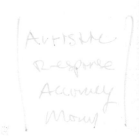

The Artistic Standard (Rhetoric Is Poetic)

The artistic standard focuses on means, on the ways in which rhetoric is poetic. The word *aesthetic* comes from the Greek word *aisthetikos*, which means "pertaining to sense perception." This original meaning is retained in the word *anaesthetic*, which refers to substances like chloroform or novocaine that cause total or partial loss of sensation. The artistic or aesthetic standard is a measure of how skillfully, artistically, or creatively a rhetorical act attempts to alter perception, create virtual experience, attract and hold attention, and induce participation and identification. It is not a measure of how well an act achieves its purpose (that would be the *response* standard), but rather of how creatively a rhetor responds to the obstacles faced, of how inventively a rhetor fulfills the requirements or expectations of form.

For example, although there is little evidence to suggest that Angelina Grimké's speech at Pennsylvania Hall (see Chapter 8) achieved its immediate purpose (*response*), we nevertheless rate it high on artistic grounds because she was extremely creative in responding to an extraordinarily difficult situation. Most rhetors would

- Aesthetics (Artistic standard)
- Effects (Response standard)
- Truth (Accuracy standard)
- Ethics (Moral standard)

Figure 11–1
*Evaluation
Criteria*

"throw in the towel" if confronted by a disruptive audience that ridiculed them and their cause, a target audience that viewed itself as powerless, and a VIP audience that was complacent or threatened by their aims and that disapproved of their gender, faith, and affiliations. In this case the critic must recognize how many challenges exist and anticipate limited response. Despite that obstacle-filled situation, however, one can applaud Grimké's skill in responding to her rhetorical context. How clever to enact the very argument you wish to advance (women can be effective public advocates) and to disarm your audience's resistance with a stunning array of argumentative and language strategies that taken together invest the cause with godliness! Moreover, the capacity of her speech to arouse our admiration attests to its enduring power, a strong indicator of aesthetic merit.

Many rhetorical acts examined in this book, such as Robert F. Kennedy's impromptu speech in Indianapolis delivering the news of MLK's death (Chapter 5), Dr. Martin Luther King Jr.'s "I've Been to the Mountaintop" and Abraham Lincoln's "Gettysburg Address" (Chapter 2), Frederick Douglass's "What to the Slave Is the 4th of July?" (Chapter 7), and Franklin D. Roosevelt's "Pearl Harbor War Speech," (Chapter 14) deserve high artistic ratings. Each is a gem poetically. Each is an elegantly framed rhetorical response to events difficult to understand. Each attempts to create virtual experience and induce participation in refreshing and inventive ways. The artistic standard demands analysis of techniques, means, and strategies. These can be assessed with or without external evidence that a discourse achieved its goal. The artistic standard also reveals those works that have the capacity to endure through time as models of rhetorical action because they are deeply moving, eloquent, and original.

Edwin Black, for example, featured an address, a kind of sermon, that John Chapman made in Coatesville, Pennsylvania, on August 18, 1912, the one-year anniversary of a particularly cruel lynching in that town.[1] It was delivered in an empty store to an audience of three: "a lady friend, an elderly Negro woman, and an unidentified man, believed to be a local spy" (79). Obviously, it had no great effect; it was not included in anthologies of great speeches, nor was it noticed or praised when it was delivered. In analyzing its artistry, Black writes:

> Chapman would have us perceive the event as a scene in a morality play. The play itself is the history of this country, seen as the death-through-sin and the potential rebirth through purification of a whole people. . . . the lynching is seen as a ritual murder, and the appropriate response to it is a religious experience. We are able, through this response, to view the lynching unequivocally as a crime, and yet we do not hate the criminals, for we feel ourselves to be responsible. (87)

In other words, although inspired by a specific event, Chapman's artistry enables him to transcend the incident that was the impetus for the speech and the moment of its delivery to invite us white U.S. Americans to see ourselves as members of the lynch mob and to redeem ourselves through undergoing an experience of guilt and repentance.

That is artistry at its best. The limitations of the artistic standard are evident when we turn our attention to advertising and admire the skills of those who exploit the strategic resources of verbal and visual language in order to manipulate us politically or commercially. Rating the cleverness of Super Bowl ads has become such a popular pastime that websites devoted exclusively to evaluating them sprout like weeds during and immediately after the football game. Such uses of artistry may trouble us, but the artistic standard does not provide a basis for judging the purposes or ends of rhetorical action.

The Response Standard (Rhetoric Is Pragmatic)

The *response standard*, the evaluation of a rhetorical act in terms of its effectiveness, reflects the demand that rhetoric be pragmatic. This evaluative standard assumes that every rhetorical act must communicate, induce participation from an audience, and affect perceptions, beliefs, and attitudes. Unless some reaction occurs, the act must be judged a failure.

Effects are difficult to isolate and verify, however. It is difficult to separate responses to one act from responses to other rhetoric that precedes and follows it. Most influence is the result of a campaign or of a series of experiences. Similarly, it is hard to measure just what the audience response was. Clapping may reflect relieved courtesy; questionnaires report only what people say occurred; the size and nature of the response may be greatly affected by the medium in which an act is presented; some websites either don't tabulate browser visits or update the number of "hits" they receive; other websites claim to do so, but there is no way to verify their count. Regardless, the number of "hits" tells us little about whether or not the content of the website somehow influenced or persuaded viewers. DVRs have played havoc with measures for recording TV viewership (e.g., Nielsen ratings) for advertisers. For these reasons, it is usually difficult to determine accurately the effects of a given rhetorical act.

Examples of diverse discourses that have met with resounding success include the Harry Potter books by J. K. Rowling, which became the biggest publishing phenomenon ever, occupying an unprecedented number of weeks at the top of the *New York Times* best-seller list; ad campaigns such as "Got Milk?" "Absolut Vodka," and "Benetton," which have won coveted industry awards for impact; Billy Graham, whose inspirational sermons on tours across the globe spanning six decades have won him international acclaim; *The Sopranos* for their many years as some of the most-watched shows on TV; and YouTube, whose video clips are viewed more than 100 million times a day, have made it hands down the most popular website, even eclipsing the viewership of TV networks.

The effects standard is sometimes at odds with the artistic standard. Many highly successful films are panned by critics. Recently, for all its box office success, *The Hobbit* received cool artistic reviews. Similarly, highly successful TV ads use techniques that drive viewers to the mute button, and the development of recording devices such as TIVO reflect audience resistance to some kinds of advertising.

The effects standard also raises ethical problems. Applied strictly and in isolation, it would applaud rhetoric without regard for its accuracy or social consequences. By such a measure, the finest rhetorical works would be speeches of Adolf Hitler who inspired an entire nation to believe in Aryan superiority and the elimination of all Jews! Advertising that persuades teenagers to smoke or drink alcohol despite serious health hazards also raises ethical problems. Similarly, popular and funny beer ads, such as "Here We Go" ads for Bud Lite that run during collegiate sporting events make subtle and disturbing connections between sport and alcohol consumption among young people. Clearly, the effects standard cannot be used alone; other standards need to be used with it. The starting point of much analysis, however, is an attempt to explain why and how demonstrable effects were produced.

The Accuracy Standard (Rhetoric Is Problem Solving)

The *accuracy standard* measures the similarity between the "reality" presented in a rhetorical act and "reality" as presented in other sources; that is, it is concerned with *truth*. In this case the critic tests the accuracy and typicality of evidence in the discourse against other sources known to be well informed and compares the arguments selected against the pool of arguments available. Rhetoric is a part of social decision making. If we are to make good decisions, we need the best evidence available, and we need to examine all the relevant arguments. For this reason, considerations of adequacy and accuracy always are important.

But this standard also has limitations. Rhetoric is problem solving; the truths of rhetoric are social truths, truths created and validated by people. There is no simple way to verify all rhetorical claims or to validate all rhetorical arguments. The occasions best suited to rhetorical deliberation are those in which well-intentioned, informed people disagree. A good critic has to acknowledge conflicting evidence, varying interpretations, and competing perspectives and must recognize that no simple judgment about the truth of most acts can ever be made. In addition, no discourse is ever long enough to tell the whole truth, and the constraints of space and time, which are inherent to rhetoric, complicate strict application of this standard.

"Hurricane Katrina: Our Experiences" by Larry Bradshaw and Lorrie Beth Slonsky in Chapter 1 is an example of the difficulties in applying the truth standard. On one level, the essay scores high on accuracy—after all these are the very words of officials, police officers, and others. And the essay is detailed and relatively long, suggesting that accuracy is more important than attention span. On another level, however, the essay raises questions. Are these experiences typical? Do these reports accurately represent what occurred? Insofar as they mirror other information about conditions in New Orleans after Hurricane Katrina, they will be accepted as true, but they are also reports from a limited perspective.

The excerpt from the final speech by former Senator Dale Bumpers defending President Clinton in his impeachment trial in the Senate (Chapter 5) illustrates the importance of and the difficulties in applying a truth standard—in this case, the difficulties in deciding what the founders meant by the phrase "high crimes and misdemeanors." The media-hyped antitobacco website designed by youth for youth to warn viewers about the lies and hypocrisy of "Big Tobacco" appropriated a potent domain name: The Truth.com. The Questions for Analysis at the end of this chapter—an answer to a question posed to Malcolm X to explain the meaning of "The Ballot or the Bullet"—will invite you to make difficult judgments, especially those based on truth standards.

In some contexts audiences receive help in trying to assess facts. Ad Watch campaigns that run during elections focus primarily on truth claims. These are important critical segments in the news, especially effective in catching and preventing outright distortions, but the reality is that all ads contain omissions, creative editing, and half-truths. *FactCheck.org* and *FlackCheck.org* perform a similar function for the online community.

In one respect, this standard conflicts with concerns for effects. Discourses that tell the whole truth, as far as that is possible, and adhere to strict, technical accuracy are likely to be suitable only for experts. In fact, if the truth standard were applied strictly, nearly all rhetorical acts would be judged inadequate, and the finest pieces of rhetoric would be those directed to an elite group of specialists. Given rhetoric's popular character and its role in social and public decision making, this standard alone would not be an appropriate basis for evaluating rhetorical action.

One of the most controversial and confounding events illustrating the challenges of applying the truth criterion was the shooting of an African American teenager named Trayvon Martin in Sanford, Florida, by George Zimmerman, a member of a Neighborhood Watch group. Leonard Pitts, a reporter for the *Miami Herald*, a syndicated columnist who won a Pulitzer and is noted for extraordinary journalistic storytelling, wrote a column in which he described what he believed had occurred:

> It happened like this. He was visiting his father, watching hoops on television. At half-time, he left his dad's townhouse in a gated community and walked to a 7-Eleven for snacks. There was a light drizzle and he was wearing a sweatshirt and jeans. On the way back, he drew the attention of George Zimmerman, captain of the Neighborhood Watch. Zimmerman, who is white, called police from his SUV and told them he was following a "suspicious" character. The dispatcher promised to send a prowl car and told Zimmerman to stay in his vehicle. He didn't. When police arrived, they found him with a bloody nose and Martin face down on the grass not far from his father's door, a gunshot wound in his chest.[2]

Other reports call many of these statements into question. For example, Zimmerman is elsewhere identified as having a Latina mother. An editorial in the *Washington Post* of March 20, 2012, suggested that Zimmerman had stalked Martin and that a witness had observed two men fighting just before the shooting. That same editorial also claimed that Martin's girlfriend, who had apparently been talking with him by cell phone at the time of the shooting, heard someone struggling with Martin.[3]

President Obama responded to these events on Friday, March 23, 2012, in unusually personal terms: "I can only imagine what these parents are going through. . . . If I had a son, he'd look like Trayvon."[4] Konrad Yakabuski, writing from Sanford, Florida, describes the situation this way: "The volatile alchemy that provoked such national outrage over the death of an innocent black teen in a hoodie has many elements. They include Sanford's seemingly Keystone cops, Florida's permissive gun laws, and the state's controversial 'Stand Your Ground' legislation that its critics call a license to kill."[5]

These fragments from the ongoing national conversation about these events problematize any and all truth claims. The first story describes an innocent teenager killed by an overeager member of a Neighborhood Watch group when punched in the nose. Conflicting accounts support or deny Zimmerman's claim of acting in self-defense. Obama's statement personalizes the issue in ways that suggest that any black teenager in a hoodie could be the target of white violence. A local reporter calls the competence of local police into question, notes slow response by legal authorities, and the possibilities created by permissive gun laws and "Stand Your Ground" laws that make it difficult to distinguish self-defense from unprovoked attacks.

These columns and our commentary merely touch the surface of the complex issues in this case. Ask yourself how, amid conflicting claims and testimony, the "truth" of these events can be known.

The Moral Standard (Rhetoric Is Powerful)

The *moral standard* is necessary because rhetoric is powerful and thus has significant ethical dimensions. It judges whether rhetoric helps or harms, whether it promotes social harmony or discord. It evaluates the social consequences of rhetorical action—both its purposes and the means by which they are achieved. It judges the long-term consequences of rhetoric for society (What happens to a political system in which voting decisions are made on the basis of thirty-second television commercials?) and for future rhetorical action (How can we communicate about complex issues if norms for rhetorical action are limited to the short segments typical of commercial and cable television programming?) as well as how these are affected by new technology (How can we vote intelligently if political advertisers exploit the visual capacities of television and the unregulated congestion of cyberspace to prompt us to draw false conclusions?). Obviously, such judgments are highly controversial, and in some cases they are directly related to the truth criterion.

Many and diverse rhetorical acts have come under heavy ethical scrutiny by politicians and advocacy groups for promoting excessive sex and violence, incivility, discrimination, and illegal activity, or for contributing generally to society's moral decline. A wide sample of these include gangsta rap music, Internet porn sites, *Doom* video games, shock jock Don Imus's and Howard Stern's morning shows—both of which were canceled by networks for their offensiveness; then later reinstated—Ann Coulter's insults, Louis Farrakhan's speeches on racial separatism, and Fred Phelps and his followers for picketing soldiers' funerals with offensive language about gays and God's wrath. Ethical judgments are subjective; they require us to balance legitimate competing claims. There are limits on First Amendment freedoms, for example, but we ought to fight to see that only absolutely essential limits are set. Ethical evaluation requires that you take a close look at opposing views and at the social consequences of the ideas advocated. Then ask yourself whether you have just defined as ethical only what is reformist or supports the status quo or what supports your point of view.

A good example for judging rhetoric using all four standards of evaluation is the classic political campaign spot for Lyndon Johnson in the 1964 presidential campaign: "The Daisy Spot." Created by media guru Tony Schwartz, the ad revolutionized political advertising in this country (Figure 11–2).

Aesthetically, the ad was an aural and visual masterpiece that responded inventively to rhetorical obstacles. The specter of the Kennedy assassination (only eleven months earlier) still loomed large. Politics had lost its innocence. Lyndon Johnson, the vice president who became president, was not a particularly likable candidate. He was a Texan, rough around the edges, whose manner was a sharp contrast to JFK's smooth, northeastern style. Schwartz, then still an obscure ad creator, convinced the Johnson campaign that he could create an ad that would solve the candidate's serious political problems and capitalize on his opponent's (Senator Barry Goldwater) one major weakness: speaking glibly in ways that could frighten voters. Johnson bought it, and history was made. The commercial's content went like this: A little girl is sitting in a field counting petals on a daisy. In a cute way, she stumbles in her counting. As her count reaches ten, the visual motion is frozen, zooms in to the child's eye, then the viewer hears an ominous countdown. When the count reaches zero, we see a nuclear explosion and hear President Johnson say, "These are the stakes, to make a world in which all God's children can live or to go into the darkness. Either we must love each

Figure 11–2
"The Daisy Spot" Ad

VOTE FOR PRESIDENT JOHNSON
ON NOVEMBER 3.

Courtesy of the Democraztic National Committee

other or we must die." As the screen goes to black at the end, white lettering appears stating, "Vote for President Johnson on November 3." The ad doesn't pack much power when you just read the words. But this ad gave birth to negative advertising via a clever enthymeme (it never says Goldwater will push the nuclear button, but it prompts viewers to think it); it was the first spot to use real children's voices as opposed to adults imitating children; it introduced natural sound (the actual countdown of a missile test); it used a fast-moving color and light scheme and a plethora of camera angles. Just four years earlier, the 1960 election had been marked by black and white, preproduced jingles, cartoon images, and slow visual pacing. The Daisy Spot taught us that it is much more important for a voter to feel a candidate than to see him. In all, the Daisy Spot was in a league of its own.

The response it evoked was huge even though the ad aired only once on NBC's "Monday Night at the Movies." It created such controversy that the networks refused to run it again. A firestorm of protest erupted from Republicans who claimed that the spot accused Senator Goldwater of being trigger happy (although nowhere in the spot is Goldwater even mentioned). Goldwater's approval ratings plunged, and he never recovered. Goldwater himself credited this ad with contributing to his political defeat. The Daisy Spot is still referred to as the single most effective political ad ever produced.

Ethically, the ad was troublesome and teaches us that rhetorical ingenuity is not always synonymous with high moral standards. The sinister associations created by the ad in the minds of viewers between Goldwater and Armageddon frightened even the networks. Fearing legal retribution, they canceled future ad placements.

On truth grounds, the ad was difficult to evaluate because it was slippery. There are no facts or figures to dispute. There are no explicit claims. There are only frightening feelings and sinister associations created in the minds of viewers. Previous campaign rhetoric made the ad's enthymematic premise at least plausible. Goldwater had stated that he supported the use of tactical atomic weapons. The ad invited viewers to recall those startling admissions and contemplate the idea that he might actually use nuclear weapons in Vietnam. Special constraints weighed heavily on the ad's truth quotient.

SPECIAL CONSTRAINTS

Rhetorical evaluations must be modified in terms of the special pressures created by the context and the occasion. These special pressures or constraints (a constraint is something that limits, restricts, or regulates) include (1) *competing rhetorical action*, (2) *preceding or subsequent events*, (3) *the media of transmission*, and (4) *expectations and requirements created by the occasion*. Each of these should be examined to see if it leads us to qualify or refine our judgments about artistry, response, accuracy, and morality. The first two constraints will be treated here, the latter two in subsequent chapters.

Competing Rhetorical Action

Very few rhetorical acts occur in isolation, and many are part of campaigns and movements. But campaigns include competition from other persuaders—political candidates or advertisers—and movements are protests against the status quo, which will be defended by its supporters. In other words, much rhetoric occurs in a competitive environment, and it has to be judged in relation to its competition. It's nice to receive an award for excellence in advertising, for example, but it's equally important to know how well you did against competing products.

Political campaigns illustrate how competition modifies judgments. As we write, we have completed another political season, including debates among those who sought to be the Republican nominee for the presidency in 2012. Republican candidates included former Senator Rick Santorum, former House Majority Leader Newt Gingrich, Representative Michelle Bachmann, Representative Ron Paul, Texas Governor Rick Perry, former CEO of Godfather's Pizza Herman Cain, and former Governor Mitt Romney (MA). These candidates had to be assessed in comparison to each other and in relation to different formats and time limits. Later, the eventual Republican presidential nominee, Mitt Romney, and President Barak Obama were compared in a series of three debates. The powerful Daisy Spot must be assessed against its "low-tech" ad counterparts of the 1960s and against the kinds of brash rhetoric uttered by Goldwater during the campaign.

Comparison is an integral part of assessing rhetorical acts. As you evaluate, consider the choices available and then examine the ways in which those choices were limited by opponents, by competing positions, or by events and issues. Ask yourself what was possible, given the situation. Given the opposition, what was the best strategy? Given competing persuaders, what role was possible, what purpose was reasonable? Pay special attention to attempts to respond to issues, charges, and opponents. These should help you notice one kind of constraint that limits rhetorical action.

Preceding or Subsequent Events

A rhetorical act is always one in a series of events. The meaning of a rhetorical act is not an absolute or a given; its character and meaning are always, in part, a function of the context in which it occurs. Evaluation needs to include an awareness of events that preceded and followed it because these may explain the act and modify its import. When Bono, the rock musician from the group U2, first decided to call attention to the plight of Africa, few believed he would become such an expert on third-world health issues that even world leaders would agree to meet with him. His admirable role as an international social activist (earning him a Person of the Year award by *Time* magazine) has spurred other celebrities, such as Angelina Jolie, Oprah Winfrey, George Clooney, and Jay-Z (a.k.a. Shawn Carter), to pursue noble international ventures as well. This phenomenon is more than a bandwagon effect. Consumers of media judge the rhetorical action of others by what has gone before.

Many examples of rhetorical acts illustrate these principles. In 1948 Margaret Chase Smith of Maine was elected to the Senate after four terms in the House of Representatives. As her career in the Senate began, Senator Joseph McCarthy (R-WI) was fanning the flames of the "Red Scare" by announcing that Communist spies had infiltrated the highest levels of the government, including the State Department. Although she was concerned about the issue, Chase Smith began cautiously to ask McCarthy for specific details, names, and numbers; McCarthy repeatedly avoided answering her questions. After seeking the advice of journalist friends, she drafted a speech that objected to McCarthy's tactics but that never mentioned his name. She added a final statement of principles that was signed by six other Republican senators. On June 1, 1950, she addressed the Senate and delivered what came to be known as her "Declaration of Conscience," asking her Senate colleagues to "do some soul-searching . . . on the manner in which we are using or abusing our individual powers and privileges."[6] Unless the reader knows about these prior events, the meaning of her words is not clear, and the excited reaction to her speech cannot be understood.

What has come to be called Richard Nixon's "Checkers Speech" (named for his children's dog Checkers, which was mentioned in the speech) is another example. Unless you know that Nixon had been accused of misusing funds given by wealthy supporters and was being pressured to resign as the vice-presidential candidate by the Republican National Committee, and that presidential candidate Dwight Eisenhower withheld his support even after Nixon was cleared of the charges by an audit and a legal opinion, and that his entire political future hung on whether he could generate an extraordinarily massive response from the audience, you are likely to view the speech as highly emotional and sentimental, a tearjerker. But when you know the events that preceded it, the speech takes on a slightly different hue.

Earl Spencer's eulogy for his sister, Princess Diana, can only be fully appreciated if you know the troubled story of her life as a former Royal. From run-ins with the Queen, to episodes of bulimia, from the paparazzi's obsession with her, to the way in which she met her tragic death, the speech artfully "dances" between an uplifting memorial and a political statement.

As discussed earlier, the obstacle of cultural history is a long-term view of the problem of preceding events. In light of the past, a rhetor may be expected to develop a new argument, take a new perspective, develop a new role, or respond to unforeseen events. This is illustrated by substituting the phrase "climate change" for "global warning," and using the phrase "gun security" instead of "gun control" in responding to the killings at Sandy Hook Elementary School in Newtown, Connecticut.

Subsequent events can have various effects that complicate assessment. Assessing the final speech of Dr. Martin Luther King Jr. is difficult, for example, without being affected by what now seem to be his prophetic statements about his death. Similarly, in a little-known speech in 1962 in Newport, Rhode Island, President John F. Kennedy said of his family: "We are tied to the ocean. And when we go back to the sea, whether . . . it is to sail or to watch it, we are going back from whence we came."[7] These words took on special poignancy after John F. Kennedy Jr. lost control and crashed his single-engine plane into the sea with wife Carolyn Bessette and her sister aboard. That speech was reintroduced to millions of the U.S. public by TV commentators, and a few of its words were splashed across a six-page, full-color pullout in *Time* magazine in the wake of the accident. Subsequent events transformed those statements into memorable words that we interpret as having special significance.

Subsequent happenings can also become a truth standard against which to measure the claims of speakers. The tobacco companies now find themselves in court admitting that nicotine is addictive and that smoking causes lung cancer, emphysema, and other fatal diseases—contradicting thirty years of advertising and legal statements—in a desperate plea to reduce the enormous punitive damages awarded by jury verdicts against them. Similarly, the passage of time is the ultimate determinant of ethical judgments. Are certain rap lyrics or video games or websites really dangerous? Did Elvis Presley's startling new brand of rock and roll, complete with gyrating hips, corrupt his adoring fans? A contemporary ad campaign for a financial service ridiculed that idea, although it was taken quite seriously in the 1950s and 1960s. Furthermore, the ability of some rhetoric to withstand the test of time is clear evidence of artistic excellence. Thus, Lincoln's Gettysburg Address is no longer merely a speech made to honor those who died in the battle at Gettysburg; it remains an enduring commemoration of all those who have given their lives in battle for this nation. As time passes, you may be forced to take account of two different judgments: that of the immediate audience and that of history.

Agency

Agency is the term that identifies the ability of individuals or groups to achieve the ends they desire. From reading this book, you might gain the mistaken idea that rhetors are powerful people, agents who can change the world with a single speech. Such a notion ignores all the factors that give a rhetorical act its power. First, there is cultural history. Malcolm X, for example, uses the phrase, "the ballot or the bullet," but that phrase first appears in U.S. history in a famous speech by Patrick Henry and later was used in a speech by Abraham Lincoln. In all of these cases it captured a dramatic choice: change will come either through political processes or violence—war or revolution. In addition, Malcolm X's power as a speaker came from hearing his father, a Baptist minister, preach, and from earlier efforts by African Americans such as David Walker, Frederick Douglass, Marcus Garvey, Mary Church Terrell, and Ida B. Wells, among others. Malcolm X could not succeed as a speaker and activist apart from a supportive movement; as a lone voice, he would have cried in the wilderness with no one to hear him.

Every rhetor builds on and appropriates from the past, a process the Romans called *imitatio*, and is buoyed by past efforts and by being part of a group effort and by cultural values, such as equality, that bolster his demands. The agency of President Lyndon Johnson in gaining passage of the Civil Rights Act in 1964 grows out of the prior efforts of the Rev. Dr. Martin Luther King Jr. and his coworkers—recall Johnson's use of the phrase "we shall overcome" from that movement's anthem in his speech to Congress in support of that bill. Reportedly, Martin Luther King wept when he heard it uttered.

Conversely, none of this should be read as denying the special talents of individuals who find the words to make ideas from the past live again. The genius of Lincoln was his ability to use cultural resources from the nation's past and from the Bible and forge them into memorable words that captured the moment and urged listeners to act in ways consistent with "the better angels of their nature." Note, however, that even these powerful words could not prevent a civil war.

At the same time, rhetorical resources can be perverse or malign. The legacy of U.S. racism persists and fuels the "hate speech" that devastates people of color and encourages violence against them. Here, too, individuals in white supremacist groups energize the devils of our nature and our past.

Individual speeches can mobilize audiences, especially as speakers become living examples of what they advocate. Robert Kennedy exemplifies the painful process of redirecting one's efforts away from anger expressed destructively to energy focused on bringing social and political change. Sheryl Sandberg, Chief Operating Officer at Facebook, makes herself a model for women in the 2011 graduating class at Barnard urging them to find agency, to be unafraid, and to strive to achieve "the big dream." Sandberg's speech highlights the slow process by which equal rights for women are achieved. She calls attention to the failure of women over the past thirty years to assert themselves to take advantage of opportunities that now exist. As she notes, an important element in that resistance are the cultural norms about women's roles that women have absorbed and are loath to challenge in order to be all they can be.[8]

Talented individual speakers make a difference, but their impact rests on links to cultural history, cultural values, and the organized efforts of others. Attempting to assess the effects of rhetorical acts requires an astute analysis of all of the historical-cultural factors that facilitate and impede their efforts.

Theodore Olson's essay making a case for gay marriage (see Chapter 10) illustrates this slow process. In the 1960s groups of gay men and women formed and briefly published journals that shared their experiences and problems and connected individuals. But the beginning of the gay rights movement was what is called the Stonewall Riot of 1969, the explosion of resistance to ongoing police harassment at a bar in Greenwich Village patronized primarily by gay men. That explosion brought the oppression of gays into the public arena, fostered organization and group efforts to end discrimination against gay men and women in employment and housing and, ultimately, to overturn laws that made their sexual activity illegal. From those beginnings, there has been an ongoing effort to remove restrictions on gay men and women in the military, starting with "Don't Ask, Don't Tell," passed during the Clinton administration, to the current elimination of restrictions on gay men and women in the military. That has progressed to efforts to legalize gay marriage, and the recent

Supreme Court ruling of June 2013 on the federal Defense of Marriage Act (DOMA). Finally, in his inaugural address of January 21, 2013, President Obama referred to the principle "that all of us are created equal" and stated that it "is the star that guides us still; just as it guided our forebears through Seneca Falls and Selma and Stonewall."[9] Here Obama links the 1848 woman's rights convention that was the beginning of women's organized efforts to gain their rights, the1969 Selma to Montgomery March ("Bloody Sunday") for voting rights in 1965, and the beginnings of the gay rights movement in 1969. Similarly, Olson's essay links the effort to legalize gay marriage to fundamental cultural values and draws comparisons to other efforts to expand human rights, illustrating the ways in which the rhetoric of an individual depends on history and culture to be successful.

 MATERIAL FOR ANALYSIS

The rhetorical act for analysis is a statement made in response to a question. That statement is a shorter version of the speech, "The Ballot or the Bullet," that was delivered many times in 1964 by Malcolm X, formerly a minister of the Nation of Islam. Texts of the speech as delivered in Cleveland and Detroit can be found on the Web and in collections of his speeches.

Born Malcolm Little in Omaha, Nebraska, in 1925, Malcolm moved with his family of eight several times to escape death threats aimed at his father, a Baptist minister who was a Civil Rights activist. In 1929, in Lansing, Michigan, their house was burned to the ground, and two years later his father was murdered. His mother, emotionally traumatized, was committed to a mental institution, and Malcolm and his seven siblings were split up among orphanages and foster homes.

Although Malcolm was a good student in his early years, he dropped out of high school, went to Harlem, and by the 1940s was involved in narcotics and gambling. Convicted of burglary in 1946, he was incarcerated for seven years during which time he furthered his education and converted to the Muslim religion and joined the Nation of Islam.

When he was paroled in 1952, he was a devoted follower of the Islamic leader Elijah Mohammad. He dropped the name "Little" and chose "X" to signify his lost tribal name. By 1959, he had established himself as an articulate minister and spokesman for the Nation of Islam. His oratorical brilliance is largely credited with swelling the membership ranks from 500 in 1952 to 30,000 in 1963! After leaving the Nation of Islam in 1964, he went on a pilgrimage, the Hajj, to Mecca and became a Sunni Muslim; he also founded the Muslim Mosque, Inc. and the Organization of Afro-American Unity. That trip had a major impact on his thinking, particularly because his experiences made him realize that not all whites, particularly those in other nations, were racists.

As racial tensions mounted during the early Civil Rights movement and the organizations he formed challenged the leadership of Elijah Muhammad, he became a marked man. He rarely traveled without bodyguards. On February 14, 1965, his home where his wife and four daughters lived was firebombed. Two weeks later at a speaking engagement in New York, three gunmen—all members of the Nation of Islam—rushed Malcolm onstage and shot him dead. He was 39.

Malcolm X's volatile, short-lived rhetorical career was characterized by a charismatic message prompting African Americans to recognize that white society oppressed black people from recognizing their full potential, and urging them to become united politically in order to challenge their unjust conditions.

Malcolm X, impromptu remarks on his widely acclaimed speech, "The Ballot or The Bullet," delivered 1964

"Ladies and gentleman, Minister Malcolm X discusses the ballot or the bullet. Minister Malcolm, what do you mean by the ballot or the bullet?"

1   "Well, as our people, the Afro-Americans, become politically mature they become very much aware of the recent trend in political elections. They say that every time there is an election recently there is always a recount; that whites are so evenly divided politically that in many areas the race is so close that they have to count the votes all over again to see who got in office.

2   You had a recount where the governor was concerned in Massachusetts or in Minnesota or in Rhode Island and the same thing was so close between President Kennedy and Nixon that they had to count the votes all over again and our people are beginning to see this and they also realize that any minority group that has a block of votes is able to determine who will be the next mayor or who will be the next governor or who will be the next president or who will be the next congressman or the next senator. And this enables them to see the strategic position that they are in.

3   Also they realize that it was the black vote that put the present administration in Washington, D.C. It was the black vote here in America that put a Democratic administration in Washington, D.C., and despite the fact that it is admitted by students of political science that the twenty-two million Afro-Americans were the ones who put the present administration in power in Washington, D.C., the present administration has put us last; we put them first, but they put us last. And you may say, "Well, why do I say this?" Because they've been down there for four years and are only just now getting around to civil rights legislation or doing something about the violation of the civil rights of the twenty-two million Afro-Americans who put them in power.

4   Now despite the fact that they claim that they can do nothing about this when you look at the structure of the senators and the congressmen in Washington, D.C., or the two political parties, we can see whether the congressmen are concerned, two hundred fifty-seven of them are Democrats and only one hundred seventy-seven of them are Republicans. That means that the Democratic Party controls two-thirds of the House of Representatives. And where the senators are concerned there are sixty-seven Democratic senators and only thirty-three Republicans that control two-thirds of the Senate. And despite the fact that they control two-thirds of the House and the Senate and are able to pass all the other types of legislation that come up, when it

comes to the rights of the black people in this country who put them in power, they always have some kind of alibi to give the Negro to try and explain why they have not been able to deliver or keep their promises or the promises that they made when they were running for office. And the alibi that they usually use is they say that the Dixiecrats tie things up. Well, there was a time when black people were politically immature; that they thought it was the Dixiecrats who were keeping the Democrats from fulfilling their promise. But today as Negroes become politically mature, they can see that a Dixiecrat is nothing but a Democrat in disguise. That you've got to be a Democrat before you can be a Dixiecrat. And as our people begin to see this, they are also able to see that it is actually a coalition of southern Democrats along with the northern Democrats who actually play a giant political con game.

5   A good example of this, recently when I was in Washington, D.C. watching the senators' filibuster, I noticed that in the back of the senate room there was a huge map on the wall showing the states where most of the Negroes lived. And in each one of those states where the majority of the Negroes were living, the senator from that state was involved in a filibuster, which meant that he had to filibuster in order to keep those Negroes from getting voting rights. Because as soon as the Negroes in the southern states get voting rights, they will vote out of office the present racist segregationists who are posing as senators in Washington, D.C. And once the Negro gets the vote and he can oust these southern senators and southern congressmen, then that means the present committees that govern the direction that this government takes in its foreign and domestic policy will be changed because the committee chairmen will be changed. And in many instances they'll have a black senator or black congressman.

6   The including of black people into the governmental system automatically will mean that the political philosophy of the government will change, the political direction of the government will change, and it will have an effect on the economy of this particular country.

7   In fact, the twenty-two million Afro-Americans are in a position to bring about a bloodless revolution where America is concerned because if America gives complete voting rights and voting power to every person on this continent it will include overnight a block of twenty-two million Afro-Americans who have a unique political and economic philosophy. So this means that America for the first time in history represents a country that can actually involve itself in a bloodless revolution.

8   All other revolutions in history have been bloody. The Russian Revolution was bloody; the Chinese Revolution was bloody; the French Revolution was bloody; the Cuban Revolution was bloody. Revolutions historically are always bloody. Now America is in a unique position to involve herself in a bloodless revolution by giving the twenty-two million Afro-Americans the ballot. And if they don't give the twenty-two [million] Afro-Americans the ballot, and make possible a bloodless revolution, then they are going to force the Afro-Americans to use the bullet and there will be a bloody revolution.

9   And this is what I meant when I say "the ballot or the bullet." It's the same thing that Patrick Henry meant when he said, "liberty or death!"

Questions for Analysis

1. How would you rate this speech using an aesthetic standard of evaluation? Consider how Malcolm X uses many of the language strategies discussed in Chapter 7. Consider the form of this speech—impromptu remarks at a press conference. Locate an audio or video recording of Malcolm X's "The Ballot or the Bullet" on the World Wide Web. How does delivery and vocal quality factor into an aesthetic evaluation?

2. How would you rate this speech using a truth standard of evaluation? Note how many statistics, anecdotes, and other statements of fact that Malcolm X uses as support material for his arguments on voting inequities between blacks and whites in this country and the systematic discrimination against blacks that is perpetuated in the U.S. political process. How does assessing accuracy and typicality in this rhetorical act underscore some of the difficulties with the truth criteria as discussed in this chapter?

3. How would you rate this speech using an ethical standard of evaluation? Note that many U.S. Americans, especially whites, were frightened by his confrontational rhetorical choices, including what they perceived to be real threats of violence. Look at the incendiary line at the end of this speech from which the speech gets its title. But look at it in context of the whole and its placement at the end. Is your ethical critique at all tempered? In what ways is it strategic that he uses a famous Patrick Henry line in support of his militant policies? How do your religious beliefs affect your ethical assessment of this speech? Of its rhetor? (Malcolm X was a Muslim minister and a former spokesman for the radical "Nation of Islam.")

4. How would you rate this speech using an effects standard? How do arguments (see Chapter 5 for various types) work together in this rhetorical act that would explain the intense and varied reactions to it? Removed from the 1964 political climate, does this speech still evoke a powerful response from you today? Why or why not? Are there preceding or subsequent events in this country or in your area that might affect your reaction to the speech? The full-length "Ballot or the Bullet" became Malcolm X's signature speech. He gave it many times in different variations to many different audiences, some supportive, some hostile. He received heavy media coverage. Even today, speech critics have rated the longer version of this speech as one of the top ten speeches of the twentieth century. On what bases do you think this speech wins such high effects approval ratings? Check out biographical work on Malcolm X and the longer, more well-known, version of "The Ballot or the Bullet" on the World Wide Web for additional information on the speech and its impact on the 1960s political climate in this country.

EXERCISES

Critical Thinking Exercises

1. As a class, arrange to attend a movie together, or rent it to view at home. Be prepared to discuss it in an agreed-upon class period. Give the movie a separate evaluation using all four criteria: aesthetics, effects, truth, and ethics. Compare your results with the results of other class members in group discussions. After exchanging judgments, can you see why evaluating rhetoric is fraught with challenges? How does evaluating a film along different lines help you appreciate it better? Which standard of evaluation was the most difficult for you to apply? Why?

Analytical Writing Exercises

2. Evaluate a website of your choice by writing an analytical essay using the Website Critique questions below. The Website Critique is designed to help you fulfill all the critic's responsibilities when judging discourse. Recall from Chapter 2 that criticism is a process that requires, first, careful description, second, recognizing aspects of the rhetorical problem, and finally, making evaluations based on four separate criteria.

    a. *Identifying Information.* What is the subject matter? What search engine did you use? Why? What is the URL address of your website? Where does it appear on the list of websites related to this subject?

    b. *Purpose.* What is the primary rhetorical purpose of the website? What is the controlling idea or thesis? Where are these purposes most clearly realized? Why is this purpose significant?

    c. *Audience.* Who is the target audience for this website? Where can this be verified? Why is this audience targeted?

    d. *Persona.* What role does the creator of this website play? Is it easily discernible or not? Do you know who created the website? Is it singularly or corporately authored? What specific credentials are provided to enhance the ethos of the site's creator? Is the website well maintained, and is it sufficiently sophisticated (visuals, links, portals) to enhance the rhetor's persona?

    e. *Tone.* What is the prevailing attitude projected by the website? How do visuals, word choice, punctuation, layout and design (basic and technical features of visual rhetoric) contribute to the "feel" of the website? Where is this most prevalent? Why is this attitudinal quality important?

    f. *Evidence.* What evidence (VASES) does the website use to substantiate its claims? Does the website use lots of evidence? Little evidence? Sufficient evidence for its subject matter and its target audience? How are the strengths and weaknesses of the types of evidence demonstrated? Where are good excerpts to document these types of evidence? Can you account for the type and amount of evidence used in the website?

    g. *Structure.* What is the prevailing organizational structure (sequential, topical, logical)? How does the organizational structure support or challenge the prevailing value identified for it? Does the website have links? Are they easy to navigate, or do they take you places without any way of getting back? Does the website have organizational coherence? Why do you suppose the website is designed in this manner?

    h. *Strategies.* Choose ONE aspect of strategy (language, argument, or appeals) to critique. If language, what language strategies are evident? Where? Why? If argument, what argument types are evident? Where? Why? If appeals, what values underscore the rhetoric? Sources of audience captivation? Where? Why?

    i. *Evaluation.* How do you rate this website on aesthetic grounds? Why? How do you assess this website on truth grounds? Can you? How do you judge this website on ethical grounds? Why? How do you evaluate this website based on effects? Do you know how many persons visited the website? Do you know what publicity it has received from being listed as links on other websites? Is this a website you will visit again?

Portfolio Entry 10: Evaluation

3. Evaluate your rhetorical acts according to the four criteria discussed in this chapter: aesthetics, truth, ethics, and effects. Can you proclaim a single winner? In what ways were these judgments easy? Difficult? Respond in two to three pages.

Strategic Speaking Exercises

4. Craft a two- to three-minute speech to formulate belief around the thesis: "The best movie to see this year is _____." Use all four standards of evaluation to convince your audience that your film is a winner. Vote on a class winner.

NOTES

1. Edwin Black, *Rhetorical Criticism: A Study in Method* (1965; Madison: University of Wisconsin Press, 1978). Chapman's address and Black's analysis are found on pp. 79–90.

2. Leonard Pitts, "Teen's Death Raises Painful, Pressing Question," *Chicago Tribune*, March 18, 2012. Reprinted with permission from Tribune Media Services.

3. See "In Trayvon Martin Case, A Search for Answers," *Washington Post*, March 20, 2012. Available online at http://articles.washingtonpost.com/2012-03-20/opinions/35446180_1_trayvon-martin-george-zimmerman-attacker. Accessed 6/23/13.

4. Ken Thomas, "Obama: 'If I had a son, he'd look like Trayvon,'" The Associated Press, Sunday, March 24, 2012, *Waterloo Region Record*, p. A10.

5. "Killing Echoes an Uglier Time in America," *The Globe and Mail*, March 31, 2012, p. A21.

6. The text of Smith's speech is available online at http://www.americanrhetoric.com/speeches/margaretchasesmithconscience.html. Accessed 10/18/13.

7. The text of Kennedy's speech is available online at http://home.comcast.net/~ceoverfield/sea.html.

8. See Sheryl Sandberg, "Barnard College Commencement Address," May 17, 2011. Available online at http://barnard.edu/headlines/transcript-and-video-speech-sheryl-sandberg-chief-operating-officer-facebook.

9. Barack Obama, "Second Inaugural Address." Available online at http://www.usatoday.com/story/news/politics/2013/01/21/obama-inaugural-address/1851731/.

Chapter 12

Understanding Visual Rhetoric

I mages that aim to influence us are inescapable (see Figure 12–1). Sculpture, picket and traffic signs, religious and political symbols, YouTube videos, smartphone apps, films, television programming, photographs, computer icons, websites, paintings, posters, print ads, architecture, dance, parades, corporate logos, billboards, and many other visual events enrich and clutter our symbolic landscape. This chapter examines the special characteristics and constraints of analyzing rhetorical acts that are primarily visual. In Chapter 3 you were introduced to nonverbal features of speechmaking and how to use visual aids appropriately. In public speaking, the visual aspects of rhetoric are secondary. Such nonverbals as sustained eye contact, natural gestures, and erect posture are designed to enhance, not substitute for, the verbal message. Visual aids such as PowerPoint or Prezi slides should be used sparingly and not overshadow the rhetor's words.

Visual rhetoric as examined in this chapter, however, means that the image is the entire or the dominant persuasive message. Words, if used at all, are relegated to caption status; they are handmaidens to the images. However, to study visual rhetoric carefully is not to study images or artifacts in isolation from larger contexts in which an audience might encounter them. As Bruce Gronbeck reminds us: "visuality always has been integral to rhetorical consciousness."[1] A sophisticated critique of messages that magnify the visual and minimize the verbal requires specialized knowledge of visual principles, production techniques as they relate to the elements of descriptive analysis, and the problems such rhetoric poses for evaluation.

Figure 12–1
Visual Rhetorical Images

AP Images

AP Images/Nick Ut

Black Russian Studio/Shutterstock.com

AP Images/Jeff Widener

©Daryl Lang/Shutterstock.com

Courtesy of NASA

Joe Rosenthal/ Historical/Corbis

Bettmann/Corbis /AP Images

Allstar Picture Library/Alamy

Gamma-Rapho/8851/Getty Images

PRINCIPLES OF VISUAL RHETORIC

Three principles or observations about visual rhetoric anchor the critical perspective advanced here. First, *visual messages are pervasive and threaten to eclipse the influence of the spoken and written word in the twenty-first century*. Children today spend seven times as much time watching television as reading. Video stores outnumber libraries three to one in most cities. A majority of adults can readily discuss the last film they saw but have some trouble recalling the last speech they heard face to face and unmediated, and they cannot remember when they last finished a book—even as an e-reader! Educators now refer to children as visual learners and embrace visual pedagogy (art, dance, video, and the like) to teach subjects ranging from history to health. More than 60 percent of our grocery store purchases are impulse buying, which is primarily a result of packaging—the way the product looks and its placement on the shelves. Ronald McDonald is second only to Santa Claus as a recognized icon in the United States. At sporting events, in concert halls, political rallies, even in our houses of worship, eyes turn away from the real event as soon as images begin to move on giant screens.

Some critics insist that television itself has been transformed since the 1980s from a word-based rhetoric with minimal production values to a visually based mythic rhetoric that uses sophisticated production techniques to project an extreme self-consciousness of style.[2] Even waging war is now a visual business and a primary way in which people have formed opinions about the war on terror.[3] Recent empirical studies have substantiated the powerful effects of print news photographs on shaping viewers' reduced support for the U.S. presence in Iraq.[4] Visual rhetoric is pervasive, in part because it is powerful. Lester Olson, Cara Finnegan, and Diane Hope remind us that "visual rhetoric affects the whole range of our activities in public life": how we see, remember, memorialize, confront, resist, consume, commodify, govern, and authorize.[5] It is central to creating national identity and collective memory. Collective memory is our shared sense of the past. It is "created through the extended circulation and appropriation of images over time" and shapes audience expectations and memories of historical events. Photos, in particular, often act as a "repository of complex and conflicting beliefs and attitudes about American identity,"[6] and as they become "iconic," they become especially powerful for publics because they acquire a kind of "secular sacredness" about who we are and what we value.[7]

The second principle of visual rhetoric is that *visual messages are volatile, eliciting positive and negative responses simultaneously*. They are ambivalent, complex, "unstable articulations" that allow for "elasticity" in making connections and assigning meaning.[8] The familiar expressions "Seeing is believing" and "A picture is worth a thousand words" capture their high ethos appeal. Gordon Parks, the pioneer African American photographer for *Life* magazine, filmmaker, and civil rights activist, said of the volatility of pictures:

> I have come to believe that no art form transforms human apathy quicker than that of photography. Having absorbed the message of a memorable photograph, the viewers' sense of compassion and newfound wisdom come together like two lips touching. And it is an extraordinary thing when an unforgettable photograph propels you from an evil interlude to the conviction that there must be a better day.[9]

Paul Messaris, a scholar of visual literacy, writes, "Photographs come with an inherent guarantee of authenticity that is absent from words." He relates a story from the civil rights movement that captures poignantly the authority and trust we place in visual rhetoric. Dr. Martin Luther King Jr. stood alongside a photographer watching a policeman beat a young civil rights worker. The photographer became so upset at what he was filming that he stopped, poised to intervene. King reminded him of the importance of his work: "Unless you record the injustice, the world won't know that the child got beaten. . . . I'm not being cold blooded about it, but it is so much more important for you to take a picture of us getting beaten up than for you to be another person joining in the fray."[10]

King, no doubt, learned that lesson painfully from a tragic moment in the infancy of the civil rights movement. In 1955 a fourteen-year-old boy named Emmett Till was brutally murdered by two white brothers in Mississippi for allegedly flirting with a white girl. The all-white, all-male jury later confessed that not a single one of them doubted that the defendants were guilty, yet emerged within an hour of deliberations to proclaim the brothers not guilty. But it was not the corrupted verdict that outraged a nation and galvanized the black community, as much as it was Emmett Till's mother's decision to hold an open casket funeral and to have her slain son's body photographed for all the world to see how his murderers had left his body pulverized—all for daring to speak to a white girl. Christina Harold and Kevin Michael DeLuca examine the ways in which these photographs of Till's mutilated body were a "crucial visual vocabulary" that "articulated the ineffable qualities of American racism in ways words simply could not do and served as a political catalyst for black Americans" to band together and demand change.[11] Killian Jordon, senior editor of *Life* magazine, summed up the power of a great visual by saying simply: "It tells the truth. It documents. It makes a statement: Life will never be the same."[12]

Other maxims, however, remind us of the dark side of visuals. "Do not be deceived by appearances," "Do not judge a book by its cover," and from the Bible: "Cursed be the man who makes a graven or molten image." Perception and knowledge, appearance and truth, often are at odds with each another. Plato spent a lifetime telling us as much. Journalism educator Mitchell Stephens captures the negatives of visual rhetoric succinctly:

> Images look real but are fake. They pretend to be what they are not. They lie. The portrait is a mute, lifeless substitute for the person; the idol, a primitive and superficial knockoff of the god. But that idol is also attractive and easy to see. It can distract from the more profound but more amorphous glories of the god.[13]

The advent of digital manipulation—almost anyone can perform edits via photoshop and experiment with graphic flourish on instagram—has made the negative influences of visuals even more prominent.

Despite its distracting and even dangerous implications, the enchantment and ease with which visual rhetoric is digested leads to the final premise: *Visual messages are efficient, emotional, and enthymematic in the way they persuade*. "Images," Stephens continues, "are marvelously accessible."[14] We can grasp images quickly and process the ideas they suggest with greater efficiency. The symbols you see in Figure 12–2 demonstrate this concise feature. For viewers young to old, crossing all educational levels, and transcending language and literacy, these symbols communicate quickly and effortlessly—especially important in a fast-paced world that demands multitasking and quick decision making.

Images exude emotion. They "sear great events in the public memory and wring revelation from small, private moments," says *Life* magazine.[15] They are

Figure 12–2
Visual Rhetorical Symbols

© Cengage Learning

pleasing to the eye. Art historians John Walker and Sarah Chaplin observe that pleasure and pain are a central part of the experience of visual culture. These emotional states are the means by which visual culture seduces us.[16] Gallagher and Zagacki have examined the emotional depth of photographs, concluding that their emotionality is rhetorical in three ways: photos evoke common humanity by capturing moments of enactment, creating identification, and forcing us to reexamine taken-for-granted ideas. At its most potent, visual rhetoric enables viewers to experience "epiphanic moments"—a single powerful image can fuse issues, ideas, longings, and values.[17] The montage of news photos at the beginning of this chapter illustrates the emotional appeal of visual rhetoric in all its highs and lows, from the exhilaration of a sporting triumph (Jamaican Usain Bolt being proclaimed the fastest man in the world at both the Beijing and London Olympics), to the horror and sadness of national tragedy (terrorist-directed planes crashing into the World Trade Center; the mass murder of 22 first graders and teachers at Sandy Hook Elementary in Newtown, Connecticut; JFK Jr. saluting the bier of his assassinated father). Nick Ut's Pulitzer-prize winning image of a naked, screaming Vietnamese girl in the aftermath of a U.S.-ordered napalm air strike hastened the end of the Vietnam War. Its emotional horror so tormented the U.S. army captain who ordered the air strike that he personally sought out the girl, Kim Phuc, to seek her forgiveness.[18] Examining the special conditions that made "accidental napalm" an iconic photo, Hariman and Lucaites contend that the photo's composition (the basic and technical elements are described later in this chapter) captures not just the horror and trauma of war but the moral incoherence and failure of the Vietnam War. The photo's disturbing message to the U.S. public is one of betrayal, and no amount of discursive policy rationalization can soften that agonizing truth.[19]

Complex causes that have difficulty gaining much traction among a wider public have been energized by emotional images. Fourteen-year-old Malala Yousatsai of Pakistan became the new face of education for girls around the world after she was shot in the head and neck by the Taliban for her outspoken views about the importance of education for girls in her country. "I am Malala" is now the official name of the robust

U.N. petition to support education for girls worldwide, and she has been nominated for the Nobel Peace Prize.

Images invite viewers to draw their own persuasive conclusions; they do not argue explicitly. As such, they can create associations in ways that would be too audacious or laborious to say or write. The enthymematic power of visual rhetoric is illustrated in another iconic image of the Vietnam War—the Kent State shooting as photographed by John Filo on May 4, 1970. Shortly after Richard Nixon announced that the United States was invading Cambodia, hundreds of campuses exploded in protest. At Kent State University, the ROTC building went up in flames. In the protests that followed on that campus, the Ohio National Guard shot thirteen students, killing four. Filo's photograph captured this horrible scene but, of more importance, the disturbing visual performed a potent proposition according to Hariman and Lucaites. These scholars maintain that this picture "seriously wounded American society's basic sense of legitimacy" because our government is not supposed to shoot its citizens for gathering in free assembly or for speaking and demonstrating against the policies of one's government. In effect, the photograph was an "inventional resource for animating moral deliberation."[20] The way in which this visual worked enthymematically to articulate the sentiments of the antiwar movement points to a larger value of visual rhetoric for social movements and other out-groups. For rhetors with little access to "big media," visual rhetoric (particularly in the form of protests, marches, boycotts, dress, and now an array of social media platforms, etc.) has always been a vital tool for establishing agency and civic engagement. In rhetorical acts of confrontation and resistance, visual display factors prominently as a medium of expression.

More contemporary examples of the subtle argumentative power of iconic images involve two U.S. statues. First was the public outcry over the changes proposed in a bronze statue memorializing the three firefighters who struggled to raise a flag late in the afternoon on September 11 in the smoldering disaster site of the World Trade Center. The statue was commissioned to honor the 343 comrades they had lost that day. The original photo (see Figure 4–3 in Chapter 4), reminiscent of the iconic Iwo Jima flag raising (see Figure 12–1), touched a responsive chord in viewers around the world, The 2001 photo was strangely and powerfully similar to the World War II flag raising because both photos captured a heroic deed of courage, grit, teamwork, and unflagging patriotism at a historic moment marked by the darkness of the threat against us. But a year later when the statue commemorating the photo was ready to be commissioned, the three white men who raised the flag were replaced by one black, one white, and one Hispanic firefighter. There was so much protest over the statue's change—"political correctness run amok" as many New Yorkers complained—that the bronze statue was never unveiled.

Second, when the Martin Luther King Jr. monument was unveiled, it depicted the revered civil rights leader carved in a thirty-foot piece of granite titled "The Stone of Hope." The sculpture of King with arms folded and a stern facial expression resembles, for some, an ancient Egyptian pharaoh. "I was a drum major for justice, peace and righteousness" is the carved quotation attributed to King. Controversy erupted immediately. Complaints ranged from King appears too towering and confrontational—more mighty pharaoh then compassionate prophet—to the wording attributed to King being taken out of context (the drum major line was a paraphrase of some comments King made in 1968, and King is known for so many other rousing lines it seemed peculiar to paraphrase this one), to the lack of recognition of his Christian ministry, and finally to the fact that the commissioned artist was Chinese, not a U.S. citizen.

Despite the unintended meanings that visual enthymemes can provoke, advertisers rely on enthymematic images. Recall from the previous chapter the enthymematic message of the "Daisy Spot." One of the first ads ever produced that capitalized on the idea that sex can sell anything was a 1965 Noxzema commercial in which a beautiful Swedish blonde whispers, "Men, nothing takes it off like Noxzema," to striptease music. That commercial is still ranked as one of the top ten commercials of all time for suggesting what could not be verbalized.[21] The ambiguity of visual rhetoric also means that it can produce an excess of meaning, something philosopher Umberto Eco calls "the fatal polysemy of images."[22] What do the plumes of smoke from the *Challenger* space shuttle (see Figure 12–1) communicate to those who were not born during this tragic turning point in U.S. space history? The abstractness of much postmodern art has generated humor from some and protest from others for its seemingly limitless interpretations. Clearly, the enthymematic qualities of images cut both ways.

VISUAL MESSAGES AND ELEMENTS OF DESCRIPTIVE ANALYSIS

With these principles of visual rhetoric in mind, some of its special features can be introduced and analyzed. Just as we would not criticize a musical score by referrng only to notes from the treble clef, we cannot analyze visual rhetoric using only a few perceptual cues. The rhetorical ability of any visual field is, to a great degree, a function of the artistic and production techniques used in its creation.[23] Two sets of specialized grammars will be introduced here: (1) *basic elements of visual communication* and (2) *technical elements of the camera*. The first set of specialized features covers a wide range of visual phenomena; the second set applies only to media. Both are vital to understanding the rhetorical force of a visual's purpose, audience, tone, persona, structure, evidence, and strategies (Figure 12–3).

Figure 12–3
Visual Rhetoric and Descriptive Analysis

PURPOSE Create virtual experience

AUDIENCE Visual learners are transcultural

PERSONA Medium is the messenger

TONE Vivid, sensory, design sensitive

STRUCTURE Associative and spatial

EVIDENCE Visuals

STRATEGIES Appeals to human condition argument, enthymeme

© Cengage Learning

At least four paired elements compose the core of visual messages: (1) *figure and ground;* (2) *shapes and space;* (3) *balance and direction;* (4) *color and lighting.*[24] Visuals insist that we determine the relationship between the subject and its background if we are to understand its purpose. Scenic backdrops confer meaning on the primary object. Our perception is altered greatly depending on whether a person's face is framed in a police lineup on *America's Most Wanted* or in a "Look Who's 40" lineup in the local newspaper. The three basic shapes of images—square, triangle, and circle—conjure up distinct emotions. Typically, square-shaped objects connote straightness, honesty, and sometimes dullness. Triangular images tend to suggest conflict and action. Circular forms frequently project warmth and security. Consider the expressions: "He's a square"; "It's a love triangle"; "She has a circle of love and support." Remember, though, that these are not fixed associations, and variations do not mean that the shapes lack artistic merit. The size, scale, and number of these shapes are related to how space is used. Lots of white space has often been associated with luxury, higher class, and independence; cramped space sometimes suggests the opposite. Contrast grocery ads with high-end cosmetic ads for expensive products. Examined in combination, shape and space are strategies that help us confer meaning on an image, especially in regard to such elements as purpose and tone.

Balance and direction are perceptual cues that help us organize a visual. Images present themselves as either symmetrical or asymmetrical—arranged equally or unequally on both sides of an imaginary line in the middle of a visual field. Symmetry is designed to suggest formality and is visually comforting; asymmetry tends to suggest informality and creates dissonance. Further, visuals direct our eyes to move in certain directions. Unlike the act of reading, which requires the same horizontal left-to-right eye movement, the act of perceiving has no automatic start and end point. Ads, for instance, sometimes want us to start with the copy and move to the visual or vice versa.

Color and lighting affect mood and contribute greatly to how visuals create virtual experience. Even our language reinforces this. "She has a sunny disposition"; "He's blue today"; "I see red, I'm so angry"; "He's down to earth"; "You get a gold star"; "There's a silver lining to the story"; "We're a green corporation—environmentally friendly"; "We're unsure; it's a gray area." Black-and-white photos are described as "classic"; polarized issues are depicted as "black and white"; Rainbow colors have suggested unity, righteousness, and gay rights. When Oreo posted a Facebook photo of its iconic cookie filled with rainbow icing, the cookie entered the political arena. The image, posted to commemorate the one-year anniversary of New York legalizing same-sex marriage, was taken to be Oreo's endorsement of liberal ideals. This new rainbow colored icing sparked a backlash from conservatives. Thousands called for a boycott of Nabisco, Oreo's parent company. On the opposite end of the spectrum a petition emerged to convince Oreo to continue to produce the rainbow-filled cookie.[25]

Lighting can heighten or diminish the intensity of an image. Flat lighting (no shadows) diminishes intensity; textured lighting (varied lights and shadows) heightens intensity. Contrast the lighting in a doctor's waiting room with that in a sports bar, an educational program with a horror flick.

More specialized technical features of visual rhetoric include (1) *focus,* (2) *angle,* (3) *shot sequencing and movement,* (4) *editing,* and (5) *sound.*[26] The sharpness or fuzziness of an image helps us interpret mood and our relationship to an image. Hard focus is objective and distancing; soft focus is subjective and intimate. Pictures on identification cards are hard focus (unless they are flubbed); glamour portraits are soft focus.

Angle, the position of the camera relative to its subject, projects the camera's persona and positions the viewer in relationship to the object. Media critic Joshua Meyerowitz reminds us that low-angle shots suggest power and authority; level shots connote a peer relationship with the viewer; high-angle shots are used to show that someone is small or weak.[27] Focus and angle are especially useful strategies for examining persona–audience associations.

Moreover, the type of shot (super close-up, close-up, medium close-up, medium shot, wide shot) is used strategically to alter our perceptions of an image. Close-ups project intimacy and encourage viewers to feel empathy. Television reporters are seldom shot in close-ups in order to maintain the aura of impersonal objectivity; protesters, on the other hand, sometimes try literally to get in the camera's face.[28] To move images, the camera has about as many options as a roller coaster. It can zoom, pan, tilt, roll, dolly; it can be stationary or handheld. To sequence images in such a way as to invite enthymematic response, the camera can adopt a volatile montage structure—the juxtaposition of different images that stimulates a new meaning in the viewer's mind.[29] Music videos have demonstrated the rhetorical potency of this montage structure. Each picture looked at separately is rather benign; when edited together with fast cuts, these images take on a whole new, and often subversive, meaning. Sometimes editing is smooth and seamless (as when dissolves and fades are used); other times editing is disruptive and jarring (as when wipes and jump cuts are used). At all times, editing is vital to the pacing and rhythm of a visual. Shot selection and sequencing also act as important proofs for the visual's purpose.

Finally, sound (sound effects, natural sound, music, narration, dialogue) envelops the viewer in a pleasing virtual reality, establishes a mood, and becomes a visual poetics. The natural sound used in the "Daisy Spot" was startlingly real to viewers and heightened the ominous juxtaposition between innocence and evil that the ad was trying to convey. Actor Charlton Heston was the spokesperson for a host of corporations owing, in part, to his authoritative, soothing voice. Famous ad jingles—from Alka Seltzer's "pop, pop, fizz, fizz, oh, what a relief it is" to Budweiser's "Whaaaaas Uuuuuuup"—use alliteration, rhythm, metaphor, personification, onomatopoeia (it sounds like what it is), and a host of other poetic devices to ratchet up the emotional quotient of the visual message.

Taken together, these basic and technological features give us the tools and a vocabulary to analyze visual rhetoric in a sophisticated and meaningful way. Television critics in the industry and in academia have used these elemental and technical features of visual messages to make powerful rhetorical analyses of popular shows ranging from *Leave It to Beaver, All in the Family*, and *M*A*S*H* to *Survivor, Modern Family, Once Upon a Time*, and *The Big Bang Theory*. For instance, a body of research now concludes that early TV shows adopted a utilitarian approach to the relationship between the shows' narratives and their production techniques, meaning that aesthetic and technological features were camouflaged and predictable (always an establishing shot to a medium shot) and distancing (close-ups rarely were used). Contemporary shows, on the other hand, adopt a more rhetorical approach, a "more aggressive use of the camera."[30] Everything from tighter control of screen space, varied lighting, disruptive edits juxtaposed with whip pans, to handheld cameras and wide experimentation with angles produce a chaotic visual image that overwhelms dialogue and heightens visual spectacle.[31]

PROBLEMS OF VISUAL RHETORIC

One of the things you probably noticed in the application of elements of descriptive analysis to basic and technological features of visual messages is that the terms *audience* and *persona* undergo major transformations. A viewer is different in some ways from an audience. A camera is different from a speaker or writer. Because images are made to be seen, they demand lookers, but unlike other forms of rhetoric, they do not demand an acknowledgment that a viewer exists. As Walker and Chaplin conclude:

> We enjoy images voyeuristically: we can look at a scene as if we were peering into a room through a one-way mirror. Fundamental to the appeal of visual media is...that we can watch to our heart's content without ourselves being observed.[32]

Witness the huge hit series, *Survivor*, one of the most voyeuristic shows ever produced. Or consider the voyeuristic appeal of YouTube. Accessible whenever you want, you can search for images of everything from dumb animal tricks, spectacular performances, or goofball tricks to how to fix just about anything. The South Korean sensation Psy made YouTube history by hitting a superviral milestone: 1 billion views for his "Gangnam-style" music video.

These voyeuristic experiences typically are solitary, which diminishes our influence over the rhetorical act. Stephens observes that in visual culture "we, the audience, have no influence on anything that transpires. Shows proceed entirely without us. As the pawn of such large, intractable forces, a viewer can end up feeling somewhat small."[33] That diminished influence led many early rhetorical theorists to believe that rationality and the deliberative process actually were subverted by visual display;[34] yet for visual media, the viewer is an economic agent. Despite references to television viewers as "couch potatoes," they are not seen as passive voyeurs by sponsors; rather, they are conceived as active buyers and discriminating consumers.[35]

Other audience-related problems with visual rhetoric begin with misperception. The gross oversimplification of visuals leading to distortion is a by-product of an image's wonderful efficiency and potent emotionalism. This concern already has been discussed in the section dealing with principles of visual rhetoric, but other dimensions of this problem need to be noted. We tend to process complicated events and issues, such as war, in all-too-simplistic terms. The U.S. public had no interest in the Kosovo conflict until pictures of ethnic Albanians herded into cattle cars, reminiscent of scenes from Nazi Germany, hit the national press and the airwaves. Outrage erupted. Until a graphic picture of a U.S. GI tortured and killed and dragged through the streets of Somalia found its way into our living rooms, the U.S. public supported peacekeeping there. The abortion debate was reignited and has resulted in tougher abortion restrictions in many states because horrible pictures and videos of third-trimester abortions (labeled "partial-birth abortions") have been shown to elected officials.

The chaos that followed after Hurricane Katrina was captured in pictures of despair and hopelessness from residents on rooftops, looting in New Orleans, scuffles between refugees and police, and charges of racial discrimination based on who received the first provisions. Whether representative of the debacle or not, these images created the view that our elected officials at all levels (local, state, federal) were inept and insensitive. The public outcry demanded accountability in the form of special hearings on Capitol Hill. Those Katrina images that conveyed government ineptitude were still lingering with great persuasive force seven years later in the aftermath of Hurricane Sandy. Elected officials and government agencies, especially FEMA, scrambled to be more effective, compassionate, and camera-savvy—though with mixed success.

When domestic and international policy is made by agents of change solely or in large measure based on pictures, we have reason to be concerned. Neil Postman, an inveterate critic of visual rhetoric, once said glibly: "It is implausible to imagine that anyone like our twenty-seventh President, the multi-chinned, 300-pound William Howard Taft, could be put forward as a presidential candidate in today's world" because the shape of a man's body is just as relevant to an audience enamored by visuals as the shape of his ideas.[36]

A subject-related problem emanating from visuals is a lack of cultural history. The lack of context, which leaves viewers guessing or reinforcing their existing beliefs, is a by-product of an image's ability to persuade enthymematically. In other words, visuals create insulated viewers comfortable with their own ideological conclusions, which raises the uncomfortable question: do visuals always tell the truth? Consider antiabortion protestors who carry signs displaying grisly photos of aborted fetuses. Do these photos lie or tell the truth? What role does context play in determining this kind of picture's truth or falsehood? Was the abortion performed as the result of a vicious rape? Was the mother's life threatened by delivery? Was the fetus severely deformed? What's the rest of the story? Photos are a form of evidence, but, as columnist Randy Schofield notes, "some assembly is required." Photos alone cannot take the place of argument and reasoning. Some photos attempt to shock and manipulate by short-circuiting argument. That's one of the reasons the Bush White House fought to suppress photographs of the flag-draped coffins of military personnel killed in Iraq and of the abuses at Abu Ghraib prison. The administration understands the power and the limitations of visuals—they excite deep feelings, but they cannot tell the whole truth by themselves.[37]

Lacking a way to communicate critical context, pictures can also lose their punch. Consider the button in Figure 12–4.

When we showed it to a class of freshman students, they interpreted it variously. All recognized the "no" circle, now common on traffic markers, that something is prohibited. But just what was prohibited was unclear. One person said, "No more hang-ups." Another said, "Don't keep me hanging." Yet another said: "I've seen that sign in hotel rooms discouraging guests from using the fire alarm sprinkler nozzle to hang clothes! Only one person was certain. She recognized the button as one distributed by the National Abortion Rights Action League (NARAL) and translated it as "No more illegal, unsafe abortions." Because the button is highly abstract, it is ambiguous. For that reason, visual rhetoric works best with viewers who are "true believers"—those who already agree. An ideal viewer for the button is a member of NARAL who recalls the higher rates of maternal death and sterility that resulted from illegal abortions performed under unsanitary conditions and with improper instruments, such as a coat hanger.

Figure 12-4
Ambiguous Signs

The persona of visual rhetoric is equally complex. Viewpoint is located in the camera. The camera's operator can move from an objective or subjective role, a dominant or diminished role, by pushing a button. Like the Wizard of Oz, if you strip away the technological bells and whistles of the visual rhetor, you are often unimpressed by what is left. Does this mean that the rhetor's reputation is not important? (Who is the camera operator, film director, artist, or sculptor?) Can we read a visual message carefully without knowing whether a veteran or novice videographer shot it? If a right- or left-wing, male or female, Caucasian or ethnic minority, straight or gay artist sculpted it? Even written rhetoric comes with bylines and sometimes pictures of the writer. Visual rhetoric dwarfs the importance of the human rhetor. As Ronald Reagan once quipped, "I like photographers—you don't ask questions."[38] To alter a famous saying by the Canadian cultural scholar Marshall McLuhan, "The Medium Is the Messenger."

Finally, visual rhetoric is difficult to judge. How do we know, for instance, if nondiscursive rhetoric is effective, if our traditional ways of finding out require subjects to be articulate in the discursive mode? To be sure, we will always have Nielsen ratings, Google hits, and box office numbers, but what about the effects of other visual phenomena? Can focus group members articulate how an ad campaign, a memorial, or a corporate logo works for them? Because most visual rhetoric is absorbed by solitary viewers, a sense of collective support or rejection is difficult to achieve. A corollary to the standing ovation is difficult to find when people are observing a magazine ad, whizzing by a billboard, or contemplating a piece of modern art.

How do we censure unethical images when they only suggest harm but do not spell it out explicitly? Should Benetton, the hip Italian clothier, be punished for its ads on billboards and websites that humanize death row inmates in soft focus mug shots, show graphic violence, film an AIDS patient's last breath? It is difficult to prosecute potentially harmful visual messages when the "proof" is not in the pudding but in someone's head. Still, voices of protest do work. R. J. Reynolds's hip spokes animal, Joe Camel, was roundly criticized by educators for making kids think smoking is cool. The pressure worked, and Joe disappeared.

How do we judge the truthfulness of a photo when digital manipulation makes it virtually impossible to detect alteration? The picture of O. J. Simpson in Figure 12–1 calls attention to truth issues. In 1994, *Time* magazine placed defendant O. J. on its cover after the opening of "the trial of the century," in which he was charged with the murders of his wife and her friend. The only problem was that the picture was digitally altered. Simpson's face was purposely darkened—a retouching practice that has become increasingly common. To many readers, this digital alteration made him appear more sinister-looking. In this case the alteration was discovered and raised public awareness of the technique. Interestingly, *Time* will no longer allow us to reproduce the digitally altered cover, only a corrected cover image that you will find at the beginning of this chapter. But what about other, more covert, alterations and acts of staging? In the film *Wag the Dog,* the use of visual deception was raised to comic proportions, but the film underscores just how far technology can take us in transforming visuals into mass falsehoods.

How do we evaluate aesthetics without getting lost in or mesmerized by all the fancy footwork that technology has to offer? The richly satiric *Colbert Report* on Comedy Central begins humorously with an overproduced opening complete with soaring eagles, waving flags, and dizzying graphics that mock the sensationalism of televised special reports. It is challenging to balance an artistic appreciation that is sensitive to techniques but that does not lose sight of the narratives these techniques support. Meaningful aesthetic judgment requires critics who are literate in both word content and technical grammar—no small feat. These questions concerning the perils of judgment and the complex rhetor–viewer relationship expose the volatility of visual rhetoric and underscore the importance of recognizing its special constraints if we are ever to understand how visuals influence.

 MATERIAL FOR ANALYSIS

See the photo montage of key moments in U.S. culture at the beginning of this chapter. Choose one or more and address the following questions.

Questions for Analysis

1. What feelings do you have about these pictures? Must you have lived through these events for them to be meaningful to you? How do they support the three principles of visual rhetoric discussed in this chapter?
2. How does each picture create virtual experience and alter perception? How does each serve an instrumental or a consummatory purpose? Do some measure up better than others in achieving these purposes?
3. What is the general tone of each? How do basic elements and technical features of visual rhetoric contribute to tone?
4. Can you discern a target audience for each picture? Is it nondiscriminating? Is there a consumer interest? Do these pictures invite voyeur tendencies?
5. Which appeals are primary? Are they universal or culture specific? How do they help you form enthymematic responses?
6. Can you imagine another pictorial composite (angle, color, focus, shot sequence, balance, figure/ground, etc.) in which the reaction to the picture would be quite different?
7. Does the organization or individual credited for the photograph (persona) influence the credibility of the picture? How?
8. Do these twelve pictures, representing very different eras, events, and contexts but presented together (montage structure), influence your reaction to any one of them? How?

EXERCISES

Critical Thinking Exercises

1. Psychologists tell us that color choice is directly related to mood states. Examine several websites or print ads and discuss how color contributes to the tone of the site.

2. Color associations are cultural. In one recent Japanese election, one candidate for the post of prime minister chose the color pink to identify him. His supporters wore pink baseball caps and pink sweaters, draped the rostrum from which he spoke with pink material, and handed out literature that featured the color pink. Would you advise a candidate in the United States to select pink as his or her color? Why might pink have different connotations in Japan?

3. If you own a camera without a zoom lens, you know how frustrating it is to take shots of people. Find six to

twelve photos of people you have taken that represent some of the different types of shots presented in this chapter. How does the type of shot affect the rhetorical value of your pictures?

4. Divide into groups. Each group is required to record a desired music video. Discuss how montage structure works to create certain enthymemes. Are any of these subversive? Are production values of the video pleasing? Disturbing? Explain.

5. Body piercing, tattoos, jewelry, hats, and T-shirts often become visual rhetoric. Explain how these work as popular and concise expressions of people's beliefs. Are any of these body symbols ambiguous? Is that an oxymoron, or might that be strategic? Why?

6. As a class, Google "Madonna's meat dress." Discuss what was so jarring about this visual display of dress? Why did it receive so much media attention? How did it help or harm advocates for vegetarianism, the ethical treatment of animals, and food safety? How did other contextual factors of occasion enhance or diminish her outlandish attire?

Analytical Writing Exercises

7. The tribute or "support ribbon" is a familiar visual symbol that communicates a message efficiently (see Figure 12–2). Look up the April 20, 2007, issue of the *Virginia Tech Collegiate Times* (www. collegiatetimes.com). The cover story is a simple, powerful visual of a support ribbon with hundreds of questions embedded in it dealing with all the unanswered questions that lingered five days after the rampage of killings by a disturbed student gunman on that campus that left thirty-three dead. Write a short (500-word) analytical essay that examines how that visual display conveys the enormity of the tragedy without overwhelming the reader or being insensitive to its many victims? How does the visual story illustrate the principles of visual rhetoric? Do you see any of the problems of visual rhetoric in the way the ribbon is used? What other visual choices might have created ethical dilemmas for the student journalists?

8. Critique the Ad Council ad shown in Figure 12–5 ("Help Delete Online Predators"), a visual rhetoric campaign to support the National Center for Missing and Exploited Children.

   Your three- to four-page critique should consider these questions:

   a. How does the ad conform to the descriptive analysis of visual rhetoric? (See Figure 12–3.)

   b. What special audience or subject challenges does the ad confront? How well does the visual meet those

Figure 12–5
Help Delete Online Predators

Courtesy of the Ad Council and The National Center for Missing & Exploited Children

challenges? What other problems of visual rhetoric do you see in this ad?

   c. How do the captions interface with the visual? Are they complementary? Competitive?

   d. Rate this piece of visual rhetoric on aesthetics, truth, and ethics.

9. Critique the following magazine covers for provocative visual rhetoric factors: (1) *Time* magazine's May 21, 2012 issue, "Are You Mom Enough?"; (2) *Time* magazine's April 18, 2008, issue, "How to Win the War on Global Warming"; and (3) *The Atlantic Monthly*'s July/August 2012 issue "Why Women Still Can't Have It All." A simple Google search will reveal all three. How do these three issues illustrate the three principles of

visual rhetoric? What sorts of problems do you think each of these covers presents for some viewers? Rate these covers for aesthetics, ethics, truth, and effects.

Portfolio Entry 11: Visuals

10. Compare and contrast the ways that your three rhetorical selections use visuals to advance their purpose. Are words central to the rhetorical acts, or are they reduced to caption status? Which principles of visual rhetoric are most apparent? What essential and technical aspects of visual rhetoric are important to your selections? Explain. How do they relate to audience? Structure? Strategies? Tone? Persona? Evidence? (If visuals are not included, speculate in one to three pages how the selections could be enhanced with a visual component.)

Strategic Speaking Exercises

11. Prepare a three- to four-minute visual speech on a controversial policy issue. Your aim is to formulate belief with pictures alone. As with other speeches that demand visual aids, you will need approval by your instructor for the images you wish to use to "tell your side of the story." With your slides (jpeg images on PPT slides or iMovie or cataloging pictures on "Flicker" or some other slide show software program), select and organize images only (no text other than captions) that best represent your point of view. After your presentation, ask the class to write down what they think your thesis was. Share answers. Does audience reaction match your intended purpose? Reflect further on your experience by discussing the following: What challenges artistically, technically, and rhetorically did you face with such an unusual speech assignment? How might your visual speech be enhanced with a musical score? With voice-over narration? How does this exercise illustrate the three principles of visual rhetoric? The problems of visual rhetoric?

NOTES

1. See Bruce Gronbeck as quoted in Lester C. Olson, Cara A. Finnegan, Diane S. Hope. eds., *Visual Rhetoric: A Reader in Communication and American Culture* (Los Angeles: Sage, 2008), p. 2.

2. See a host of media literacy sites for studies on the prevalence of media culture, including www.medialiteracy.com; for consumer behavior and visual consumption, see Arthur Asa Berger, *Seeing Is Believing* (Mountain View, CA: Mayfield Publishing, 1998), p. 31. For a "top ten" listing of cultural icons, see A&E Network series, *The T.V. Ad*, July 2000; the argument that television programming has adopted a more self-conscious visual style is made by John Thornton Caldwell, *Televisuality: Style, Crisis, and Authority in American Television* (New Brunswick, NJ: Rutgers University Press, 1995), p. 4.

3. See for instance, Dana L. Cloud, "To Veil the Threat of Terror: Afghan Women and the Clash of Civilizations in the Imagery of the U. S. War on Terrorism," *Quarterly Journal of Speech*, 90 (2004): 285–306. As reprinted Lester C. Olson, Cara A. Finnegan, and Diane S. Hope, eds., in *Visual Rhetoric: A Reader in Communication and American Culture* (Los Angeles: Sage, 2008), p. 397. Cloud maintains, for example, that the photo essays on Time.com encourage viewers to adopt a paternalistic stance toward Afghan women and to "interpret the war as a moral clash between good and evil and between persons who are essentially reasonable and people who are fundamentally irrational."

4. Michael Pfau et al., "The Effects of Print News Photographs of the Casualties of War," *Journalism & Mass Communication Quarterly*, 83:1 (Spring 2006): pp. 150–158.

5. Lester C. Olson, Cara A. Finnegan, and Diane S. Hope, eds., *Visual Rhetoric: A Reader in Communication and American Culture* (Los Angeles: Sage, 2008). p. 2.

6. Hariman and Lucaites as quoted in *Visual Rhetoric*, p. 177; and Olson et al. p. 100.

7. Osborne as quoted in *Visual Rhetoric*, p. 122.

8. Hariman and Lucaites as quoted in *Visual Rhetoric*, p. 177; Edwards & Winkler as paraphrased in *Visual Rhetoric*.

9. Gordon Parks as quoted in Victoria Gallagher and Kenneth Zagacki, "Visibility and Rhetoric: Epiphanies and Transformations in the *Life* Photographs of the Selma Marches of 1965," *Rhetoric Society Quarterly*, 37:2 (2007): p. 116.

10. Paul Messaris, *Visual Persuasion* (Thousand Oaks, CA: Sage, 1997), p. 141.

11. Christina Harold and Kevin Michael DeLuca, "Behold the Corpse: Violent Images and the Case of Emmett Till," in *Rhetoric & Public Affairs*, 8:2 (Summer 2005): p. 265.

12. Killian Jordan, "Editor's Note," in the "Collector's Edition, Great Pictures of the Century," *Life* (October 1999), p. 10.

13. Mitchell Stephens, *The Rise of the Image, the Fall of the Word* (Oxford: Oxford University Press, 1998), p. 60.

14. Stephens, *The Rise of the Image*, p. 61.

15. *Life*, Collector's Edition, Great Pictures of the Century," p. 16.

16. John A. Walker and Sarah Chaplin, *Visual Culture: An Introduction* (Manchester: Manchester University Press, 1997), p. 150.

17. Gallagher and Zagacki, "Visibility and Rhetoric," p. 113.

18. Louise Steinman, "The Girl in the Photo," salon.com, August 3, 2000.

19. Robert Hariman and John Louis Lucaites, "Public Identity and Collective Memory in U.S. Iconic Photography: The Image of 'Accidental Napalm,'" *Critical Studies in Media Communication*, 20:1 (March 2003): 35–66. See also *No Caption Needed: Iconic Photographs, Public Culture, and Liberal Democracy* (Chicago: University of Chicago Press, 2007).

20. Hariman and Lucaites, "Dissent and Emotional Management in a Liberal-Democratic Society: The Kent State Iconic Photograph," *Rhetoric & Society Quarterly*, 31 (2001): 5–32.

21. The ad was rated the sixth best ad of all time according to Arts and Entertainment Network, *The TV Ad*, July 2000.

22. Umberto Eco, *The Search for the Perfect Language*, trans. James Fentress (Oxford: Oxford University Press, 1995), p. 174.

23. One of the first researchers to enunciate this clearly was David Barker, "Television Production Techniques in Communication," *Critical Studies in Mass Communication* (September 1985): 234–246.

24. Many production scholars have conceptualized these components. I have taken the liberty of pairing them. For a good overview, see Berger, *Seeing Is Believing*, pp. 53–66.

25. Nick Carbone, "Top 10 Memes of 2012" at Time.com. http://newsfeed.time.com/2012/12/04/top-10-news-lists/slide/rainbow-oreos/print/.

26. Berger, *Seeing Is Believing*, pp. 83, 97–99.

27. Joshua Meyerowitz, "Multiple Media Literacies," in Horace Newcomb, ed., *Television: The Critical View*, 6th ed. (Oxford University Press, 2000), pp. 425–438.

28. Meyerowitz, "Multiple Media Literacies," p. 430.

29. Messaris, *Visual Persuasion*, pp. 168–169.

30. See Barker. "Television Production Techniques in Communication."

31. Caldwell, *Televisuality*, p. 64.

32. Walker and Chaplin, *Visual Culture*, p. 101.

33. Stephens, *The Rise of the Image*, p. 127.

34. Hariman and Lucaites, "Public Identity and Collective Memory," p. 35.

35. See Caldwell, *Televisuality*.

36. Neil Postman, *Amusing Ourselves to Death* (New York: Penguin, 1985), p. 7.

37. Randy Scholfield, "Photos Show Only Part of the Truth," *Wichita Eagle*, October 14, 2005, p. 9A.

38. Ronald Reagan as quoted in Gordon Jackson, *Watchdogs, Blogs and Wild Hogs: A Collection of Quotations on Media* (New Media Ventures, Spokane, Washington: 2006).

Chapter 13

Understanding the Medium of Transmission

T his chapter is a primer in how media technologies influence our messaging behavior and shape the way we send and receive rhetorical acts. It is designed to heighten mindfulness of how we engage media texts so that we may become discerning citizens rather than blind consumers. Once we know how the very technologies we use to transmit rhetorical acts influence the form, content, and reception of those acts, we become better equipped to navigate the digital frontier from a critical perspective.

Understanding the medium of transmission builds on the fundamentals, resources, and special constraints presented in earlier chapters. It takes the elements of descriptive analysis, the rhetorical problem, and standards of evaluation and asks questions such as these: How do media invite our assent? What are the promises and the perils of media as influence peddlers in the digital age? How does the medium of communication (newspaper, radio, television, computers, smartphones) affect the rhetorical message? The overriding premise of the chapter is: *Media are powerful because they pervade our culture, carry moral authority, and acquire special influence through their means of transmission.*

MEDIA AS RHETORICAL CONSTRUCT

A number of fundamentals about mediated rhetorical influence lie at the heart of the field of media literacy. These concepts function as theoretical anchoring points for educators and practitioners (Figure 13–1). For students, they address the "why" or "so what" questions that arise when we seek to "decode" mediated messages.

All media messages are constructed. We understand this idea better with social media than with established media. Of course, we say a YouTube video or Facebook post is created and thus personalized by the user. But what about news? Coverage of unfolding events are shaped by the media outlet, the reporter, photographer, or editor assigned and are affected by the day of the week the story airs or is published. The idea that journalists "cover the story" is a bit misguided. Journalists actually co-create a story. Because media messages are constructed, it is important to get your news and information about the world from a wide array of sources.

Media messages use a language with its own rules. "DIKU that F2F still WFM." "I need a v.o. and a p.o.p. with natsound on that top story." Do you know what those two sentences mean in media-speak? Unlike the mechanics of writing or the rules of speaking, media messages play by their own rules. Media has its own specialized grammar. We examined several grammatical rules as they pertain to visual messages in Chapter 12 (figure/ground; space/shape; color/lighting; balance/direction; focus; angle; shot sequence and movement; editing; and sound). Texting and tweeting has its own lingo. Photoshop and Instagram enable sophisticated ways to digitally alter photographs. The language of media is not just different and enriching in other ways compared to face-to-face communication. It is also lacking in basic nonverbal and contextual features, creating greater possibilities for miscommunication. Understanding how mediated messages are produced and published will go a long way in recognizing its influence, artistry, and ethical constraints.

Different people experience the same media messages differently. We understand that fans of different sports teams often see a game differently, and the same holds true of media messages. Based on age, background, gender, income level, schooling, religious, and ethnic orientation and many other more personalized traits, media consumers will

1. Media messages are constructed.

2. Media messages have their own language rules.

3. Media messages are experienced differently by different people.

4. Media are driven by profit.

5. Media have embedded values.

6. Media are pervasive and carry high authority.

7. "The Medium is the message."

Figure 13–1
Fundamentals of Media Literacy

see, hear, and remember different elements of a mediated message. Media literacy researcher George Gerbner studied how the elderly who were heavy TV consumers developed a "mean world syndrome" when other younger adult viewers with the same heavy diet of TV did not. Currently, the Supreme Court is examining the constitutionality of a California ban on selling or renting violent video games for children under age eighteen based on the argument that freedom of speech (in this case the corporate speech of the gaming industry) is filtered very differently (and dangerously) by minors than by adults.

Media are primarily driven by a profit motive. Media are businesses that need many customers to stay alive. Without advertisers or underwriters, there is no information and entertainment at your fingertips. That is true for established media and now for social media. When you use the search engine Google to access a website, invariably you will be subjected to a series of online (pop-up and banner) ads. When you watch a video online, even on a news source site, you must first watch a commercial. Gaming online is free for the first few times, and then you're often charged a user fee. If we recognize that media are businesses, we can better understand why efforts to ramp up the entertainment quotient of all programming is so important. Even the most sobering and complex topics (for example, health care reform) must be treated in the media in an entertaining way so that lots of people tune in, log on, and stay around! If viewers and surfers are bored or are required to do too much "heavy lifting," media enterprises collapse.

Media have embedded values and points of view. This goes one step beyond the idea that media messages are constructed. It recognizes that many media outlets and special programming have established points of view (for example, conservative or liberal)—think MSNBC versus Fox News; Disney versus PBS. Without sampling a variety of media messages, you may mistake a particular point of view as "the way it is." Further, you may be prone to thinking and responding to your own views as expressed on blogs, chat rooms, and so forth in ways that create a cozy, but insular "echo chamber" in which your ideas are never debated but only confirmed. In 2010, President Obama told the graduating class at the University of Michigan, "if you're somebody who only reads the editorial page of *The New York Times*, try glancing at the page of *The Wall Street Journal* once in a while. If you're a fan of Glenn Beck or Rush Limbaugh, try reading a few columns on the Huffington Post website."[1] As media companies grow larger through mergers, they become less diversified. As a result, this principle of media becomes even more pronounced.

Media are pervasive and carry high moral authority; "the medium is the message." These concepts have particular implications for us as rhetorical critics. These remaining media literacy concepts will be the special focus of the rest of this chapter.[2]

MEDIA AND HIGH ETHOS APPEAL

Mass media and social media are powerful because they pervade our culture. It wasn't always that way. Gutenberg invented the printing press in 1440. It was 435 years later to the next milestone—the telephone in 1875. Forty-four years later, along came radio.

Twenty years later television was invented. In the 1970s and 1980s pagers, mobile, satellite, and wireless phones and large, slow, home computers arrived. The Internet was born in the 1960s but wasn't really publically available until 1992. Think of how technology has changed in the past twenty years! Now we have video chat, text messaging, a cell phone on nearly every hip, and most of us can't imagine communicating without email. Each day we're bombarded with more than 5,000 advertising messages. We have access to 800 channels via satellite dish; 600 million users subscribe to Facebook; more than 500 YouTube links are tweeted every minute. As a whole, Americans eight to eighteen increased their consumption of all media from 6 hours and 19 minutes each day in 1999 to 7 hours and 38 minutes each day by 2010. Experts now predict that Generation Y users (currently ages ten to seventeen) will spend close to one-third of their lives (23 years, 2 months) online![3] It really has become like trying to take a sip of water from a fire hose.[4]

Now try to imagine a day without exposure to media. One of the exercises at the end of this chapter invites you to turn off your favorite communication technology for forty-eight hours and record the kind of "withdrawals" you experience. If you are like most people, this will be a challenging assignment.

Media are extraordinarily influential because they acquire intellectual and moral authority. We are loath to admit this and much prefer to engage in media bashing. The newspaper is a "rag" that prints "yellow journalism" and is only good for "lining bird cages." Television is "the boob tube," a "vast wasteland," even "chewing gum for the eyes." Radio personalities are referred to as "shock jocks," and as a medium radio has been accused of spewing forth more subversive discourse and propaganda than any of its media counterparts. The Internet has been called a "conspiracy connection," a "congested web," or "a cybertrap" where anarchy rules and "cyberbullies" flourish. Others have warned that the Internet creates a "digital divide" between the haves and have-nots; linguistic confusion between "digital natives" and "digital immigrants"; and a troubling chasm between parents and children. Its hyperlink and personalization features intensify insular, echo-chamber "tribal discourse" first made popular by talk radio. Even the fascination with zombie culture has been attributed to the "always on" screen fixation of social media. Throughout history we often have "killed the messenger." Since the time of the early Greeks, bad news has often resulted in scapegoating the courier. In some sense, media have intensified that phenomenon by encouraging viewers, listeners, and subscribers to "sound off" on their opinion lines, Internet polls, and Twitter walls to capture what is "trending" in media culture.

Although media bashing is commonplace and we are loathe to admit that we are "tethered to social media,"[5] the influence of media on our lives is undeniable. For many, media are more credible and trustworthy than family, places of worship, and real (as opposed to virtual) interpersonal relationships. Media critic Neil Postman long ago argued that television had become the command centre of our culture an analog to what the medieval church was in the fourteenth or fifteenth centuries. For anything to be legitimate, it had to come through television."[6] Another way of documenting the media's influence is to recognize just how frequently it validates experience. Individuals who have witnessed crimes, for instance, often report that it was not until they saw, heard, or read the news of the event that the experience became real, that they believed it actually happened, and that it was important.[7] For many teens, a dating relationship is not real until a status change has been noted on Facebook. Extreme examples even suggest that virtual relationships are becoming more satisfying than physical ones—such as the football star from Notre Dame whose sense of dating involved an exclusive online relationship that never physically existed; it was a hoax! We know that children between the ages of eleven and seventeen will communicate online with persons they have never met eleven times more frequently than their face-to-face communication time with parents over the course of a lifetime.[8] Teens would rather go to YouTube for how to fix a tire than ask a parent! A 2011 survey of media habits observed that a smartphone is often the first object touched by a modern owner when he or she wakes up in the morning and the last thing touched before going to bed.[9] The high moral authority of media is here to stay. The Internet itself has changed the face of activism (crowdsourcing), crime (online predators), politics (online fund-raising, advertising), journalism (blogging citizen journalists), education (distance learning and open courseware), business (e-commerce), health care (medical diagnostic phone apps and websites), and human relationships (e-dating).

How did media personalities, digital friends, and search engines come to replace parents and priests as voices of authority? Why are we more comfortable in a chat room with strangers than in the town square with our neighbors? More likely to be a radio caller or tweet a response than be a speaker at city hall? Norman Rockwell's famous "Freedom of Speech" portrait is a quaint reminder of rhetoric in a relatively unmediated age. Part of the answer lies in the special rhetor–audience relationship that media creates.

The rhetorical process outlined in Chapter 1 suggests a single source (a rhetor) and a single receiver (an audience). When the masses replace an individual receiver and a corporate, anonymous, or depersonalized source takes the place of an in-the-flesh rhetor, the meaning of messages is altered significantly. Although some aspects of this unique relationship were discussed in Chapter 12 in the context of visual messages, other features need to be emphasized here.

In mediated communication, neither party to the rhetorical act knows entirely who the other is. One of the most iconic cartoons from *The New Yorker* about this special quality of the Internet said it best. As a dog is perched on a chair preparing to go online, he looks down at his fellow canine and says: "On the Internet, no one knows you're a dog." The veil of secrecy media erects is liberating. Employees can craft messages and conduct office business in their pajamas from home or in the stands of their kids' games. One might think that this anonymity would result in a lot of confusion and miscues in sending and receiving messages. On the contrary, as scholars John Fiske and John Hartley note, it is this inability to know the other that "imposes a discipline on the encoders which ensures that their messages are in touch with the central meaning systems of the culture and that the codes in which the message is transmitted are widely available."[10] In other words, mediated messages must be and are easy to process and thus speak to the receiver, whoever he may be.

The persona of the mediated message is fragmented and sometimes multivoiced. The rhetor's role in mediated discourse may be identified with an image, voice, signature, tag line or byline of an individual, but it may also include a chorus of professionals including advertisers, corporate owners, general managers, program and technical directors, gatekeepers, editors, image consultants, and Web masters. That there is no single authorial identity of the media communicator inflates the concept of "persona" and extends its influence. The image on our screen, the voice over the airwaves, the mug shot of the columnist, the hashtag identifier of the tweet, the "avatar" of our gaming identity, the status update on our Facebook page, or the signature of the Web master operates as a "front," a fragment that is devoid of other communicative cues that engage the full array of our senses. The notion of "digital incarnation"[11] takes the concept of ethos and identification to a whole new level. The audience of the mediated message is referred to broadly as "the masses," "followers," "subscribers," or "surfers"; optimistically as "cybercitizens" and "digital activists," and, more darkly, as "stalkers," "creepers," or "cyberbullies." Specifically, the immediate audience is defined in a physical sense as *receptors*. We are "viewers," "listeners," "readers," or "surfers"— terms that heighten our roles as active, sensory beings. The sheer deluge of messages we are exposed to means that the real audience obstacle in a mediated world is inattention. As columnist Nicholas Carr has observed: "Once I was a scuba diver in the sea of words. Now I zip along the surface like a guy on a Jet Ski."[12] We are not readers in the traditional sense. Users today "power browse."[13]

The target audience of mass-mediated messages capitalizes on this active, sensory component. Although stereotyped as "couch potatoes" or "zombies," the audience of mediated communication targeted by a corporate persona is imagined as anything but passive or inert. Rather, media rhetors envision their receptors as active buyers or *discriminating consumers* who fit economically desirable demographic categories.

The created audience is a critical concept in mass-mediated rhetoric. Media rhetors must create a role for their large consumer base. They must convince the masses to be willing accomplices in creating consumer culture. They must invite us to become packaged and delivered to advertisers, to welcome appeals to materialism, not shun them.[14] In so doing, media rhetors make a bargain of sorts. They do not engage in class warfare or pander to movers and shakers (hence, a VIP audience is irrelevant), and they give us some control—or at least the illusion of control—over the message. With the remote control in hand, or with the click of a mouse, or the turn of a dial or page, or with the DVR-ing of a show, the audience-as-willing-consumer "calls the shots." Mass audiences are impatient for "the hook" that prompts them to stick around and absorb the message. Media rhetors know this and try to track our changing tastes with countless surveys and ratings instruments (e.g., Arbitron, Nielsen, Gallup, and Google Analytics). Audience members are also more likely to assume this created role because they are anonymous; and because they are anonymous, they can surrender to their *voyeuristic tendencies*. There is a certain luxury in knowing that a rhetor is not watching you personally and that "tuning out" a message will not hurt anyone's feelings, just as tuning in a message will not require you to explain to anyone your media consumption habits, one reason that pornography sites on the Internet are visited by millions of people.[15]

THE MEDIUM IS THE MESSAGE

One of the "Ps" of rhetoric examined in Chapter 1 maintains that "rhetoric is powerful" because it can help or harm. Media show that this can be a double-edged sword. *Media create many paradoxes for us*. Various media platforms enable us to give enormous amounts of information more quickly, but now we have an "information glut," "data fatigue," and don't know how to process it all. Media make us less provincial, more a "global village" in sharing news from all over the world, yet media consumption is one of our most solitary and lonely activities. Media give us convenient, nonstop coverage of the lives of VIPs, yet usurp our right to privacy. The mass media bring a nation together (coverage of celebrations and tragedies), yet they also divide us (coverage of wars, conflict, scandal, and crime). Media educate us on a range of topics in such a way that we can take charge of everything from our health to our wealth. But media also has been implicated in everything from an increase in violence and aggressive behavior in youth, to hate crimes in adults, a "mean-world syndrome"[16] that can lead to depression in the elderly, attention-deficit disorder in toddlers, incivility in our elected officials, and a debasing of our values that leads many to immoral and unhealthy behavioral choices (smoking, drug abuse, teenage sex, truancy, cutting, suicide, divorce, bigotry, domestic violence). Professor Sherry Turkle of MIT captures the special paradox of social media in her book *Alone Together*. She writes:

> [W]e nurture friendship on social networking sites and then wonder if we are among friends; we are connected all day, but are not sure if we have communicated; we insist our world is increasingly complex, yet we have created a communication culture that has decreased the time available for us to sit and think uninterrupted. . . . We go online because we are busy but end up spending more time with technology and less time with each other. . . . The ties we form through the internet are not, in the end, the ties that bind. But they are the ties that preoccupy.[17]

It is no surprise, then, that as social media increasingly becomes the "go to first" medium, critics would be divided into opposing camps: "cyberevangelists" and "cyberskeptics." Cyberevangelists, such as Bill Gates, tell us that "the internet is becoming the town square for the global village of tomorrow" and we should be thrilled that for the first time in human history it is possible for everyone online to have a voice in shaping digital culture, including our ability to access, adapt, create, copy, and distribute words, sounds, and images all on the same devices.[18] Cyberskeptics such as Professor Turkle and best-selling author and columnist Malcolm Gladwell remind us that "all that glitters is not gold." From underperforming search engines and untrustworthy wikis to the regression to "tribal" communication; from the distractions that lead to shortened attention spans to the "slacktivism" that results from those who perform the effortlessness of signing a mass petition on Facebook and assume it's as effective as more traditional collective action demands; cyberskeptics remind us that this new medium of transmission may be brilliant, but also brilliantly disturbing. In the Material for Analysis at the end of this chapter, Gladwell articulates his concerns about social media in a compelling story about why successful social movements will not be tweeted.

The promises and the perils of media can be better understood by looking closely at how a channel uniquely filters a message. *Because the medium (the channel) is such an important, but taken-for-granted, rhetorical dimension of the message, it invites our assent in seductive ways.* As aspiring media critics, it is important for you to know that the individual medium of expression has benefits and limitations. This requires recognition that the medium itself is a constraint. Chapter 12 suggests that the medium is really part of the messenger. In terms of the rhetorical problem, there are many rhetor-related obstacles in mediated communication. Each transmission source has a prior ethos. It has a specific reputation for helping and for hindering an audience in its entertaining, profit-seeking mission (Figure 13–2).

The print media (especially newspapers) still cling to an authoritative reputation for their (1) *linearity*, (2) *permanence*, and (3) *in-depth coverage*. Our talk demonstrates how much we value that kind of discursive expression. Children are told to "toe the line," "walk the straight and narrow," and to follow a "clean line of thought." On the other hand, we are told, "avoid circular reasoning," and "don't make waves."[19] A "reader" often chooses to consume the news via this sense receptor because she can glance back over the page, pause, reflect, read again, and save and retrieve the article

Figure 13–2

Medium of Transmission

	Primary Strengths	Primary Weaknesses
Newspaper ©RTimages/Shutterstock.com	Discursive authority	Dated
	Permanent	Requires literacy
	In-depth coverage	Costs consumer directly
		Takes time to digest
Radio ©Sandra van der Steen/Shutterstock.com	Intimate medium	Nonvisual
	Reaches most segmented audiences	Coarse discourse
	Decline in community engagement	
Television ©ndphoto/Shutterstock.com	Largest audience	Lacks depth and perspective
	Visual storytelling	Sensational
		Not childproof
Internet ©Günay Mutlu/iStockphoto.com	Convergence capabilities	No gatekeepers
	Empowers users	Overdependency

for another time. This is a huge advantage over the other ephemeral and mostly disposable media. The print media also are especially suited to fulfill the rhetorical purpose of explaining the who, what, where, when, and in particular, the how and why of an event. By contrast, a thirty-minute local newscast does not even begin to cover the amount of information that is presented on the front page of a newspaper. In its glory days (1800–1920s) before the competition moved in, print journalism enjoyed preeminent status as the single media source of daily information.

The print media have many limitations. Newspapers (1) *are dated*, (2) *require literacy*, (3) *cost the consumer directly*, and (4) *take time to digest*. If you rely on a newspaper for weather, you know how frustrating dated information can be. If you want to know who won an election, a game, or the lottery, you don't turn to the newspaper first. Increasingly, reading literacy is a problem in maintaining healthy newspaper subscriptions as more and more people identify as visual learners. Even among those who say they like to read, many complain they do not have time to read a paper every day. And then there is the irritant of the cost factor; unlike basic radio or TV, the medium bills you directly for its message. This cost feature has nearly decimated some newspaper and magazine chains. By 2009 much press was being given to "how to save your newspaper." Print journalist Walter Isaacson, capturing the frustration of many in the newspaper industry, said:

> When I used to go fishing in the bayous of Louisiana as a boy, my friend Thomas would sometimes steal ice from those machines outside gas stations. He had the theory that ice should be free. We didn't reflect much on who would make the ice if it were free, but fortunately we grew out of that phase. Likewise, those who believe that all content should be free should reflect on who will open bureaus in Baghdad or be able to fly off as freelancers to report in Rwanda under such a system.[20]

Radio has a colorful and checkered history in mass media lore. *Its primary strength is that it can achieve intimacy with a more sharply delineated demographic profile of listeners who remain loyal.* It was also the first portable medium, before iPads and smartphones enabled us to take our computer technology with us. President Franklin Roosevelt was the first to realize the value of connecting with the citizenry via radio. He reached millions of Americans instantly in his "fireside chats." The medium enabled him to "chat" with Americans as citizens, peers, and members of a common national family united in their efforts to combat the perils of the Great Depression. Listeners could hear his confidence, steadiness, and optimism. They could feel the warmth of his delivery. His New England accent became recognizable and comforting. Roosevelt's detractors, such as Senator Huey Long of Louisiana and Father Charles Coughlin of Detroit, developed their own radio shows and wooed millions of disadvantaged Americans to be fearful of his policies. The fame of these two radio hosts marked the beginning of a colorful relationship between subversive discourse, charismatic personalities, and the airwaves. Intimacy between rhetor and audience can still be achieved today, as is evident in the popularity of "talk radio"—the second most popular format behind country music. "Callers" and listeners alike become fiercely loyal to their show's host (a real boon for advertisers). Rush Limbaugh's listeners, for instance, call themselves "dittoheads." Although in its infancy radios were not portable, they are today. With car, boat, shower, and clock radios, and Internet radio stations that stream on our smartphones, the medium can accompany us throughout our daily lives. Radio's deficiencies did not become evident until the advent of television. Suddenly, *its nonvisual character was a disadvantage.* Why merely listen to someone if we could see and listen? Television also stole the immediacy that radio once claimed over print. Radio has maintained a loyal base, but at a price. Today radio is blamed for much of the coarseness in our discourse (shock radio) and the vulgarity of our music (the explosion of alternative music stations). As satellite radio has raised its appeal to increasingly smaller niche musical tastes for a price, media critics have traced the precipitous decline in such subscribers being engaged in their local communities. A strength of traditional radio stations was their high civic engagement and the profiling of home-grown talent. Satellite radio severs connections to community, and radio hosts have no place they call "home." Radio also holds the dubious distinction of being the medium most heavily regulated by the federal government.

Television is still the preeminent medium. *It captures the largest audience faster than any other medium. The visual nature of its message invites our assent in especially satisfying ways.* As detailed in Chapter 12, visuals are captivating because they are efficient, emotional, and enthymematic. Television can entertain us better than any other medium because the use of moving pictures makes creating virtual experience effortless. With the advent of twenty-four-hour news stations and advanced remote technology, TV takes us "up close and personal" anywhere on the globe at any time. Even in 1960, when TV viewership was relatively new, the influence of moving visuals was dramatic in the first televised presidential debate between John F. Kennedy and Richard M. Nixon. Both candidates were seasoned debaters and well versed on the issues, but in terms of a style compatible with television, Kennedy was better prepared. Nixon looked pale and ill (in fact, he had recently been hospitalized); he wore heavy makeup and was visibly sweating. He was not as clean-shaven as Kennedy. He glanced nervously at a clock in the studio. Kennedy, on the other hand, appeared to enjoy the setting. Smiling and relaxed, his tanned youthfulness was now perceived as a strength, not a weakness. Not surprisingly, viewers believed Kennedy won the debate by a wide margin. Interestingly, some research suggests that Americans who listened to the debate on the radio thought Nixon had won.

Televised presidential debates are still huge media events today—a kind of Super Bowl of American democracy. In the 2012 election, a whopping 67 million Americans tuned in to the first debate, and two-thirds of Americans continue to indicate that viewing the debates helps them decide who to vote for and helps them actually cast a ballot.[21] We also know that unlike 2008, more money was spent in both presidential candidates' campaigns on TV ads than online or in print combined. One million TV ads (up 40 percent from 2008) cost both campaigns more than $1 billion because 55 percent of Americans still get their news from TV.[22]

The limitations of television have been widely documented. Three are worth examining here: (1) *Television programming lacks depth and perspective,* (2) *it converses in sensationalism,* and (3) *it is not childproof.* Because the screen is two-dimensional, reporters look as large as the burning buildings by which they stand. Even though TV sets in homes have become larger, sharper, and thinner, the screen cannot reflect the actual scope or magnitude of a scene. Over time, this compact view blunts our reaction to triumphs and tragedies. Content concerns create other distorted perspectives. The average sound bite, or direct quotation of what a person said, went from eighteen seconds in 1982 to five seconds in 2000. It's difficult to speak intelligibly in that amount of time, let alone explain something clearly. Even the sixty-second ad is a rarity, giving way to thirty-second and even fifteen-second varieties. Because television dramatizes what it covers, it is prone to sensationalism. Ads tell us that you can lose your friends if you eat the wrong potato chips. Sitcoms show us that family conflict can be resolved in twenty-two minutes. The news tells us, "If it bleeds, it leads." Sports coverage captures "the thrill of victory and the agony of defeat," but not the tedium of training, studying one's opponent, and the mind games or strategies between points, downs, or innings. Educators and parents have long voiced concern that television is an "open-admission technology."[23] Television offers the same information to adults and children. The screen has a mesmerizing effect on even small children. Print, on the other hand, shelters the child. A parent can read about a grizzly murder in the morning paper or on an ipad and not have to worry about anyone else being exposed to the message. If the TV is on, parents may find themselves fumbling for answers to a child's concerned question: "Who is he shooting?"

The Internet, of course, is the heir apparent to media dominance in the twenty-first century. The technical makeup of the computer captures newspaper, radio, and TV in its "web of influence" and projects each in a new, user-friendly form. Its primary strengths are (1) *its convergence capabilities* and (2) *the ways in which it can empower media audiences.* The Internet has developed "streaming" capacities for radio signals and TV images. Online newspapers have been around for several years. Now, with a click of a mouse or a thumb swipe on a smartphone, the media consumer can engage in "one-stop shopping." She can check her Facebook and Twitter feed, read her favorite blog and morning paper online while eating breakfast, listen to her favorite radio station while paying bills or buying online, and watch only those features of the six o'clock newscast that interest her when she comes home from work at 7:00 p.m. with her children in tow! The Internet is a media supermarket, and like a discriminating shopper, you can "fill your cart" with the products (stories) you want. Not surprisingly, these strengths make the Internet "hot property." More and more Americans are using the Internet on their smartphones. Truly, we are now mobile, digital communicators 24/7.

This leads to the Internet's limitations, many of which were articulated by the cyberskeptics earlier in this chapter. But taken as a whole, what remains an overriding downside of the Internet has most to do with its infancy as a medium of transmission: (1) *Because there is no official gatekeeper, near anarchy rules communication behavior on the Internet.* We are flooded with information that is true and false, helpful and dangerous, dated and current, simplified and complicated, crude and sophisticated. In short, getting information from the Internet is like the "Wild West," a new frontier of digital space that has yet to be "harnessed." You may drown in a sea of information and never slake your thirst. Adding insult to injury, you may have jeopardized your privacy if you gave out personal information on a nonsecure site or posted something on your Facebook page that could get you fired. Some tips for navigating in this treacherous environment are presented in Chapter 3, especially in relation to how to judge a website's credibility. The legal landmines of Internet law are new and vexing. The digital frontier pits rights to privacy, intellectual property, and safety against the public's right to know, open access, and free speech. At one end of the spectrum are cases such as the rape trial in Steubenville, Ohio. Online activists pressured law enforcement to speed up the process of indicting the offending high school football players by posting online all sorts of personal information of some of those charged with the crime and even those prosecuting the crime. They also mobilized both virtual and actual protests to attract big media attention. At the other end of the spectrum are cases such as the genius MIT student and founder of Reddit, who, as a fierce open-access advocate, downloaded nearly 5 million academic papers from a pay-walled database. He was arrested for it and faced thirty-five years in prison and a $1 million fine when he killed himself. These cases represent the chasm of values in the digital frontier. They stretch our traditional notions of civil liberties, police protection, due diligence, the right to a fair trial, and the power of public opinion.[24]

Rhetors with commercial interests from all four media recognize that they have rhetorical problems in terms of their reputations. Internet services are producing more sophisticated search engines, virus checks, and privacy alerts; they are even encouraging legal sanctions against some website content. Television executives have bowed to pressure to rate family entertainment, they have experimented with family-sensitive news formats, and they actively encourage viewers to check out their websites for more in-depth coverage. Radio stations have become partners of television stations, especially in weather-casting, and have welcomed Web-casting as a way to shore up a dwindling audience base and to reemphasize their portability. Newspapers now hire graphic artists as journalists to cater to the visual consumer, encourage readers to go online to capture up-to-date information, and post mug shots of their columnists to invite a more intimate bonding with readers.

MEDIA CAMPAIGNS AND MOVEMENTS

Political campaigns and movements for social and political change are profoundly affected by the kinds of traditional mass media coverage they receive and the new social media platforms they exploit. In some ways campaigns and social movements are alike. All seek to persuade and arouse audiences to action. All extend over a period of time. Because they seek to reach relatively large audiences, they must repeat their messages often so their target audiences will see and hear them, and they need to develop a slogan or central idea that prompts audiences to remember their messages.

There are some differences. An ad campaign has no clear ending. You can buy a product anytime and anywhere it is available. By contrast, political campaigns end on election day, and, except for states that have early voting or voting online or by mail, you have to act—to vote—on that day at a designated place. A product that gains even a 5 percent market share can be a roaring success; by contrast, a candidate must gain a majority or sometimes at least a plurality of votes cast—a much stiffer requirement.

Like ad campaigns, social movements extend over time. They have defined "stages" such as inception, resistance, mobilization, maintenance, and termination. These stages are accompanied by clear rhetorical tasks, such as articulating grievances, recruiting members, staging protests, achieving outcomes, and disbanding. Generally, a movement's tasks are accomplished by leaders who exhibit different qualities. Movements need leaders who are prophetic (can articulate a compelling ideology and vision), charismatic (can engage and energize the rank and file and the opposition), and pragmatic (can organize and strategize how movements recruit and retain members, raise sufficient funds, influence policy makers, affiliate with third parties, etc.). A diversity of leadership expertise is usually necessary to carry a movement from one stage to the next—stages that can take months, years, or decades.[25]

The campaign for woman suffrage, for example, began in 1848, but all U.S. women were not enfranchised until ratification of the Nineteenth Amendment in 1920—a struggle that lasted seventy-two years! Along the way, key rhetorical leaders of the movement (Elizabeth Cady Stanton was its philosopher; Anna Howard Shaw its charismatic recruiter, and Carrie Chapman Catt it's shrewd pragmatist) engaged the rank and file in overcoming formidable audience, subject, and rhetor resistance; gaining adherents; seizing momentum; facing setbacks; and savoring success.[26]

Social movements can be hurt and helped by their treatment in the media. The first woman's rights convention, held at Seneca Falls, New York, in July of 1848, benefited greatly from hostile newspaper coverage. The women who attended were described as "a rebellious group of aged spinsters," and "Amazons" who "demoralize and degrade" their sex. They were particularly pleased when the *New York Herald* printed the entire "Declaration of Sentiments," a manifesto that summed up their grievances in a form similar to the Declaration of Independence, even though its editor James Gordon Bennett referred to the convention as "a gathering of crazy old women who want to abolish both the Bible and the Constitution."[27] All of this coverage gave the movement valuable publicity and enabled those who had not attended to understand just what the woman's rights movement sought to accomplish.

As newspaper reaction to the Seneca Falls convention illustrates, media coverage often distorts events and treats movements as undesirable disturbances of public order. In *The Whole World Was Watching: Mass Media in the Making and Unmaking of the New Left*,[28] Todd Gitlin uses coverage of the New Left, starting in the 1960s, as a way to understand how media influence movements. At first, he argues, the media ignore new political action groups; then they selectively emphasize novel, controversial, and, hence, "newsworthy" aspects of their activities that distort movement efforts. Gitlin argues that any movement is disparaged because journalists assume that political demonstrations disrupt what is the legitimate social order, reflecting a strong U.S. cultural bias against collective action, no matter what the cause. In the case of the New

Left, media coverage converted leaders into celebrities, estranging them from others in the movement; inflated and dramatized public statements into revolutionary rhetoric and militancy; and, thus, translated more moderate efforts for change into extremism. Consider how this same big media treatment has affected other more contemporary social movements in North America such as Occupy Wall Street and Idle No More, and movements at the other end of the political spectrum, such as the Tea Party movement. How have these movements been portrayed by mass media in terms of their healthiness to the political order? Examine how these movements have been depicted visually, what journalists have been assigned to cover their activities, what amount of airtime and column space they've received proportionate to other political happenings, and how their leaders have been profiled.

We know that deeply entrenched cultural traditions can influence media coverage of social movement events. Research bears this out. For example, rhetorical critic Bonnie J. Dow analyzed TV news reports (ABC, NBC, and CBS) of the Women's Strike for Equality held on the fiftieth anniversary of women's enfranchisement, August 26, 1970. She concluded that all three networks relied on negative stereotypes linking women and visual pleasure. Network news framed the strike as sheer spectacle and as absurdist entertainment rather than reasoned protest. Repeatedly, network coverage reduced the movement to the trope of "bra-burning," which never occurred (bras and girdles were thrown into a trash can at a demonstration against the Miss America Pageant).[29]

Unlike some TV news coverage, popular entertainment programming has tended to treat movements and causes more charitably. The gay rights movement, for instance, has been assisted by TV series that feature gays in positive, successful ways. Beginning with *Will and Grace* and *Queer Eye for the Straight Guy* to more recently *Modern Family*, television series today depict gay life as normal, credible, and attractive. Internationally, social movements have also received positive attention via TV entertainment. In Saudia Arabia, social satire on TV often tests the fault line between modernity and tradition. A new comic trial balloon called *Hush Hush* that advocates for women's rights in a comedic way was created for Ramadan, the Muslim holiday season. In one episode of the show, *Hush Hush* portrays women driving in Saudi Arabia. (Women are not allowed to drive there.) But the satire makes the taboo seem less problematic.[30] In Canada, the award-winning CBC comedy *Little Mosque on the Prairie* has for six years attracted a loyal fan base in eighty-three countries. Set in a small town in Saskatchewan, the show derives its humor from exploring the interactions of the Muslims (both its conservative and liberal Islamic characters) with the non-Muslim townsfolk (Christians and others). The show tackles such issues as whether a Muslim woman still has to cover her hair if the only man who can see her is gay, whether Muslims can participate in the odd Canadian sport of curling, or whether a Muslim woman's scarf is always a solution to a bad hair day. Even when the show drifts into more political fare, such as when one of the characters claims to have been unable to attend a conference in the United States because he was wrongly placed on a "no-fly" list, it turns out he was simply afraid of flying and it was a convenient foil. The title of the show is a clever paraphrase of the classic, wholesome American book and TV drama series, *Little House on the Prairie*, about a pioneer family settling the West.[31]

Movements can be helped or harmed by TV depictions, but what of movements that rely on the power of social media? What's their staying power? The characteristics of social media would seem to privilege the success of social movement discourse (Figure 13–3). Social media is *interactive* (not top-down communication), allows for

Figure 13–3
Our Digital
Rhetorical
Universe

asynchronous connections (participate on your own time), happens in *real time* (stay on top of breaking news), *empowers* users (make an immediate impact), *converges* platforms (can easily participate on multiple devices), and *narrowcasts* (captures the "True Believer" easily). In some ways, social movements have exploited these features of social media. For example, in the past decade, political unrest in Kenya, Uganda, Tunisia, Somalia, Egypt, Lybia, and Iran has seen disenfranchised citizens turn to social media to rise up against repressive regimes. According to professors John Palfrey and Urs Gasser of Harvard, social media enables activists to "harness the Internet's power to render more transparent the actions of a specific government," and it provides a way for ordinary citizens to come together and participate actively in real-time, becoming empowered in their micro-mobilization efforts without fear of immediate physical reprisal.[32] Others have noted that social media are tools that enable revolutionary groups to lower the costs of participation, organization, recruitment, and training as they can reach thousands of adherents with a single Facebook post or Twitter feed, enabling a massive call to action in seconds.[33]

Stories of the way social media has hastened political activism abound. For instance, "the Arab Spring"—a string of protest movements from Egypt, Libya, and Yemen that all used Twitter and Facebook to promulgate their unrest—actually began in the remote country of Tunisia. A 26-year-old Tunisian vegetable vendor set himself on fire after police stole produce from his stand. The suicide of the man, a college graduate unable to find work within his field of study, triggered a revolution in his home country that spread across the Arab world via tweets, texts, photos, videos, and posts. As one Egyptian activist said about the success of the Arab Spring: "We use Facebook to schedule our protests; Twitter to coordinate and YouTube to tell the world."[34]

The Kony 2012 YouTube video was another story that showcased the power of social media to energize digital citizens the world over to promote the capture of an obscure Ugandan war criminal, Joseph Kony, of the Lord's Resistance Army. Produced by the group Invisible Children, this short film traced the reign of terror in Uganda that involved using children as prostitutes and soldiers to advance the corrupt regime. Seen by 100 million people on YouTube and Vimeo, it became the fastest-spreading viral video produced by a social movement of its time. And it picked up the support of a host of celebrities from Rihanna and Nicki Minaj to Bill Gates.

Occupy Wall Street is another success story of social media advancing social movements, this time beginning in North America. To protest the financial crisis, a group calling itself "the 99 percent"—made up of those who didn't fit into the top 1 percent of earners in the country—set up shop in New York City's Zucotti Park in September 2011. The movement called for tighter regulations on Wall Street and bank reform. It started on Wall Street but quickly grew to other parts of the country. It captured the imagination of college students, who having been made aware of Occupy via social media, then worked to stage sit-ins and sleep-ins on campuses. The #Occupy hashtag was set up on Twitter. Skype was used to hold conference calls between different Occupy groups from all over the world. Facebook and Meetup helped Occupy members coordinate and call meetings. In just a few short weeks, social media made it possible for Occupy Wall Street to go from the Big Apple to the rest of the world.

Yet despite the natural affinities of social media fueling contemporary social movements that the aforementioned examples suggest, a good deal of evidence points to a more sputtering relationship. Social media also exhibits characteristics that work against movement success. First, any single virtual cause must compete in a veritable cauldron of cybercauses for the attention of the fatigued surfer. The data smog of the "twittersphere," for instance, risks any single protest being buried after a short exposure time. The Kony 2012 video was viewed by millions and prompted thousands to sign Facebook petitions, but it disappeared as quickly as it came, in part because of counter-videos and tweets that challenged some of its factual legitimacy.

Second, the ease with which social media can sign up converts means that early recruitment numbers look good, but long-term retention is a real problem. Social media demands little from movement adherents. Dubbed "slactivism" by Internet researcher Evgeny Morozov, social media tends to cultivate "feel-good online activism that has zero political or social impact."[35] In the Material for Analysis essay in this chapter, Malcolm Gladwell observes: "social media activism is built on weak-ties" and weak ties don't lead to high-stakes activism. Papic and Noonan conclude:

> The key for any protest movement is to inspire and motivate individuals to go from the comfort of their homes to the chaos of the streets and face off against the government . . . [social media] does not necessarily motivate them to physically hit the streets and provide fuel for a revolution.[36]

Third, in its propensity to promote peer-to-peer interactivity around causes, social media creates a leadership vacuum. It does this in several ways. The platform is well-equipped to fling open a movement to instant, widespread membership. But this means that a call for action often spreads like wildfire before a movement is sufficiently prepared, its ideology articulated, and its leaders identified and groomed. In addition, the very leaders who get a movement off the ground via social media are often ill-equipped to assume the rhetorical tasks of strategically moving causes forward. As Papic and

Noonan note: "Protest movements are rarely successful if led from somebody's basement in a virtual arena. Their leaders must have charisma and street smarts, just like leaders of any organization."[37] Finally, even if movements have effective leaders in place, social media can diminish their leadership effectiveness by exposing their whereabouts to authorities (although there are ways to mask IP addresses by using proxy servers). Social media is open to everyone—including dictators looking to crack down on dissidents. In Egypt, nearly forty leaders of the uprising were arrested early on in the protest through their Internet activities.[38] Social media is designed to build networks—not leaders, not platforms, not organization, and not rhetoric that strikes responsive chords in enough adherents to sustain a movement's aims.

In a larger sense, other media challenges arise when social movements that agitate for change over many years must create a context that embraces adaptation. When the woman's rights movement began in 1848, it was essential to produce messages that defined goals and announced their program, which produced the Declaration of Sentiments asserting "that all men *and women* are created equal," followed by a list of resolutions identifying the specific grievances that were their chief targets. Elizabeth Cady Stanton, one of the convention conveners, made a speech setting forth the major arguments for change buttressed by detailed evidence. Stanton's last public speech "The Solitude of Self," delivered in 1892, was very different from her speech at Seneca Falls. One reason for the difference in rhetorical strategy was her long experience; another was that she and others had been making arguments for woman's rights and suffrage for many years, arguments now familiar to members of Congress and state legislators, the agents of change with the power to enact laws giving women rights to their earnings, to own property, to guardianship of children, to make contracts, and to ratify an amendment to enfranchise women. Accordingly, she chose to do something radically different, something that would surprise legislators so much that they would listen and perhaps reexamine their positions on these issues. In other words, think of campaigns and movements as contexts that require adaptation by speakers and writers at different stages in their development and to the kinds of coverage they receive in the media.

Political campaigns pose similar problems. Candidates need to have a memorable slogan, logo, or song and use a particular color on signs and bumper stickers and campaign literature, which differentiates them from others. Candidates need to "stay on message," consistently expressing key positions that define their campaigns. When candidates travel from place to place, the audience is new, so candidates must repeat their messages, but the reporters who cover them have heard it all before and tend to disparage what isn't "news," and to wait for the gaffe or oddity that will make headlines. This "wait for the gaffe" mentality is especially enticing for cable news, which must fill airtime 24/7. That mass media fosters this insatiable need for the new, provocative, outrageous, and scandalous creates significant problems for candidates: they face two audiences, fresh faces in new places and jaded journalists. How can they adapt to both—stay on message and gain good coverage?

A candidate's message is like the woman's rights Declaration of Sentiments— a basic statement of position, a manifesto for this candidate's campaign. The websites of candidates who seek to be their party's nominee are good examples of the effort to create such a message, and the Internet enables them to modify it to respond to current happenings. Candidates also seek agents of change, those who can vote and are more likely to, which explains the special efforts to reach older people, party members, or people with strong views on specific issues. Because young people are less likely to vote, their concerns may not be addressed. Poor people who work long hours also find it harder to vote, given the times that polling places are open and where they are located. Ad campaigns also target particular groups, such as children whose tastes run to sugary cereals, but they also target parents who can buy the cereal, hoping that they will ignore the dental and obesity problems that sugary foods tend to promote.

Social movements often are energized by "tipping point" events. The various gun control advocates in the United States were galvanized and came together to demand reform after the mass killings at Sandy Hook Elementary School in Newtown, Connecticut, in 2012. The collapse of Wall Street and the exposure of criminal deceit, from the excesses of Bernie Madoff to the mismanagement of funds by Lehman Brothers and Goldman Sachs beginning in 2008, were the catalyst events for the beginning of the "Occupy" movement. In presidential primary campaigns, some events can create momentum; an unexpected ability to raise large amounts of money or a surprising showing in the Iowa caucuses or the New Hampshire primary can prompt donors to give money, attract campaign workers, and make a candidate think that she or he has a real chance to win. These are moments when rhetorical action is likely to be particularly effective because it is buttressed by reactions to these events.

As you evaluate tweets, Facebook pages, letters to the editor, op-eds, editorials, columns, speeches, and journalistic coverage of rhetoric in campaigns and movements, and as you participate in such campaigns and movements as a speaker or writer, as a critic you should also be alert to the need to balance repetition with problems created by familiarity with arguments (see material on persuasive arguments theory in Chapter 5). Think, too, about how you can use dramatic attention to movement goals as evidence, how you can use examples that make issues personal and salient for audiences. Become a regular reader of op-eds and letters to the editor, and begin to identify why these were selected for publication and what it is about the best that makes them seem particularly effective.

In a cluttered media landscape, successful campaigns and social movements must not only have articulate and personable leaders or representatives to carry the cause through its changing iterations, they must also have a clear and consistent message that identifies and differentiates them from others. Knowing how to separate one's cause from the competition requires knowing how to target audiences persuasively. Movement rhetors often employ sophisticated market research to help them understand who is most susceptible to their messages or who can be or can influence agents of change (buy products, vote, picket, demonstrate, organize neighborhood "coffees"). They rely on logistics. Social movements need headquarters, workers, a plan of action, websites and Web managers, and bloggers to respond to emails and update material. And, of course, all movements must learn to face opposition, manage issues, and plan for crisis. Parity products (brands that are functionally equivalent) appeal to the same customers; candidates compete with other candidates for swing votes; and social movements prompt resistance from groups and organizations that will be affected by the changes the movement seeks. Accordingly, differentiation is vital: Why should I buy this product or vote for this candidate rather than another? Why should I vote at all? Why do I need this product? Why should I give to this cause? Why should I continue to give to this cause (say, for example, the Live Strong Foundation) when its leader (Lance Armstrong) is embroiled in a doping scandal? Responding to competitors or opposition groups via media is vital. Candidates must respond to attacks; products face comparative advertising; social movements must defend themselves against attacks that changes are too radical, costly, disruptive, impractical, and that their undesirable side effects outweigh their advantages.

As a critic of mediated campaigns and movements, you will find that judging their successes and failures is a tricky business. This chapter has presented you with specialized knowledge to help you unpack their complexities. First, by introducing you to principles of media literacy, you have gained an appreciation of media as a powerful rhetorical construct that carries high ethos appeal, and whose messages are highly influenced by its particular medium or platform. Second, by recognizing some of the special audience, subject, and rhetor-related rhetorical challenges, you are better prepared to offer fair and unbiased evaluations of mediated messages (on aesthetics, truth, ethics, and effects grounds). Third, by understanding the special elements of social movements as mediated rhetorical processes, you are equipped to conduct descriptive analyses with greater sophistication. Understanding the medium of transmission from the point of view of the rhetoric of social movements enables you to practice campaign advocacy or be a political journalist with keener insights into what messages work and why.

 MATERIAL FOR ANALYSIS

Small Change: Why the Revolution Will Not Be Tweeted[39]

by Malcolm Gladwell

1   At four-thirty in the afternoon on Monday, February 1, 1960, four college students sat down at the lunch counter at the Woolworth's in downtown Greensboro, North Carolina. They were freshmen at North Carolina A. & T., a black college a mile or so away. "I'd like a cup of coffee, please," one of the four, Ezell Blair, said to the waitress. "We don't serve Negroes here," she replied.

2   The Woolworth's lunch counter was a long L-shaped bar that could seat sixty-six people, with a standup snack bar at one end. The seats were for whites. The snack bar was for blacks. Another employee, a black woman who worked at the steam table, approached the students and tried to warn them away. "You're acting stupid, ignorant!" she said. They didn't move. Around five-thirty, the front doors to the store were locked. The four still didn't move. Finally, they left by a side door. Outside, a small crowd had gathered, including a photographer from the Greensboro *Record*. "I'll be back tomorrow with A. & T. College," one of the students said.

3   By next morning, the protest had grown to twenty-seven men and four women, most from the same dormitory as the original four. The men were dressed

in suits and ties. The students had brought their schoolwork, and studied as they sat at the counter. On Wednesday, students from Greensboro's "Negro" secondary school, Dudley High, joined in, and the number of protesters swelled to eighty. By Thursday, the protesters numbered three hundred, including three white women, from the Greensboro campus of the University of North Carolina. By Saturday, the sit-in had reached six hundred. People spilled out onto the street. White teenagers waved Confederate flags. Someone threw a firecracker. At noon, the A. & T. football team arrived. "Here comes the wrecking crew," one of the white students shouted.

4   By the following Monday, sit-ins had spread to Winston-Salem, twenty-five miles away, and Durham, fifty miles away. The day after that, students at Fayetteville State Teachers College and at Johnson C. Smith College, in Charlotte, joined in, followed on Wednesday by students at St. Augustine's College and Shaw University, in Raleigh. On Thursday and Friday, the protest crossed state lines, surfacing in Hampton and Portsmouth, Virginia, in Rock Hill, South Carolina, and in Chattanooga, Tennessee. By the end of the month, there were sit-ins throughout the South, as far west as Texas. "I asked every student I met what the first day of the sitdowns had been like on his campus," the political theorist Michael Walzer wrote in *Dissent*. "The answer was always the same: 'It was like a fever. Everyone wanted to go.'" Some seventy thousand students eventually took part. Thousands were arrested and untold thousands more radicalized. These events in the early sixties became a civil-rights war that engulfed the South for the rest of the decade—and it happened without e-mail, texting, Facebook, or Twitter.

5   The world, we are told, is in the midst of a revolution. The new tools of social media have reinvented social activism. With Facebook and Twitter and the like, the traditional relationship between political authority and popular will has been upended, making it easier for the powerless to collaborate, coördinate, and give voice to their concerns. When ten thousand protesters took to the streets in Moldova in the spring of 2009 to protest against their country's Communist government, the action was dubbed the Twitter Revolution, because of the means by which the demonstrators had been brought together. A few months after that, when student protests rocked Tehran, the State Department took the unusual step of asking Twitter to suspend scheduled maintenance of its Web site, because the Administration didn't want such a critical organizing tool out of service at the height of the demonstrations. "Without Twitter the people of Iran would not have felt empowered and confident to stand up for freedom and democracy," Mark Pfeifle, a former national-security adviser, later wrote, calling for Twitter to be nominated for the Nobel Peace Prize. Where activists were once defined by their causes, they are now defined by their tools. Facebook warriors go online to push for change. "You are the best hope for us all," James K. Glassman, a former senior State Department official, told a crowd of cyber activists at a recent conference sponsored by Facebook, A. T. & T., Howcast, MTV, and Google. Sites like Facebook, Glassman said, "give the U.S. a significant competitive advantage over terrorists. Some time ago, I said that Al Qaeda was 'eating our lunch on the Internet.' That is no longer the case. Al Qaeda is stuck in Web 1.0. The Internet is now about interactivity and conversation."

6   These are strong, and puzzling, claims. Why does it matter who is eating whose lunch on the Internet? Are people who log on to their Facebook page really the best hope for us all? As for Moldova's so-called Twitter Revolution, Evgeny Morozov, a scholar at Stanford who has been the most persistent of digital evangelism's critics, points out that Twitter had scant internal significance in Moldova, a country where very few Twitter accounts exist. Nor does it seem to have been a revolution, not least because the protests—as Anne Applebaum suggested in the Washington *Post*—may well have been a bit of stagecraft cooked up by the government. (In a country paranoid about Romanian revanchism, the protesters flew a Romanian flag over the Parliament building.) In the Iranian case, meanwhile, the people tweeting about the demonstrations were almost all in the West. "It is time to get Twitter's role in the events in Iran right," Golnaz Esfandiari wrote, this past summer, in *Foreign Policy*. "Simply put: There was no Twitter Revolution inside Iran." The cadre of prominent bloggers, like Andrew Sullivan, who championed the role of social media in Iran, Esfandiari continued, misunderstood the situation. "Western journalists who couldn't reach—or didn't bother reaching?—people on the ground in Iran simply scrolled through the English-language tweets post with tag #iranelection," she wrote. "Through it all, no one seemed to wonder why people trying to coordinate protests in Iran would be writing in any language other than Farsi."

7   Some of this grandiosity is to be expected. Innovators tend to be solipsists. They often want to cram every stray fact and experience into their new model. As the historian Robert Darnton has written, "The marvels of communication technology in the present have produced a false consciousness about the past—even a sense that communication has no history, or had nothing of importance to consider before the days of television and the Internet." But there is something else at work here, in the outsized enthusiasm for social media. Fifty years after one of the most extraordinary episodes of social upheaval in American history, we seem to have forgotten what activism is.

8   Greensboro in the early nineteen-sixties was the kind of place where racial insubordination was routinely met with violence. The four students who first sat down at the lunch counter were terrified. "I suppose if anyone had come up behind me and yelled 'Boo,' I think I would have fallen off my seat," one of them said later. On the first day, the store manager notified the police chief, who immediately sent two officers to the store. On the third day, a gang of white toughs showed up at the lunch counter and stood ostentatiously behind the protesters, ominously muttering epithets such as "burr-head nigger." A local Ku Klux Klan leader made an appearance. On Saturday, as tensions grew, someone called in a bomb threat, and the entire store had to be evacuated.

9   The dangers were even clearer in the Mississippi Freedom Summer Project of 1964, another of the sentinel campaigns of the civil-rights movement. The Student Nonviolent Coordinating Committee recruited hundreds of Northern, largely white unpaid volunteers to run Freedom Schools, register black voters, and raise civil-rights awareness in the Deep South. "No one should go *anywhere* alone, but certainly not in an automobile and certainly not at night," they were instructed. Within days of arriving in Mississippi, three volunteers—Michael Schwerner,

James Chaney, and Andrew Goodman—were kidnapped and killed, and, during the rest of the summer, thirty-seven black churches were set on fire and dozens of safe houses were bombed; volunteers were beaten, shot at, arrested, and trailed by pickup trucks full of armed men. A quarter of those in the program dropped out. Activism that challenges the status quo—that attacks deeply rooted problems—is not for the faint of heart.

10 What makes people capable of this kind of activism? The Stanford sociologist Doug McAdam compared the Freedom Summer dropouts with the participants who stayed, and discovered that the key difference wasn't, as might be expected, ideological fervor. "*All* of the applicants—participants and withdrawals alike—emerge as highly committed, articulate supporters of the goals and values of the summer program," he concluded. What mattered more was an applicant's degree of personal connection to the civil-rights movement. All the volunteers were required to provide a list of personal contacts—the people they wanted kept apprised of their activities—and participants were far more likely than dropouts to have close friends who were also going to Mississippi. High-risk activism, McAdam concluded, is a "strong-tie" phenomenon.

11 This pattern shows up again and again. One study of the Red Brigades, the Italian terrorist group of the nineteen-seventies, found that seventy per cent of recruits had at least one good friend already in the organization. The same is true of the men who joined the mujahideen in Afghanistan. Even revolutionary actions that look spontaneous, like the demonstrations in East Germany that led to the fall of the Berlin Wall, are, at core, strong-tie phenomena. The opposition movement in East Germany consisted of several hundred groups, each with roughly a dozen members. Each group was in limited contact with the others: at the time, only thirteen per cent of East Germans even had a phone. All they knew was that on Monday nights, outside St. Nicholas Church in downtown Leipzig, people gathered to voice their anger at the state. And the primary determinant of who showed up was "critical friends"—the more friends you had who were critical of the regime the more likely you were to join the protest.

12 So one crucial fact about the four freshmen at the Greensboro lunch counter—David Richmond, Franklin McCain, Ezell Blair, and Joseph McNeil—was their relationship with one another. McNeil was a roommate of Blair's in A. & T.'s Scott Hall dormitory. Richmond roomed with McCain one floor up, and Blair, Richmond, and McCain had all gone to Dudley High School. The four would smuggle beer into the dorm and talk late into the night in Blair and McNeil's room. They would all have remembered the murder of Emmett Till in 1955, the Montgomery bus boycott that same year, and the showdown in Little Rock in 1957. It was McNeil who brought up the idea of a sit-in at Woolworth's. They'd discussed it for nearly a month. Then McNeil came into the dorm room and asked the others if they were ready. There was a pause, and McCain said, in a way that works only with people who talk late into the night with one another, "Are you guys chicken or not?" Ezell Blair worked up the courage the next day to ask for a cup of coffee because he was flanked by his roommate and two good friends from high school.

13 The kind of activism associated with social media isn't like this at all. The platforms of social media are built around weak ties. Twitter is a way of following (or being followed by) people you may never have met. Facebook is a tool for efficiently managing your acquaintances, for keeping up with the people you would not otherwise be able to stay in touch with. That's why you can have a thousand "friends" on Facebook, as you never could in real life.

14 This is in many ways a wonderful thing. There is strength in weak ties, as the sociologist Mark Granovetter has observed. Our acquaintances—not our friends—are our greatest source of new ideas and information. The Internet lets us exploit the power of these kinds of distant connections with marvellous efficiency. It's terrific at the diffusion of innovation, interdisciplinary collaboration, seamlessly matching up buyers and sellers, and the logistical functions of the dating world. But weak ties seldom lead to high-risk activism.

15 In a new book called "The Dragonfly Effect: Quick, Effective, and Powerful Ways to Use Social Media to Drive Social Change," the business consultant Andy Smith and the Stanford Business School professor Jennifer Aaker tell the story of Sameer Bhatia, a young Silicon Valley entrepreneur who came down with acute myelogenous leukemia. It's a perfect illustration of social media's strengths. Bhatia needed a bone-marrow transplant, but he could not find a match among his relatives and friends. The odds were best with a donor of his ethnicity, and there were few South Asians in the national bone-marrow database. So Bhatia's business partner sent out an e-mail explaining Bhatia's plight to more than four hundred of their acquaintances, who forwarded the e-mail to their personal contacts; Facebook pages and YouTube videos were devoted to the Help Sameer campaign. Eventually, nearly twenty-five thousand new people were registered in the bone-marrow database, and Bhatia found a match.

16 But how did the campaign get so many people to sign up? By not asking too much of them. That's the only way you can get someone you don't really know to do something on your behalf. You can get thousands of people to sign up for a donor registry, because doing so is pretty easy. You have to send in a cheek swab and—in the highly unlikely event that your bone marrow is a good match for someone in need—spend a few hours at the hospital. Donating bone marrow isn't a trivial matter. But it doesn't involve financial or personal risk; it doesn't mean spending a summer being chased by armed men in pickup trucks. It doesn't require that you confront socially entrenched norms and practices. In fact, it's the kind of commitment that will bring only social acknowledgment and praise.

17 The evangelists of social media don't understand this distinction; they seem to believe that a Facebook friend is the same as a real friend and that signing up for a donor registry in Silicon Valley today is activism in the same sense as sitting at a segregated lunch counter in Greensboro in 1960. "Social networks are particularly effective at increasing motivation," Aaker and Smith write. But that's not true. Social networks are effective at increasing *participation*—by lessening the level of motivation that participation requires. The Facebook page of the Save Darfur Coalition has 1,282,339 members, who have donated an average of nine cents apiece. The next biggest Darfur charity on Facebook has 22,073 members, who have donated an average of thirty-five cents. Help Save Darfur has 2,797 members, who have given, on average, fifteen cents. A spokesperson for the Save Darfur Coalition told *Newsweek*, "We wouldn't necessarily gauge someone's value to the advocacy movement based on what they've given. This is a powerful mechanism to engage this critical population. They inform their community, attend events, volunteer. It's not something you can measure by looking at a ledger." In other words, Facebook activism succeeds not by motivating people to make a real sacrifice but by motivating them to do the things that people do when they are not motivated enough to make a real sacrifice. We are a long way from the lunch counters of Greensboro. . . .

Questions for Analysis

1. How well does Gladwell use argument and evidence to create virtual experience and alter our perception in building a case of "cyberskepticism" regarding social media and its impact on social movements?

2. Who is the target audiences of this column? How do you know? Of what significance is it that the author is a columnist for *The New Yorker* and a best-selling author of such trendy books as *The Tipping Point*, *Blink*, and *Outliers*? What persona does he play?

3. What audience obstacles does this piece attempt to combat? What subject obstacles does it attempt to combat? How successful can a single message of this limited scope be?

4. How does this piece demonstrate that "*the medium is the message*"? Discuss the specific strengths and weaknesses of print media in this regard. What if this piece were translated to another medium, say a radio interview, a YouTube video, a blog, a tweet, what might it look or sound like? What new rhetorical challenges and opportunities do these other mediums of expression pose for cyberskeptics?

5. How would you rate this piece on aesthetics? Truth? Ethics? Effects?

EXERCISES

Critical Thinking Exercises

1. Political cartoons poignantly capture cultural trends. None are more memorable and rhetorically sophisticated than *The New Yorker*. The cartoon in Figure 13–4 is one of the "classics" at capturing the highs and lows of communicating online. Combining the lessons of Chapter 12 (visual rhetoric) and Chapter 13 (medium of transmission), critique the photo along these lines:

   a. How does this cartoon illustrate the three principles of visual rhetoric from Chapter 12?

   b. How does this cartoon illustrate some of the fundamentals of media literacy?

   c. Find some political cartoons that characterize contemporary social movements. Are the movements enhanced or diminished, championed or ridiculed, by the portrayals?

2. Choose any media form (radio, TV, Internet, newspaper, smartphone) and try to live without using it for forty-eight hours. Discuss your experience in class. How difficult was this? How did it alter

Figure 13–4
The Enthymematic Power of Political Cartoons

"On the Internet, nobody knows you're a dog."

your daily habits? How dependent are you on this technology?

3. As a class, select a sitcom for viewing. Discuss what aspects of the show can be described as sensational. What aspects distort perspective? Count the number of laugh tracks that you hear. What purpose do they serve? How does the show exemplify some of the paradoxes of the mass media? How does the show address social issues or causes in liberating or restrictive ways?

4. Arrange to visit a radio station, a television station, or a newspaper. Examine how the news of the day is "manufactured." How are decisions made to give events news space? What "stories" get on the air or are in print versus on the station's website? How is the news business demystified by this tour? From understanding the decision-making processes in media news rooms, what advice can you give social movement advocates for gaining visibility for their cause?

5. The entertainment industry uses multiple channels to reach consumers. The Walt Disney Corporation, for instance, combines Web tools, retail outlets, TV and cable channels, publishing houses, recording studios, and other media in marketing its products. It is a true multinational corporate empire with incredible influence over the imagination of children all over the world. Try to find out why Disney has been picketed and boycotted in recent years. What have the issues been about? What medium of transmission has been the most frequent target of concern? Why?

Analytical Writing Exercises

6. Examine how a current event is treated by your local newspaper versus a local TV or radio station. Use key elements of descriptive analysis to write a brief analytical essay tracking the difference in coverage.

7. Write an op-ed letter to your local paper supporting or protesting a timely issue, cause, or campaign that is meaningful to you. If it is not published or is edited considerably, why do you think that happened? If it is published, what kind of response did you receive? How did your experience support or challenge the kinds of rhetorical challenges identified in this chapter for how campaigns and movements must struggle to receive fair and consistent coverage?

Portfolio Entry 12: Constraints of the Medium

8. Evaluate your rhetorical acts in terms of the strengths and weaknesses of their respective media of transmission. In two or three pages, discuss how influential the

medium is in your evaluation of the acts in terms of aesthetics, truth, ethics, and effects.

Strategic Speaking Exercises

9. Mass media require that we examine a *collective rhetor* that is generally camouflaged. Think how peculiar it would be for us to say, "I'm going to call the president of Media General, the news and technical directors, the assignment editor, the anchor, the photographer, the reporter, the satellite truck driver, and the video editor to complain about or compliment the message I just heard." Because we cannot identify the single persona of mass-mediated messages, what ethical challenges arise for newsmakers and news consumers? In small groups,

prepare a five-minute skit that humorously addresses the difficulties in conversing, debating, or generally engaging the "rhetor" of a media report.

10. Divide the class into two groups: "pro" and "con" on the issue of media coverage of violence. Choose a specific topic such as: Should U.S. media (print and broadcast) show graphic pictures of the perpetrators of mass shootings? Cover suicides? Curtail negative political cartooning and advertisements? Discuss such things as timing, placement, news value, and the special ways in which visuals persuade (Chapter 12) before formulating your position statement. Select a group spokesperson to "make the case statement" (no more than five minutes) for your group. How are the groups' arguments framed around ethical versus effects evaluation?

NOTES

1. Barack Obama, "Remarks by the President at University of Michigan Spring Commencement," May 1, 2010. Accessed 2/3/13. Available online at http://www.whitehouse.gov/the-press-office/remarks-president-university-michigan-spring-commencement.

2. See Susan Schultz Huxman, *Media Literacy Boot Camp: Focus on Social Media and the Middle School Years*. Workbook prepared with a grant from Communities in Schools, USD 259 Wichita Public Schools, May 12 and Oct 22, 2010. See also James W. Potter, *Media Literacy*, 2nd ed. (Thousand Oaks: Sage, 2001).

3. See Shirley Biagi, *Media Impact*, 2nd ed. (Pacific Grove, CA: Wadsworth, 1992); Neil Postman and Steve Powers, *How to Watch TV News* (New York: Penguin, 1992); Kathleen Jamieson and Karlyn Kohrs Campbell, *The Interplay of Influence*, 6th ed. (Belmont, CA: Wadsworth, 2006); *Media & Values Newsletters* (Los Angeles: Center for Media and Values, 1993); "TV ALERT: A Wake-Up Guide for Television Literacy." Media Literacy Workshop Kit (Los Angeles: Center for Media and Values, 1993); AP News Industry News, Press Release, August 28, 2000.

4. Tom Chatfield, *50 Digital Ideas You Really Need to Know* (London: Quercus Pub., 2010). Other sources used in this chapter for media literacy findings and statistics are from the following: Andrea Millwood Hargrave, "Media Literacy in the Digital Age," *NHK Broadcasting Studies*, 8 (2010): 189–209); Mizuko

Ito et al., "Giving and Learning with New Media: Summary of Findings from the Digital Youth Project." Digital Learning online. November 2008. www.digitallearning.macfound.org/ethnography; Jeanine Koranda and Fred Mann, "Teens Favor Text over Talk," *The Wichita Eagle*, April 26, 2010, p. 1A; Josh McDowell, *The Disconnected Generation* (Nashville, TN: Word Publishing, 2000); S. Nimon, "Generation Y and Higher Education: The other Y@K," *Journal of Institutional Research*, 13 (2007): 11, 24–41; *PBS Media Literacy Kit*. www.KPTS.org. Accessed March 10, 2010; James Potter, *Media Literacy*, 2nd ed. (Thousand Oaks: Sage, 2001); James Potter, *The 11 Myths of Media Violence* (Thousand Oaks: Sage, 2003); David G. Savage, "High Court to Hear Case of Violent Video Games," *The Wichita Eagle*, April 28, 2010, p. 1A; John Richard Schrock, "Are Video Games Causing Achievement Gap?" *The Wichita Eagle*, March 24, 2010, p. 2B; Nancy Solomon, "Schools Urged to Teach Youth Digital Citizenship," *NPR: All Things Considered*. 6 October 2010. http://www.npr.org/templates/story/story.php?storyID=130380236l; Mathew Trevett Smith, "Second Life Provides Real-World Benefits," *Faculty Focus*, May 3, 2010; "Tweens Online: Kids Rule." *New Media Age*: 10 Academic OneFile. Accessed April 14, 2010; "Tweens and Technology: Quick Stats." *Temptations of a Generation* series. Accessed April 20, 2010; "TV Alert: A Wake-Up Guide for Television Literacy, A Media Literacy Workshop Kit," *The Center for Media Values*.1993; "Video Games Cause for Concern?" *BBC News: World Edition*,

November 26, 2000. Accessed 5 May 2010, www.bbcnews.com; S. Craig Watkins, *The Young and the Digital* (Boston: Beacon, 2009).

5. Sherry Turkle, *Alone Together: Why we Expect More from Technology and Less from Each Other* (New York: Basic Books, 2011).

6. Canadian Broadcasting Corporation interview with Neil Postman, July 2, 2000. Available online at http://www. myna.com, p. 1.

7. Ibid.

8. Peggy Chassen and Carol Itulsizer, *The TV Smart Book for Kids* (East Rutherford, NJ: Dutton Press Penguin/Putnam, 1983); Michael Fortino, *There Is an Internet E-mergency* (New York: The Fortino Group, 2001).

9. Chatfield, *50 Digital Ideas You Really Need to Know*, p. 78.

10. John Fiske and John Hartley, *Reading Television* (London: Routledge, 1989), p. 81.

11. Chatfield, *50 Digital Ideas You Really Need to Know*, p. 176.

12. Nicholas Carr, "Is Google Making Us Stupid." *The Atlantic* (July/August 2008). As quoted in Mark Bauerlein, ed., *The Digital Divide* (New York: Penguin, 2011), p. 65.

13. Ibid., p. 66.

14. Kathleen Hall Jamieson and Karlyn Kohrs Campbell, *The Interplay of Influence*, 6th ed. (Belmont, CA: Wadsworth, 2006).

15. Joshua Meyerowitz, *No Sense of Place: The Impact of Electronic Media on Social Behavior* (New York: Oxford University Press, 1989); Neil Postman and Steve Powers, *How to Watch TV News* (New York: Penguin Books, 1992).

16. George Gerbner and Larry Gross, "Living with Television: The Violence Profile," *Journal of Communication* 26 (1976): 172–199.

17. Turkle, *Alone Together*, pp. 281–288.

18. Chatfield, *50 Digital Ideas You Really Need to Know*, pp. 4–5.

19. Tony Schwartz, *The Responsive Chord* (New York: Anchor, 1973), p. 7.

20. "How to Save Your Newspaper: A Modest Proposal." *Time*, February 16, 2009, p. 33.

21 Nielsen ratings as reported at WashingtonPost.com 10/4/2012.

22. Pew Research Center for the People and the Press, September 27, 2012.

23. Postman and Powers, *How to Watch TV News*, p. 148.

24. Kate Allen, "Old Fashioned Justice Crashes Digital Evangelists," *Toronto Star*, January 20, 2013, pp. A1, A12.

25. Charles Stewart, Craig Allen Smith, and Robert E. Denton Jr., *Persuasion and Social Movements*, 2nd ed. (Prospect Heights: Waveland, 1989).

26. Susan Schultz Huxman, "Passing the Torch for Woman's Rights: Elizabeth Cady Stanton, Anna Howard Shaw and Carrie Chapman Catt." In Martin Medhurst, ed., *A Rhetorical History of the United States*, Vol. 5 (East Lansing: Michigan State University Press, 2008), pp. 355–384.

27. See Alma Lutz, *Created Equal: A Biography of Elizabeth Cady Stanton* (New York: John Day, 1940), p. 52; and Miriam Gurko, *The Ladies of Seneca Falls: The Birth of the Woman's Rights Movement* (New York: Schocken Books, 1976), p. 139, quoted in Karlyn Kohrs Campbell, *Man Cannot Speak For Her. Vol 1, A Critical Study of Early Feminist Rhetoric* (New York, Praeger, 1989), pp. 67–68.

28. Todd Gitlin, *The Whole World Was Watching: Mass Media in the Making and Unmaking of the New Left* (Berkeley: University of California Press, 1980).

29. Bonnie J. Dow, "Spectacle, Spectatorship, and Gender Anxiety in Television News Coverage of the 1970 Women's Strike for Equality," *Communication Studies*, 50 (1999): 143–157. See also Bonnie J. Dow, "Fixing Feminism: Women's Liberation and the Rhetoric of Television Documentary," *Quarterly Journal of Speech*, 90 (2004): 53–80.

30. Alessandra Stanley, "TV Pushes the Limits in Saudia Arabia," *Waterloo Record*, August 25, 2012, p. C1.

31. See www.cbc.ca/littlemosque.

32. John Palfrey and Urs Gasser, *Born Digital: Understanding the First Generation of Digital Natives* (2008). pp. 255–267, as quoted in Mark Baauerlein, *The Digital Divide* (New York: Penguin, 2011), p. 191.

33. Marko Papic and Sean Noonan, "Social Media as a Tool for Protest," February 3, 2011. www.stratfor.com/weekly/20110202-social-meida-tool-protest.

34. See Patrick Meier, www.movements.org; Craig Watkins, "Social Movements in the Age of Social

Media: Participatory Politics in Egypt." http://
theyoungandthedigital.com/2011/02/18-
social-movements. See also www.mashable
.com/2011socialmedia-uprising-activism.

35. Evgeny Morozov, *The Net Delusion: The Dark Side of Internet Freedom* (New York: Perseus Books Group, 2011).

36. Papic and Noonan, "Social Media as a Tool for Protest."

37. Ibid.

38. Ibid.

39. Source: *The New Yorker*, October 4, 2010, pp. 1–9. Reprinted with permission. Paragraph numbers added.

Chapter 14

Understanding Occasion

A popular 1950s TV game show, Name That Tune, tested contestants' musical knowledge. The object was to be first to name a song after hearing only its first few notes. A rhetorical counterpart to that game might be called *Name That Occasion*. Let's see what kind of contestant you are in naming these "old chestnuts" from only the first few words:

1. "Dearly beloved, we are gathered here . . ."
2. "Your Honor, we request that Exhibit A . . ."
3. "Mr. Speaker, with all due respect to my colleague from the state of . . ."

Pretty easy game, huh? Even without hints such as who the speaker or audience is, or what the title of the speech is, or even when it was delivered, you can probably provide the answers easily. The first is from a solemn religious ceremony, maybe a wedding or even a eulogy; the second is from a courtroom setting, probably from the middle part of a trial when evidence is being presented; the third is from a political or legislative occasion, such as a heated debate on a bill in Congress.

It is important for critics to understand occasions that trigger such well-defined rhetorical expectations. For practical reasons, as discussed in Chapter 11, we can better evaluate the effectiveness and artistry of a given piece of discourse if we can compare it to others like it (preceding rhetorical action). For philosophic reasons, we discover that as symbol users we are creatures of convention. In other words, we are comforted by the "ghosts" of Rhetoric Past. Even for sociological reasons, we can learn that well-defined rhetorical occasions tell us something about a culture's values. For instance, the rise of some kinds of discourse (e.g., corporate damage-control rhetoric) or the decline of others (e.g., Fourth of July orations) is a clue to the communal needs of a society at any given time.

This chapter documents our reliance on rhetorical precedents, introduces the classical origins of *rhetorical genres*, and examines instances when rhetoric does not neatly conform to the implicit "rules" of a given occasion. Applications will be made to the three-part conceptual core of this book: elements of descriptive analysis, the rhetorical problem, and standards of evaluation. In sum, this chapter gives you the knowledge and tools to act as a discerning analyst when confronted with the special constraints of rhetorical occasions.

OUR GROUPING IMPULSE AND ARISTOTLE'S RHETORICAL GENRES

It seems that by their very nature, human beings have a need to categorize, pigeon-hole, label, form clusters, set parameters, typecast, discriminate. The naming function of language (as discussed in Chapter 7) demands it. Our grouping impulse starts early. From a scientific perspective (recall from Chapter 1 that even a "perspective" is a discriminating function), we want children to learn that dogs are different from cats, mammals different from amphibians, vegetables different from fruits. From a sociological perspective, we learn to categorize young people as "nerds" or "jocks," "teacher's pet" or "class clown." Politically, we learn to distinguish among Republicans and Democrats and Independents and to be aware of voting blocs such as "evangelicals" and "soccer moms." From a religious perspective, we learn the difference between Christians, Jews, Muslims, and Buddhists. Every time you fill out a survey that asks demographic questions (age, sex, occupation, economic bracket, ethnicity, and religious, political, or professional affiliations) you are validating the impulse to categorize.

Our need to categorize extends to rhetoric too. The labeling and explanation of rhetorical forms that endure has an ancient and venerable heritage. Long before media literacy practitioners began to encourage consumers to understand the differences between the "formulas" of the sitcom and the docudrama, between the image ad and the issue ad, and to lobby the entertainment industry to adopt rating systems to assist us in our discriminating media tastes, Aristotle said to his students, "The species . . . of rhetoric are three in number; for such is the number [of classes] to which the hearers of speeches belong" (1358a).[1]

Specifically, Aristotle described three types or genres of rhetoric: (1) *deliberative* rhetoric dealing with future policy, which emerged in legislatures and dealt with expediency/inexpediency or practicality/impracticality issues; (2) *forensic* rhetoric dealing with criminal charges and punishment of past behavior, which emerged in the law courts and dealt with justice/injustice; and (3) *ceremonial* or *epideictic* (from *epideixis*, to show forth or display) rhetoric dealing with a person, place, or idea in the present moment, which emerged on special occasions and dealt with praise/blame (1358b).[2] Everywhere he looked in Athenian society, Aristotle saw these types of speech on a regular basis. Some became classics: Demosthenes's political oratory, "On the Crown"; Socrates's trial on the charge of corrupting the youth recorded in Plato's *Apology*; and Pericles's funeral oration (*epitaphios logos*) for the Athenian soldiers who

	Forensic (judicial)	Deliberative (political)	Epideictic (ceremonial)
Aim	Justice/injustice	Expediency or inexpediency	Praise or blame
Time	Past	Future	Present
Issue	Questions of fact	Questions of policy	Questions of value
Audience	Jurors	Voters	Observers

Figure 14–1
Aristotelian Genres

fell in the Peloponnesian War. It is a remarkable testament to the endurance of these types of speeches that they are still commonplace in the twenty-first century! To be ure, our speech genres are more complex and varied than in Aristotle's day, but these three groupings are still standard bearers in our culture (Figure 14–1).

Every social group needs rules to live by, the laws that are a result of deliberation; inevitably, some will break these rules, which requires forensic determinations of guilt and punishment; and because both are divisive—we disagree about what rules are best and about guilt and punishment—we need the healing brought about by ceremonial discourse.

Epideictic or ceremonial rhetoric, tied to specific occasions, demands special kinds of evaluation because of the requirements and expectations created by these occasions. Typical examples of epideictic rhetoric are inaugural addresses, Fourth of July speeches, commencement addresses, awards ceremony rhetoric, and eulogies. Such speeches appear on occasions that recur at regular intervals, and our experience with such rhetoric and the traditions that have developed around them create special constraints on rhetorical action. For each kind of occasional address, distinct expectations exist.

In general, however, epideictic rhetoric is closer to the *nondiscursive* than to the discursive end of the continua of rhetorical action. Its very name suggests its *consummatory purpose*; that is, we are to celebrate or commemorate the occasion, and speakers are expected to display their artistic skills and be judged on their performance. The language of such rhetoric tends to be formal, poetic, and figurative. Structurally, it is likely to explore various aspects of a feeling or attitude. The occasions themselves suggest that supporting materials are likely to emphasize what is psychologically appealing and what reflects cultural values. Finally, such addresses are more likely to develop ritualistically, another indicator of their close ties to occasions, than to provide logical arguments.

The eulogy (*eu* = well, *logos* = to speak; in short, to praise) is one kind of epideictic rhetoric. It appears on the occasion of a burial or memorial service as a result of a death. The death of any person, especially one we love and admire, forces us to confront our own mortality, and such deaths, especially violent deaths and those of children, disrupt the human community of which the deceased were a part. The eulogy meets certain very basic human needs. These can be specified in terms of the elements of descriptive analysis. Its purpose is fourfold: (1) *It acknowledges death early in the discourse.* (2) *It keeps the deceased at the center of the discourse.* (3) *It reunites the sundered community.* (4) *It immortalizes the deceased.* It shifts the relationship between the living and the deceased to suggest that although dead in the flesh, the deceased lives on in spirit—in children, good deeds, or in principles—reassuring the living that a kind of immortality exists for all of us. The tone of the eulogy is personal (death is an intimate matter) and somber, and it frequently uses language strategies, such as metaphors of rebirth, to express the idea of immortality. The persona of the eulogist is camouflaged.

Figure 14–2
*Eulogistic Rhetoric
and Descriptive
Analysis*

PURPOSE	Maintain action Reknit community, honor deceased, recall core values
AUDIENCE	Community of believers
PERSONA	Camouflaged, collective moral voice
TONE	Reverential, formal, unifying, uplifting
STRUCTURE	Emphasis on present tense, loose chronology
EVIDENCE	No proof required, used for amplification only
STRATEGIES	Language: formal, elegant, poetic Appeals: traditional values; "materializing the spiritual and spiritualizing the material" Arguments not needed

© Cengage Learning

Support material or "proof" is not necessary because the audience is already a community; what would ordinarily be evidence is used here to illustrate and amplify. Because of its consummatory purpose, the structure of a eulogy must emphasize the present, glorify the past, and hold out hope for the future. If a eulogy is to satisfy and comfort the audience, it must perform these functions in some way (Figure 14–2).

Eulogies disappoint us when they do not meet our expectations. In terms of the rhetorical problem, the subject obstacle of *cultural history* looms large. All too often, eulogies fail to conform to cultural norms, to be reassuring in their familiarity, to be part of a long-standing rhetorical tradition. A popular self-help book today reminds people to avoid this major pitfall. Author Roger Rosenblatt, sternly warns: "It's not about you. If you're giving a eulogy, try to focus on the deceased!"[3] Another related cultural history pitfall is that eulogies sometimes wander into controversial territory. However, doing so is potentially inappropriate because arousing controversy prevents the reunification of the community. A classic example of this violation occurred when Senator Charles Percy bluntly advocated gun control and an end to the war in Vietnam—both highly controversial issues—in a eulogy for Senator Robert F. Kennedy, who died of gunshot wounds in 1968. He shocked the audience and violated audience expectations and failed to perform the eulogistic function of unification. In other words, the characteristics of the eulogy become bases for evaluating this particular kind of occasional rhetoric.

The presidential inaugural address is another example of epideictic rhetoric, although the requirements for such a speech are less rigid and specific. Still, we expect the president to speak on this occasion (the Constitution does not require it) and to perform these rhetorical functions: (1) *reunify the nation*, because the inauguration follows a long and divisive political campaign, we expect the newly elected president to reunify the nation; (2) *rehearse traditional values*, because this is an occasion tied to fundamental national values (the speech is now given after the presidential oath of office has been administered), we expect the president to rehearse those values for us and make them vivid and appealing for us again; (3) *enact the presidency*, because we fear the power of the executive, we expect presidents to be humble, to admit limitations, and to ask for the help of Congress, the people, and God in their efforts to govern. And yet we expect presidents to show vigor and vision—to welcome the challenges of executive power. Enacting the presidency is a *rhetorical tightrope* of sorts, and finally, (4) *set forth guiding principles* for the incoming administration because this is the beginning of a new administration and we expect presidents to indicate the philosophy and tone of their administration, to suggest in broad terms the foreign and domestic policies that are of primary importance. Presidential inaugural addresses vary greatly, but these criteria can be used to evaluate how well a president meets audience expectations.[4]

These rules of the eulogy and inaugural are also bases for distinguishing competent from outstanding efforts. In terms of standards of evaluation, we can judge effectiveness by the degree to which a given inaugural or eulogy pays homage to its identifying rhetorical markers. Use these criteria, for example, to compare a contemporary inaugural to that of John Kennedy. In the Material for Analysis section, you will be asked to evaluate a eulogy (President Ronald Reagan's *Challenger* eulogy) based on its implicit rules. In each case, go further and ask if the speech not only met audience expectations but also met them in ways that were deeply moving, adapted to the occasion, and highly original; in short, is it aesthetically pleasing?

We can judge artistry by the way in which the discourse weaves conventional rhetorical choices with inventional or innovative ones. This is tricky business. Think back to the opening "*Name That Occasion*" excerpts. They are dull. An artistic eulogy must meet the expectations for its form (conform to the demands of cultural history) but do so in fresh, not predictable ways (show an individual stamp of authenticity). On the other hand, we have considerable practice in doing this. We expect regular television programming to be predictable; sitcoms, for example, are supposed to be funny, with each episode complete in itself, but when a particular show becomes too predictable, we stop watching it. Long-running sitcoms illustrate the combination of the predictable and innovative. *Friends* and *Seinfeld* are good examples, and it's fun to watch them even now in reruns.

Like the epideictic genre, deliberative or political discourse dealing with the expediency of future policy issues also plays to audience (voter) expectations and presents special rules for evaluation. Typical examples of deliberative discourse are political campaigns, debates, party platforms, keynotes, congressional legislative hearings, special interest group lobbying, and citizen petitions. Presidential rhetoric flourishes in the deliberative sphere, which includes press conferences, State of the Union addresses, veto messages, signing statements, and war rhetoric.

War rhetoric is a particularly challenging subform of deliberative discourse that warrants special attention here. In addition to the extraordinary demands that wars require of nation-states (sacrifice, money, long-term public support), our nation's founders were fuzzy over jurisdiction on war making. So when you ask, Who has the power to wage war, Congress or the president? the answer in the Constitution is purposely conflicted. Article one says only Congress "has the power to declare war . . . to raise and support Armies . . . provide and maintain a Navy. . . ." Article two designates the president as "Commander in Chief of the Army and Navy of the United States and of the militia of the states." The result, as David Kennedy, constitutional historian at Stanford University, says, is that "the founders crafted an invitation to perpetual conflict between Congress and the President."[5]

Capturing the paradox of war rhetoric that our constitution presents, presidential rhetoric scholars Kathleen Hall Jamieson and Karlyn Kohrs Campbell have identified several recurring challenges in the war addresses of U.S. presidents: how to request assistance of Congress without capitulating the upper hand; how to play commander-in-chief without sounding like a dictator; how to portray the country as a defender, not an aggressor; whether to name the hostility "war" or "conflict"; whether to seek unanimity of purpose without throttling dissent; whether to give a war speech before or after intervention; how to convey urgency without scuttling thoughtful deliberation; and whether to present a truthful narrative without being deceptive.[6]

This rhetorical minefield has created a deliberative subgenre that requires the greatest of rhetorical maneuvering. In terms of the elements of descriptive analysis, the rhetorical conventions that characterize U.S. presidential war rhetoric include a purpose, which is to justify military action as unavoidable; a commander-in-chief persona; a serious, controlled, forceful, and urgent tone; a short but compelling narrative structure proclaiming that a threat from a specified adversary imperils the nation; dramatic, "forced choice" language (either/or; good/evil); appeals to urgency, sovereignty, nationalism, God, and patriotism; deductive reasoning and argument from principle prevail; evidence is sparse; the immediate audience consists of the nation, allies, and even the enemy; the target audience is the nation; the created audience is a united and committed citizenry; and agents of change are the Congress and military and diplomatic corps (Figure 14–3). You will have an opportunity to examine presidential war speeches from a generic perspective in the Material for Analysis later in this chapter.

Figure 14–3
War Rhetoric and Descriptive Analysis

PURPOSE	Initiate action
	Justify military action
AUDIENCE	Target: the nation
	Created: unanimity of support
	Agents of change: Congress, military
PERSONA	Commander-in-chief
TONE	Serious, controlled, urgent, forceful
STRUCTURE	Narrative
	A threat-imperils-the-nation storyline
EVIDENCE	Downplayed and subsumed by superior persona
STRATEGIES	Language: dramatic and dichotomous
	Appeals: urgency, sovereignty, nationalism, God, patriotism
	Argument: justificatory, causal and deductive

© Cengage Learning

GENRE VIOLATIONS AND RHETORICAL HYBRIDS

What happens when the rules of a genre are purposely violated? We may laugh at the brazenness of twisted form. James Thurber's satiric adaptation of Little Red Riding Hood (see Chapter 6) and James Finn Garner's *Politically Correct Bedtime Stories* are good examples. We may smile wryly at the irony in bumper stickers like Practice Senseless Beauty and Random Acts of Kindness. We may wince at the bumbling effort to fulfill an epideictic address. In the film *Four Weddings and a Funeral,* Hugh Grant makes a fool of himself in trying to offer a toast to the groom. We may even frown, groan, and stick out our tongues and blow—which is what young children do when we have read aloud to them *The Paper Bag Princess* by Robert Munsch.[7] Yet all of these rhetorical acts are alike in their aim to entertain by turning convention on its head.

Some rhetorical acts, however, violate audience expectations in order to agitate more powerfully for a cause, jolt audiences out of their complacency, and receive media attention (if it's deviant, it's news). Elizabeth Cady Stanton's "The Solitude of Self" (1892), can be appreciated for its ability to disarm legislators precisely because it violated standard norms of deliberative address. Expecting to hear another argumentative treatise on the merits of woman suffrage, Stanton's audience was in for a real surprise. Her speech contained no proper introduction, no resolution to argue, no evidence to substantiate a policy, no plea that legislators act like agents of change, and no logical form. Yet its nondiscursive purpose (a dramatic expression that each human is unique, alone, and self-sovereign), haunting tone, narrative structure, artistic language, and appeals to the universal experiences of us as humans gave the speech such empathic force that her audience of male legislators reacted with stunned, contemplative silence. The speech created such a stir that Stanton was asked to give it on two other occasions. This major rhetorical violation worked because of an intractable cultural history problem. Leaders of the woman's rights movement had already spent fifty years delivering countless deliberative speeches explaining why women should have the right to vote. Sadly, they had gained little and still faced much resistance. Further, Stanton herself was in the twilight of her career at age seventy-six and had the stature to create a speech that completely defied categorization, ruled out refutation, and perfected persuasion. Stanton had learned from bitter experience that chivalry was a comforting worldview for many people at the time and could not be refuted in logical ways. (How do you formulate an argumentative treatise to make men feel less superior and women less inferior?) Engaging in some rhetorical deviance was her way to jolt agents of change out of their complacency and agitate more powerfully "on another plane" for woman's rights.

Forty years earlier, Frederick Douglass, a freed slave from Maryland, took the same rhetorical tack in agitating for the antislavery cause. His Fourth of July address delivered in Rochester, New York, on July 5, 1852, is a model of elegance (see Chapter 7), but it is also a classic in terms of the ways that the epideictic genre can be subverted in the name of protest, in part by tactics that initially appear to meet expectations before shifting gears. Rather than praise and honor Americans, he shamed and scolded them; rather than idealize a glorious past, he held up the Constitution for ridicule; rather than look optimistically to the future, he saw gloom and doom. Although Douglass risked bodily harm in delivering such a sacrilegious speech, its vitriolic content attracted media attention and helped make him a leader in the antislavery cause.

These two speeches on behalf of woman's rights and civil rights are not isolated examples of generic surprises. In fact, minority rhetors who champion unpopular causes are much more likely to use a *rhetoric of subversion*. In order to combat huge audience obstacles when facing powerful elites who are committed to maintaining the status quo, disenfranchised rhetors must sometimes ruffle feathers rhetorically and resort to shock tactics.[8] In 1968 at the Mexican City Olympics, two U.S. track stars in the 200 meter run, Tommie Smith and John Carlos (gold and bronze medalists, respectively), shocked the nation and the world at the victory ceremony by standing barefoot with heads bowed and a single black-gloved fist raised during the national anthem. The athletes described the gesture as a tribute to their ethnic heritage and a protest over race relations and police brutality against African Americans in this country. Both athletes were banned from the Olympic Village and sent home by the International Olympic Committee (IOC) and the U.S. Olympic Committee. Michael Moore shocked the Academy Awards in his acceptance speech for *Bowling for Columbine* by chastising President Bush and calling him a "fictitious president" waging a war "for fictitious reasons." Thirty years earlier Marlon Brando refused the Oscar to protest Hollywood's treatment of Native Americans. In these cases audiences were visibly agitated. In the early 1990s, a group of female artists called The Guerrilla Girls drew attention to the long-standing privileging of male artists and male-owned art galleries in this country by showing up at black-tie art show openings across the country in gorilla costumes!

Most rhetors who step outside the security of a standard rhetorical form do so more timidly than the preceding rhetors and only under special circumstances. We call these rhetorical acts *hybrids*. Like a hybrid crop such as Turkey Red wheat, which combines two strains of grain for a heartier yield, rhetorical attempts to combine genres can endure. Nevertheless, rhetorical hybrids can look and sound quirky. The key to a rhetorical act that wants to fold deliberative rhetoric into a eulogy, for example, is to consider the following: (1) *Does the occasion, such as the manner of death, invite a deliberative subform?* If a young person has died senselessly at the hands of a drunk driver, for example, expressing a desire to support the efforts of MADD or SADD is understandable. (2) *Were the deceased and the eulogist in agreement on the policy issue?* If you had a friend who died as a result of being shot with a handgun but who was an avid member of the NRA, you would be ill-advised to promote tougher gun control, even if you as the eulogist supported that cause. (3) *Is the policy promoted as a tribute to the deceased?* If you suggest that people of good faith should show compassion to persons with AIDS at a funeral for an AIDS victim, it must be phrased as a tribute to that individual. (4) Finally, and most critical, *is the deliberative theme introduced in such a way that the epideictic features of the address clearly predominate?* Is it seven-eighths ceremonial in nature? Is there ever a moment in reading, listening, or viewing a tribute when you wonder, What happened to the deceased? You will have a chance to examine a eulogistic hybrid along these lines in the Material for Analysis later in the chapter.

THE APOLOGETIC GENRE AND THE MEDIA AGE

Some genres are so complex and "high stakes" that they require the kind of rhetorical maneuvering found in politicized tributes. One such animal is what Aristotle called an *apologia*—or what we label today as the rhetoric of self-defense, image repair, or crisis management. Even Aristotle was puzzled about how to categorize the speech of self-defense. He never dignified the rhetorical form by giving it separate "species" status, but he noted that an apologia shares features from all three classical genres. As in *forensic discourse*, apologists must ask for revised judgments of their past actions. They must redefine the reality portrayed by their accusers and deal in *questions of fact*—Was an act (misdeed, crime) committed? But apologists are not performing in a courtroom in front of jurors and a judge and so do not seek justice. As in *deliberative discourse*, apologists must wrest argumentative control over the alleged misdeed from the hands of their accusers if they wish to survive and recover politically or economically. But apologists are not appealing to voters per se, nor do they aim to present *questions of policy* in problem-solution form to make an expedient case. Thus, as in *epideictic discourse*, apologists engage in image repair, seeking to restore their honor by treating *questions of value* in front of observers who exercise their voyeuristic tendencies in what can best be described as a spectacle of rhetorical grace or awkwardness under fire. But apologists are consumed with the past, not the present, and the ceremonial expectations of voicing noncontroversial themes to an audience of a community of believers does not describe the apologia either. It is indebted to all three genres, but its allegiance to none makes the apologia challenging to create and critique.

In terms of elements of descriptive analysis, the purpose of an apologia reflects its multifaceted heritage (Figure 14–4). As epideictic discourse, it aims to alter perception (repair an image). As forensic rhetoric, it aims to explain (revise the reality portrayed by the accusers), and as deliberative speech, it aims to formulate belief (seek vindication). The audience is the lay public, but we fondly—and with the assistance of media—cast ourselves in the role of "moral guardians" in a public, not legal, trial either to exonerate or censure the beleaguered rhetor. The apologist's persona must exude morality and trustworthiness. Rhetors often project a kind of "noble victim"

PURPOSE	Alter perception, repair image
AUDIENCE	Lay public empowered as "jurors" in a public setting to exonerate or censure
PERSONA	Noble victim, honorable public servant; self-referencing is prominent
TONE	Defensive, contrite, controlled, intimate, candid
STRUCTURE	Short, expedient, narrative components
EVIDENCE	Self as "expert" is primary; all types of proof appropriate
STRATEGIES	Language: straightforward Arguments: bolstering, corrective action, confession, denial, differentiation, jurisdiction, shift blame, transcendence Appeals: morality, fairness, compassion, purification, vindication

Figure 14–4
Apologetic Rhetoric and Descriptive Analysis

© Cengage Learning

self-defense. The tone is contrite, intimate, and candid, but it can often be defensive, serious, and counteraccusatory too. Structurally, apologias are seldom gems of cohesiveness or intricacy. Serious accusations demand timely responses. The poetic features of rhetoric are often exchanged for the pragmatic. But lots of evidence, especially in terms of personal testimony, and strategies, especially arguments and appeals, are well suited to the form. Specifically, scholars have identified the following recurring arguments in apologias: (1) *bolstering* character ("We are a good and noble company"; "I am an honest and trustworthy person; consider my whole record."); (2) *denial* ("The charge is completely false"); (3) *differentiating* this act/actor from others ("Yes, certain incidents did occur, but consider the circumstances"); (4) *transcending* the immediate occasion or issue/attack ("Let's take a fresh approach. The real thing we should be discussing is . . ."); (5) *attack the accuser or shift the blame* ("Consider the source!" "It's a smear tactic by my opponent!" "The press is overstepping its boundaries"); (6) *corrective action* ("We will repair the damage"); and (7) *confession* ("I'm sorry.")[9]

Apologetic rhetoric abounds in political, religious, sports, and corporate arenas. An avalanche of high-profile crises has flourished in this country. Richard Nixon's "Checker's Speech" and his multiple Watergate defenses, Ted Kennedy's "Chappaquiddick Address," Ronald Reagan's "Iran-Contra apologia," and Bill Clinton's damage control efforts in the "Lewinsky scandal" suggest that politicians have been most vulnerable to crisis response rhetoric. But televangelists charged with extortion, Catholic priests charged with sexual abuse of young boys, and Scientologists charged with unethical, cultlike recruitment tactics remind us that even in the most moral of arenas, image repair discourse has flourished.

Our fascination with and near worship of sports has brought with it uncompromising scrutiny as well. In "America's game," we have Pete Rose of the Cincinnati Reds banished from the Hall of Fame for his betting on the game and Barry Bonds of the San Francisco Giants caught up in the steroids scandal as he chased Hank Aaron's home run record. In each case, their speeches of self-defense failed. In the Tour de France and Olympic Games we have world class athletes, such as Lance Armstrong, called to explain why they failed drug tests and the IOC itself called to explain its bidding practices in selecting host cities. In the college ranks we have Division I football and basketball programs forced to defend their recruitment tactics to the NCAA, individual coaches forced to explain their abusive behavior toward players, and players forced to explain their academic fraud or "point shaving" scams. Indeed, sports apologia has become a sport in itself.

Corporate rhetors in both the profit and nonprofit sector have seen the sharp rise of this rhetorical genre and know they are not immune. Many corporate cultures rehearse plans for responding to crisis. Crisis plans, damage control teams, and consultants with specific skills in how to repair a corporation's image in the wake of damaging accusations are now regularly part of public affairs and communication divisions. Organizations have many models of success (Tylenol and the cyanide poisonings; Chrysler and the federal bailout; the United Way and CEO fraud; Pepsi and the syringe scare, The *Washington Post* and a reporter's plagiarized Pulitzer prize-winning article, to name but a few). They have even more models of failure (the *Exxon Valdez* oil spill; Dow Chemical and the manufacturing of napalm; Dow Corning and silicone breast implants; Sears and auto repair fraud; Union Carbide and the Bhopal disaster; Enron, Arthur Anderson, and WorldCom bankruptcies for unethical accounting practices; and FEMA and the Department of Homeland Security for its incompetent handling of Hurricane Katrina, for example).

Use of the genre of apologia is not restricted to politicians, public figures, and heads of corporations; the form is of equal importance to students and teachers. In Frank McCourt's *Teacher Man: A Memoir*,[10] he tells the story of being handed a note by one of his students explaining his absence the day before. The note was a detailed, wildly creative narrative. As he explains, the harried parents of his students say to their children, "Write the note and I'll sign it," and the result was that he had a drawer full of excuses that revealed that his students were "capable of the finest American prose: fluent, imaginative, clear, dramatic, fantastic, focused, persuasive, useful." McCourt copies and distributes some as objects of study; then he invites the class to concoct excuses for absences, but they quickly and enthusiastically proceed to new subjects: an excuse from Adam to God, from Eve to God, for Lucifer's seduction of Eve, for Judas, Attila, Al Capone. Unexpectedly, the principal and the superintendent of schools visit his class. McCourt is sure that he will be reprimanded; instead, he is praised for "his energetic and imaginative teaching." The principal has some reservations about encouraging students to write excuses for evil people and criminals, but adds, "It's what lawyers do, isn't it? And from what I've seen in your class, you might have some promising future attorneys in there."

We have on rare occasion excused students for turning something in late because the stories they told were so wildly, improbably, disarming and filled us with delight. We have often refused to accept late work from students who offered lame excuses. Consider how you might use the apologia, and consider the critical standards your instructor might use in evaluating the excuses that you offer.

That rhetors from diverse arenas are sometimes forced to "air their dirty rhetorical laundry" in public invites questions. Why is it that you are more likely to read, watch, or hear an apologia in the next month than a eulogy, a debate, or a trial? Part of the answer lies in the rise of media (recall Chapter 13). Media have blurred distinctions between public and private lives in their need to play journalistic watchdog (a role consumers praised media for performing in uncovering illegal activities in the Watergate affair), fulfill commercial obligations (the more dirt you can dig, the higher the ratings), and satisfy our desire for entertainment (vilifying scapegoats is cathartic). Another part of the answer lies in the evolution of our concept of citizenship. No longer passive, faceless masses, today individuals identify with an activist NIMBY (not in my backyard) outlook. If you suspect foul play at your workplace, you can seek protections and become a whistle-blower. If you suspect a product defect, you can alert the Consumer Product Safety Commission. If you wonder why your local, state, or federal representative never returns your phone calls, you can tip off your local media to do an investigative piece.

The genre of apologia should remain a keen interest of rhetorical critics, no matter its ebb and flow. It is a genre that is unlikely to decay. In civilized society, people must fight with words, not clubs. The genre is keenly connected to the double-edged sword of democracy. Only in a democracy can people demand public accountability of prominent figures, and only in a democracy must public figures engage in a sometimes painful, embarrassing form of discourse that reveals to the whole world their human foibles. The genre's symbolic power and historical persistence are tied to its rhetorical complexity. The litmus test for success is this: Who tells the better story, the accuser or the apologist? It is a high-stakes rhetorical battle that apologists cannot afford to lose. It is the ultimate symbolic test of grace under pressure for a public figure. The genre is a public purging of sins and a reaffirmation of the ethical norms of a society often presented in theatrical proportions to bring pleasure to spectators; it is the most intimate form of secular discourse. The purging of sins in public can be ennobling and cathartic. The visual media are especially equipped to provide the excess and exaggeration that this type of theater demands. The psychological appeal of the genre is best summed up by communication scholar Edward Corbett:

> What perversity is there in the human psyche that makes us enjoy the spectacle of human beings desperately trying to answer the charges leveled against them? Maybe secretly, as we read or listen [or watch or log on], we say to ourselves, "Ah, there but for the grace of God go I."[11]

 MATERIAL FOR ANALYSIS I

On January 28, 1986, with swirling media attention and NASA optimism, the space shuttle *Challenger* was launched with seven crew members, including the first non-astronaut, a school teacher, Christa McAuliffe. With the world and many children watching, the *Challenger* exploded a little over one minute into the flight. What the Kennedy assassination was to the baby boomers, the *Challenger* tragedy became to generation X'ers. People remember where they were when they saw or heard the news of the crash. That millions of schoolchildren were watching the launch in their classrooms only added to the anguish of this national loss. Americans were simply unprepared for a space tragedy of this magnitude.

NASA had experienced problems in the past. In the first *Apollo* launch, three astronauts were killed in a fire on the launching pad, but the program was in its infancy. When *Apollo 11* landed on the moon, we forgot about the risks, and faith in NASA grew. Three astronauts were almost lost on *Apollo 13*, but their mission ended successfully. From 1967 until the *Challenger* disaster, NASA had never lost an astronaut.

Reasons for the disaster began to circulate almost immediately, although the official report of the explosion would not be released for four months by a presidential commission investigating the incident. Finger-pointing at NASA was swift and harsh. Technical problems in the design of the O-ring seals, which caused the crash, had been known for almost a decade. A general lack of communication at NASA prevented the concerns from being taken seriously. Further, NASA was charged with being overly concerned with commercializing its program—whipping up public support and public funds—by initiating the teacher-in-space idea. The campaign to make the launch entertaining and educational deemphasized the calculated risks of manned space exploration. NASA's foray into public relations turned into a nightmare.

President Ronald Reagan, an enthusiastic supporter of space exploration, was faced with the task of confronting a national tragedy, dealing with the accusations of technical incompetence, bureaucratic oversight, and a kind of zealotry that led to the death of a civilian, all on very short notice. Reagan was scheduled to give the State of the Union Address that same evening. He scrapped those plans and instead gave a tribute that merged subtle deliberative themes into the epideictic genre.

President Ronald Reagan's *Challenger* Tribute, January 29, 1986[12]

1   Ladies and gentlemen. I planned to speak to you tonight to report on the State of the Union. But the events of earlier today have led me to change those plans. Today is a day for mourning and remembering. Nancy and I are pained to the core by the tragedy of the shuttle *Challenger*. We know we share this pain with all of the people of our country. This is truly a national loss.

2   Nineteen years ago, almost to the day, we lost three astronauts in a terrible accident on the ground. But we've never lost an astronaut in flight; we've never had a tragedy like this. And perhaps we've forgotten the courage it took for the crew of the shuttle but they, the *Challenger* seven, were aware of the dangers and overcame them and did their jobs brilliantly.

3   We mourn seven heroes: Michael Smith, Dick Scobee, Judith Resnik, Ronald McNair, Ellison Onizuka, Gregory Jarvis, and Christa McAuliffe. We mourn their loss as a nation together.

4   The families of the seven—we cannot bear, as you do, the full impact of this tragedy but we feel the loss and we're thinking about you so very much. Your loved ones were daring and brave and they had that special grace, that special spirit that says, "Give me a challenge and I'll meet it with joy." They had a hunger to explore the universe and discover its truths. They wished to serve and they did—they served all of us.

5   We've grown used to wonders in this century; it's hard to dazzle us. For 25 years the United States space program has been doing just that. We've grown used to the idea of space, and perhaps we forget that we've only just begun. We're still pioneers. They, the members of the *Challenger* crew, were pioneers.

6   And I want to say something to the schoolchildren of America who were watching the live coverage of the shuttle's takeoff. I know it's hard to understand that sometimes painful things like this happen. It's all part of the process of exploration and discovery; it's all part of taking a chance and expanding man's horizons. The future doesn't belong to the fainthearted. It belongs to the brave. The *Challenger* crew was pulling us into the future, and we'll continue to follow them.

7   I've always had great faith in and respect for our space program, and what happened today does nothing to diminish it. We don't hide our space program; we don't keep secrets and cover things up. We do it all up front and in public. That's the way freedom is, and we wouldn't change it for a minute. We'll continue our quest in space. There will be more shuttle flights and more shuttle crews and, yes, more volunteers, more civilians, more teachers in space. Nothing ends here. Our hopes and our journeys continue.

8   I want to add that I wish I could talk to every man and woman who works for NASA, or who worked on this mission, and tell them: "Your dedication and professionalism have moved and impressed us for decades, and we know of your anguish. We share it."

9   There's a coincidence today. On this day 390 years ago, the great explorer Sir Francis Drake died aboard ship off the coast of Panama. In his lifetime the great frontiers were the oceans, and a historian later said, "He lived by the sea, died on it, and was buried in it." Well, today we can say of the *Challenger* crew, their dedication was, like Drake's, complete. The crew of the space shuttle *Challenger* honored us by the manner in which they lived their lives. We will never forget them nor the last time we saw them this morning as they prepared for their journey and waved goodbye and "slipped the surly bonds of earth to touch the face of God."

10   Thank you.

Questions for Analysis

1. How does this speech conform to the general requirements of epideictic speaking when the seven elements of descriptive analysis in this chapter are applied to it? Does this speech demonstrate the four recurring eulogistic themes? How well? What do you think are some of the distinctive qualities that Ronald Reagan brings to the conventional demands that a eulogy makes?
2. What language strategies do you see in this eulogy? (See Figure 7–2.) Which are primary? Do they work to complement key eulogistic themes? How? What questions of value emerge in the address about U.S. character and innovation? Are they time-bound or timeless? Explain.
3. Locate a recording of the address (in your library, or on Internet sites such as AmericanRhetoric.com). How do Ronald Reagan's pitch, rate, volume, vocal variety, enunciation, posture, eye contact, and facial expression enhance the eulogy? Can you see from this aspect of the address alone why Ronald Reagan was sometimes called "The Great Communicator"? Why might nonverbal and visual aspects of rhetoric be more important for the epideictic genre than other genres?
4. Given what you know about some of the controversial issues that emerged in the media almost immediately after the crash, how does Reagan incorporate deliberative themes in the tribute? What specific paragraphs do this? Are the various positions that Reagan takes enthymematic? Explain. How well do you think this speech adheres to the guidelines proposed in this chapter for how to merge deliberative elements in epideictic rhetoric tastefully?
5. The president of the United States has many roles to play. In the event of a national loss, the president must play the role of moral leader, a fitting epideictic persona, yet the president is still the leader of the free world, and any major media address by the president is scrutinized for political implications. Because NASA is closely tied to what Aristotle called "matters of the state," is President Reagan obligated to introduce political themes in this eulogy in ways that others are not?
6. In science museums, I-MAX theaters, website albums, and the like, the *Challenger* crew has been memorialized. How do the principles of visual rhetoric discussed in Chapter 12 enhance the features of the epideictic genre? Locate one visual tribute from the crash and discuss the ways that the basic or technical features of visual rhetoric work in that piece to create the appropriate mood of epideictic discourse.

What rhetorical problems can visual tributes create? What is the power and the limitation of the familiar picture showing cascading plumes of smoke (see Figure 12–1) in terms of fulfilling the purpose of epideictic rhetoric?

7. In February 2003, seventeen years after *Challenger*, and not quite two years after 9/11, another NASA mission ended in tragedy. The *Columbia* space shuttle disintegrated upon reentry, killing all seven astronauts on board and spreading tons of debris over Texas and six other states. President George W. Bush faced a strikingly similar rhetorical situation as Reagan. Locate Bush's speech tribute to NASA and the *Columbia* astronauts. Compare the ways that Bush uses eulogistic themes and larger epideictic requirements to respond to the *Columbia* disaster. Compare rhetorical challenges including locations, audiences, larger political contexts, and presentation styles. Who performs the better tribute? Why? What special challenges does Bush face?

MATERIAL FOR ANALYSIS II

"Pearl Harbor War Speech," December 8, 1941[13]

Franklin D. Roosevelt

1   Yesterday, December 7, 1941—a date which will live in infamy—the United States of America was suddenly and deliberately attacked by naval and air forces of the Empire of Japan.

2   The United States was at peace with that nation and, at the solicitation of Japan, was still in conversation with the government and its emperor looking toward the maintenance of peace in the Pacific.

3   Indeed, one hour after Japanese air squadrons had commenced bombing in Oahu, the Japanese ambassador to the United States and his colleagues delivered to the Secretary of State a formal reply to a recent American message. While this reply stated that it seemed useless to continue the existing diplomatic negotiations, it contained no threat or hint of war or armed attack.

4   It will be recorded that the distance of Hawaii from Japan makes it obvious that the attack was deliberately planned many days or even weeks ago. During the intervening time, the Japanese government has deliberately sought to deceive the United States by false statements and expressions of hope for continued peace.

5   The attack yesterday on the Hawaiian Islands has caused severe damage to American naval and military forces. Very many American lives have been lost. In addition, American ships have been reported torpedoed on the high seas between San Francisco and Honolulu.

6   Yesterday, the Japanese government also launched an attack against Malaya.

7   Last night, Japanese forces attacked Hong Kong.

8   Last night, Japanese forces attacked Guam.

9   Last night, Japanese forces attacked the Philippine Islands.

10   Last night, the Japanese attacked Wake Island.

11   This morning, the Japanese attacked Midway Island.

12   Japan has, therefore, undertaken a surprise offensive extending throughout the Pacific area. The facts of yesterday speak for themselves. The people of the United States have already formed their opinions and well understand the implications to the very life and safety of our nation.

13   As commander in chief of the Army and Navy, I have directed that all measures be taken for our defense.

14   Always will we remember the character of the onslaught against us.

15   No matter how long it may take us to overcome this premeditated invasion, the American people in their righteous might will win through to absolute victory.

16   I believe I interpret the will of the Congress and of the people when I assert that we will not only defend ourselves to the uttermost, but will make very certain that this form of treachery shall never endanger us again.

17   Hostilities exist. There is no blinking at the fact that our people, our territory, and our interests are in grave danger.

18   With confidence in our armed forces—with the unbounding determination of our people—we will gain the inevitable triumph—so help us God.

19   I ask that the Congress declare that since the unprovoked and dastardly attack by Japan on Sunday, December 7, a state of war has existed between the United States and the Japanese Empire.

Questions for Analysis

1. How does FDR's war speech fit the expected purpose of war rhetoric: justification of military action?
2. How does FDR come across as a commander-in-chief? Is the tone of his address compatible with the persona; is the mood serious, forceful, confident, and urgent?
3. In terms of conventional organizational structure, does FDR craft a compelling narrative that establishes an imperiled nation? A specific adversary? How does he show that exhaustive efforts have been tried to restore peace nonmilitarily? Does he seek unanimous commitment for the cause?

4. Who is the target audience? Does he address the enemy? Our allies? Where does he urge Americans to be united in purpose? Does he speak to military or diplomatic forces?
5. Do you see much rational evidence in this speech? Psychological evidence?
6. What especially dramatic and forceful language devices does FDR use in painting a picture of good versus evil? What emotional appeals are used to rally the nation? What general and specific arguments are used to fulfill the requirements of form? Do you see fallacies? What ethical issues present themselves in looking at how FDR uses strategies to go to war with Japan?
7. What tensions do you see in the speech (based on the eight challenges identified in the chapter to explain the paradox of war rhetoric and the conflicting constitutional demands)? How well does FDR craft a speech that is aesthetically pleasing and ethically sensitive to the paradox that war rhetoric presents?
8. A critic, Hermann Stelner, analyzed the word choices in this address, and he argued that these characterizations made it easier for Americans to accept the idea of placing Japanese immigrants and citizens into internment camps.[14] Look carefully at the words that FDR uses to characterize the Japanese and evaluate the evidence for that claim in the speech.
9. On October 7, 2001, President George W. Bush gave a war speech to the nation justifying our military engagement in Afghanistan in response to the perpetrators of 9/11. Locate that speech and compare Bush's rhetorical choices with FDR's. Does Bush more or less conform to the requirements of war rhetoric? In what ways is his war address different from Roosevelt's? After viewing the video or audio clips of both speeches, how does presidential persona and presentation style affect your assessment of each speech? Which speech addresses the tensions of war rhetoric most clearly?

EXERCISES

Critical Thinking Exercises

1. Here is a passage from Earl Spencer's tribute to his sister Princess Diana at her funeral in Westminster Abbey in September 1997. Identify the key eulogistic themes. How does it capitalize on one of the many controversial points surrounding Diana's life and death—that she was stripped of her royal title after divorcing Prince Charles—and show signs of being a rhetorical hybrid (merging deliberative elements)? Is this tasteful?

> Diana was the very essence of compassion, of duty, of style, of beauty. All over the world she was a symbol of selfless humanity, a standard-bearer for the rights of the truly downtrodden, a truly British girl who transcended nationality, someone with a natural nobility who was classless, who proved in the last year that she needed no royal title to continue to generate her particular brand of magic.

2. Attend a commencement. Rate the commencement address in terms of the basic epideictic elements. Interview three to five people afterward. Did they like it or not? Why? Do their responses echo some of the audience expectations of the genre that you have learned?

3. As a class watch the ceremonies for the Academy Awards, the Grammys, the Tonys, or the Emmys. Rate the acceptance speeches in terms of conformity to epideictic themes. Did you see any rhetorical hybrids (deliberative themes merged in epideictic address)? Did the merger work? As a class, vote on a winner.

4. Video tributes sometimes accompany or even take the place of speech tributes. What are their special rhetorical strengths and weaknesses at fulfilling the requirements of epideictic form (recall Chapter 12)?

5. The following are excerpts from corporate apologia. Identify the apologetic argument type (bolstering, denial, differentiation, transcendence, attack the accuser, corrective action, confession) that you see in each:

a. "The completely ridiculous and false story that the President of the *Procter & Gamble* company appeared on a talk show to discuss the company's connection to Satanism has been resurfacing in your area. It is a variation of the lie that was spread in 1990. None of this is true." (*Procter & Gamble*, press kit)

b. "We're part of your community and thousands of others all over the country. We have a shared interest in safety. For us, just like you, it's always safety first." (*Domino's Pizza*, flyer)

c. "There is a difference between United Way of America and United Way of the Plains." (Open letter, local *United Way*)

d. "Finally, and most importantly, I want to tell you how sorry I am that this accident took place. We at Exxon are especially sympathetic to the residents of Valdez and the people of the state of Alaska."(Open letter, *New York Times*, Exxon)

e. "From the outset, I believe all of us have been deeply upset and revulsed by the statements that were made on our air about the young women who represented Rutgers University in the NCAA Women's Basketball Championship with such class, energy and talent. Those who have spoken with us the last few days represent people of goodwill from all segments of our society—all races, economic groups, men and women alike. In our meetings with concerned groups, there has been much discussion of the effect language like this has on our young people, particularly young women of color trying to make their way in this society. That consideration has weighed most heavily on our minds as we made our decision, as have the many e-mails, phone calls and personal discussions we have had with our colleagues across the CBS Corp. and our many other constituencies. I want to thank all those who came to see us to express their views. We are now presented with a significant opportunity to expand on our record on issues of diversity, race and gender. We intend to seize that opportunity as we move forward together." (CBS Chief Executive Leslie Moonves's statement announcing the firing of U.S. radio host Don Imus for remarks about the Rutgers women's basketball team.)

Analytical Writing Exercises

6. Here are two passages from presidential inaugural addresses. The first is from John Kennedy's inaugural; the second from Bill Clinton's first inaugural. Write a 500-word essay that compares and contrasts them in terms of the four themes of presidential inaugurals. Is one the "ghost" of the other? Explain.

JFK's Inaugural Address

In your hands, my fellow citizens, more than in mine, will rest the final success or failure of our course. Since this country was founded, each generation of Americans has been summoned to give testimony to its national loyalty. The graves of young Americans who answered the call to service are found around the globe. Now the trumpet summons us again—not as a call to bear arms, though arms we need; not as a call to battle, though embattled we are; but a call to bear the burden of a long twilight struggle, year in, and year out, "rejoicing in hope, patient in tribulation"—a struggle against the common enemies of man: tyranny, poverty, disease, and war itself. Can we forge against these enemies a grand and global alliance, north and south, east and west, that can assure a more fruitful life for all mankind? Will you join in that historic effort? In the long history of the world, only a few generations have been granted the role of defending freedom in its hour of maximum danger. I do not shrink from this responsibility; I welcome it. I do not believe that any of us would exchange places with any other people or any other generation. The energy, the faith, the devotion which we bring to this endeavor will light our country and all who serve it—and the glow from that fire can truly light the world. And so, my fellow Americans, ask not what your country can do for you; ask what you can do for your country.

Clinton's First Inaugural Address

My fellow Americans, you, too, must play your part in our renewal. I challenge a new generation of young Americans to a season of service—to act on your idealism by helping troubled children, keeping company with those in need, reconnecting our torn communities. There is so much to be done—enough, indeed, for millions of others who are still young in spirit to give of themselves in service, too. In serving, we recognize a simple but powerful truth: We need each other. And we must care for one another. Today, we do more than celebrate America;

we rededicate ourselves to the very idea of America. An idea born in revolution and renewed through two centuries of challenge. An idea tempered by the knowledge that, but for fate, we—the fortunate and the unfortunate—might have been each other. An idea ennobled by the faith that our nation can summon from its myriad diversities the deepest measure of unity. An idea infused with the conviction that America's long heroic journey must go forever upward. And so my fellow Americans, as we stand at the edge of the twenty-first century, let us begin with energy and hope, with faith and discipline, and let us work until our work is done. The Scripture says, "And let us not be weary in well-doing, for in due season we shall reap, if we faint not." From this joyful mountaintop of celebration, we hear a call to service in the valley. We have heard the trumpets. We have changed the guard. And now—each in our own way, and with God's help—we must answer the call.

Strategic Speaking Exercises

7. The following accusatory scenarios invite you to respond by crafting "mock" apologies. Form groups of four. Together construct a fitting response to the charge leveled against you. A primary argument strategy is suggested for each scenario. Choose a group spokesperson to give a one-minute speech of self-defense to the class. Vote for a winner. How did nonverbal features (posture, eye contact, facial expression, gestures, body movement, and so on) factor into your assessment of whether to exonerate or censure?

a. Situation 1: You have been accused of cheating on an exam in this class. Two witnesses have testified to the accuracy of the charge, claiming specifically that you brought crib notes and had a detailed test code written on the bottom of your shoe. (Tip: Frame your response around transcendence)

b. Situation 2: You have been charged with reckless driving by some of your peers who believe that you may also have been driving while under the influence of alcohol—though the charges have not been empirically verified by anyone. (Tip: Frame your response around differentiation)

c. Situation 3: Rumor has it that you have failed to observe the visitation hours in the women's/men's dorms on several occasions this semester. (Tip: Frame your response around denial)

d. Situation 4: You were seen by two campus security persons shouting obscenities out of your dorm window at 2:00 a.m. last Friday. (Tip: Frame your response around bolstering)

8. Bring an apologia to class (sports, religious, political, corporate). It may be in the form of an advertisement, a speech, a video news release, newsletter, or website segment, flyer, or the like. You have two to three minutes to give an oral critique to show its indebtedness to the classical genres. How is it like forensic discourse? Deliberative discourse? Epideictic discourse? Which genre is it most like? Does it resemble expectations for a typical apologetic message as judged by the seven elements of descriptive analysis? What special problems are posed in critiquing written apologetic discourse, especially in terms of evaluating persona?

NOTES

1. Aristotle, *On Rhetoric: A Theory of Civic Discourse,* trans. George A. Kennedy (New York: Oxford University Press, 1991), p. 47.

2. Aristotle, *On Rhetoric,* pp. 47–48.

3. Roger Rosenblatt, *Rules for Aging* (San Diego: Harcourt, 2000).

4. For extended discussion of inaugurals, see Karlin Kohrs Campbell and Kathleen Hall Jamieson, *Deeds Done in Words: The Genres of Presidential Governance* (University of Chicago Press, 1990), pp. 14–51.

5. David Kennedy, "Founders' Fuzziness." *Time,* January 29, 2007, p. 21.

6. Campbell and Jamieson, *Deeds Done in Words,* "War Rhetoric," pp. 101–127.

7. This story pokes fun at the classic mold of the prince coming to save the princess from a horrible dragon. The princess in Munsch's book must save the prince by outsmarting a dragon. She succeeds, but once rescued the prince demands that she leave him to fetch more appropriate princess attire (the dragon had destroyed her home and clothes, and she is only wearing a paper bag). The princess tells him that he is arrogant and runs off by herself to live happily ever after.

8. This thesis is developed in Karlyn Kohrs Campbell, "Inventing Women: From Amaterasu to Virgina Woolf," *Women's Studies in Communication,* 21:2 (1998): 111–116.

9. See especially W. A. Linkugel and B. L. Ware, "They Spoke in Defense of Themselves: On the Generic Criticism of Apologia," *The Quarterly Journal of Speech*, 59 (1973): 273–283; W. L. Benoit, *Accounts, Excuses, and Apologies: A Theory of Image Restoration Strategies* (Albany: University of New York, 1995); and S. S. Huxman and D. Bruce, "Toward a Dynamic Generic Framework of Apologia: A Case Study of Dow Chemical, Vietnam, and the Napalm Controversy," *Communication Studies*, 46 (1995): 57–72.

10. Frank McCourt, *Teacher Man: A Memoir* (New York: Scribner, 2005), pp. 83, 84, 90.

11. Edward P. J. Corbett, Foreword, in Halford Ross Ryan, ed., *Oratorical Encounters: Selected Studies and Discourses of Twentieth-Century Political Accusations and Apologies* (New York: Greenwood, 1988), p. xi.

12. Ronald Reagan, "Space Shuttle 'Challenger' Tragedy Address," January 28, 1986. Accessed 1/31/13. http://www.americanrhetoric.com/speeches/ronaldreaganchallenger.htm paragraph numbers added.

13. Franklin Delano Roosevelt, "Pearl Harbor Address to the Nation," December 8, 1941. Accessed 1/31/13. http://www.americanrhetoric.com/speeches/fdrpearlharbor.htm; paragraph numbers added.

14. Hermann G. Stelzner, "'War Message,' December 8, 1941: An Approach to Language," *Communication Monographs*, 33 (1966): 419–437.

Epilogue

WHAT IS RHETORIC?

As far as anyone can determine from extant Greek sources, Plato coined the word *rhetoric* to distinguish what he taught, which he called philosophy, from what was taught by sophists, who trained young men to speak well in the assembly and courts, a circumstance that may explain some of its negative connotations.[1] *Rhetoric* (also *rhema* = word; *rhetor* = public speaker) comes from the Greek verb *eiron*, from which we derive the word *irony*, the trope for saying one thing and meaning something else, a trope that exploits the gap between what we can express in language and what we feel, experience, and believe.

Plato recognized this gap. In the dialogue *Cratylus* he wrote that truth cannot be expressed in literal or factual language, and his great truths emerge in metaphor and myth: the story of the cave in the *Republic*, the allegory of the Isles of the Blessed in *Gorgias*, the metaphor of the chariot, horses, and charioteer for the soul, and the myth of the invention of writing in the *Phaedrus*, for example. The French philosopher Jean-Paul Sartre captured the dilemma of language when he wrote, "*La loi de toute rhétorique, c'est qu'il faut mentir pour être vrai,*" or, loosely translated, "The law of all rhetoric is that you have to lie in order to tell the truth."[2] Sartre's comment calls attention to the need to shape language artfully, to exaggerate, embellish, dramatize, in order to find ways to communicate some part of our ineffable, indescribable internal experiences to others.

From ancient times, there have been two disparate or conflicting reactions to the gap between words and reality, language and human experience. One is represented by Plato, whose story of the soul's journey describes a process in which, in being born, we forget the truths or forms that we glimpsed in the heavens. His dialogues show Socrates struggling to overcome that forgetfulness or amnesia in order to lead those he questions to what he calls *anamnesis*, the recollection of the great truths, the forms, perceived by our souls prior to birth. This, of course, echoes other stories of the loss of paradise, of an Eden in which there was perfect communication and complete understanding.

The other response is what Kenneth Burke refers to as the Blessed Fall,[3] which treats language as the source of all human creativity and invention, and equally of all human deceit and division, and the cruelty that arises out of alienation and separation. The Greek Isocrates and the Roman Cicero describe speech as the faculty that lifted us out of savagery and enabled us as humans to cooperate in order to create all the good things that make our lives better, all that we call civilization, a word that refers, of course, to the creation of communities and the use of symbols to induce cooperation. Ironically, the cost was our almost infinite capacity for evil, our ability to hate others, to deceive them, to be willing to sacrifice them on the altar of our beliefs. One of the earliest sophists, Gorgias, wrote a speech, the "Encomium of Helen," about the famous and beautiful woman whom many blamed for the terrible Trojan War—and please note, women often have been blamed for the human fall from perfection (e.g., the biblical Eve and the Greek Pandora). In that discourse Gorgias discusses the power of speech, a power that he claims *feels* as great as necessity, although, of course, it is not.

Why are we vulnerable to such power? Gorgias's answer is that our memories are faulty; our perceptions are partial or biased; our interpretations of the same events differ; we draw differing conclusions from experiences. Because of these limitations, we are vulnerable, open to the words of others, which exploit our faulty memories, our limited perceptions, and our varied understandings, inferences, and predictions. These can be used to persuade us, even against our interests, through what Edward Bernays, the founder of public relations, called the "engineering of consent,"[4] a process of molding public opinion by which we come to support policies and practices that are inimical to our values and dangerous to us, but beneficial to others, often those with the resources to disseminate sophisticated messages repeatedly in attractive and appealing ways via mass media.

As an example, consider the pervasive use of European models in advertising in Japan; in fact, it is rare to see an Asian face in anything except local advertising. One commentator notes that in anti-Korean and anti-Chinese comic books, that sell well in Japan, the Japanese characters are drawn with Western features, whereas Koreans and Chinese look stereotypically Asian.[5] That suggests that the Japanese want to look different, which is reflected in using cosmetic surgery to alter their eyes and by dying their hair brown, which has become fashionable among young Japanese.

In other words, rhetoric is the study of the ways that truths are socially constructed through language, including the ways that Japanese come to see themselves. Such truths are not Plato's eternal forms; they are what the Greeks called *endoxa*, opinions, the shared beliefs or common sense of a culture, society, or people.

It might seem that rhetoric is the whole study of language; in one sense, that is true. I do not intend to claim the world for rhetoric, however. Rhetoricians study public discourse of all types—literary, political, scientific, philosophical, and commercial—in order to discover *the knowledge that emerges out of practice*. For example, for many years I have studied the public discourse of U.S. presidents.[6] Much of it is dull, pedestrian, and verbose, but the study of it all enables critics to understand the ways that presidential speeches and proclamations threaten or imperil the institution, contribute to its stability, and facilitate or inhibit presidential power. Bob Woodward's *Plan of Attack*,[7] a report on the process leading to the U.S. invasion of Iraq, repeatedly comments that "policy is made in speeches," illustrated vividly by President Bush's speech at the West Point graduation in 2002 in which he subtly introduced the idea of preemptive war as an appropriate defensive military policy.

Such scholarship on discursive practices has produced a considerable amount of work on genres, which are discursive events that occur repeatedly under particular conditions, and are speeches or writings of types that audiences recognize and for which they have highly developed expectations and evaluative criteria. Examples are opening speeches to parliament, U.S. presidential inaugurals, and even pedestrian letters of recommendation.[8] This kind of analysis has been extended to the practices of other institutions, such as business enterprises, with careful study of vision statements, annual reports, and the like, all of which as individual documents usually are quite dull, but as bodies of practice are essential parts of understanding how institutions sustain themselves and manage change. The greatest challenge is always justified and explained as mere continuity.

I have explored Franklin Roosevelt's December 8, 1941, speech in which he invited the U.S. Congress to declare that, owing to the attack on Pearl Harbor, a state of war existed between the United States and Japan. It is quite different from other speeches seeking declarations of war because of the attack. What is of particular interest is the way in which the Japanese are characterized in the speech—as deceptive, treacherous, and double-dealing. These characterizations made it seem more likely that Japanese immigrants and Japanese Americans would be willing to become spies and to commit sabotage. Such assumptions led to an Executive Order that sent most Japanese in the United States to internment camps.[9]

Those who teach courses in literature study discursive practices in similar ways, although the materials they work with tend to be less dull, pedestrian, and verbose. Literary theory is the study of patterns of practice. Wayne Booth's *Rhetoric of Fiction*[10] is a study of the role of narrative choice in the structure and development of novels, of the ways in which different kinds of narrators manage and influence the responses of readers. John Ciardi's *How Does a Poem Mean?*[11] is a rhetorical study of the artful ways in which poetry creates experience, particularly the ways in which the interaction of form and content shape readers' responses. Whether you call such work literary criticism or literary theory or rhetorical analysis, I hope that you can perceive the affinity and similarity between studies of how language works in political, scientific, and commercial discourse with the ways in which language works to achieve dramatic and literary ends. Kenneth Burke, who was a music critic as well as a literary and rhetorical critic and theorist, made rhetoric central to the study of literature, literature as argument, narrative voice as persuasion, poetry, novels, and drama as a special kind of "equipment for living."[12]

There is an important difference in emphasis in poesis and rhetoric, however. In poetry, novels, and other literary works, the aim is vicarious experience; the end is an enlarged sense of and feeling for the human condition. In rhetoric, the aim is choice and *praxis*, action in the here and now. That is why rhetoric tends to be blunt, argumentative, and emotional, seeking to mobilize passions that generate behavior. At their extremes, the contrasts are dramatic; at some moments they converge, as when someone calls on us to act in ways consistent with the best that we can be, with what U.S. President Abraham Lincoln called "the better angels of our nature." A recent article in the *New York Times* discussed the problems created by the secret police in the country of Jordan and included an interview with a poet, who had been arrested and jailed for the public performance of his work. In that interview the poet, Mr. Qudah, said that "'expressing topical ideas through poetry is an Arab tradition. . . . It is like music, you are making a speech but in a musical way. . . .'" Still, Mr. Qudah notes, "You cannot form a political party by reciting poetry."[13]

WHY STUDY RHETORIC?

Why, then, study rhetoric? We study rhetoric to understand how language works—in different ways in different languages—to explore the resources in language that make ideas memorable and appealing, that create unforgettable, powerful experiences, whether in sublime literary works or public speeches or in advertising that exploits visual, auditory, tactile, olfactory, and kinesthetic languages and symbols.

A second reason to study rhetoric is to understand the history of thought, illustrated, for example, by historian Benedict Anderson's studies of *Imagined Communities*,[14] which explore the historical and symbolic factors that contributed to the rise of nationalism in the nineteenth century. Anderson offers this "definition of the nation: it is an imagined political community," and he explains, "It is *imagined* because most of the members of even the smallest nation will never know most of their fellow-members, meet them, or even hear of them, yet in the minds of each lives the image of their communion" (6). He quotes historian Ernest Gellner as saying, "Nationalism is not the awakening of nations to self-consciousness: it invents nations where they do not exist."[15] In particular, Anderson notes,

> It is imagined as a *community*, because, regardless of the actual inequality and exploitation that may prevail in each, the nation is always conceived as a deep, horizontal comradeship. Ultimately it is this fraternity that makes it possible, over the past two centuries, for so many millions of people, not so much to kill, as willingly to die for such limited imaginings. (7)

Such scholarship is closely related to rhetorical studies of constitutive rhetoric, the kind of speech that creates and sustains community, which has been vividly illustrated by the discourse of former President Hugo Chávez in the country that he strategically and rhetorically renamed the Bolivarian Republic of Venezuela. Chávez wished to wear the mantle of the great South American liberator and to claim that his government was a seamless continuation of the revolution that Simón Bolivar and others began early in the nineteenth century.

In addition, I do not think it is possible to understand Western ideas and ways of thinking without some familiarity with the cultures of ancient Greece and Rome, which have had such a powerful influence on Christianity and on the political thought and educational systems of Europe and the United States. The rediscovery of Greco-Roman classical works, facilitated by the cultural flowering of studies by Arabic scholars, spread ideas that fueled the European Renaissance, ideas with considerable power still. The essence of those ideas was the liberal arts, a system of education grounded in the *quadrivium*, the four-part curriculum of mathematics, geometry, music, and astronomy, and the *trivium*, the three-part curriculum composed of grammar, logic, and rhetoric. Rhetoric was the capstone, the means by which to demonstrate competence or mastery of knowledge. Only when students could *articulate* what they knew were they considered fully educated. Speech was an index of character; producing cogent public discourse was an index of an ordered, disciplined mind.

Why, then, has rhetoric fallen into disrepute? Strangely enough, I no longer am sure that it has; studies of rhetoric are sprouting in many disciplines—in economics, political science, and cultural studies, among others. Nonetheless, there is still considerable hostility to it as a concept and to its study. The charge that some discourse is mere rhetoric, empty rhetoric, bombast, bloviation, or demagoguery reflects a quite human detestation and fear of artful language. I believe this reaction is directly related to a desire to suppress awareness of that nasty persistent gap between words and our felt reality, between language and human experience, a gap that unavoidably catapults us abruptly into rhetoric, which is the skillful, artful effort to bridge that divide.

I do not know if the word *rhetoric* can be rescued from its negative associations, but I believe that the study of how language works its wiles, how it influences us, is vital to understanding culture and politics in the broadest sense. In some ways it is hard to sell rhetoric to others because rhetoric reminds us of our defects: our bad memories, our biases, our disagreements, and our vulnerability to seduction of all sorts—we protest foolishly that we remain unaffected by advertising, for example. What we forget, of course, is that rhetoric is equally about our virtues, about our ability to create powerful dramatic works, literary and political, all of which tell lies that transport us far beyond our humdrum daily lives. In *The Well-Tempered Critic*,[16] Canadian literary theorist and critic Northrop Frye writes of great political rhetoric as "high style in ordinary speech," exemplified by the words of U.S. President Abraham Lincoln at Gettysburg; Joseph Welch's simple but profound challenge, "Have you no sense of decency?"; to the excesses of U.S Senator Joseph McCarthy; the Sermon on the Mount in the book of Matthew in the New Testament; and the dignity with which a New Orleans mother explained her reasons for sending her white child to an unsegregated school (44–45).

I study rhetoric in order to understand what it means to be human, to swim in language, and to use and be used by it. I share with Isocrates and Cicero the view that it has enabled us humans to create all that makes our life good, but I share with Plato the belief that it has the capacity to foster and to rationalize the greatest of human evils.

Karlyn Kohrs Campbell

NOTES

1. Edward Schiappa, *The Beginnings of Rhetorical Theory in Classical Greece* (New Haven: Yale University Press, 1999).

2. Peter France, *Rhetoric and Truth in France, Descartes to Diderot* (Oxford: Clarendon Press, 1972), p. 33.

3. Kenneth Burke, *The Rhetoric of Religion* (Boston: Beacon Press, 1961).

4. Edward Bernays, *The Engineering of Consent* (Norman, OK: University of Oklahoma Press, 1955).

5. See Norimitsu Onishi, "Ugly Images of Asian Rivals Become Best Sellers in Japan," *New York Times*, 19 November 2005. Accessed 11/21/05. http://www.nytimes.com/2005/11/19/international/asia/19comics.html?_r=1&n=Top/Reference/Times%20Topics/People/O/Onishi,%20Norimitsu&oref=slogin.

6. K. K. Campbell and K. H. Jamieson, *Presidents Creating the Presidency: Exercising Rhetorical Power* (Chicago: University of Chicago Press, in press).

7. Bob Woodward, *Plan of Attack* (New York: Simon and Schuster, 2004).

8. Mikhail M. Bakhtin, "The Problem of Speech Genres," in C. Emerson & M. Holquist, eds. *Speech Genres and Other Late Essays* (Austin: University of Texas Press, 1986), pp. 60–102.

9. See Hermann G. Stelzner, "'War Message': December 8, 1941: An Approach to Language," *Quarterly Journal of Speech*, 33 (1966): 419–437.

10. Wayne Booth, *Rhetoric of Fiction*, 2nd ed. (Chicago: University of Chicago Press, 1983). Originally published 1961.

11. John Ciardi, *How Does a Poem Mean?* (Boston: Houghton Mifflin, 1959).

12. See Kenneth Burke, *The Philosophy of Literary Form: Studies in Symbolic Action* (Baton Rouge: Louisiana State University Press, 1941); *A Grammar of Motives* (New York: Prentice-Hall, 1945); *A Rhetoric of Motives* (New York: Prentice-Hall, 1950).

13. Neil MacFarquhar, "Heavy Hand of the Secret Police Impeding Reform in Arab World," *New York Times*, 14 November 2005. Accessed11/14/2005. http://www.nytimes.com/2005/11/14/international/middleeast/14jordan.html.

14. Benedict Anderson, *Imagined Communities*, Rev. ed. (London & New York: Verso, 1991).

15. Ernest Gellner, *Thought and Change* (London: Weidenfield & Nicholson, 1964), p. 169; cited in Anderson, *Imagined Communities*, p. 6.

16. Northrop Frye, *The Well-Tempered Critic* (Bloomington: Indiana University Press, 1963).

Index

Marx, Karl, 257
Maslow, Abraham, 208
McCarthy, Joseph, 273, 349
McCourt, Frank, 335
McKibben, Bill, 87–94, 231
McLuhan, Marshall, 293
McMurtry, Larry, 11
media. *See also* social media;
    television
  apologetic genre and, 332–336
  development history of,
    300–301
  ethos and, 300–303
  Internet, 307–308
  language of, 299
  as message, 303–308
  moral authority of, 300–302
  narrowcasts, 311
  persona and, 302
  political campaigns in, 306–315
  print, 304–306
  radio, 306
  as rhetorical construct, 299–300
  target audiences for, 303
  transmission methods, 305
  voyeurism and, 303
Melville, Herman, 128
memorization, 42–43, 47
Mencken, H. L., 4
Messaris, Paul, 284–285
metaphors
  connotations and, 184–185,
    188
  figurative language and, 173–174
metonymy, 123, 185, 188
Meyerowitz, Joshua, 290
Michelman, Kate, 157–158
Miller, Zell, 125
A Million Little Pieces (Frey), 148
Moby Dick (Melville), 128
Mohammad, Elijah, 276
Monroe, Alan H., 154
Moore, Michael, 332
moral authority, of media, 300–302
moral standards, for evaluation,
    270–272
more or less argument, 116
Morozov, Evgeny, 312

Mothers Against Drunk Driving
    (MADD), 167
Mother Teresa, 209
motivated sequences, 154
movement, as nonverbal cues, 67

name-calling argument, 133
naming, 166–168
narrative sequence structures, 146
narrowcasts, 311
The Nation, 131
needs, of audiences, 208–209
negating, 170–171
negative definition, 103
The Negro on the American Frontier
    (Porter), 13
New England Journal of Medicine,
    177
new media, topical structure in,
    149–150
Nixon, Richard, 186, 253, 273,
    287, 306–307, 334
non sequitur, 133
nonverbal cues, 64, 66–67
numerical transitions, 62
Nussbaum, Martha, 23n4

Obama, Barack, 118–119, 182,
    272
  Father's Day speech, 216–227
  use of allusion for, 187
objectivity, rhetoric and, 3
occasion, 325–336
  ethos influenced by, 256
  eulogy, 327–328
  rhetorical genres and
    deliberative, 326, 329–330
    epideictic, 326–329
    eulogy and, 327–328
    hybrids of, 331–332
    violations of, 331–332
  rhetors influenced by, 256
  war rhetoric, 329–330
Occupy Wall Street movement,
    312
Olive, Print, 13
Oliver Twist (Dickens), 10

Olson, Lester, 284
Olson, Randy, 3
Olson, Theodore, 261, 275
onomatopoeia, 188
On Rhetoric (Aristotle), 4–5, 86,
    116
operational definition, 103
oral style, in language, 174
organization
  audience as influence on,
    153–159
    conclusions, 156–159
    introductions, 155–156
    outlining, 159–161
  logical structures in, 150–153
  outlining, 142–144
    audiences as influence on,
      159–161
  sequence structures in, 144–146
  of thesis, 141
  topical structures in, 148–150
  as type of argument, 140–141
outlining, 57–58
  audiences as influence on,
    159–161
  deductive structure for, 159–160
  inductive structure for, 160
  in organization, 142–144
    audiences as influence on,
      159–161
    development of ideas, 143
  refutative structure for, 160–161
  sequence structures, 144–146
  story diagrams, 147
  three-sided structure for, 160
  two-sided structure for, 160–161
Oxford Classical Dictionary, 49
Oxford English Dictionary, 49
Oxford International Dictionary, 49

Palfrey, John, 311
Palin, Sarah, 168, 240
parallelism, 182–183, 188
Parks, Gordon, 284
participation
  enthymemes and, 259–260
  persuasion and, 257
  for rhetors, 259–261